AF575640

Catherine Kernan E. Ashley Rooney with Laura G. Einstein and Janice C. Oresman

SINGULAR AND SERIAL

Contemporary Monotype and Monoprint

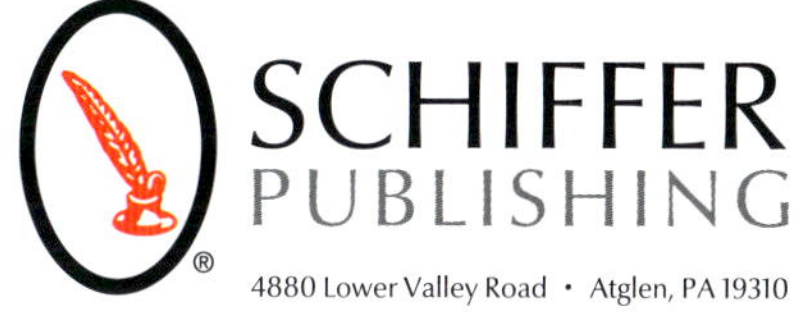

Other Schiffer Books on Related Subjects:

Contemporary American Print Makers, E. Ashley Rooney and Stephanie Standish, foreword by Susan J. Goldman, ISBN 978-0-7643-4691-0

Harry Bertoia Monoprints, Nancy N. Schiffer, ISBN 978-0-7643-3850-2

50 Contemporary Women Artists: Groundbreaking Contemporary Art from 1960 to Now, John Gosslee and Heather Zises, eds., foreword by Elizabeth Sackler, ISBN 978-0-7643-5653-7

Copyright © 2019 by E. Ashley Rooney and Catherine Kernan

Library of Congress Control Number: 2018959400

All rights reserved. No part of this work may be reproduced or used in any form or by any means—graphic, electronic, or mechanical, including photocopying or information storage and retrieval systems—without written permission from the publisher.

The scanning, uploading, and distribution of this book or any part thereof via the Internet or any other means without the permission of the publisher is illegal and punishable by law. Please purchase only authorized editions and do not participate in or encourage the electronic piracy of copyrighted materials.

"Schiffer," "Schiffer Publishing, Ltd.," and the pen and inkwell logo are registered trademarks of Schiffer Publishing, Ltd.

Designed by Molly Shields
Cover design by Molly Shields
Type set in Swis721 Lt BT/ZapfEllipt BT
Front cover images: Sue Heatley, *Milky Lava Moon*, 2017; Paul Deruvo, *Parents*, 2010.
Back cover images: Richard Bosman, *Stove on Fire*, 2017; Sara Greenberger Rafferty, *Paynes* III, 2016; Inka Essenhigh, *Gene*, 2010.

ISBN: 978-0-7643-5727-5
Printed in China

Published by Schiffer Publishing, Ltd.
4880 Lower Valley Road
Atglen, PA 19310
Phone: (610) 593-1777; Fax: (610) 593-2002
E-mail: Info@schifferbooks.com
Web: www.schifferbooks.com

For our complete selection of fine books on this and related subjects, please visit our website at www.schifferbooks.com. You may also write for a free catalog.

Schiffer Publishing's titles are available at special discounts for bulk purchases for sales promotions or premiums. Special editions, including personalized covers, corporate imprints, and excerpts, can be created in large quantities for special needs. For more information, contact the publisher.

We are always looking for people to write books on new and related subjects. If you have an idea for a book, please contact us at proposals@schifferbooks.com.

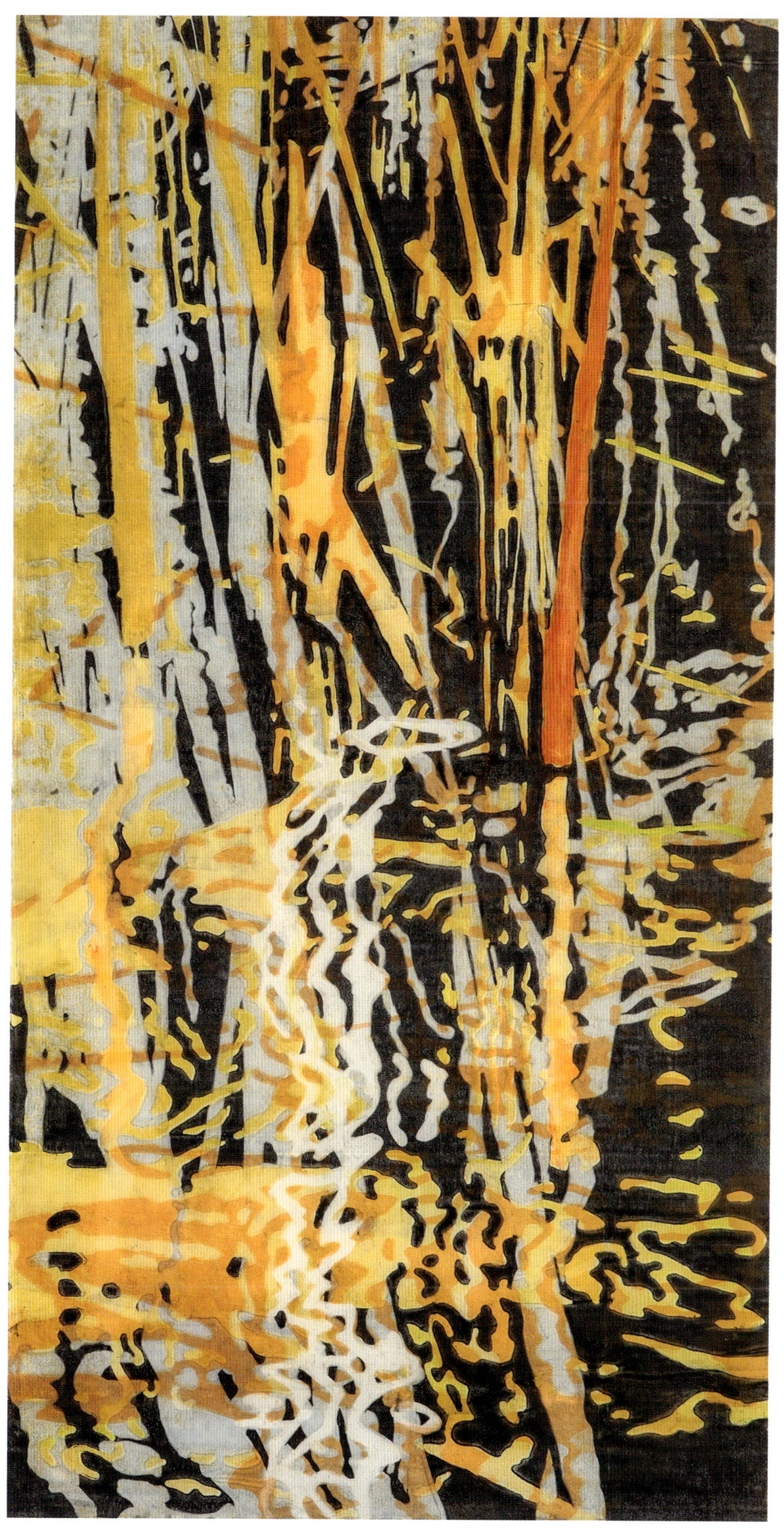

Catherine Kernan. *Tracking #7*. Offset woodcut monoprint with Akua soy-based inks.

CONTENTS

PREFACE

Catherine Kernan

This long-overdue book, *Singular and Serial: Contemporary Monotype and Monoprint*, presents some of the many ways today's artists are making one-of-a-kind prints. Single transfers and "variant editions," alternatively known as monotypes and monoprints, are part of a long tradition. More recent radical experimentation has opened the floodgates for artists to make prints in any way imagination suggests and new technologies allow. When Ashley Rooney approached me to assemble a book on monotypes and monoprints, I welcomed the chance to examine some of the innovations that make these forms a highly accessible and relevant visual language for our time.

In 1986 John Cage passed burning paper through a press in order to create undeniably singular prints, thereby establishing a standard of outrageousness rarely equaled in printmaking. When Willie Cole makes prints by pressing a hot iron on paper, he appears unconcerned with categories and definitions. These and many other unorthodox practices have proliferated, blurring boundaries between traditional types of printmaking. The distinctions seem functional only in relative terms.

In her book *Ink, Paper, Metal, Wood,** Kathan Brown addresses singular prints clearly and directly. She recognizes all singular prints but accepts monoprint as the most functional and inclusive term for prints that are neither monotypes nor variants of a conventional print. Although not universally adopted, Brown's terminology is the most convincingly inclusive to me as a practicing artist.

Singular and Serial: Contemporary Monotype and Monoprint showcases the work of artists who live and work in the United States and whose practice includes singular prints. Although not exhaustive, the selection is diverse, with a wide variation in backgrounds, ages, regions, and technical approaches. For "true" monotypes, the artists use a variety of materials (e.g., oil paint, ink, watercolor, crayons, and pencils), often in a very painterly way on a smooth, unworked surface. Monoprinters commonly work with etched plates, trace and offset transfers, collage, woodcut, digital media, screen print, photosensitive plates, and all manner of stencils. Many build up sculptural surfaces from which to print. Our selection of images is characterized by freewheeling and improvisational, as well as more traditional, approaches.

Within the field of printmaking, editions have long been evaluated for their technical consistency and closely controlled printing. Monotypes and monoprints are now celebrated and valued for their uniqueness and variations, for their dance with chaos, and for evidence of the artist's direct participation. Monotype, varied editions spun off from editionable plates, and monoprints continue to grow in stature as a personal counterpoint to the dominance of the computerized image.

Two experienced curators, Janice C. Oresman and Laura G. Einstein brought to this project their depth of knowledge, wide-ranging connections, and discriminating judgment. Their backgrounds in curating, collecting, and art history provide a counterbalance to my view from the studio. Their participation is critical to this project's value and success. As we considered work from individual artists, galleries, print publishers, and independent studios, every choice sparked analysis and negotiation. Our differing visions and understandings of monotype, varied editions, and monoprint became a topic of productive and ongoing discussion as we curated the images.

Enriched by our different training, experiences, and professional platforms, *Singular and Serial: Contemporary Monotype and Monoprint* is a guide to some of the issues and intricacies of contemporary one-of-a-kind printmaking. To printmakers, teachers, collectors, dealers, curators, and art lovers, it offers a wealth of visual material as well as the thoughts of individual artists about their process and motivations for making singular prints.

---

* Brown, Kathan. *Ink, Paper, Metal, Wood* (Chronicle Books, 1996), 252–257.

ACKNOWLEDGMENTS

All the images in this book are courtesy of the artists who created them. We offer thanks for their willingness to contribute and supply the needed writing, image files, and captions.

Many friends, colleagues, and print professionals contributed to bring this book into being. To all of them, we offer thanks:

Sirarpi Heginian Walzer, for suggesting me to Ashley Rooney

Ashley Rooney, for inviting me to undertake the project and for her incredible patience

Janice C. Oresman and Laura G. Einstein, for writing their essays that evidence enthusiasm for the medium and knowledge of the print world

Clifford S. Ackley, for reading my essays and making astute edits

Artists Dan Welden, Robert Andrew Parker, and Bill Jacklin, for discussions that led to valuable insights

Joan Peterdi, for discussions and historical perspective

Roberta Wadell, for pointing me to Susan Tallman's definition of monotype and monoprint

Jane Glaubinger, for raising the issue of terminology and explaining her point of view

Joann Moser and Kathan Brown, for their insightful and thorough books on printmaking

All the artists who submitted but whose work we were not able to include, for the effort they made, and for making prints

The patient and helpful contacts at print publishers and studios are due my sincere thanks. They include Anders Bergstrom at Hauser & Wirth; Alice Wu at Kala Institute; Brian Rumbolo at Carolina Nitsch; Andrew Mockler at Jungle Press; Bridget Casey at Mary Ryan Gallery; David Cost and Michael McCabe of The Fourth Dimension Studio; Dusica Kirjakovic at Lower East Side Printshop; Jen Dragon of Cross Contemporary Art; Jim Stroud of Center Street Studio; Kim Schmidt and Bridget Casey at Mary Ryan Gallery; Mari Marks Mondanelli and Jesse France at Highpoint Printmaking Center; Miranda K. Metcalf at Davidson Galleries; Sona Pastel-Daneshgar and Paula Panzchenko at Tandem Press; Roseanne Colachis at Shark's Ink; Rachel Gladfelter at Pace Prints; Peter and James Pettengill and Alyssa Robb at Wingate Studio; Peter Colon at DC Moore; Norm Stewart of Stewart & Stewart; Marjorie Van Dyke and Deborah Freedman at VanDeb Prints; Kerry Santullo and Kirsten Flaherty at Dieu Donné; Tamsin Doherty and Marisa Stockton at Brand X Editions; and Nick Ryan at William Havu Gallery.

I extend deep and heartfelt thanks to my longtime partners in print, Jane Goldman, Randy Garber, Mary Sherwood, and Ilana Manolson; to my brilliant daughter, Josephine; and to my generous and supportive friend John Powell.

INTRODUCTION

The Monotype and Monoprint Traditions

Laura G. Einstein

"Why do it on a plate, and print it, instead of painting it directly on the paper?"[1] This is an important question for the monotype and monoprint traditions. As *Singular and Serial: Contemporary Monotype and Monoprint* has been put together, and after long discussions with renowned curator and collector Janice C. Oresman and painter-printmaker Catherine Kernan, I have reached conclusions that might help establish criteria for examining, clarifying, and updating terminology in common use. In the end, this book applauds the creative impulses of the artists who work in the printmaking medium.

Monotype refers to a print that was drawn or painted on a clean, unworked surface and printed. Monoprint, on the other hand, refers to a singular impression with combined repeatable and unique techniques. The history of these two printmaking approaches has been well documented over time. Although the terminology might be confusing, the history of their development is not.

From earliest time, artists have created singular images that reflect their own impulses, whatever the medium, whatever the tools. Printmaking, with its use of inks, pressure, paper, and tools, is a physical endeavor that requires different skills than does painting. Most artists who are printmakers rarely create just one image; most often work simultaneously both in painting and printmaking because printmaking has unique qualities that can be captured only within this particular technique. In French, *peintre-graveur* (literally, painter-printmaker) suggests the artist's facility with both. Artists discussed in this book make it clear that painting informs printmaking and printmaking informs painting. Artistic impulse is paramount.

As a definition and for simplicity's sake, monotype is the transfer of an image from one surface to another. Artist Dan Welden told me, "A monotype is essentially a one-of-a-kind creation on an untouched surface, which is then transferred to another surface." The direct transfer of a fresh painting or drawing, either liquid or solid, this process is meant to yield just one ("mono-") print ("type").[2] Monoprint, however, incorporates potentially repeatable elements or matrices such as stencils and stamps and allows for interventions and modifications within the given form, allowing it to retain the status of being a unique and singular print and the "mono" designation. A monoprint may also include other printmaking techniques or mixtures of them or both, such as lithography, etching, engraving, woodcut, screen print, and digital processes. Both monotype and monoprint retain "mono" as a prefix, since they both present a singular impression.

Susan Tallman, in 1996, makes the following distinctions:

> Monotype is a unique print that is made by painting or drawing on an unmarked plate, which is then run through the press . . . whereas monoprint is a unique variant of a conventional print.[3]

Unorthodox and radical innovations currently taking place in the studios of printmakers suggest a need to expand these definitions. To begin an understanding of the two processes, it is vital to set out the history of the monotype/monoprint processes.

Monotype[4]

The first written description of the monotype process was alluded to in 1821 by the distinguished print cataloguer Adam Bartsch in his discussion of the method used by the Genoese painter and etcher Giovanni Benedetto Castiglione (1609–1664), who "liberally coated a polished copper plate with oil color . . . [and] had it printed on paper." Bartsch did not give the technique a name, referring to it as "imitating aquatint."[5] The term "monotype" first appeared in print in 1881 in an *Art Journal* publication, referring to the works by American artists Albion Harris Bicknell, Charles Alvah Walker, and William Merritt Chase.[6] Many other American artists worked in monotype, including Maurice Prendergast. However, it was the French artist Edgar Degas (1834–1917) who would make a profound impact on the monotype stage to the present day.

It was the manipulation of plate tone in the seventeenth century that was important to the development of the monotype process through the nineteenth century. Many artists throughout Europe were experimenting with printer's inks to suggest atmospheric effects. The etchings and painted prints of Hercules Segers[7] (1589/90–1633/40) and Rembrandt (1606–1669) provided an early reference point for what ultimately happened in monotype. Segers himself was a painter and etcher, using tone to enliven his etchings.

Although Castiglione is credited with inventing monotype,[8] many other artists throughout Europe were experimenting with the process and plate tone. Unknown to Castiglione, the Belgian artist Anthonis Sallaert (1590–1650), a Flemish baroque painter, draftsman, and printmaker active in Brussels, was simultaneously creating prints in a similar fashion. In a *Print Quarterly* essay from 1988, Martin Royalton-Kisch writes, "there is a chance that they anticipate those of the 1640s by the presumed inventor of monotype, Giovanni Battista Castiglione,"[9] referring to eleven monotypes extant from Sallaert at the time that he published the article. Joann Moser comments about Castiglione's manipulation of the plate and use of tone:

> Most of Castiglione's monotype compositions were composed directly on the plate . . . it was the subtractive wiping away of ink from the polished copper-plate surface entirely covered with ink that is notable within these impressions. A sharp tool, probably of wood, incised white lines in the dark background, and a stiff brush appears to have created some gray areas of the design. In later monotypes Castiglione used rags, fingertips, and possibly swabs, as well as a blunt tool like a reed or bamboo pen, to create white lines or to wipe away the ink.[10]

Degas was equally innovative in the nineteenth century. In the celebrated exhibition of monotype titled *The Painterly Print: Monotypes from the Seventeenth to the Twentieth Century* at The Metropolitan Museum of Art in 1980, Degas was considered to have done "more than any other artist to make the medium an important and viable artistic process; his innovative researches alone added another dimension to the historical chronology of the painterly print."[11]

A monotype by Degas titled *The Ballet Master* (1874–75) in the National Gallery of Art, Washington, DC, carries Degas's signature and that of another French artist, Vicomte Ludovic Lepic (1839–1889), who introduced Degas to the monotype process.[12] Lepic said, "The artist who used etching should be a painter or draughtsman who uses the needle and the rag as another uses paintbrush and pencil. . . . With a stroke of the finger or a dirty rag full of ink, I make a beautiful proof where the consummate practician only produces a

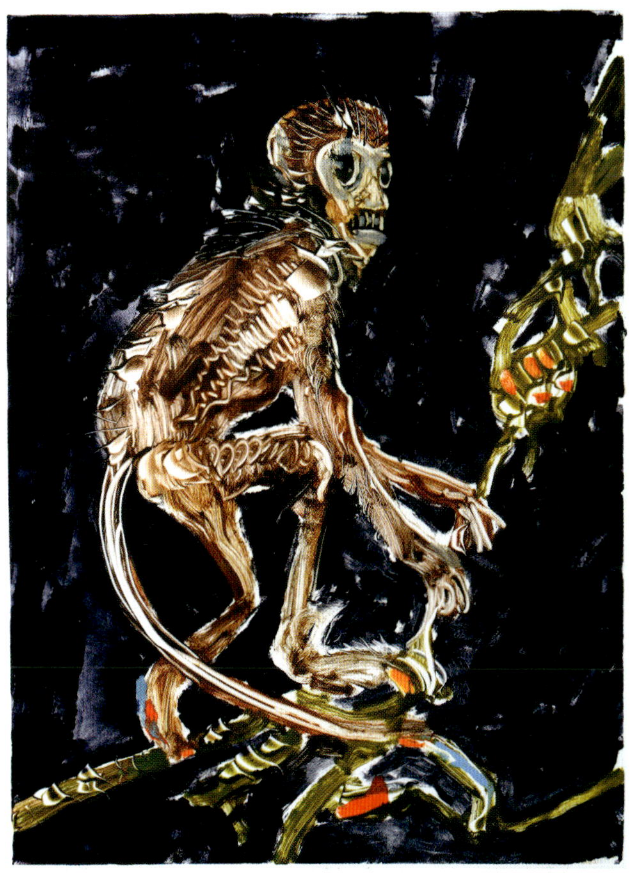

Robert Andrew Parker. *Monkey Dreams*. Monotype. 2015. *Image courtesy of Don Heiny*

dry, graceless plate."[13] In this shared work by Degas and Lepic, the work is done with greasy printer's ink on an unetched plate. Lepic is referred to as the unrepentant amateur with a positive addiction to inking. He discovered, as had all other etchers who printed their own plates, that each impression could be made unique by inking the plate anew for each printing.[14] This expansion of the use of printer's inks is pivotal to the development of the monotype tradition.

Degas made over 300 works in monotype during two discrete bursts of activity. The first lasted from the mid-1870s to the mid-1880s, a period during which he worked with black printer's ink and composed contemporaneous urban subjects; the second was a shorter campaign in the early 1890s, when he used pigmented oil paint to depict real and imaginary landscapes in images that verge on abstraction.[15] In 1968 the Fogg Art Museum, in Cambridge, Massachusetts, exhibited seventy-nine monotypes by Edgar Degas. The fact that monotype printmaking had a resurgence during the impressionist years in France—the last quarter of the nineteenth century—conveys immediately why this medium is so attractive to expressive painting and printmaking.

To many painter-printmakers, the "painterly print"[16] or monotype is as important as it was to Degas. Bill Jacklin, for instance, states that painting informs his printmaking. Jacklin, who first trained as a printmaker and then turned to painting, started making monotypes in the late 1970s. He said the following in an interview with me:

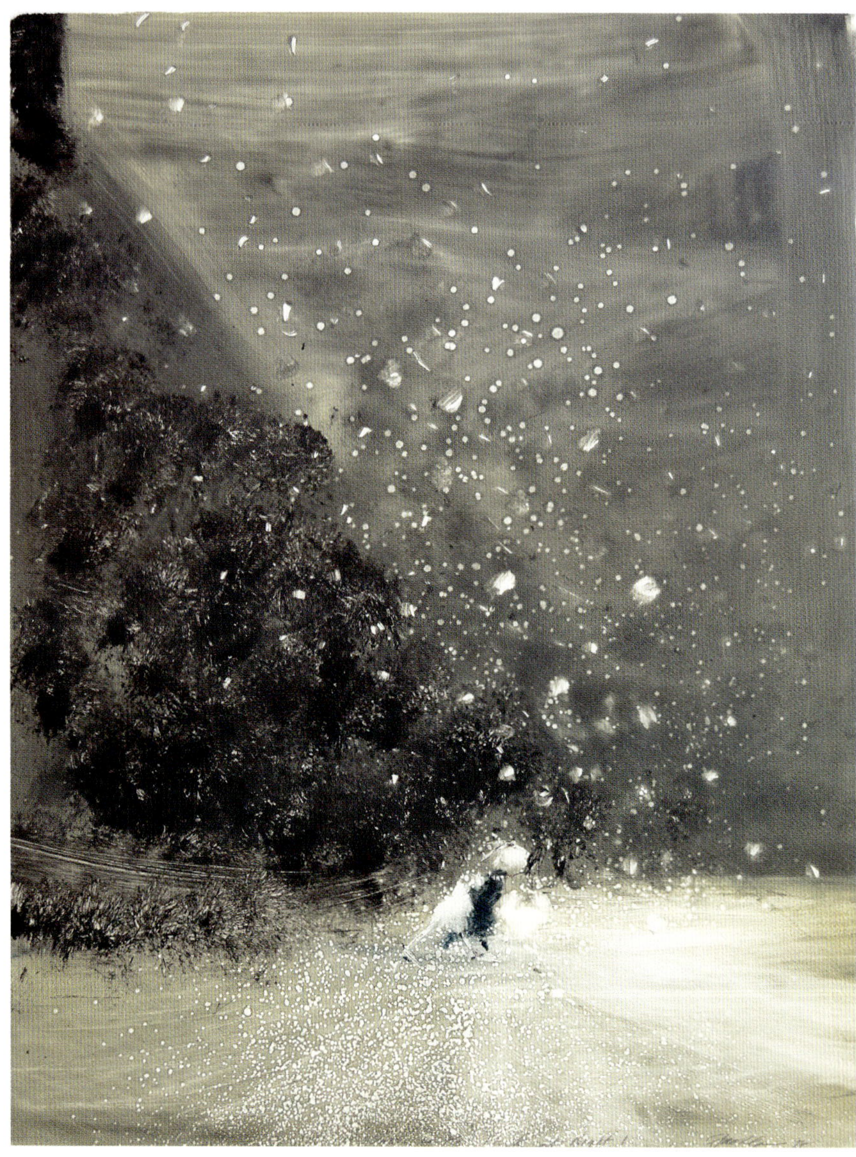

Bill Jacklin. *Snow in the Park at Night*. Monotype. 2018.

> The practice of making monotype has given me a vehicle to develop ideas while simultaneously working on a painting. I move back and forth between the press and the canvas, adjusting both compositions at the same time.

Robert Andrew Parker mused in a recent conversation

> Monotypes are easy and are technically the least demanding of the print processes. I like seeing how things look in reverse and the strange markings that you can do. My monotypes came about by accident from my own sketchbook. I started rubbing my pencil against paper and using both sides of the paper. I love the quality of Paul Klee's line. For him, the line has its own look. For me, the pencil is a sharp object that picks up ink from another surface that I can use to make marks on a page.

In the end, it falls upon the creativity of the artist to select those materials that will best create and enliven or texture the desired image. Monotype for the most part is esteemed for its spontaneous look—as a vehicle to depict energy, life, and motion with a painterly stroke of oil pigment. It can be a lush and saturated approach that is appealing for its gestural nature and the mark making that comes through in the finished product. The *New York Times* art critic Roberta Smith referred to monotypes as "the most seductive of all print mediums."[17]

Monoprint

Dating back to the early fifteenth century, printmaking involved hand coloring by the craftsmen who were making woodblock prints. Printmaking artists strive to create singular works of art with additive effects that include hand coloring and myriad other techniques to create a sought-after result. "The monoprint process combines fixed matrices, such as woodblocks, with direct hand work, and is often simply a unique variant of an otherwise editionable work."[18] Dan Welden expands on this explanation by adding, "Monoprint can employ all traditional methods; that includes direct hand work, either during or after the impression is made. The final work is a 'variant of an otherwise editionable work.'" To continue in this vein, Susan Tallman wrote, "hand-applied marks and unrepeatable variations became increasingly common through the decade: hand-colored prints were made by Mel Bochner, Claes Oldenburg, Pat Stier, Wayne Thiebaud, and Andy Warhol."[19] Renowned artist and printmaker Gabor Peterdi commented on the use of hand-colored prints as follows:

> As no two hand-colored prints are exactly alike, they are as unique in their way as monoprints. The argument of most printmakers against hand coloring is that the artist should accept the limitation of his medium and respect it. A print shouldn't try to be a painting. While I agree with this principle, I don't like to see it turned into a dogma. Artists should have the freedom to express themselves without restrictions. Ultimately, only the quality of the work matters.[20]

Known for their interpretive use of handmade papers, the noted papermaking and printmaking facility Dieu Donné commissioned Katherine Bradford to create twenty-five variants collectively titled *Superheroes and Divers* for their 2014 Paper Variables edition program. Bradford used a stencil to position paper pulp that was then pressed; the stencil became the matrix itself. The repeated images are each gouache on a sheet of pigmented linen pulp on a cotton base. Bradford commented in her essay in this publication:

> Using templates, one for the silhouette of a soaring diver, another for his boots and another for his cape, I was able to locate a flying figure in the center of each handmade 14" × 11" piece of paper. Then the real fun began . . .

The viewer is free to discern whether this is, in fact, a monoprint or a creative use of paper pulp itself for the composition. Should this work be considered a sculpture rather than a monoprint? Again, it is up to the viewer to decide.

During our last meeting, Welden commented to me as he was selecting the "right" work for this publication:

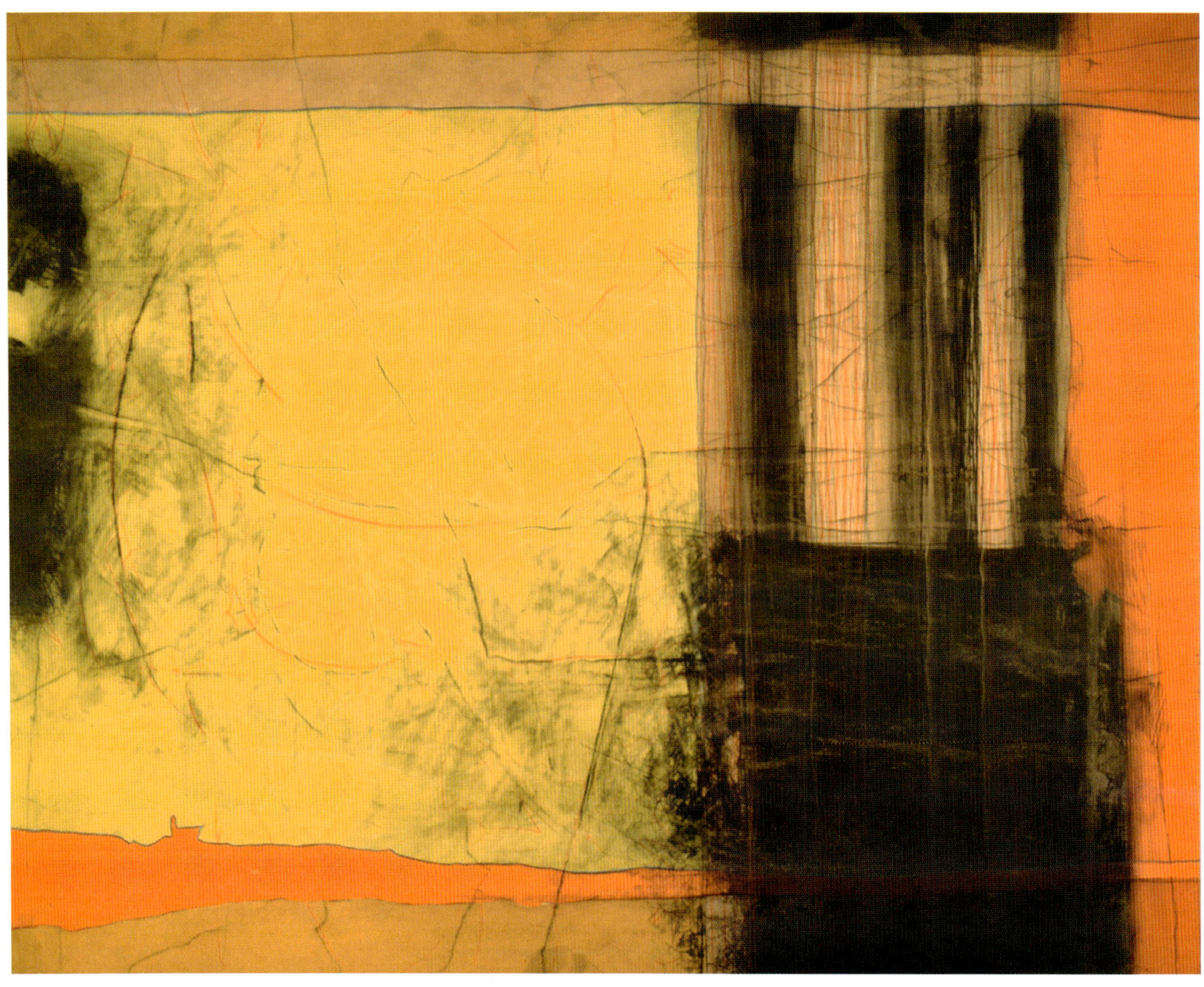

> *Red Pepper Massage* incorporates a combination of Solarplate etching with oil- and soy-based ink, one intaglio impression with three screen-printed layers of color, with water-based ink, Prismacolor pencils, and graphite. The concern for technique was never in question. This work is a monoprint. This work comes about through my own experimentation and exploration. I attempt to find the solution through various materials, ending in an "edition variable," one-of-a-kind image . . .

It is clear that the sky's the limit in terms of possibilities inherent in monotype and monoprint. One can no longer state definitively that monotype is more viable than monoprint with its variants and combined techniques and tools. Both have a place within the accepted practices that printmaking offers. Both monotype and monoprint—each a printed form—communicate the singular aesthetic impulses of the artist—whether through a one-only unique print or a series of unique variant prints, or entirely singular impressions each unlike any others. Dan Welden made a comment that I will use in closing: "It is important to me to allow the senses to appreciate the art, rather than 'pigeonhole' the artist and the technique."

Singular and Serial: Monotype and Monoprint includes examples of some of the many innovations in monotype/monoprint studio practices. The seventy-one contributing artists represent a wide diversity in technique, subject matter, and style.

Dan Welden. *Red Pepper Massage*. Monoprint with oil-based and Akua soy oil-based inks, screen print, Prismacolor pencils, and Solarplate intaglio on Hahnemühle paper. 2014. *Image courtesy of Nina M. Souther*

Notes

1. Gabor Peterdi, *Printmaking* (New York: Macmillan, 1959, rev. 1971 and 1980), 326.
2. Colta Ives, David W. Kiehl, Sue Welsh Reed, and Barbara Stern Shapiro, preface and acknowledgments to *The Painterly Print: Monotypes from the Seventeenth to the Twentieth Century*, ed. Margaret Aspinwall (New York: The Metropolitan Museum of Art, 1980), ix.
3. Susan Tallman, *The Contemporary Print: From Pre-pop to Postmodern* (London: Thames and Hudson, 1996), 297.
4. Those interested in the development of monotype will look to publications such as *The Painterly Print*, published by The Metropolitan Museum of Art in 1980; Joann Moser's publication titled *Singular Impressions: The Monotype in America*, published for the National Museum of American Art by Smithsonian Institution Press in 1997; and Jodi Hauptman's *Degas: A Strange New Beauty*, published by the Museum of Modern Art, New York, in 2016.
5. Moser, *Singular Impressions*, 1 and n1 referencing Adam Bartsch, *Le Peintre Graveur*, vol. 21 (Vienna, 1821), 39–40.
6. Moser, *Singular Impressions*, 1.
7. As reflected in the 2017 exhibition at The Metropolitan Museum of Art titled *The Mysterious Landscapes of Hercules Segers*.
8. Tallman, *The Contemporary Print*, 297.
9. Martin Royalton-Kisch, "A Monotype by Sallaert," *Print Quarterly* 5, no. 1 (March 1988): 60. Note that the name Giovanni Battista Castiglione rather than Giovanni Benedetto Castiglione as the artist has been quoted earlier in this essay.
10. Moser, *Singular Impressions*, 3–4.
11. Barbara Stern Shapiro, "Nineteenth-Century Masters of the Painterly Print," in *The Painterly Print*, 32.
12. Hauptman, *Degas: A Strange New Beauty* (New York:The Museum of Modern Art, 2016), 14.
13. Eugenia Parry Janis, "Setting the Tone—the Revival of Etching, the Importance of Ink," in *The Painterly Print*, 19 and n36, where Janis discusses and translates terms used by Gavarni and Lepic.
14. Janis, "Setting the Tone—the Revival of Etching, the Importance of Ink," 18 and n30, stating that no other etcher, either in France, England, Germany, or Italy, arrived at anything approximating the extreme application of Lepic's experiments at this time.
15. Hauptman, *Degas: A Strange New Beauty*, 14.
16. The Metropolitan Museum of Art, *The Painterly Print: Monotypes from the Seventeenth to the Twentieth Century* (New York: The Metropolitan Museum of Art, 1980), title of the exhibition and catalogue.
17. Roberta Smith, "Edgar Degas: A Strange Beauty," *New York Times* in *Art & Design*, March 24, 2016.
18. Tallman, *The Contemporary Print*, 142.
19. Ibid., 143.
20. Peterdi, *Printmaking*, 331.

Laura G. Einstein is Manager of the Mezzanine Gallery at The Metropolitan Museum of Art. She has more than thirty years' experience in curating and museum work. Einstein has worked as Interim Head and Assistant Curator of the Asian Art Department at Yale University Art Gallery. She has also served as Executive Director at the Center for Contemporary Printmaking in Norwalk, Connecticut, and as an Educator at The Glass House in New Canaan, Connecticut.

THE LURE OF MONOTYPES

Janice C. Oresman

What is a monotype? Is it more a drawing than a print? Ask around and you will get many different answers. In fact, printers keep coming up with innovative means of making monotypes that are establishing new definitions for the process. Basically, it is a drawing with paint or ink on a nonabsorbent flat surface such as metal or Plexiglas. When run through the printing press, the drawing medium is transferred to a sheet of paper and comes out in reverse just like a print. If any medium remains on the plate, a second sheet can be pulled, resulting in a ghost image or cognate—or more poetically, a *fantomé*. Because there is no matrix remaining, the impression stands alone—a unique and uneditioned print.

There is a certain unpredictability in the creation of a monotype because of the pressure exerted in printing. Artists seem to like those "accidents" as much as they like the rich and tactile surfaces. Some choose broad swaths of paint to provide images that can be widely expressive. Others favor smaller quick strokes that can be more of a shorthand approach, still giving all the information needed. A reductive method of erasing from rather than adding to the composition is another quick and easy means of completing the work before the paint goes dry.

Anything that makes a mark can be used in the process. Paintbrushes are most often used, as are brayers (rollers), knives, rags, Q-tips, and fingers, to name a few. In any case, many artists find the monotype to be a perfect process for their ideas in terms of flexibility, texture, and especially adventure.

The monotype is certainly not breaking news. It is a process that has been around for centuries, with most artists trying their hands at it, if only once. Traditionally, monotypes served as preparatory sketches for larger oil paintings. But still lifes and landscapes have been the dominating subjects over the years, with artists using available domestic imagery. Some of the first monotypes were made by transferring a drawing to a small piece of paper under the pressure of the bowl of a spoon or a hand. In these explorations of the medium, the artist was in charge of the entire process. Much, including the size of the paper, has changed since these very personal endeavors.

I had always been intrigued by monotypes, but it was not until Colta Ives's exhibition "The Painterly Print," at The Met in 1980, that I realized they had a life of their own. That catalogue became a textbook on the subject, a fine volume that I recommend to anyone interested in the subject.

It took another major exhibition and catalogue to give monotypes a jump start once again. Published in 1987, *Singular Impressions: The Monotype in America* by Joann Moser should be required reading on the subject. From then on, there appeared to be a proliferation of monotypes and experiments with the technique that led to a new tentative definition: monoprint.

In their essays for this book, Laura G. Einstein and Catherine Kernan have described the monotype process and some of the important artists who included it in their repertoire. As a print collector and curator, I had been drawn to strict definitions of the various printing techniques. Yet, the more I engaged in a dialogue with monotypes, the freer I became with my response and the more I sought them out.

In 2015, I was invited to curate a monotype exhibition at the International Print Center New York (IPCNY). I was delighted to fill a space with exciting work by well-known artists, as well as by artists whose interest in monotype might be new. But something else was sneaking in: the addition of elements and hand drawing that made me question the difference between monotype and monoprint. I wanted to keep the definition pure for the sake of my exhibit.

This book investigates twenty-first-century work, but it was certainly propelled by certain earlier artists who counted monotype as a major part of their work: Romare Bearden, Mary Frank, Matt Phillips, and Michael Mazur were a few of the frontrunners. Of this esteemed group, only Mary Frank, who persists with her work in monotype, is still living. These artists mostly created monotypes on their own, but today more and more work with master printers in studios devoted to printmaking. Large presses and increased physical assistance make for more collaborative and adventurous results.

Artists seem to favor certain categories of monotypes. One is narrative. Richard Bosman is a fine example of an artist using a sequence of prints to create an exciting event on paper. He renders the combustion of a stove in flame-like color. One can imagine Bosman loading thick paint on a plate and hurrying along from plate to plate to complete this fiery story.

Another category harks back to the serenity of turn-of-the-century art. Richard Segalman illustrates this mood very well as he uses muted tones to enter into a charming and serene environment, whether in the privacy of a home or a happy summer outing. Figures turned away keep us from entering the scene, where it remains as quiet as possible. Neither in costume nor demeanor are his figures made of solid stuff. This

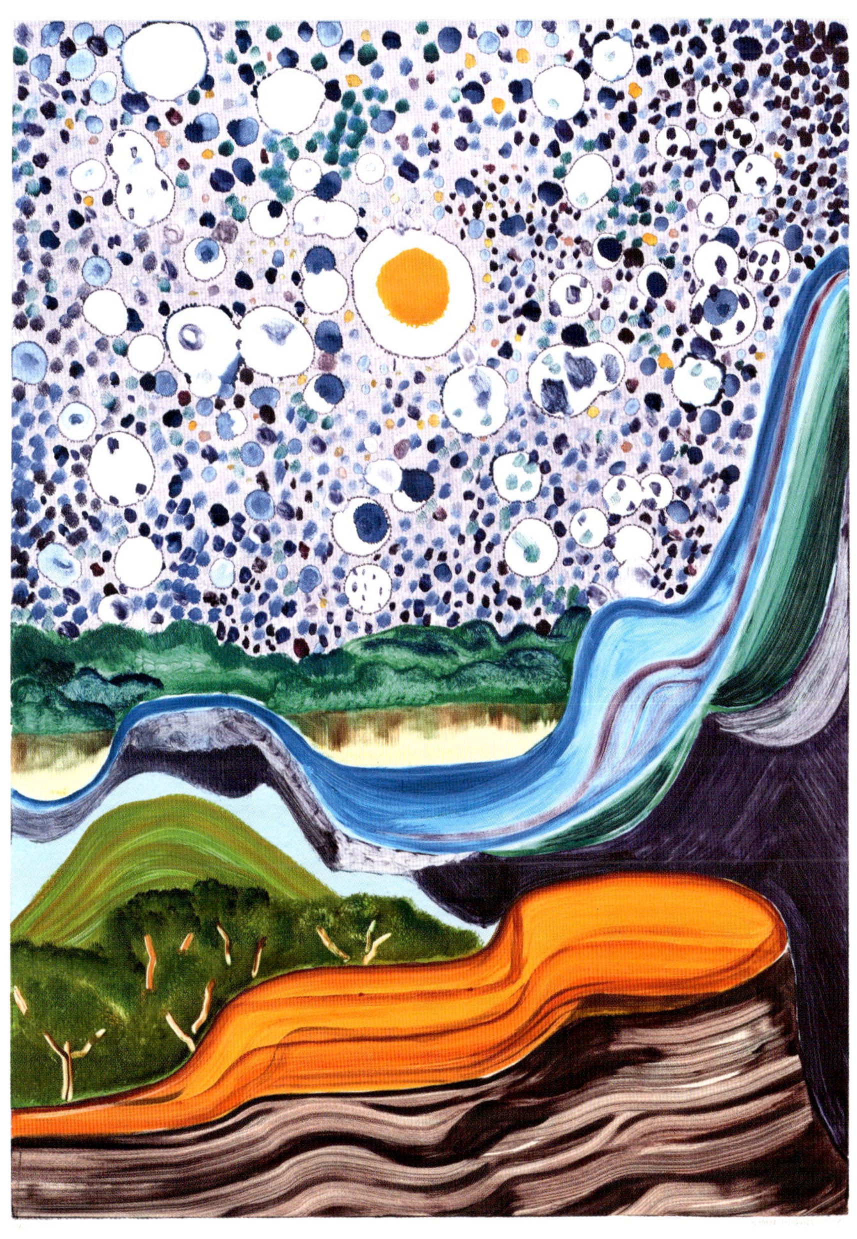

Shara Hughes, *The Stars Don't Lie*. Monotype with oil-based ink. 2018. *Image courtesy of Pace Prints*

poetic element is typical of earlier art that still persists, especially in monotypes.

Inka Essenhigh extols the mystery of ancient legends in the manner of the surrealist artists of the twentieth century. She unleashes that passive moodiness of Segalman with more fluid swirls of paint that pull you into the spin both physically and psychologically.

Interpreting landscape is another favorite subject of artists engaged with monotypes. Degas and his contemporaries were interested in mood. Excessive color would distract from that. More recent landscapes are depicted in bright colors, often fanciful and always dynamic. Shara Hughes fits this description. Broad gestures and tiny circles of color that come from oil dripped on the plate before running it through the press animate her true monotypes. The result is a jewel-like quality that enlivens the surface of an unidentified and magical landscape.

Landscapes similarly become looser, more nonspecifically gestural, and more painterly in the hands of artists such as Gregory Crane, who uses as a starting subject his own backyard in Brooklyn. Gregory Amenoff addresses his monotypes with colors that are thick with paint, applied in a very aggressive way. Color bleeds into color in the press. By contrast, Stuart Shils applies paint with a knife, flattening out the surface to give further credence to an imaginary architectural setting. H. Peik Larsen reverts to a hazy and mysterious landscape more in an older tradition.

Still life, the very personal and quiet subject of earlier monotypes, explodes in the work of contemporaries. Donald Traver, Judith Linhares, Valentina DuBasky, and Susan Schmidt fix on an

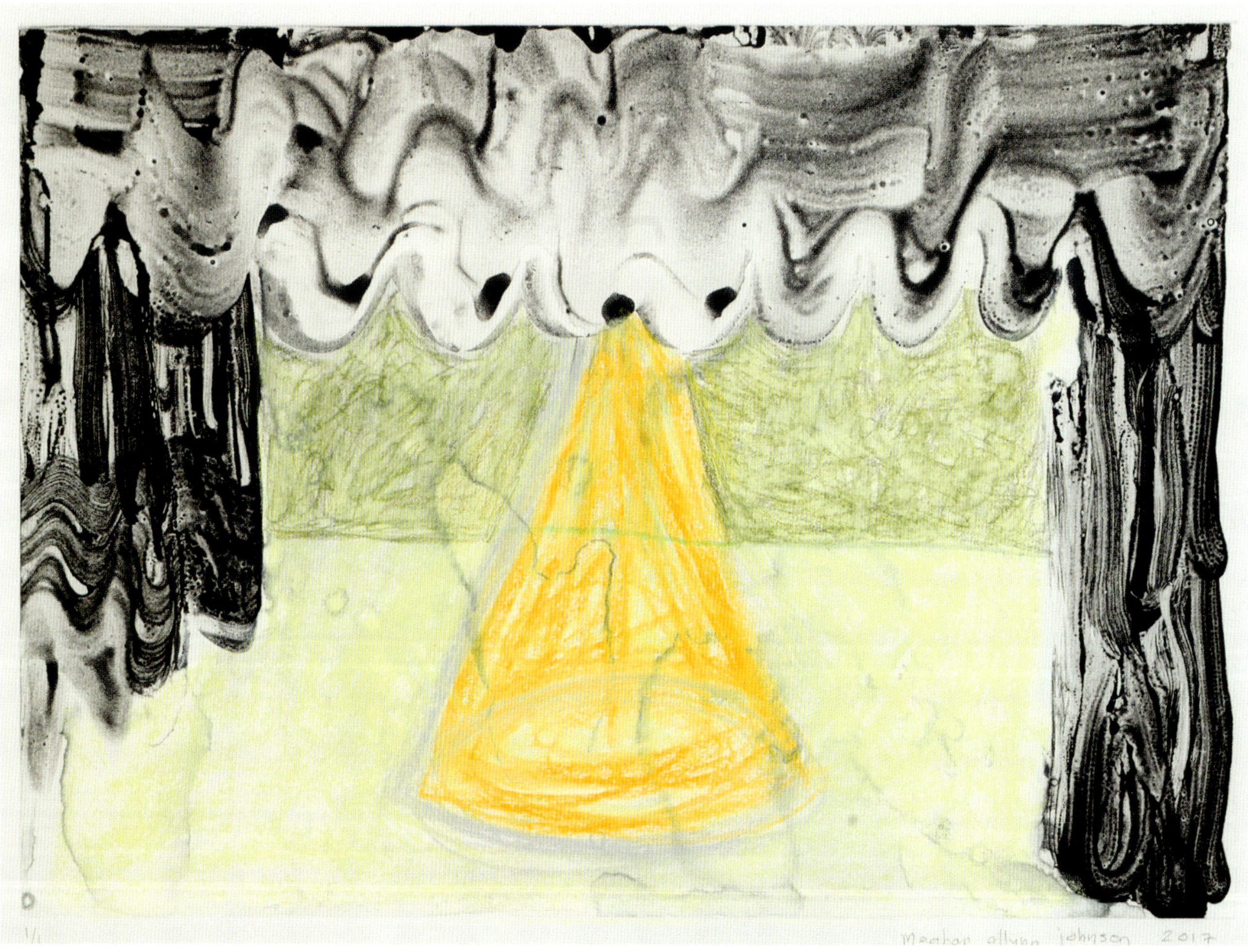

Meghan Allynn Johnson. *Stagelight 2*. Watercolor monotype. 2017. *Image courtesy of David Knut Projects*

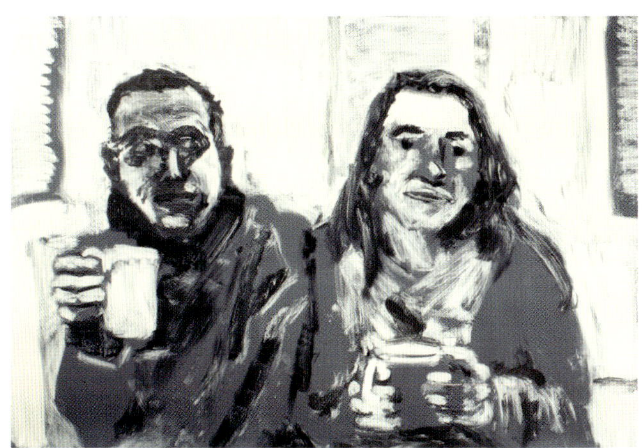

image and investigate it over and over. The speed of monotypes affords quick responses to compositions that appear to have endless possibilities of expression.

It is not surprising that abstraction should have an enormous appeal for artists favoring monotypes. Approaching the plate with gusto and expressing gestures that are not planned but simply occur is a pleasant experience that is totally unselfconscious. Eric Aho represents this group well. The viewer cannot decipher the meaning of his work but can be overwhelmed with its dynamism. Rita Ackermann is another who keeps her meaning to herself.

Jim Stroud, a master printer from Milton Village, Massachusetts, has recently worked with Carrie Moyer, Eva Lundsager, and Marcus Linnenbrink on monotypes. Nondescript shapes bump into each other as they float on the surface. Not just monoprints but monotypes are being subjected to new adventures all the time.

Paul DeRuvo's portrait of his parents is a compendium of all that is traditional in a monotype. His subject is close-up and personal. He has taken the shorthand route, indicating hands by slashes, faces by smudging, and clothing by wiping. Resisting color, he has paid homage to artists of another era who respected the need to move rapidly and focus on the subject rather than the coloration. Meghan Allynn Johnson's work follows his lead with her inventive uses of reductive drawing.

There was a huge response to the 2015 show at MoMA, *Edgar Degas: A Strange Beauty*. The catalogue, which revealed his affection both for monotype and monoprint, contained 176 images of his work. As we are exposed to examples of artists of the past using the monotype process in exciting ways, we are also seeing more innovative monotypes and monoprints in the art world of today. The latter employ a myriad of materials that overwhelm the tradition of pure monotypes.

Our subject is very exciting to us. It is our hope that readers will share this enthusiasm as they look thoughtfully at the images in this book and read the artists' responses to their own work. Making discoveries for ourselves certainly leads to a greater appreciation of the subject at hand and at the same time enriches our understanding and appreciation of the art of our own time.

As for me, I am still true to *True Monotype*, but I have an open mind about the future as seen in *Singular and Serial: Monotype and Monoprint* and look forward to it eagerly. After all, beauty is beauty no matter how it is defined.

Janice C. Oresman is a print collector and curator with a special devotion to monotype. She is on the Visiting Committee of the Smith College Museum of Art and the Prints and Drawings Department of The Metropolitan Museum of Art. She is a trustee emerita of the International Print Center NY (IPCNY), the Smithsonian Archives of American Art, and Smith College. She is particularly enthusiastic about today's collaboration of artists and printers whose work she sees during regular visits to studios and galleries.

Paul DeRuvo. *Parents*. 24" × 36".
Monotype. 2010.

RITA ACKERMANN

New York, New York

I studied printmaking at the Art Academy of Budapest during my first year there, because it was almost impossible to get accepted into the painter's program. At that time, I recognized monotypes as primitive and direct, and it appeared to be the most humble way of printmaking. After that year in the printmaking program, my interest shifted toward painting; since then, I have been devoted to the directness, immediacy, and—most importantly—the freedom of painting.

Working with monotypes introduced me to a specific type of immediacy where I learned to experiment with the idea of chance, forcing me to let go of any controlled decisions. The procedure of adding and erasing paint on the monotype plate has a similar feeling to blind painting, because one can never be sure of the print's final outcome.

In my practice, it is important to face the uncertainties in each and every work I create. The piece must be continually questioned, until it can conquer its own failure and be elevated to an unknown territory where it can then be called artwork. The action of monotype printing fuels my studio practice with inspiration of a newly gained confidence of risk taking.

ALL PHOTOS ARE COURTESY OF HAUSER & WIRTH. PUBLISHED BY THE ARTIST AND PRINTED BY MAURICE SANCHEZ AT DERRIERE L'ETOILE STUDIOS.

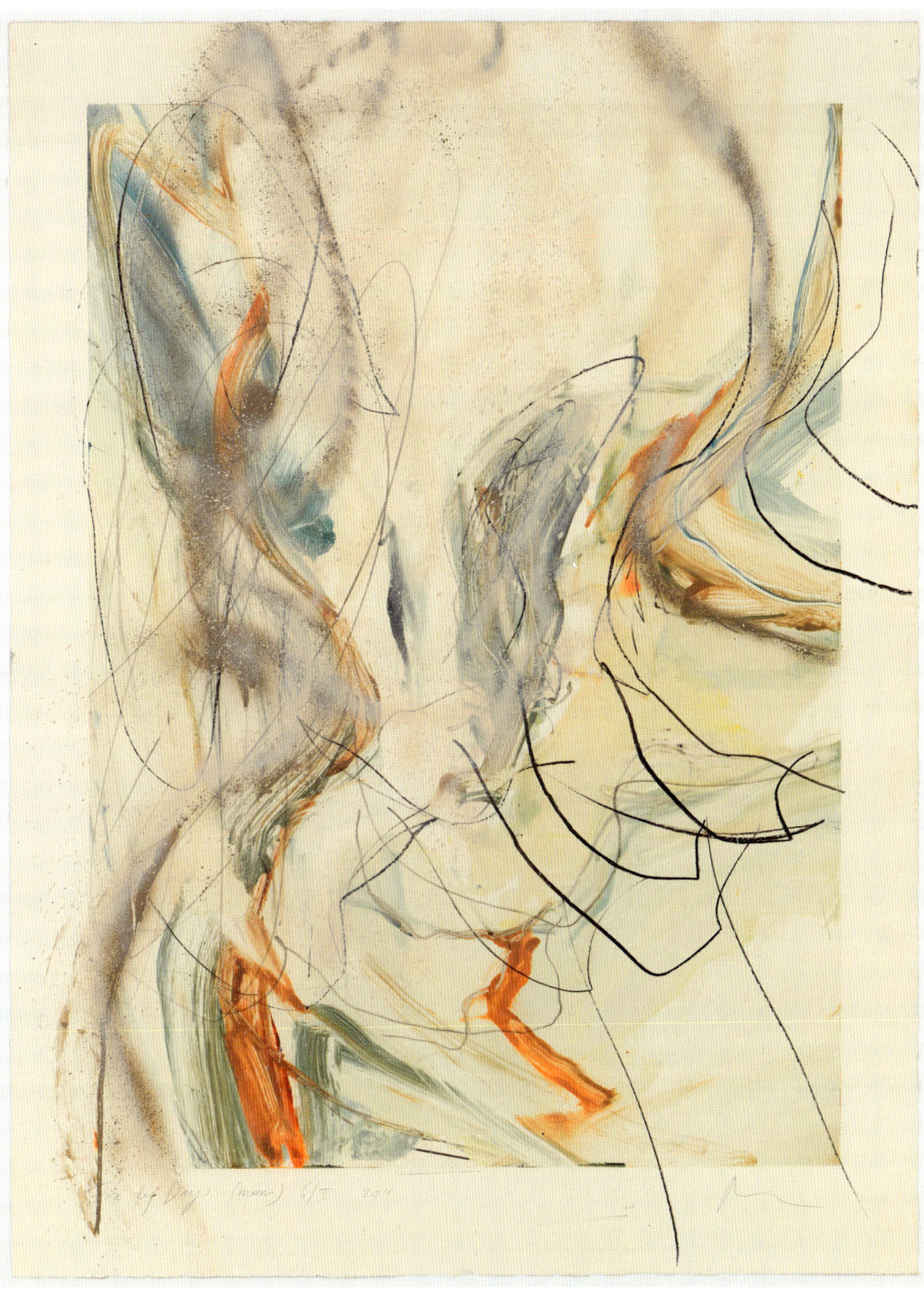

Fire by Days. Monotype with oil-based ink. 36" × 27". 2011.

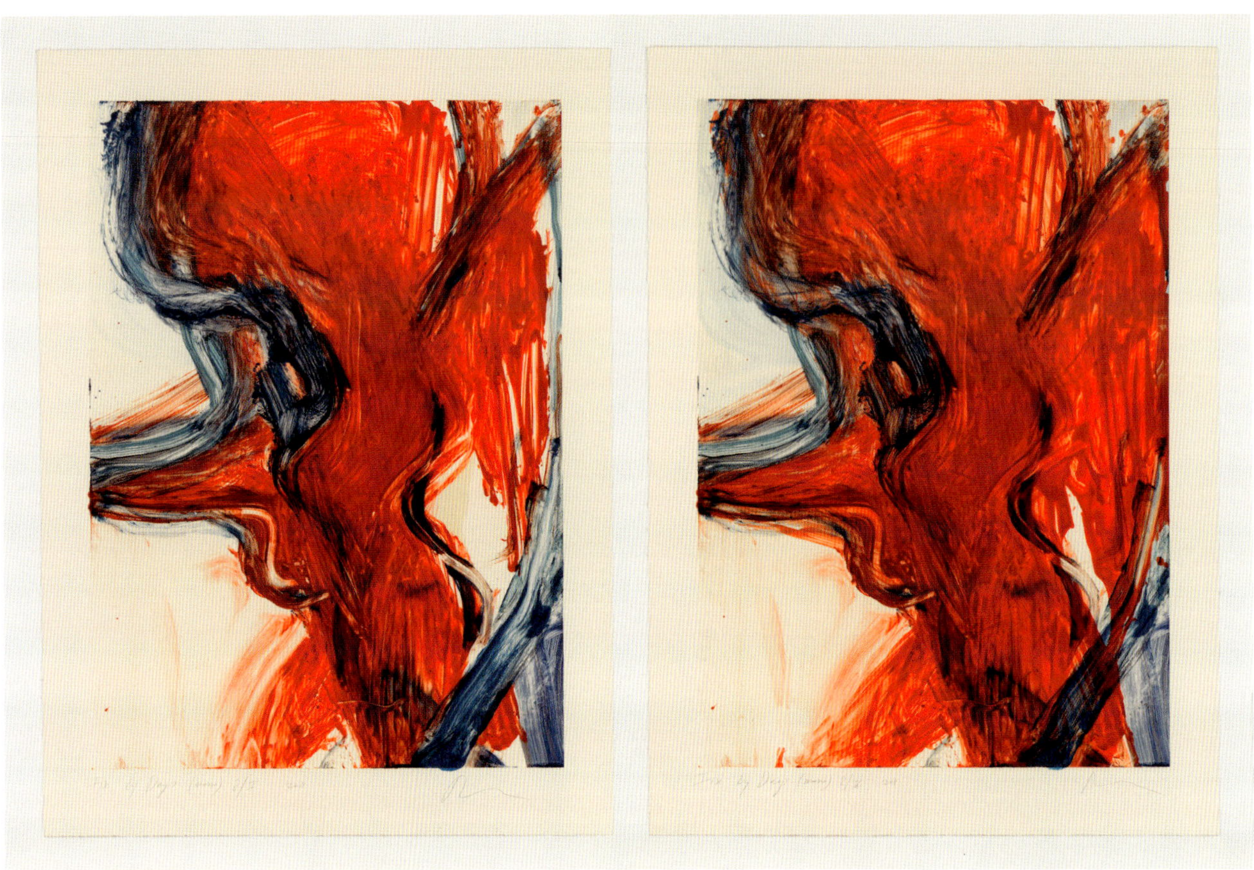

Fire by Days. Monotype with oil-based ink. 33" × 24". 2011.

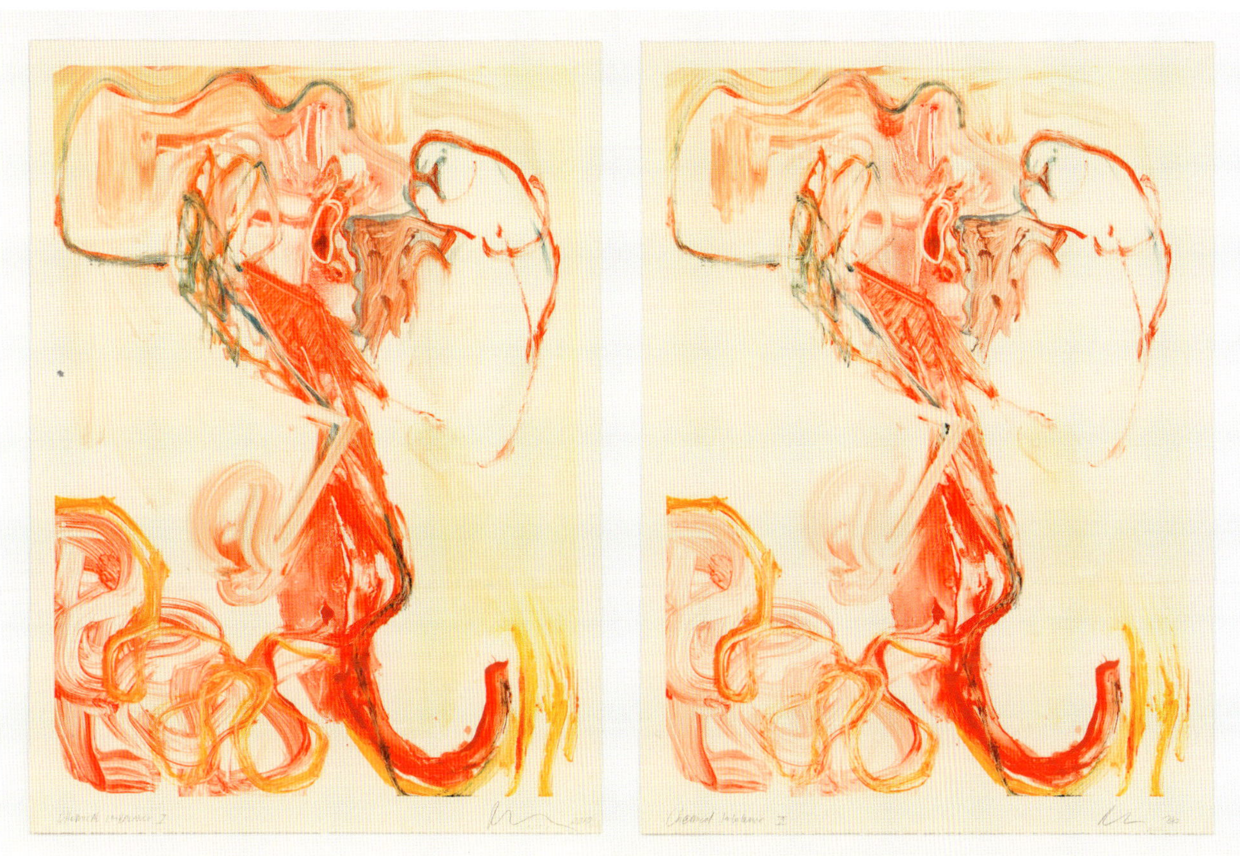

Chemical Imbalance I and III. Monotype with oil-based ink. 33" × 24.5". 2010.

ERIC AHO

Saxtons River, Vermont

The ghost—that delicate second or third impression from an inked monotype plate—might be one of the most beautiful and elusive of the medium's many painterly qualities. As a printmaker, Degas prized the delicate chiaroscuro of his cognate impressions and incorporated these increasingly fainter sheets, which served as quick templates to which he could later add pastel or gouache, as one of his chief tools. For my own work in monotype, the ghost is the link between successive images extending to a tonal train of thought. Like Degas, the ghost conjurer, I build up my monotypes through several subsequent states, with each resulting in a ghost impression. Traces of marks from previous states are then set in contrast to new layers of rich ink, varying in viscosity, then pressed finally into one surface simultaneously revealing and concealing the glow of the paper. Similar to Degas, I'm also after qualities in the monotype that float between the worlds of intention and incident, wherein even an accident becomes a desired effect.

Although I'm now primarily a painter, I began as a printmaker. Phenomenology, history, landscape, and the sensory exchange between the natural and painted world are at the forefront of my interests. The monotype, an indelible element of my artistic foundation that blurs the boundaries of painting and drawing, is an ethereal counterbalance to the materiality of painting.

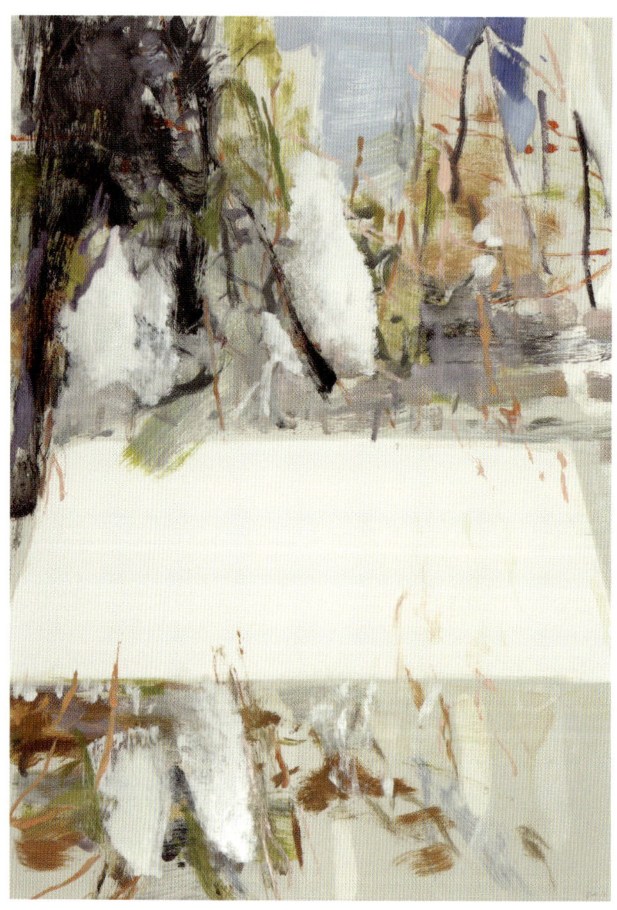

Covert Set 2-B. Monotype with oil-based inks. 29.5" × 41.75". 2010.

PHOTOS ARE COURTESY OF DC MOORE GALLERY, NEW YORK. PUBLISHED BY THE ARTIST. PRINTED BY MARINA ANCONA AT 10 GRAND PRESS.

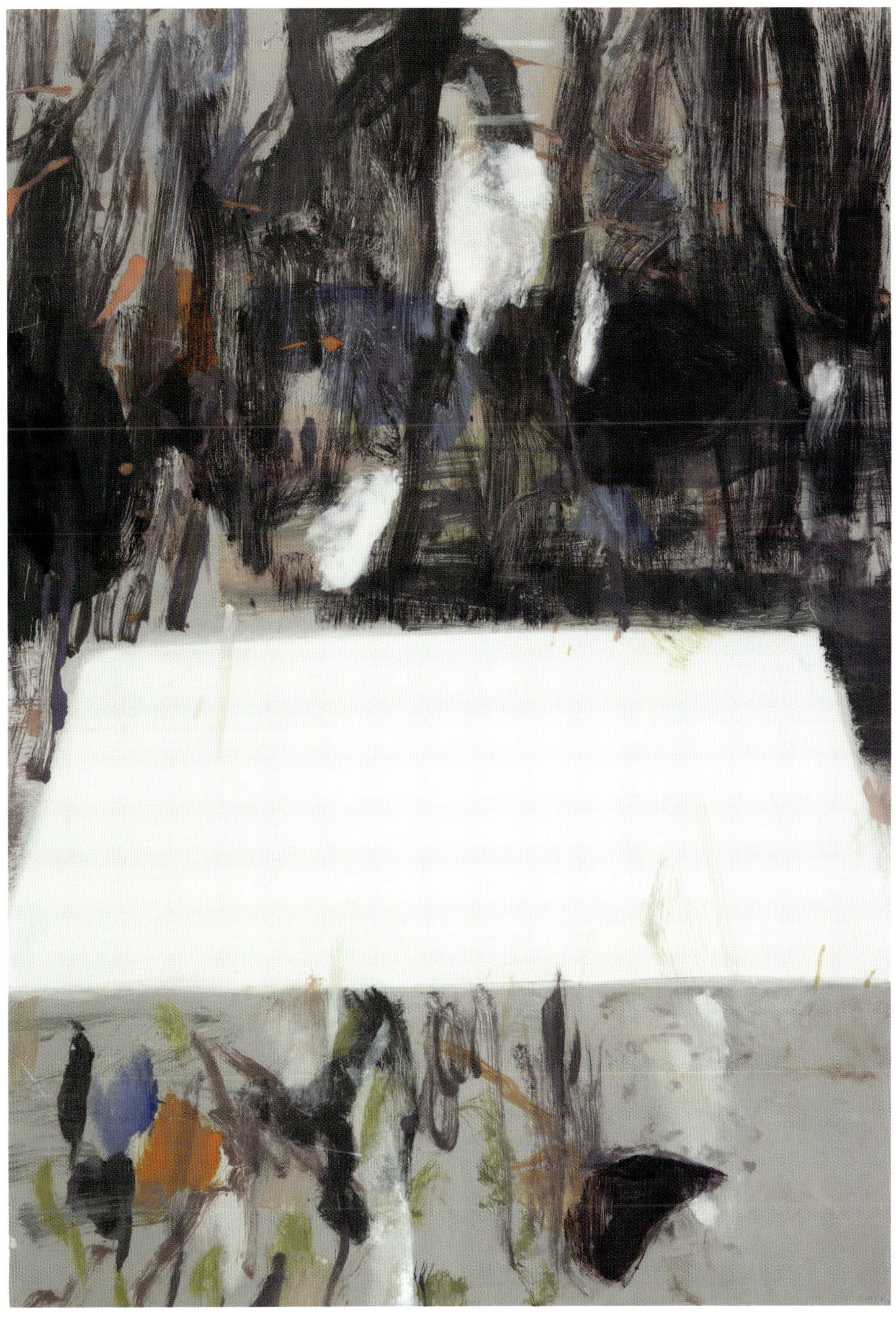

Covert Set 2-D. Monotype with oil-based inks. 29.5" × 41.75". 2010.

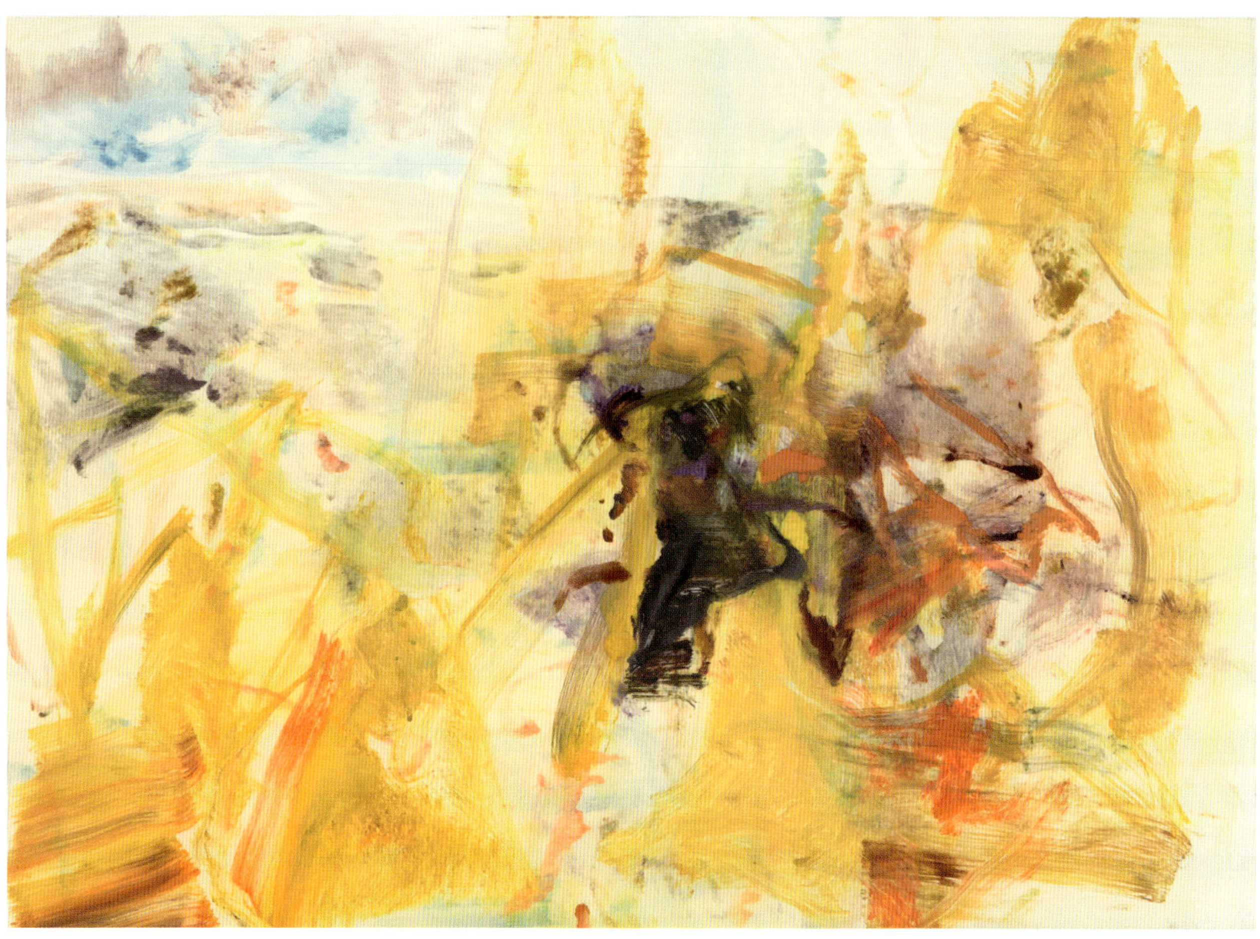

>
Translation 6. Monotype with oil-based inks. 29.5" × 41.75". 2013.

Translation 4. Monotype with oil-based inks. 29.5" × 41.75". 2013.

Translation 14. Monotype with oil-based inks. 29.5" × 41.75". 2013.

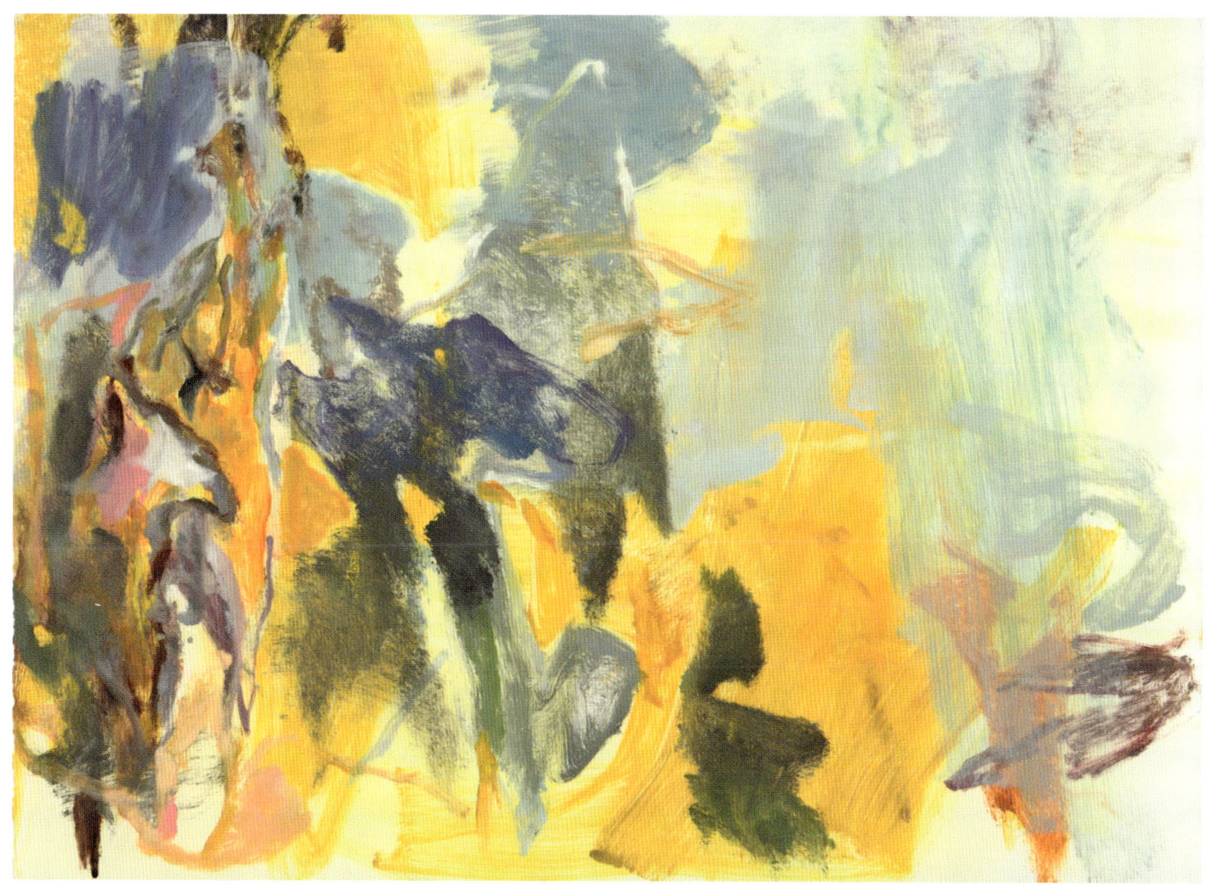

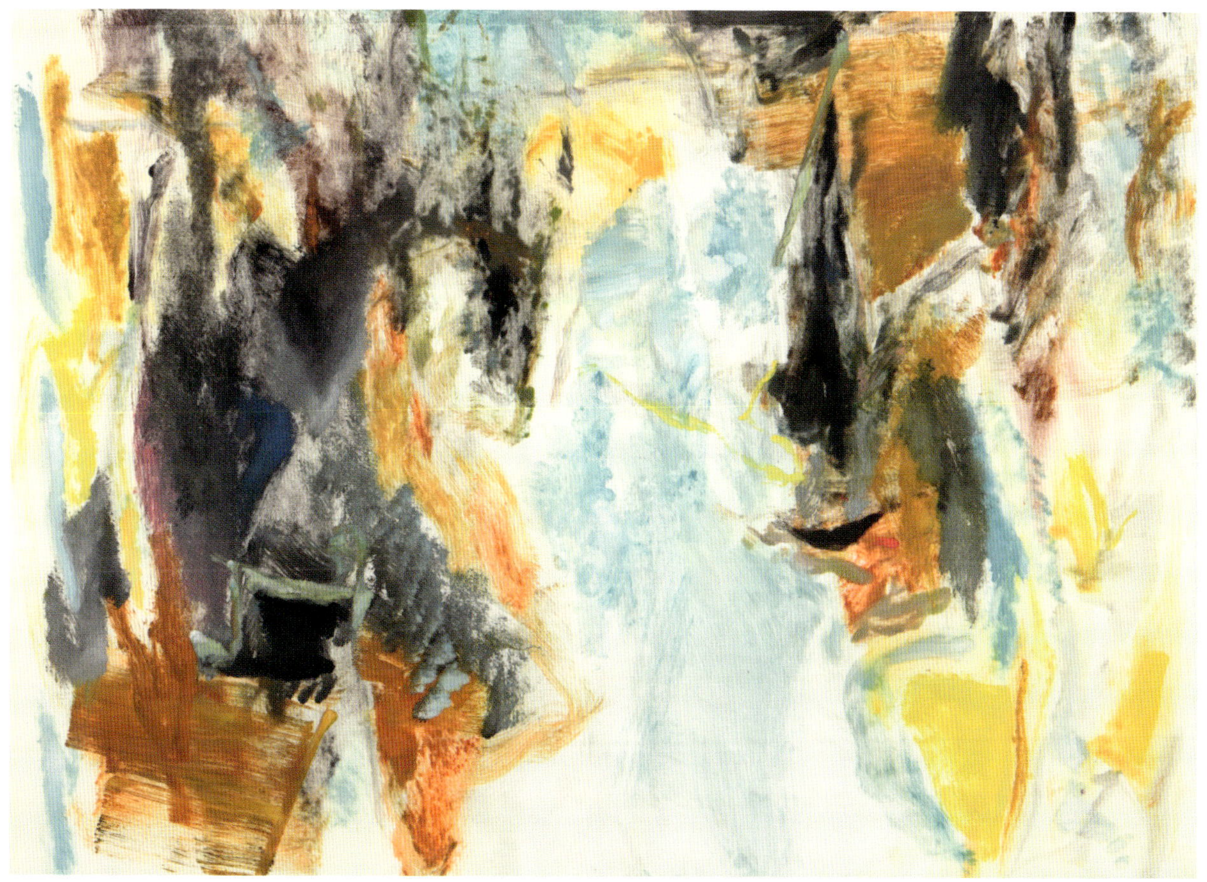

GREGORY AMENOFF

New York City & Ulster County, New York

For virtually all my early career in the 1970s and 1980s, I constructed my paintings with an extremely heavy impasto. Hence, they were almost entirely opaque and for the most part devoid, by design, of a sense of light. My preoccupation was rather on materiality and a sense of gravity. In the late 1980s, master printer Maurice Sanchez of Derriere L'Etoile studios suggested I come in to make monoprints. Maurice and I had collaborated on a group of lithographs, but I had never tried my hand at the monotype process. Our work together continued for nearly twenty years.

From the very first prints I made, I realized the power of transparency and its attendant luminosity. That realization came at a time when I was ready for a change in my paintings; the weight and opacity felt like a burden rather than an inspiration. Within a year of my first monoprint session with Maurice, I literally turned my painting process upside down. I dismissed oil paint from my studio and began working with water-based paint applied in thin layers, with a goal toward capturing the airy luminous (backlit) presence so naturally available in the production of monoprints. Although I returned to painting with oil, the experience I gained from making monoprints continues to influence my work.

PUBLISHED AND PRINTED BY THE ARTIST AND STEVE KURSH AT STEVE KURSH PRESS.

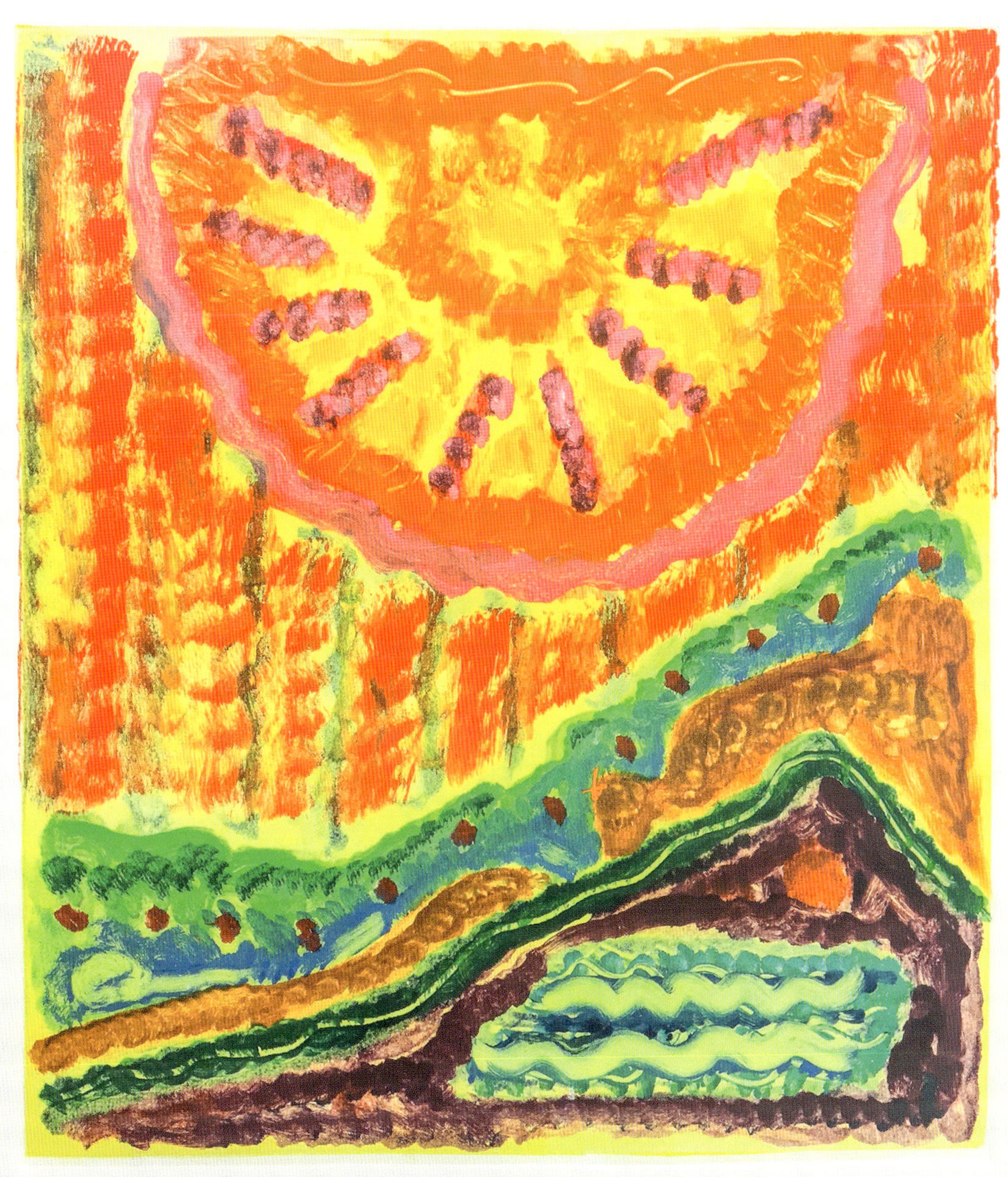

Untitled. Monotype with oil-based inks.
25" × 24". 2017.

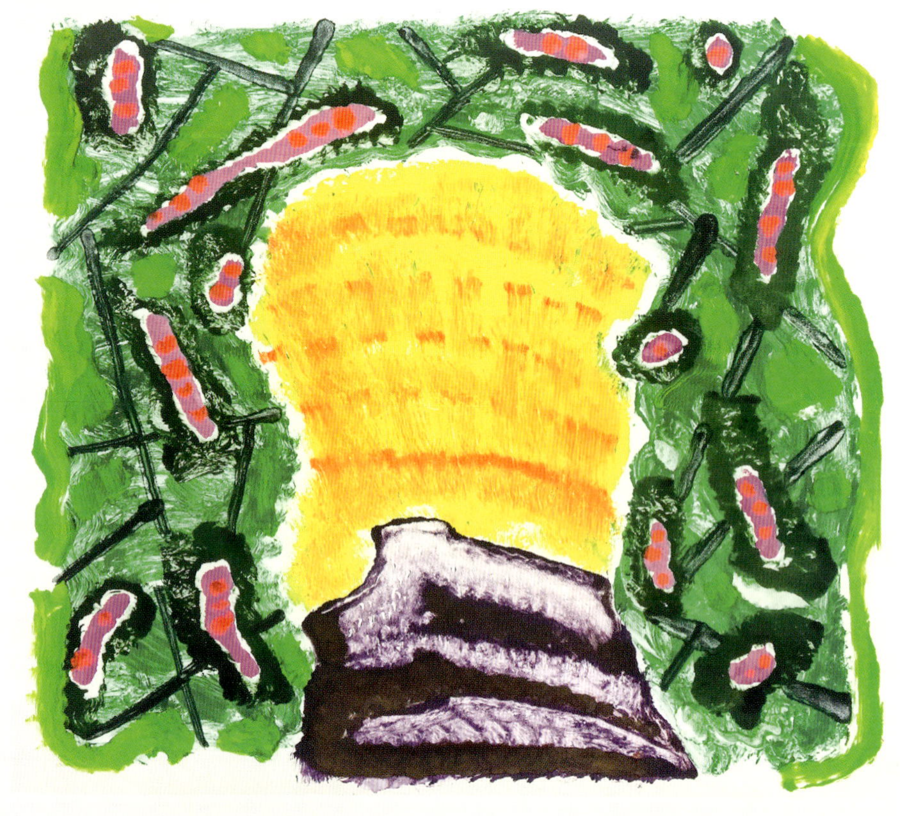

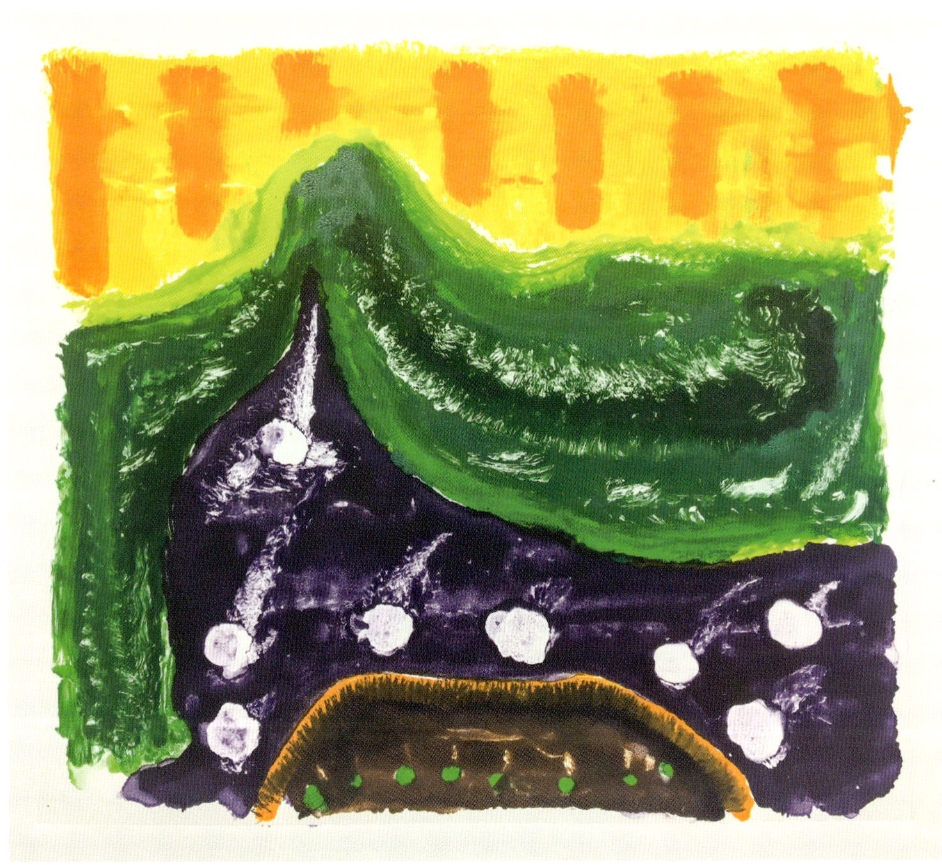

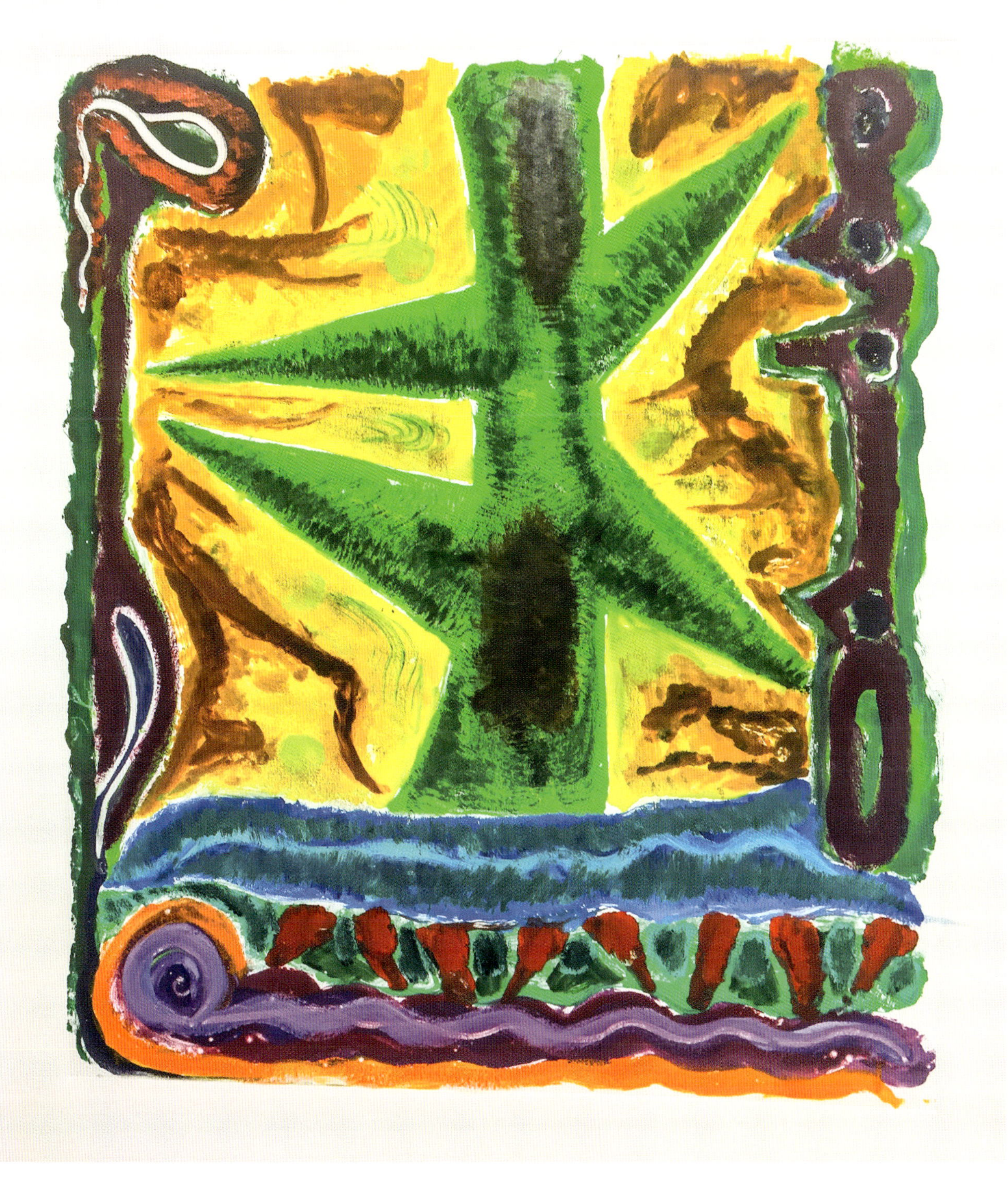

<
Untitled. Monotype with oil-based inks.
25" × 24". 2017.

Untitled. Monotype with oil-based inks.
25" × 24". 2017.

Untitled. Monotype with oil-based inks.
25" × 24". 2017.

R. ANTHONY ASKEW

Santa Barbara, California

As a fine artist with specialties in printmaking and painting, I am naturally drawn to monotypes. Monotype allows me to work directly on the plate in brushed, wiped, and rolled layers, and there is always visual excitement when the process reveals what the press transfers to the paper.

The ability to include selected images and papers with chine collé adds another dimension to the monotype. The papers are dampened, coated with wheat paste, laid onto the painted plate, and then included in the printing. Finding and collecting papers and images to combine in the printing process is both challenging and rewarding.

The optimism and zeal that life holds for me is a gift of the monotype process. I am grateful to work in the studio of master printer Michael McCabe in Santa Fe, New Mexico. He is a gifted artist and instructor: I am indebted to his friendship.

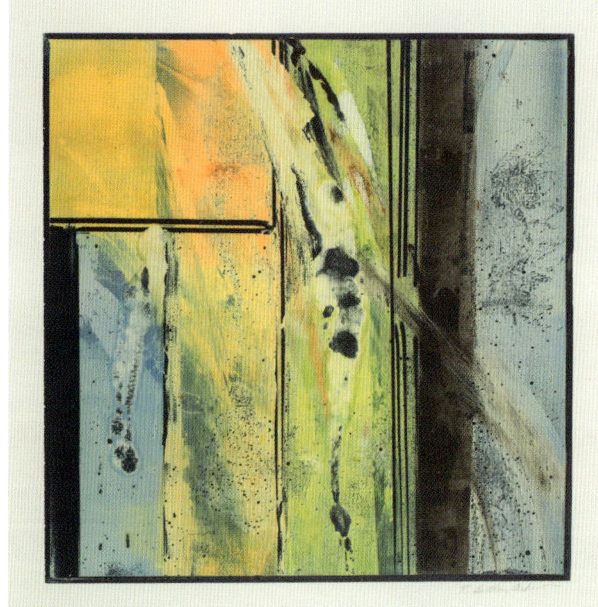

Redolent Sea. Viscosity monotype with oil-based inks on Arches 88 paper. 16" × 16". 2017.

ALL IMAGES ARE COURTESY OF CHRIS RUPP. PUBLISHED BY THE ARTIST. PRINTED BY MICHAEL MCCABE AT FOURTH DIMENSION STUDIO.

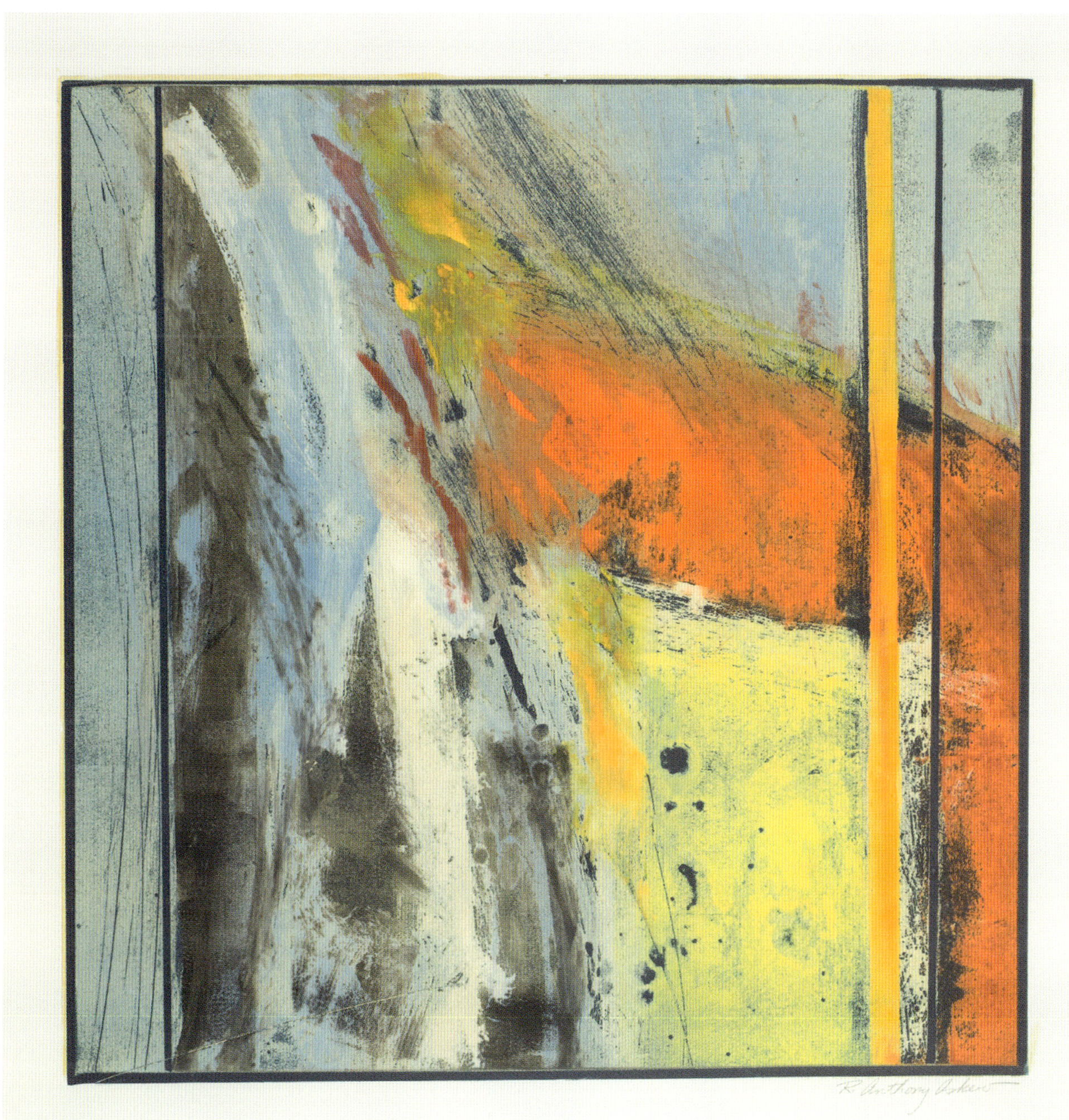

Morning Rife. Viscosity monotype with oil-based inks on Arches 88 paper. 16" × 16". 2017.

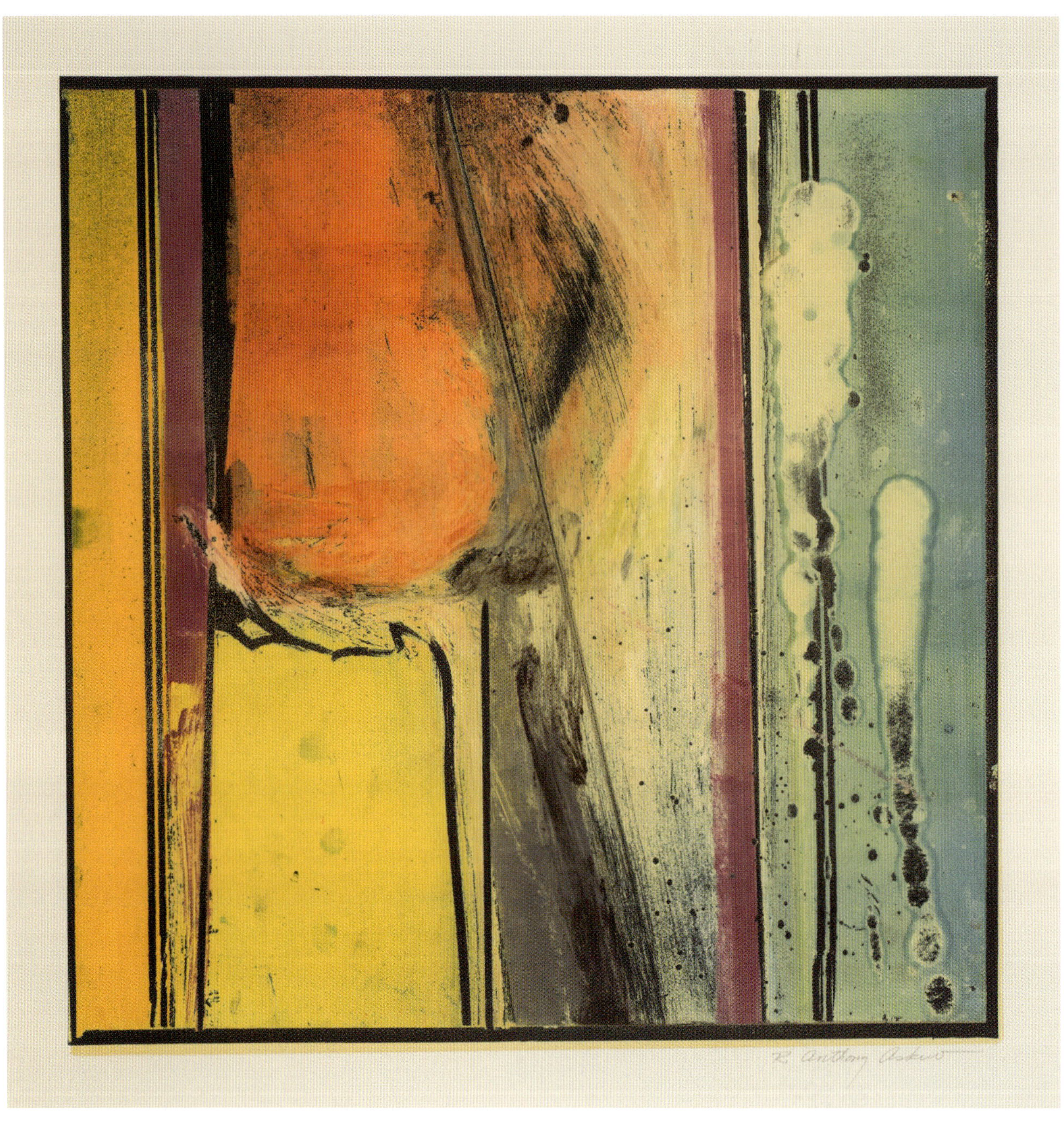

>
First Light. Viscosity monotype with oil-based inks on Arches 88 paper. 16" × 16". 2017.

Dominion. Viscosity monotype with oil-based inks and Solarplate intaglio on Arches 88 paper. 16" × 16". 2017.

Felicity. Viscosity monotype with oil-based inks on Arches 88 paper. 16" × 16". 2017.

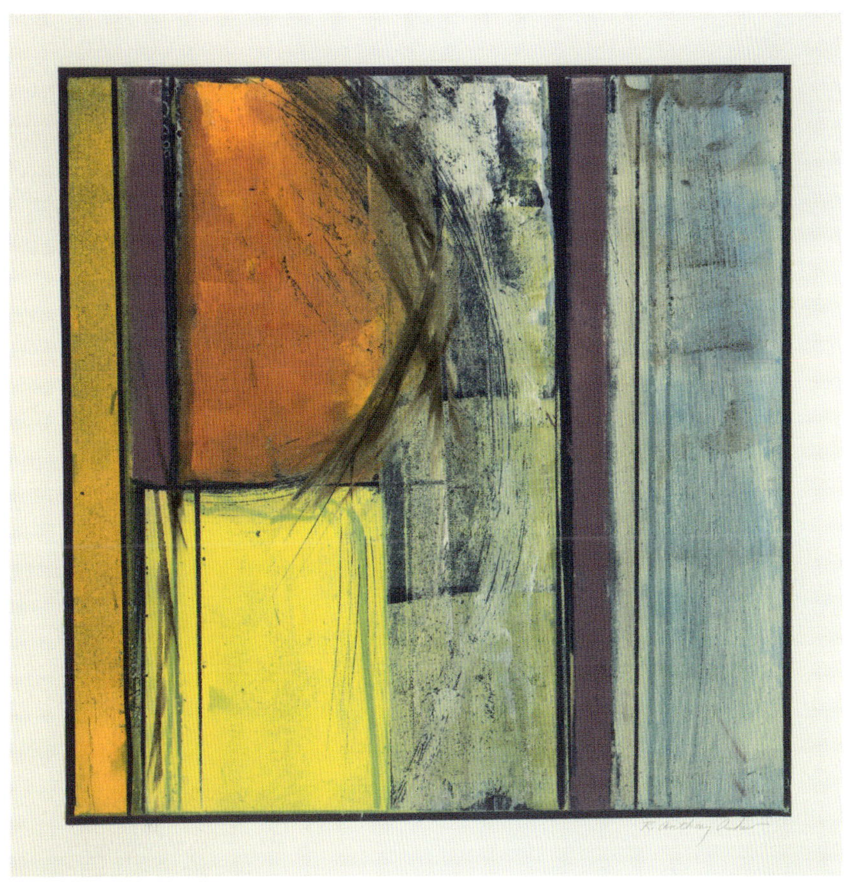

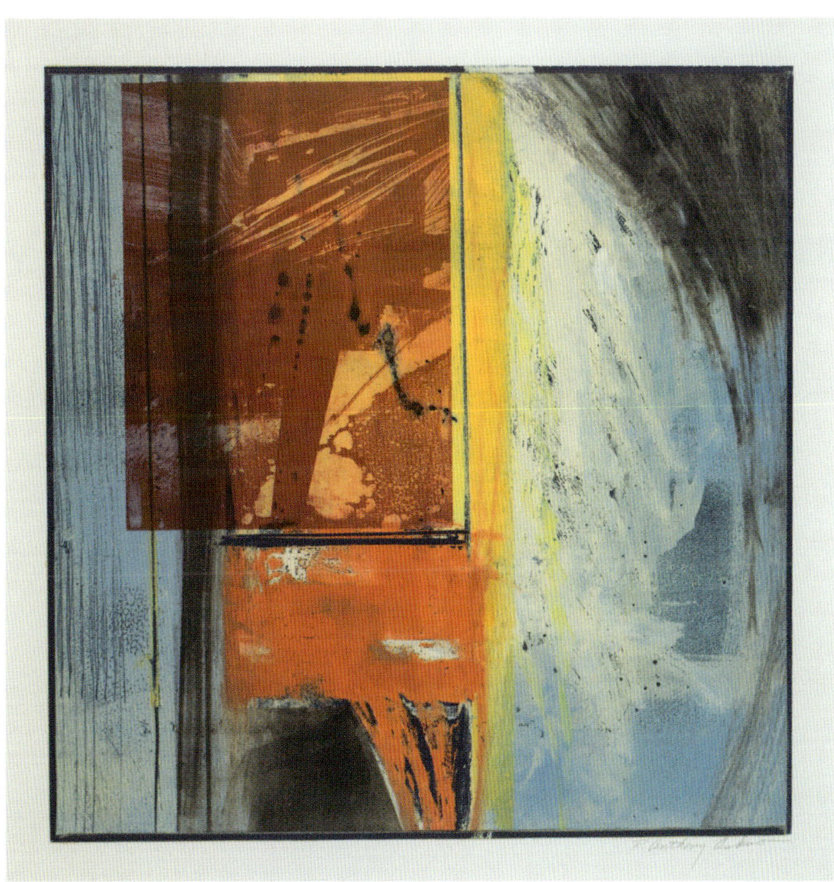

ANDREA BELAG

New York City & Far Rockaway, Queens, New York

The materiality of paper and the transparent layers of paint give monotypes light. I often adapt a configuration from a watercolor drawing or oil painting, but I make adjustments to the scale and for the new surface. I have to reimagine color relationships in the print, and I discover a new range of hues through layers of printing. The white paper is a brilliant surface, and I am now going full circle by bringing that light into my larger oil paintings.

The printing process changes what I have painted on the plate, and it adds an element of chance to the process. Monotype becomes the meeting of the known, the adapted, and the improvisational.

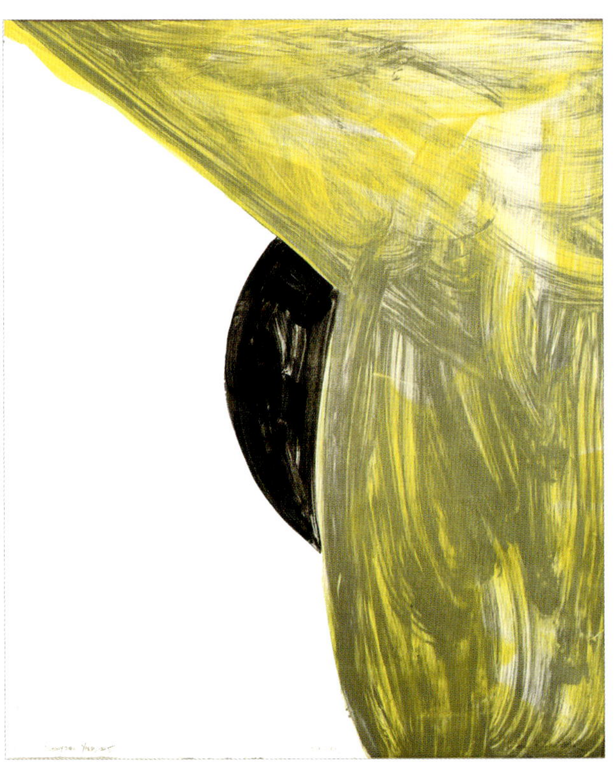

Sunnyside Yards 5. Monotype with oil-based inks. 33.75" × 29.5". 2016.

PUBLISHED BY VANDEB EDITIONS. PRINTED BY MARJORIE VANDYKE AT VANDEB EDITIONS.

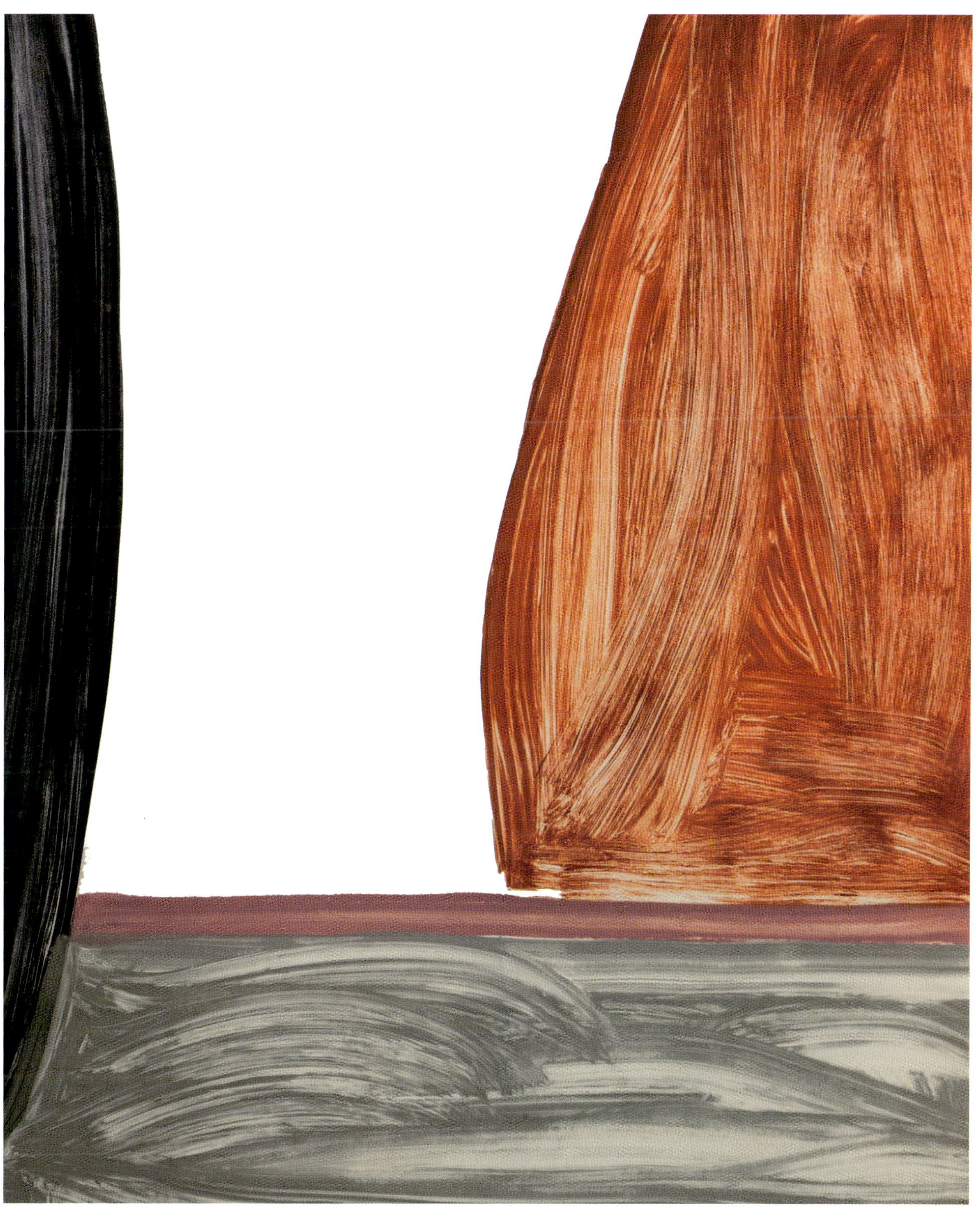

Sunnyside Yards 4. Monotype with oil-based inks. 33.75" × 29.5". 2016.

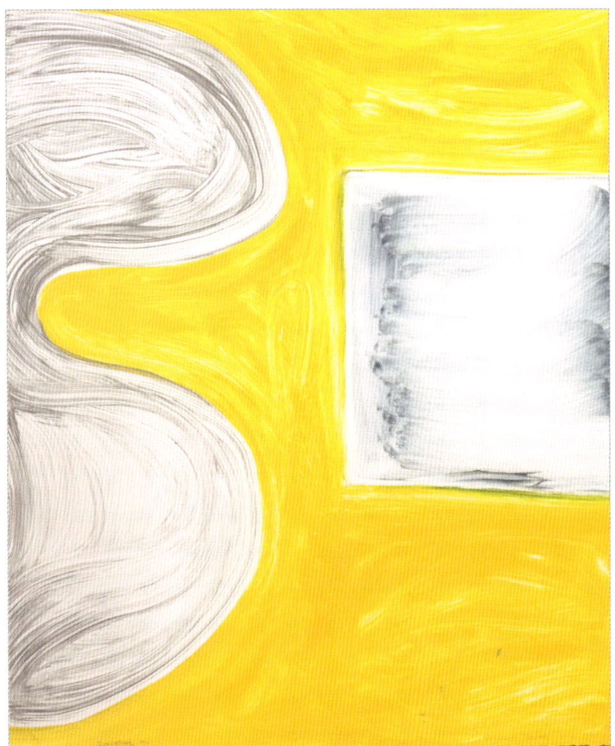

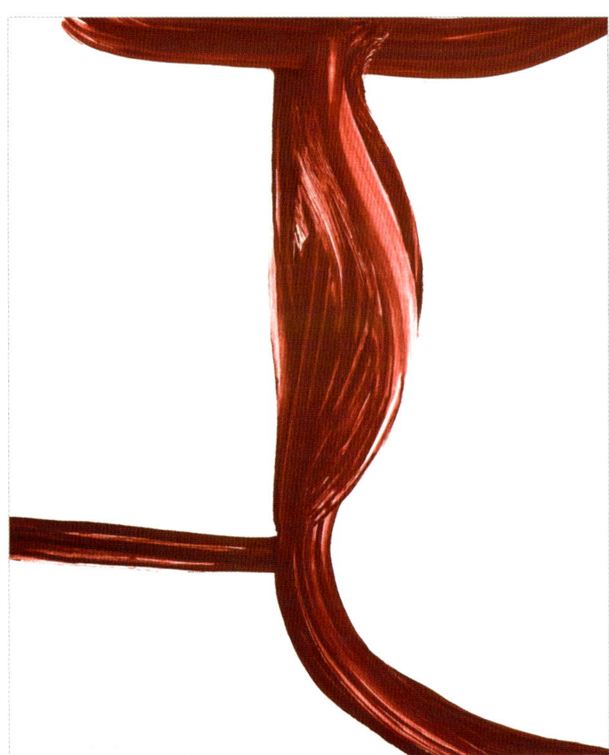

Sunnyside Yards 12. Monotype with oil-based inks. 33.75" × 29.5". 2016.

Sunnyside Yards 21. Monotype with oil-based inks. 33.75" × 29.5". 2016.

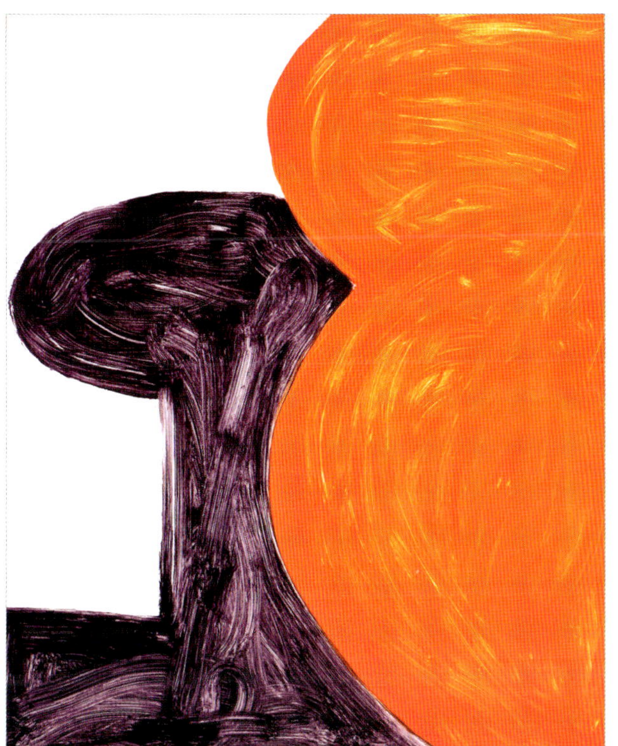

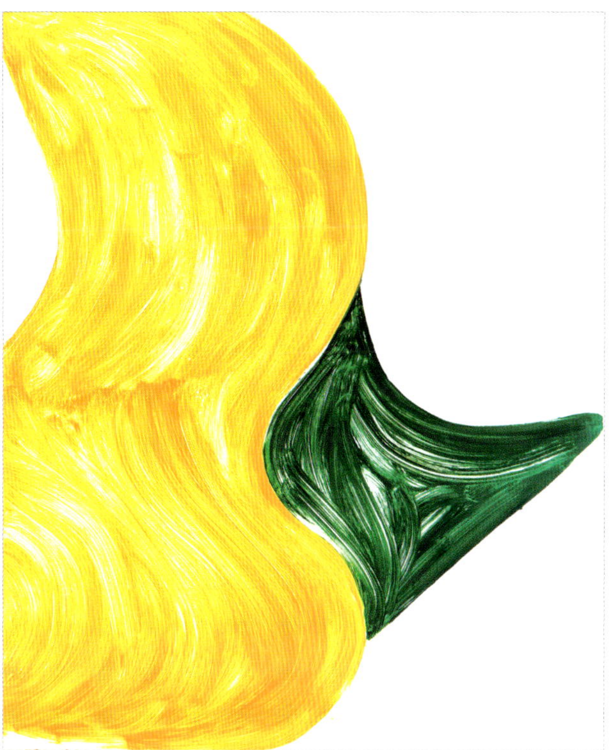

Sunnyside Yards 23. Monotype with oil-based inks. 33.75" × 29.5". 2016.

Sunnyside Yards 27. Monotype with oil-based inks. 33.75" × 29.5". 2016.

RICHARD BOSMAN

Esopus, New York

I have always loved making prints, although I think of myself primarily as a painter. With monotypes, the relationship to painting is as close as it could possibly be. What I find particularly compelling about the monotype is that it makes fluidity visible. It's always exciting and surprising to see what's painted on the plate transferred to paper. I want the images to be as immediate and direct as possible, and using oil paint with extender makes each individual brushstroke visible on the surface of the paper. I love that energy and speed, which relates to contemporary life, can be captured this way.

I am interested in narrative and am drawn to images of foreboding. Although there is no clear plot, viewers can make any number of story lines. I use sources in popular culture, and my pictures are culled from film, comic books, and the internet. I like them to have some ambiguity of meaning; I often incorporate a story that exists outside the picture frame—much like a film still. I am attracted to dramatic images, which have often been the subject of art and are reflected in contemporary media.

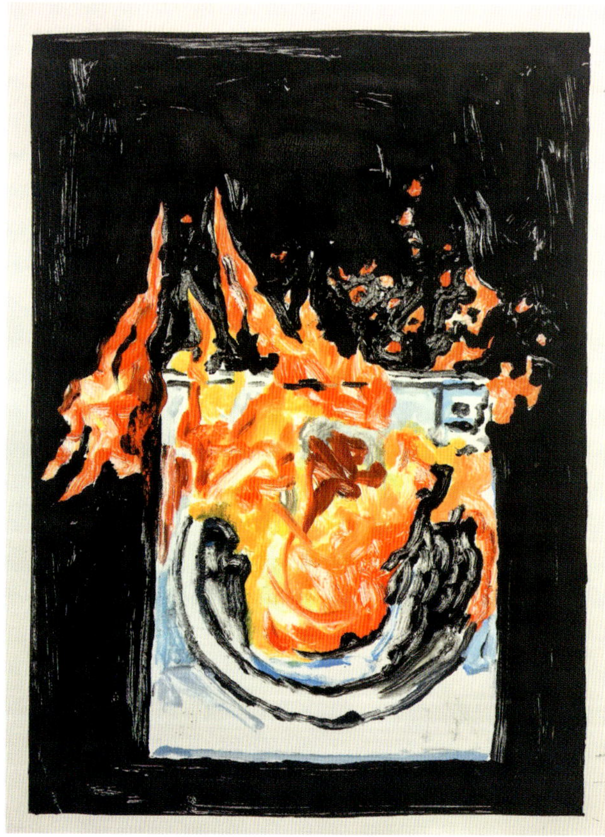

Dryer Fire. Monotype with oil-based inks. 24" × 18". 2017.

ALL PHOTOS ARE COURTESY OF JEN DRAGON, CROSS CONTEMPORARY ART. PUBLISHED AND PRINTED BY THE ARTIST.

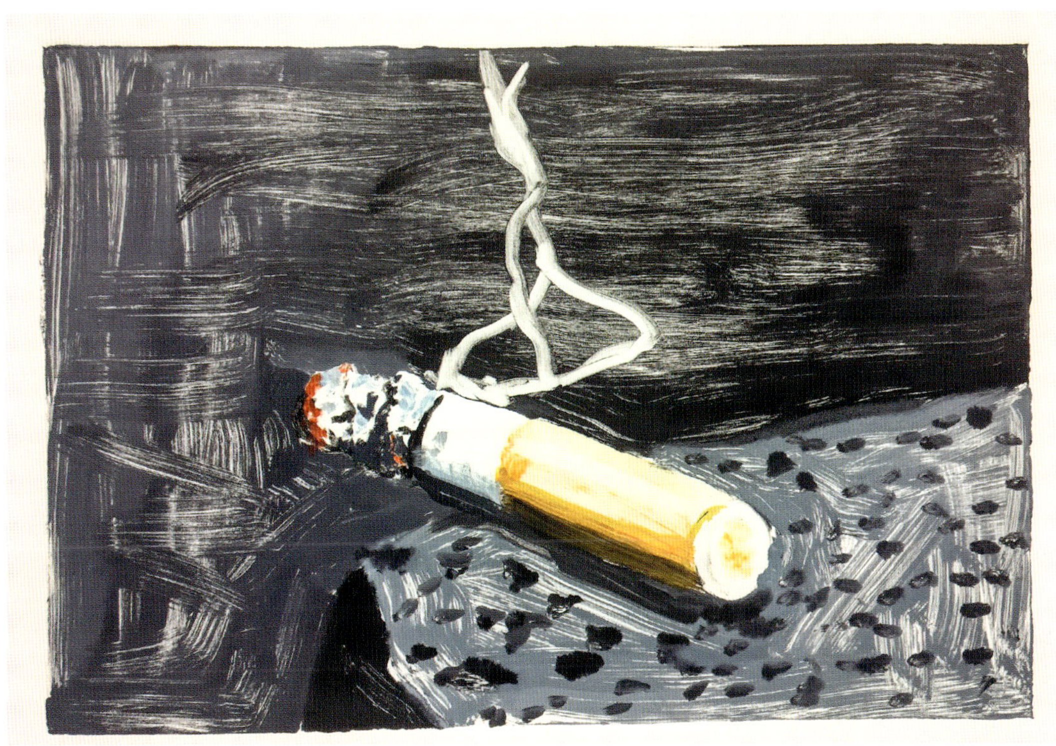

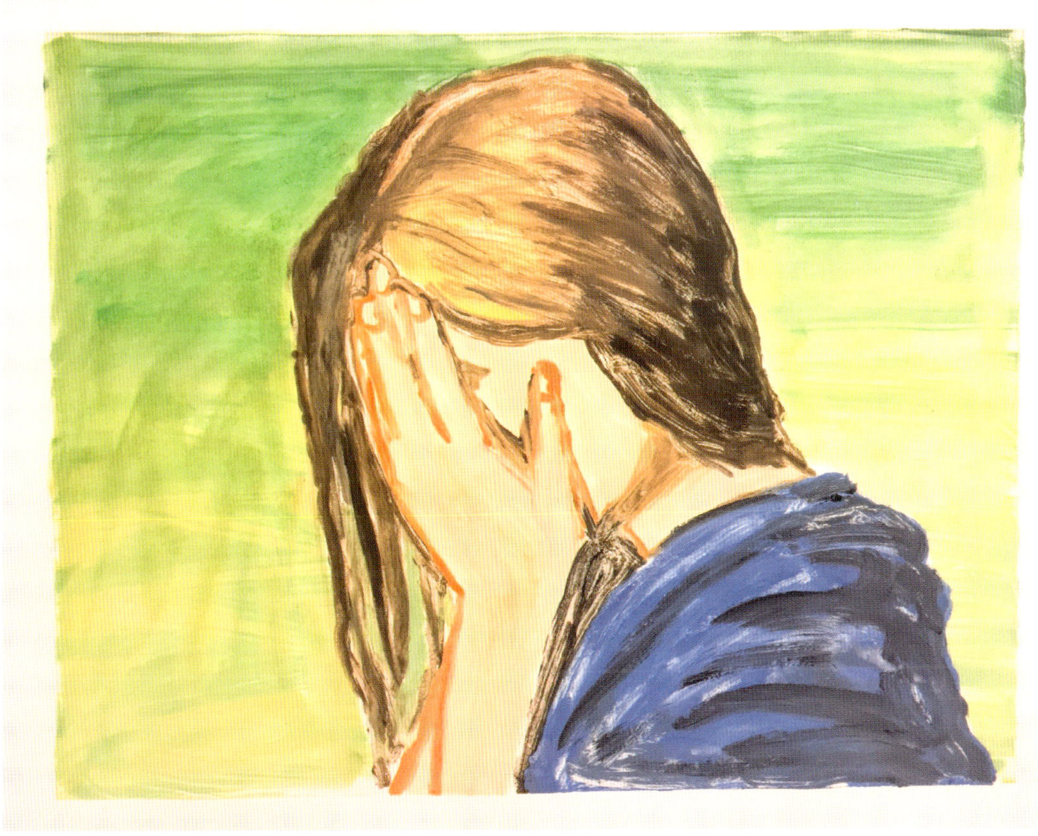

∧
Gasp. Monotype with oil-based inks. 24" × 18". 2017.

∨
Crying Woman. Monotype with oil-based inks. 18" × 24". 2017.

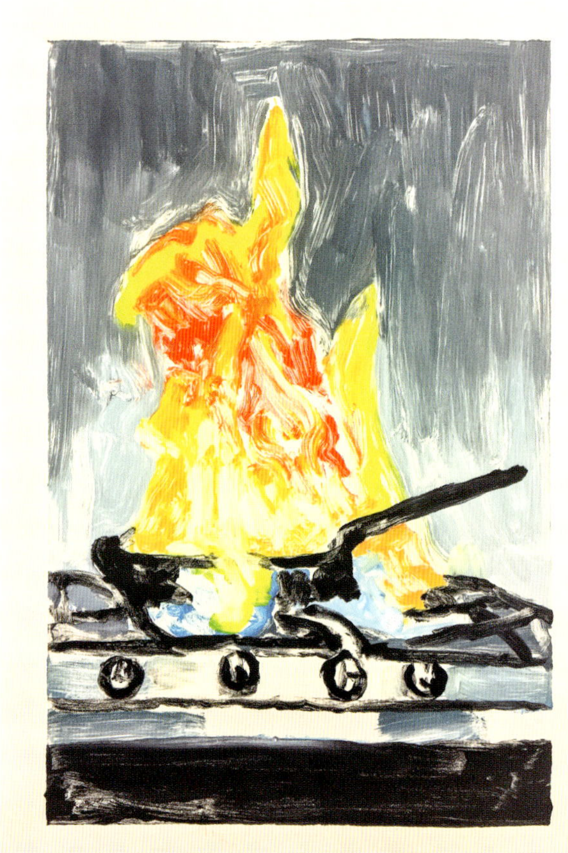

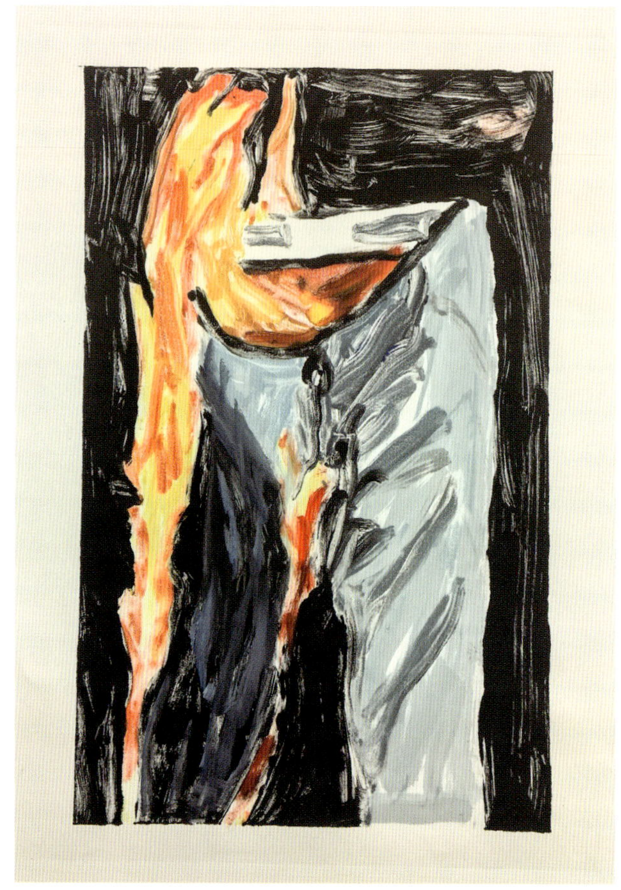

Stovetop Fire. Monotype with oil-based inks. 20" × 14". 2017.

Pants on Fire. Monotype with oil-based inks. 20" × 14". 2017.

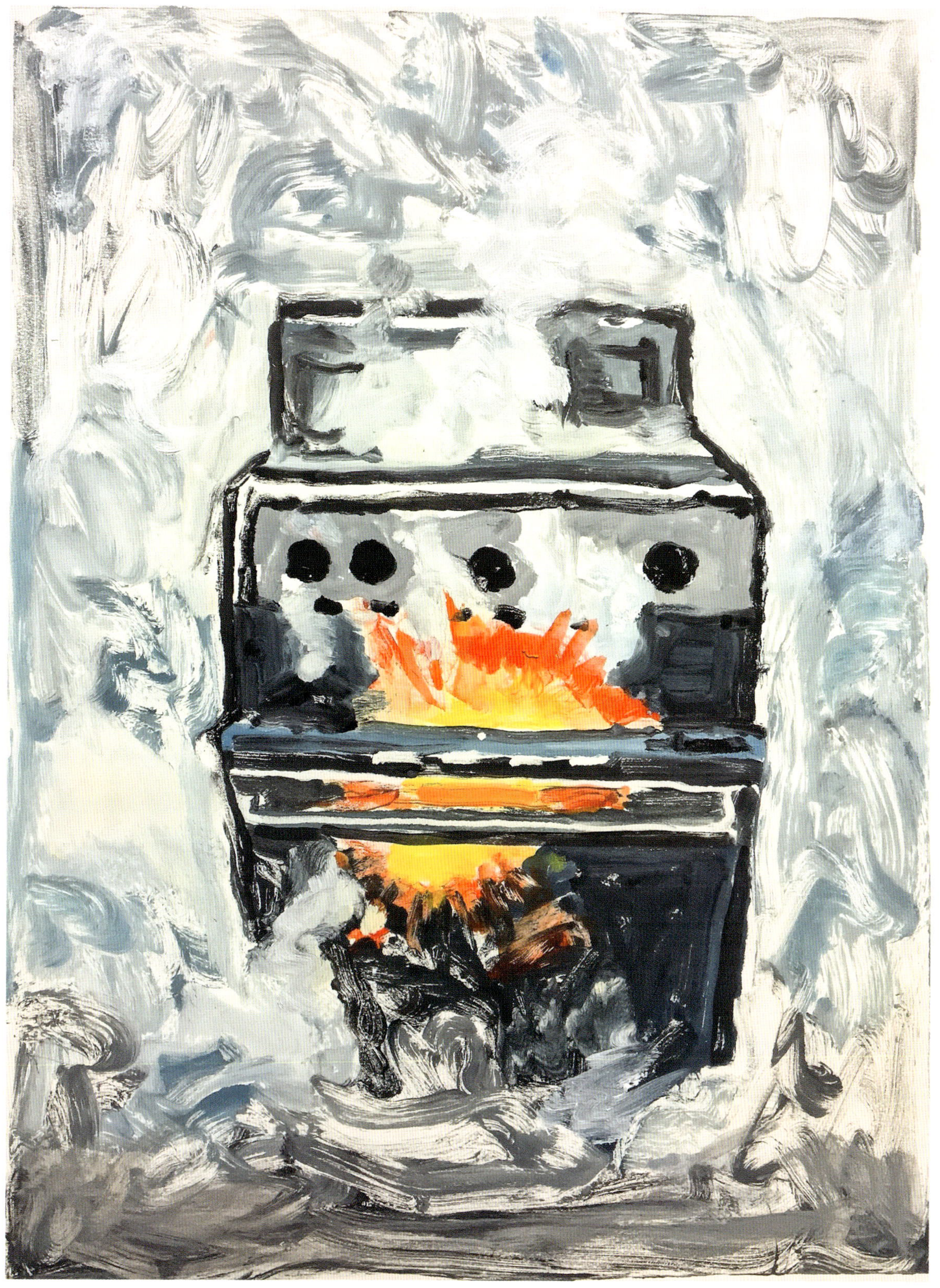

Oven Fire. Monotype with oil-based inks. 18" × 24". 2017.

BRAD BROWN

San Francisco, California

In 2012, I worked at Shark's studio in Holualoa, Hawaii, on a group of colorful monotypes titled *'Okina*. The *'okina* is the Hawaiian representation of the glottal stop, a separation of doubles. The monotypes in this series are doubles, divided into upper and lower halves. I worked on two plates simultaneously. Both plates came together to form the image. Where the plates meet at the join, there is a "kiss"; this is literally the crux of the matter. In these prints, there is a simultaneous division and unity: the halves are joined and remain separate.

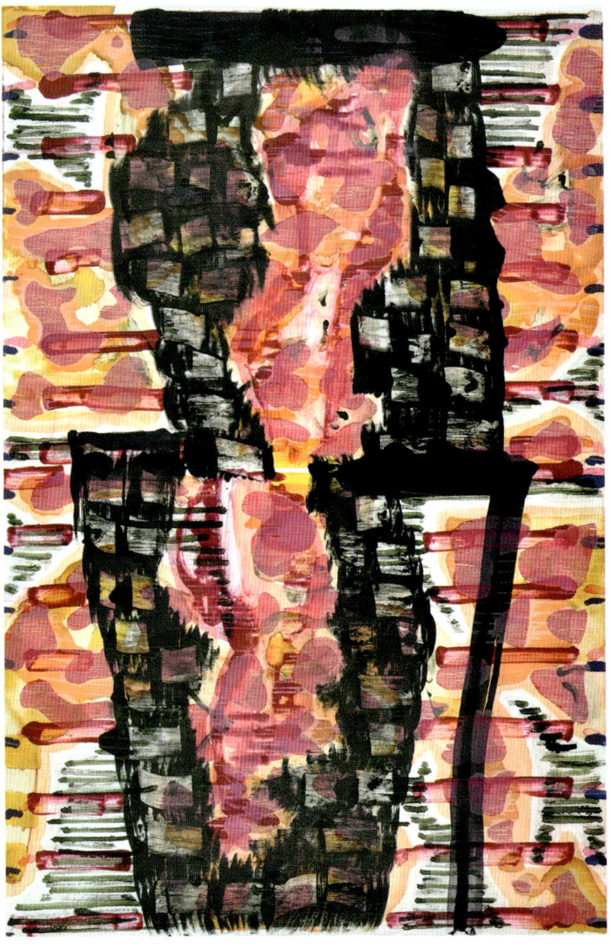

'Okina #32. Monotype with oil-based inks. 22.25" × 15". 2012.

ALL PHOTOS ARE COURTESY OF BUD SHARK. PUBLISHED AND PRINTED AT SHARK'S INK BY BUD SHARK.

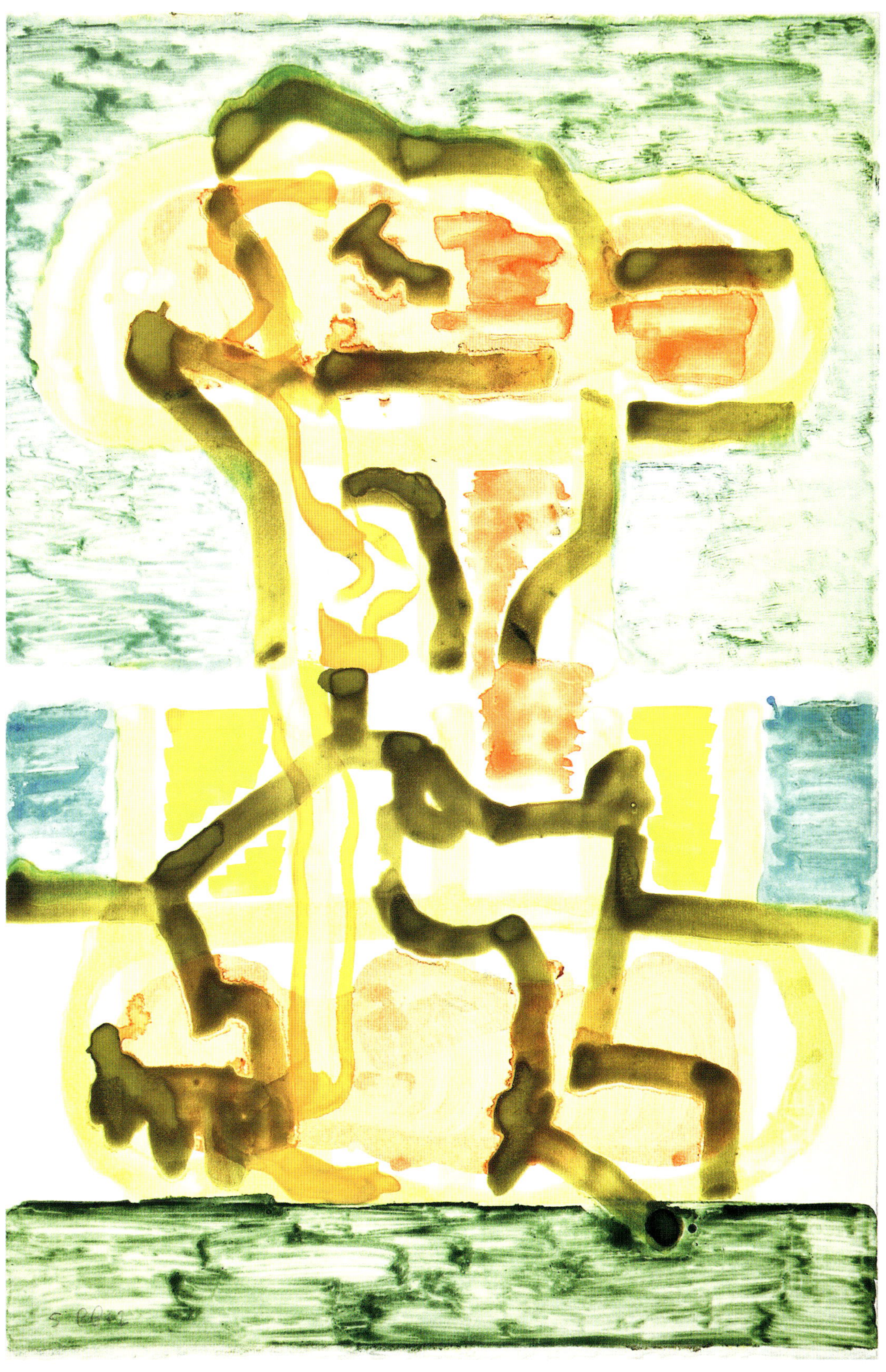

'Okina #5. Monotype with oil-based inks. 22.25" × 15". 2012.

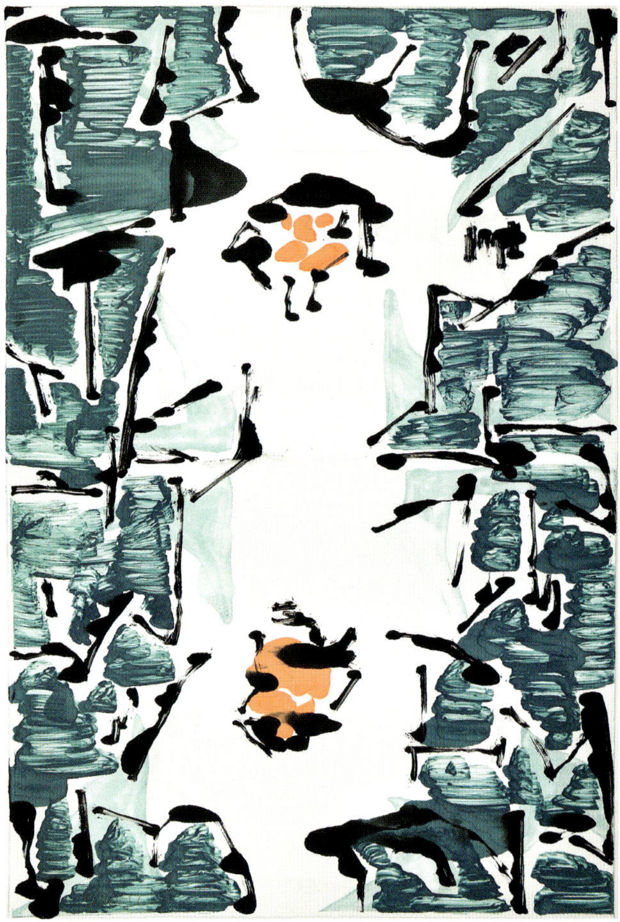

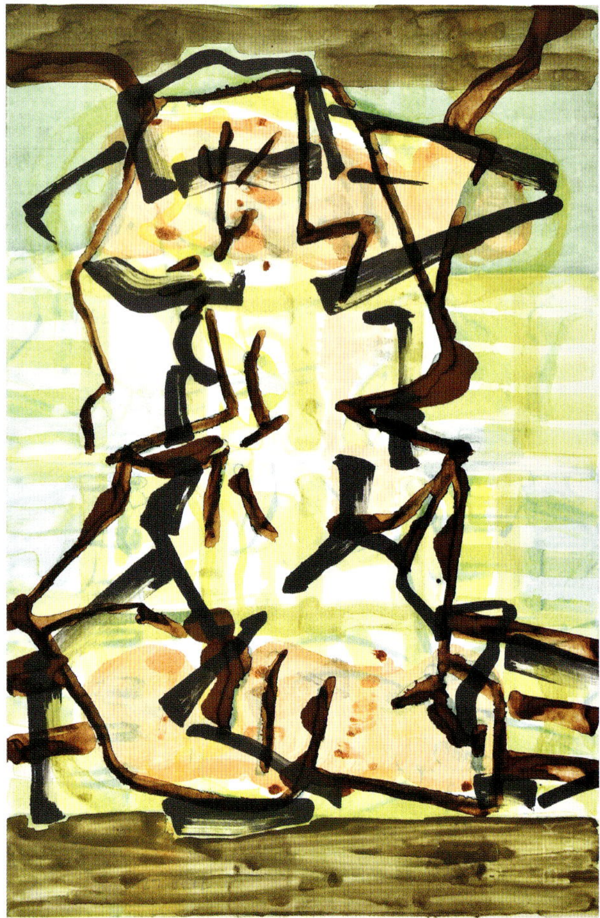

'Okina #12. Monotype with oil-based inks. 22.25" × 15". 2012.

'Okina #27. Monotype with oil-based inks. 22.25" × 15". 2012.

GREGORY CRANE

Brooklyn, New York

One of the most important elements in making a painting is orchestrating the parts toward a greater effect. The process of turning an observation into a painting begins to get more and more abstract as I translate what I see. This translation, or distillation, is the "basic anatomy" of a painting. I'm attracted to nature more for what I imagine it to be. Metaphor becomes the driving force behind the painting, making it more vivid, more alive. I want the painting to be more than just what it looks like.

I first began using the monotype process as a tool toward developing my larger oil paintings. I found it an excellent way of reviewing the image I was considering. The process allows me to work out all the formal elements that compose a painting, such as composition, light effect, form, and color. The monotype is pulled from a Plexiglas plate that has been prepared to accept oil color. In three to four hours, I can have a finished print that possesses an aspect of vitality and spontaneity all its own. Over the years of printmaking, I have come to appreciate and value these unique immediate qualities of the monotype.

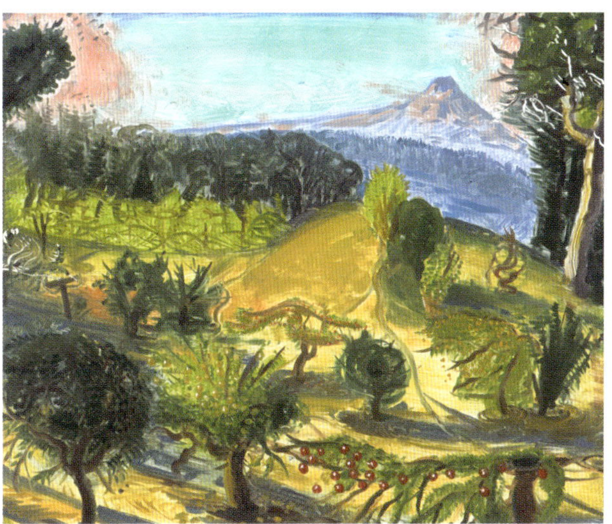

Mike's Orchard. Monotype with oil-based inks. 20" × 25". 2002. *Photo is courtesy of Cheryl Pelavin*

PUBLISHED BY PELAVIN EDITIONS. PRINTED BY CHERYL PELAVIN AT CHERYL PELAVIN FINE ARTS.

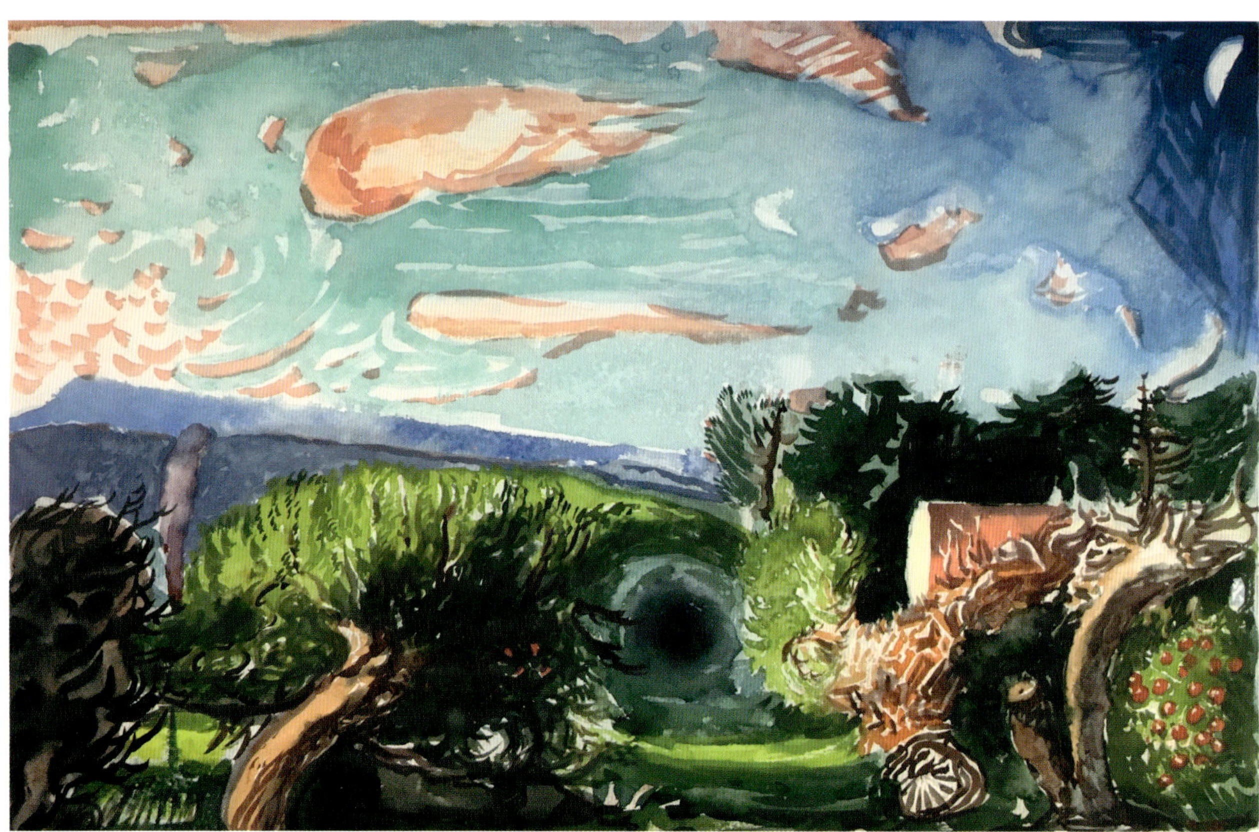

Orchard & Water Tank. Monotype with oil-based inks. 16" × 28". 2008. *Photo is courtesy of Russ Spitkovsky*

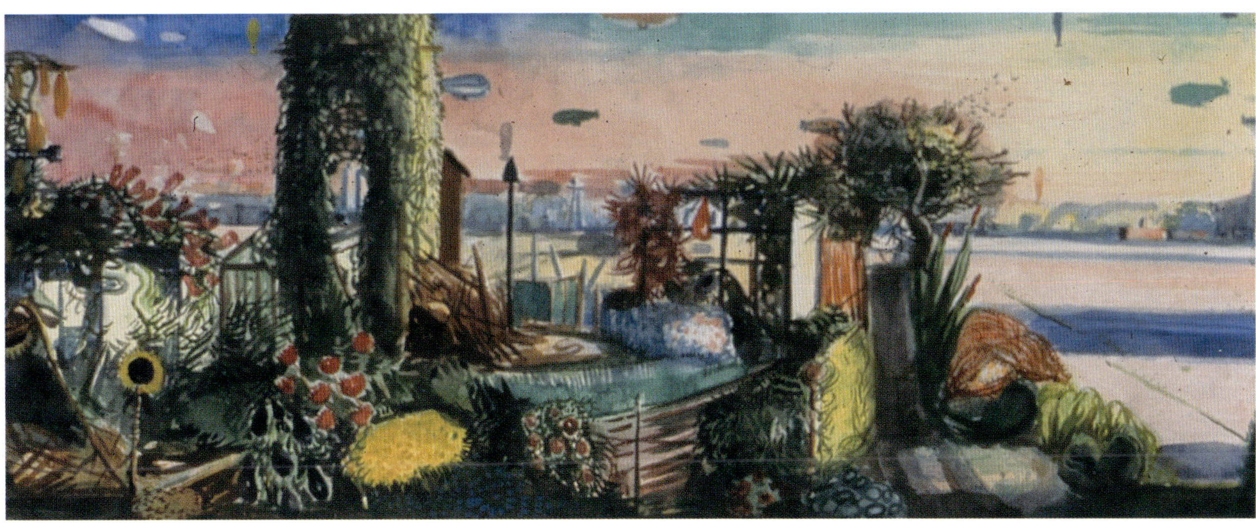

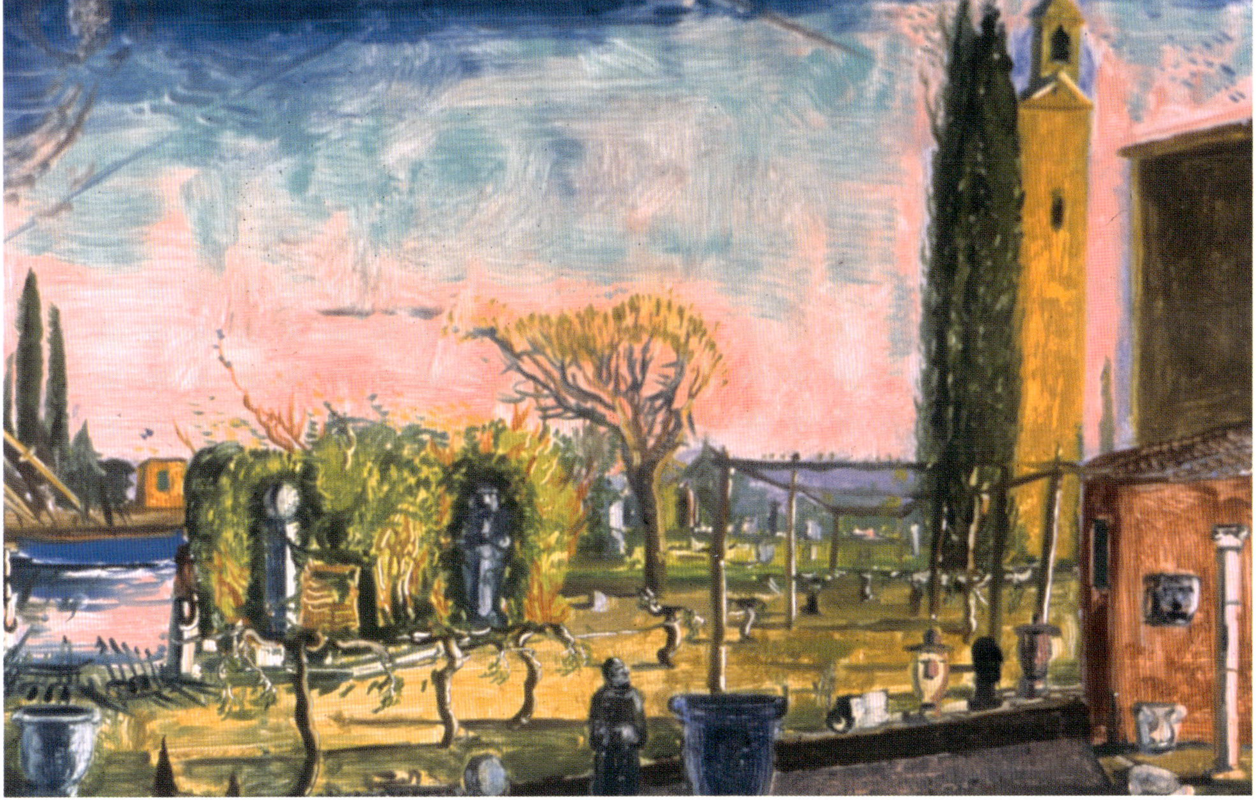

∧

Blimps & Balloons (A Memorial). Monotype with oil-based inks. 16" × 32". 2008. *Photo is courtesy of Cheryl Pelavin*

∨

Torcello with Statues. Monotype with oil-based inks. 18" × 32". 2004. *Photo is courtesy of Cheryl Pelavin*

PAUL DERUVO

Norwalk, Connecticut

My love for printmaking began on an improvised setup in my father's photography studio, after learning about the reductive monotypes that underpinned Degas's pastel drawings and seeing the wheat-pasted linoleum cuts of the street artist Swoon. I am eternally grateful that shortly after being introduced to printmaking, I had the opportunity to begin apprenticing at the Center for Contemporary Printmaking, under Anthony Kirk, a master printer who introduced me to the transmutative power, nuance, and possibilities available to those who practice the art of fine printing.

My images address intimacy, gender, and love as it appears in our daily lives. Through the devotional act of rendering and the craft of fine printing, I hope to reclaim part of the history of representation and find expression for a shared moment of compassion.

Monotype allows me to create images reductively, by first rolling a thin, even layer of ink onto copper or plastic and then carefully removing and manipulating that ink with dry brushes and rags to reveal the luminosity of the paper. In this way, the image slowly takes form on the plate; each time as the image emerges, it transports me back to the developing trays in the darkroom of my father's photography studio, where I devoted myself, for the first time, to a mysterious process.

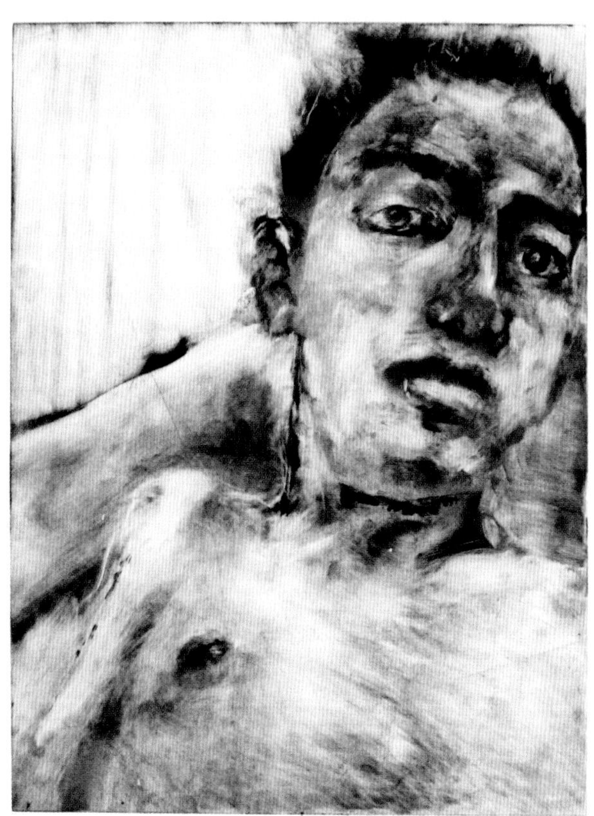

Varient. Monotype with oil-based inks on Hahnemuhle copperplate paper. 12" × 9". 2012.

PUBLISHED AND PRINTED BY THE ARTIST.

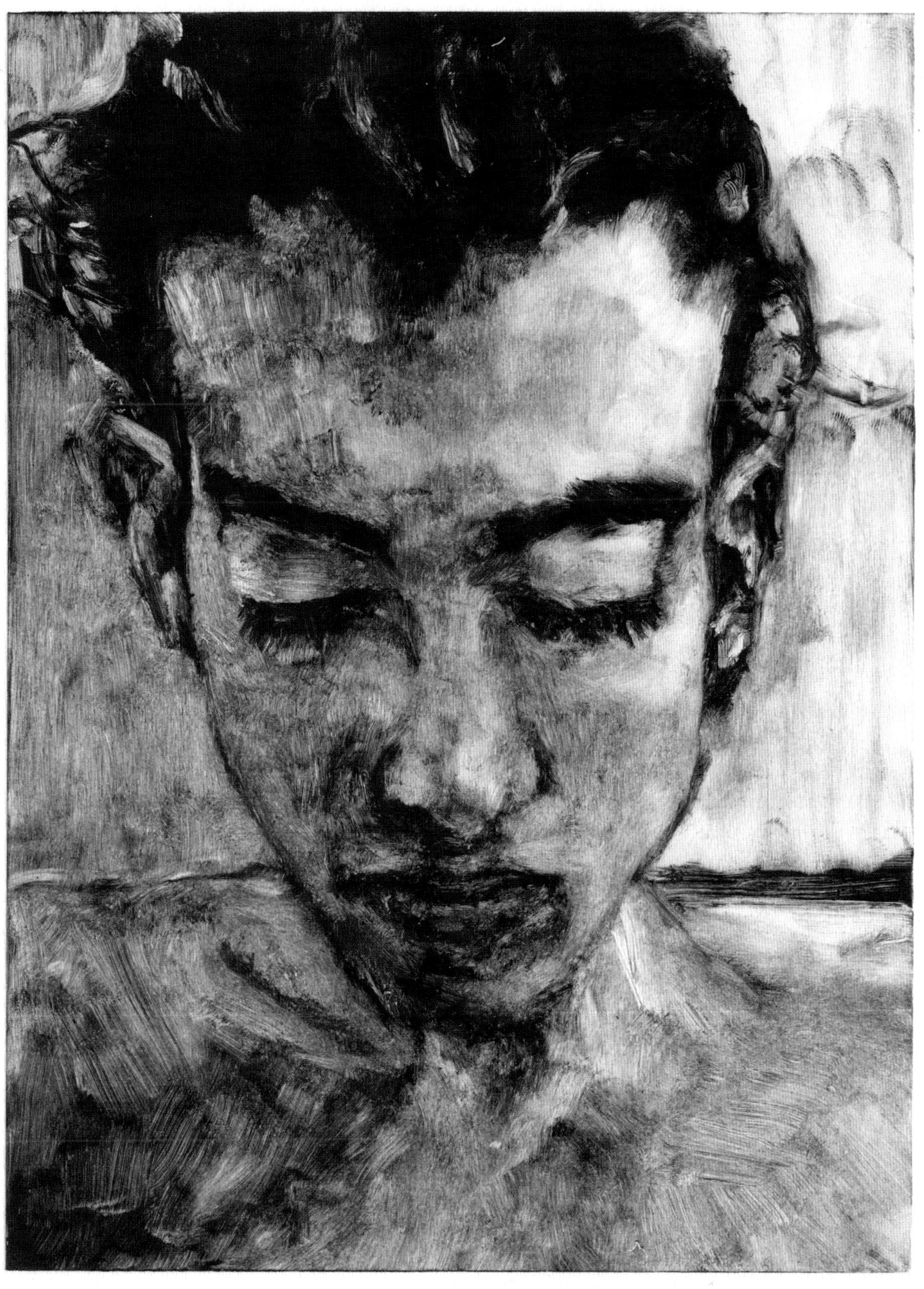

Love and Isolation I. Monotype with oil-based inks on Hahnemuhle copperplate. 12" × 9". 2012.

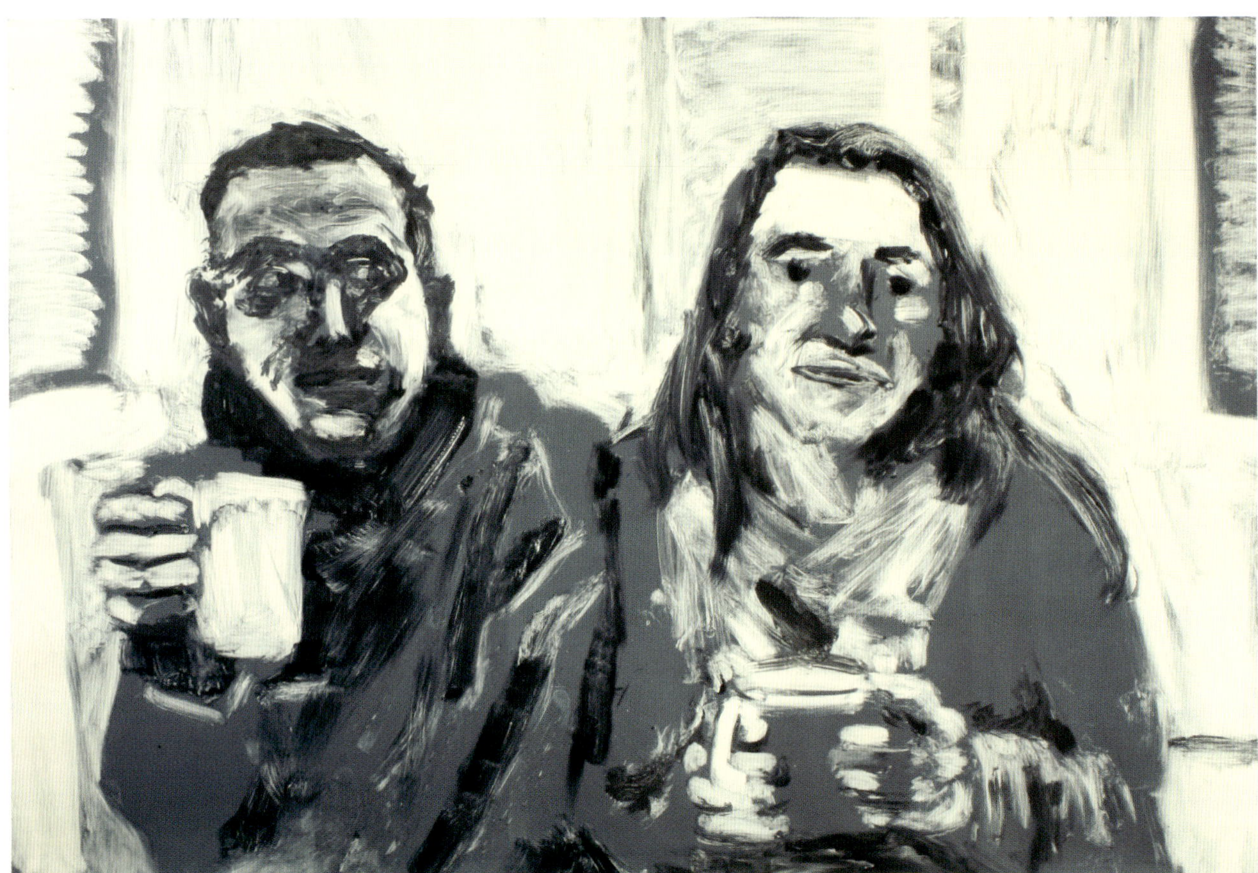

Parents. Monotype with oil-based inks on Rives heavyweight paper. 24" × 36". 2010.

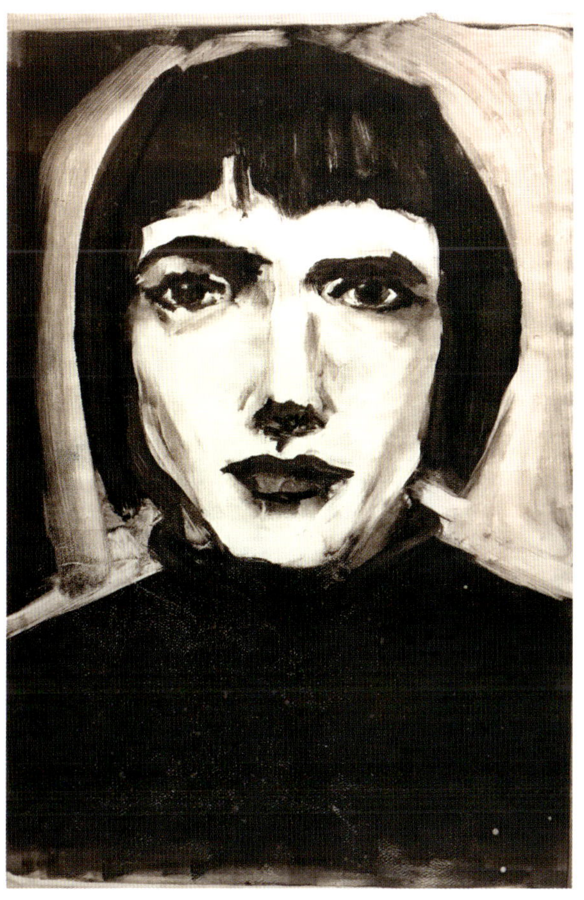

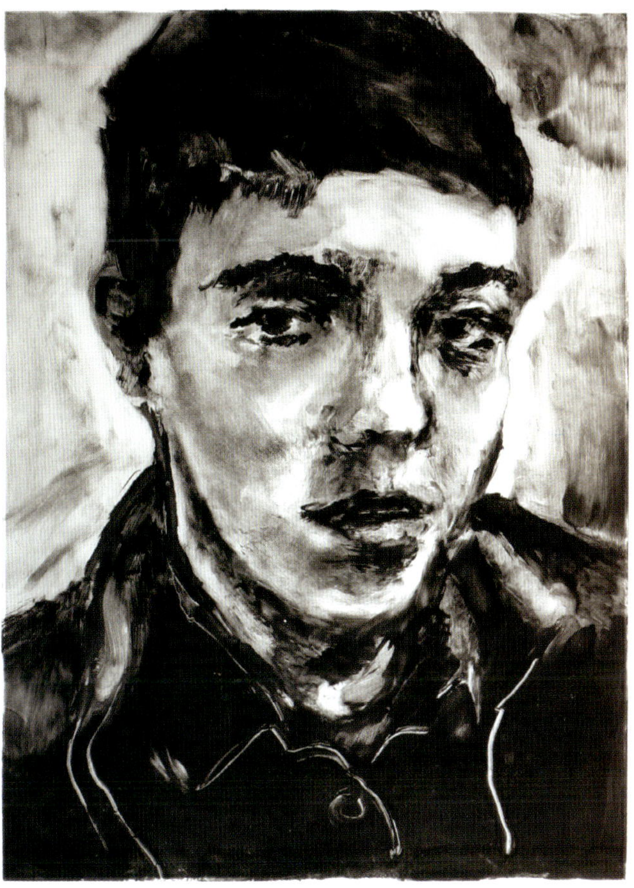

In Drag 1. Monotype with oil-based inks on pastel paper. 16" × 12". 2012.

Portrait. Monotype with oil-based inks on Hahnemuhle copperplate paper. 16" × 12". 2012.

VALENTINA DUBASKY

New York, New York

Monotype is a central part of my art. My monotypes, paintings, and works on paper are closely related, with influence and inspiration flowing between all three. My recent series of monotypes, Silk Route–inspired birds created at Tandem Press, are inspired by my travels on the Silk Routes, where I researched Buddhist cave painting and ancient art to prepare for my own "modern-day, cave-wall" artwork.

At Tandem Press, I began by creating monotypes directly on the plate. In a process that combines gesture and tactility, improvisation and experimentation, the possibilities for combining techniques become an exciting part of a collaborative process. The recent monotypes incorporate encaustic, handwork, and chops made from my line drawings.

Monotype is open, fluid, and completely contemporary; therefore, it is an ideal medium to explore new meanings. Monotype also includes the element of time, which makes the results of creating a monotype nearly immediate. It is possible to have a dialogue with the finished monotypes while creating new ones. I know of no other medium that can do all this in quite the same way. With monotypes, the artist can create, respond, and create again.

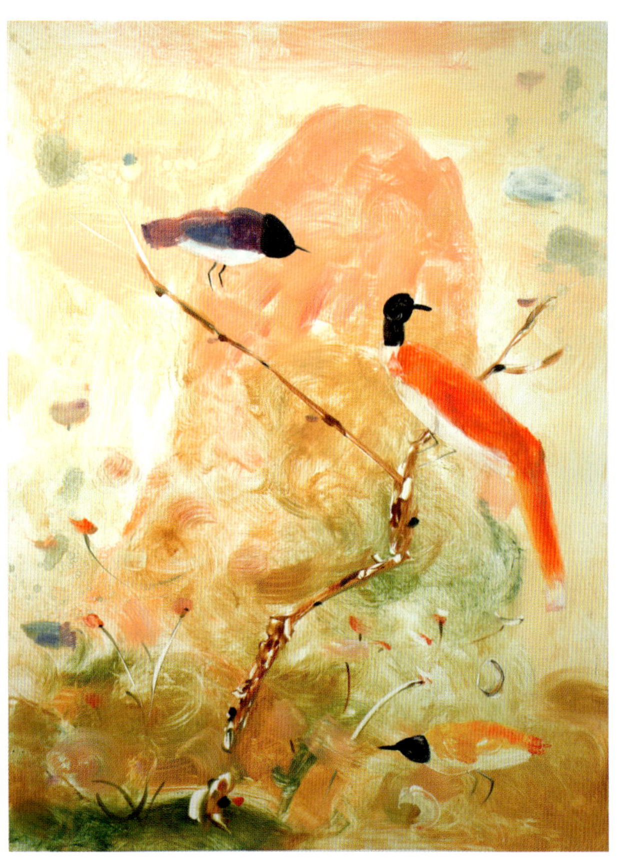

Adagio Mountain Birds. Monotype with oil-based inks. 53.75" × 41.25". 2013.

ALL PHOTOS ARE COURTESY OF TANDEM PRESS. PUBLISHED AND PRINTED AT TANDEM PRESS.

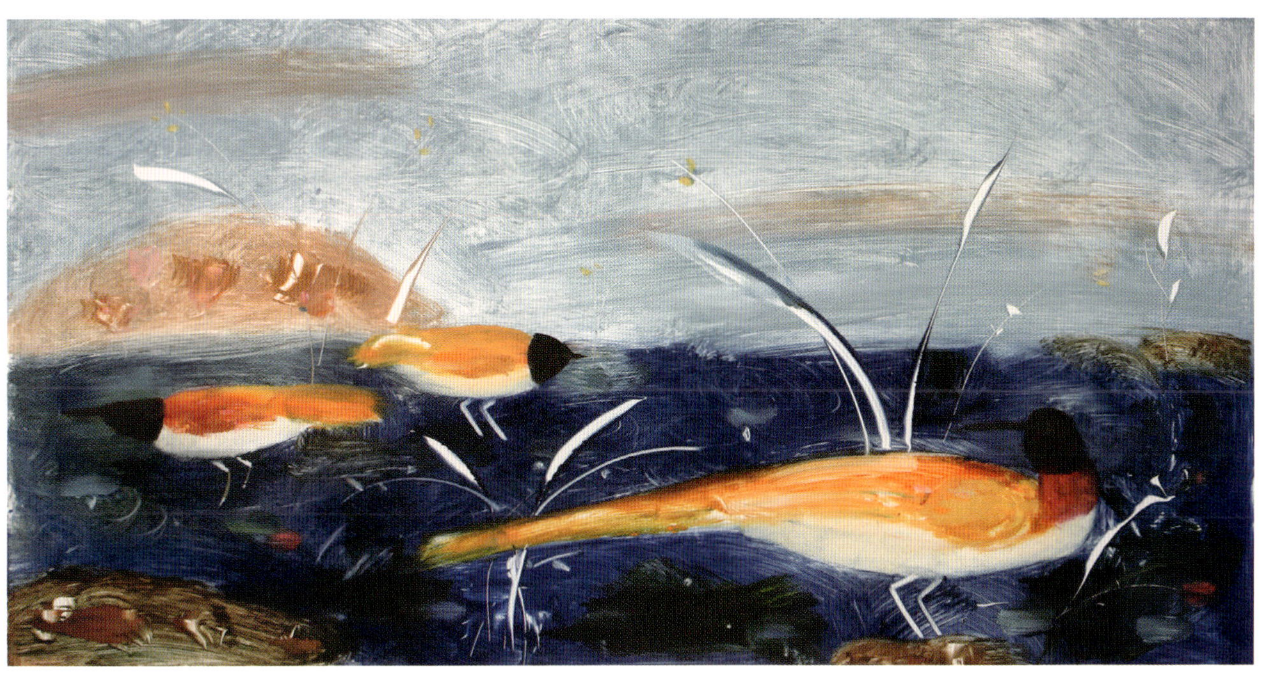

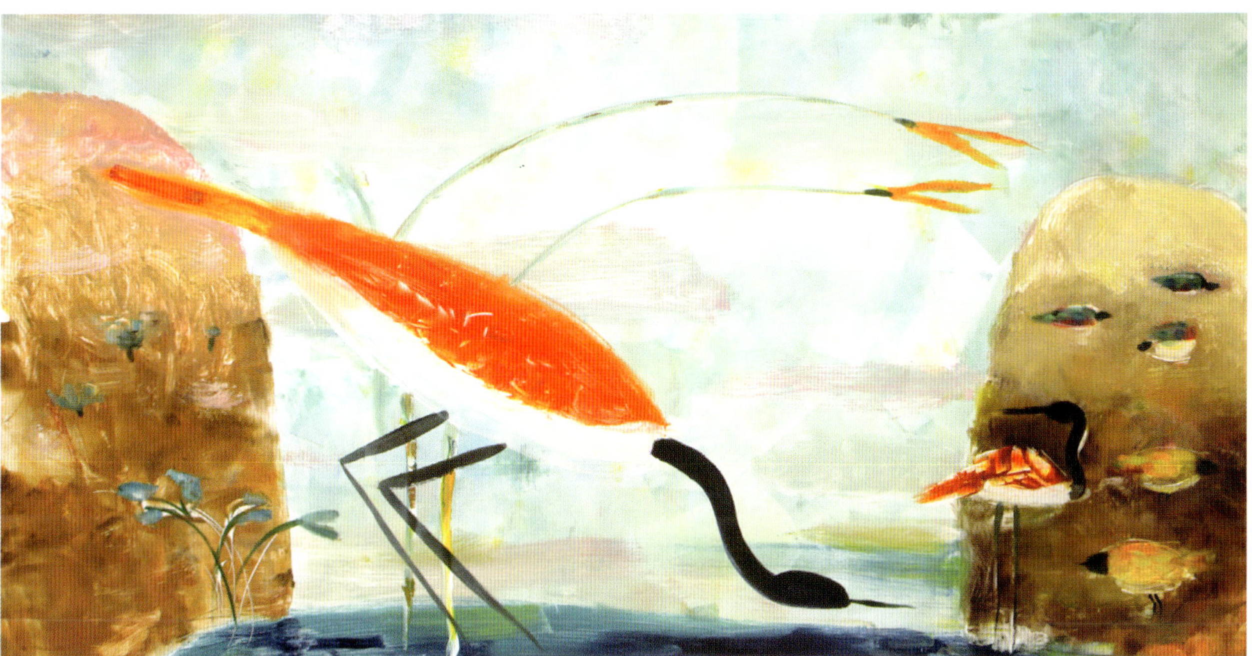

∧
Blue Meadow with Amber Birds. Monotype with oil-based inks and collage. 26.25" × 45.5". 2013.

∨
Cliff Site with Red Heron. Monotype with oil-based inks and collage. 26.25" × 45.50". 2013.

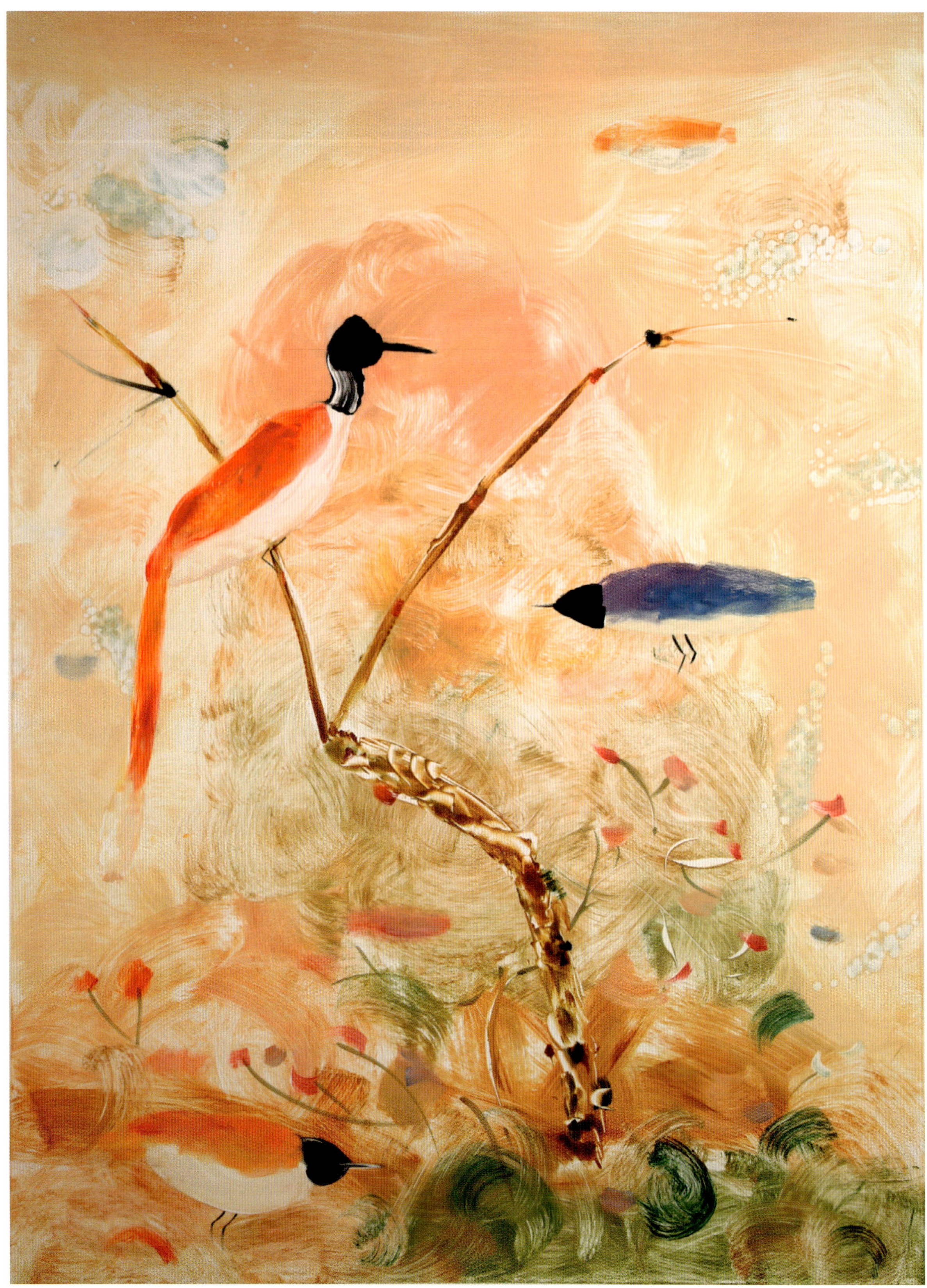

Allegro Mountain Birds. Monotype with oil-based inks. 53.75" × 41.25". 2013.

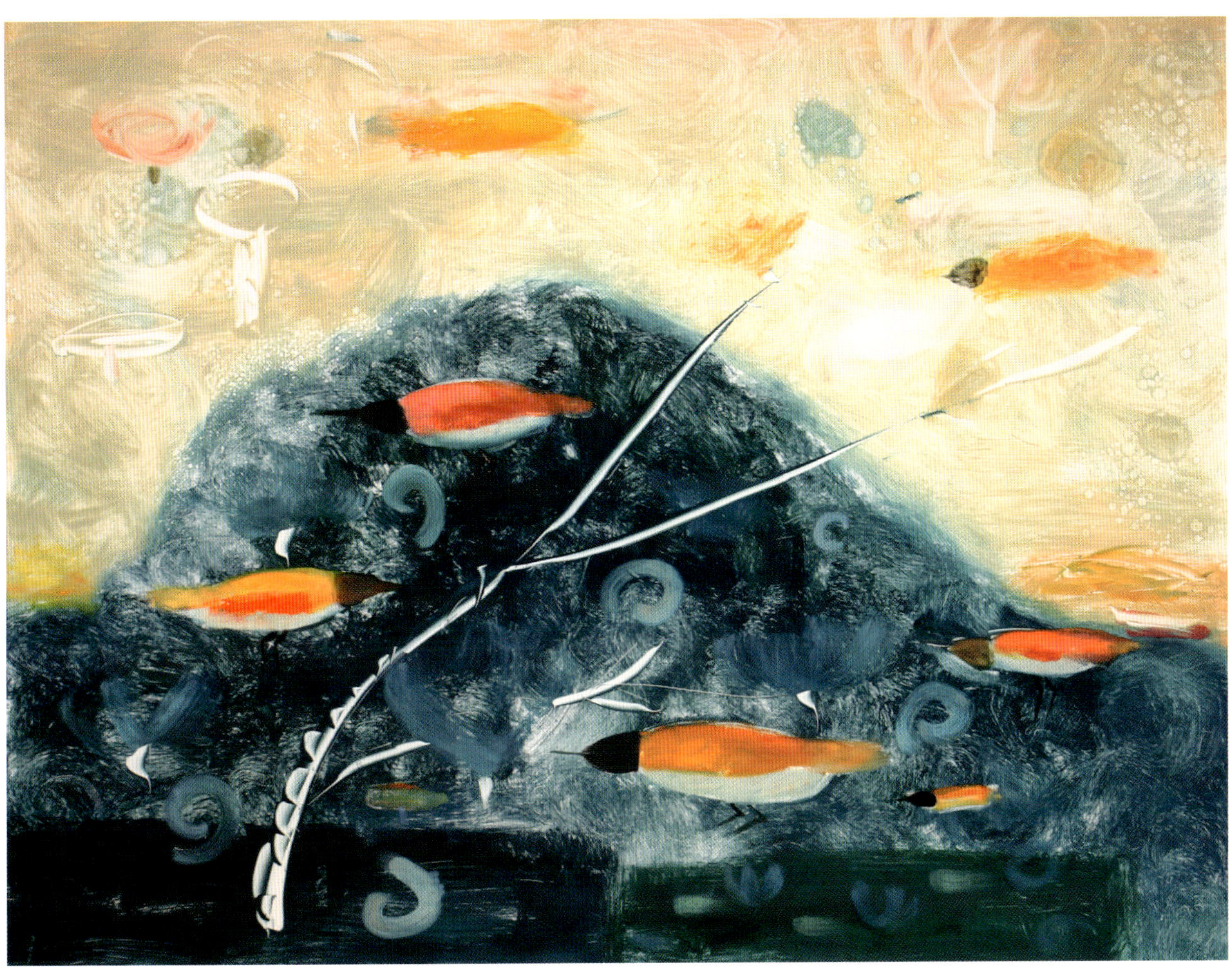

Rhythm Mountain Birds. Monotype with oil-based inks. 53.75" × 41.25". 2013.

INKA ESSENHIGH

New York, New York

My new monoprints and editioned etchings reference many different mythologies, from fairy tales to Greek tragedies, as well as the spiritual side of nature. I use these mythic settings as jumping-off points, letting go of the original meaning and capturing the narrative, which I then filter through my own internal dreamscape. I make the imagery mine while referencing the season in which the work was created.

Sunshine. Painted monotype printed from a steel matrix. 23.5" × 20.75". 2010.

Sea God. Painted monotype printed from a steel matrix. 23.5" × 20.75". 2010.

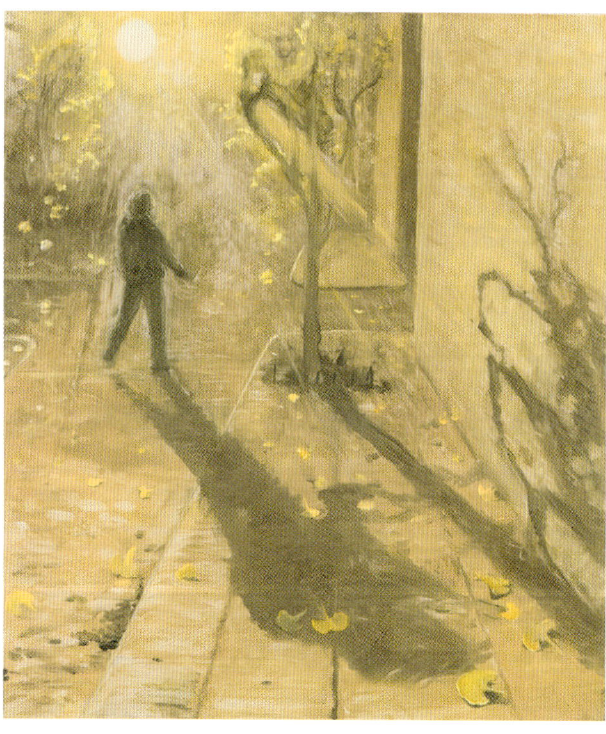

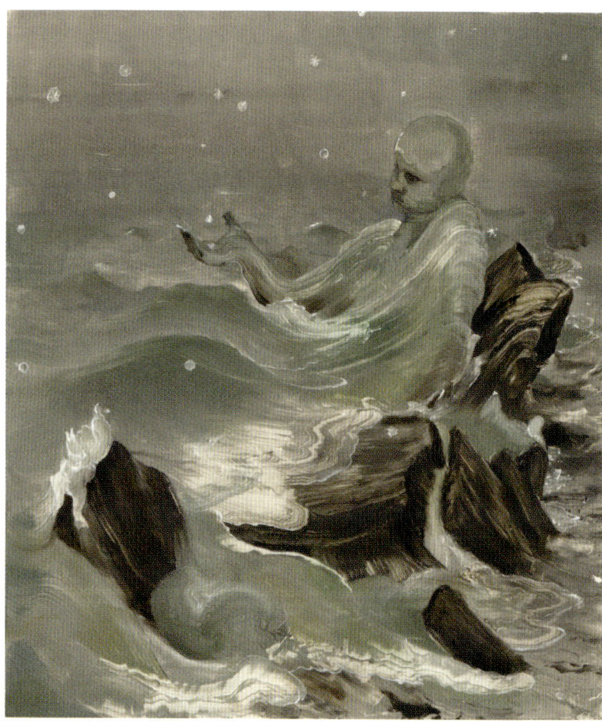

PUBLISHED BY PACE PRINTS. PRINTED AT PACE EDITIONS, INC., BY BILL HALL, ANN ASPINWALL, AND KATHY KUEHN.

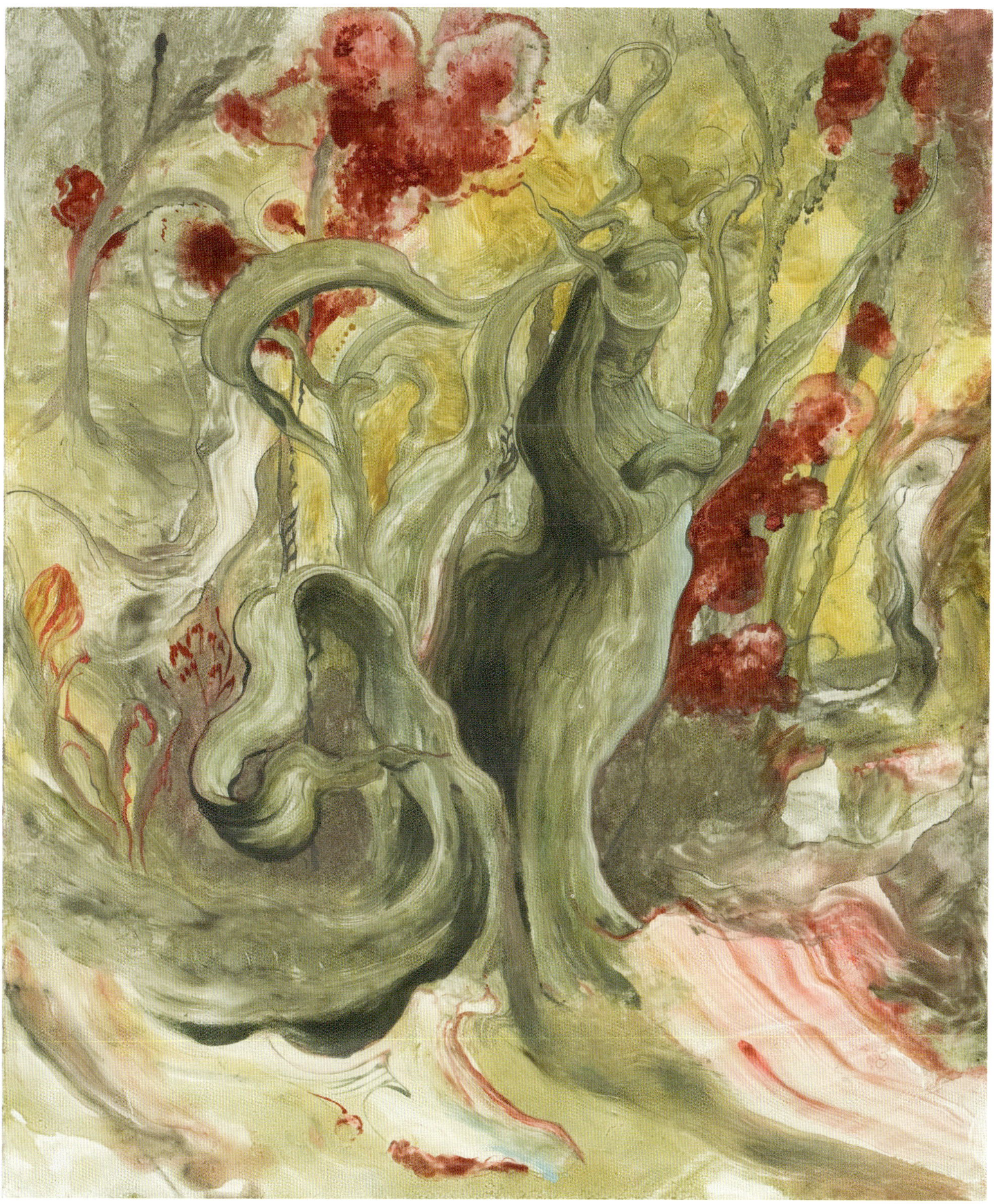

The Trappers. Painted monotype printed from a steel matrix. 18.5" × 16.25". 2010.

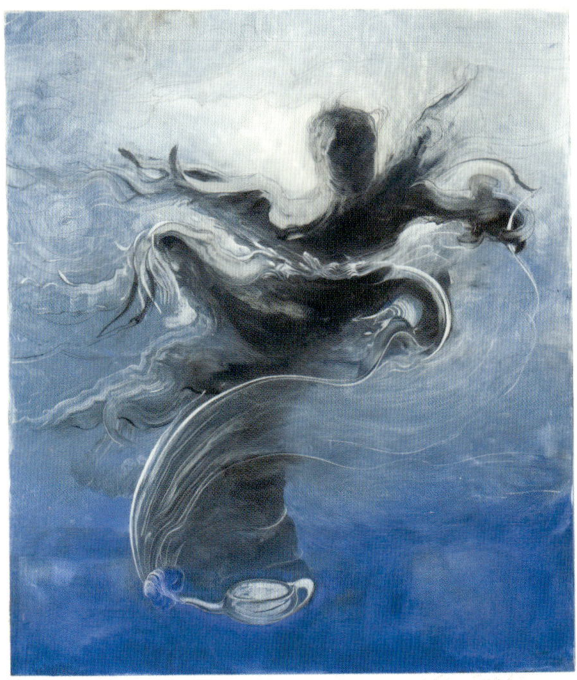

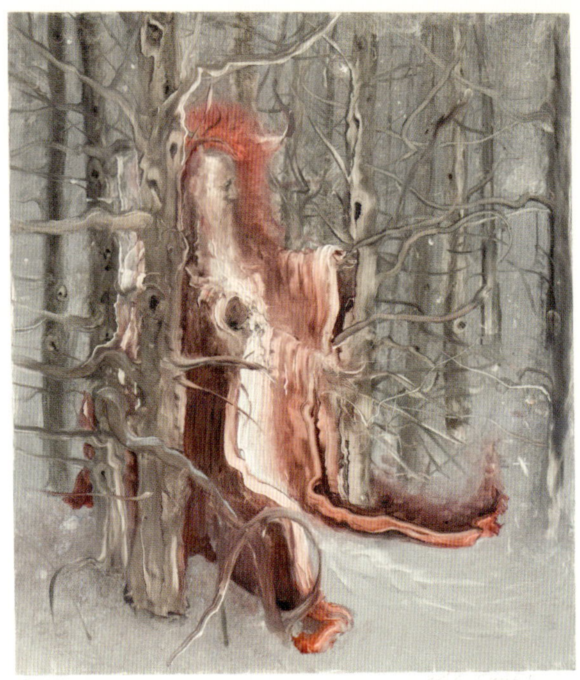

Gene. Painted monotype printed from a steel matrix. 23.5" × 20.75". 2010.

Saint in the Snow. Painted monotype printed from a steel matrix. 23.5 × 20.75". 2010.

LIZA FOLMAN

Brookline, Massachusetts

My work is often created in response to the built environment, from my immediate urban surroundings to the remains of ancient cultures. I am interested in expressing the suggestive absence of humanity in the structures we build, as well as the effects of the passage of time on surfaces and places. It is that relationship between ephemerality and endurance that inspired this work.

This series of monotypes was initially developed following an artist's residency in Brittany and then extended through subsequent visits to Ireland and Wales. In exploring the ancient stone sites indigenous to those areas, I found dolmen structures, which are megalithic tombs, initially covered by earth and then exposed over time by the elements. The remaining stones seem to have an innate mystery, which resonates with the drama of the windblown local landscape. I was deeply moved by their mix of strength and fragility, as well as the tension in the sculptural relationships between the stones. With their enormous, tenuously balanced stones, built by hand with great effort and ingenuity, dolmens have survived millennia and will, no doubt, outlive our contemporary constructions.

The monotypes were developed from sketches and photographic references created on site, though landscape elements are often invented. Most images were passed through the press multiple times to add depth, color, or both.

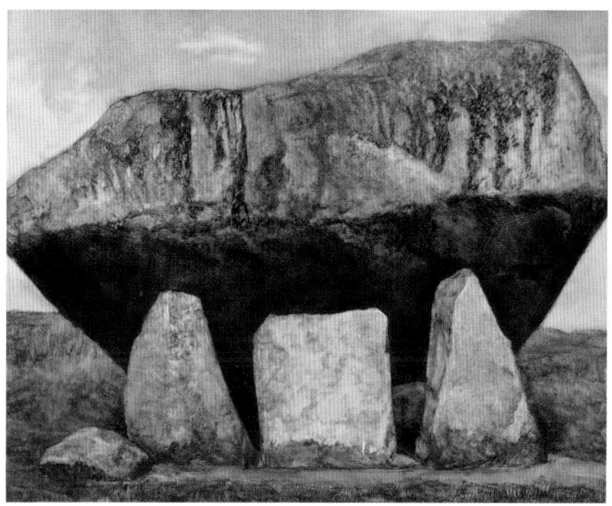

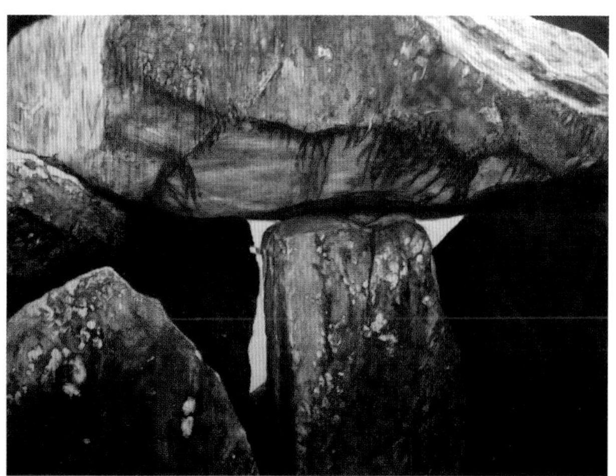

Irish Geometry. Monotype with oil-based inks. 16" × 20". 2011.

Balance. Monotype with oil-based inks. 18" × 24". 2012.

PUBLISHED AND PRINTED BY THE ARTIST.

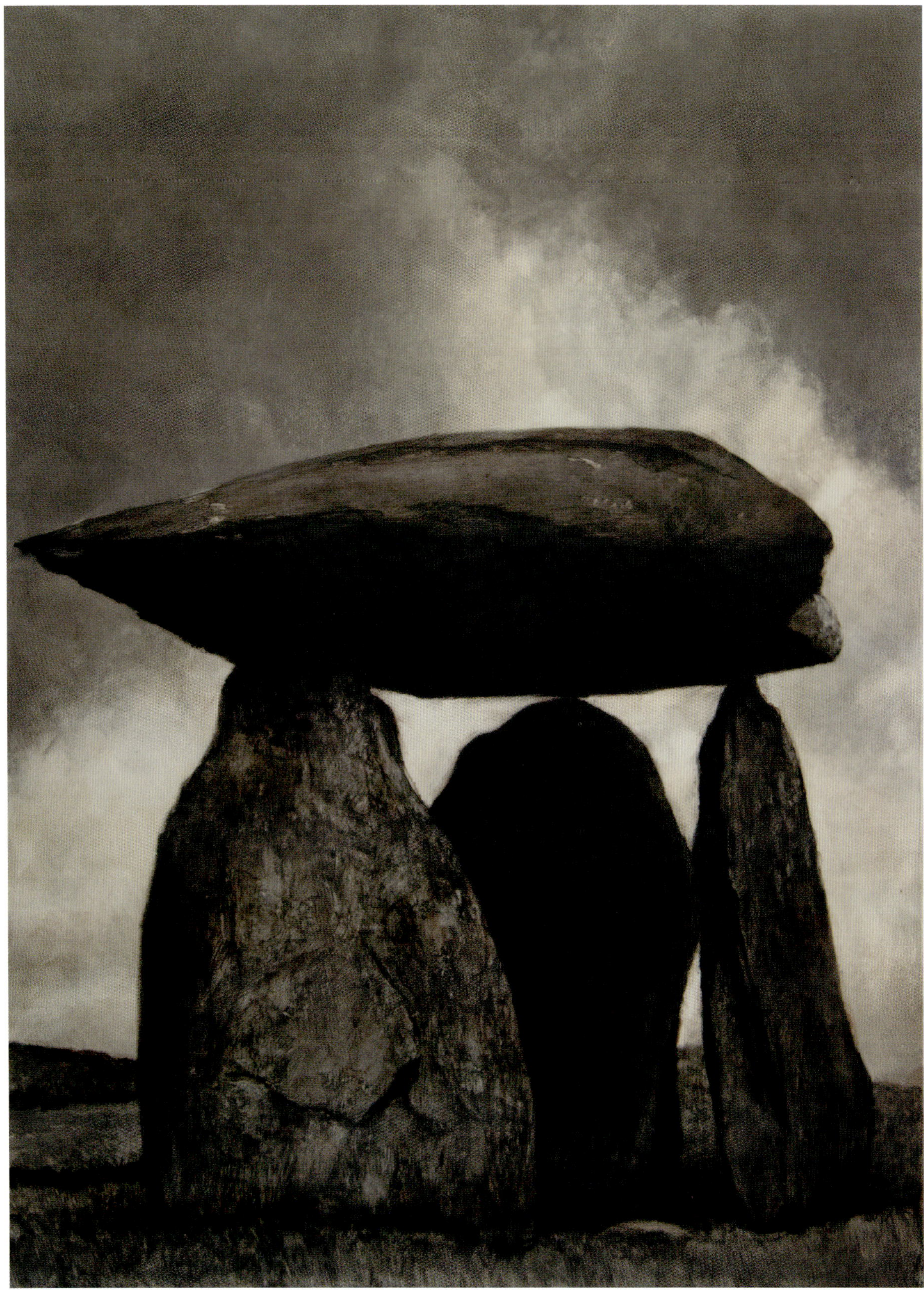

Tripod. Monotype with oil-based inks.
24" × 18". 2013.

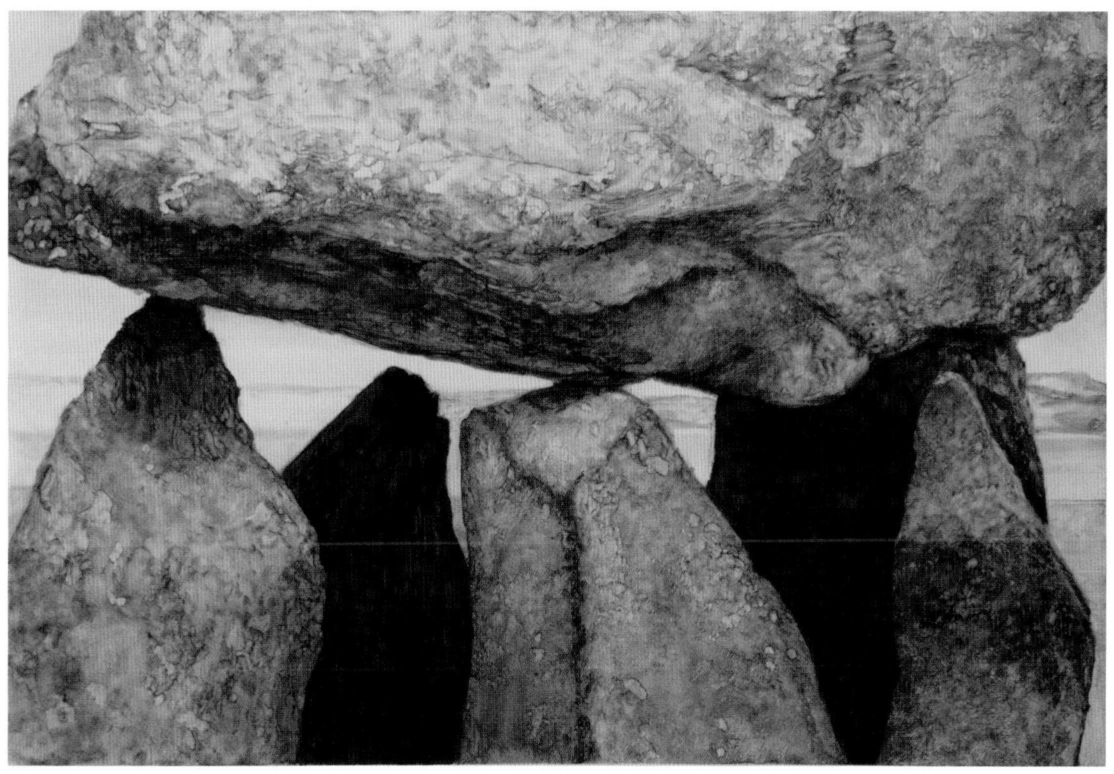

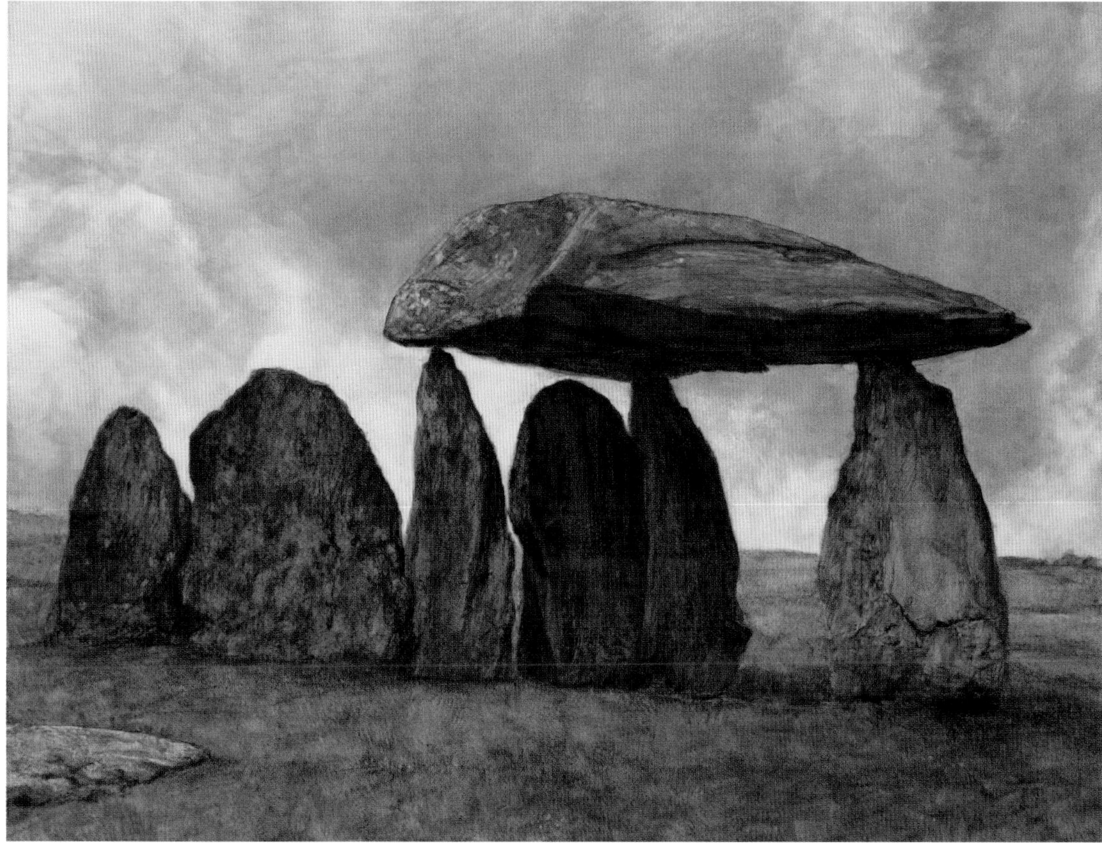

Λ
Touchstones. Monotype with oil-based inks. 16" × 20". 2013.

V
Procession. Monotype with oil-based inks. 18" × 24". 2013.

NANCY FRIESE

Cranston, Rhode Island

After the Storm. Watercolor monotype. 33" × 27". 2015.

Arbor View. Watercolor monotype. 19" × 24". 2017. *Photography is courtesy of Scott Lapham and Cade Tompkins Projects*

A monotype carries the punch of a painting with the oneness of a print. A watercolor monotype shows the wide, tactile world through a seamless embedded image. Pressure, watercolor, and paper mix into fixed fluid marks in watercolor monotypes. During the building of watercolor monotypes in open air, the watercolor strata dry quickly. The translucent sheets of large color areas are stacked with those of smaller linear structures. It is easy to add density and shifts of color or to remove and adjust areas. Overlays of color and wet shapes laid down beside dry shapes are the basic methods.

In printing, transfer is almost complete. The multiple layers of watercolor sink into the paper in unity. The luminous print appears integrated, smooth, and still, no matter the subject. Dynamic watermarks are captured and exaggerated. The look of immediacy is powerful. The trajectory of monotypes remains in the private realm; singular and swift, simple and solid. Hovering between drawing, painting, and printmaking, the monotype allures us one by one. It is reversed, lodged, and distinct and has useful and logical processes moving backward and forward. A watercolor monotype is portable, mobile, and durational. The printing surfaces may be created over years before the dampened paper pulls the image off in the press in minutes. It is an accommodating medium.

My nature prints are perceptually painted from places near at hand of sites that remind me of the ephemeral past or pull me to the vibrant present. They become greater ideas through the printing.

PUBLISHED BY THE ARTIST, CADE TOMPKINS PROJECTS, OEHME GRAPHICS, AND THE UNIVERSITY OF KANSAS. PRINTED BY SUE OEHME AT OEHME GRAPHICS AND UNIVERSITY OF KANSAS PRINTMAKING STUDENTS.

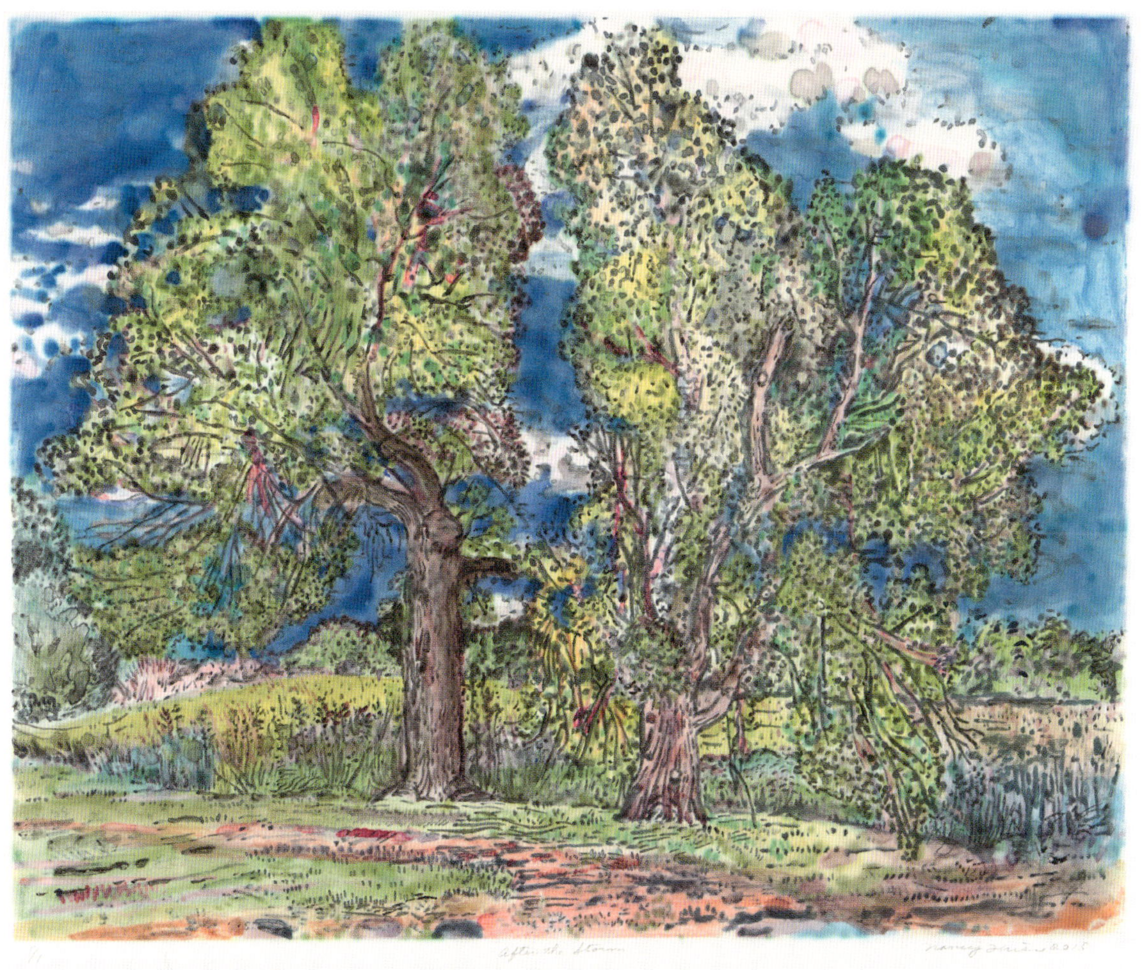

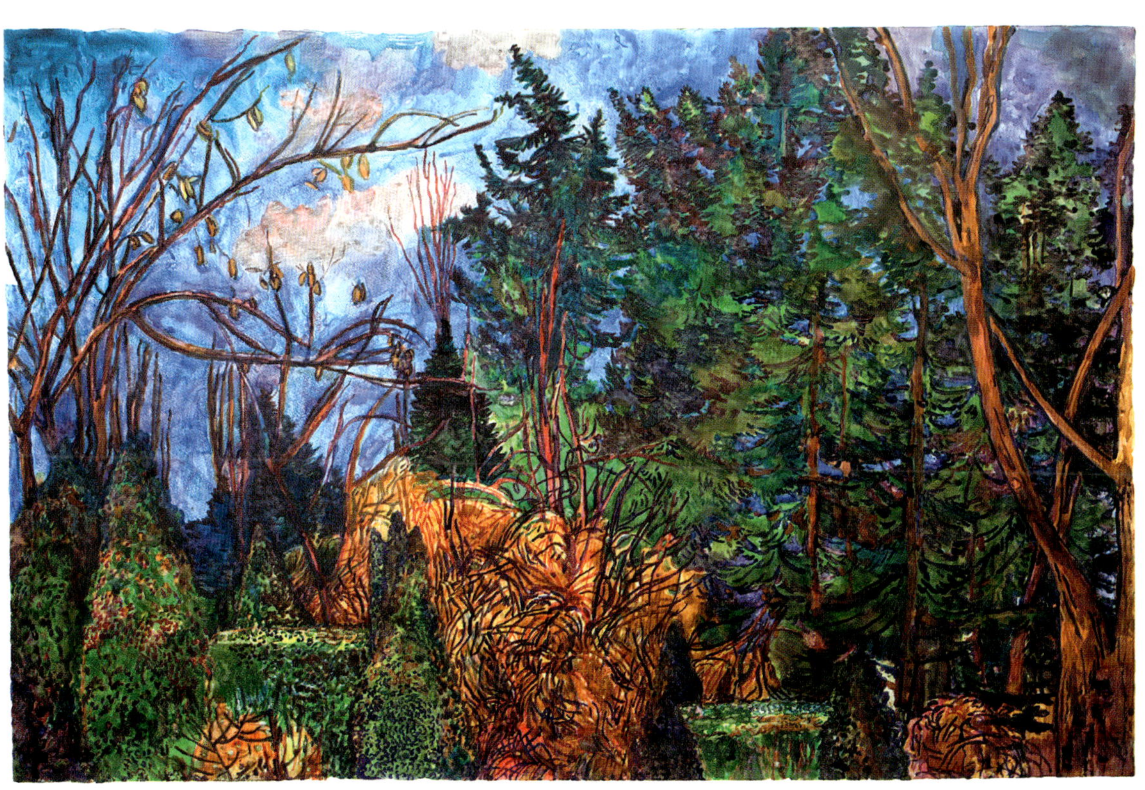

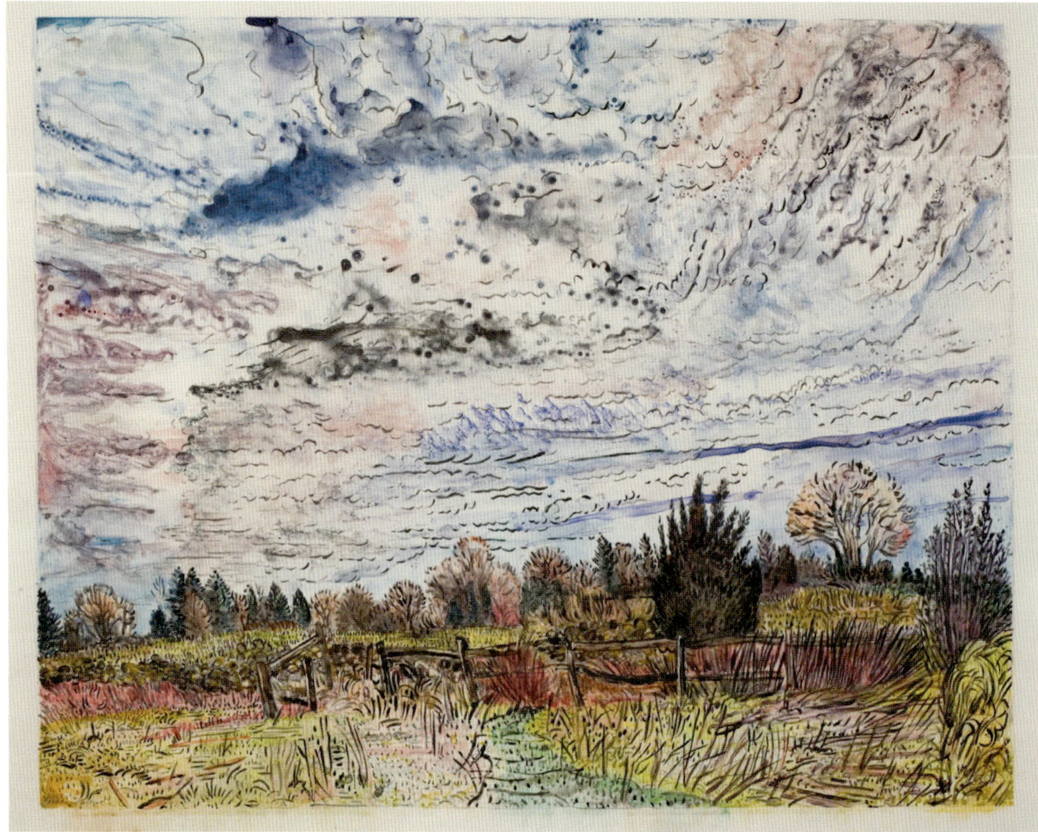

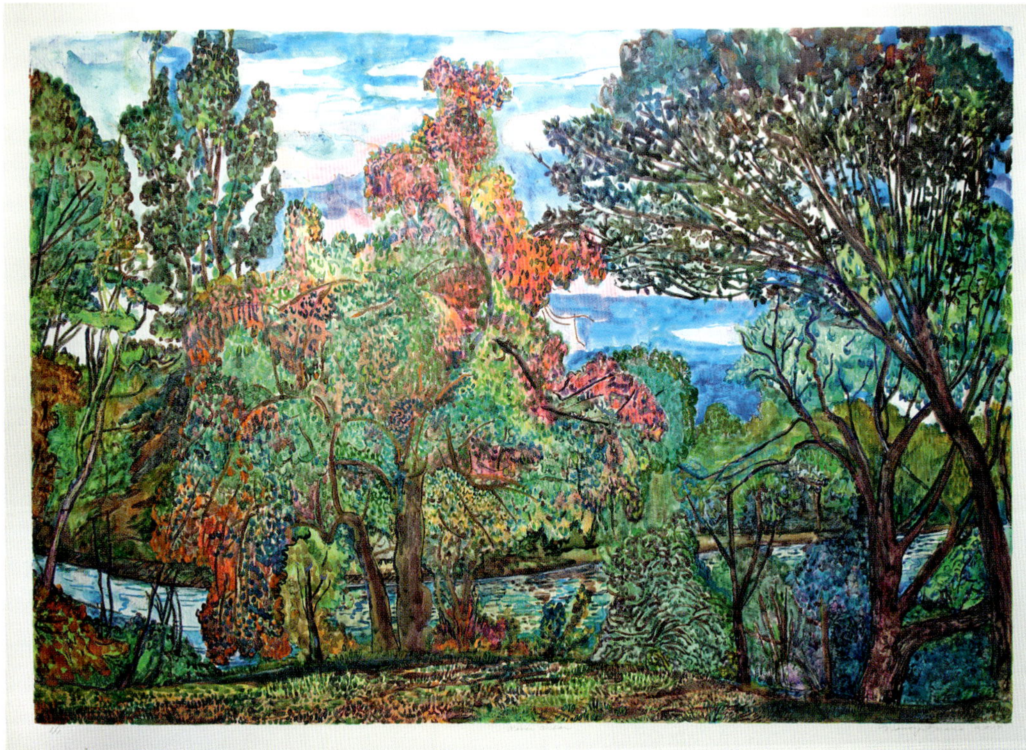

^
Avondale Preserve. Watercolor monotype. 19" × 25". 2007.

v
River Arbor. Watercolor monotype. 33" × 44". 2015.

JANE GOLDMAN

Somerville, Massachusetts

I am fascinated by technologies that extend human vision. Through microscopes we marvel at seeing the foundations of life, magnified from the cellular, molecular, and atomic levels, and at the beauty and symmetry of the zigzag, ribbon, and star shapes of diatoms.

Through the Hubble telescope, we transcend time and space, viewing images of the early universe. These technologies allow the human eye to see the previously unseen; here, seeing is believing. Paradoxically, while we base what we know on what we see, what we see and hence what we know continually changes as our knowledge increases through new technology.

Watercolor monotype most successfully expresses my aim to interpret aspects of the universe revealed through Hubble telescope images. The interactions of water, color, and gravity painted on nonporous sheet plastic, combined with the multiple layering possibilities provided by a press, result in an image that only this particular medium makes possible.

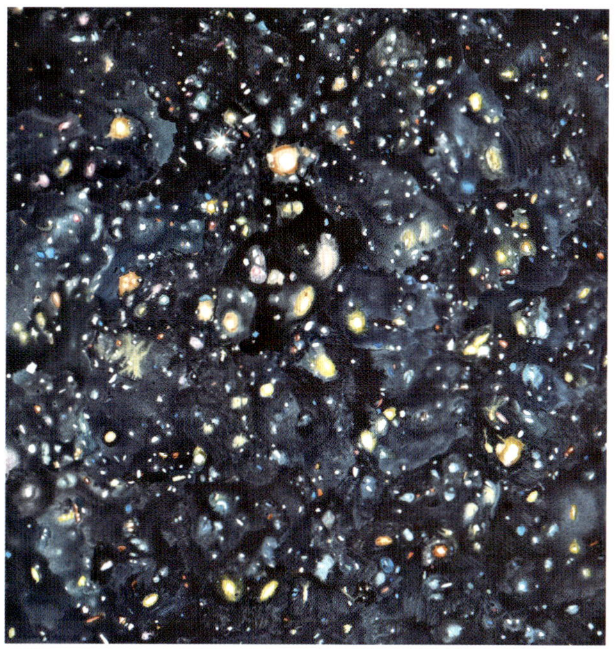

Early Universe. Watercolor monotype. 33" × 32". 2014.

ALL PHOTOS ARE COURTESY OF SUSAN BYRNE. PUBLISHED AND PRINTED BY THE ARTIST AT MIXIT PRINT STUDIO.

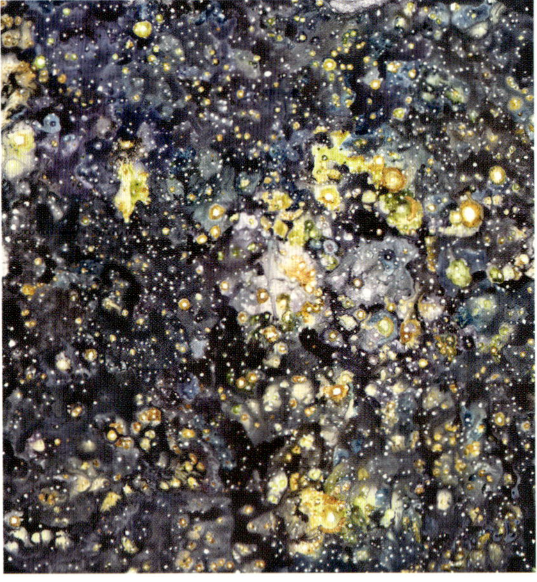

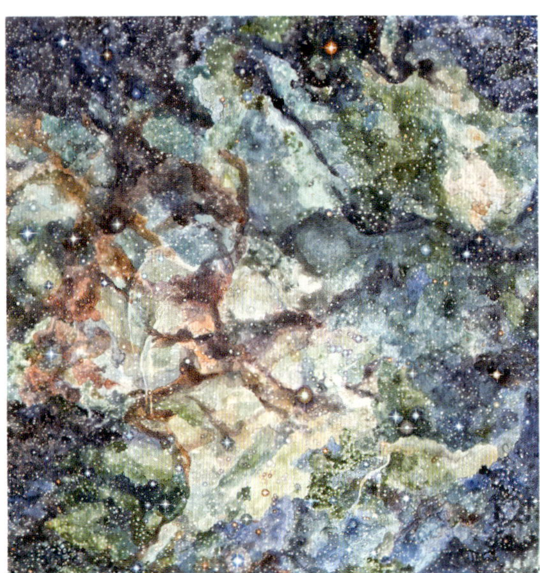

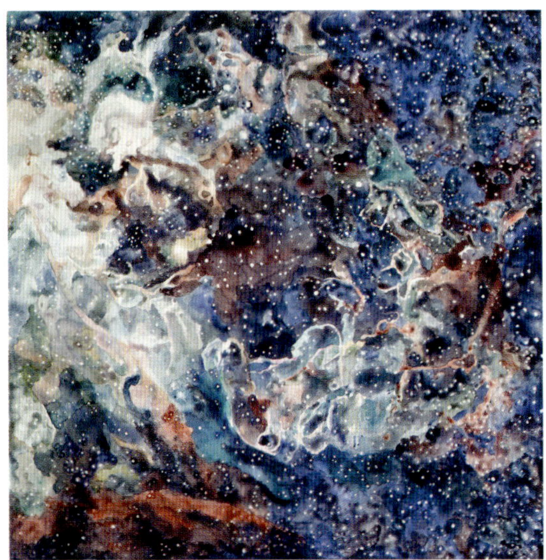

Elementary Particles I. Watercolor monotype. 33" × 32". 2014.

Emerging Cluster I. Watercolor monotype. 34" × 33". 2016.

Emerging Cluster 2. Watercolor monotype. 33" × 33". 2014.

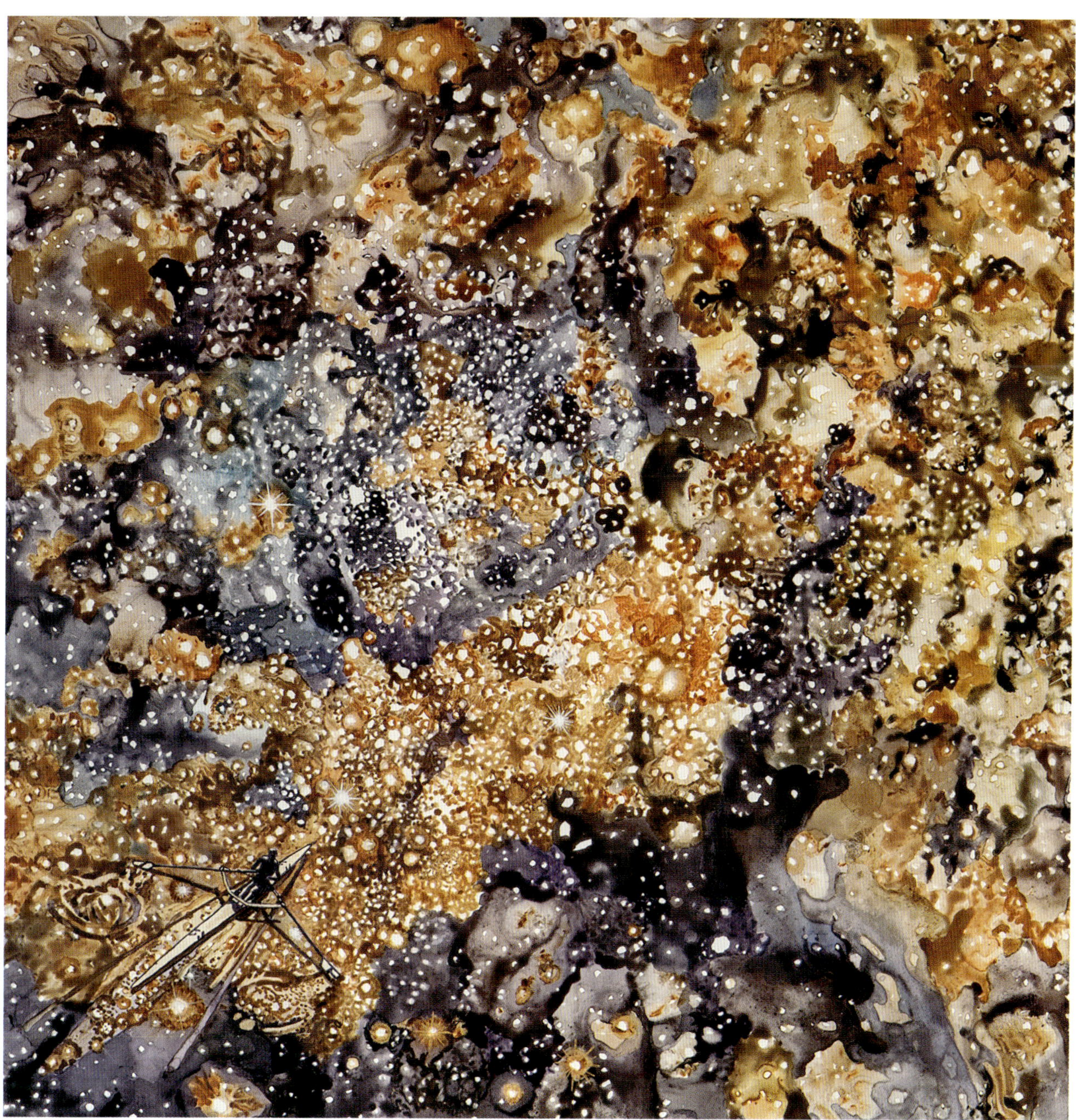

Star Sculler. Watercolor monotype. 32" × 32". 2017.

SHARA HUGHES

New York, New York

I began experimenting in the Pace Editions studio by using various printmaking techniques, including monotype. The idea of a ghost image resonated with me, and I launched into a series of monotypes for my exhibition *Surprise Anxiety* at Pace Prints, New York.

I painted shapes on an aluminum plate and passed this through the press. I then worked back on the plate, painting directly on top of the ghost image, achieving the final monotype from these layers of painting. Through this method, I was able to achieve both rich and subtle tonal ranges in my landscapes. I used brushes to paint oil-based ink on the plate but also used rags and cotton swabs both to additively and reductively work into the painting. My landscapes are created intuitively, and the shapes I initially paint on the plate are the footprints on which I build my compositions.

Through monotype making, I have learned about subtlety, patience, and letting go, as my intuitive color use was more difficult to control. When painting on the plate, colors would appear layered but would mix when run through the press. You can't get away with anything. It's like you are getting pulled over by the police and they have a spotlight on you and they see right through your soul. That's what it feels like when making monotypes.

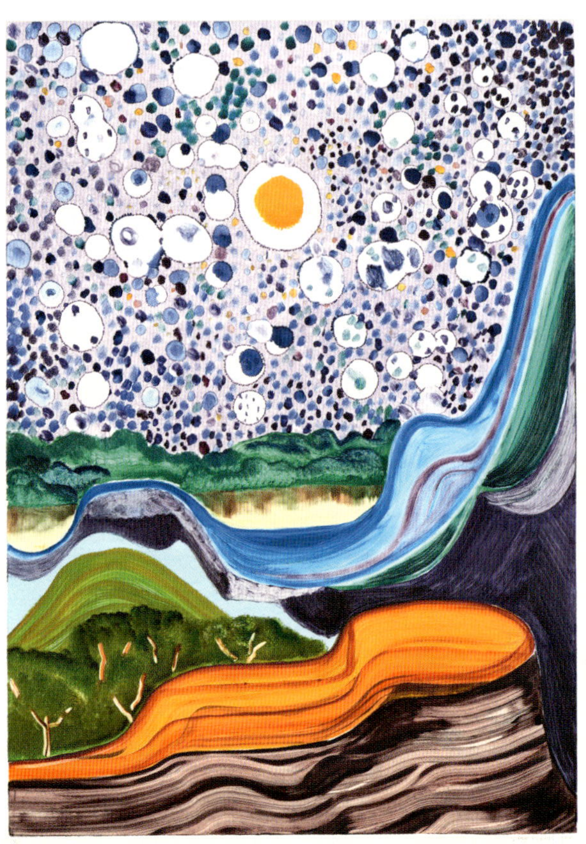

The Stars Don't Lie. Monotype with oil-based ink. 38.5" × 29". 2018.

ALL IMAGES ARE COURTESY OF PACE PRINTS. PUBLISHED BY PACE PRINTS. PRINTED AT PACE EDITIONS, INC., BY SARAH CARPENTER AND JUSTIN ISRAELS.

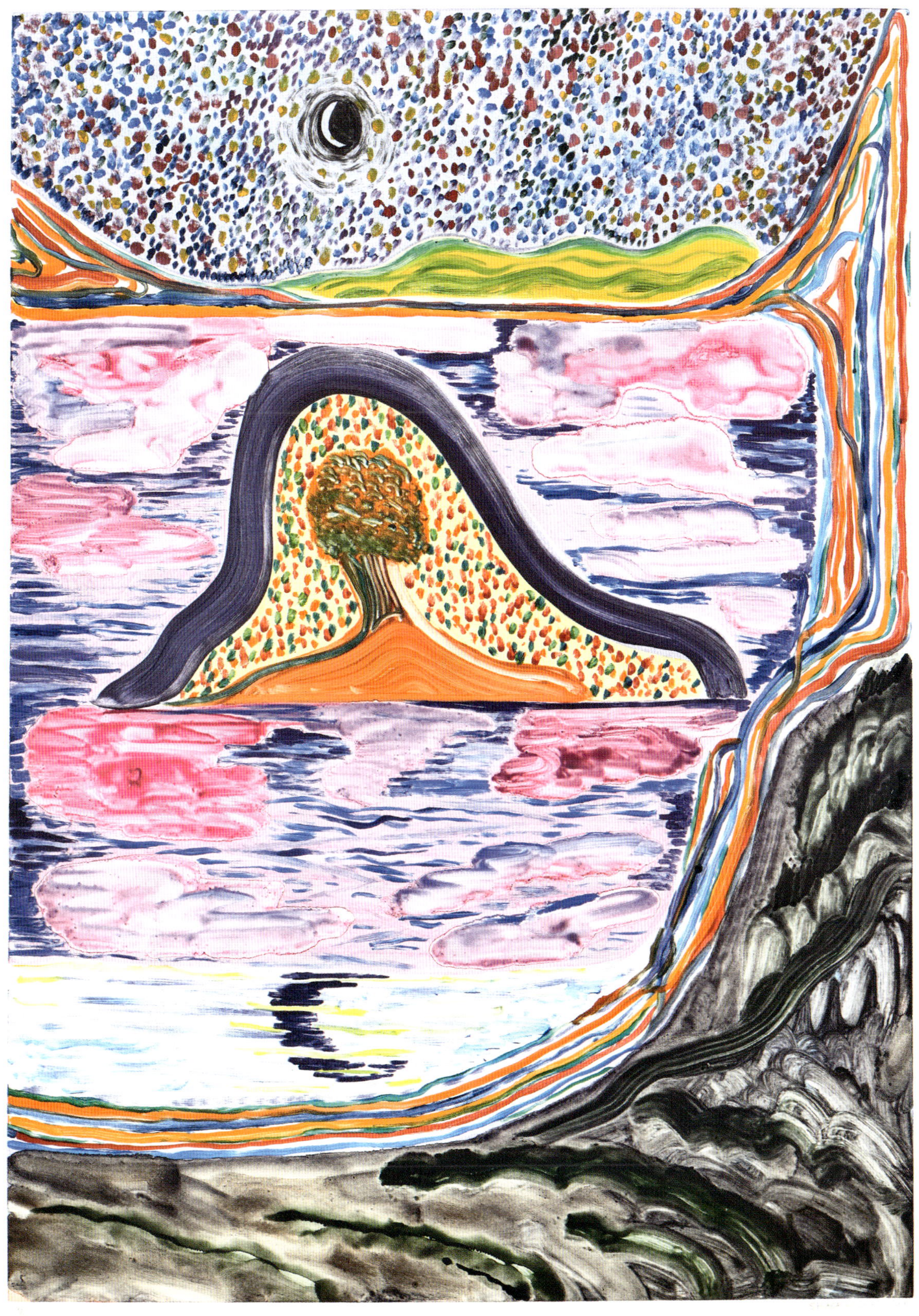

Night Out, Hide Out. Monotype with oil-based ink. 38.5" × 29". 2018.

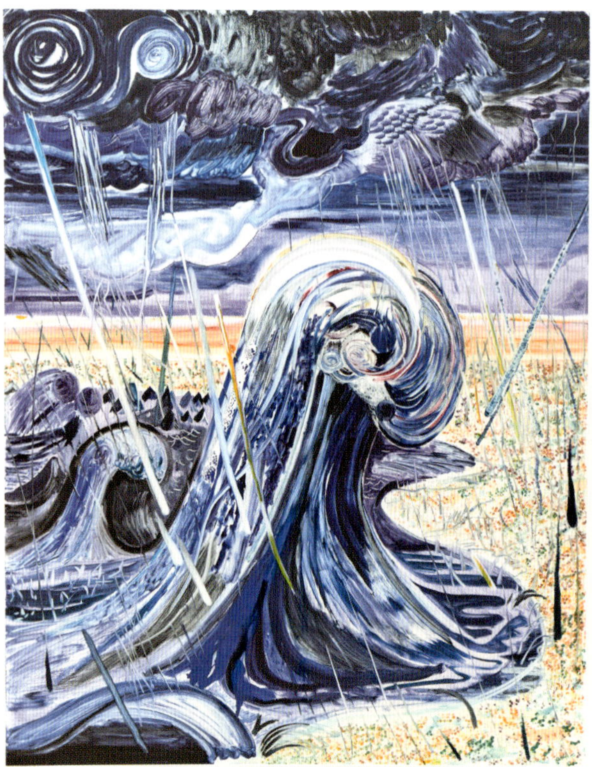

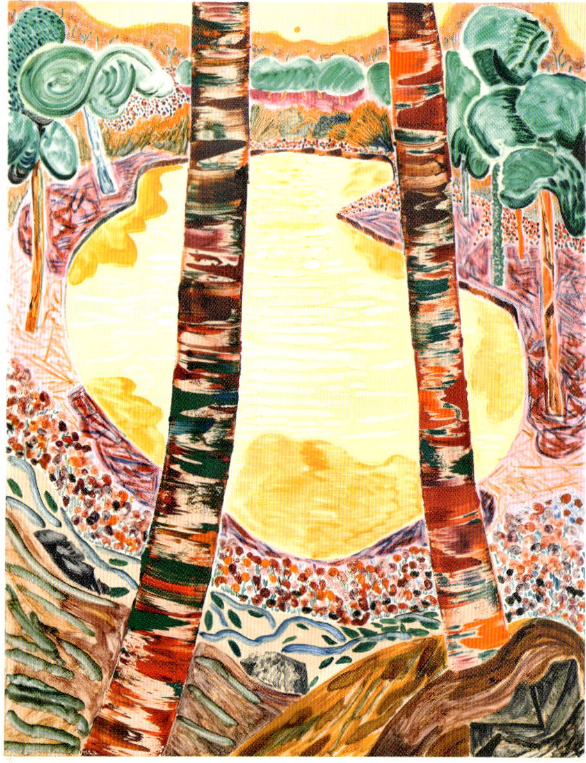

Even Your Bad Mood Is Sweet. Monotype with oil-based ink. 57" × 45.5". 2018.

Soft Dark Tide. Monotype with oil-based ink. 28" × 20". 2018.

>

Two of Us on Our Way Home. Monotype with oil-based ink. 57" × 45.5". 2018.

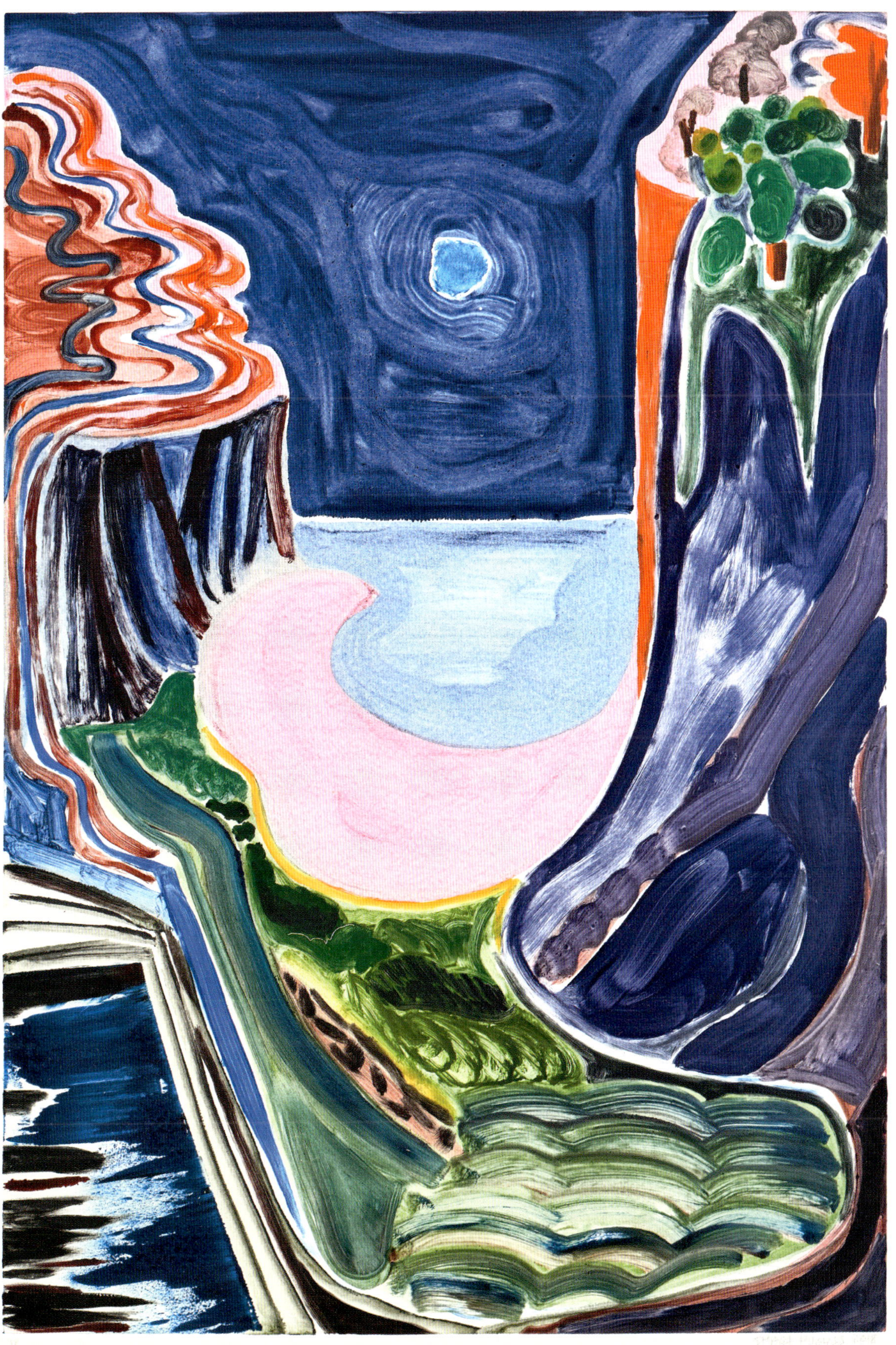

BILL JACKLIN

New York, New York

I started making monotypes in the late 1970s. I was playing with image making when it all became serious—very quickly. Monotype allows me to be myself. The practice of making monotype has given me a vehicle to develop ideas while simultaneously working on a painting. I move back and forth between the press and the canvas, adjusting both compositions at the same time. The monotypes become finished abstractions in their own right.

The monotypes are often visual ideas running ahead of the paintings that lead me to push the boundaries in painting. The nature of monotypes is that I have to work quickly; there is a great deal of risk and a lot of throwaway. Through the process, I try to find an equivalent of the energy and light that I see in my subjects—Manhattan street scenes, ice skaters, figures playing at the beach, etc. I am always looking for the magic.

Holding a visual memory in my mind, I flow with the process of making a monotype. It can be quite a volatile experience, with the interaction of the oil medium and solvents having a life of their own. I use oil paint, printer's ink, solvents, and carborundum, for its gestural nature. The spattering, a resist process, came about to show the weather. I seek to create a visual language interpreting in printed form how I see the world. It is all experiment.

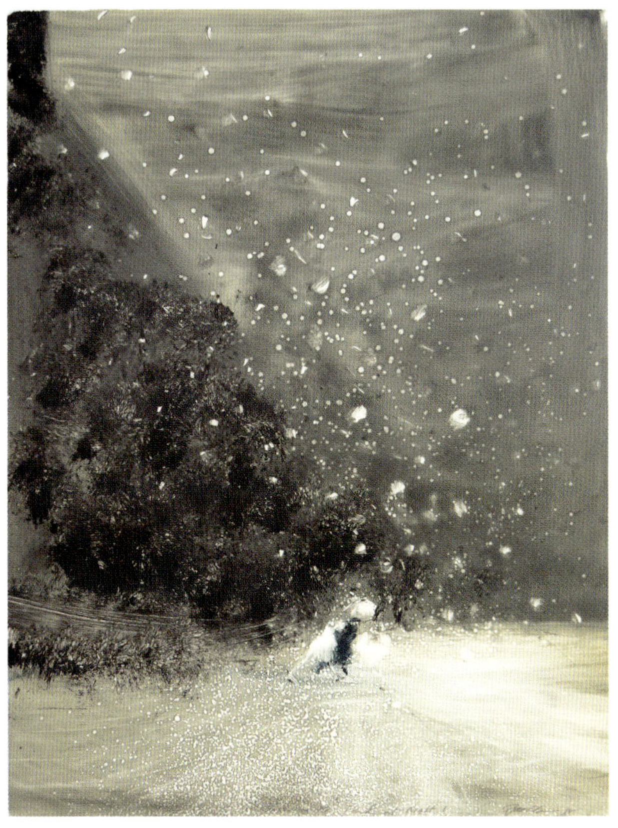

Snow in the Park at Night I. Monotype with oil-based ink and oil paints. 27.5" × 21". 2018.

PUBLISHED BY THE ARTIST. PRINTED BY THE ARTIST AND PAUL DERUVO AT THE CENTER FOR CONTEMPORARY PRINT.

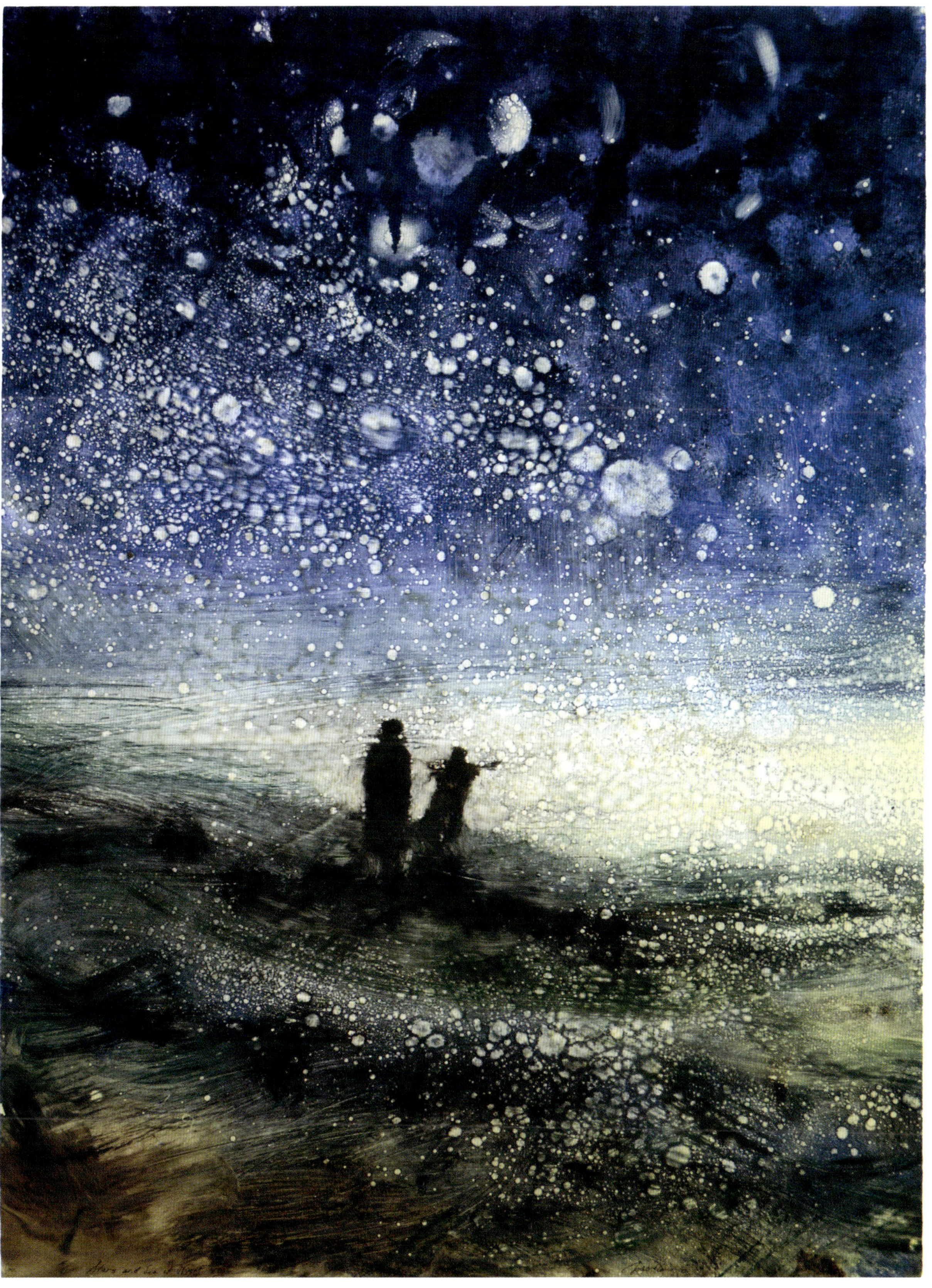

Stars and Sea at Night XIII. Monotype with oil-based ink and oil paints. 39.5" × 29.5". 2016.

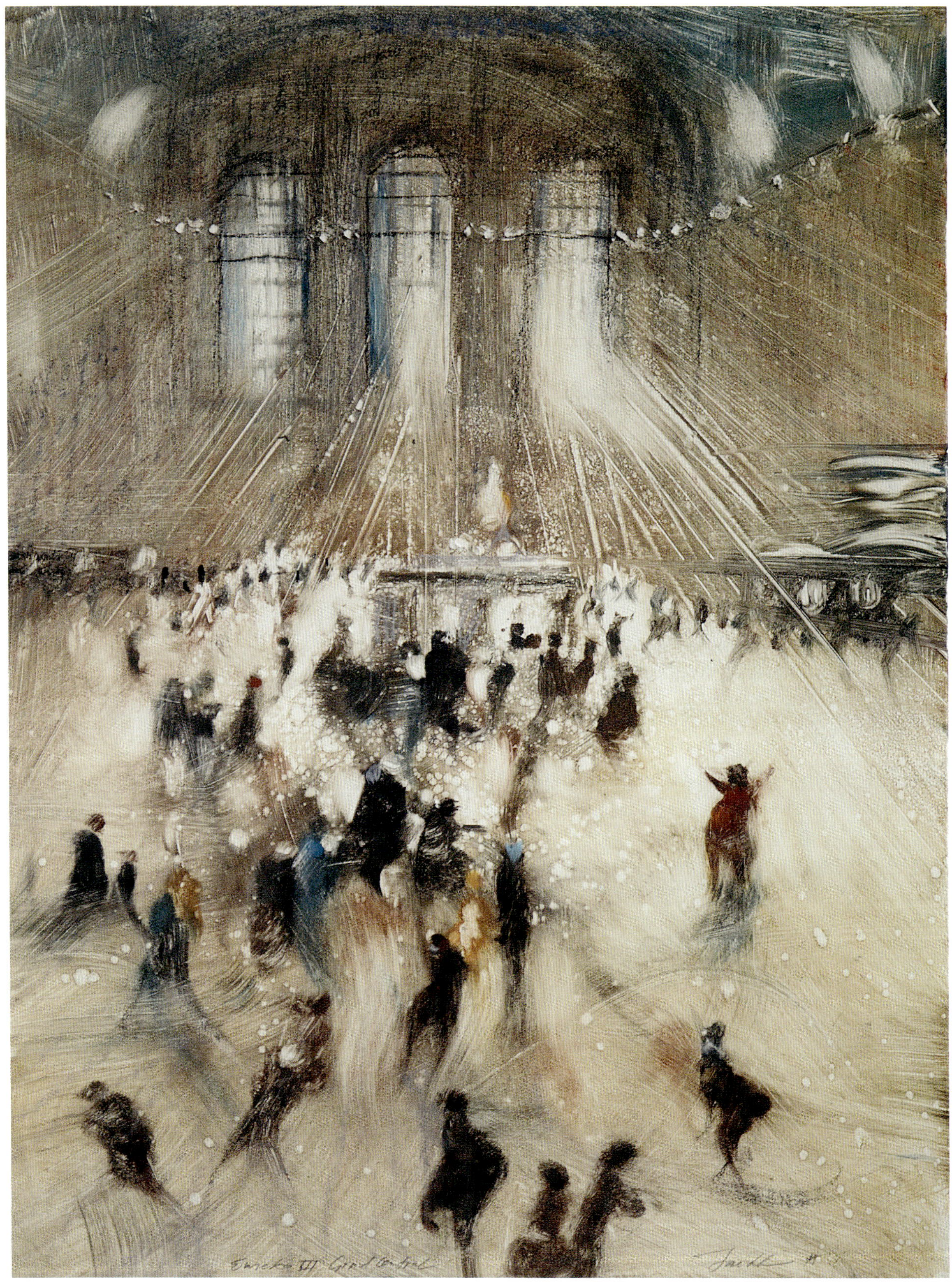

Eureka III, Grand Central. Monotype with oil-based ink and oil paints. 27.5" × 21". 2018.

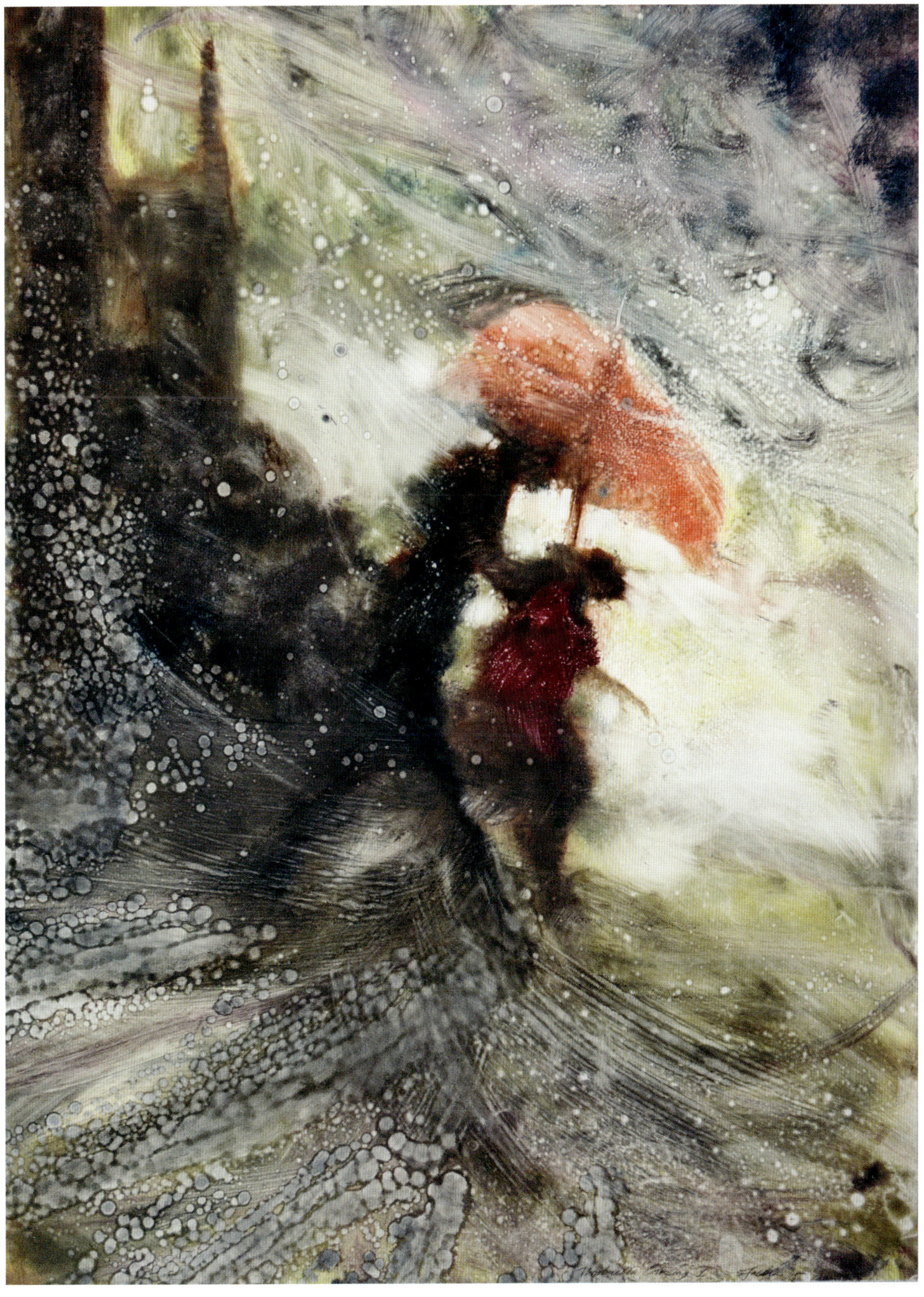

Umbrella Crossing I. Monotype with oil-based ink and oil paints. 39.5" × 29.5". 2018.

JOEL JANOWITZ

Cambridge, Massachusetts

For two years, I paid little attention to all the lumber and orange plastic fencing swaddling the trees in my neighborhood, protecting them from extensive roadwork. As these structures aged and sagged, I started to notice them and began painting and making monotypes based on this disturbing landscape. Its interactions of geometry and organic form, organization and disintegration, and neutral and intense color intrigued me and drew my work into new territory: The Protected Tree Series.

Monotypes generate ideas quickly. The spontaneity of the medium continually suggests new possibilities for my work. Moreover, immediate feedback begins as soon as one pulls a print, looks at it, responds, and begins transforming the "ghost" image remaining on the plate. I wipe, add ink, change colors, shift structure, etc., until a new print emerges.

These particular prints are viscosity monotypes. On a clean plate, I carefully paint oily inks in particular areas (e.g., the orange fencing). When I roll sticky ink over this less viscous ink, the looser ink acts as a resist, and an image emerges. Simultaneously, the brayers and rollers pick up offsets of the imagery, which I can use to build the subtlety and complexity of the plate. As I roll the brayer, the image on it keeps changing as it picks up and lays down the ink. My job is to pay attention to the plate, as the image builds, shifts, and develops, keeping the parts that resonate and wiping away the rest.

Abandon. Viscosity monotype with oil-based inks. 22.25" × 30.5". 2015.

Fenced. Viscosity monotype with oil-based inks. 30" × 40". 2016.

PUBLISHED AND PRINTED BY THE ARTIST AT MIXIT PRINT STUDIO.

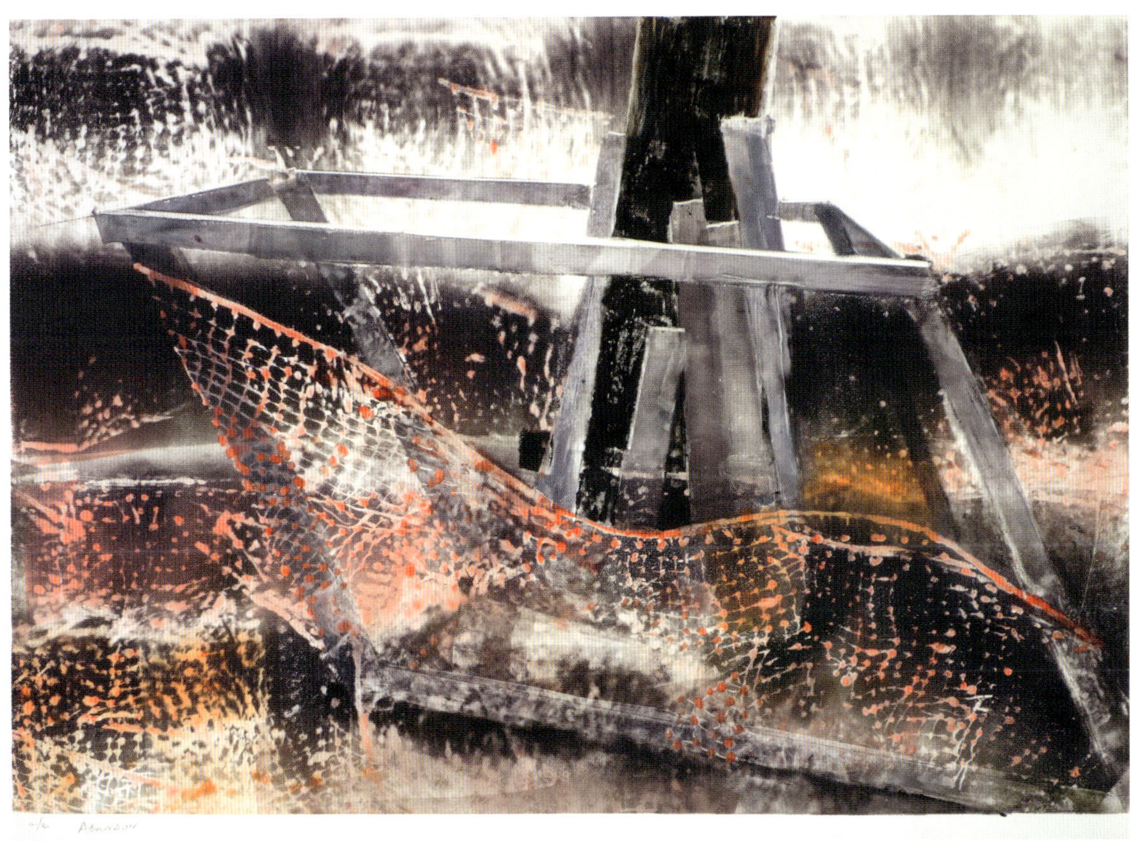

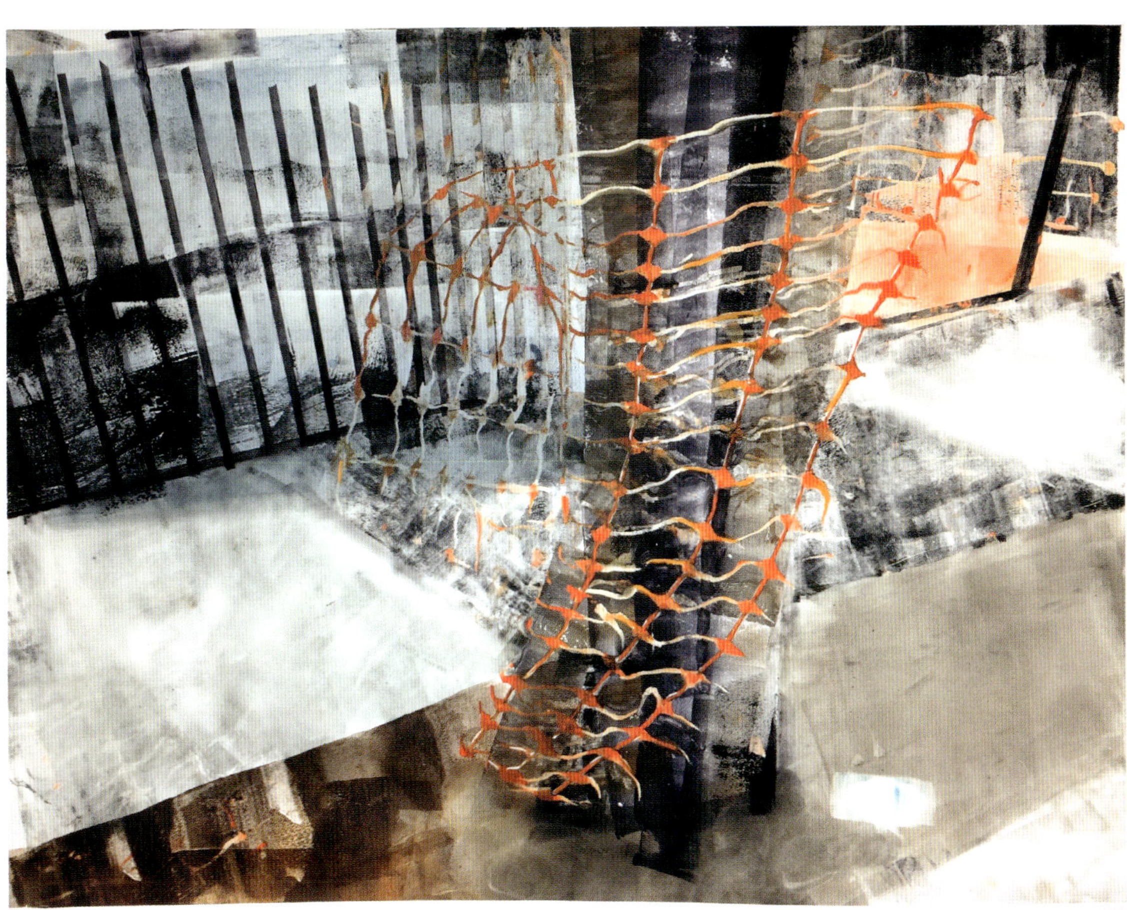

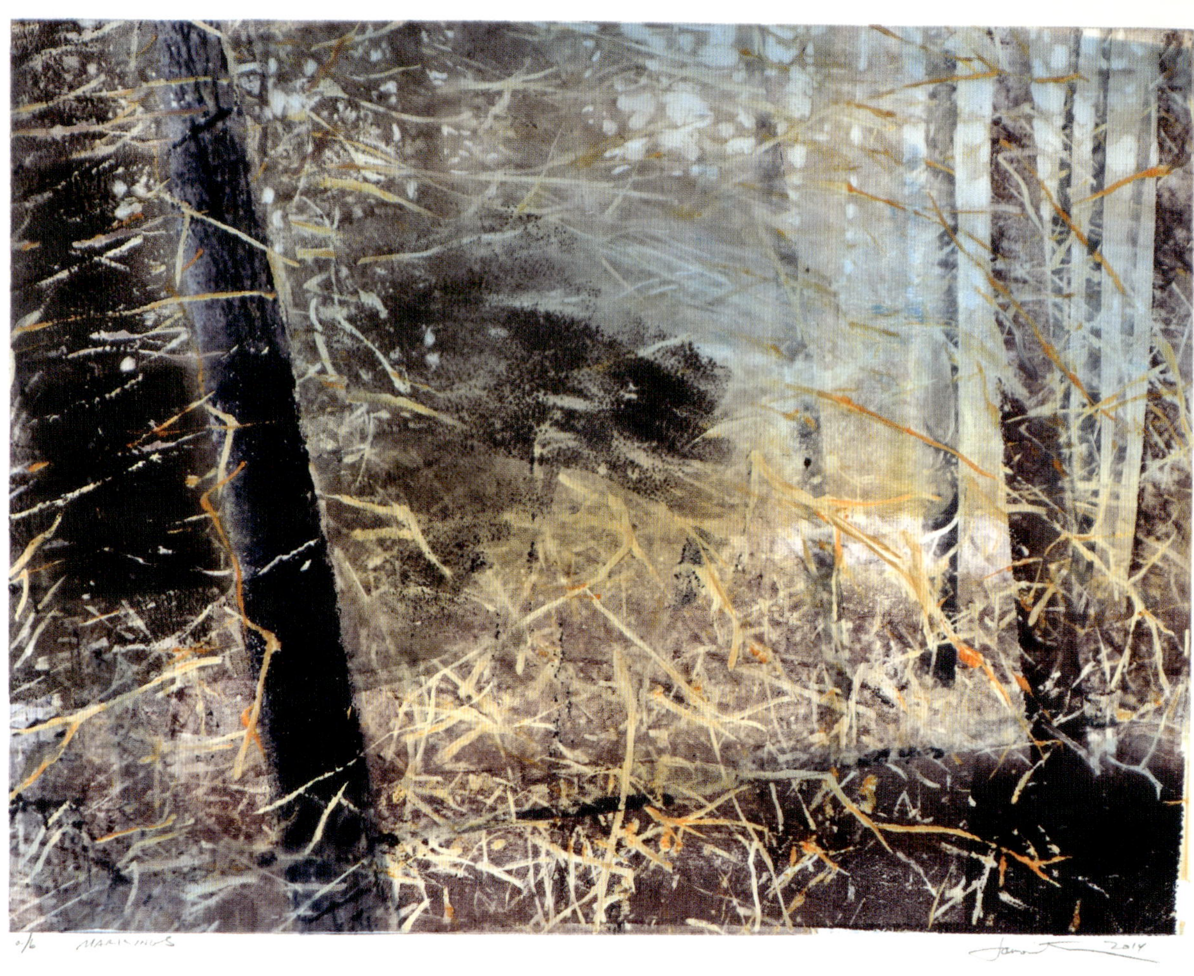

>
Mixup. Viscosity monotype with oil-based inks. 22.25" × 30.5". 2016.

Markings. Viscosity monotype with oil-based inks. 22" × 30.5". 2014.

Requiem II. Viscosity monotype with oil-based inks. 22" × 30.5". 2016.

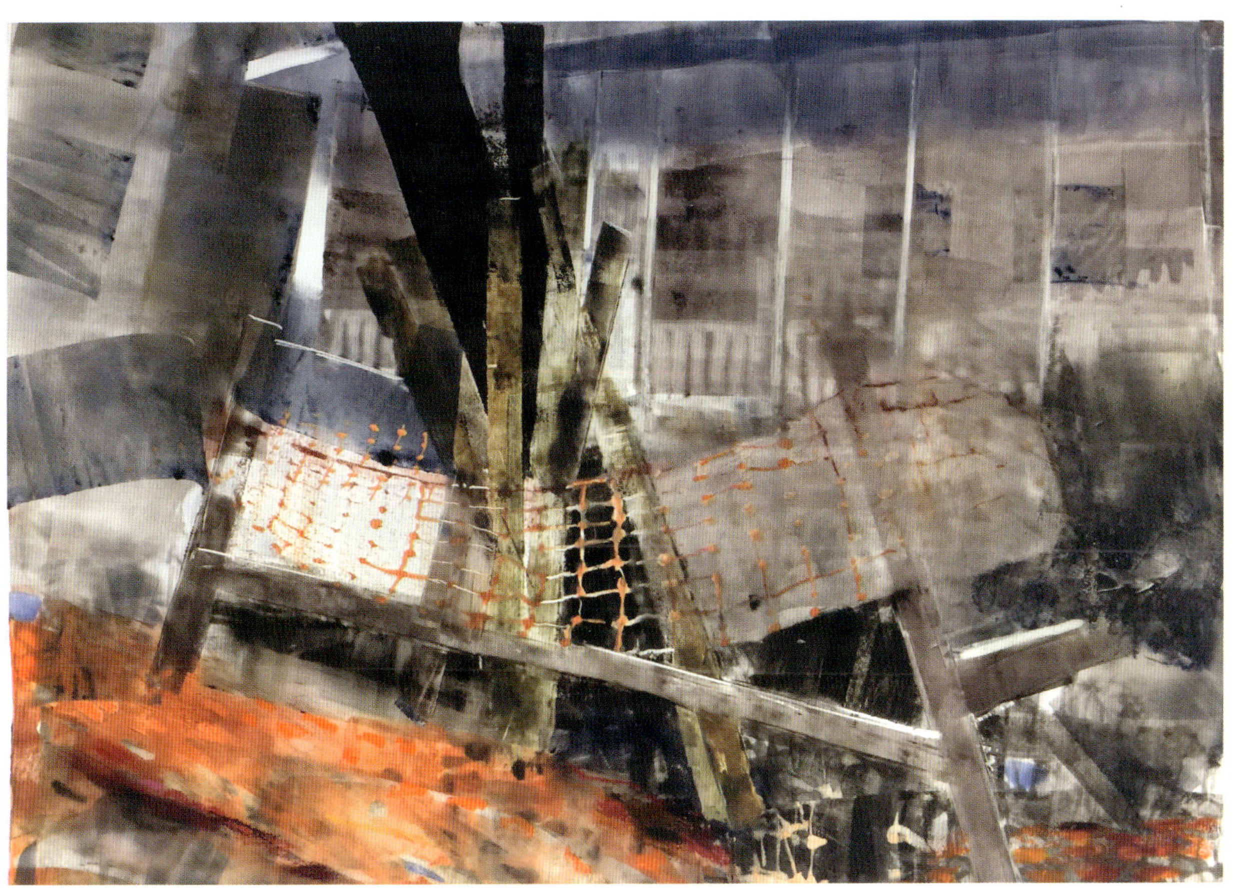

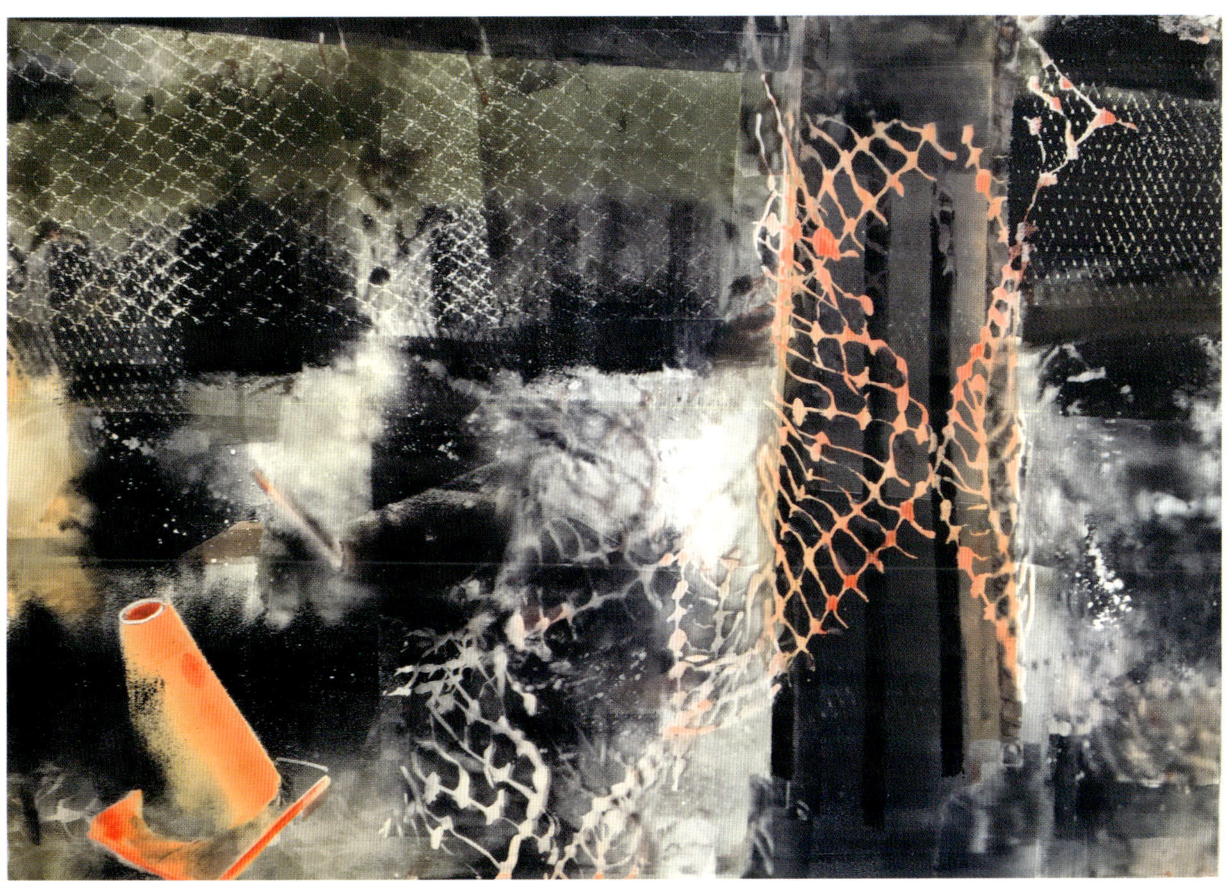

MEGHAN ALLYNN JOHNSON

New York, New York

The main output of my studio practice is in the creation of prints, drawings, and short stop-motion animation films or music videos, made using a collection of found and handmade objects. Very early animation and horror films function as a source of inspiration—notably the convention of over-the-top, unrealistic prop construction and fantastical scene development.

I play on the parallel structures of stop-motion video and printmaking, in which both time and process are flattened into the final outcome. Some of my monotypes function as 2-D works on paper, and others can be found recycled as a stage set or texture, or as part of a character or prop in my stop-motion filmmaking, which has a look of a rudimentary paper, clay, and found-object puppet theater.

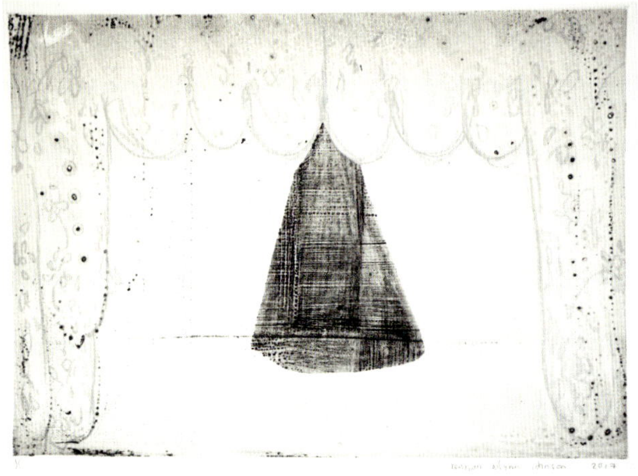

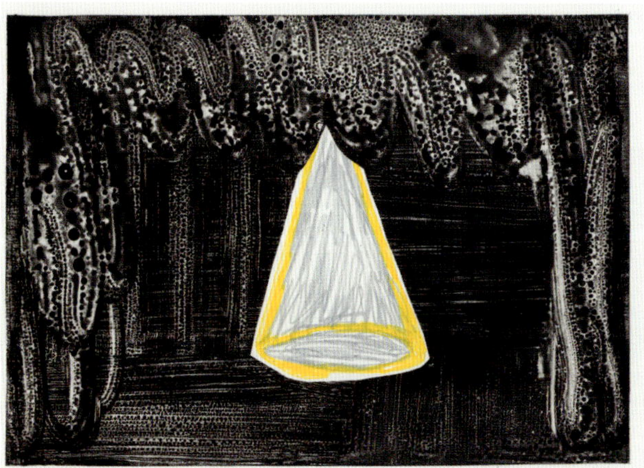

Stagelight Ghost. Watercolor monotype. 14.5" × 19.25". 2017.

Stagelight I. Watercolor monotype. 14.5" × 19.25". 2017.

ALL PHOTOS ARE COURTESY OF DAVID KRUT PROJECTS. PUBLISHED BY DAVID KRUT PROJECTS. PRINTED BY KIM-LEE LOGGENBERG AT DAVID KRUT WORKSHOP.

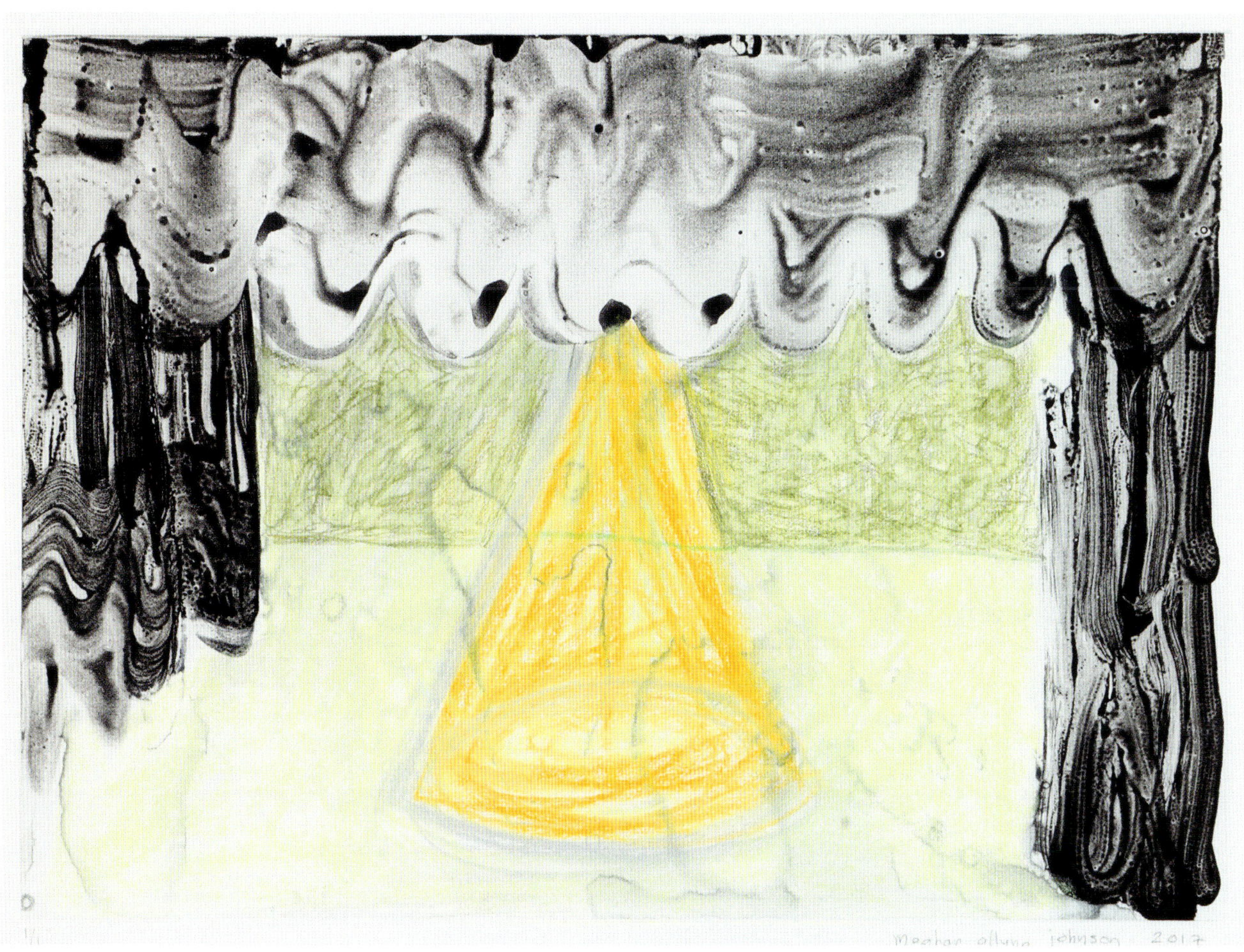

Stagelight 2. Watercolor monotype.
14.5" × 19.25". 2017.

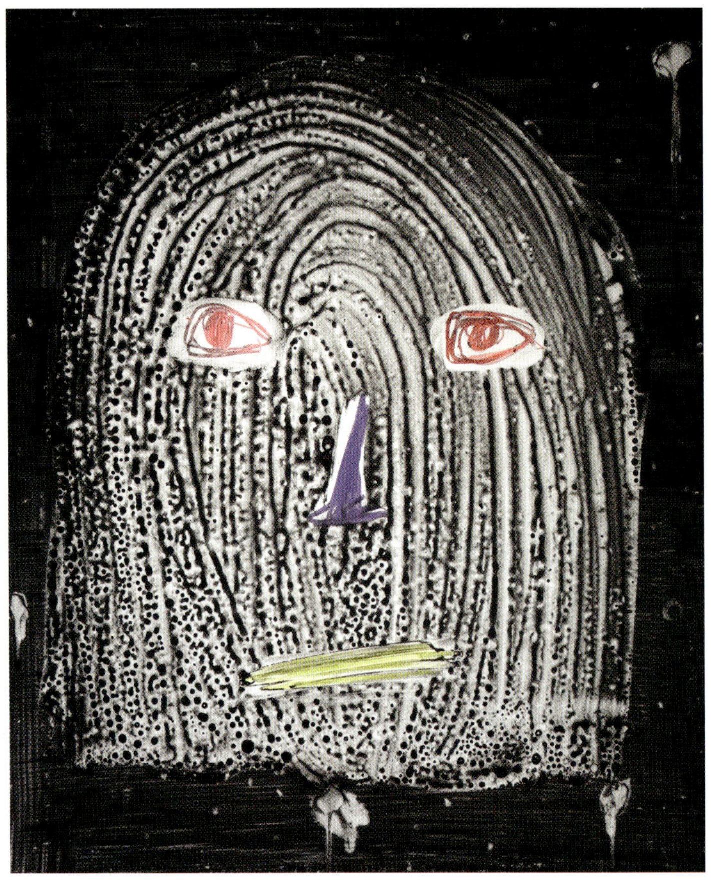

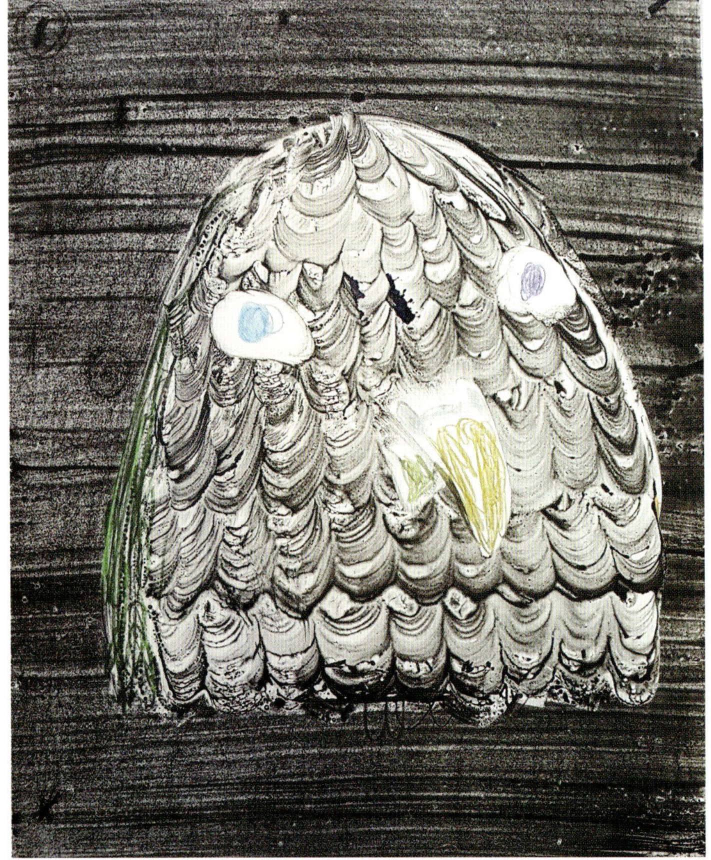

Night Spirit. Watercolor monotype. 14.5" × 19.25". 2017.

Parrot Head. Watercolor monotype. 14.5" × 19.25". 2017.

H. PEIK LARSEN

Cambridge, Massachusetts

For many years, I have had a dialogue between my paintings and monotypes as I interpret images. The iconography of elements such as tree or water is as important as are the qualities of space, light, and the energy of the moving figure. I use many of the same materials in painting and printing. The pressure from my hand and the pressure of the print press, although very different, create similar stories.

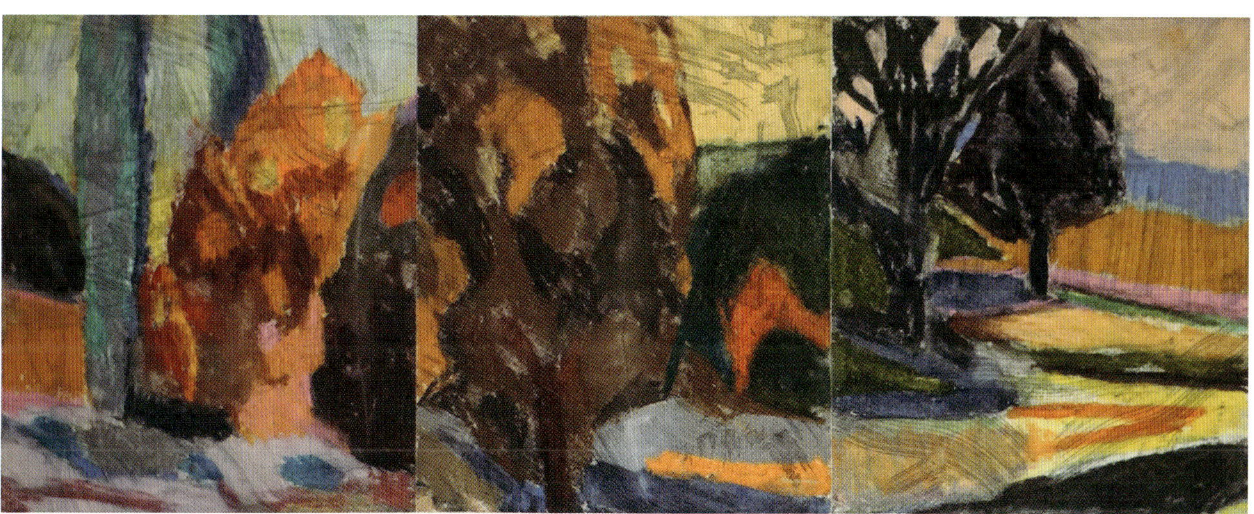

Valdorcia 4. Monoprint with oil-based ink, tint base, pastel, and etched plate. 7" × 18". 2011.

PUBLISHED AND PRINTED BY THE ARTIST AT SOME PROOF PRESS AND VES PRINT STUDIO.

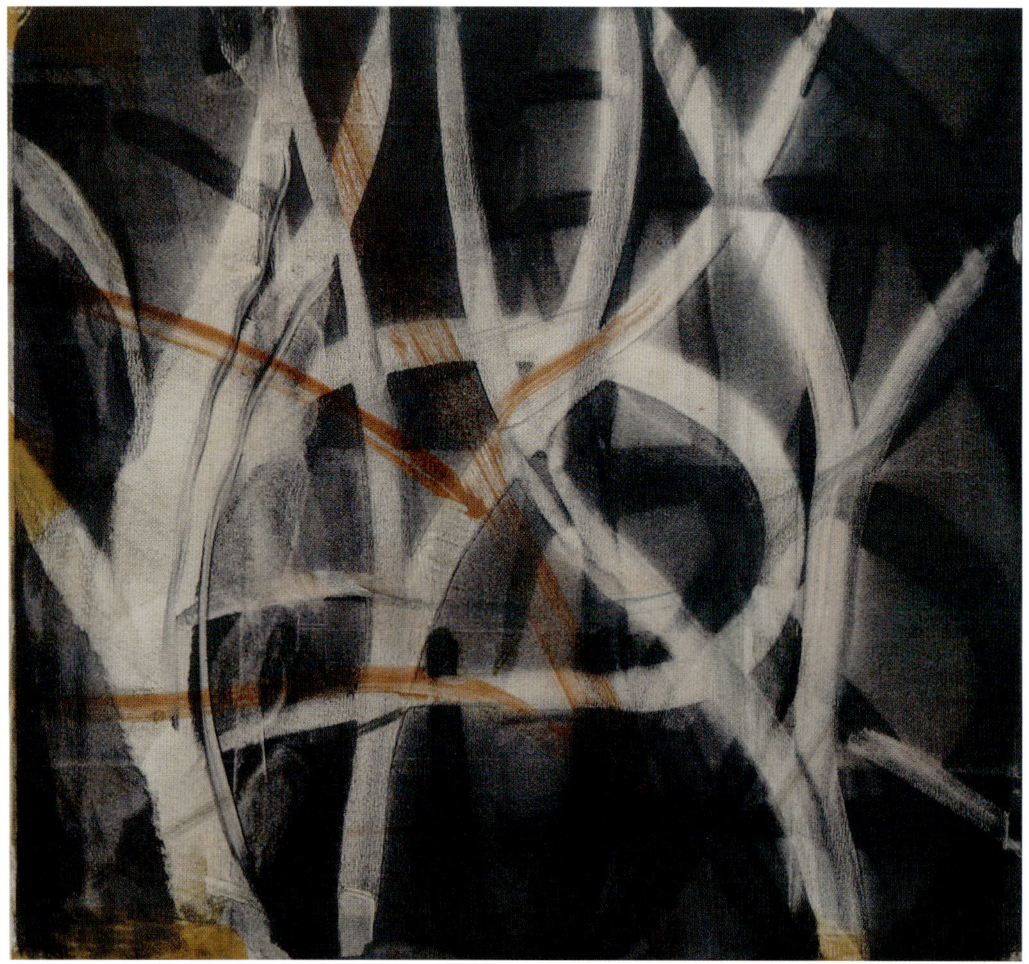

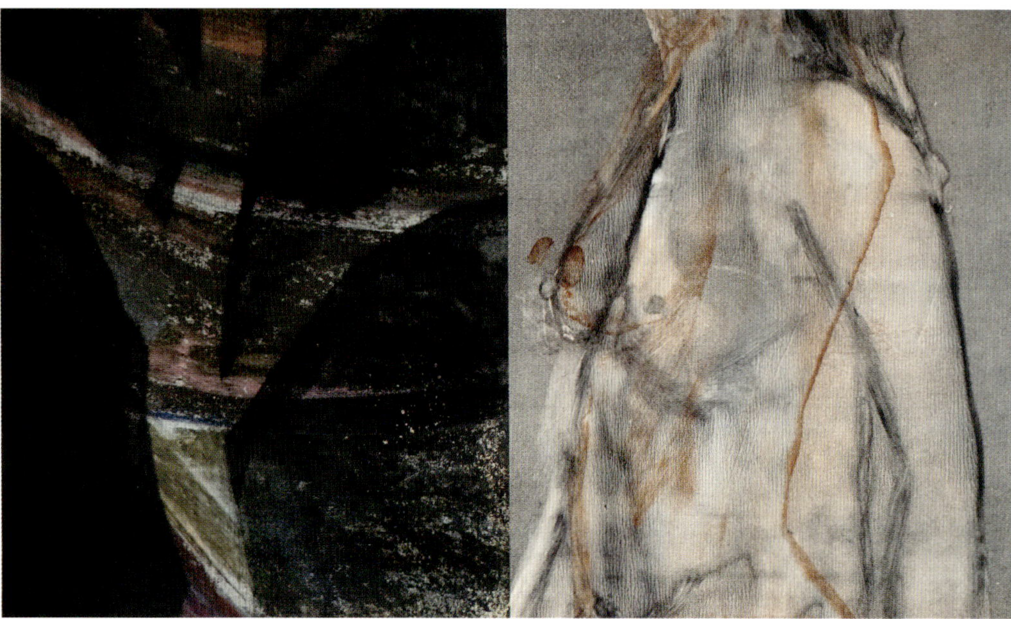

^
Arcacia III. Monotype with oil-based ink and solvent. 11.5" × 12.5". 2002.

v
2 arms. Monotype diptych. Monoprint with oil ink, tint base, pastel, and woodcut. 8.5" × 14.5". 1995.

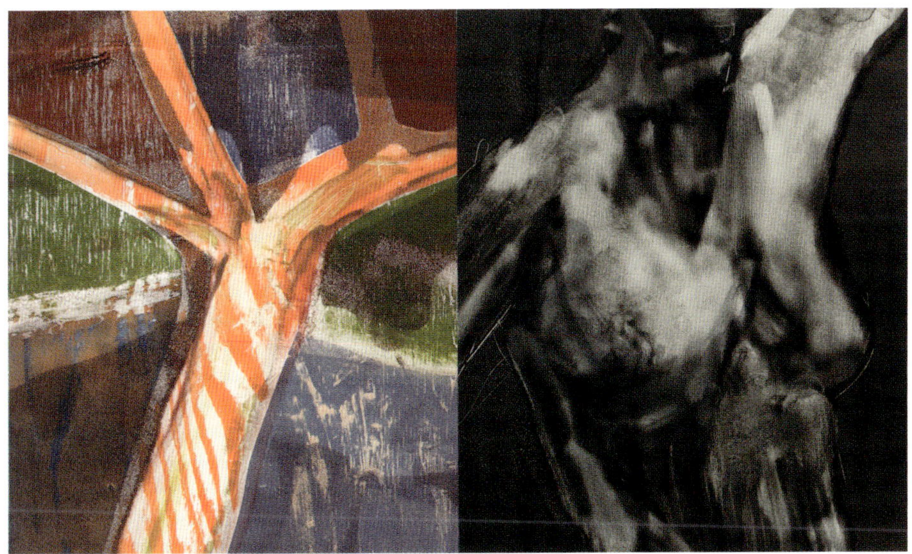

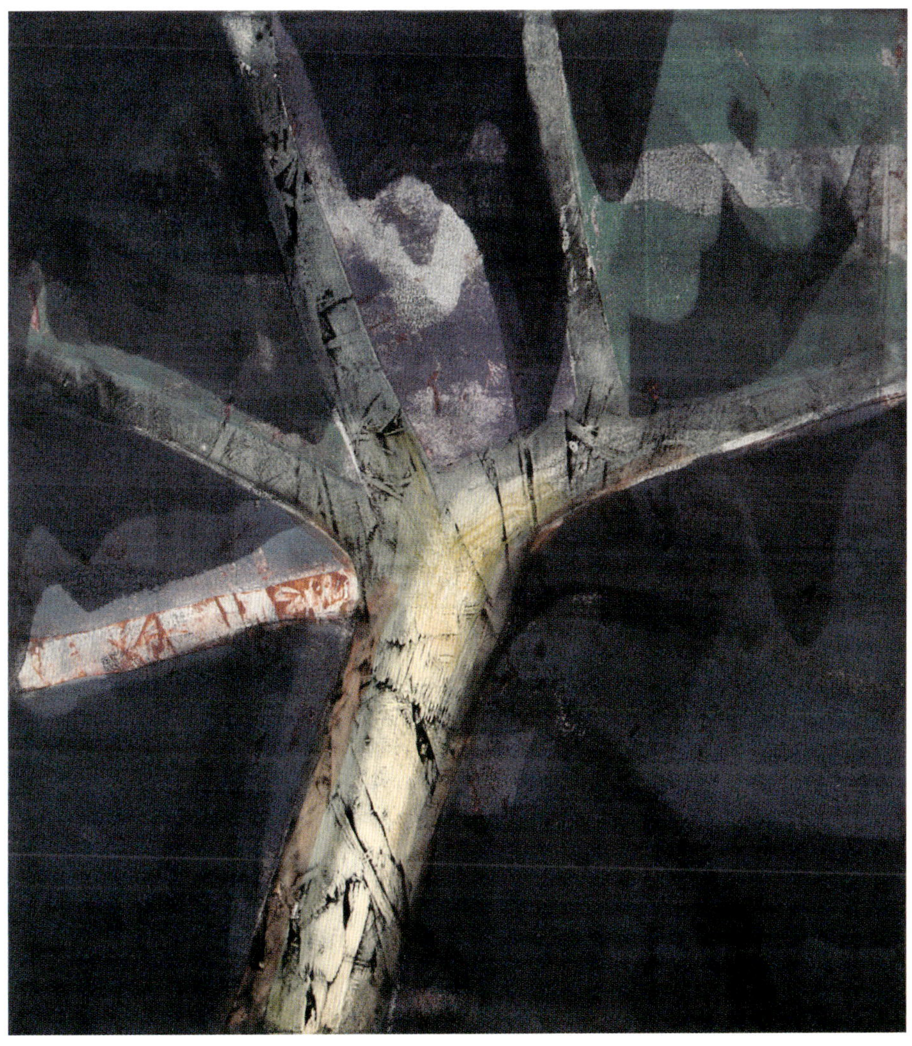

∧
Double Ilex. Monotype diptych. Monoprint with oil ink, tint base, solvent, and pastel. 8.5" × 14.5". 1995.

∨
Ilex III. Monoprint with oil ink, tint base, pastel, and woodcut. 12.75" × 11.5". 1994.

NANCY LASAR

Washington, Connecticut

My process is about layering and energizing space to create a sense of interconnection, energy, depth, and movement. Working from memory, I utilize a variety of lines and marks from tools, which I invent, along with crayons, pencils, and brushes. I strive to achieve the immediacy of direct drawing, often working on the back of the paper in what is called "trace monotype." By moving a sheet of rice paper back and forth over several inked plastic plates and drawing on the back, I can pick up layers of line and color. Images are formed without requiring a press. When completed, the rice paper is mounted face up (chine collé) to a larger sheet of white paper or adhered to panels with encaustic wax.

At other times, I compose using two overlapping drawing layers, which are printed with a press on white Western paper. I add stencils and textures to the mix. The first layer incorporates brighter hues so that when overprinted, the "light" shines through the open spaces and the images combine as one. Second and third "pulls" from the original inked plates are frequently possible. These "ghost images" can be reworked before printing again and are often very compelling. In this way, a series of related but unique prints can be created from the same matrix.

If I am lucky, acting in the moment, I find myself in a zone where things flow and connect in surprising and almost accidental ways like magic!

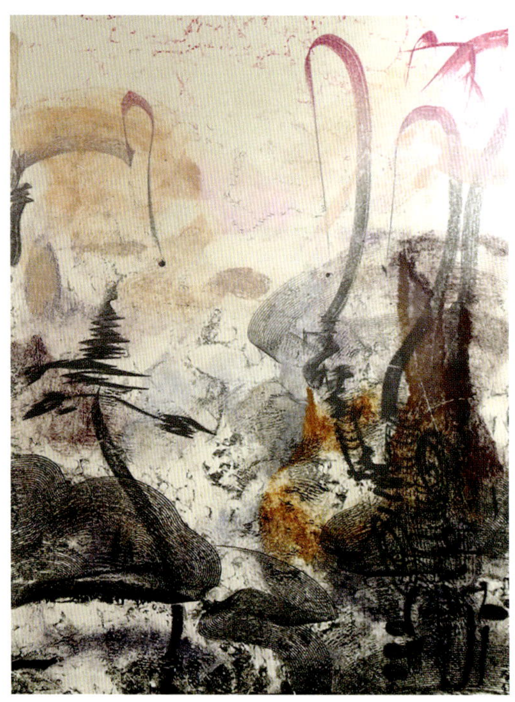

^
Mist Pine Gorge. Trace monotype with oil-based ink, carborundum, and chine collé. 31.5" × 23.5". 2014.

>
Drift. Trace monotype with oil-based ink and chine collé. 31.5" × 23.5". 2013.

Zig Zag. Trace monotype with oil-based ink. 30" × 44". 2008.

ALL PHOTOS ARE COURTESY OF TARA NUGENT. PUBLISHED BY THE ARTIST. PRINTED BY MARINA ANCONA AT 10 GRAND PRESS.

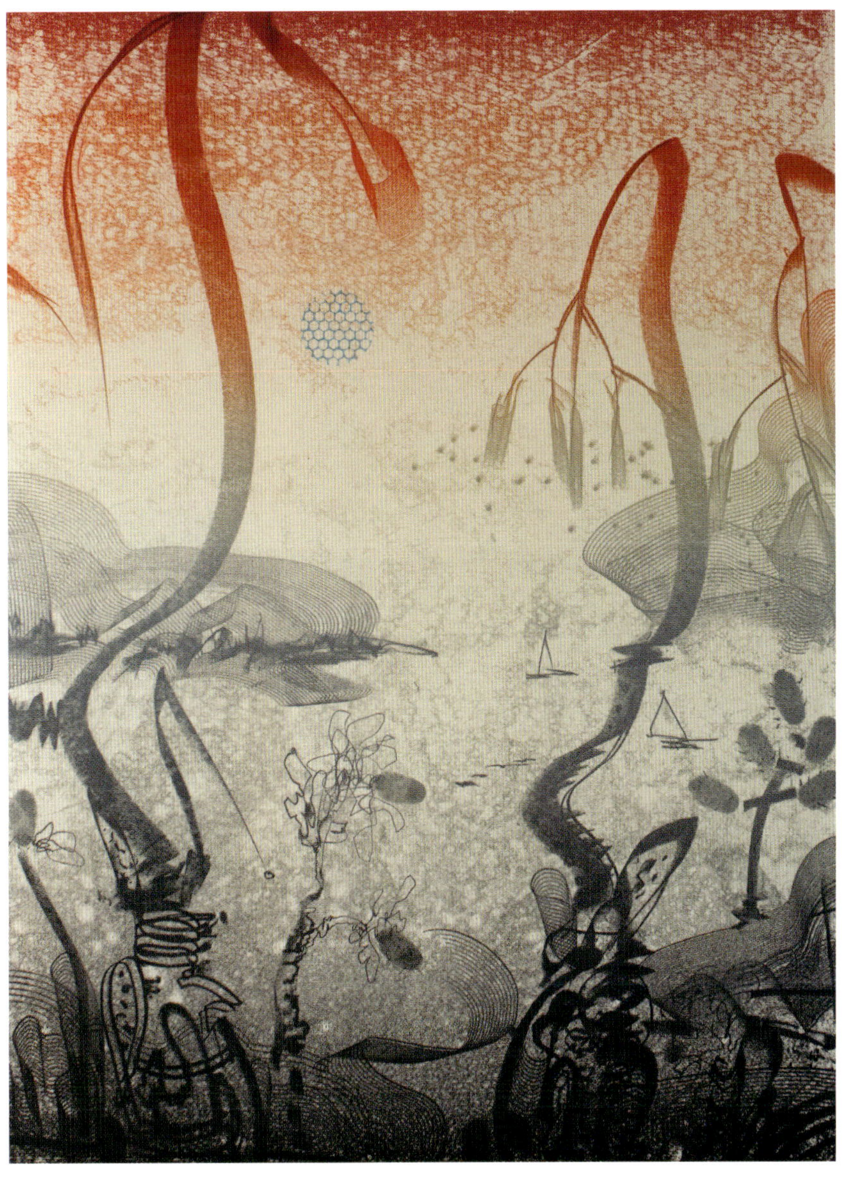

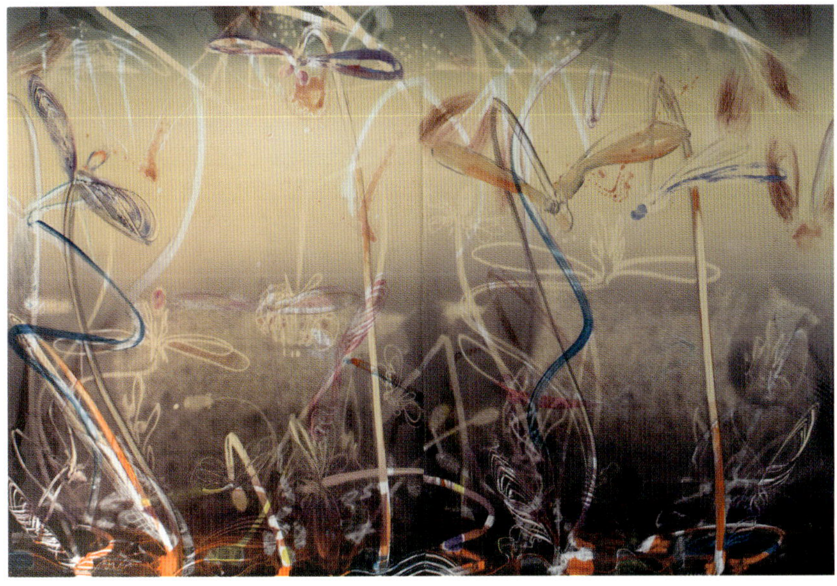

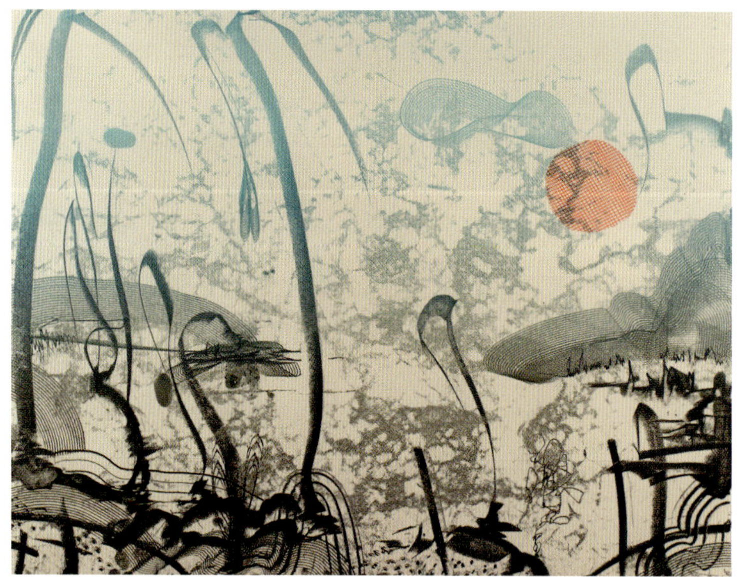

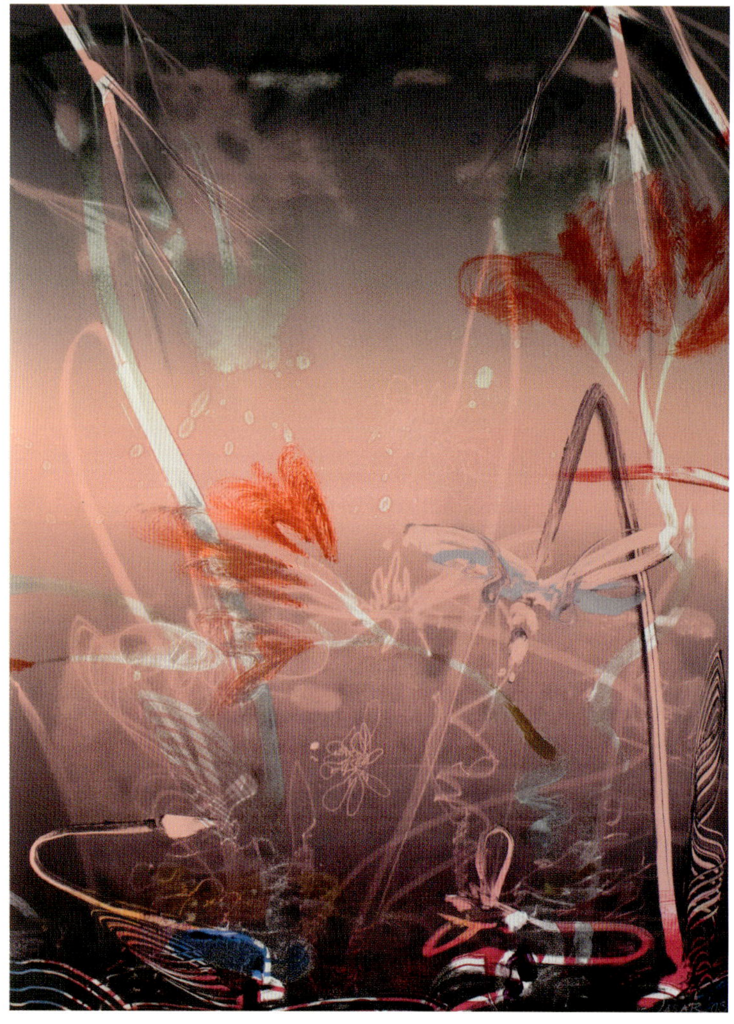

^
Warhola. Trace monotype with oil-based ink. 30" × 22". 2008.

v
Sea Grass Shore. Trace monotype with oil-based ink and chine collé. 31.5" × 23.5". 2013.

JUDITH LINHARES

Brooklyn, New York

I am always happy to be invited to make prints with a master printer, someone who knows a lot of technical information and can help you produce your best work by overseeing the process. The collaborative nature of the process always adds some new dimension to my thinking.

Monotypes, in particular, are closer in process for me to making paintings; the process involves working directly on the surface of a plate, a piece of plastic, or glass with paint, using a brush. When the paint on the plate is printed on the paper, the gesture becomes slightly simplified and enhanced; this part is always a pleasant surprise. The need to think through the image before starting is always a brain twister and a challenge. For example, if you make an image of a woman running toward the left side of the page, the image when printed will have a woman running to the right side of the page. The reversal of the image through the process can make a big difference in the appearance of the image. The need to visualize this reversal in advance is always thought provoking; using a mirror is helpful but not a perfect solution. All the surprises and challenges, plus the feedback and another pair of eyes involved in the process, always suggest new ideas and images.

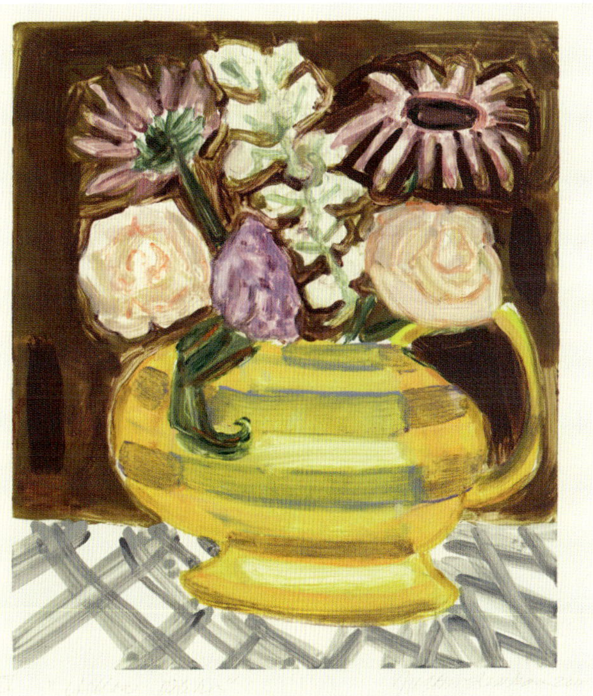

Yellow Pitcher. Monotype with oil-based ink. 18" × 15.5". 2011.

ALL PHOTOS ARE COURTESY OF ALAN WIENER. PUBLISHED BY CHERYL PELAVIN FINE ARTS AND DERRIERE L'ETOILE. PRINTED BY BRIAN PILLIOD AT CHERYL PELAVIN FINE ART AND MAURICE SANCHEZ AT DERRIERE L'ETOILE STUDIO.

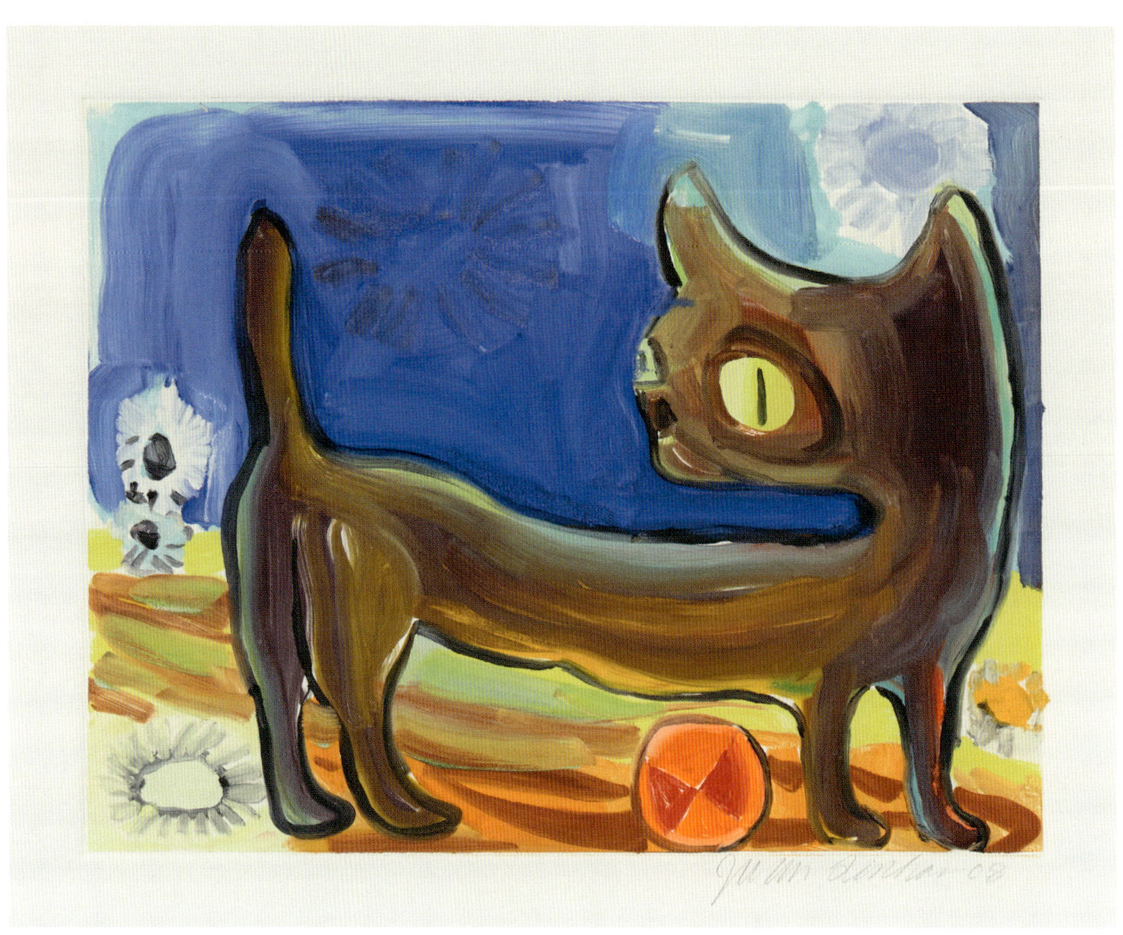

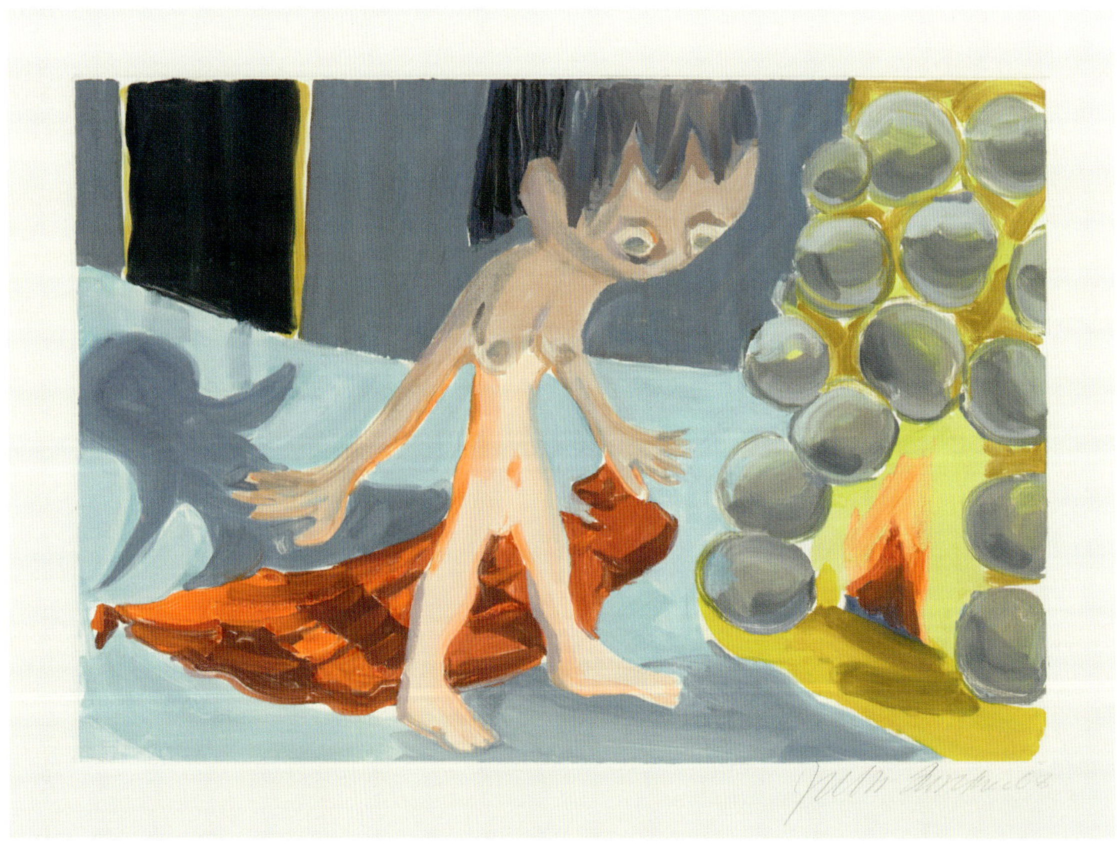

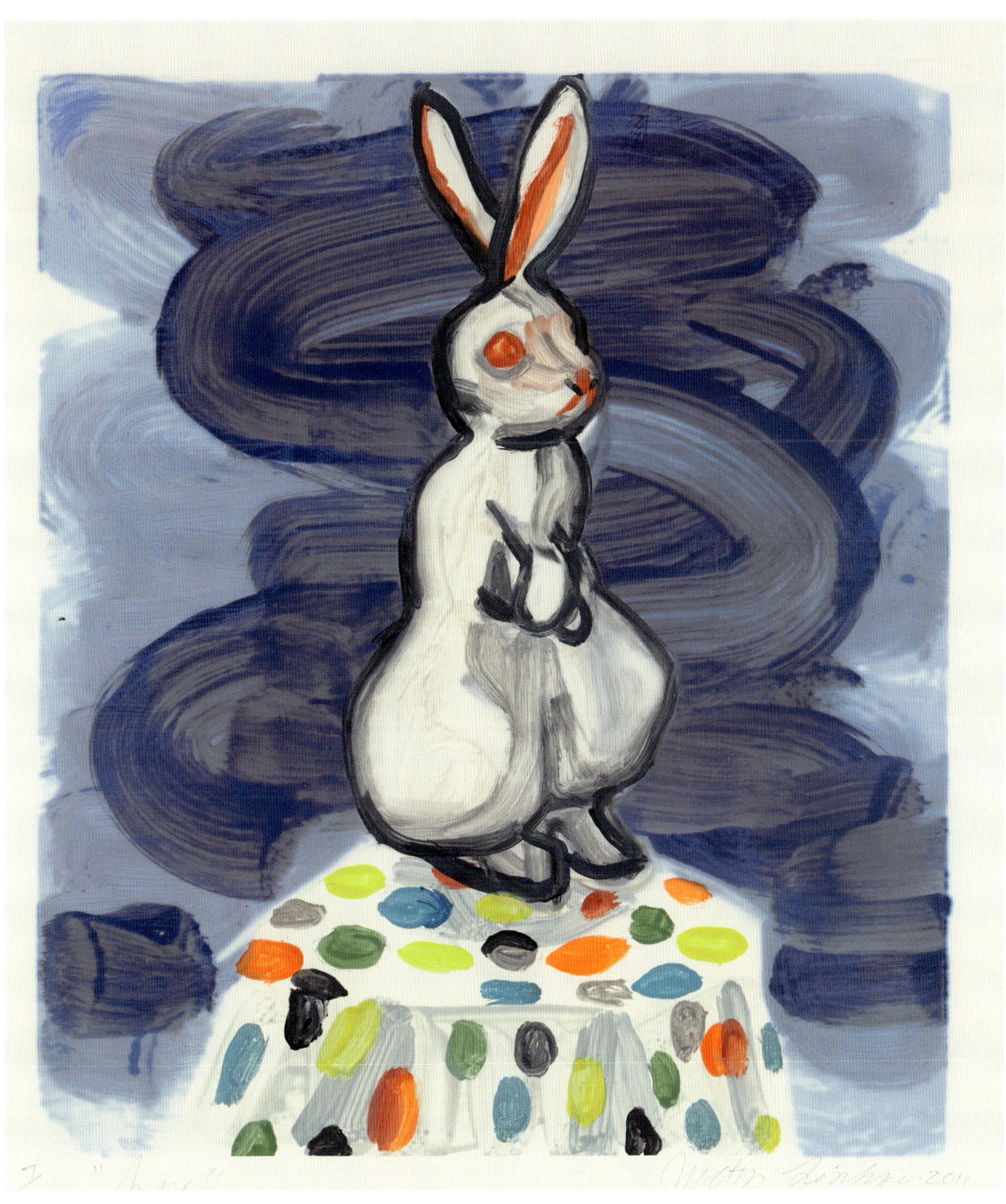

<
Cat. Monotype with oil-based ink.
18" × 15.5". 2011.

Blaze. Monotype with oil-based ink.
15.5" × 18". 2011.

Hare. Monotype with oil-based ink.
18" × 15.5". 2011.

MARKUS LINNENBRINK

Milton, Massachusetts

I had never made monotypes before working with master printer James Stroud at Center Street Studio. I wanted to find a way of working that stayed very close to my process in my own studio. We mixed up large amounts of printing ink in various colors and adjusted them in viscosity so that they would interact with each other on the press. I painted directly on the stainless-steel press bed, passing the paper through with a great deal of pressure. Each print was made with one pass. The excess ink gathered in pools after the initial print was made. A new sheet was placed on the pool of ink and run through the press in the opposite direction to create ghost prints that we titled Mudhoneys. These were often paired with the first pulls to form diptychs. Unique prints made on such large-scale sheets feel like paintings on paper and relate directly to the work in my own studio.

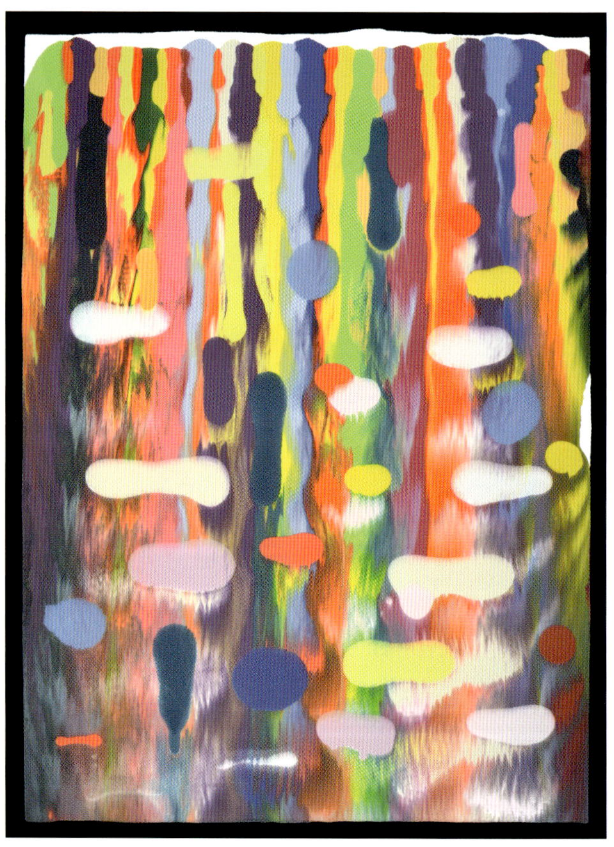

Methingksyouright,Noproblem. Monotype with oil-based ink. 48" × 35.5". 2004.

ALL PHOTOS ARE COURTESY OF JAMES STROUD. PUBLISHED AND PRINTED AT CENTER STREET STUDIO BY JIM STROUD.

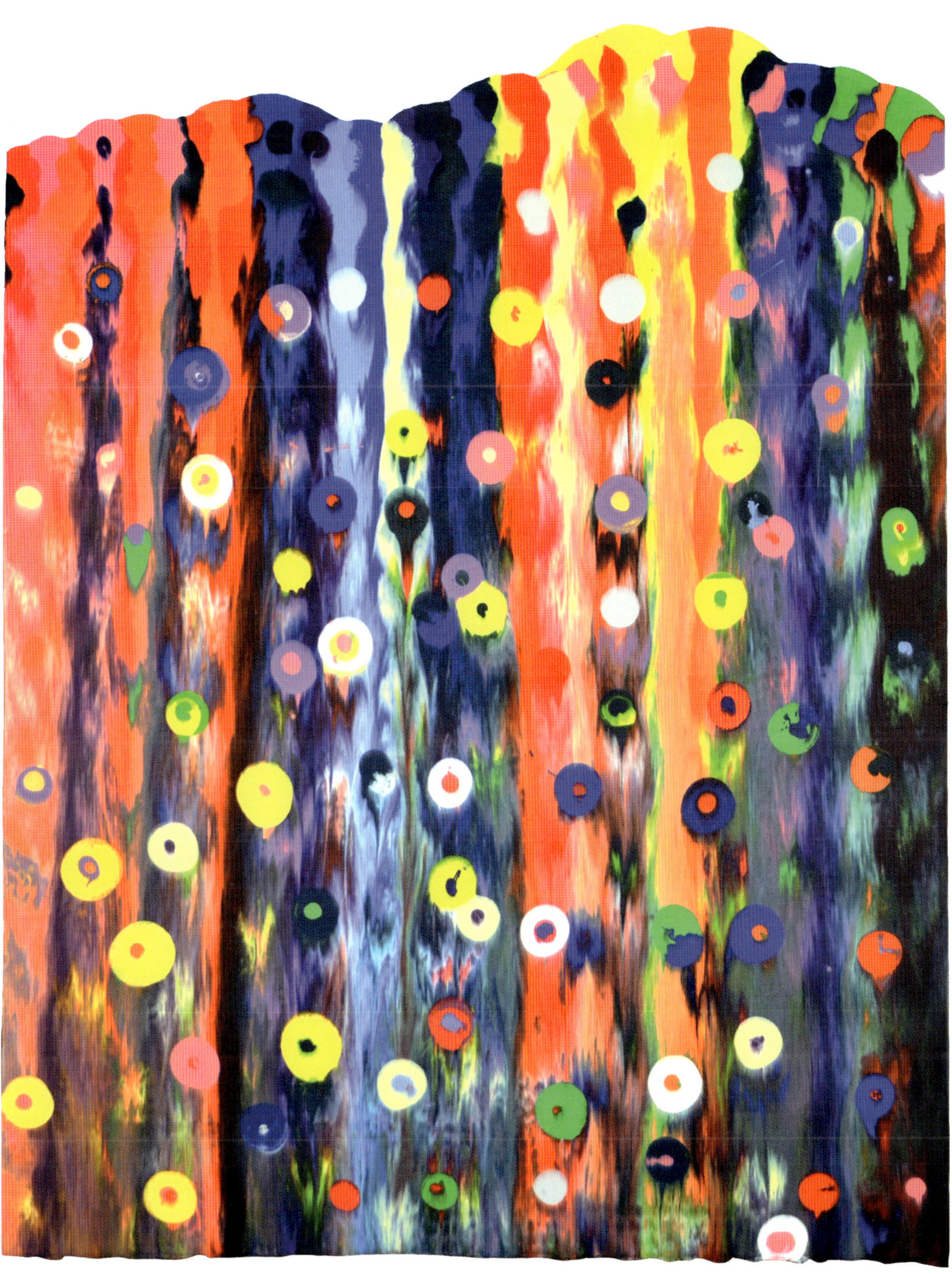

Iheardyoulooking 13. Monotype with oil-based ink. 48" × 35.5". 2013.

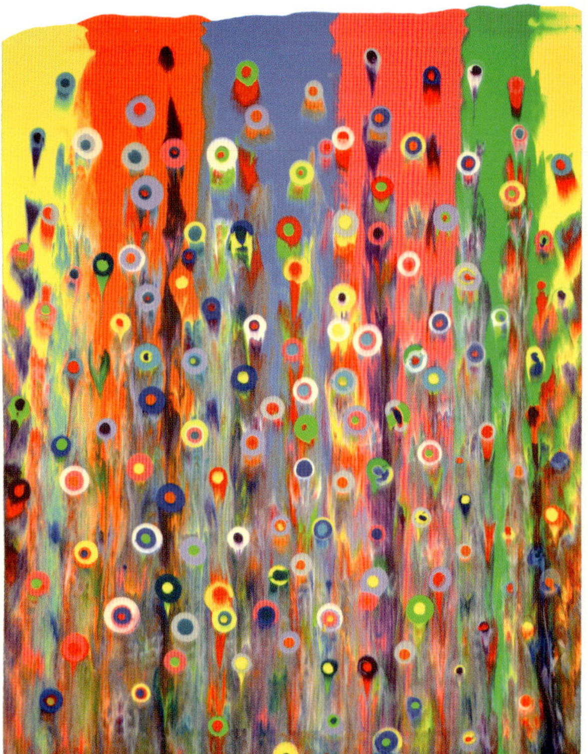

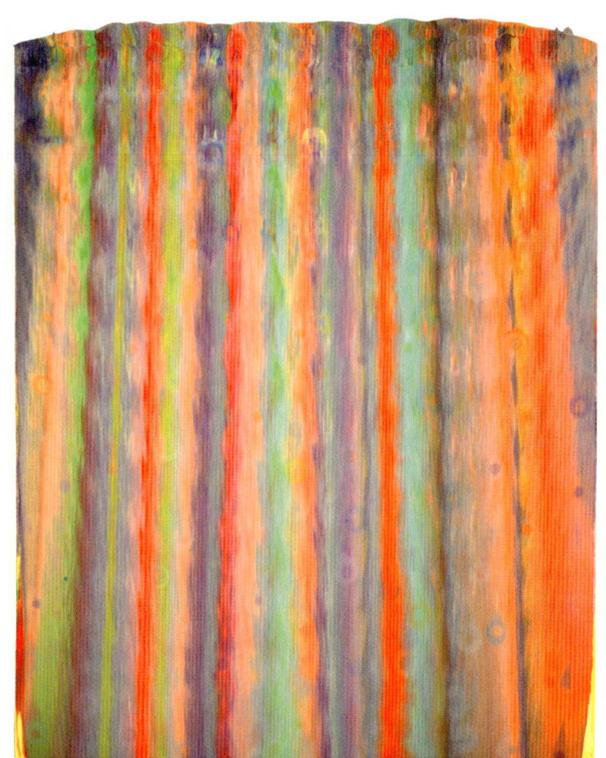

Iheardyoulooking 20. Monotype with oil-based ink. 52" × 39.5" (each image/ sheet). 52" × 79" (total diptych). 2013.

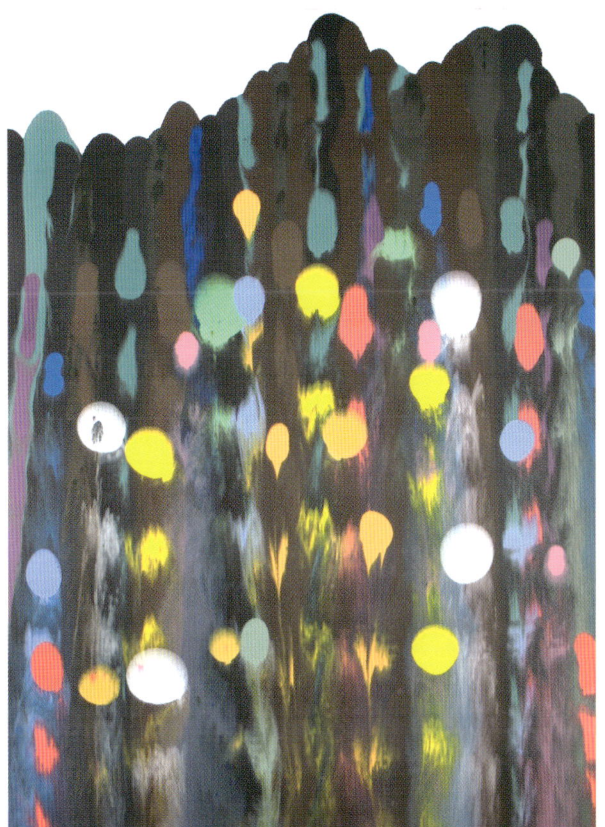

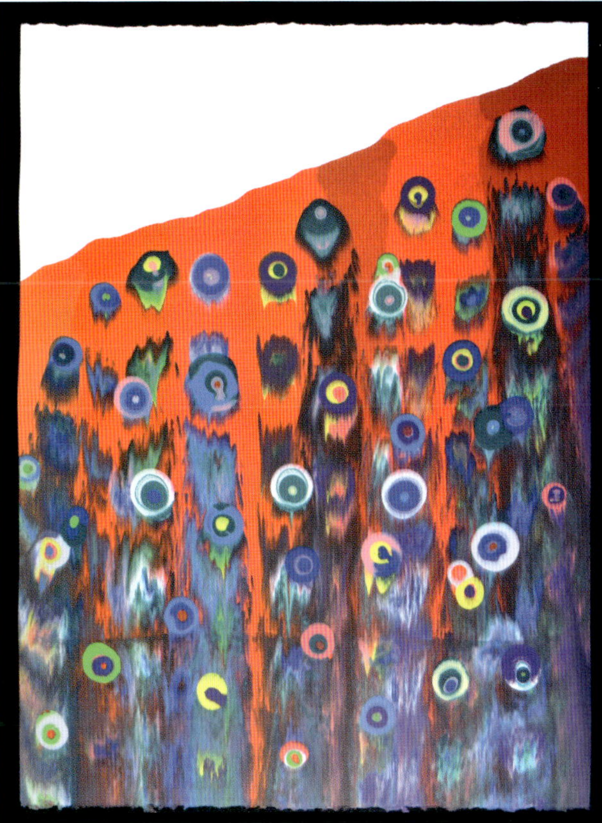

Valleyofthedolls 1. Monotype with oil-based ink. 48" × 35.5". 2009.

Iheardyoulooking(Schräg)1. Monotype with oil-based ink. 48" × 35.5". 2015.

EVA LUNDSAGER

Boston, Massachusetts

These are constellations formed of animated puddles. They are creatures, beings, stars, and planets; accumulations of paint growing out of a process that combines the accidental with the controlled and deliberate mark.

It was a joy making these; hard fought at first, slow to figure out how to work with the materials, eventually building in ease and flow, one after the other. While planning and working on these, I thought of Joan Miró's *Constellations*, which I saw in 1993 at MoMA, and as I finished them I thought of this summer's eclipse, when we all looked up at the same time.

I'm stuck to the ground, but I'm always looking up into another space, to the sky, the stars, and the planets. I see this as a vehicle for imagining other worlds, other lives, other possibilities, and other ways of existence. Imagination, putting yourself into an experience you haven't literally had, is the start of empathy. We could use more empathy right now.

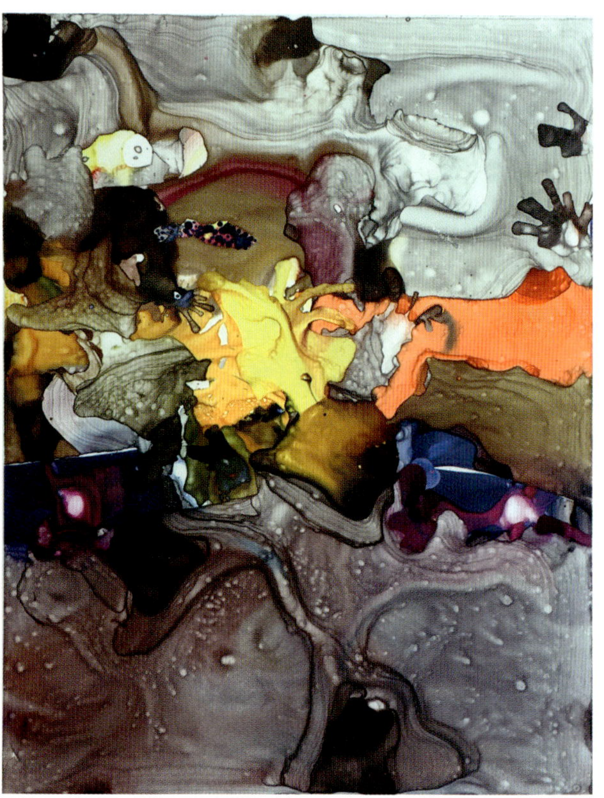

Constellation 37. Watercolor monotype. 23.75" × 18.75". 2017.

ALL IMAGES ARE COURTESY OF JAMES STROUD. PUBLISHED AND PRINTED AT CENTER STREET STUDIO BY JIM STROUD.

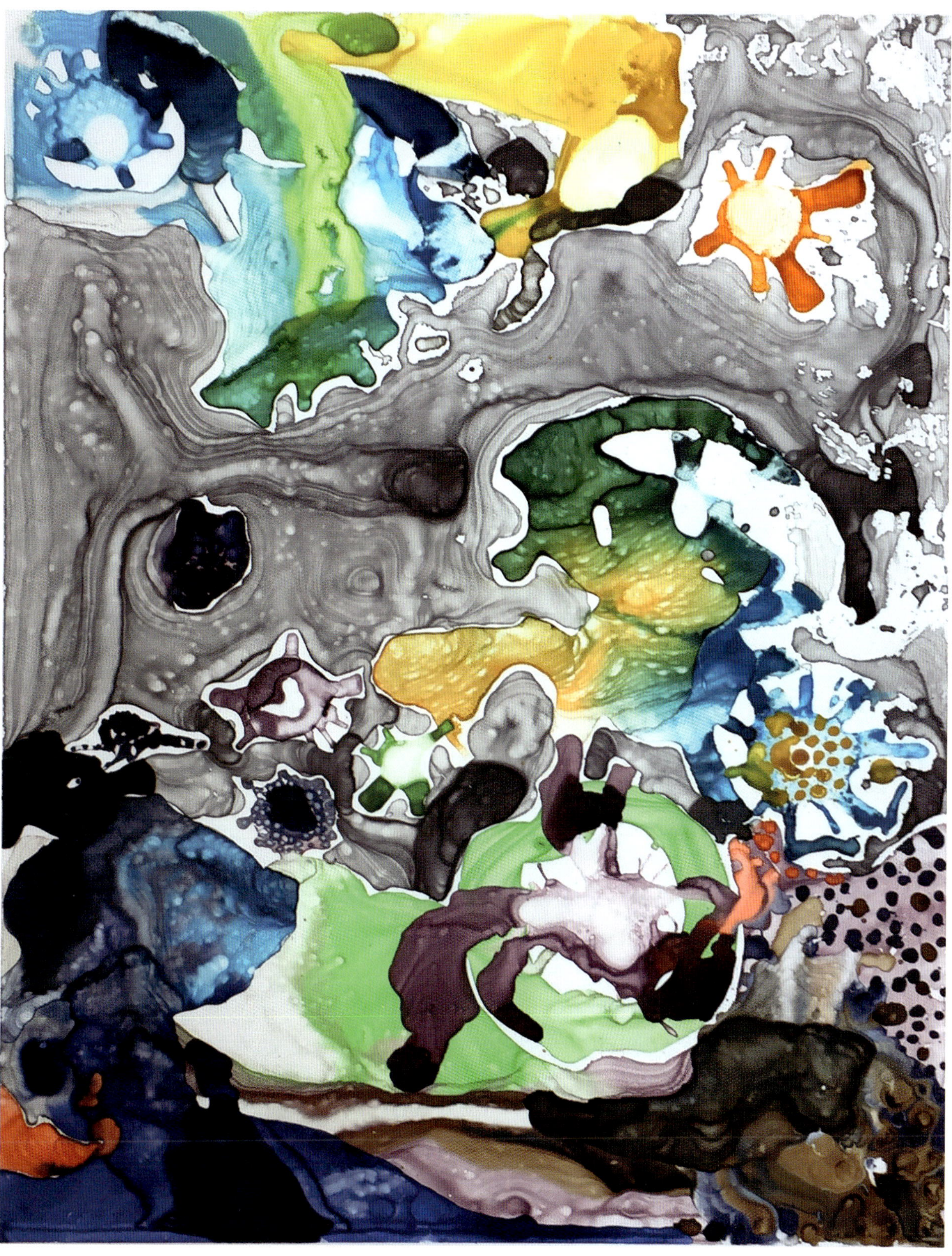

Constellation 36. Watercolor monotype.
23.75" × 18.75". 2017.

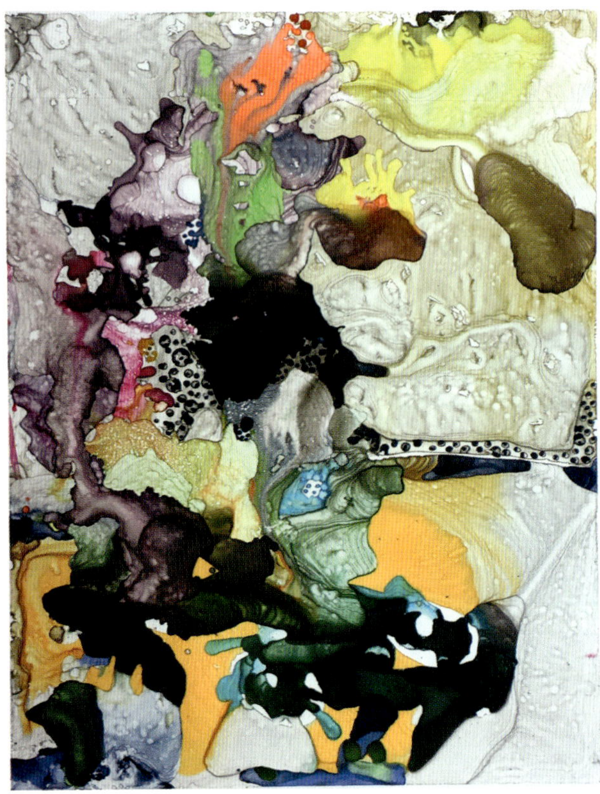

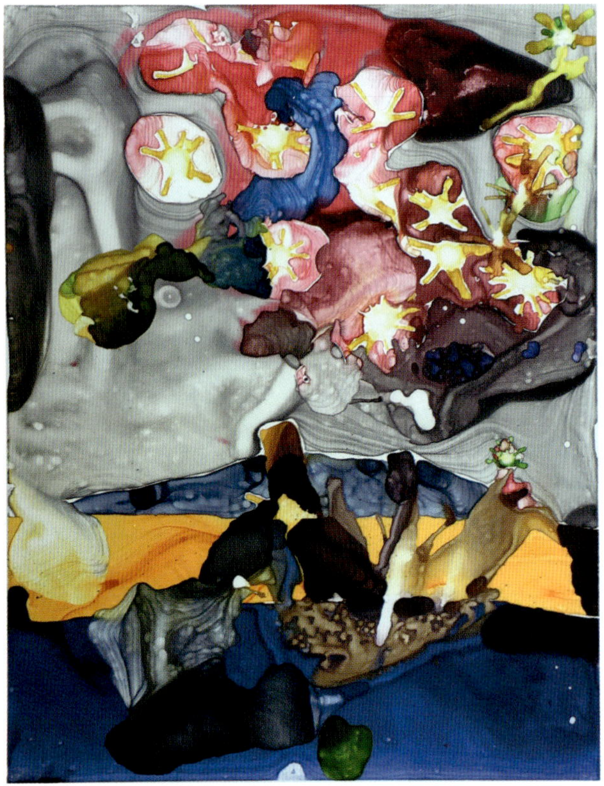

Constellation 39. Watercolor monotype.
23.75" × 18.75". 2017.

Constellation 40. Watercolor monotype.
23.75" × 18.75". 2017.

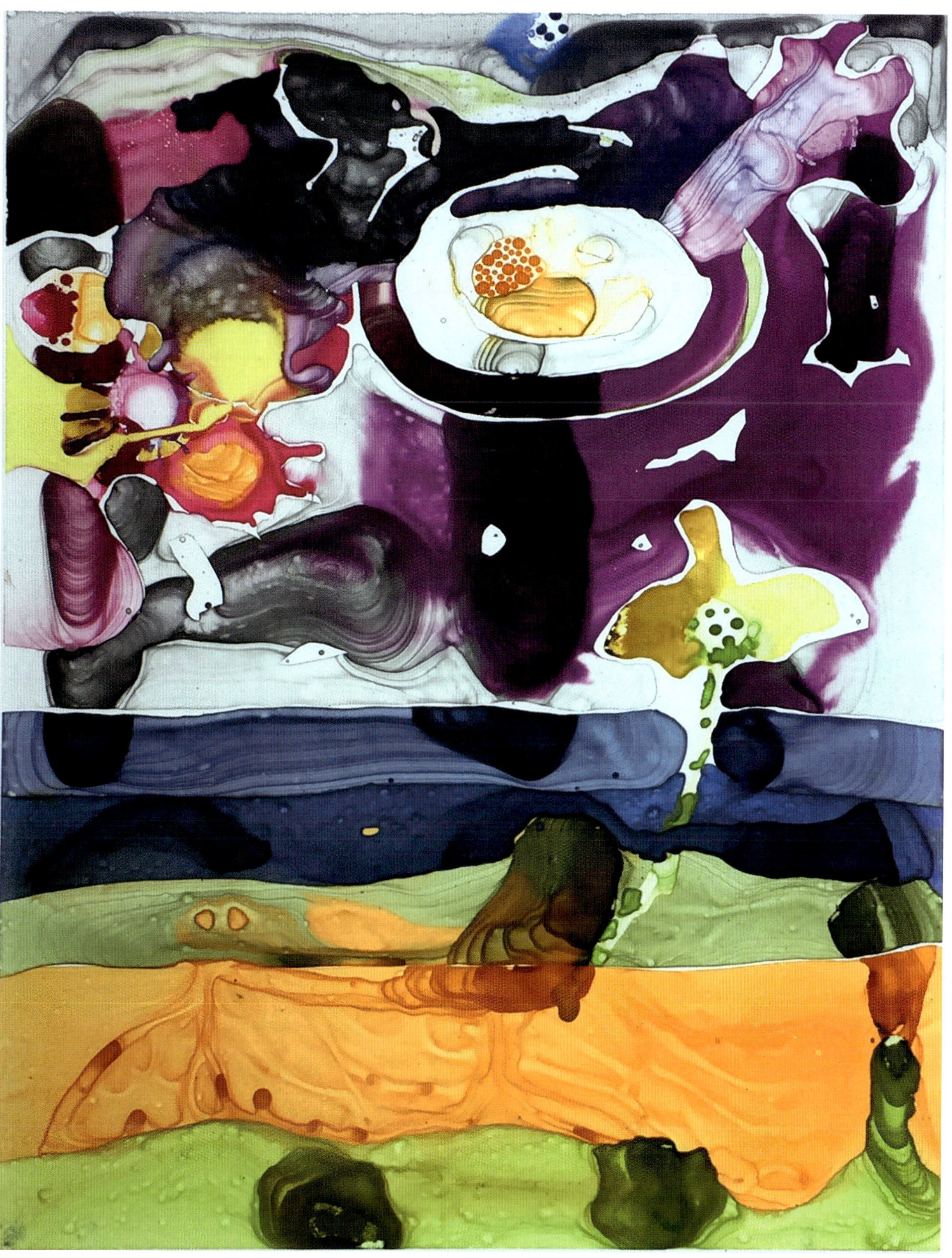

Constellation 41. Watercolor monotype. 23.75" × 18.75". 2017.

CARRIE MOYER

Brooklyn, New York

Monotypes have been critical to my evolution as a painter. For me they are a way of prying loose the preconceived notions of what can take over in the studio. The monotypes take shape quickly—one or two days as opposed to the weeks and months it sometimes takes to make a painting—so they act as a kind of sketchbook. I love tracking how clusters of ideas gather, gain critical mass, and then morph into something else across a suite of monotypes. The Rush and Roll series was all about creating unique form through the unpredictable marriage of ink and roller. Those forms that often came out looking like parti-colored Scholar's Rocks became the landscape for a dreamy narrative with the addition of woodcut and freehand drawing. The Soft Cells series was also enormously freeing and intuitive. The images came into focus slowly, through the soft buildup of stains, daubs, and precise erasures. Unlike my paintings, there were no hard-edged shapes to corral the unruly pours, just the light ministrations of fingertips and rags.

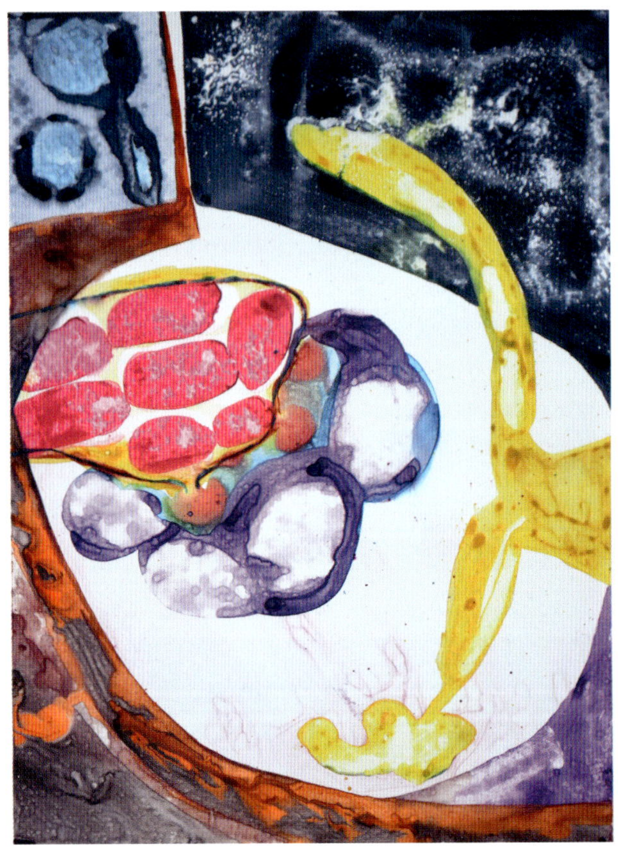

Soft Cells 3. Watercolor monotype.
18" × 24". 2014.

ALL IMAGES ARE COURTESY OF JAMES STROUD. PUBLISHED AND PRINTED AT CENTER STREET STUDIO BY JIM STROUD.

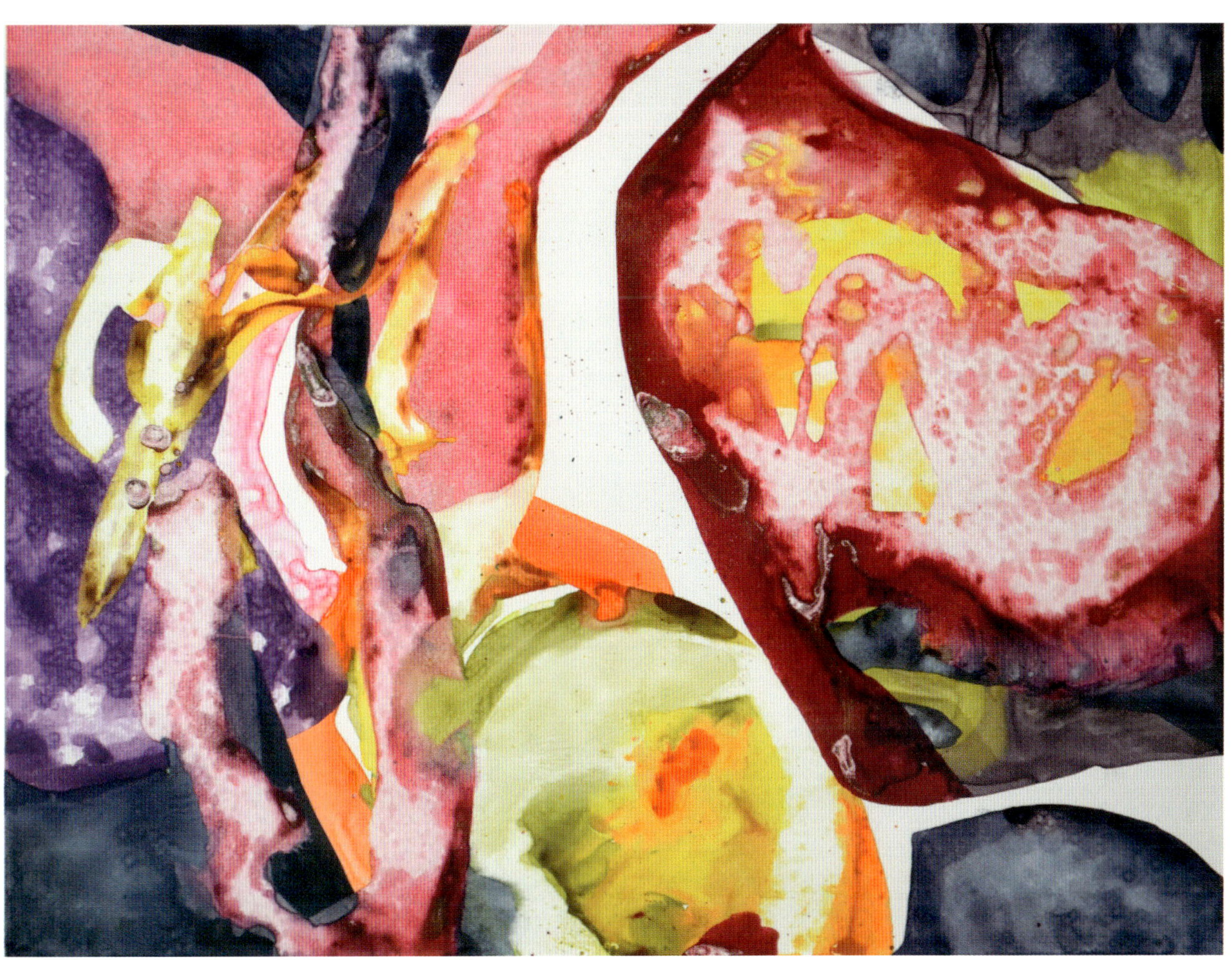

Soft Cells 4. Watercolor monotype. 24" × 18". 2014.

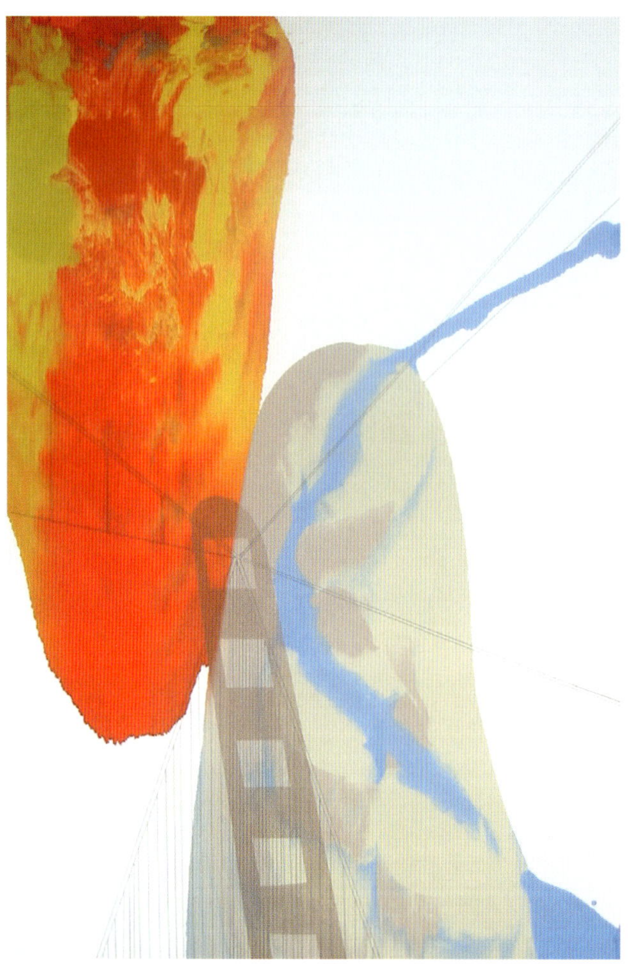

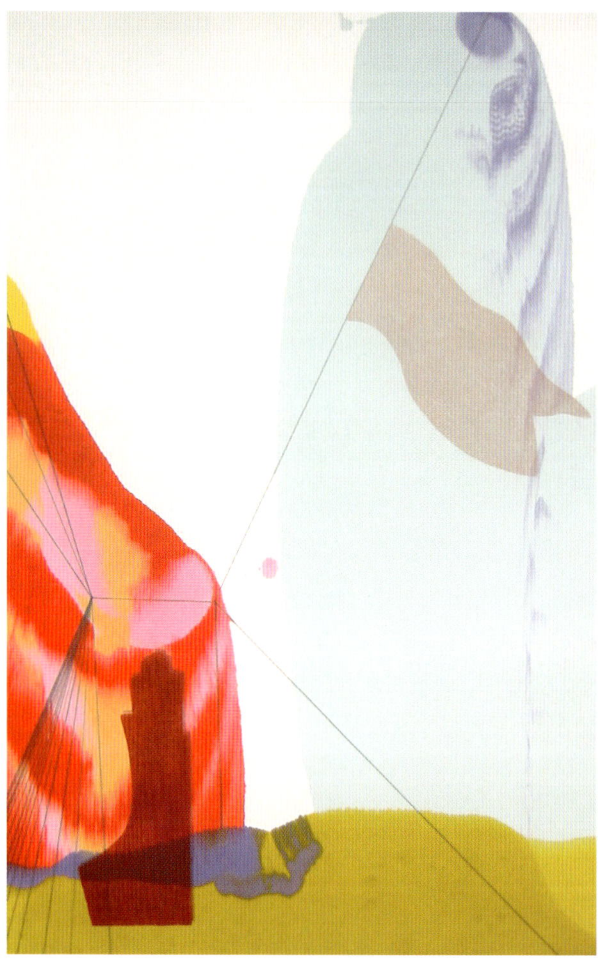

Rush and Roll 2. Monotype with graphite drawing and woodcut elements. 35.5" × 24". 2006.

Rush and Roll 11. Monotype with oil-based ink with graphite drawing and woodcut elements. 35.5" × 24". 2006.

>

Rush and Roll 7. Monotype with oil-based ink, graphite drawing, and woodcut elements. 35.5" × 24". 2006.

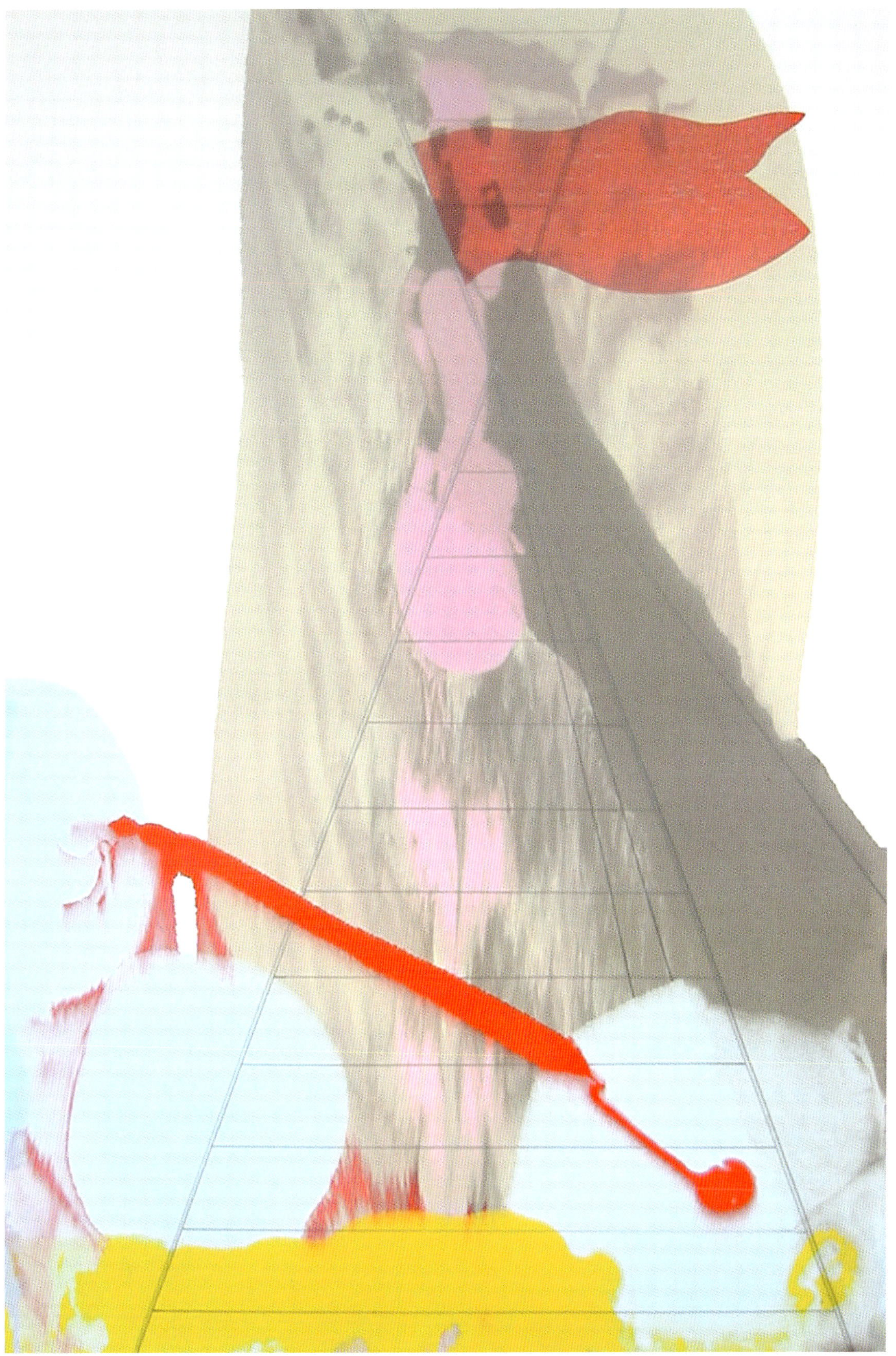

WENDY ORVILLE

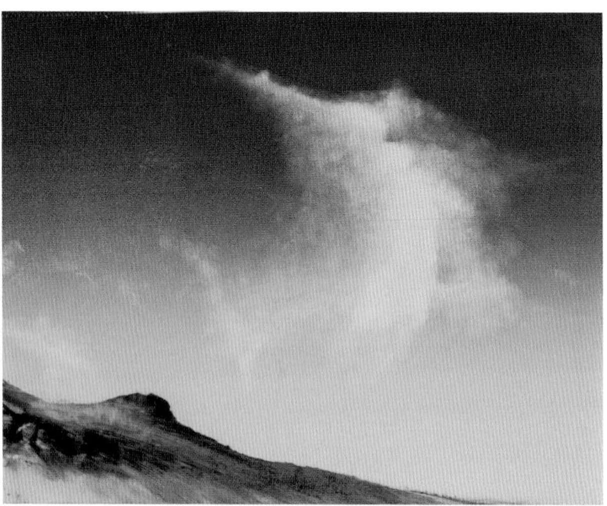

Bainbridge Island, Washington

I am drawn to vast spaces. Skies are made by wiping away forms on an inked plate with sticks and cloths—a deeply meditative and pleasurable process. I love watching clouds move across the sky, continually changing states, a focused seeing that inspires my creativity. As the daughter of a geology professor and high school biology teacher, I grew up learning that nature was both explainable and full of magic. I want my work to capture an equivalent of light and air, a caught motion, a celebration of nature's dynamism and mystery.

My intent is to reduce the landscape to essentials, evoking an emotional space that invites the viewer inside while retaining a painterly physicality and surface tension. I treat the monotype process like painting in many ways. I work to create an equivalent of light by building up translucent layers of tonal etching ink, often scratching into the surface after pulling the print from the press and adding additional marks with cut-up credit cards and brushes. Wiping away forms on an inked plate with sticks and cloths—a deeply pleasurable and meditative process—makes skies.

The challenge of making a visual and poetic equivalent of the landscape continually pushes me to explore new techniques in monotype. I have specific intentions when I work, but I also respond to what emerges on the plate and intuitively follow the image as it unfolds.

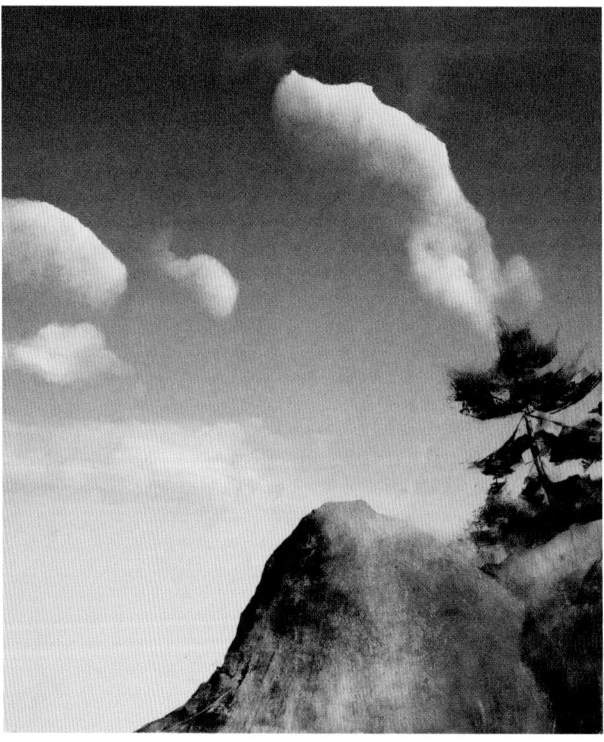

Volcano with Single Cloud. Monotype with oil-based ink. 16" × 20". 2016.

Rockaway Pine. Monotype with oil-based ink. 13.5" × 12". 2014.

ALL PHOTOS ARE COURTESY OF ART GRICE. PUBLISHED AND PRINTED BY THE ARTIST AT INKGARDEN STUDIOS.

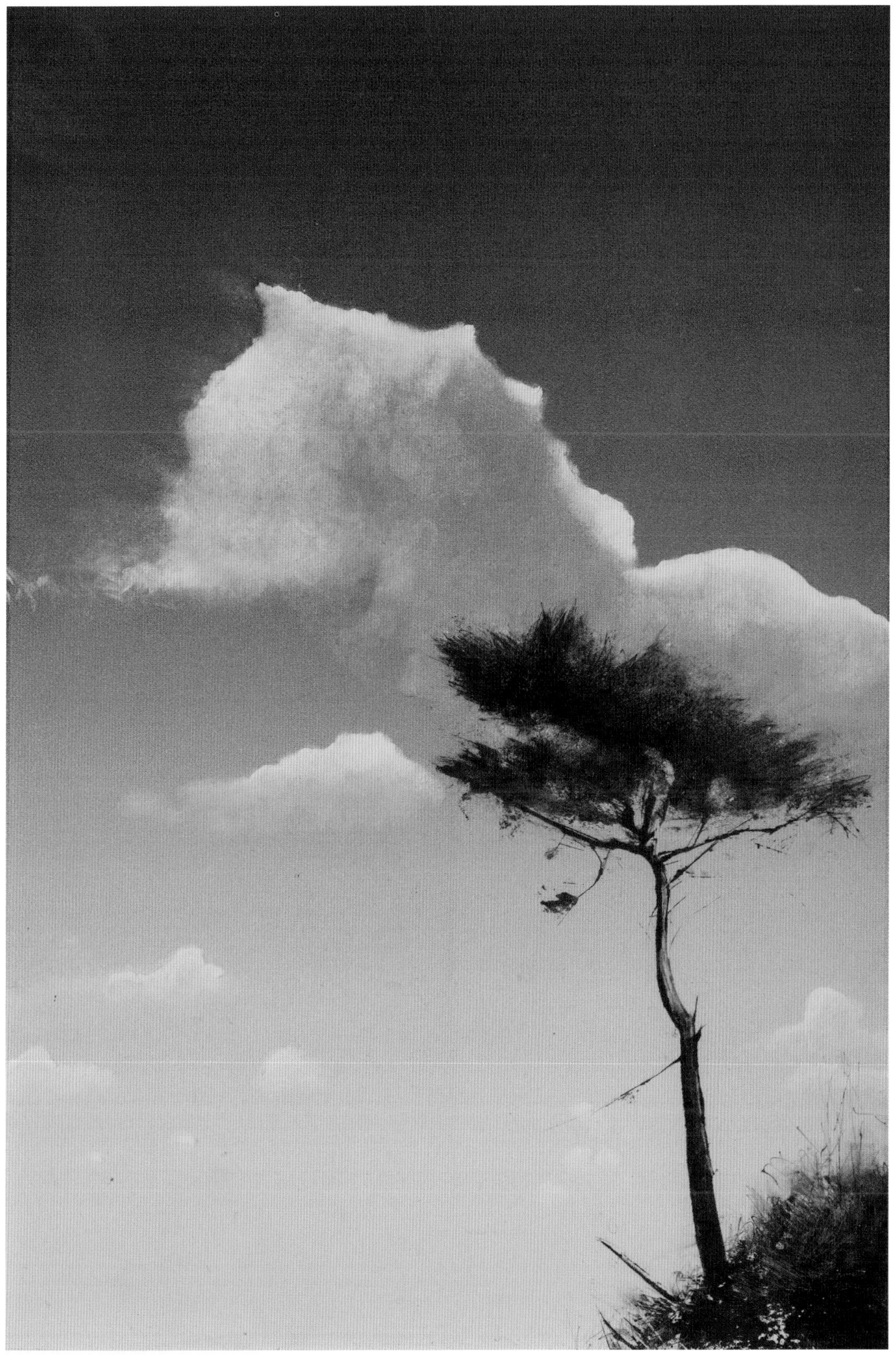

Port Townsend Fir No. 2. Monotype with oil-based ink. 19" × 13". 2016.

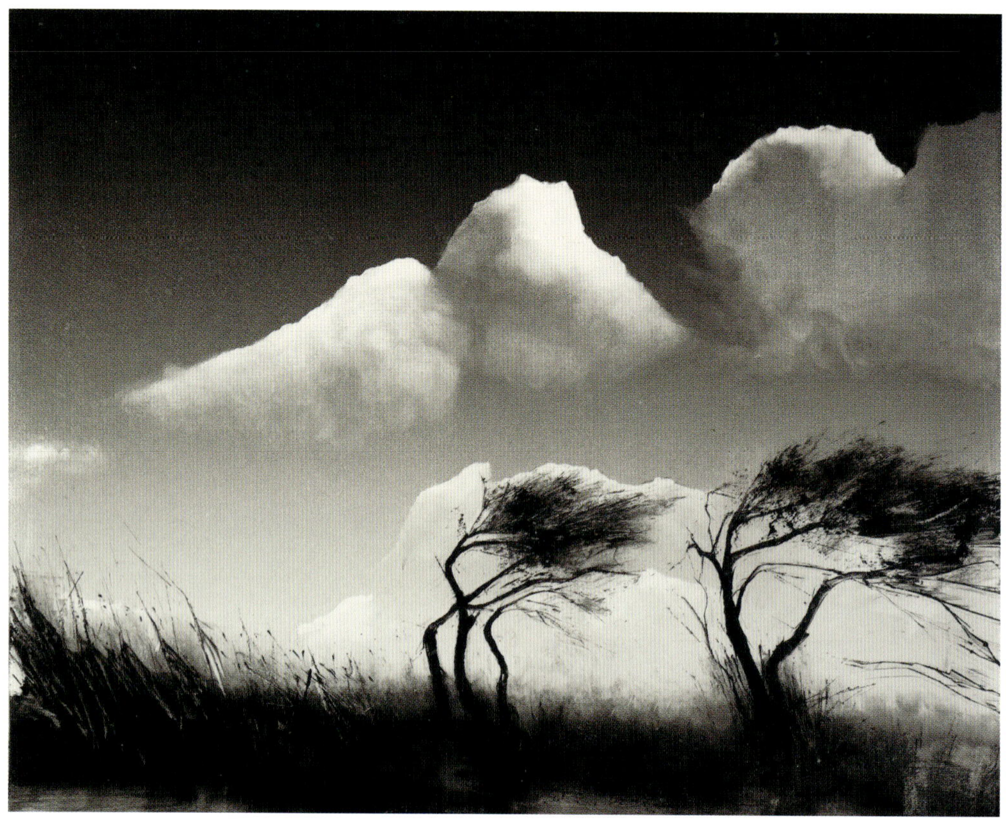

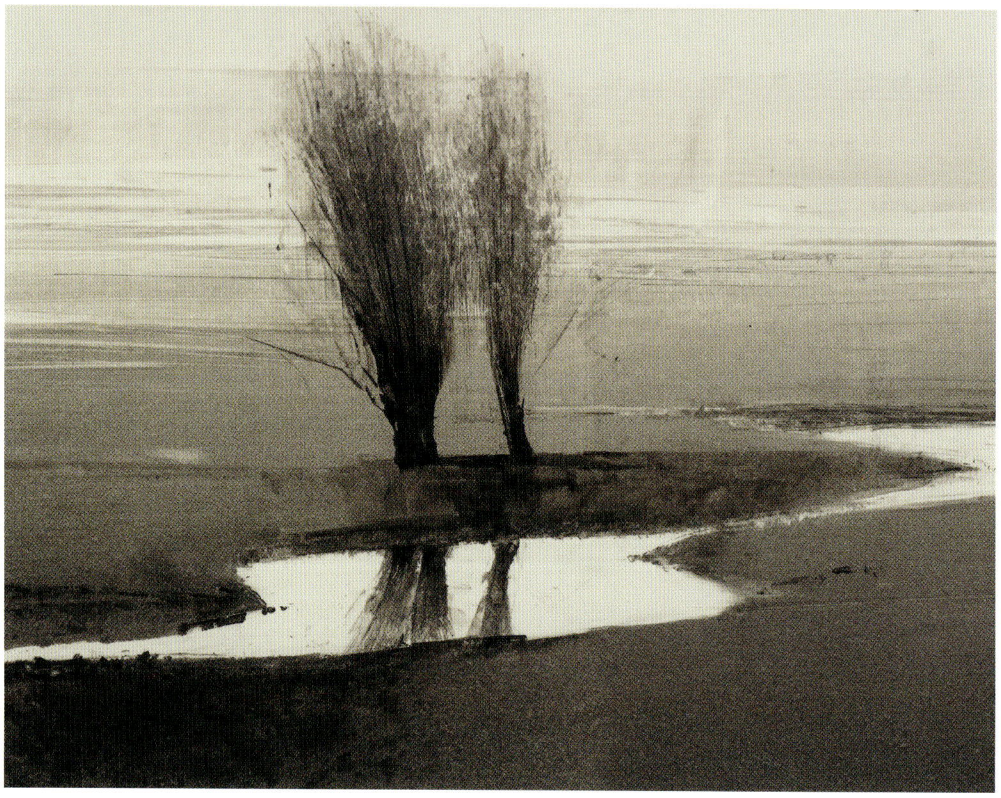

^
Refuge No. 6. Monotype with oil-based ink. 15.5" × 20". 2014.

v
Two Trees: *Nisqually*. Monotype with oil-based ink. 7" × 9". 2016.

ROBERT ANDREW PARKER

West Cornwall, Connecticut

Monotype began for me with a sketchbook and a sharpened pencil. It became an occasion to draw on a clean page on top. I did this constantly. It is paper on paper, and then I would roll up something smooth with oil, colors, and graphite. I was fascinated by the line work of Paul Klee. It is the physicality of drawing on a plate; whatever is handy that is flat, smooth, and rigid to hold a compelling image.

In my trace monotypes, I draw on the verso, flip the plate over, and then draw, with greasy materials, the image that I desire. This affords me the ability to follow my drawing in concise reverse on the proper side of the plate. I then run it through a press with paper adhered to pull an image. In the old days, it would have been easy to work with carbon paper.

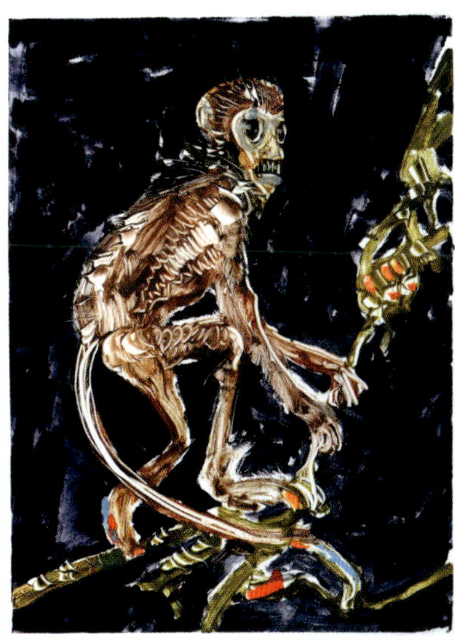

Monkey Dreams. Monotype with oil-based inks. 22" × 28". 2015.

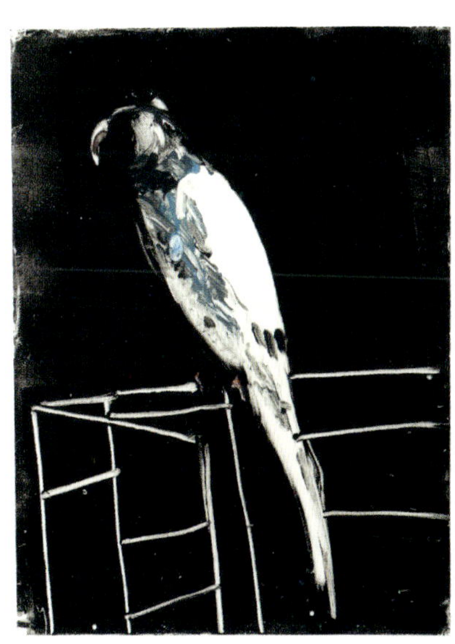

Parrot. Monotype with oil-based inks. 22" × 29.5". 2010.

ALL PHOTOS ARE COURTESY OF DON HEINY. PUBLISHED AND PRINTED BY THE ARTIST.

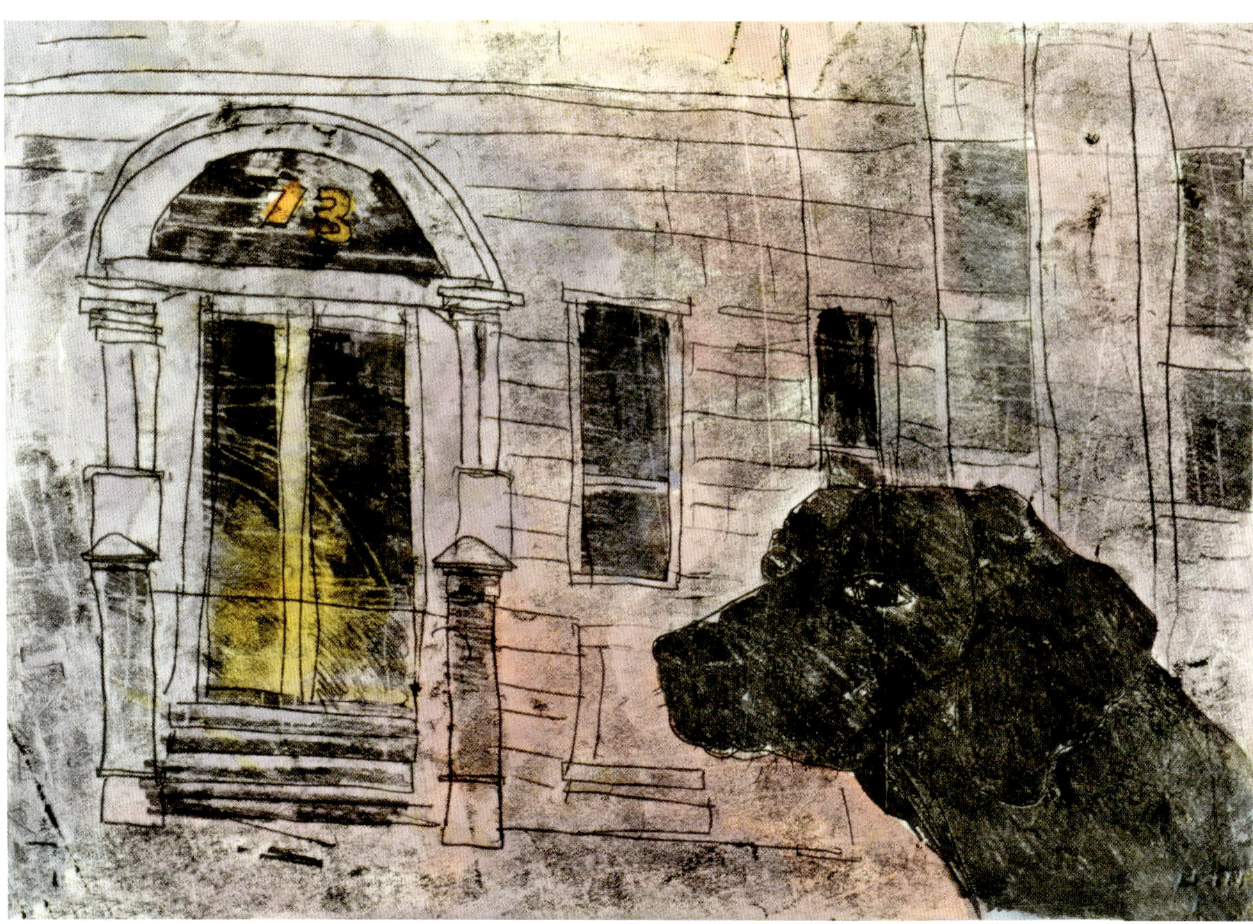

Dog in the City. Front. Trace monotype and monotype with oil-based ink. 12" × 17.5". 2000.

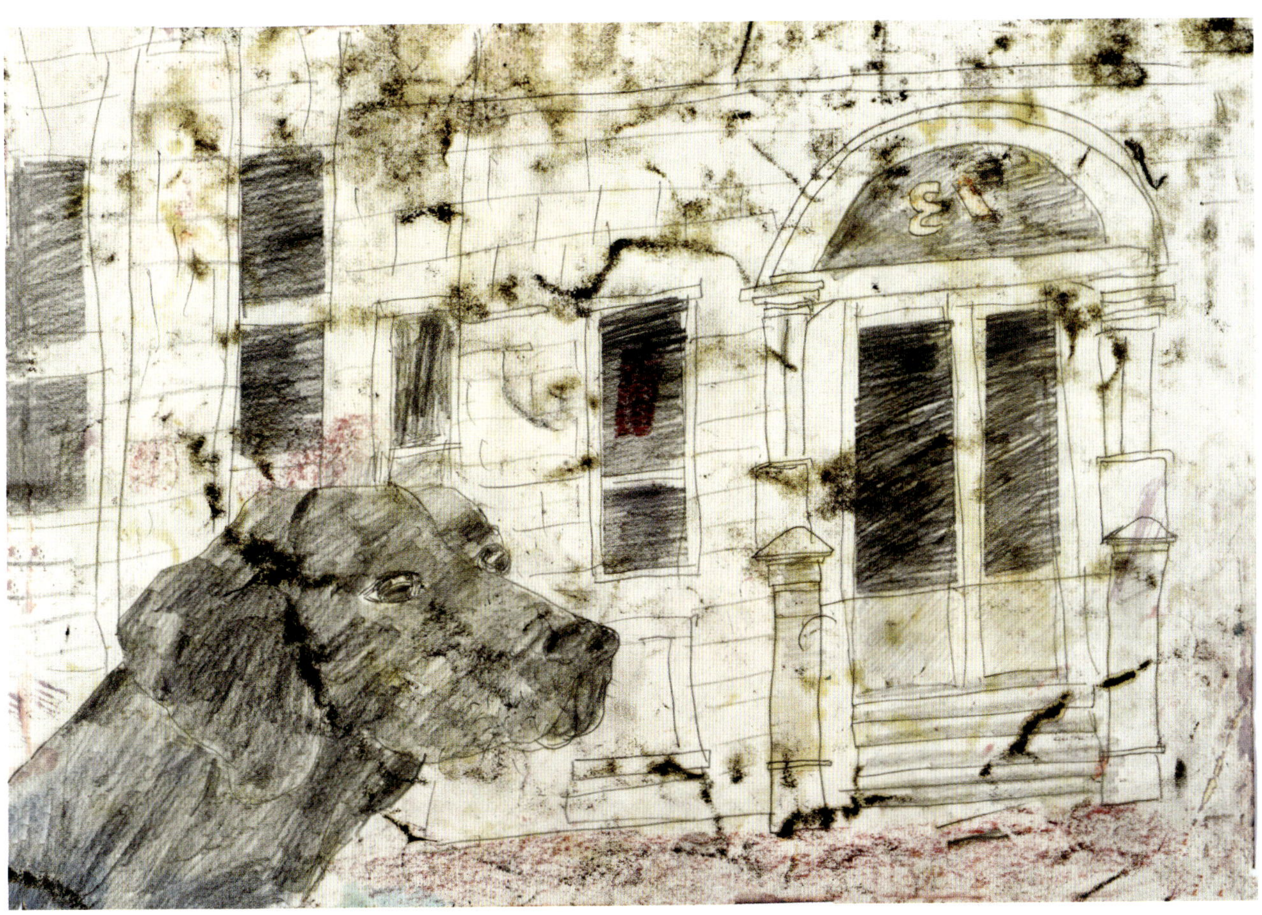

Dog in the City. Back. Trace monotype and monotype with oil-based ink. 12" × 17.5". 2000.

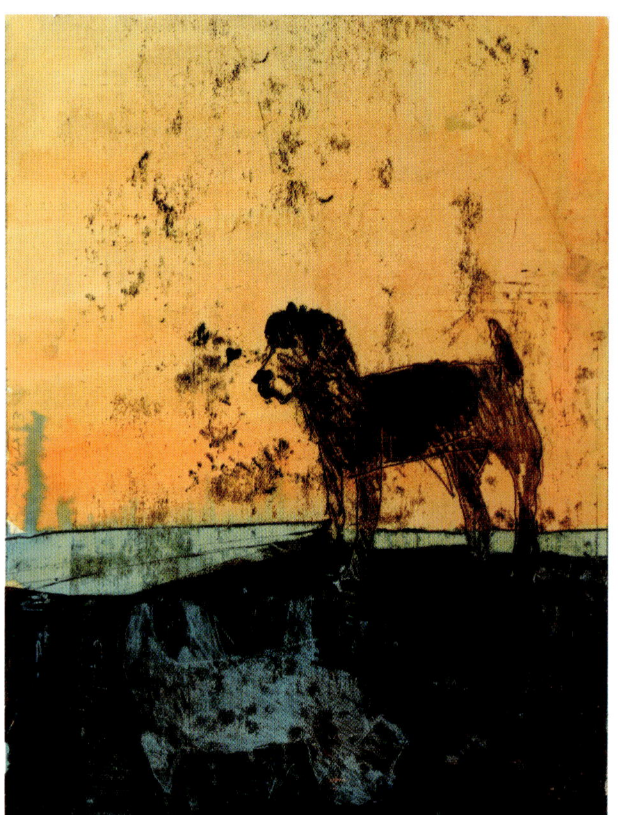

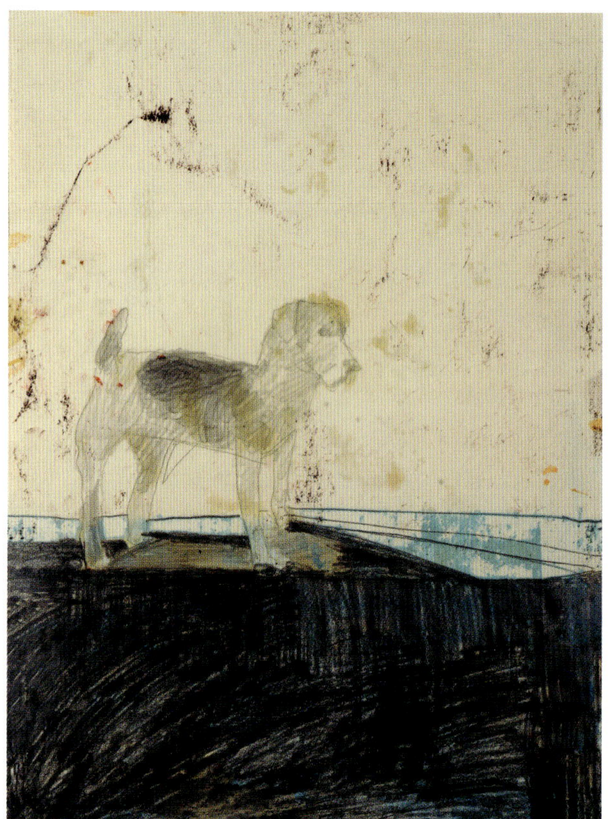

Dog at Sunset. Trace monotype and monotype with oil-based ink. 18" × 24". 2000.

Dog at Sunset. Back. Trace monotype and monotype with oil-based ink. 18" × 24". 2000.

SUSAN SCHMIDT

Cambridge, Massachusetts

In this series, I really enjoyed drawing the complex forms of woven baskets. This subject originated in an earlier project based on a fairy tale. Prominent in this fairy tale was a basket, symbolizing the entrapment of a girl and her clever escape later in the story. I wondered what the basket in the fairy tale would look like, and decided to take a closer look at that question by drawing baskets.

I found that my drawings responded to the specificity of each basket's structure. As I drew, I considered how each was constructed for particular work and shaped to one's hands. I developed my basket drawings as trace monotypes, incorporating layers and stencils. I used different viscosity inks to control the interactions between colors. The strategies of printmaking, such as layering and multiplicity, provided a way to animate the forms of the baskets. These familiar objects began to resonate with feeling as I drew them.

This series led me to draw other interwoven forms such as plants, vines, and the limbs of figures. This process of following one idea to another is uncertain, sometimes irrational, and in small moments truly exciting. This is why I make art and, in particular, why I chose the improvisational strategies of printmaking.

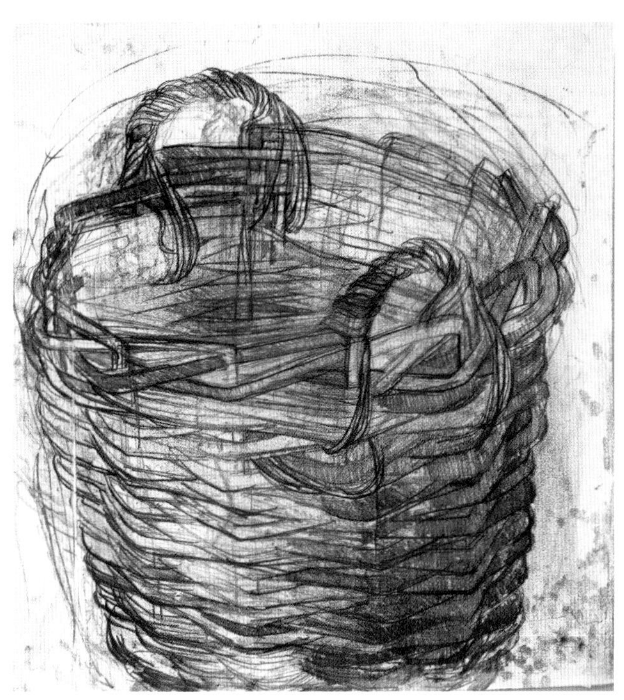

Basket of Sorrows. Trace monotype with oil-based ink. 30" × 23". 2015.

ALL PHOTOS ARE COURTESY OF BILL KIPP. PUBLISHED AND PRINTED BY THE ARTIST AT MIXIT PRINT STUDIO.

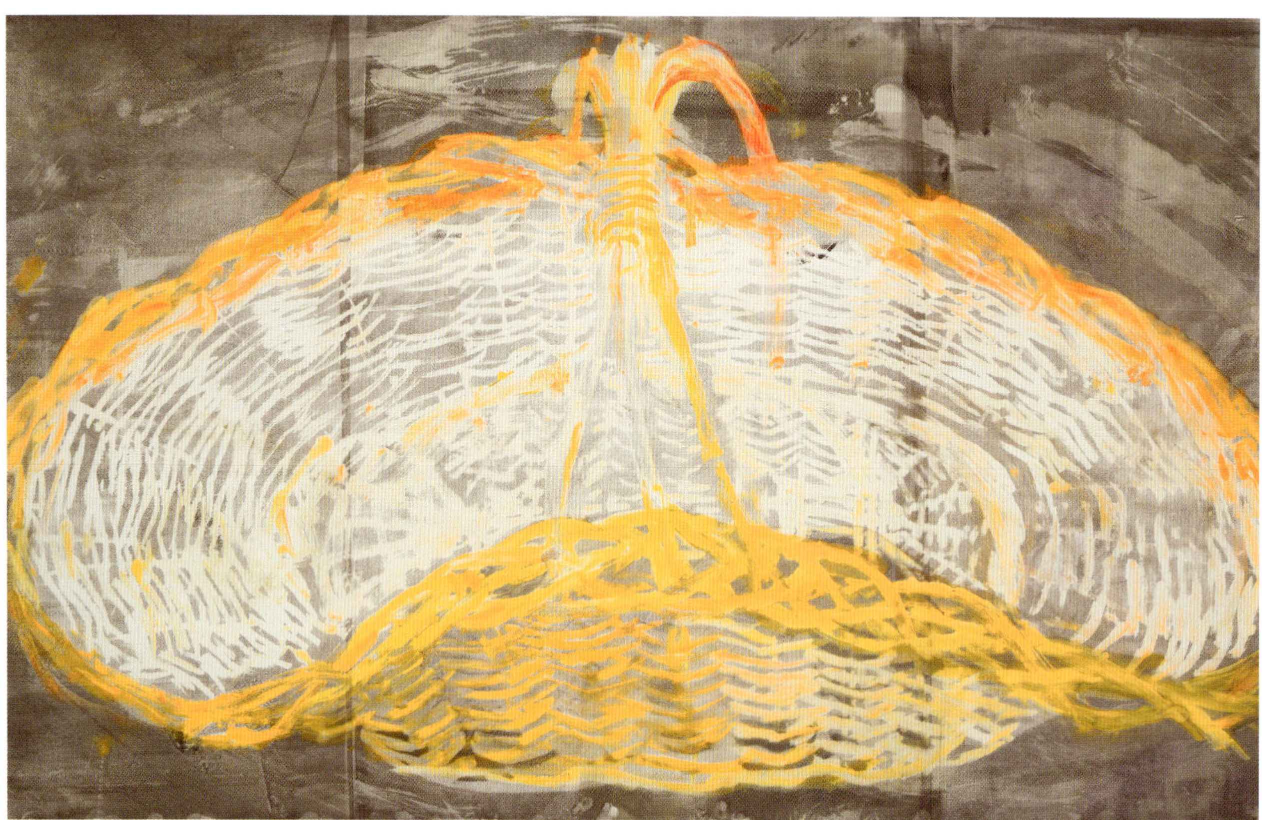

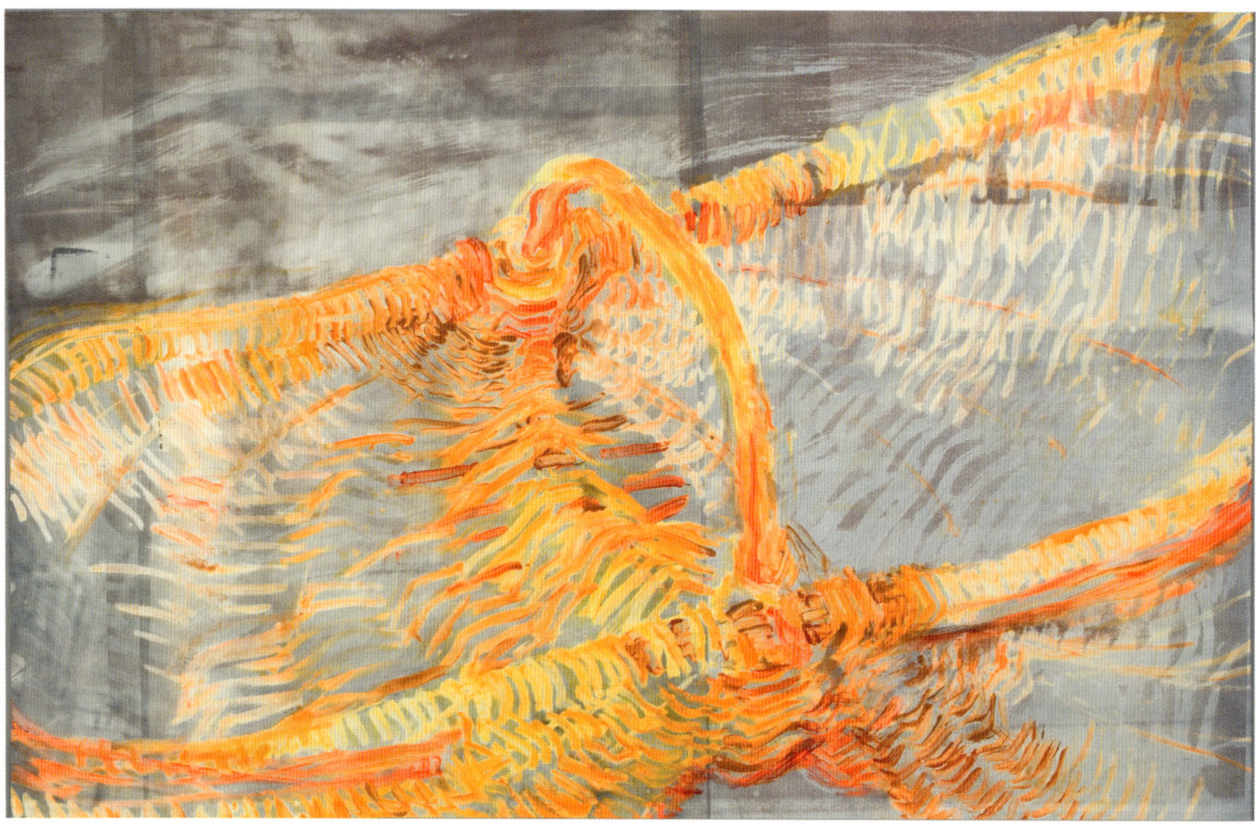

∧
Wide Mouth Basket. Monotype with Akua soy-based ink and stencil. 27" × 44". 2015.

∨
Valda's Basket 2. Monotype with Akua soy-based ink. 30" × 44". 2015.

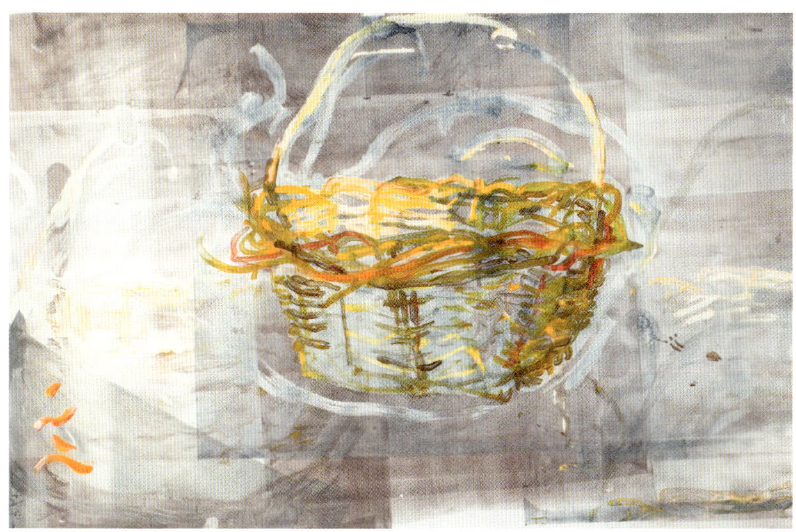

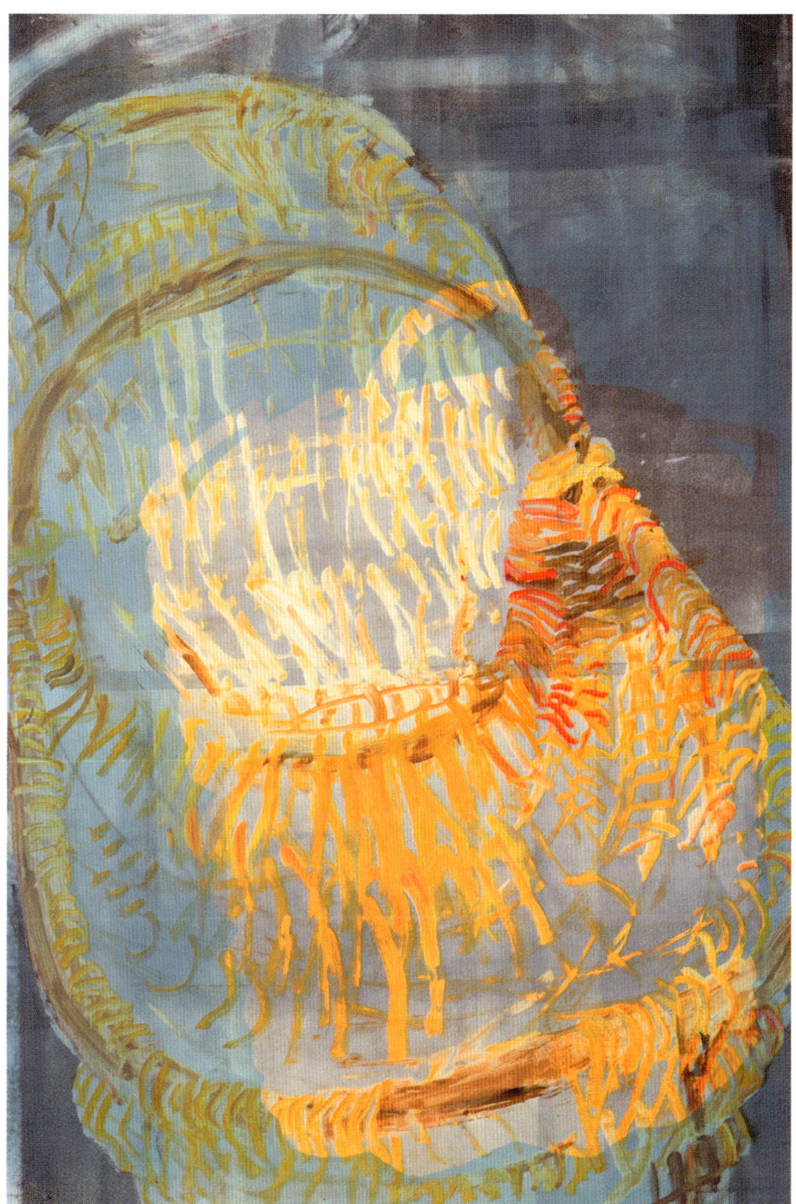

Dissolving Basket. Monotype with Akua soy-based ink and stencil. 28" × 42". 2015.

Valda's Basket 3. Monotype with Akua soy-based ink and stencil. 44" × 30". 2015.

RICHARD SEGALMAN

New York, New York

There is a saying that "When you need a teacher, they will appear." My teacher came in the guise of monotypes. I had hit an impasse with my work. Nothing I did seemed to be satisfying—watercolor, oil, pastel—all seemed to be stuck. I needed a new vision, or new eyes? Something! Then I saw a piece of work and wondered what it was. It was a monotype. Not very interested in printmaking, I passed it by. But it stayed with me. My curiosity was aroused. I had found a teacher and decided to give it a shot. Once I tried monotype, I was hooked.

I had been controlling my mediums, but the beauty of making a monotype is losing your control. It was exhilarating to let the medium become part of the message. You put all your years of work into place and then let it go. Working with a master printer is a blessing. Monotypes seem to have a life of their own. It is very exciting to be a part of such a process. Sometimes it feels like Christmas when an unexpected gift appears.

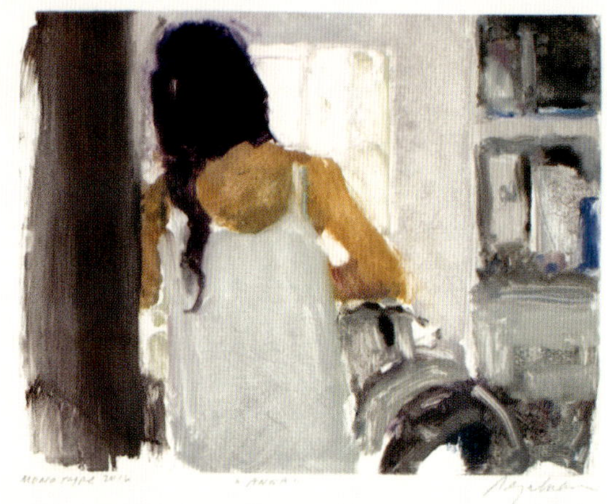

Anna. Monotype with oil-based ink. 30" × 22". 2016.

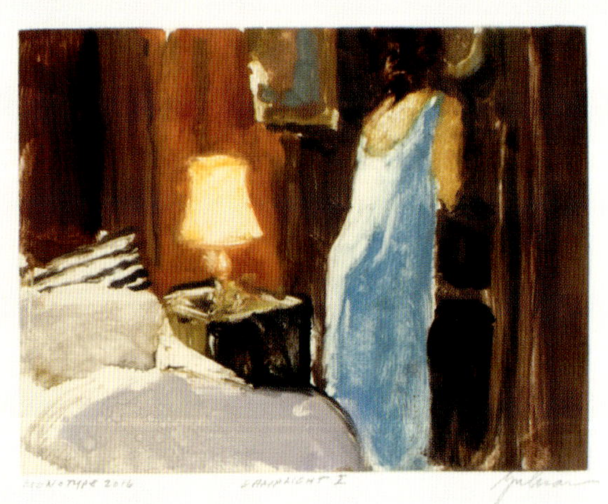

Lamplight 1. Monotype. 30" x 22". 2016.

ALL PHOTOGRAPHY IS COURTESY OF MARY RYAN GALLERY, NEW YORK. PUBLISHED AND PRINTED BY MARINA ANCONA AT 10 GRAND PRESS.

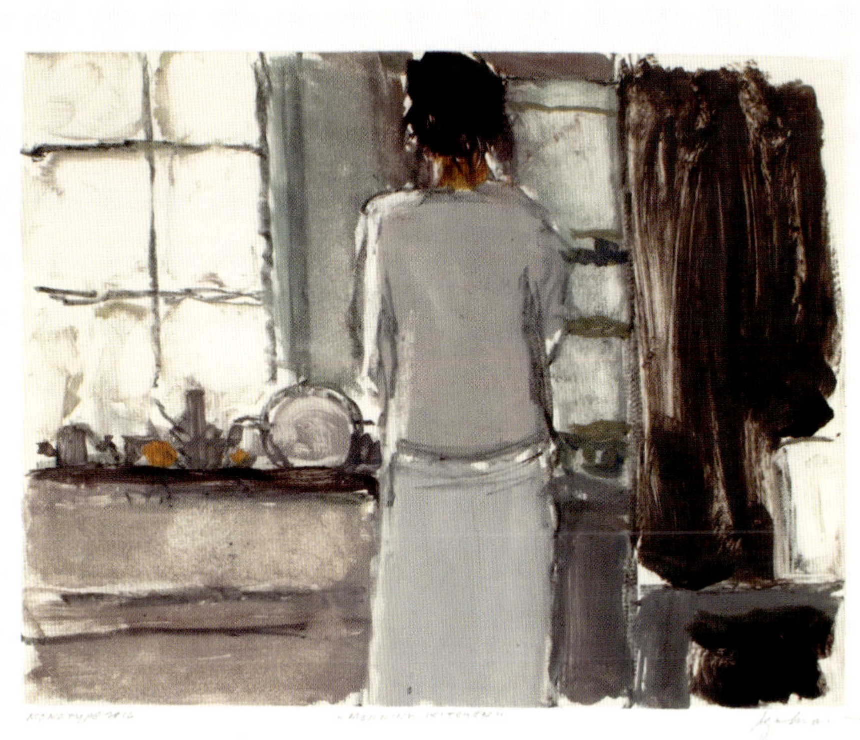

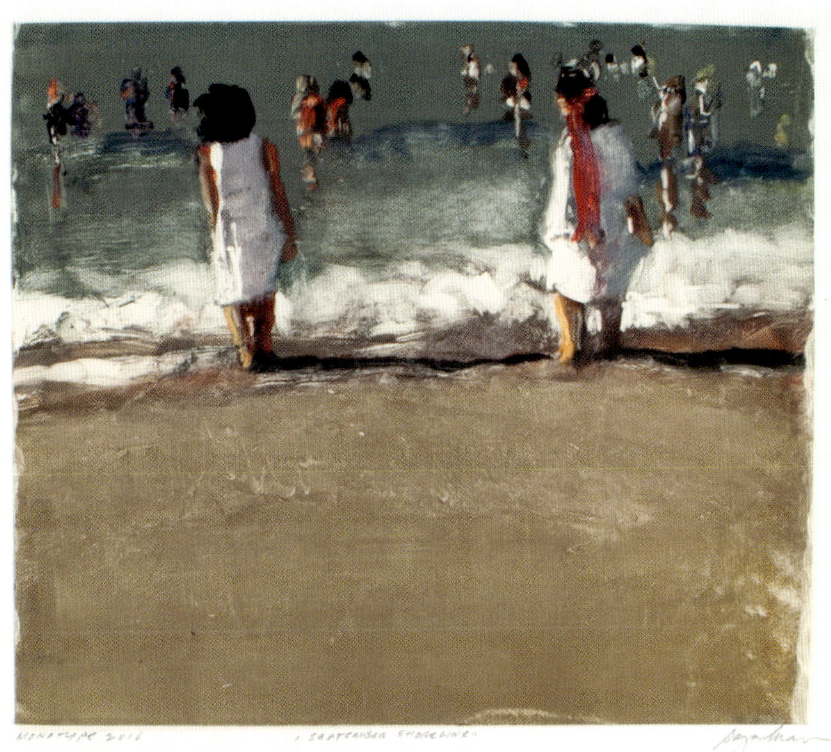

∧
Morning Kitchen. Monotype with oil-based ink. 30" × 22". 2016.

∨
September Shoreline. Monotype with oil-based ink. 30" × 22". 2016.

STUART SHILS

Philadelphia, Pennsylvania

Having been an outdoor painter for many years (one who set himself down in front of places to understand appearance and also his response to appearance), I began making monotypes in the late '90s as a way of opening the conversation about what a place *feels* like *after* the moment of engagement, *from a distance*. Compared to what had been the deep-rooted practice of direct observation, monotype allowed me to dig into an idea of exploring the residue of memory, working with my back to nature and realizing that too was a way of seeing. Having been raised as a purist who believed that images could be made only by way of immediate observation of nature, this opened many doors that shook up all of the foundational assumptions of what I had previously wanted. And as is often the case, the use of another medium as a secondary path of inquiry had a huge impact on the way I approached the large questions.

Although the process I used/use to shape the monotype image has changed dramatically over these years, there is still that element of the unknown and a quality of mystery that require quick improvisational thinking, a kind of engagement that initially was not accessible through painting. Monotype has had an indelible impact on how I approach and understand visual thinking.

Summertime in Rome, Just above Trastevere. Monotype with oil-based Charbonnel etching ink and graphite. 5.125" × 10". 2010.

A Village We Discovered at the End of a Quiet Road. Monotype with oil-based Charbonnel etching ink and graphite. 8" × 8". 2014.

ALL PHOTOS ARE COURTESY OF DAVIS AND LANGDALE. PUBLISHED AND PRINTED BY THE ARTIST.

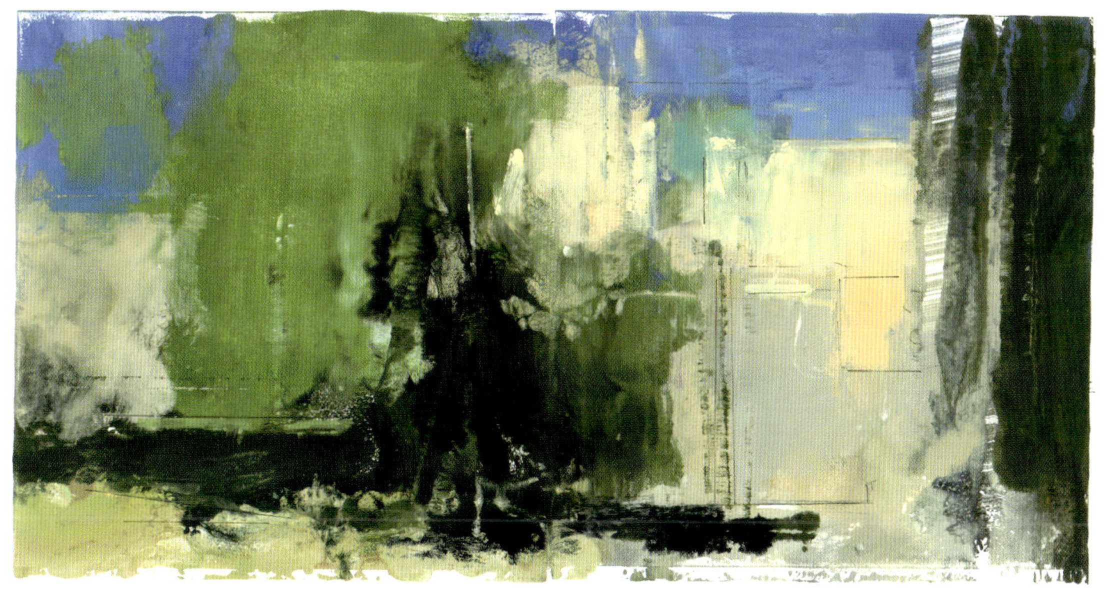

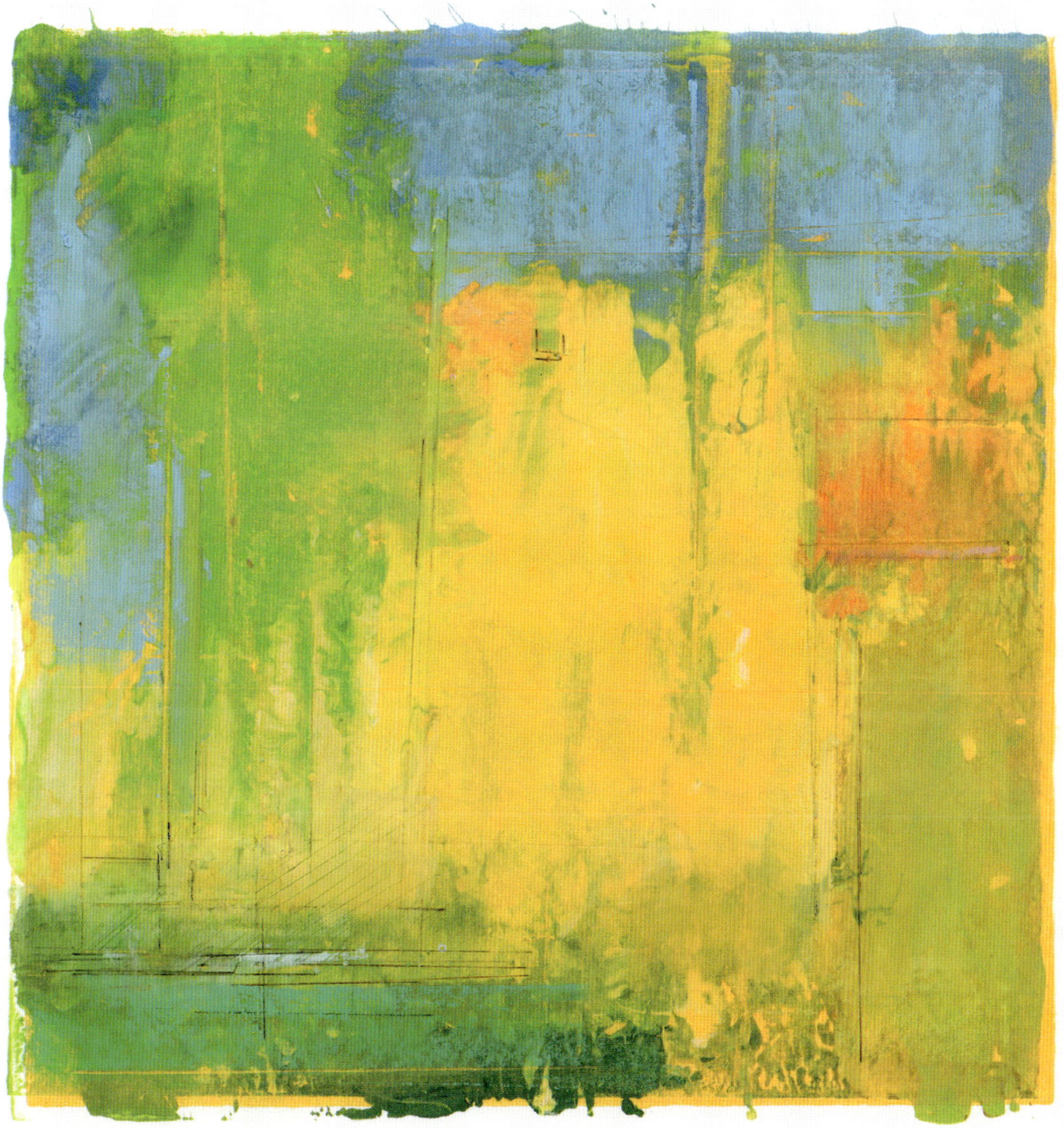

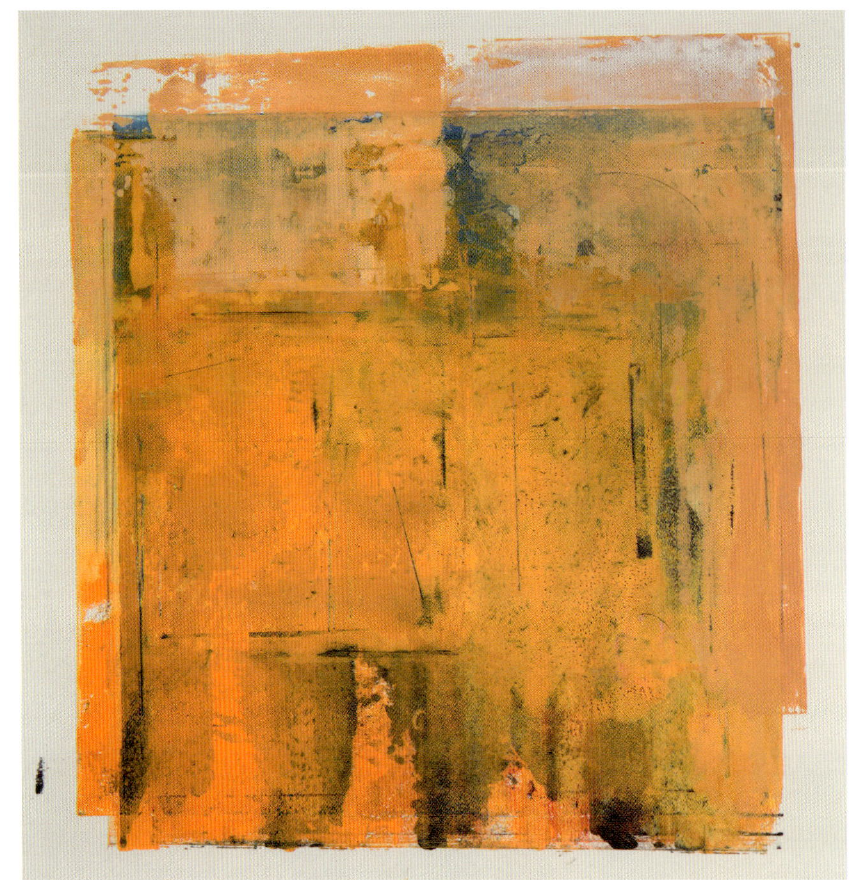

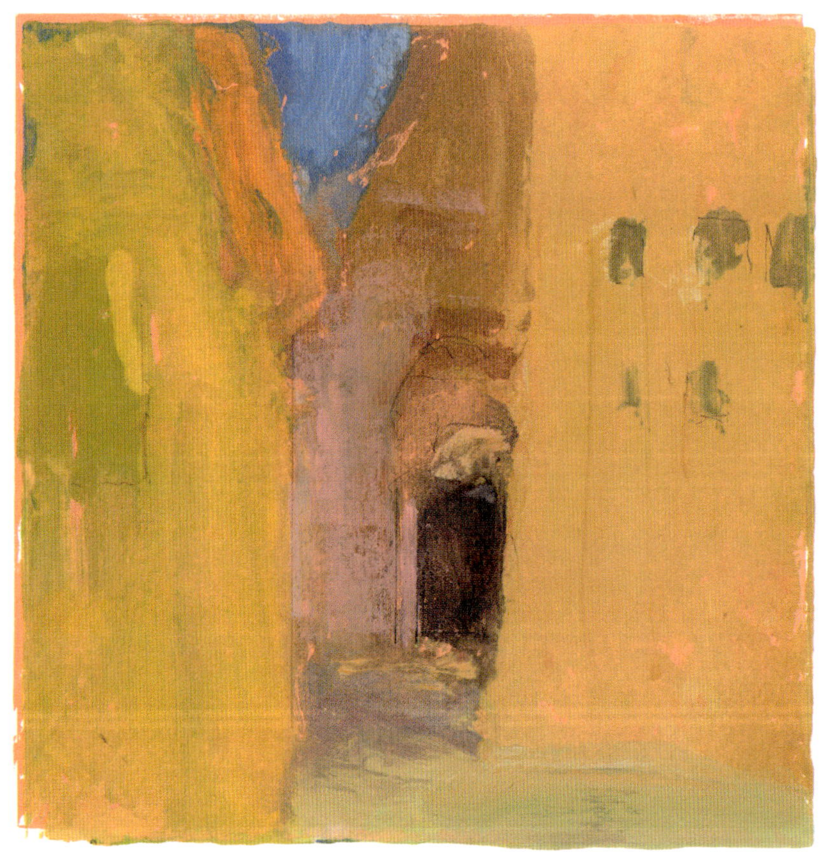

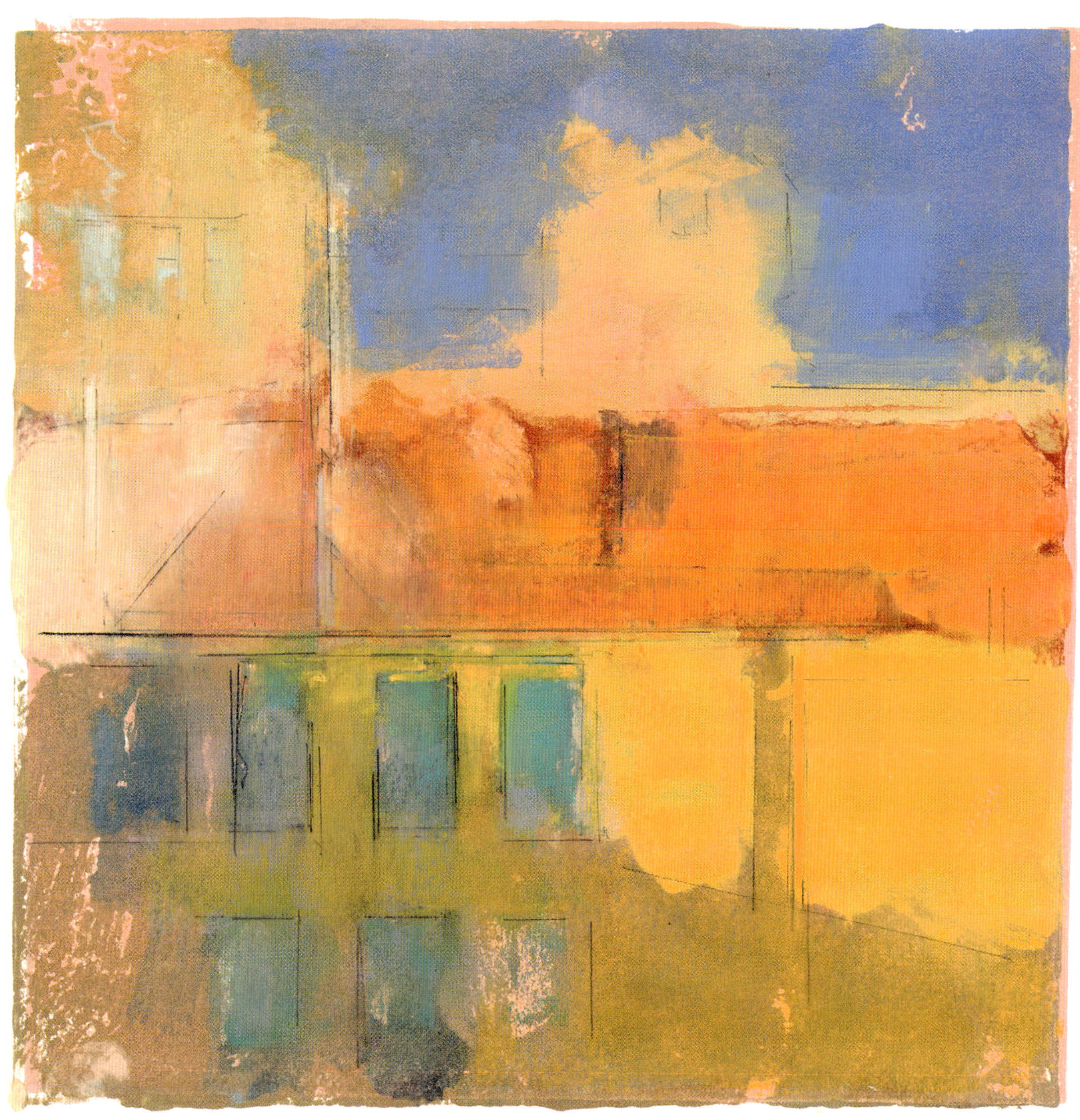

<

Afternoon Light, Walking along the Edges of Town. Monotype with oil-based Charbonnel etching ink and graphite. 9.75" × 8.08". 2013.

After Drinking Wine in Perugia. Monotype with oil-based Charbonnel etching ink and graphite. 5" × 8.5". 2007.

Fragment of Urbino. Monotype with oil-based Charbonnel etching ink and graphite. 11" × 15". 2008.

DONALD TRAVER

New York, New York

I have discovered a new clarity within the larger body of my work by creating monotypes. The medium provides narrative themes not found in making paintings. Breathing life into inanimate objects vis-à-vis stylization, "classic" pictorial representation combined with asymmetrical composition, reveals a rich source for exploration. With subjects of flora and fauna, familiar emotions turn into form.

The monotype technique is not for the faint of heart. Exhaustion has become my friend. The ultimate provocation of mirrored image, working the plate, applying the ink, and preparing the press with final pulling of the print will always bear witness to wonder. Through the monotype, I am building a cabinet of curiosities honoring the hoary elementals of this discipline.

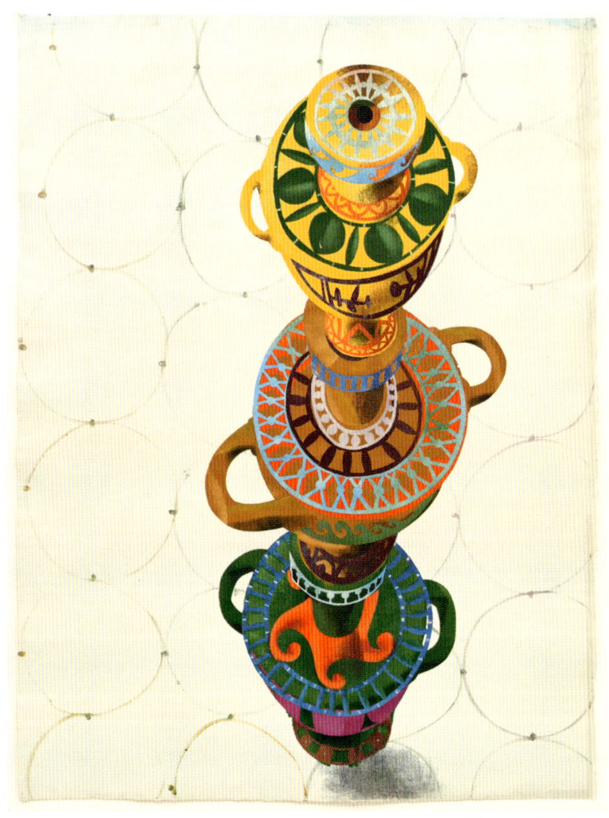

Stacked, from a Roman Floor series. Monotype with oil-based etching ink on handmade Kozo. 50" × 38". 2007–2018.

PUBLISHED AND PRINTED BY THE ARTIST AT DONALD TRAVER STUDIO.

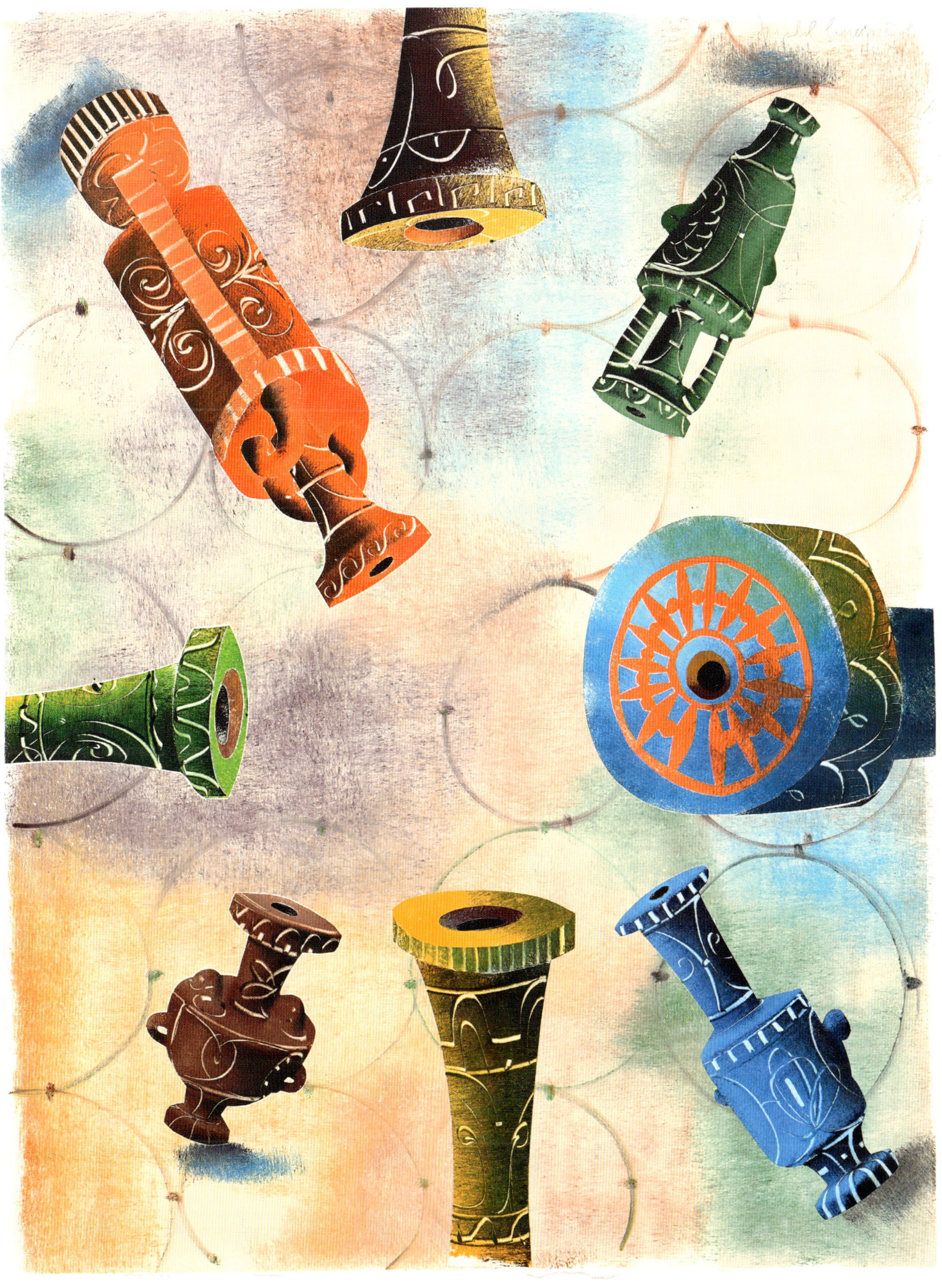

Family Gathering, from a Roman Floor series. Monotype with oil-based etching ink on handmade Kozo. 35" × 27". 2007–2018.

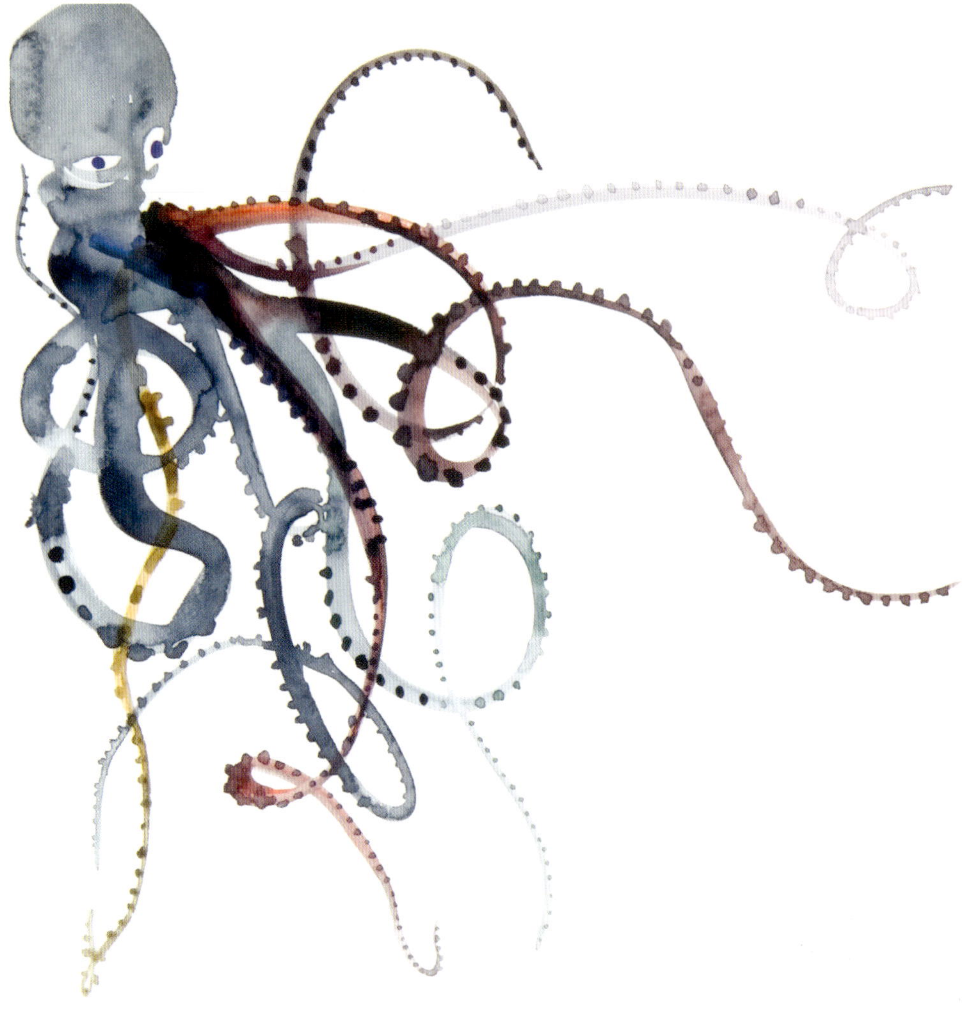

>
Fretful Self-Portrait. Monotype on handmade Kozo. 53" x 40". 2008-2018.

Self-Portrait Cornered. Monotype with oil-based etching ink on handmade Kozo. 38" × 50". 2015–2018.

Anchor Toss. Etching ink on handmade Kozo. 27" × 35". 2008–2018.

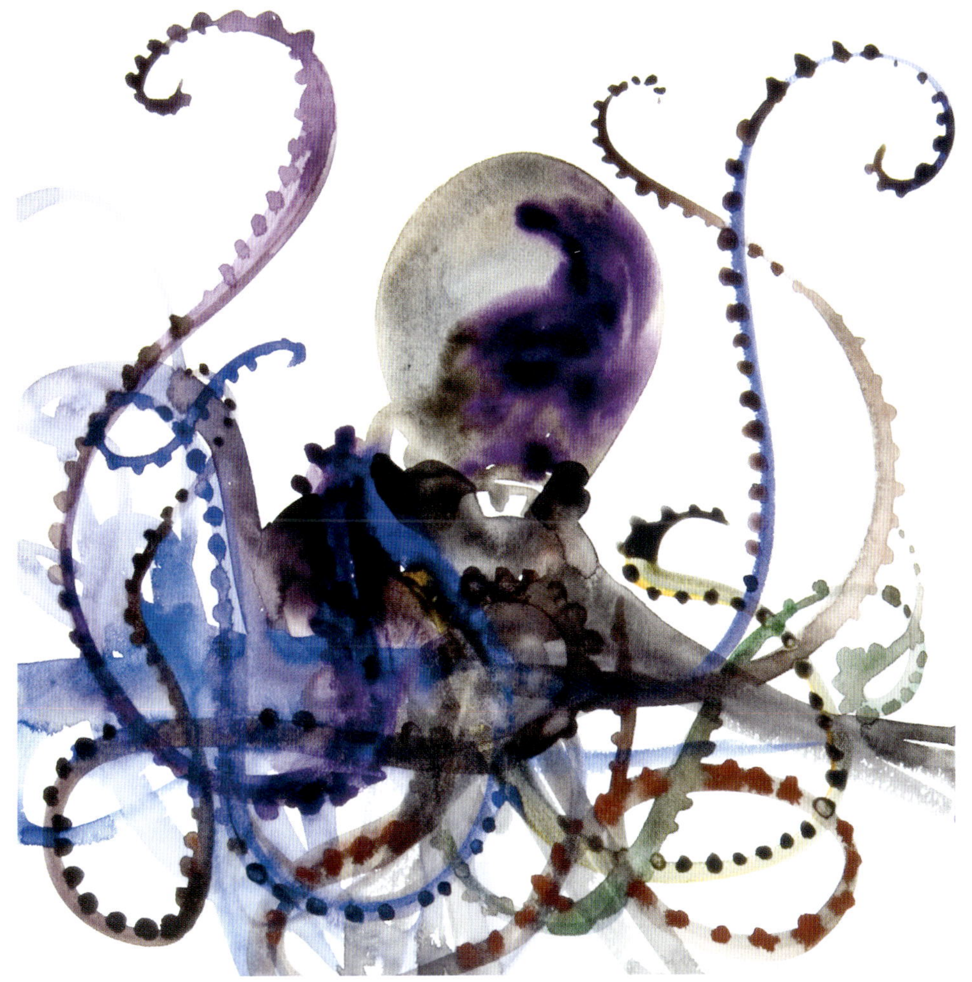

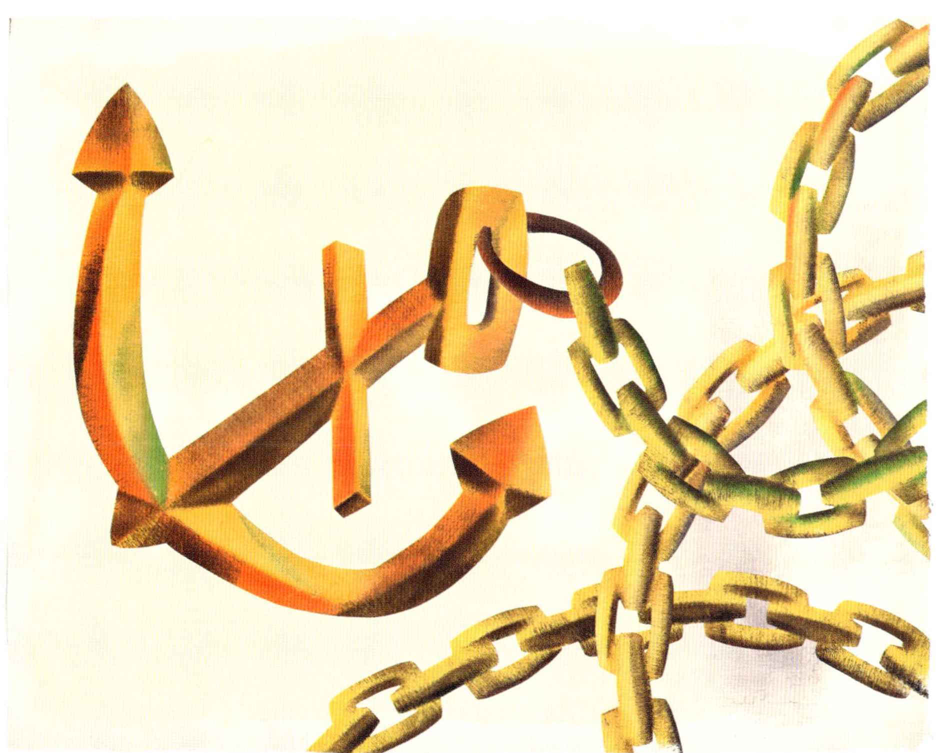

CHUCK WEBSTER

Brooklyn, New York

> First you start painting the moon, then it turns into a house. You start painting the house, it turns into a loaf of bread.
>
> —Philip Guston

I made this series at Dieu Donné Paper in 2010 as part of their Variable Editions program. We used a Mylar stencil to create a certain image, then manipulated it with pulp paint while wet and with other media once dry. I used two different stencils and moved the position on the page to indicate slight shifts in narrative and spatial dynamics. I wanted to observe how the set form became in turn an actor in a story, an oracle, an architectural plan, a mountain, or a small creature, depending on how I would alter it with pulp paint, pencil, and watercolor. We also used a very diluted pulp paint in water to give an appearance of antiquity and legend.

I work a lot using shifts in scale to create stories within the work. This variable edition was a great opportunity to work with a form and understand it in different ways.

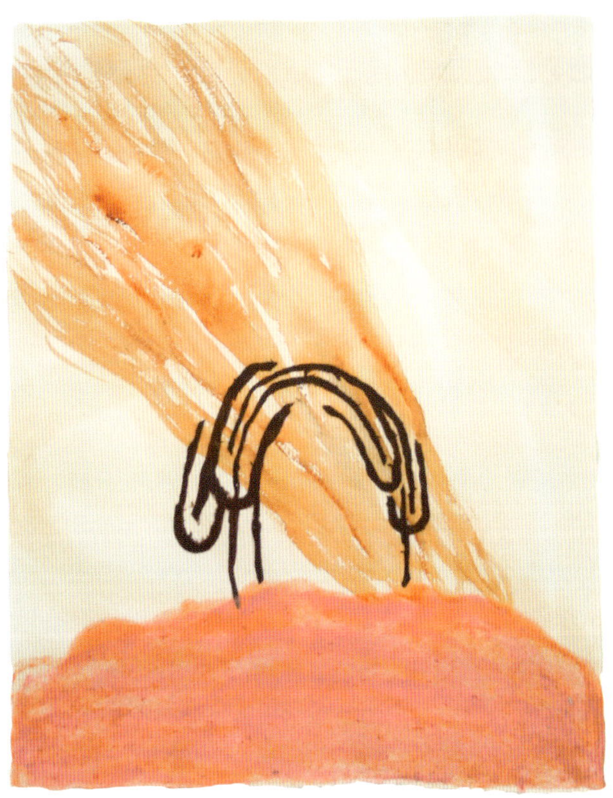

Untitled. Stenciled and freehand pigmented pulp painting series on cotton base sheet with artist hand-coloring added. 14" × 11". 2011.

ALL PHOTOS ARE COURTESY OF KIRSTEN FLAHERTY ON BEHALF OF DIEU DONNÉ. PUBLISHED AT DIEU DONNÉ PAPER MILL, INC.

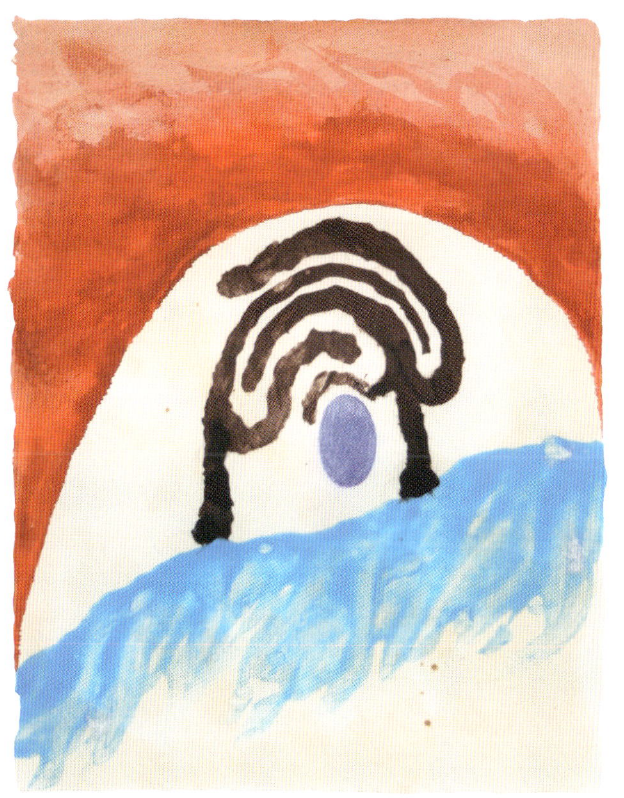

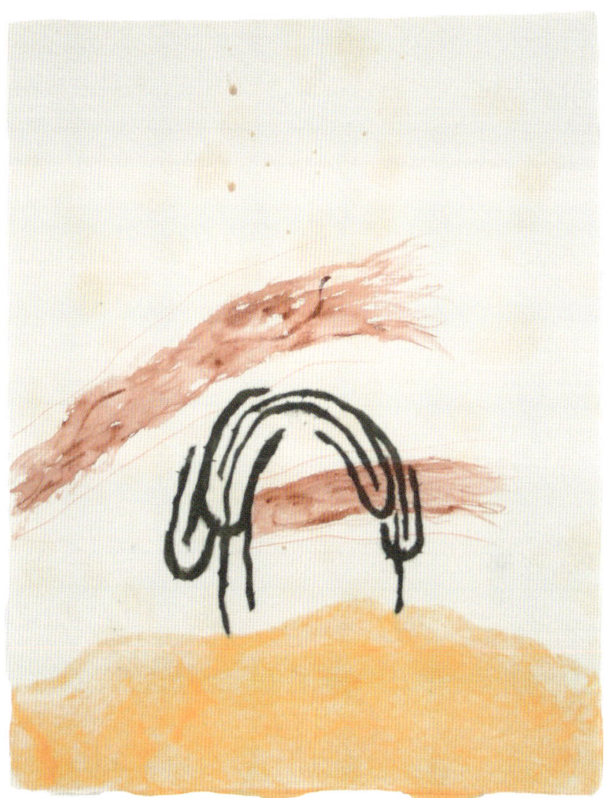

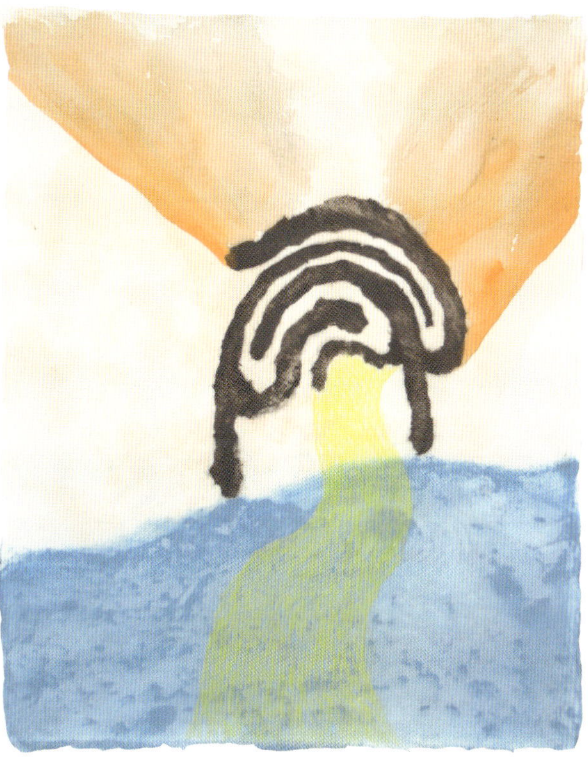

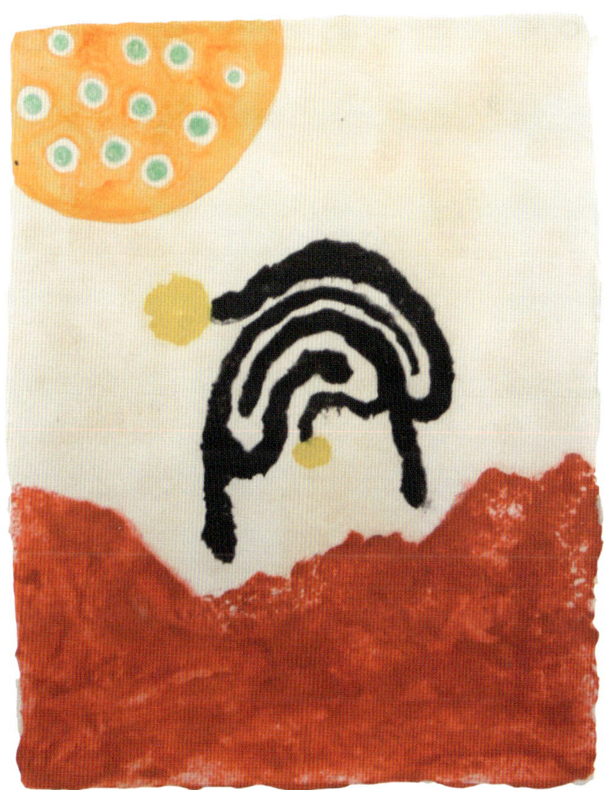

SHARON WOLPOFF

Kensington, Maryland

It is my desire to find a way of being in this world that illuminates others. Because illumination is a concept that can reveal itself in many ways, one of my favorite means of exploration is by virtue of printmaking. Specifically, I've found that the process of creating monotypes is responsive, immediate, and intuitive, and that the element of speed required to do the work can be both liberating and enlightening.

My subject matter is my day-to-day world. For example, *Brunch at Black Salt (purple) #2* is part of an ongoing series about family and friends at the table. People let their guard down over a meal, where interactions seem to glide back and forth between ritual formality and breezy family shorthand. The Comedian series was the result of a lucky night out, when I was seated right next to the stage. An endless real estate settlement inspired a series about Big Business. All of these prints are essentially illustrated notes to myself, orientation points mapping the momentum of my life.

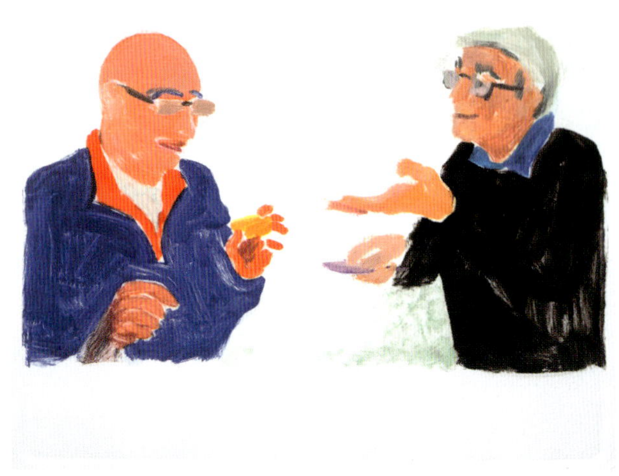

Marco and Lou and the Stinky Cheese #2. Monotype with oil-based ink. 7.75" × 10". 2016.

ALL PHOTOS ARE COURTESY OF GREGORY R. STALEY. PUBLISHED AND PRINTED BY THE ARTIST AT ANDERSON RANCH AND LILY PRESS.

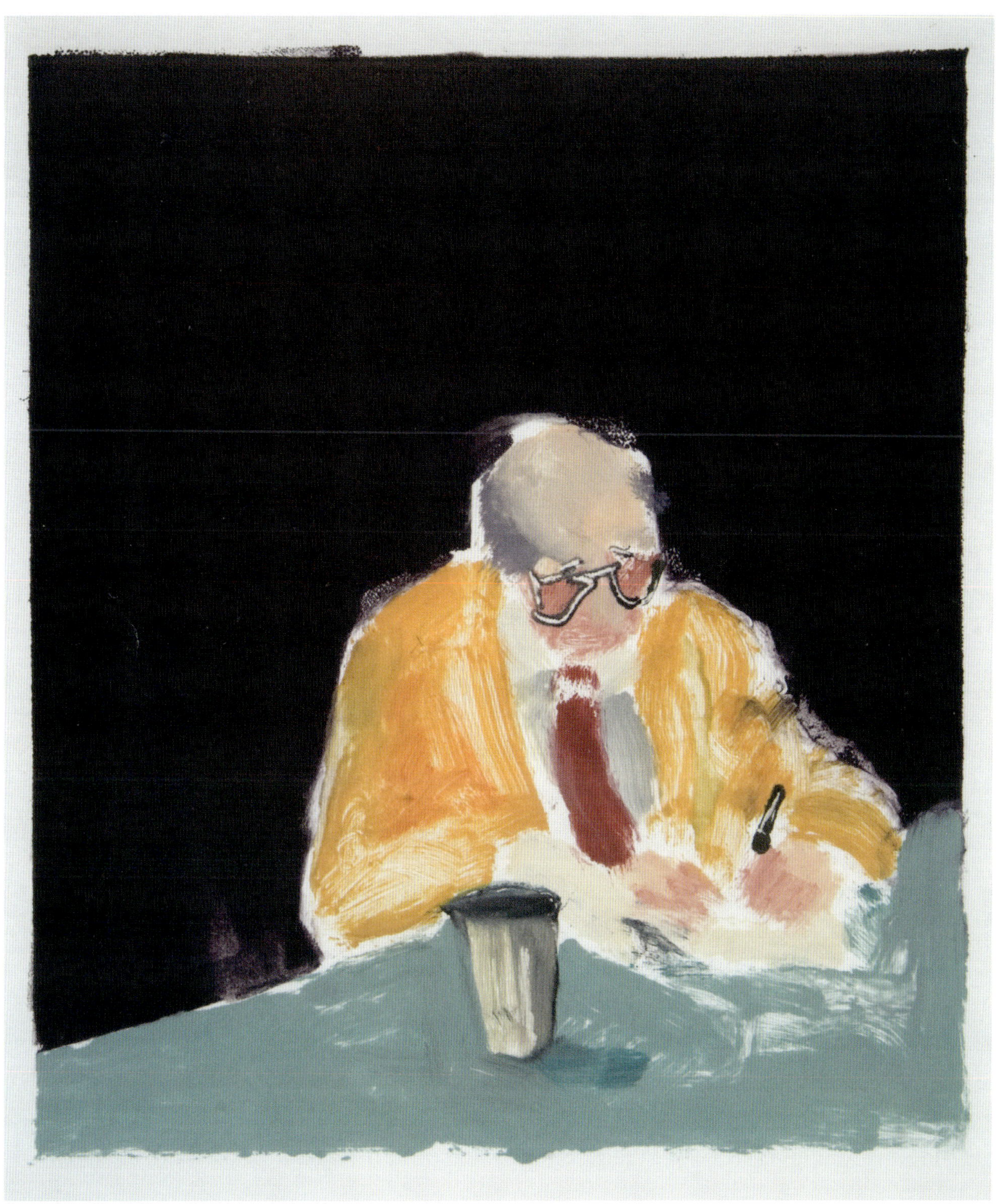

The Signature #2. Monotype with oil-based ink. 6" × 6.5". 2006.

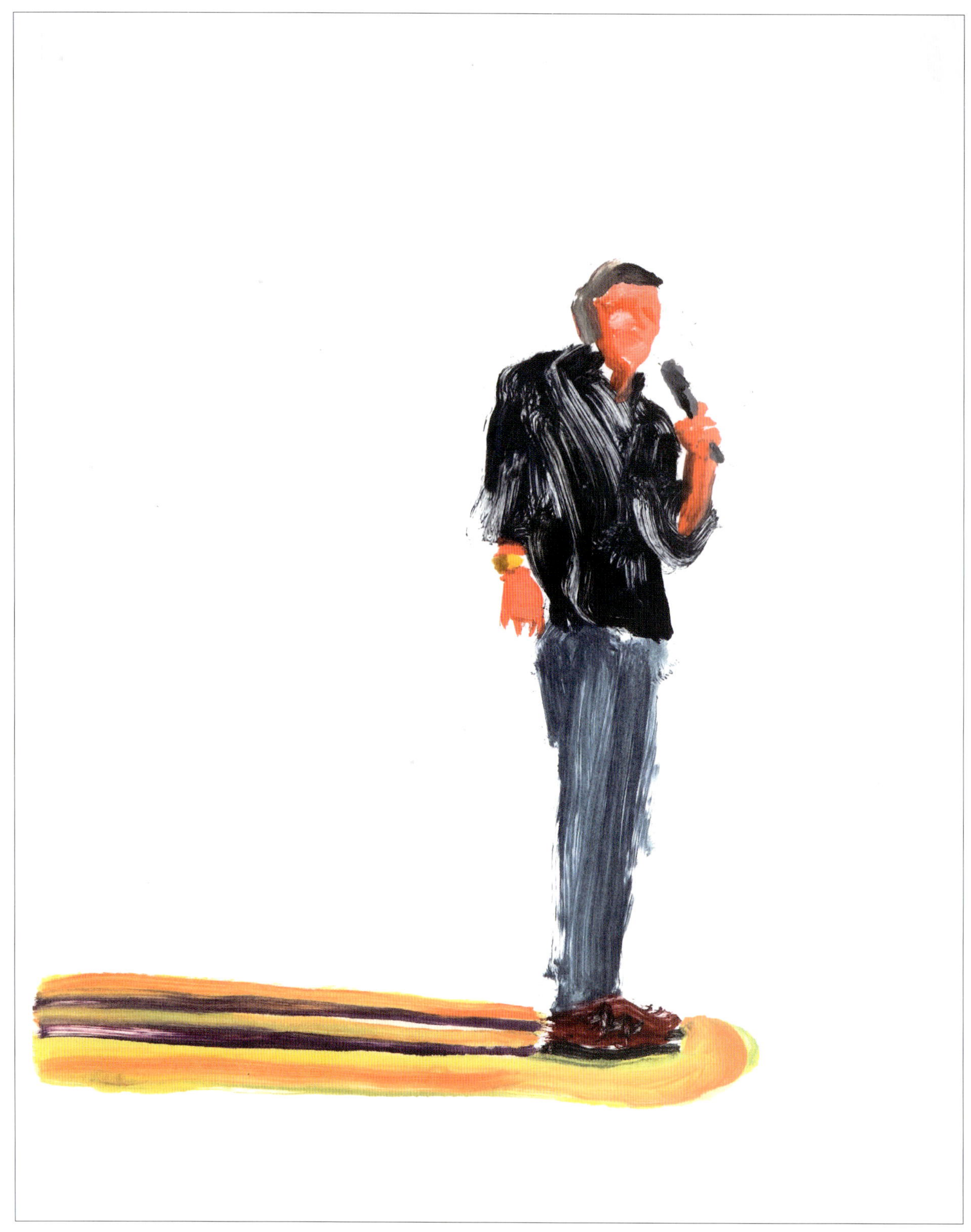

>
Brunch at Black Salt (purple) #2. Monotype with oil-based ink. 18" × 24". 2016.

The Comedian #1. Monotype with oil-based ink. 10" × 8". 2016.

The Negotiation #2. Monotype with oil-based ink. 6" × 6.5". 2006.

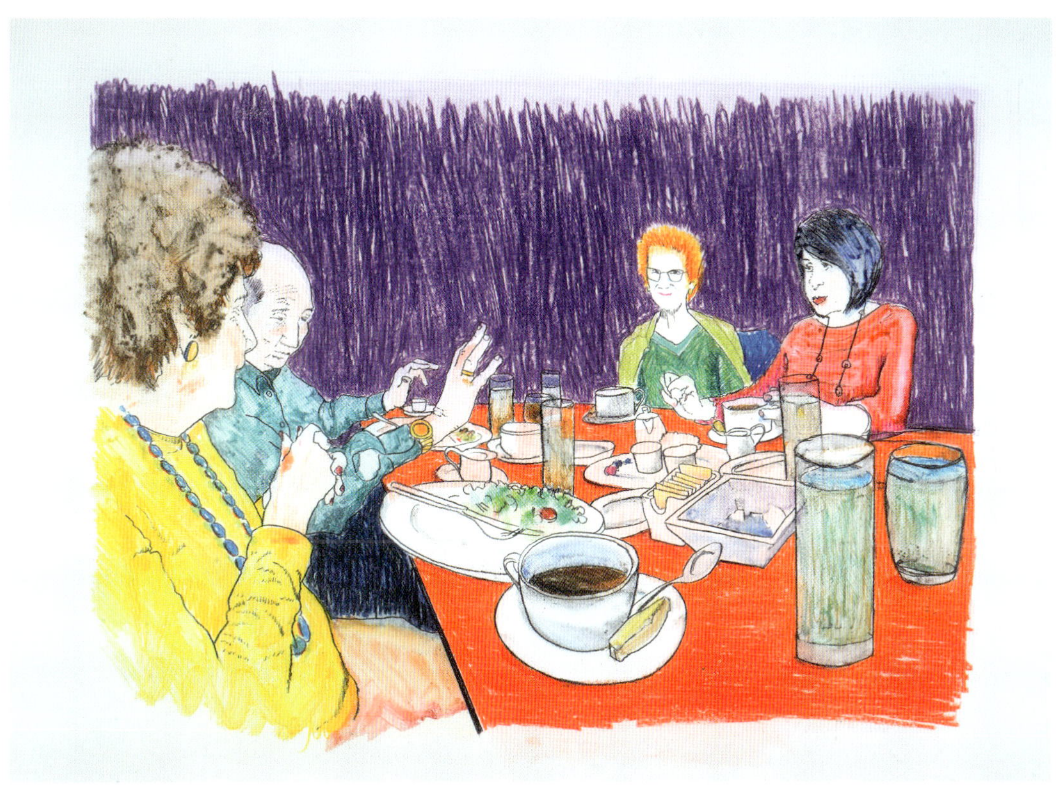

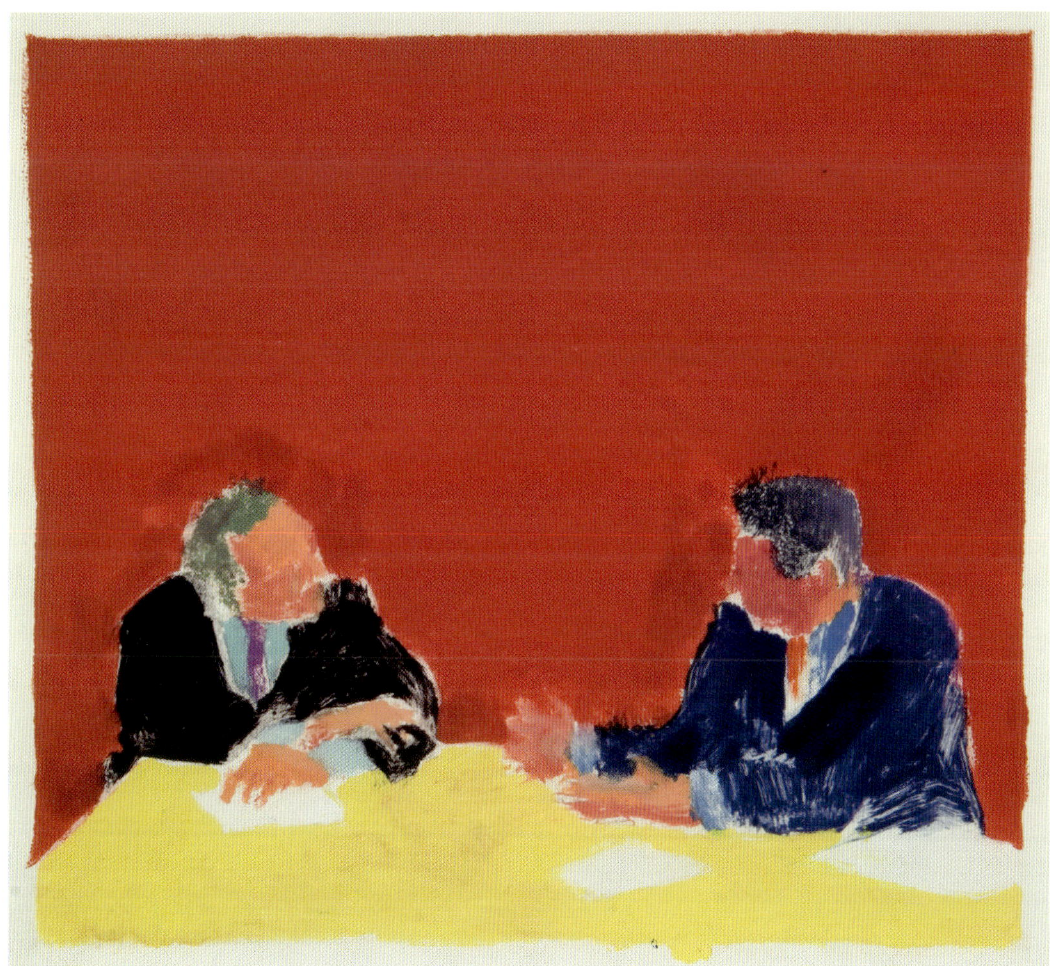

MONOPRINTS

The Choreography of Process

Catherine Kernan

The works in this section encompass monoprints and varied editions made by artists who exploit to the fullest a wide range of printmaking techniques, including many kinds of matrices and repeatable elements. With no intention of producing an edition of identical multiples, they embrace and enjoy great flexibility with regard to materials, control, and timing.

As an artist, a partner in a professional printmaking studio, a teacher, and a printmaker with decades of experience, I have witnessed the creation of many unique prints. Concurrently, I myself have made the journey from an edition printer capable of large editions to one who never makes two identical prints. As is common practice for most artists who make unique prints, I start with a particular idea or plan of action and improvise in response to what is happening on the paper as the piece progresses and the unexpected occurs. I am always prepared for a change of direction at any point.

Most artists cite the pleasure of surprise, the accidental—and the uncontrolled—aspects integral both to monoprint and monotype. Unpredictability keeps the process fresh and dynamic and requires a mental state of "be here now." There is no "proofing" stage, since every layer is critical to the print in progress. This real-time action is risky but can also lead to thrilling possibilities. The timing is also very different from its function in making multiples, or even variant editions; in many ways, it approximates the spontaneous action of painting.

Tools at hand, in the studio, I ponder how much or how little control to exert over the processes, a tension that constitutes a running internal dialogue, as I suspect it does for most monoprinters. Many questions arise: How much ink? How transparent or opaque? What viscosity? What color? How many rolls? What size roller? Which paper? Is the image ready to print? Does it need another layer? How much pressure and by what means? Should I use fingers, a wooden spoon, a baren, or the press to transfer the image? The answers are not predetermined as they are in printing editions, so every decision can either lead to paper tossed into the recycle bin, or a eureka moment of discovery.

The Fascination with Materials

The following selection of prints all incorporate elements that have the potential to resurface across multiple prints. Repeatable elements introduce some structure as counterbalance to the complete freedom of monotypes transferred from a smooth, unworked surface. They provide fixed points of reference where known and unknown collide. The dualities of fixed and fluid enhance and empower each other, partners in a visual pas de deux whose choreography alternates between imposing control and accepting the unpredictable contributions of process.

The basic plate generally in use today is plastic and is often combined with traditional matrices such as woodcuts, intaglio etched metal, lithography, screen print and/or collagraphs, or even gelatin. The choices of repeatable elements are myriad: torn paper, digital printouts, collaged printed matter, hardware store or scrapyard items, found wood, cut canvas, metal grating, string, wire, sand, or textured acrylic painting mediums. Anything that can be used to construct a matrix and inked may be literally pressed into service.

Developments in materials, such as slow-drying, soy-based inks, have changed the role of time. Whereas traditional, fast-drying, linseed-oil-based inks demand speed and quick decision making, soy-based inks extend working time to entire days or weeks, allowing the capture of more history from residual ink left on the plate or block. The implements and tools used to apply ink are those shared by painters and printmakers alike: brushes, brayers, cotton swabs, rags, combs, palette knives, scrapers, ink, oils, sandpaper, and silicone tools. Critically, printmaking is characterized by a transfer from surface to surface of some kind, most often by using pressure.

Printmaking comprises many techniques and tools. As with all art, however, quality is determined by imagery that transcends technique.

A Selection of Images

The following selection of images spans a wide variety of working practices. Each one represents an artist who has dedicated many studio hours to exploring and developing an individual way of working. With deference to all the artists, I will mention a few of them as examples of the many possible approaches.

Closest to edition prints are "variant editions," series that repeat a matrix with a simple change of inking, or the addition of handwork, with each print. For example, Sara Greenberger Rafferty adds spontaneous brush marks superimposed on a grid of etched plates. Her image of an iconic dress has personal associations of period style, accessories, and the body. The large slashes of paint that punctuate each variant suggest a confrontation with the past. This combination of a life-sized dress with the overlay of brushstrokes moves past the confines of editioned prints, to where the artist's hand converses with the matrix.

Keiko Hara marshals an array of woodcut matrices, repositioned and redeployed to create dynamic visual universes. Her *mokuhanga* prints (traditional Japanese water-based woodcut) displayed across large-scale, free-hanging panels constitute a very unorthodox use of traditional technique. The images are stable, yet they ascend and descend, advance and retreat in a cycle of time. Many of the shapes and textures reappear in different positions—in reverse, lighter or darker—activating our consciousness of the forces of growth and disappearance.

Wendy Prellwitz inks and prints worn wooden steps, hand- and laser-cut wood blocks, trace transfers, offset transfers, screen-print fragments, crumpled foil, stones, and bark, all unified by overrolling with inks mixed to different viscosities and multiple passes through the press. Her prints have the wavelike luminosity of tides and water. They entice the viewer past geometric shapes referencing architecture into vast spaces beyond where kinetic forces of horizon, ocean, and sky converge and overlie one another.

Both Jane Kent and John Schiff cut and reposition stencils to layer and lift color, creating complex spaces that embed the history of their processes. They both experiment endlessly with combinations and sequences but achieve very different results. Kent's prints are composed of diaphanous color transparencies and intriguing abstract shapes of suggestive but indeterminate identity. They balance and move with an elegant cinematic sequencing. Schiff's prints, although based on mathematical relationships, and

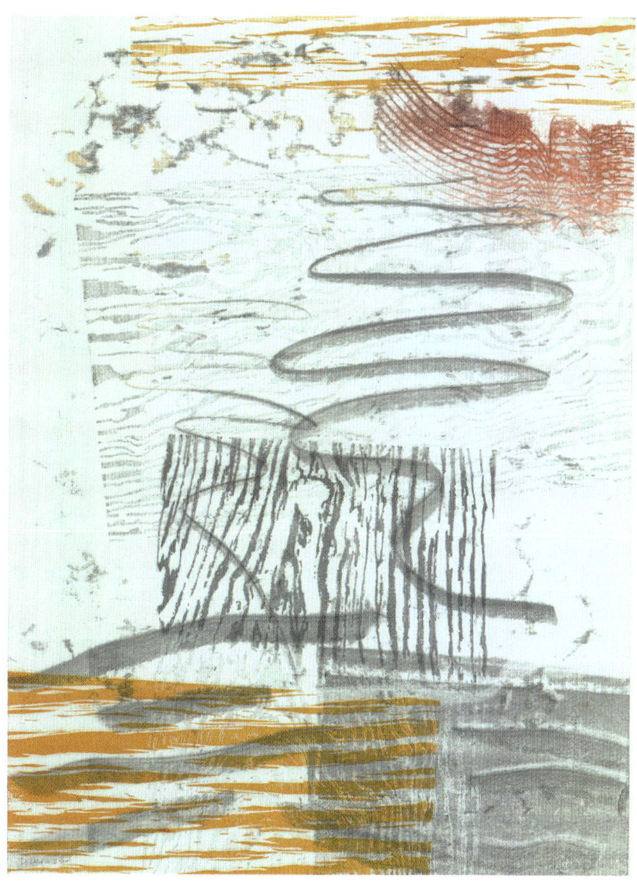

Wendy Prellwitz. *Divergence #4.* Monoprint with woodcut and soy-based ink on Kozo Asian paper. 2017.

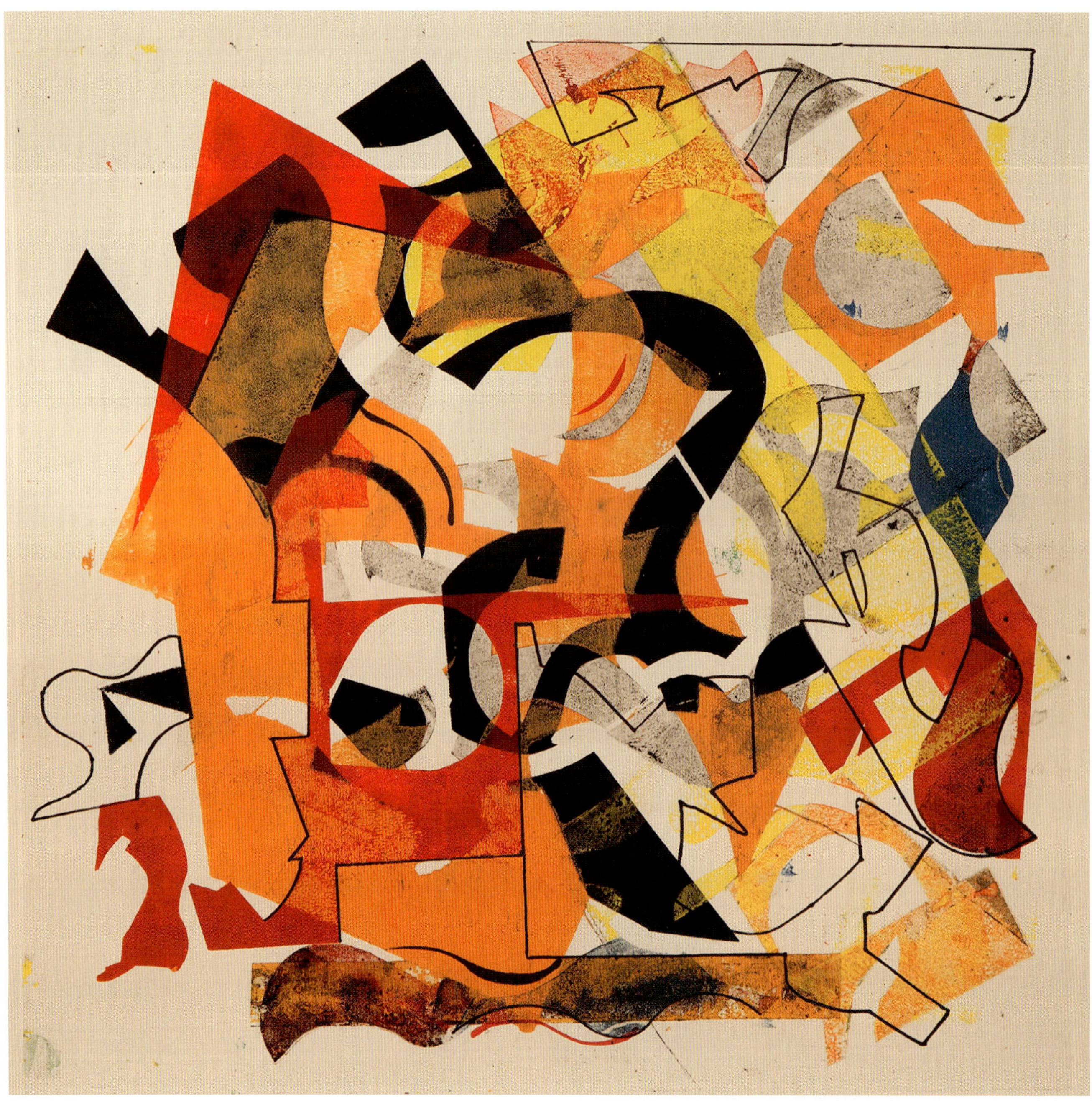

hinting at the orthogonal, are spatially complex, textural, and active, the result of overlaying stencils repeatedly without removing the residual ink. Positive and negative shapes mirror and mimic each other in dynamic compositions.

Stencils also provide the matrix for cast paper pulp pieces by Beth Campbell. Based on organizational diagrams in which branching choices lead to different possible pathways and outcomes, Campbell's choice of colors, simple shapes, and embedded dangling strings inject these "charts" with a lighthearted *joie de vivre* that corresponds to the looseness and lushness of the cast-paper technique.

Neal Ambrose-Smith considers his studio a laboratory and accordingly uses every material

John Schiff. *Infinitesimal Brevity*. Monoprint. Water-based ink and BFK Rives paper. 2017. *Image courtesy of Joel Biazzo*

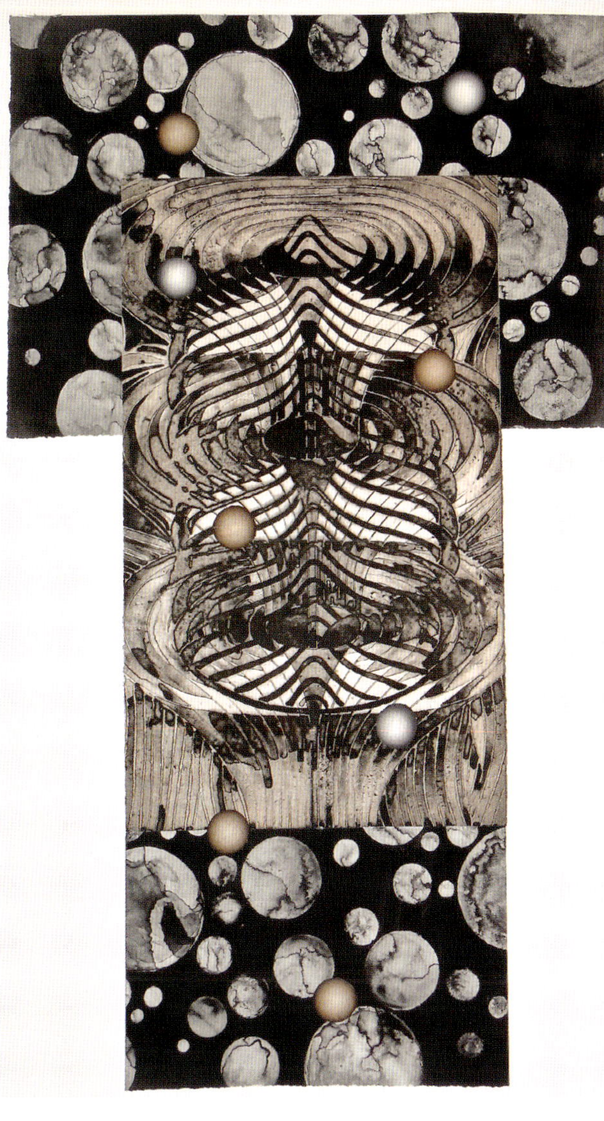

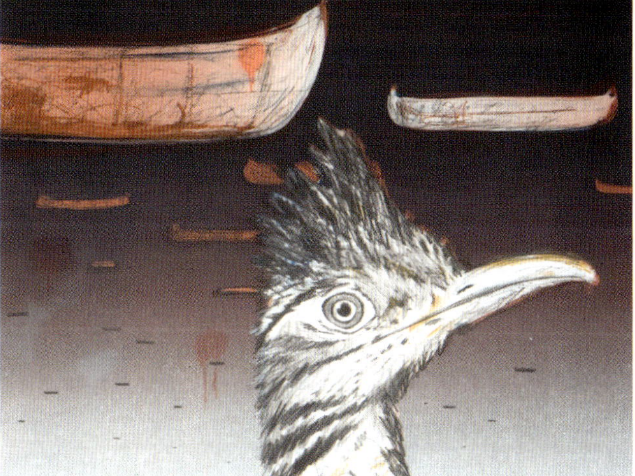

and means at hand for experimenting, including but not limited to intaglio, collage, photo plates, direct drawing, stamps, and image fragments from contemporary culture. In these particular prints, personal narratives unfold in hauntingly infinite space where iconic animals and symbols radiate the power of insight and act as personal witnesses to cultural history. Doodle drawings and stray marks lighten the mood without diluting the message.

Ryan McGinness exploits the coolly repeatable screen-print process for intensity and impact of color but combines and recombines each transfer layer in a unique sequence of hues and shapes, thereby taking advantage of and subverting traditional expectations of the medium in equal measure.

The nearly endless variety of materials available and the freedom to try everything are irresistible to the artists in this section; they relish process and follow no rules except the behavior of the inks under pressure. The prints reproduced here represent a vital segment of the larger printmaking continuum: pure painting on smooth, unworked surfaces at one end and, at the other, edition printing.

Monoprints acknowledge and accept the fragmentary, the collisions, and the discontinuities deeply ingrained in the attitude of assemblage and collage pioneered in the twentieth century and still hugely influential today. This makes monoprints particularly reflective of our contemporary culture. They show us, in fact, that printmaking is at the root of contemporary interest in digitally appropriating, repeating, recombining, and remixing images.

Steven Sorman. *from time to time*. Monoprint with oil-based inks, photopolymer intaglio, and collage on various papers. 37.62" × 22". 2017.

Neil Ambrose-Smith. *Sailor*. Monotype, graphite, and color Xerox transfer with Citra Solv. 2008.

NEAL AMBROSE-SMITH

Corrales, New Mexico

My studio is a laboratory, but probably safer than Procter & Gamble. Failed experiments and some in process are buried beneath more pressing jobs that dominate tables. I do clean, however, which is Artist Idea number 84 from my smartphone app *Artist Ideas*. Whether suspending 7-by-8-foot paintings from the ceiling to create harmonographs or attaching a print hammock to my press to create 14-foot prints, I'm always leaping to discover, which is Artist Idea number 56.

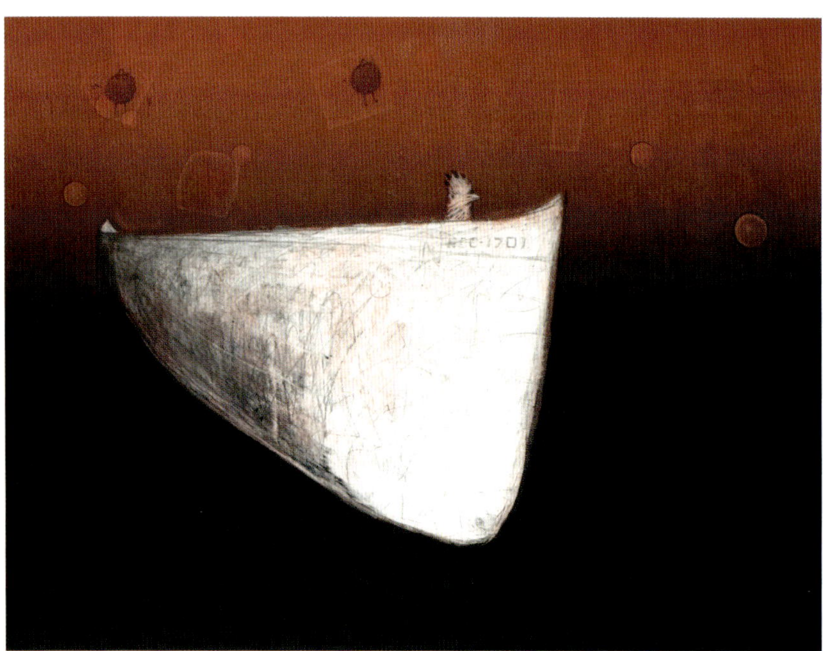

<

Going Where No Man Has Gone Before. Monoprint with Akua soy-based inks, graphite, monotype, and color Xerox transfer with Citra Solv. 22" × 30". 2008.

>

Captain, They Scrambled the Code. Monoprint with Akua soy-based inks, graphite, monotype, and color Xerox transfer with Citra Solv. 22" × 30". 2008.

Nuclear Sunset. Monoprint with Akua soy-based inks, archival pigment print, graphite, monotype, and color Xerox transfer with Citra Solv. 32" × 44". 2008.

PUBLISHED AND PRINTED BY THE ARTIST AT ANDERSON RANCH AND LILY PRESS.

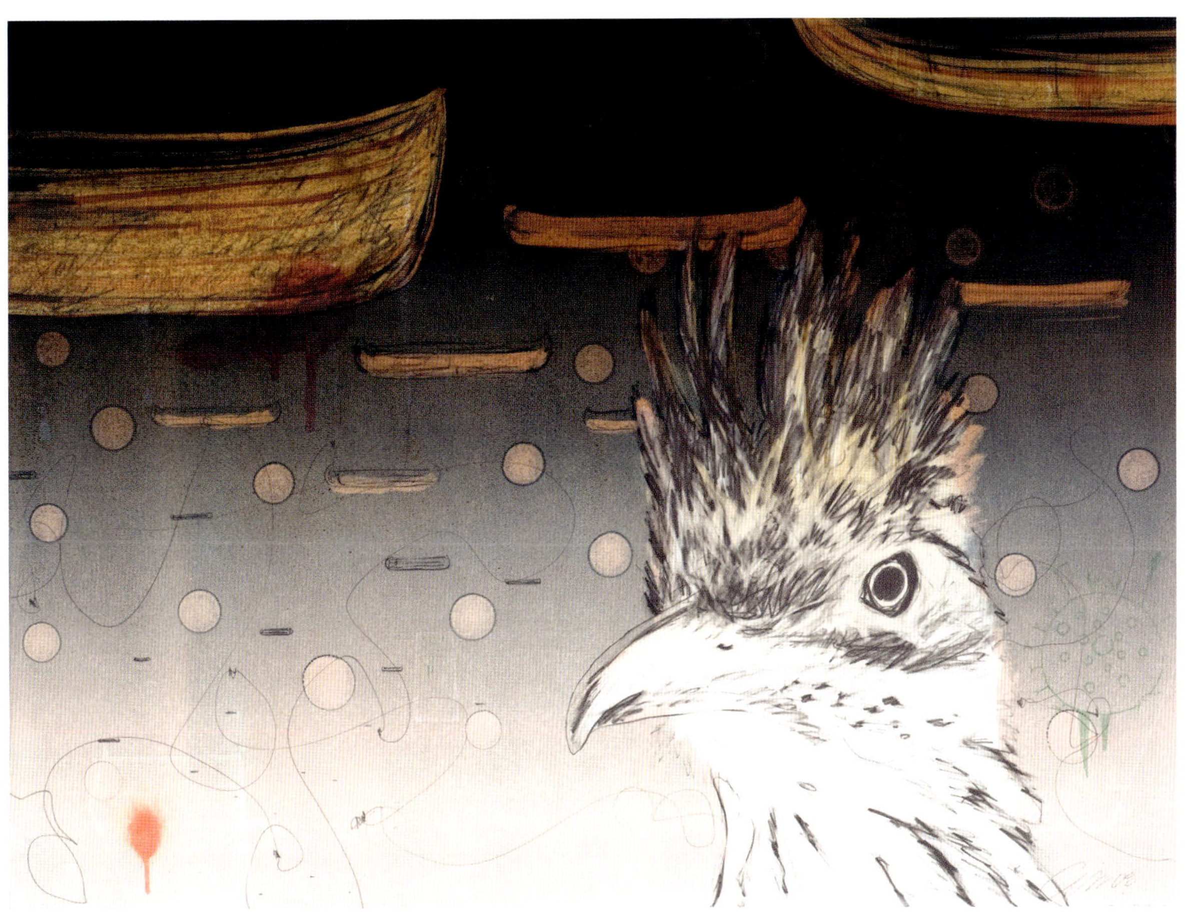

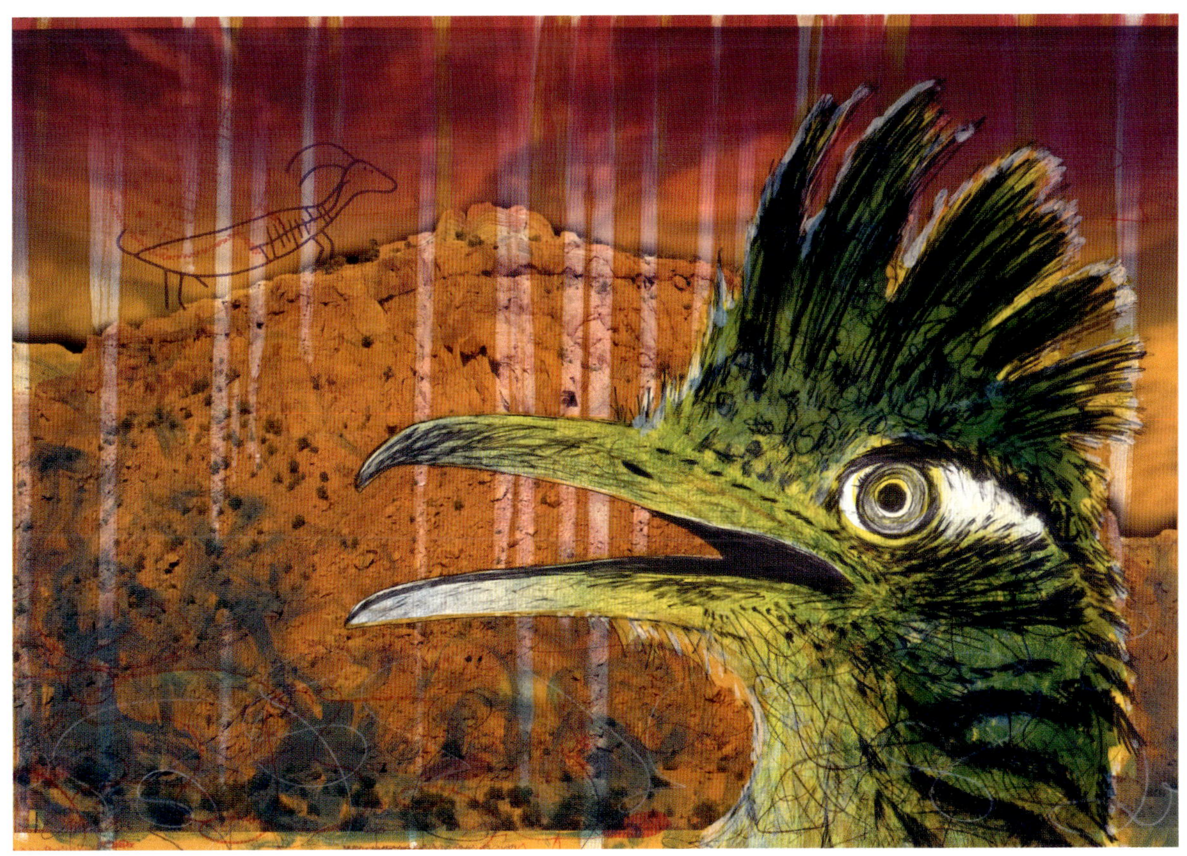

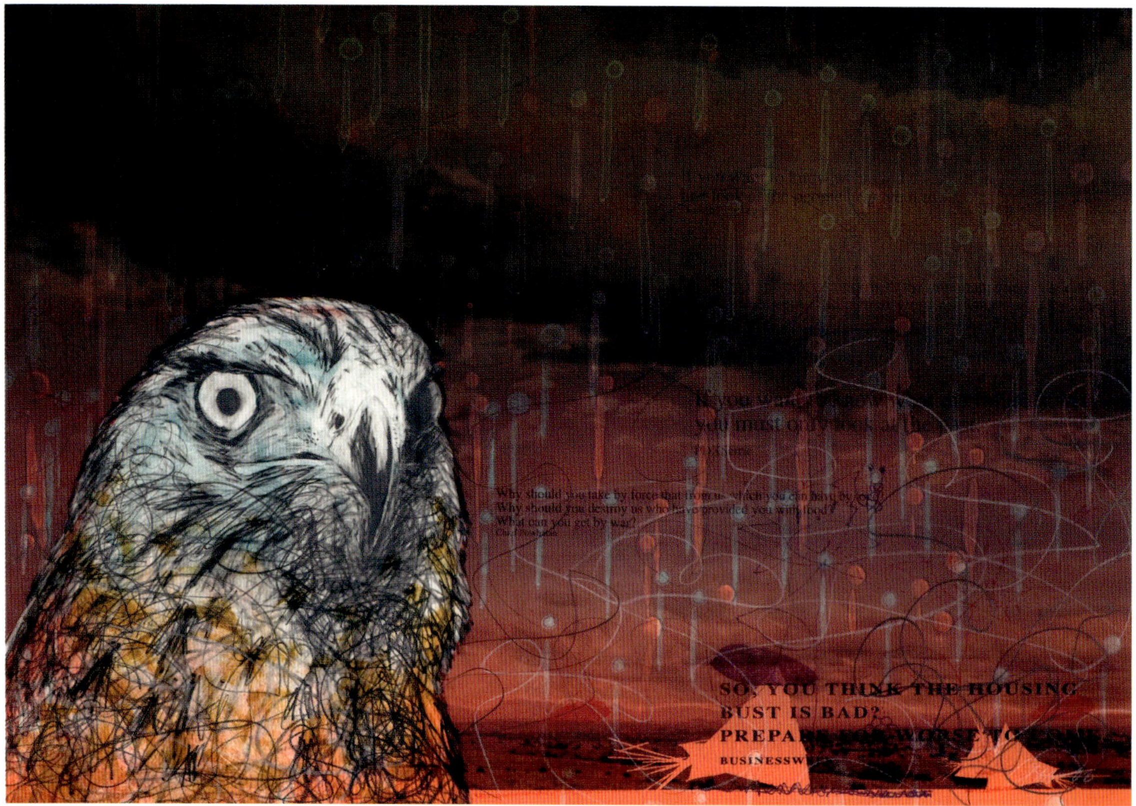

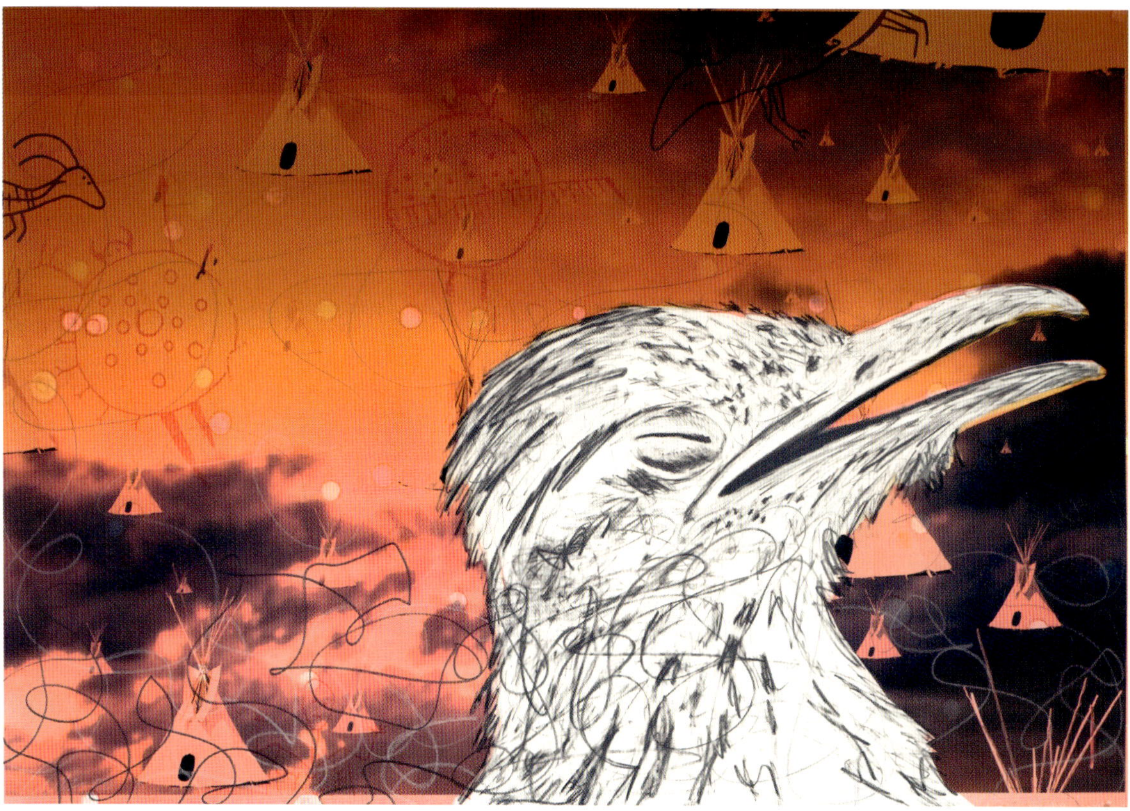

∧

Little Bird in My Head. Monoprint with Akua soy-based inks, archival pigment print, graphite, monotype, and color Xerox transfer with Citra Solv. 32" × 44". 2008.

∨

Singing the roof off. Monoprint with Akua soy-based inks, archival pigment prints, graphite, monotype, and color Xerox transfer with Citra Solv. 32" × 44". 2008.

SARAH AMOS

East Fairfield, Vermont

This body of work is primarily about fusion of land and cityscapes. I am interested in interpreting spatially dynamic, organic landscapes and my direct relationship to them. These monoprints/collagraphs use the layers of print and drawing to play with the relationship both of the new and old order and how they intersect upon impact.

The Australian landscape is the catalyst for this work. It has deep influential references to every piece. It is represented by choice of color, line, and space, bathed in sharp light with distant horizons. My work starts here as a stage where a personalized vocabulary of images is assembled, collated, and dissected. The term "landscape" is now taking on new city and spatial horizons both above and below ground.

My work is developed over a series of layers; new data is often buried deep within these histories, laminating the successive transparent waves of organic and inanimate information to each other. I have a deep interest in the distillation of these ideas. As the landscape becomes linear with clean minimalist lines, information is simplified into an ordered map system that can be easily digested and imagined. It is my mechanism to full comprehension and clarity in a climate of an overabundance of visual stimulation and brooding global forecasts.

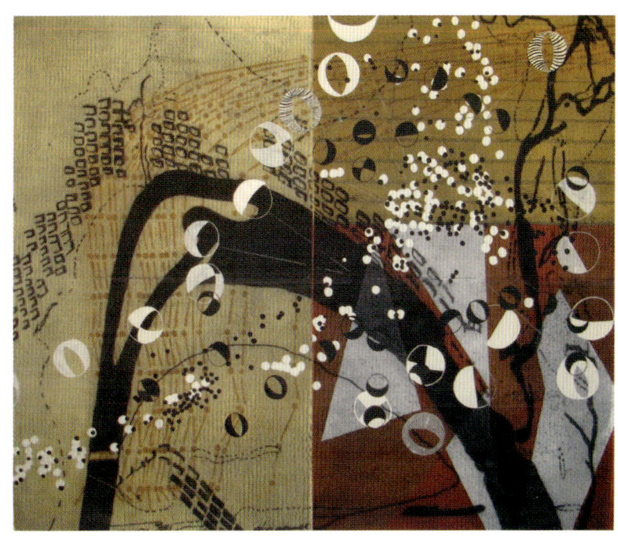

Flax. Collagraph with acrylic. 77" x 79". 2009.

PUBLISHED AND PRINTED BY THE ARTIST AT SARAH AMOS STUDIO.

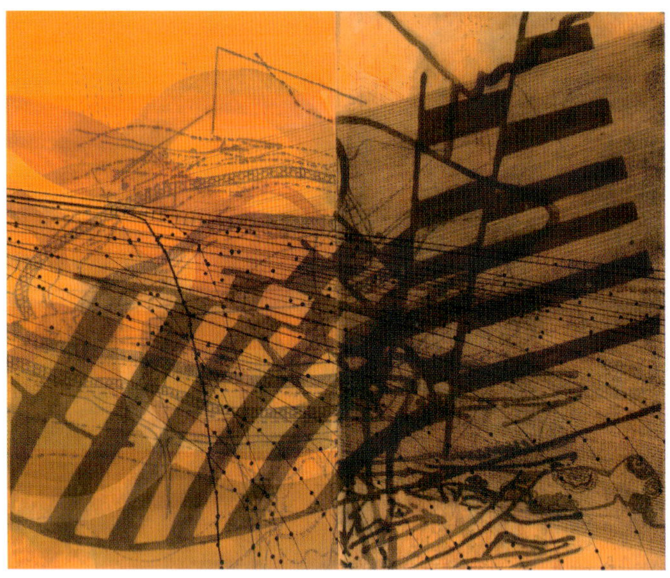

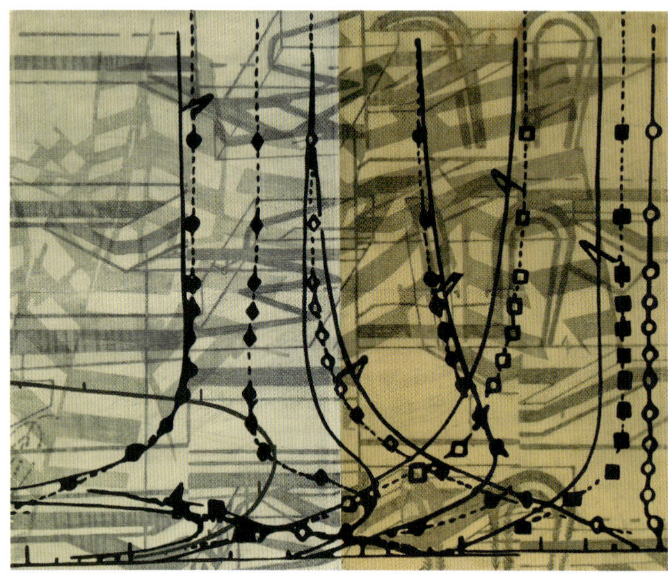

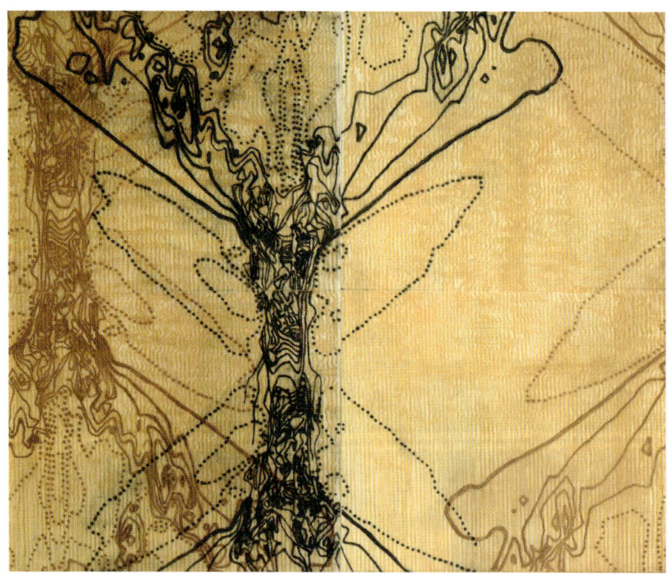

Black Viker. Collagraph with acrylic. 77" x 79". 2009.

Wide Numbers. Collagraph with acrylic. 77" x 79". 2009.

Ronbark Cicada. Collagraph with acrylic. 77" x 79". 2009.

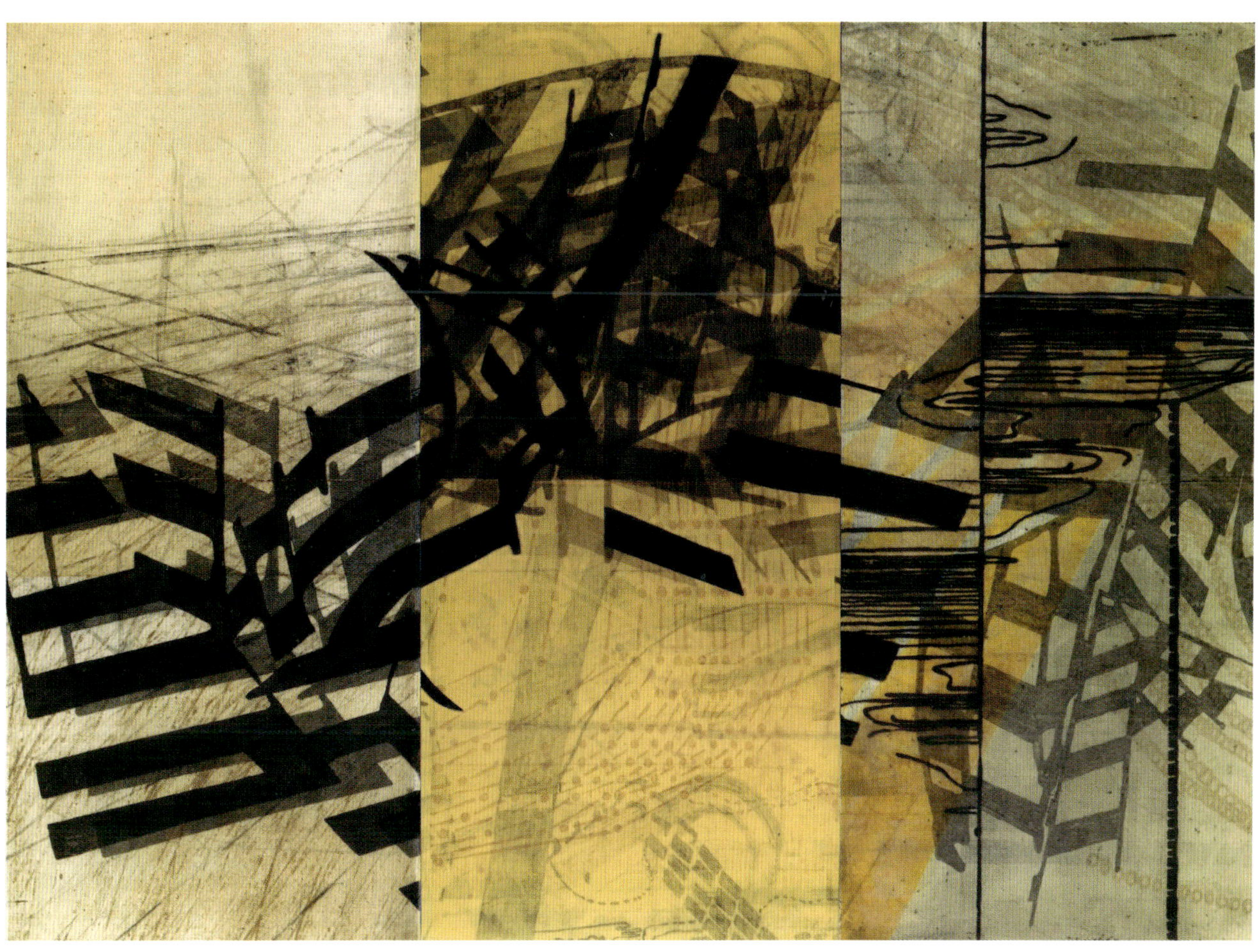

Earlier Territory. Monoprint with oil-based inks and paint, monotype, and etching. 89" × 59". 2009.

PEGGY BADENHAUSEN

Ipswich, Massachusetts

My prints are based on concepts of motion in space and lie at the intersection of color and geometry. The underlying structure of my work springs from architectural plans and dance notation, both of which represent on a two-dimensional surface the motion of the human body in three dimensions.

Combining diagrams and mark making, the regular and the spontaneous, produces unexpected juxtapositions. I find that the monotype process lends itself to this unpredictability. I encourage the accidental. The grain of the wood that I use for plates, as well as the irregularity of Japanese papers, adds to the character and individuality of the prints.

Color is a dimension in itself, and color relationships are a primary interest for me, a key connection to my environment. My work is referential rather than representational. I use colors that are specific to a landscape, an architecture, or a situation.

The combination of photographs with monotypes is a fairly recent development for me. Although I have been a photographer for decades, I have kept the two activities separate. I note, though, that my eye seeks the same thing in a photo that it does in a print. I don't take photographs specifically for a print. It seems a natural step to combine them.

Float, 3. Monoprint with oil-based etching ink and oil stick on Mulberry paper. 18" × 18". 2010.

ALL PHOTOS ARE COURTESY OF WILL HOWCROFT. PUBLISHED AND PRINTED BY THE ARTIST AT MASTWOOD PRESS.

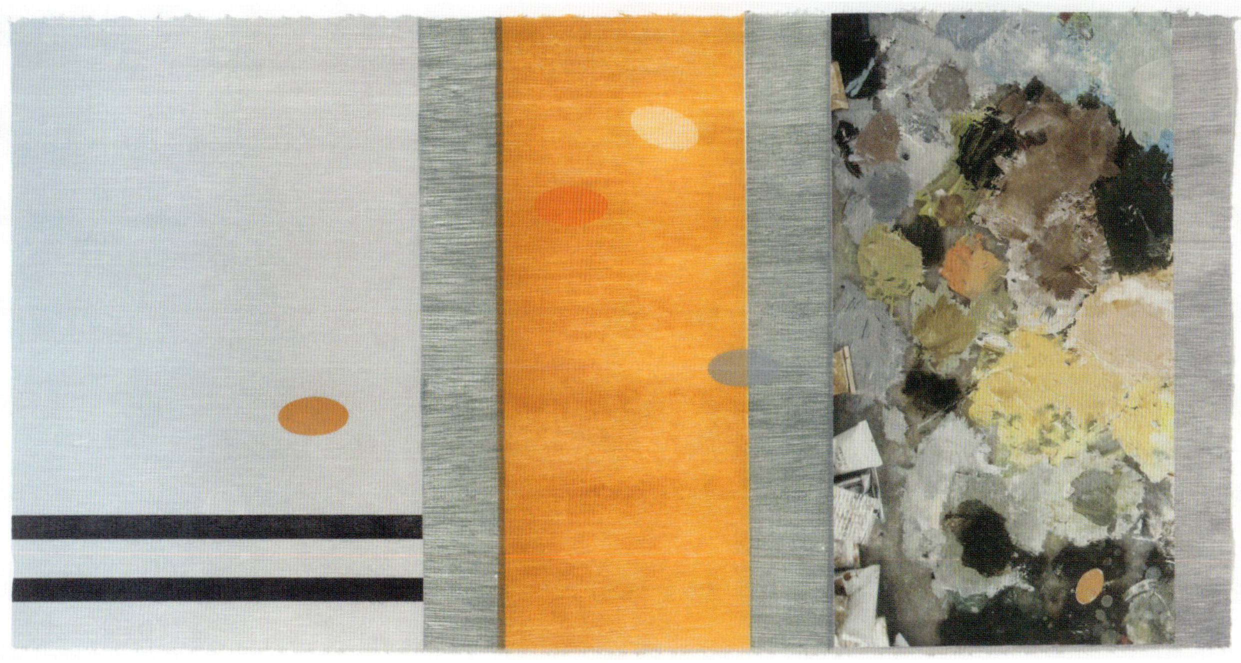

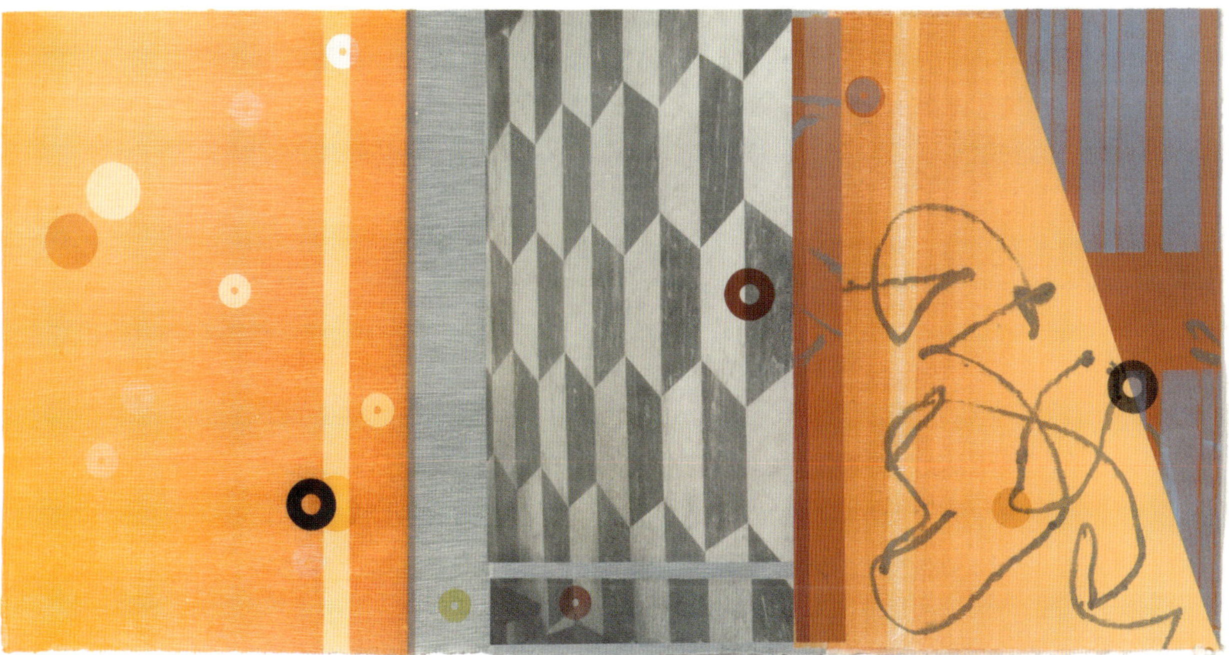

∧

Bird's Eye, 3. Monoprint with oil-based etching ink, monotype, and photographic collage on handmade Tanbo paper. 18" × 37". 2016.

∨

Bird's Eye, 4. Monoprint with oil-based etching ink, monotype, and photographic collage on handmade Tanbo paper. 18" × 37". 2017.

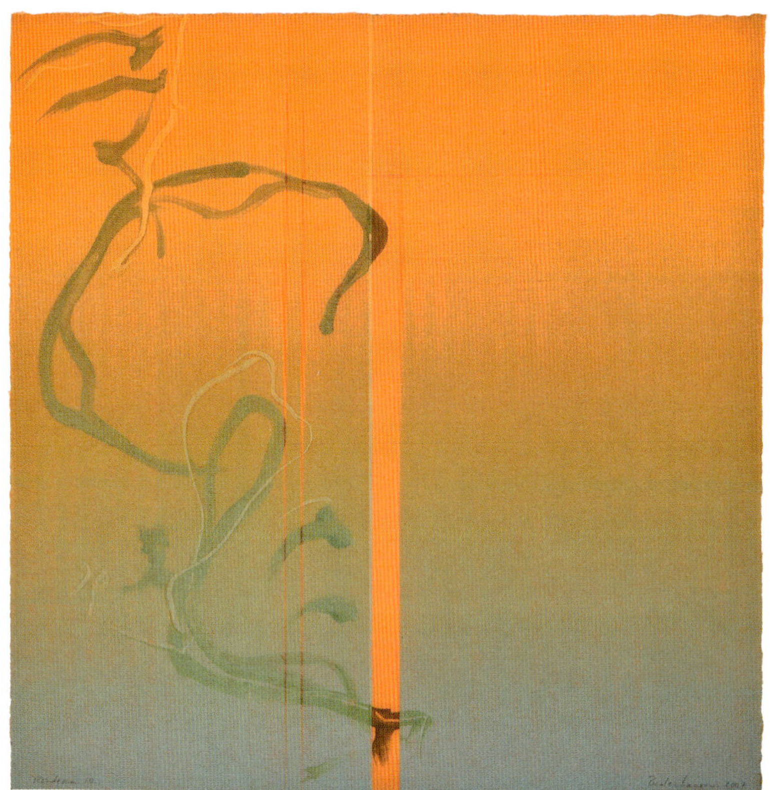

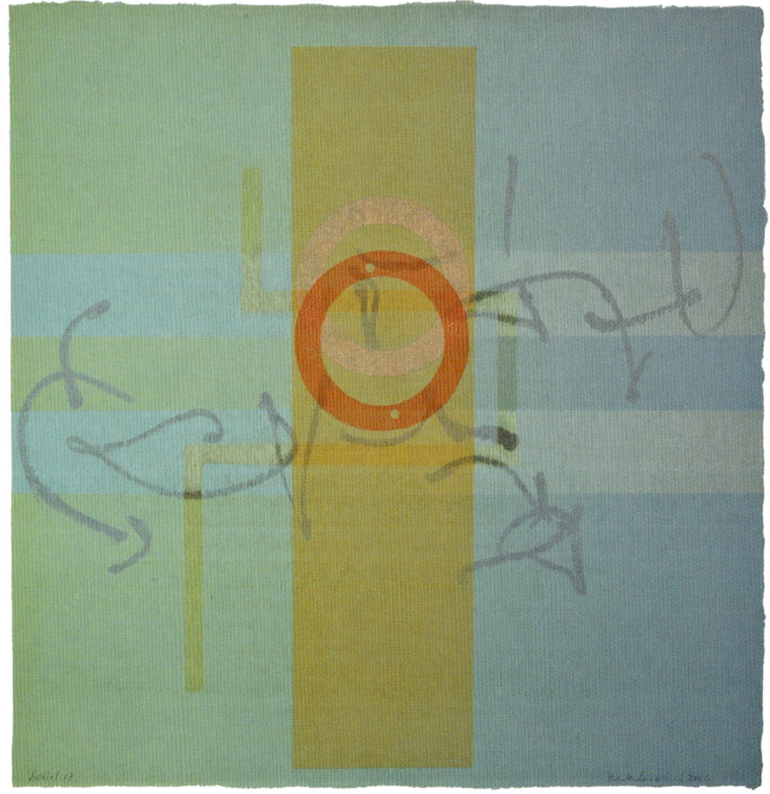

^

Rondeau. Monoprint with oil-based etching ink and oil stick on Mulberry paper. 18" × 18". 2009.

v

Aerial, 17. Monoprint with oil-based etching ink and oil stick on Mulberry paper. 18" × 18". 2007.

CHRISTINE BENEMAN

Scarborough, Maine

This series is based on architectural forms initially inspired by a late winter's walk on the High Line elevated park in New York City. The tension between the dynamic, active spaces in a reconstructed urban landscape and the undergirding logic that holds the composition together creates the fascination and mystery.

I create the print elements using collagraph plates and monotypes from hand-cut stencils. I frequently combine or cut out and layer them atop each other (or both), allowing room both for intention and improvisation. The complex and intricate proliferation of overlaid cutouts adds the excitement of unpredictability.

High Line XXI. Monoprint with Akua soy-based inks, collagraph, and monotype. 30" × 22". 2014.

Queensboro. Monoprint with Akua soy-based inks, collagraph, and monotype. 30" × 22". 2015.

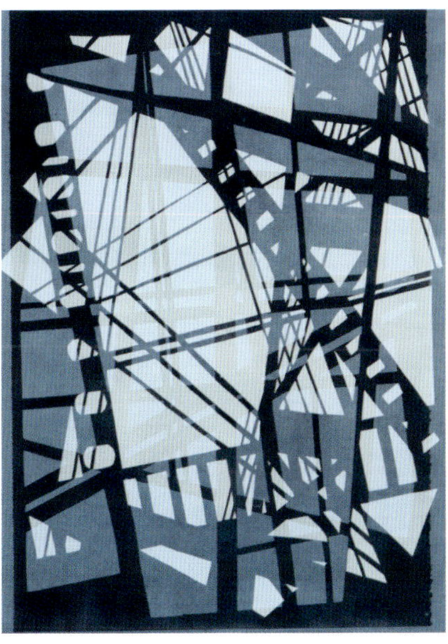

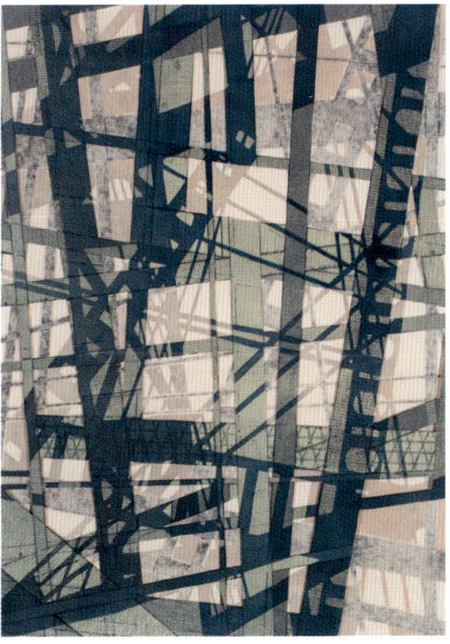

ALL PHOTOS ARE COURTESY OF JAY YORK PHOTO. PUBLISHED AND PRINTED BY THE ARTIST AT PEREGRINE PRESS.

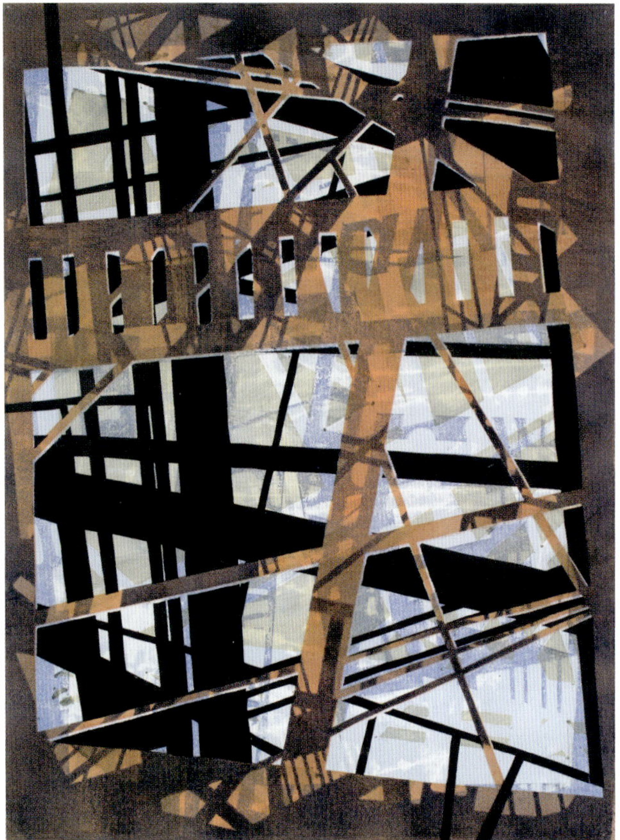

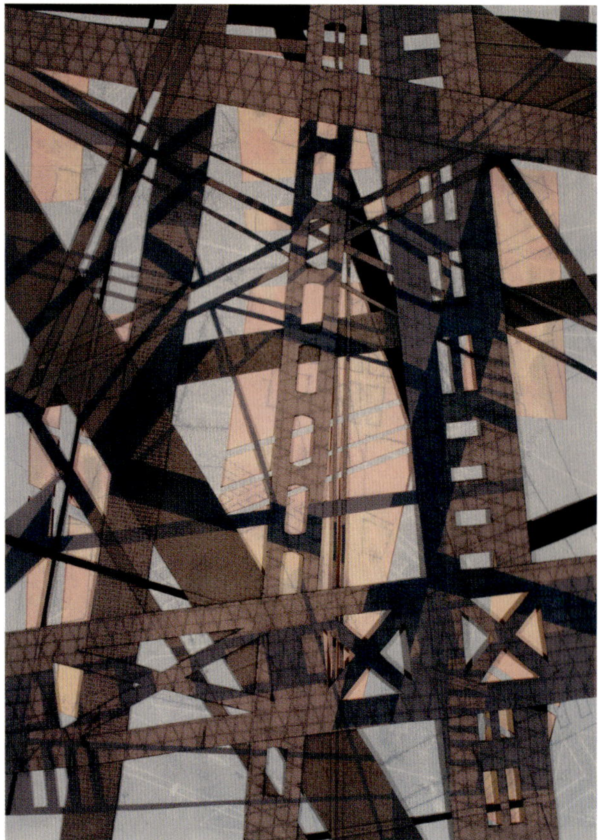

Williamsburg II. Monoprint with Akua soy-based inks, collagraph, and monotype. 30" × 22". 2015.

High Line Genesis. Monoprint with Akua soy-based inks, collagraph, and monotype. 30" × 22". 2014.

>
Construction Zone. Monoprint with Akua soy-based inks, collagraph, and monotype. 30" × 22". 2016.

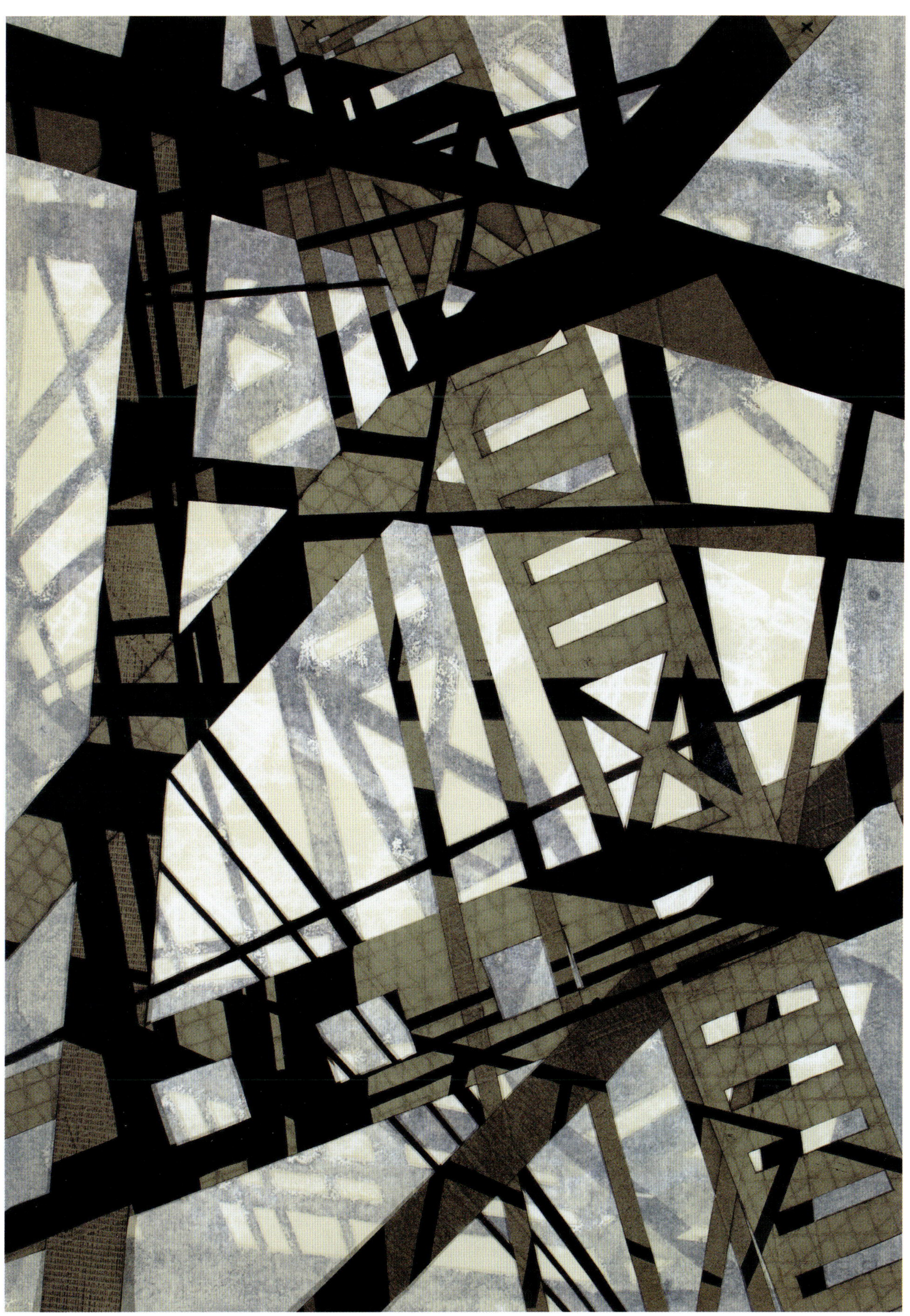

KATHERINE BRADFORD

New York, New York

Superheroes & Divers. Monoprint series with pigmented linen pulp on cotton base sheet and gouache. 14" × 11.125". 2014.

In 2014, Dieu Donné commissioned me to create twenty-five new, unique variants collectively titled *Superheroes and Divers* for their 2014 Paper Variables Editions program. Working collaboratively with studio collaborator Amy Jacobs, I used pigmented pulp to translate my painting process into a new medium. Each of the twenty-five individual works in the series features a diver or a superhero suspended midair with unique backgrounds.

Using templates, one for the silhouette of a soaring diver, another for his boots, and another for his cape, I was able to locate a flying figure in the center of each handmade 14-by-11-inch piece of paper. Then the real fun began as I invented a different sky or surrounding atmosphere for each figure, whether a flying Superman or a flying woman diver.

The longer I stayed with the project, the more possibilities for improvisation emerged. The sky area could be sprayed with hose water to create endless weather-related effects. The woman diver's bathing suit could be multicolored or any number of bright summer hues. Along the way, I stumbled on the idea of laying down a layer of thick, pigmented pulp across the bottom or top. If the color appeared along the bottom, it invariably read as landscape; if it was at the top, the paper flattened out to read as a near abstraction.

The work began to take on a rhythm as color relationships merged with the imagery. At the conclusion, I had a very satisfying fleet of buoyant characters doing my every bid.

ALL PHOTOS ARE COURTESY OF DIEU DONNÉ. PUBLISHED AT DIEU DONNÉ PAPER MILL, INC.

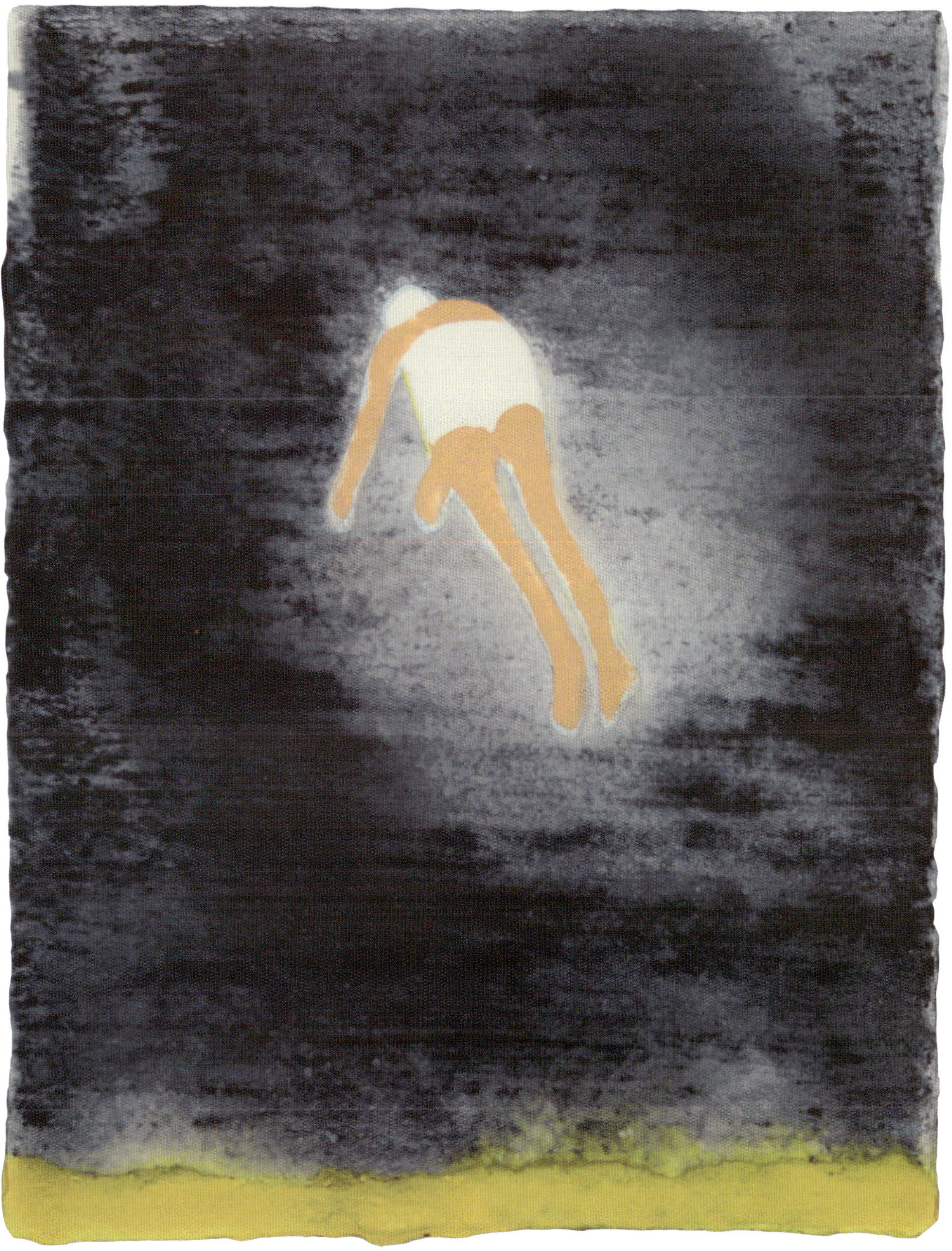

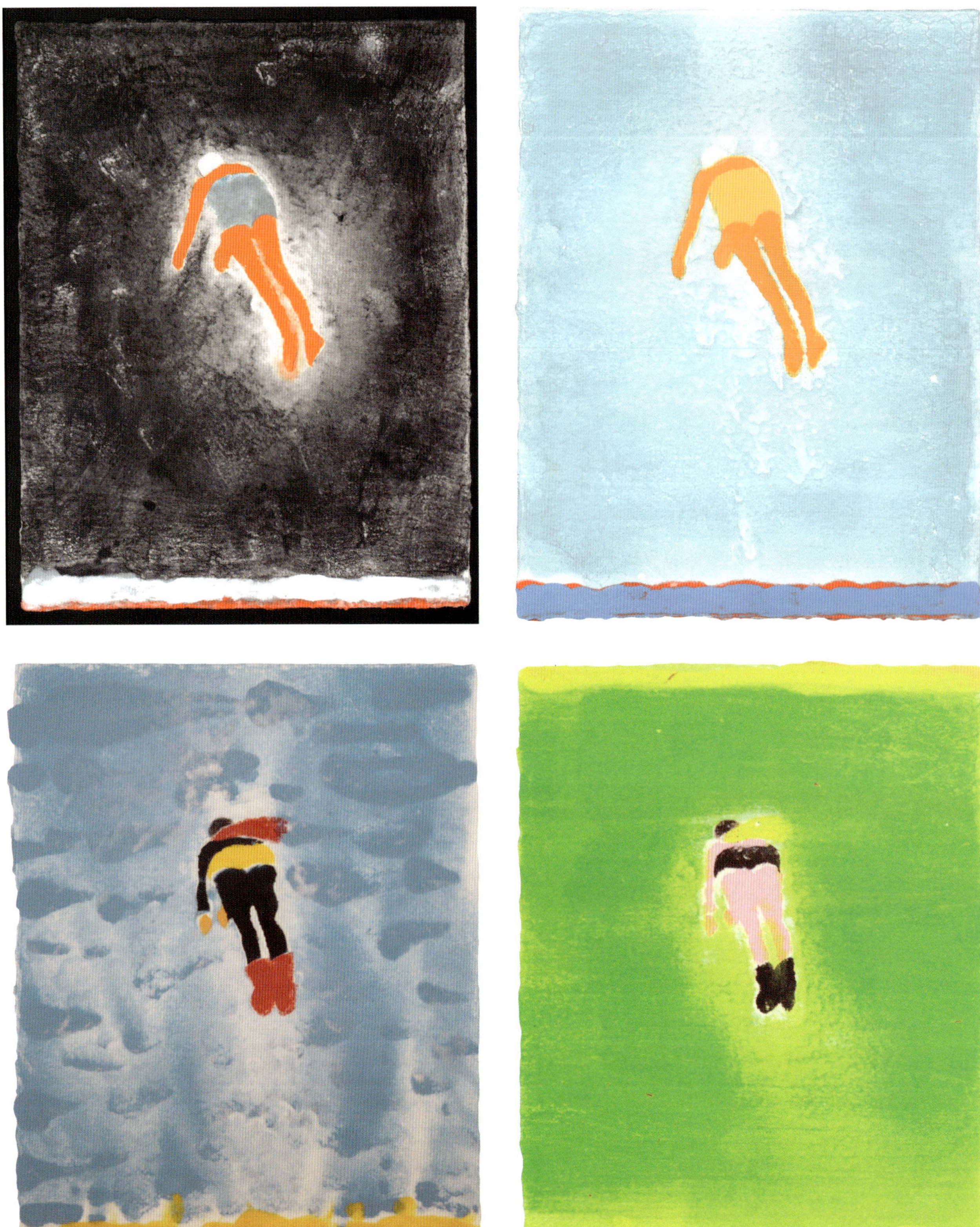

BETH CAMPBELL

Brooklyn, New York

For *Endless Outcomes*, I built on this idea of using a web of possible paths with a core point—my first hypothetical—and connecting a sequence of outcomes, as my earlier drawings and sculpture. I selected color and string combinations in an embrace of the collaboration's variable intent and laid each string composition meticulously by hand in the wet base sheets of paper. Studio collaborator at Dieu Donné, Amy Jacobs, and I then shaped deckles to create the colored mobile components and laid them into the wet composition. Finally, I applied a translucent sheet of abaca paper, promoting unique aspects of the papermaking process and enabling a contrast between the portion of the work that is determined—color and string combinations—and the length of the strings, which extend below the plane, creating an effect of unknown possibility, more and more choices.

Endless Outcomes. Monoprint series with pigmented cotton base sheet, string, abaca overlay, and pigmented linen stenciled shapes. 18" × 14.75". 2017.

ALL PHOTOS ARE COURTESY OF KIRSTEN FLAHERTY AT DIEU DONNÉ. PUBLISHED AT DIEU DONNÉ PAPER MILL, INC.

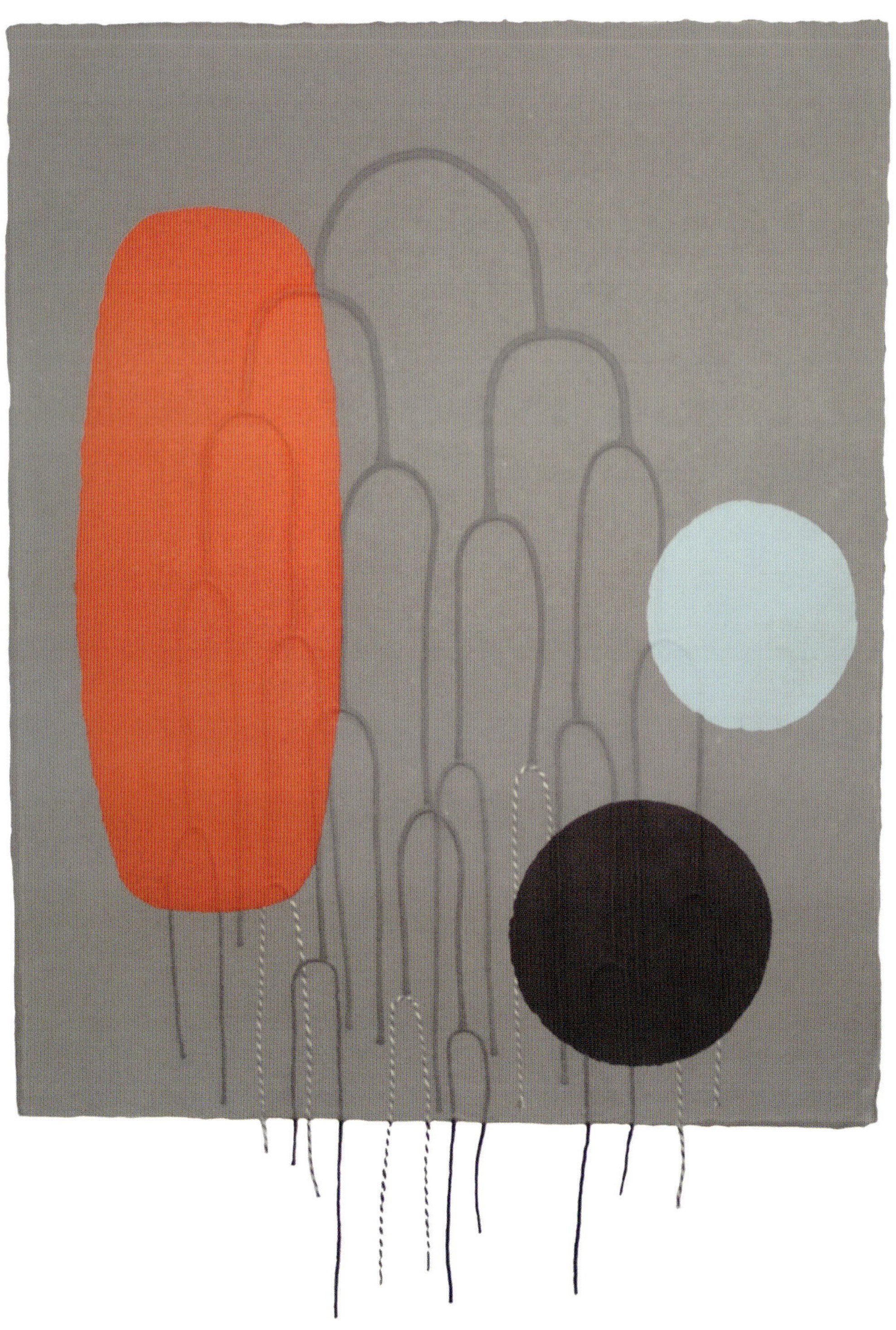

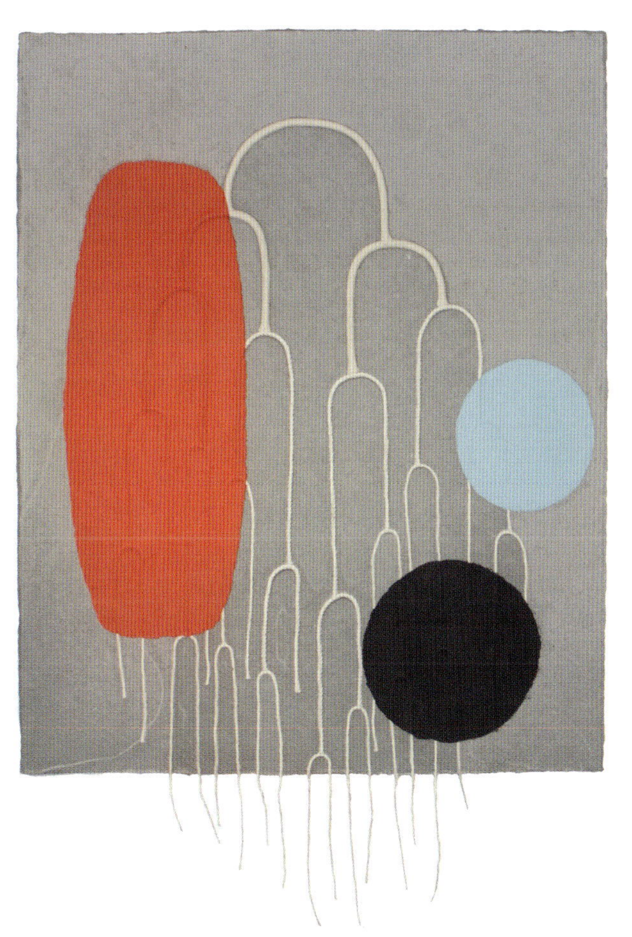

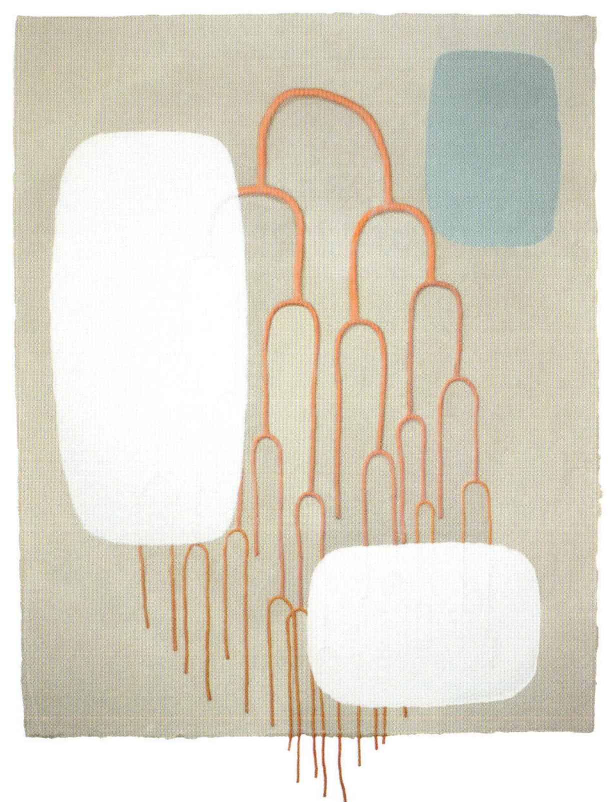

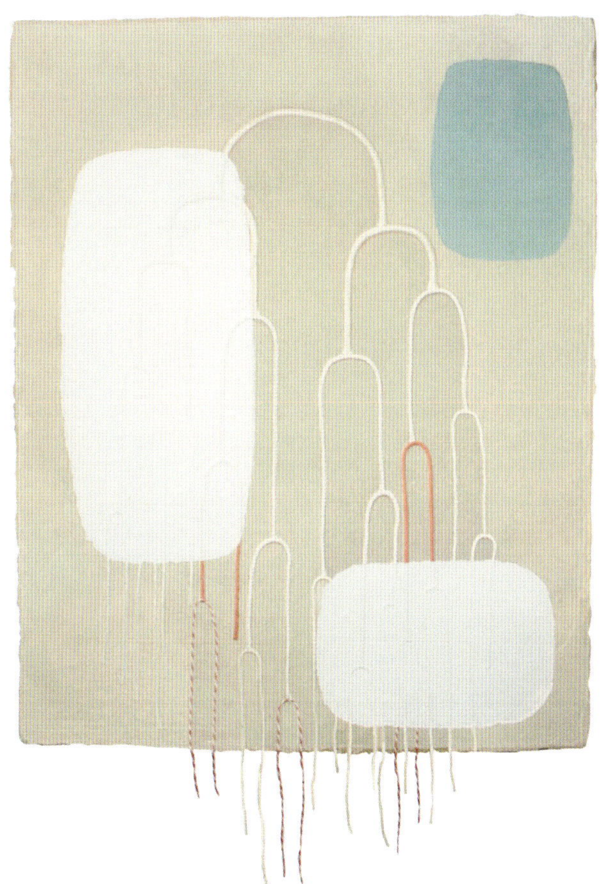

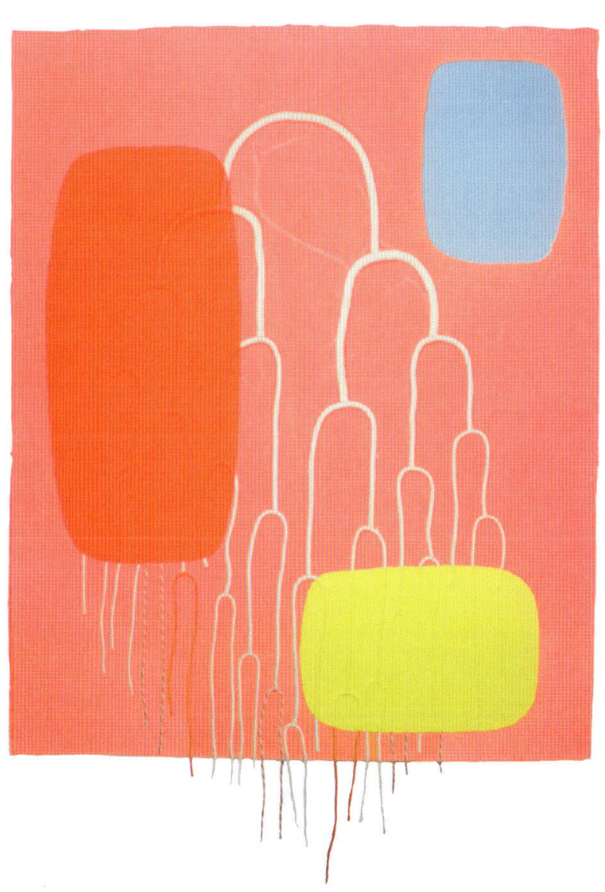

JEN COLE

Oakland, California

Monoprints offer generous scope for experimentation in the process of printing. My own process often begins with just a vague idea. I start to make marks. Some marks are intentional, and some become accidents that benefit the image. Many marks are wiped away. There are no rules in monoprinting, which is quite freeing.

Occasionally, I print a large collagraph texture over an entire piece of paper and then work back into that image with layers of ink color. Layering of translucent colors is a wonderful path to follow, rendering the visual surprise of one ink printed over another. The use of stencils and chine collé are other techniques that add dimension to my prints. Stencils hand-cut out of Mylar or acetate add repeated detail or build texture. Chine collé brings in the different element of Japanese paper. I predesign my chine collé paper and use small pieces of it in my prints as accents.

My printing involves countless additions and subtractions of marks, and many passes through the press. I usually have no clear idea about where the image is taking me, but I am attached to this process of following the muse of the print. It is most satisfying.

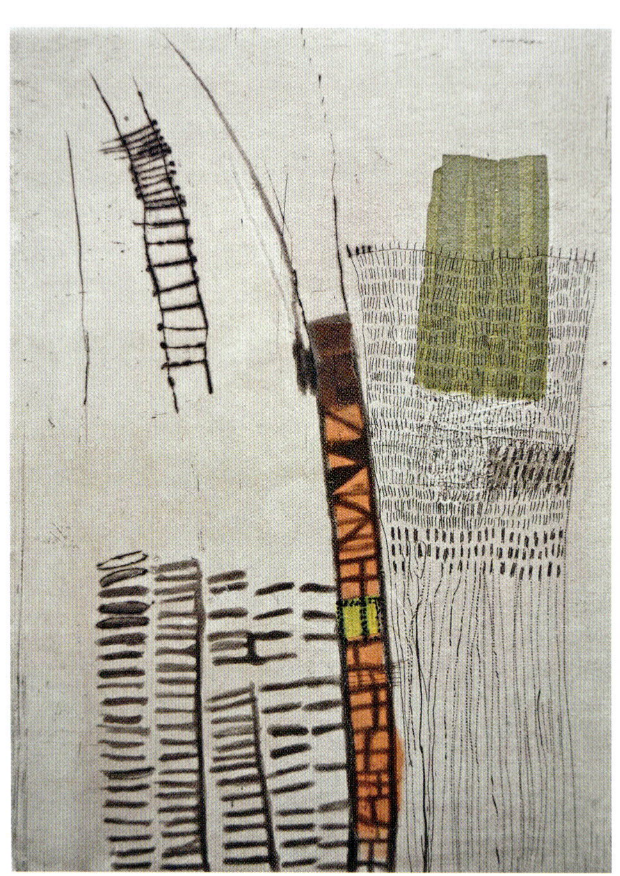

Lines to Klee II. Monoprint with oil-based inks, etching, and chine collé. 2015.

PUBLISHED AND PRINTED BY THE ARTIST AT KALA ART INSTITUTE.

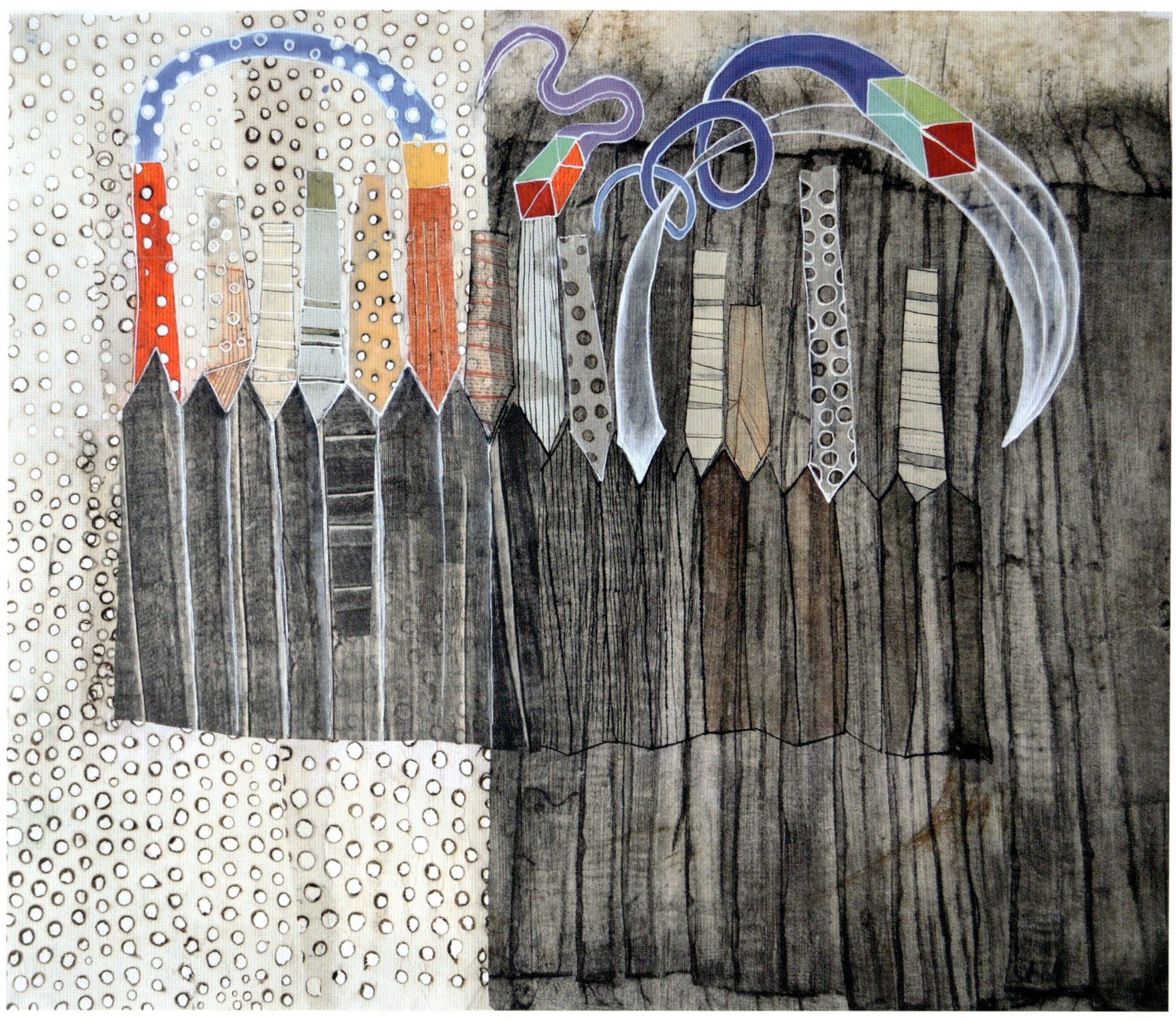

The Blue Loops. Monoprint with oil-based inks, collagraph with hand coloring. 19" × 22.5". 2016.

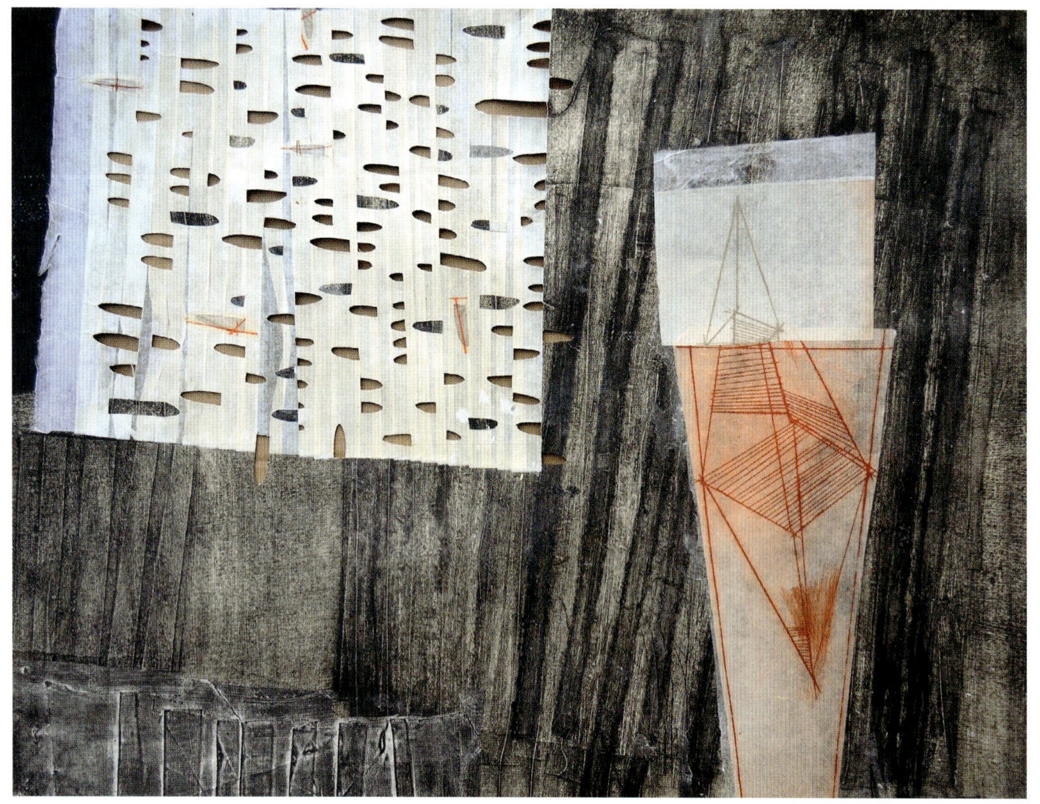

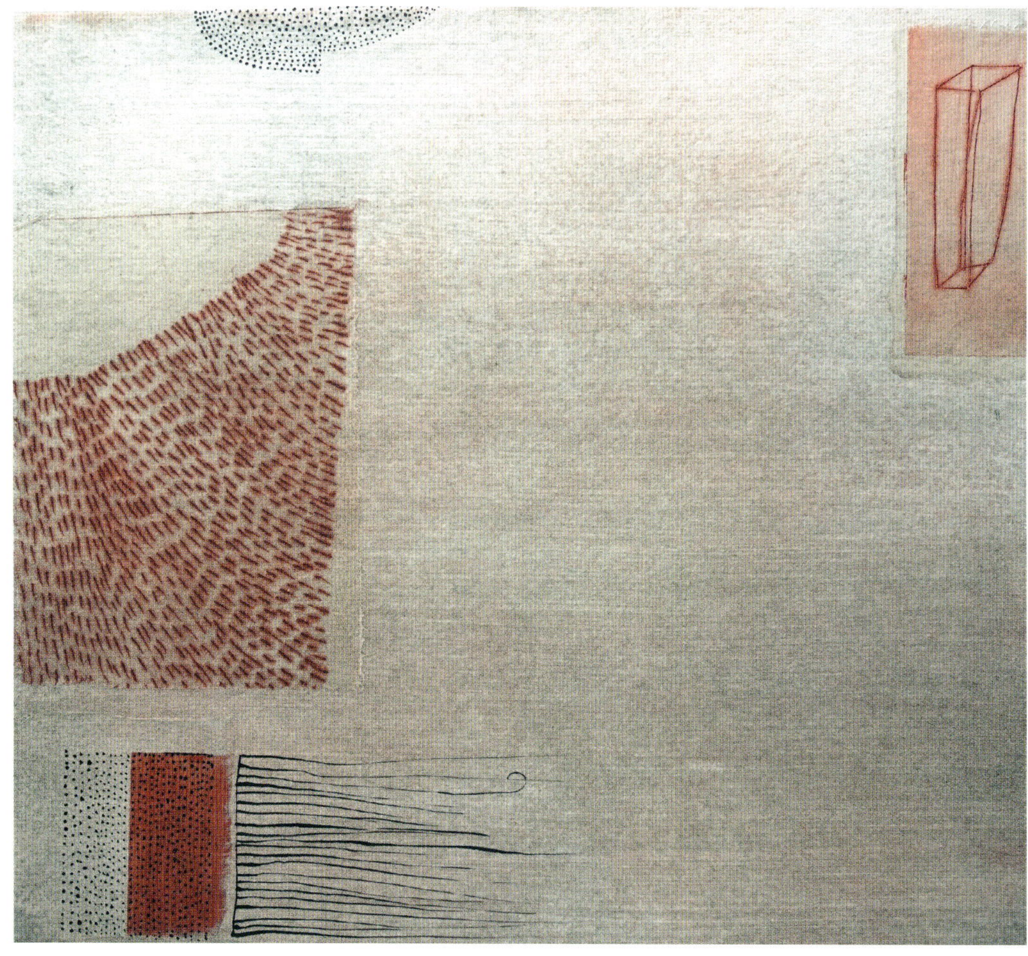

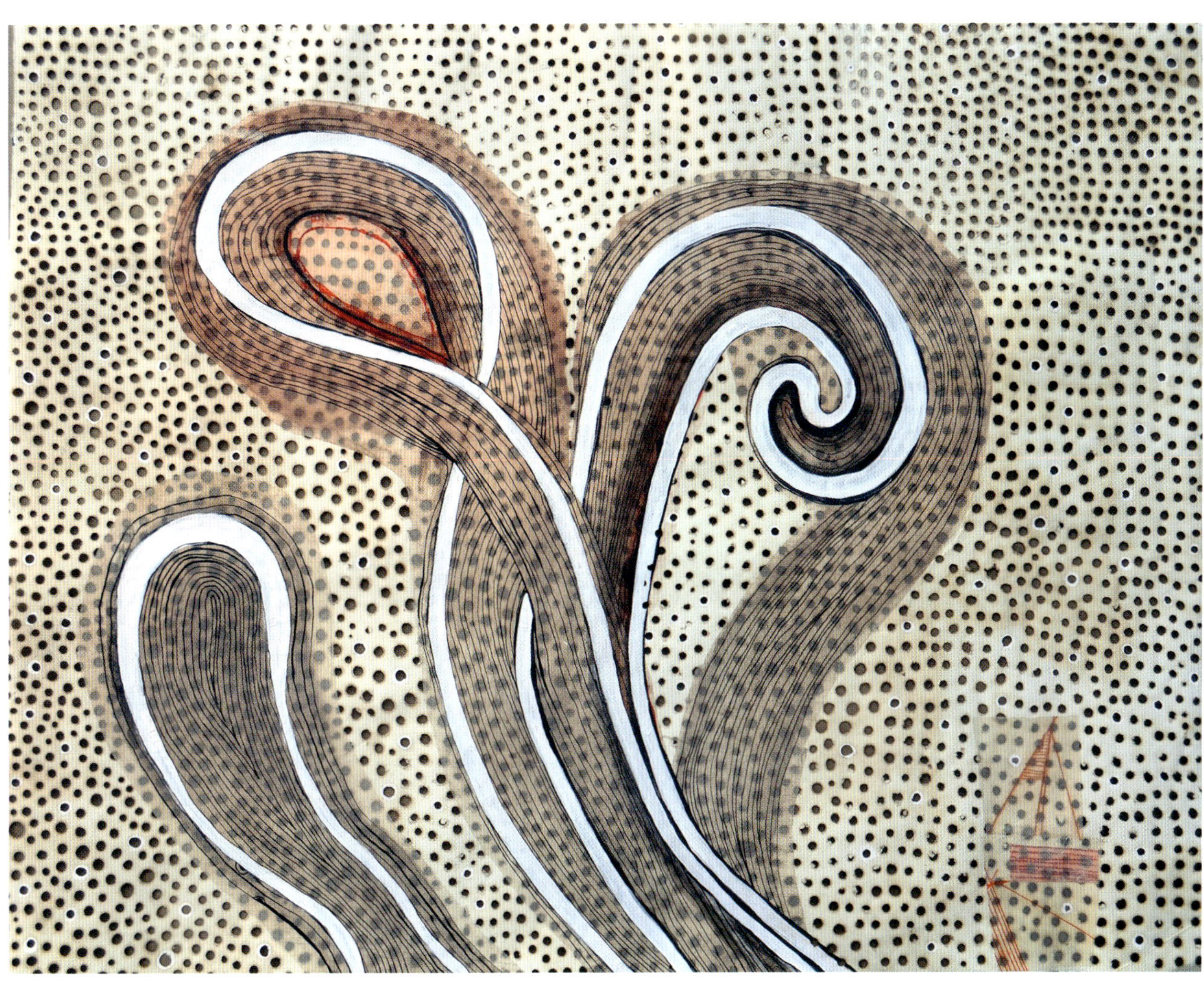

<
Real Syndrome. Monoprint with oil-based inks, collagraph with hand coloring. 18" × 25". 2017.

Low Tide. Monoprint with oil-based inks, collagraph. 2017.

Big Loops. Monoprint with oil-based inks, collage, and burnt paper. 2016.

DAVID COST

Sante Fe, New Mexico

I came to printmaking by a circuitous route. Once a career banker, then a poet, I did no art for seventy years. In 2000, I began by making simple Sumi marks—faint, quick, unconscious stabs of watercolor on paper. These marks were similar to those on the pottery I had collected for many years by the Minnesota potter Warren MacKenzie, a follower of Bernard Leach and Shoji Hamada. Out of the Japanese tradition, spontaneous, alive, they touch upon an almost indescribable essence—one of simplicity and unconscious expression.

There is where I thrive. Once in an art class, I was told I would go nowhere unless I could draw. So I drew and went nowhere. For me, the answer goes deeper. I find a seam, tap its vein, make my marks, crank the wheel, give process the nod, and delight in the print I pull.

The circles on this page I call "ceramic plates." I thought to myself, why not try to print the essence of the ceramics I love by creating plates as monoprints. Found objects also intrigue me—stones, the face of wood grains, paper, leaves, paint chips from the floor, ink blots, controlled fire, random ink drippings left on the roller—you name it—string, wire, grasses, day lilies— I've used them all in my prints. It often results in a nonintentional composition—one of chance. I believe that many of the things that must have excited John Cage also excite me. Such indirection often yields little except, perhaps, surprise. But as the poet Robert Frost once said, "No surprise to the writer, no surprise to the reader!"

I am a partner with master printer Michael McCabe in the Fourth Dimension, a Santa Fe printing studio, where we provide an affordable opportunity for artists from around the country and South America to print.

ALL PHOTOS ARE COURTESY OF JOHN VOKOUN. PUBLISHED BY THE ARTIST. PRINTED BY MICHAEL MCCABE AT FOURTH DIMENSION STUDIO.

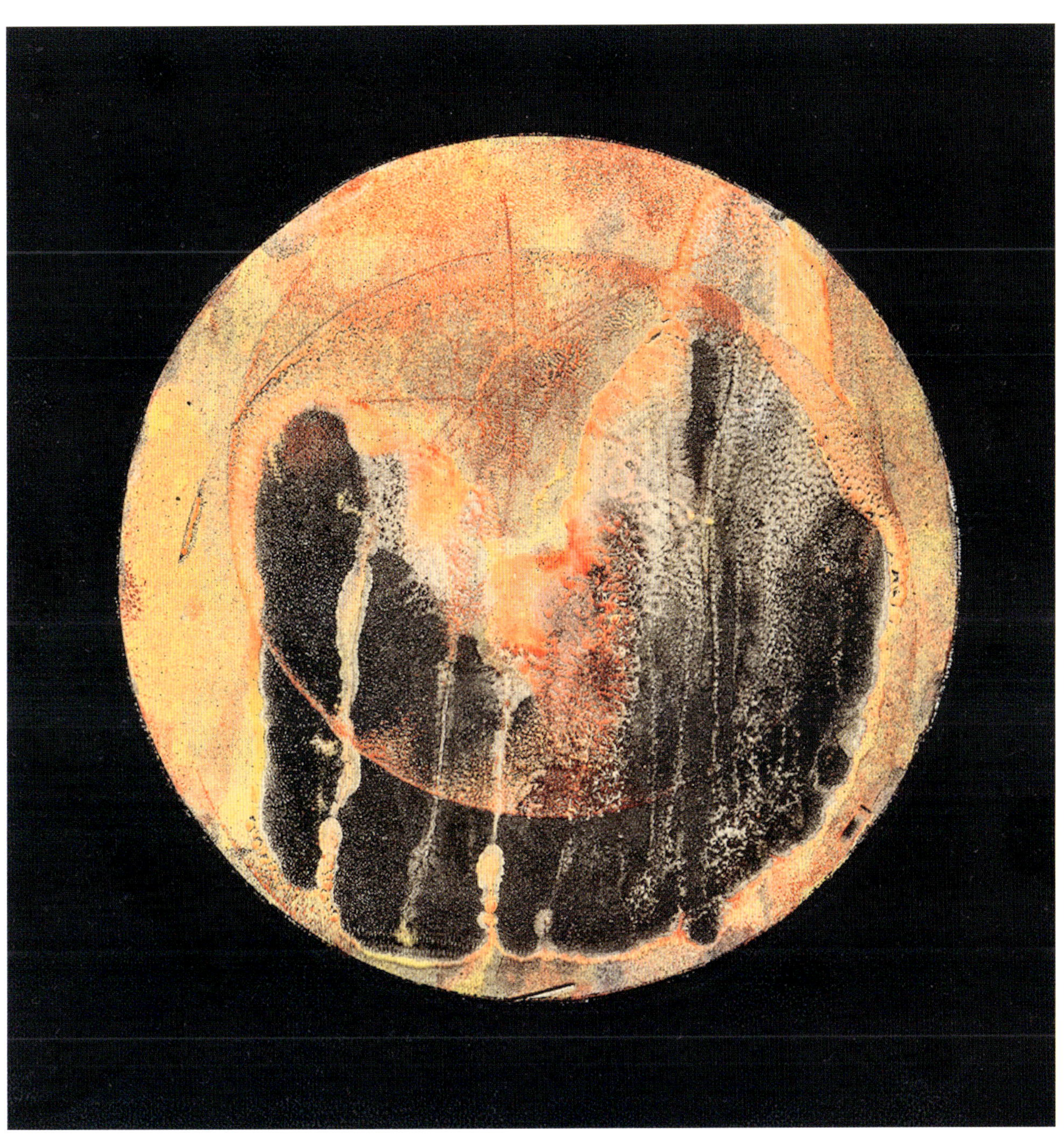

Shoji IV. Viscosity monoprint with oil-based inks. 12" × 12". 2005.

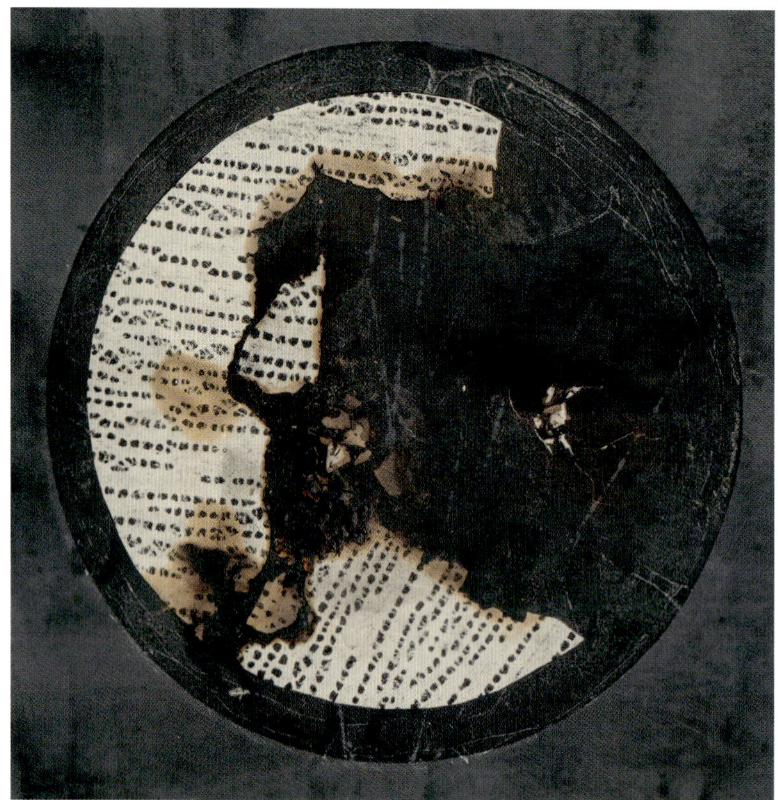

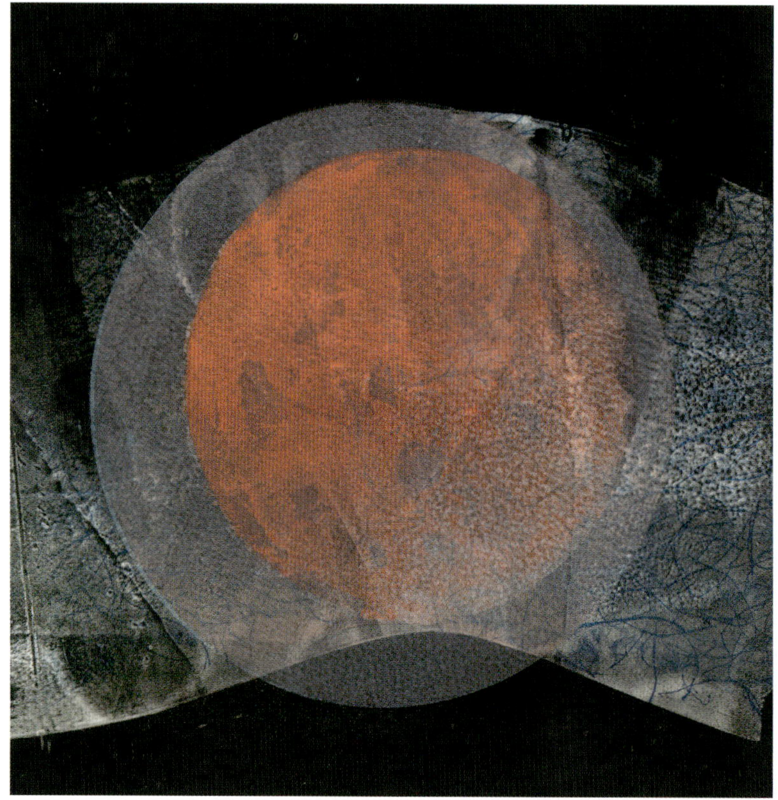

∧
Shoji V. Viscosity monoprint with oil-based inks and collage. 12" × 12". 2009.

∨
Shoji II. Viscosity monotype with oil-based inks. 12" × 12". 2006.

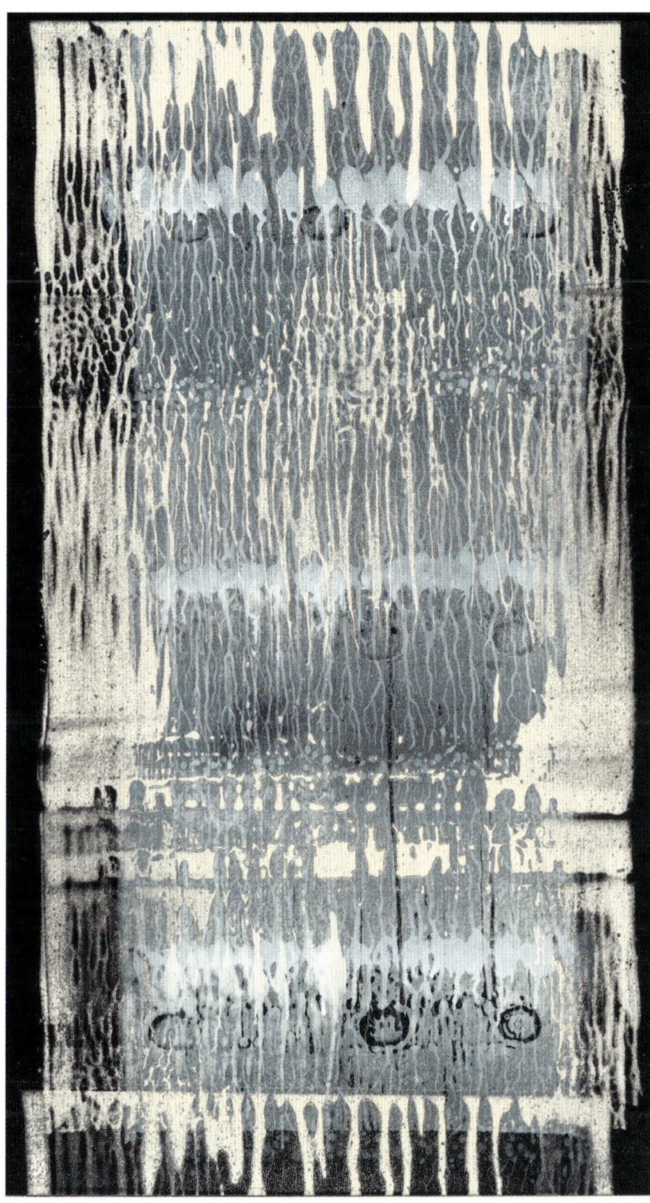

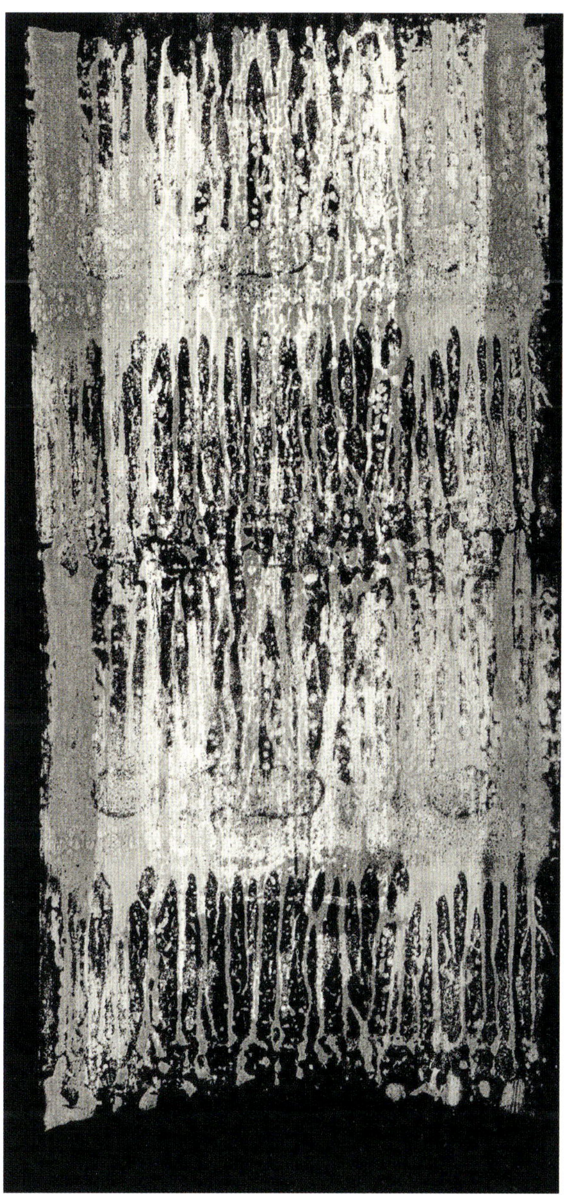

Cage I. Viscosity monotype with oil-based inks. 22" × 15". 2015.

Cage III. Viscosity monotype with oil-based inks. 22" × 8.5". 2016.

DEBORAH FREEDMAN

New York, New York

I have been making monotypes since I showed my paintings to Robert Blackburn (with whom I had studied at NYU) in the early 1990s. The paintings were of waterfalls. He suggested that I make three plates: one hard ground, one soft ground, and one aquatint, in order to create prints with various combinations. Now I had "matrixes" to work with backgrounds that were abstract and textural.

It was the perfect work method for me. It inspired me to dissect my imagery and then put it back together with endless possibilities. I have continued working with this method ever since. I have made aquatint plates with trees and used them to make hundreds of variations. I have also abandoned the matrix and made landscape monotypes, using the ghosts to increase the depth and mystery of a print.

Recently, I have made watercolor monotypes with the similar goal of creating images of depth and mystery in a discernible landscape, Making solar plates also affords another option for a matrix without using toxic solvents. Combining the solar plate with backgrounds of monotype done on vellum is also an exciting process that continues the tradition of the "painterly print": the perfect marriage of painting and printing, of which I will never tire.

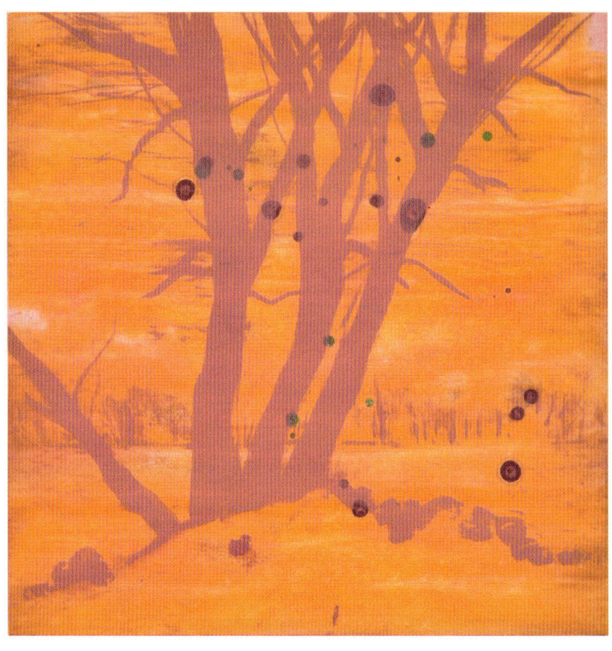

Spring Fever VI. Watercolor monotype and solar plate. 20" × 18". 2016.

>

Cold Spring IV. Solar plate. 20" × 18". 2016.

Spring Fever XIV. Watercolor monotype and solar plate. 20" × 18". 2016.

PUBLISHED AND PRINTED AT OEHME GRAPHICS BY SUE OEHME.

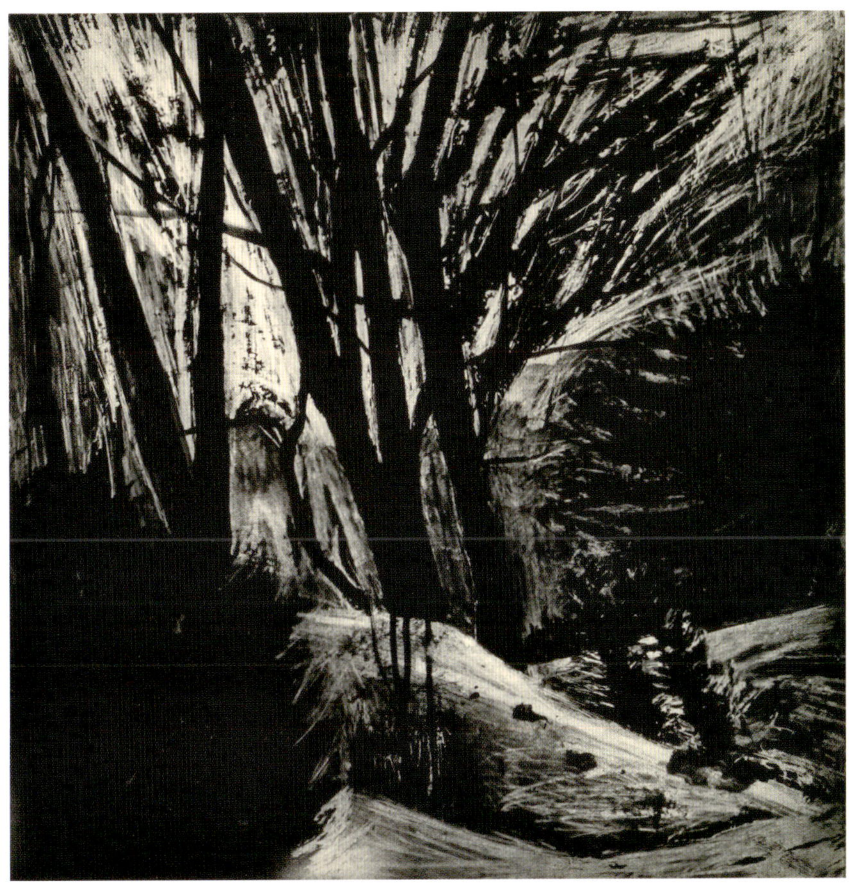

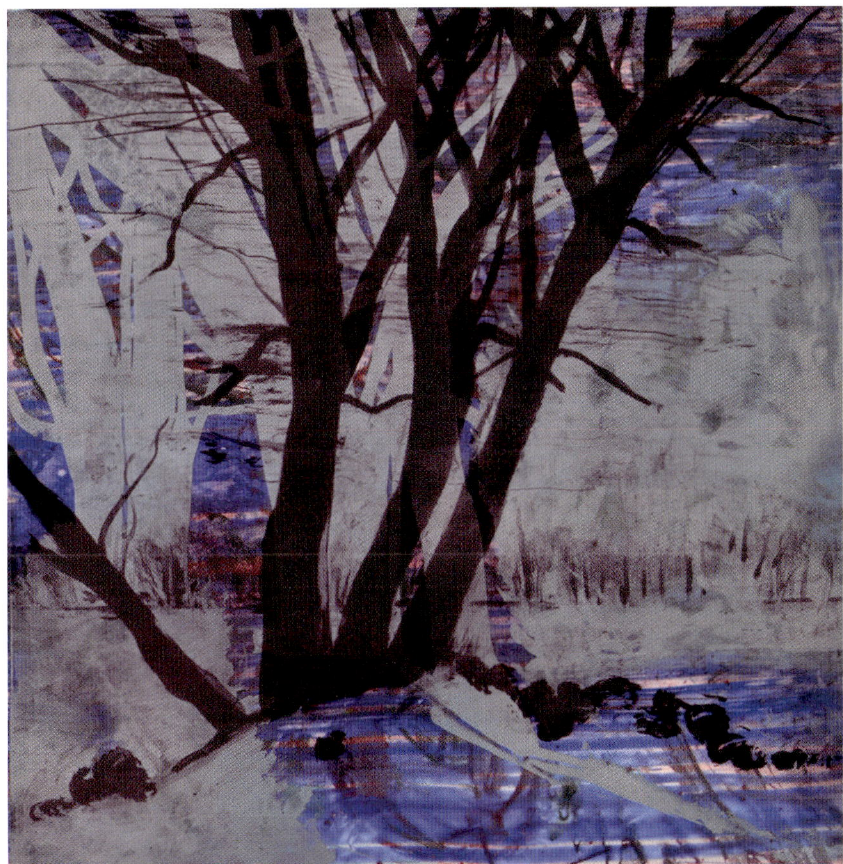

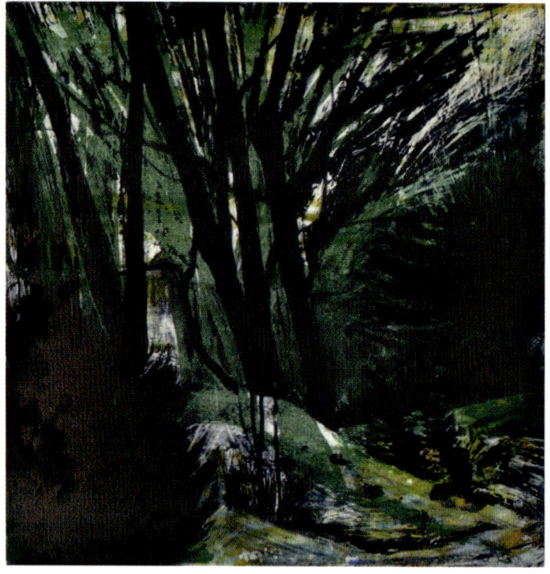

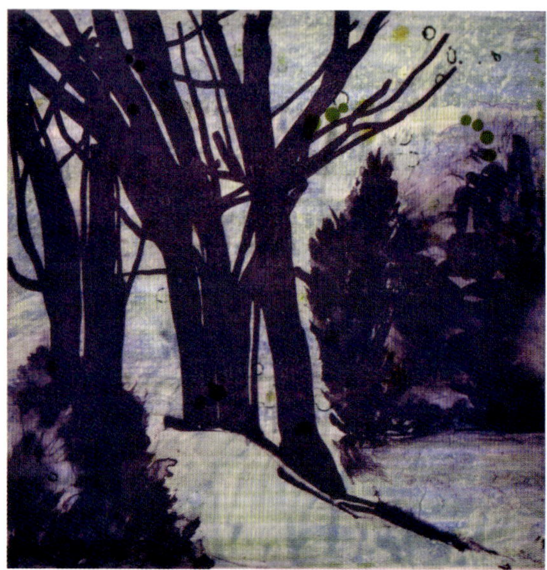

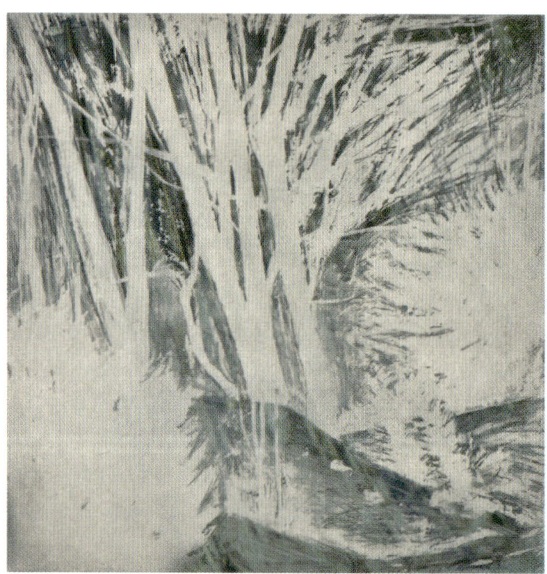

Spring Fever XV. Watercolor monotype and solar plate. 20" × 18". 2016.

Spring Fever II. Watercolor monotype and solar plate. 20" × 18". 2016.

Spring Fever III. Watercolor monotype and solar plate. 20" × 18". 2016.

DIRK HAGNER

San Juan Capistrano, California

Prints in my view are made to speak in a contemporary world; they function as something to facilitate thinking. Art goes beyond the individual expression when it connects with the human world at large, and I have chosen printmaking as the best medium to express that concept in my art. It is a natural extension to drawing. My images turn out to be multilayered, both in terms of technique and content.

I combine the rich beauty of traditional printmaking with new methods and frequently incorporate references to art and culture, and I utilize many different printmaking techniques in my work, often focusing on letterpress and relief. Even for my monoprints, I use matrices, albeit in unplanned ways.

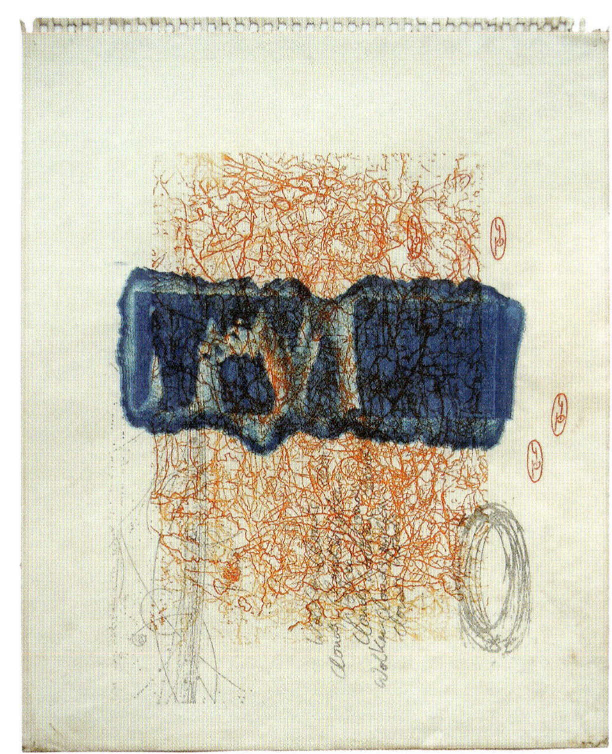

Tabulae ad Astra 4. Monoprint with oil-based ink. 16.87" × 13.87". 2015.

PUBLISHED AND PRINTED BY THE ARTIST AT INKSWINE PRESS.

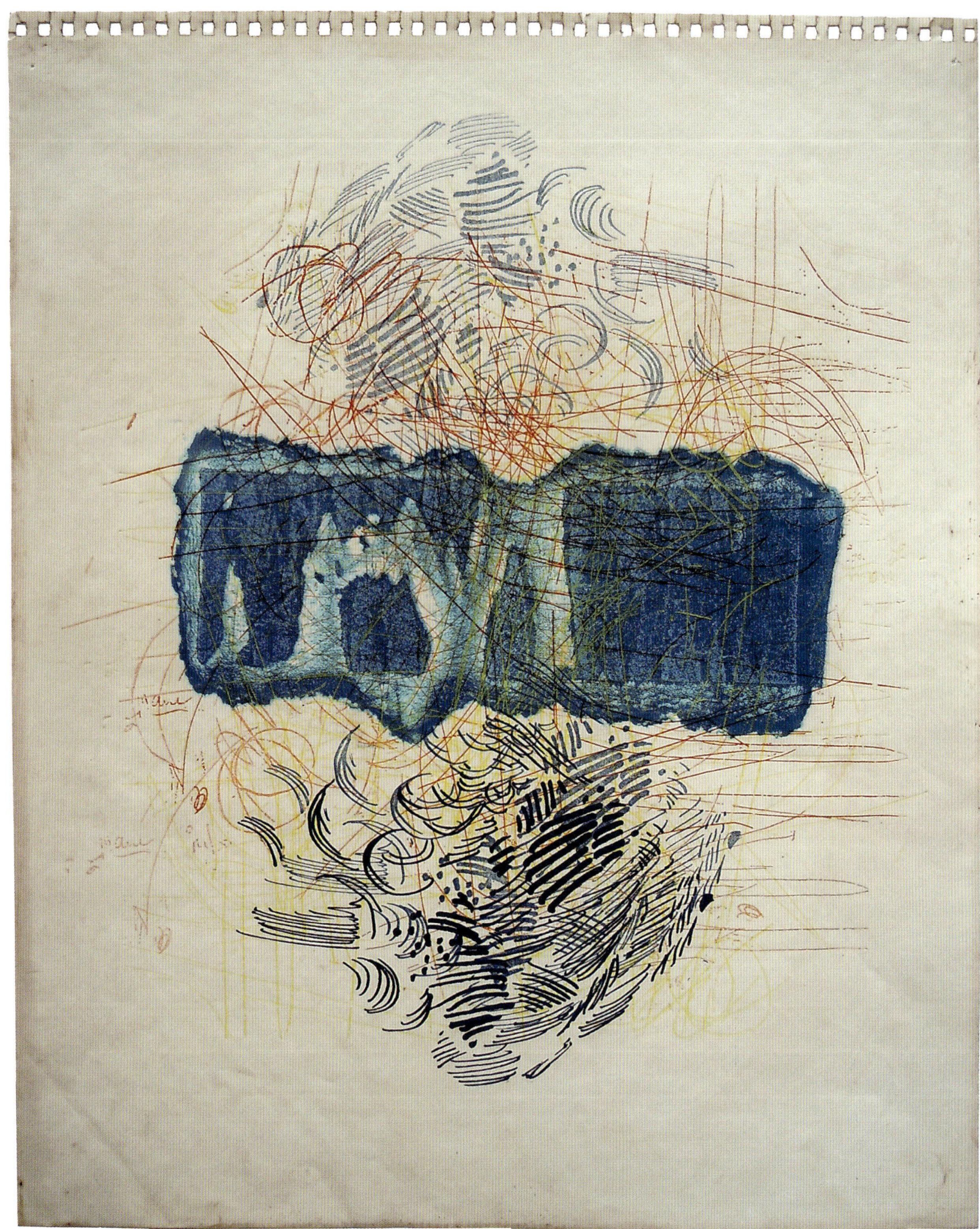

Tabulae ad Astra 2. Monoprint with oil-based inks. 16.75" × 13.87". 2015.

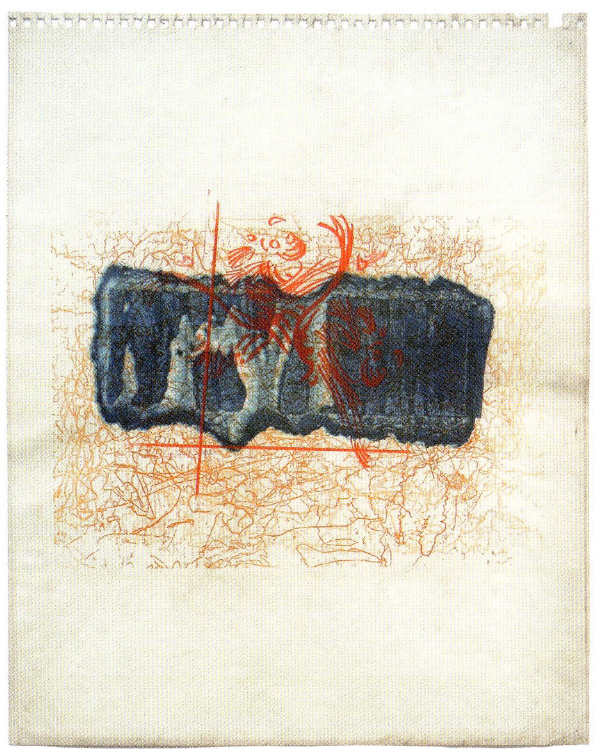

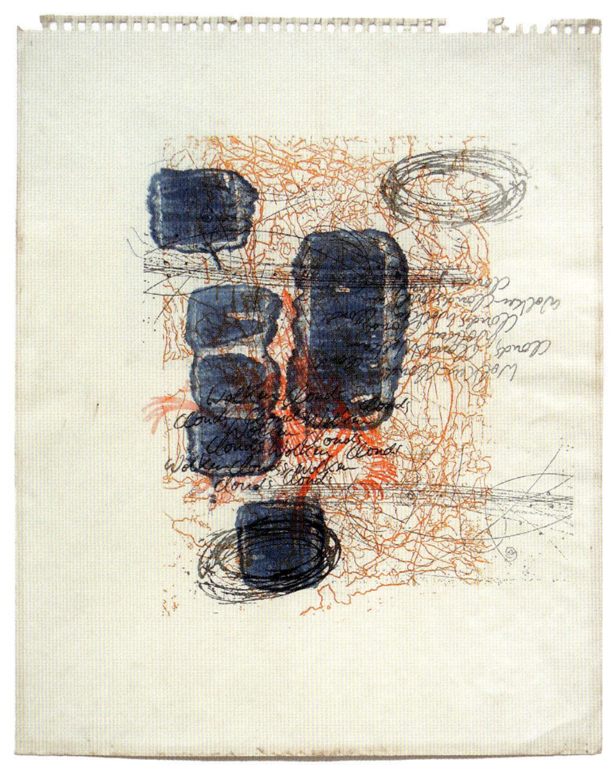

Tabulae ad Astra 5. Monoprint with oil-based inks. 16.87" × 13.87". 2015.

Tabulae ad Astra 6. Monoprint with oil-based inks. 16.87" × 13.87". 2015.

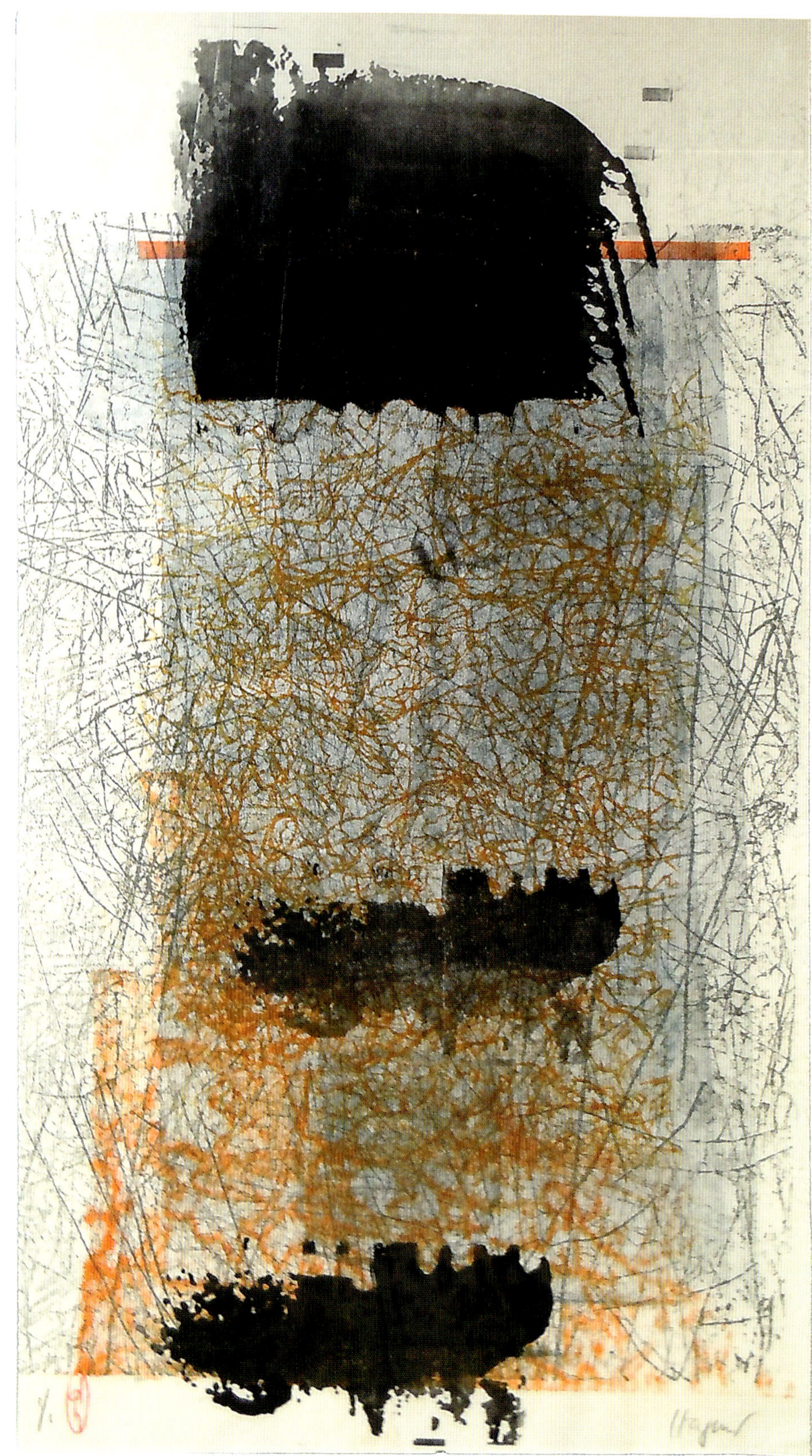

Tabulae ad Astra 3. Monoprint with oil-based inks. 14" × 8". 2015.

KEIKO HARA

Walla Walla, Washington

"Topophilia" is the given title because it conveys a sense of the place inside each human being where an exceptional inner power exists. It is our individual topophilia that connects us while at the same time cultural and political boundaries separate us. As an artist, I want to transform this topophilia into my artwork. "Verse" is another title I've given to my various explorations of stages of processing work toward "Topophilia."

Instead of an edition of identical images, I often create a series of one-of-a-kind images. Each print is a variation created by changing the registration, inking, and overlaying during the image-making process. My technique allows me to leave a clear record of my process by altering colors and their location and by making different marks and shapes for each new print. The layers of marks become fluid, resulting in a heightened potential for a new dimension of meaning. Changing light and reflection from the environment add yet another layer of printed imagery to my handprinted work.

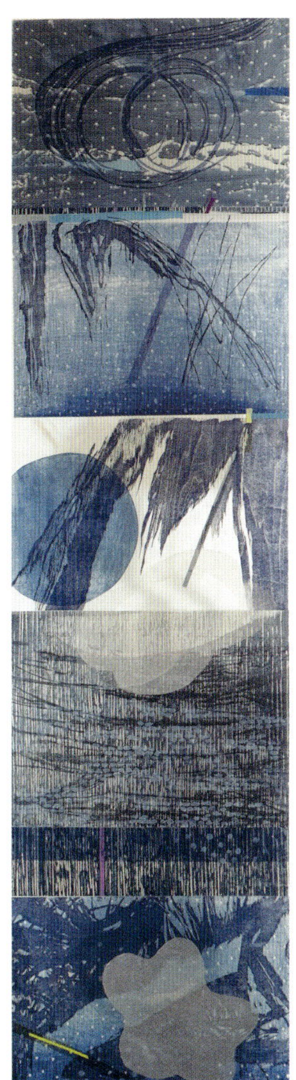

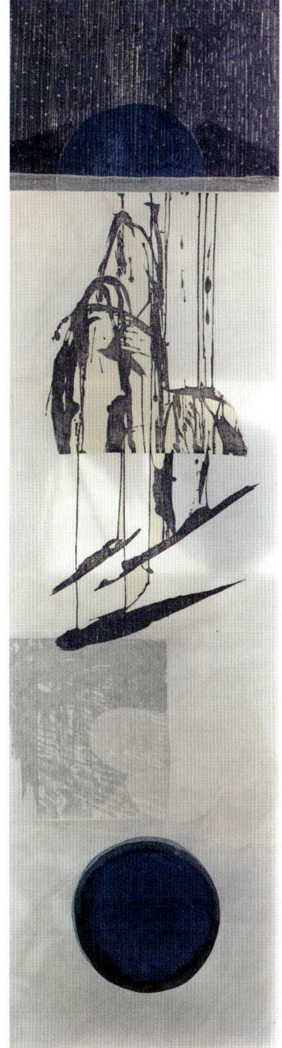

Verse Ma and Ki—Memory 7-1. Moku-hanga monoprint with collage on Washi paper. Two panels are hung back to back. 2' × 7'. 2016.

ALL PHOTOS ARE COURTESY OF COBY KUSCHALKA. PUBLISHED AND PRINTED BY THE ARTIST AT HARA STUDIO.

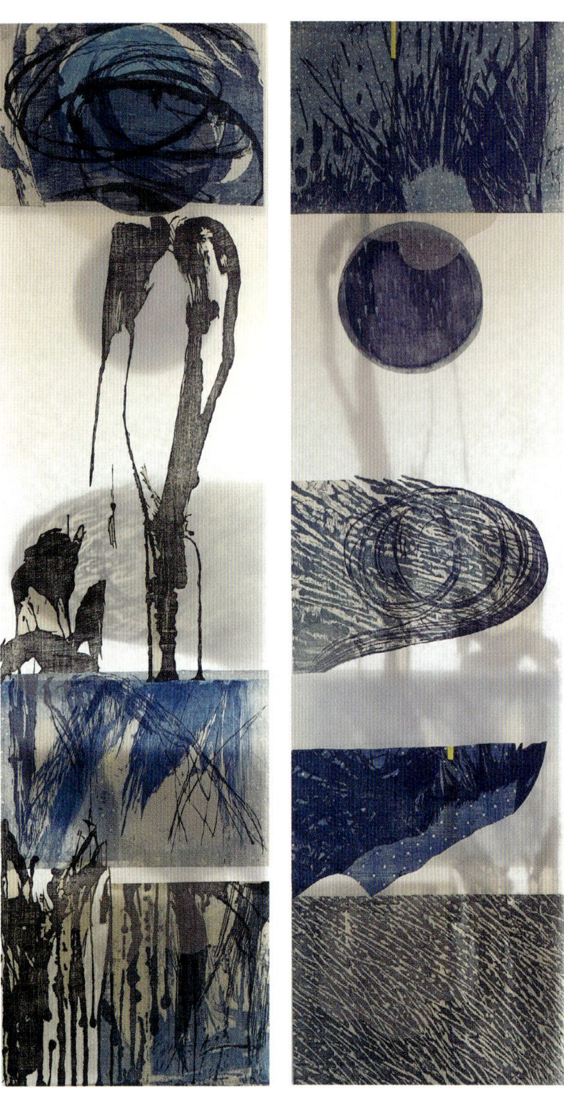

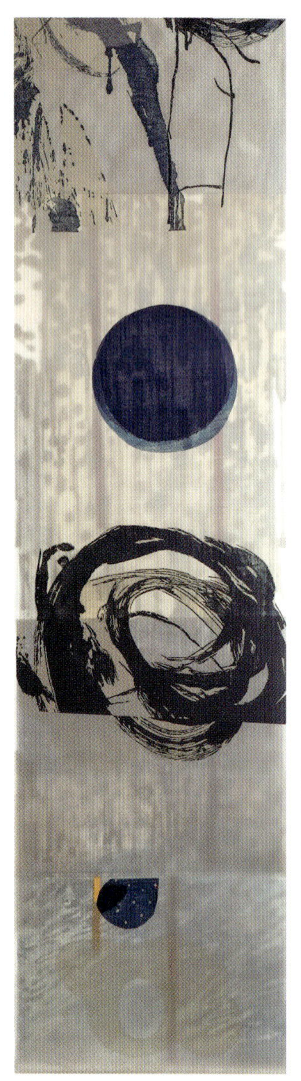

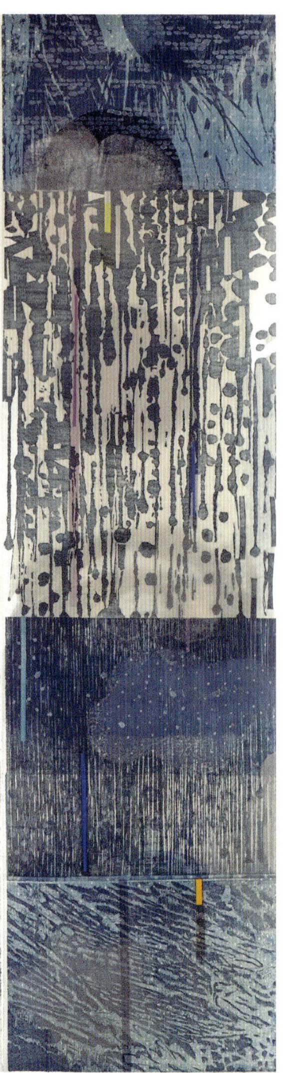

Verse Ma and Ki—Memory 7-2. *Moku-hanga* monoprint with collage on Washi paper. Two panels are hung back to back. 2' × 7'. 2016.

Verse Ma and Ki—Memory 7-4. *Moku-hanga* monoprint with collage on Washi paper. Two panels are hung back to back. 2' × 7'. 2016.

>

Verse Ma and Ki—Memory 7-3. *Moku-hanga* monoprint with collage on Washi paper. Two panels are hung back to back. 2' × 7'. 2016.

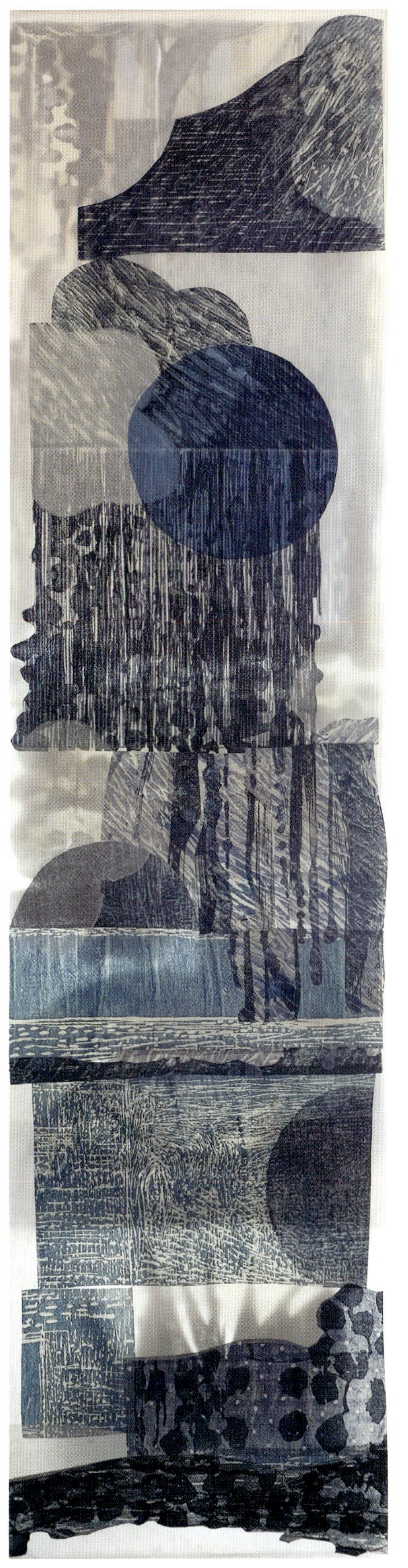

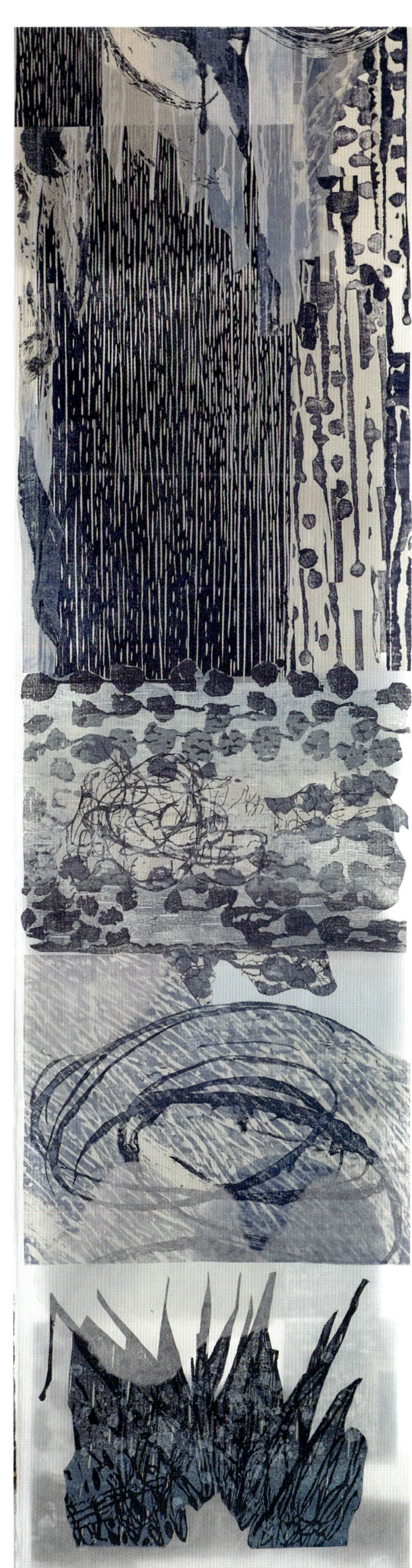

SUE HEATLEY

Richmond, Virginia

My art making is rooted in a love of the material world. The studio practice of printmaking entices my senses with the hiss of the ink as it is being rolled out, the feathery weight of paper, and the cadence of the process of layering. Carving linoleum is incredibly meditative, and the resulting image is something I simply can't achieve by any other means. The same is true of the surface where pigment melds into paper in a monotype. There's that elusive mark and subtlety that comes only through printing.

Monoprinting is especially freeing as it allows me to step away from the notion of producing an edition of prints, something I've never found particularly rewarding artistically. The combination of one-off linoleum printing with the fluid, painterly quality of monotypes provides an exciting jumping-off point for direct painting, drawing, and collage. Are the resulting artworks still categorized as prints? That is for the art historians to decide. All I know is that printmaking is the vital core of my studio practice, which I happily envision spending the rest of my life exploring.

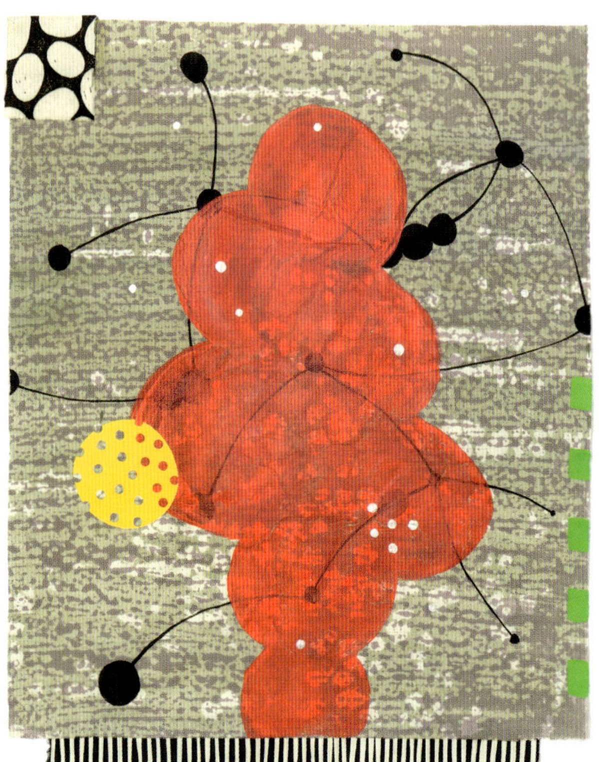

Ruby Jangle. Monoprint with water-miscible oil-based inks and water-based pigments, gouache, and collage on Kitakata paper.14" × 11.5". 2017.

PUBLISHED AND PRINTED BY THE ARTIST.

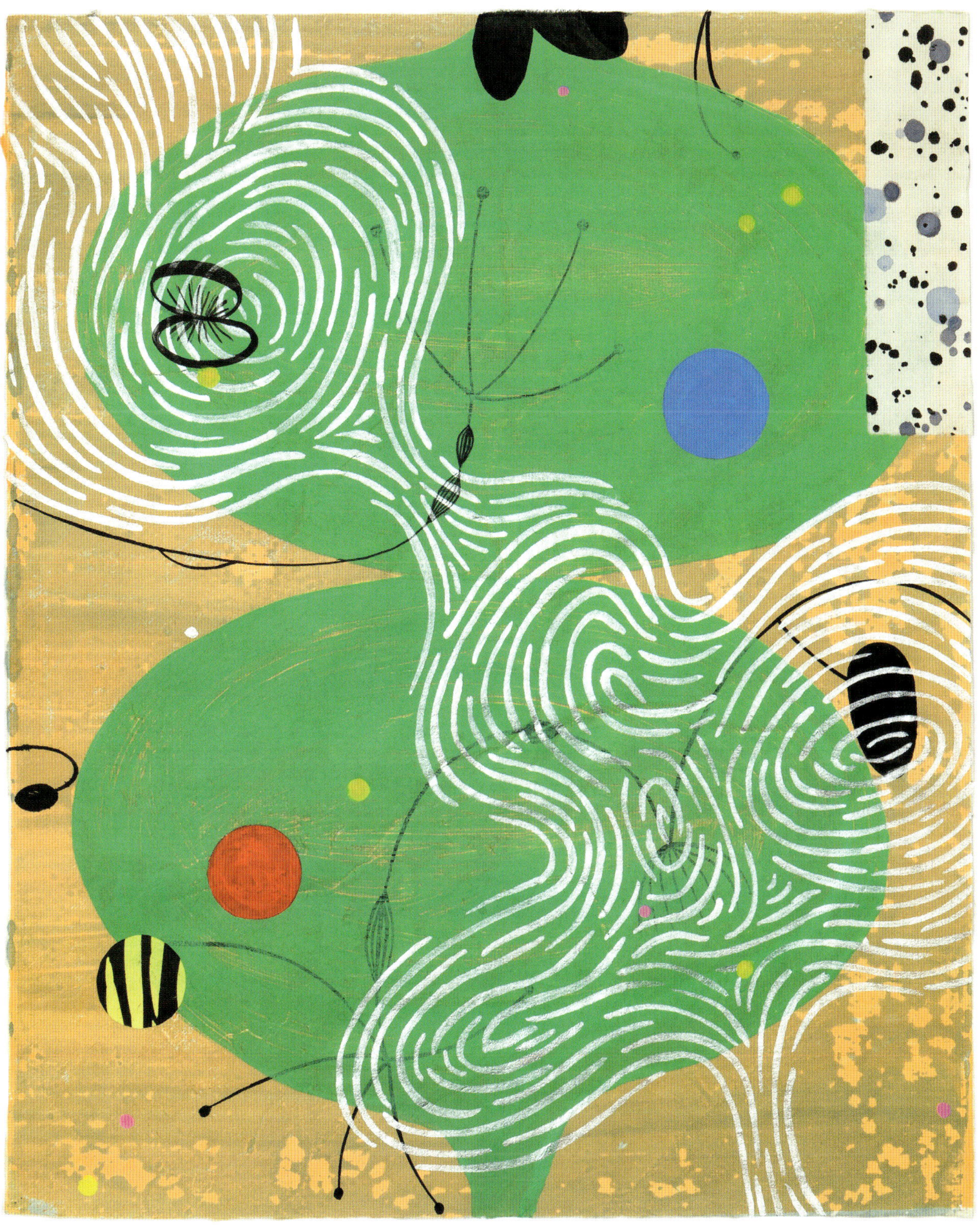

Limerick Pool. Monoprint with Charbonnel Aqua Wash water-soluble oil-based inks and water-based pigments, gouache, drawing ink, and collage on Kitakata paper. 14" × 11.5". 2017.

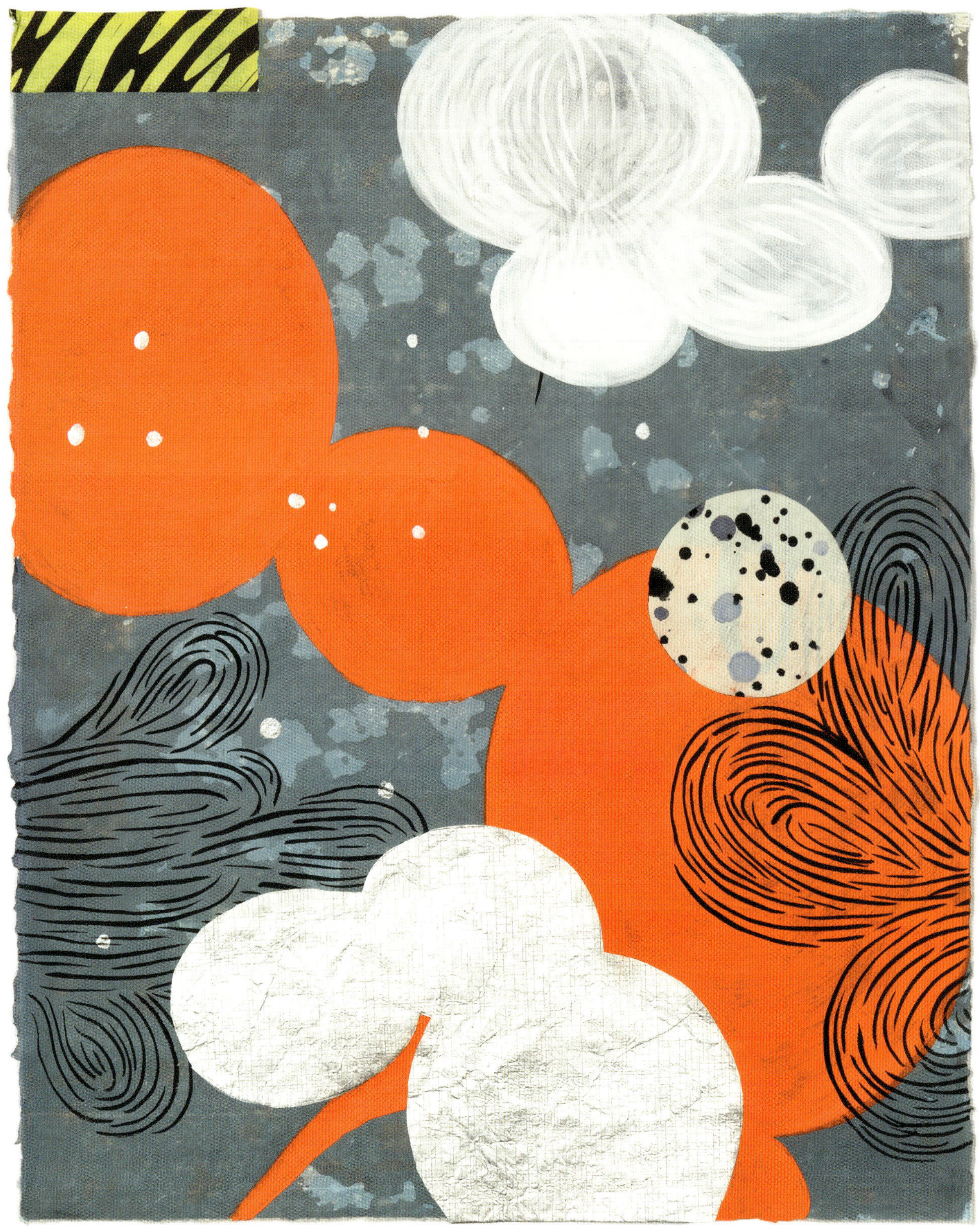

Milky Lava Moon. Monoprint with water-miscible oil-based inks and water-based pigments, gouache, Tyvek, and collage on Kitakata paper. 14" × 11.5". 2017.

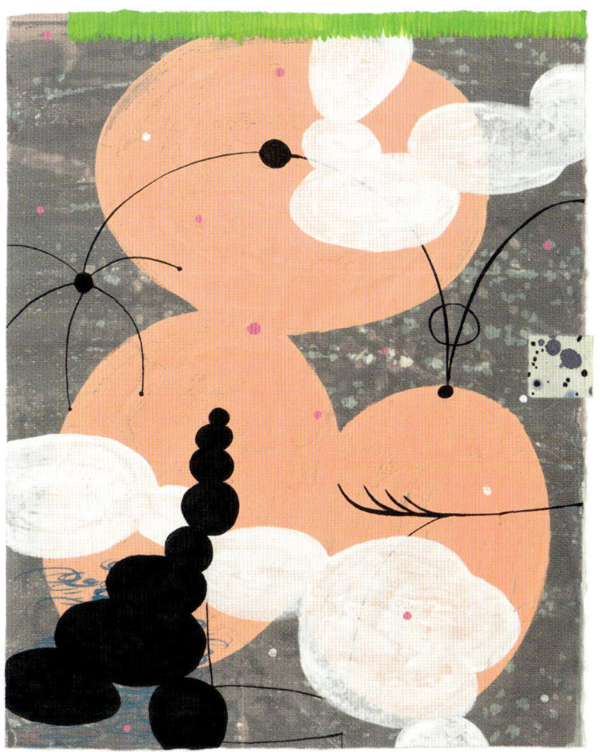

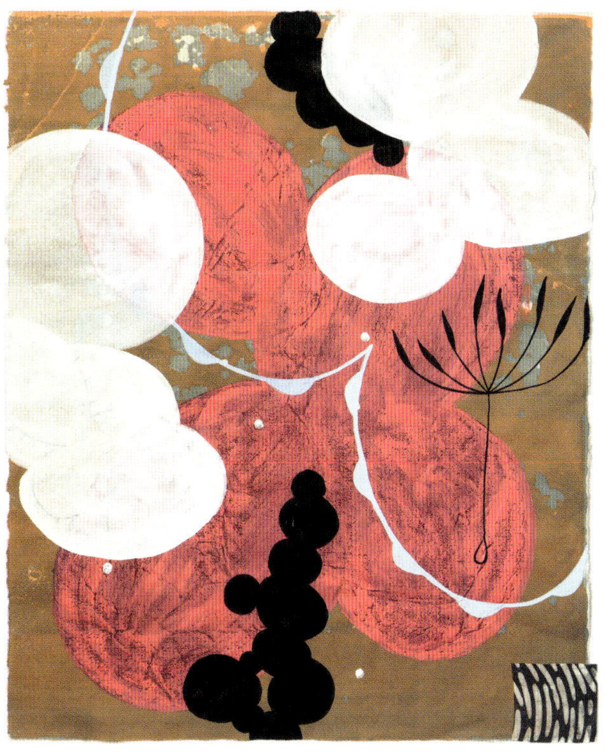

Reaching Peachy. Monoprint with water-miscible oil-based inks and water-based pigments, gouache, ink, and collage on Kitakata paper.14" × 11.5". 2017.

Sugar Jumble. Monoprint with water-miscible oil-based inks and water-based pigments, gouache, ink, and collage on Kitakata paper.14" × 11.5". 2017.

CONSTANCE JACOBSON

Boston, Massachusetts

These prints, with simple architectural elements, reference the change in my physical environment as intense urban gentrification encircles my living space, creating an uncomfortable sense of enclosure and density. The singular, house/figure structure is the vehicle, a tightly gridded, impenetrable structure that acts like a blockade. For the most part, very little light emerges from the white of the page, because of the heavy layers of alternating dark and white ink. This creates an opacity that is usually avoided in printmaking, but combined with the grid, it feels like the correct approach to convey the emotional impact of my neighborhood's conversion, as well as that of the larger, current social and political environment of unease.

I used monotype rolls, woodcut with stencils, and lithography (polyester plates) in various combinations to create this body of work.

Silence and Stealth. Monoprint with oil-based inks, woodcut, stencil, and polyester plate. 28.5" × 19.5". 2017.

Fogging. Monoprint with oil-based inks, woodcut, stencil, and polyester plate. 30.5" × 22.5". 2017.

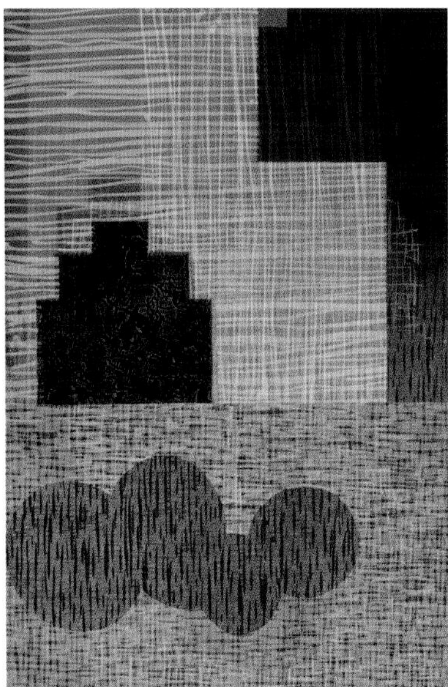

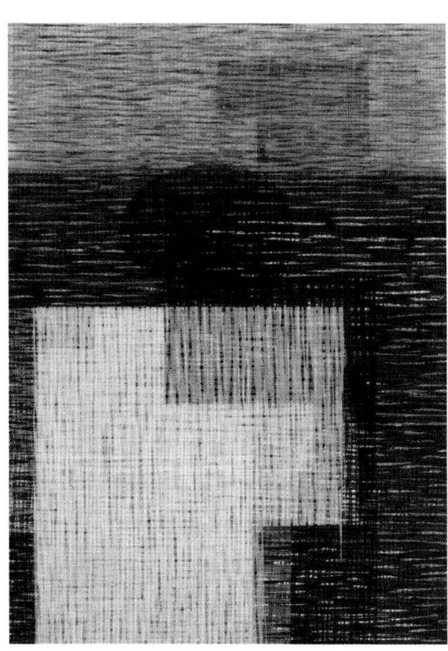

ALL IMAGES ARE COURTESY OF STEWART CLEMENTS, BOSTON. PUBLISHED AND PRINTED BY THE ARTIST AT FULL TILT STUDIO.

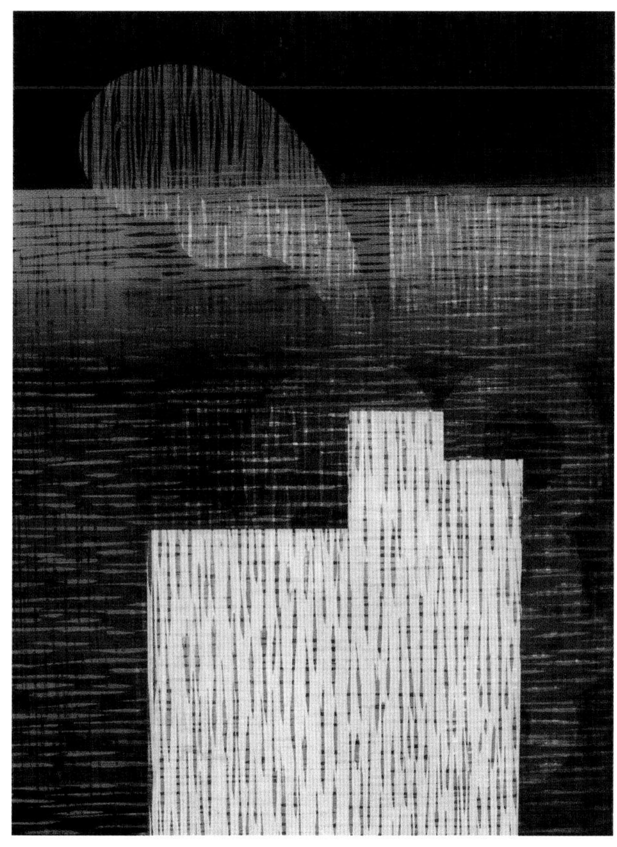

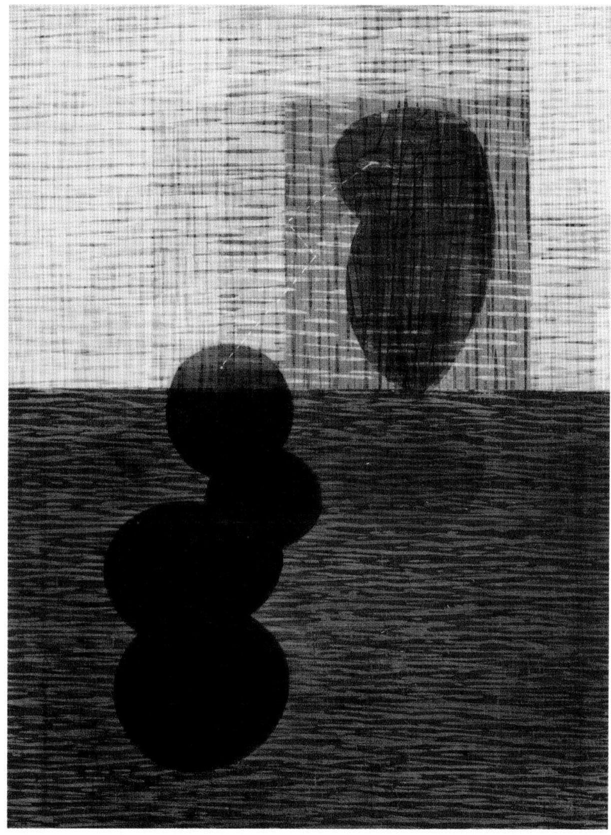

Nocturne 2. Monoprint with oil-based inks, woodcut, stencil, and polyester plate. 30.5" × 22.5". 2017.

I See You. Monoprint with oil-based inks, woodcut, and stencil. 30.5" × 22.5". 2017.

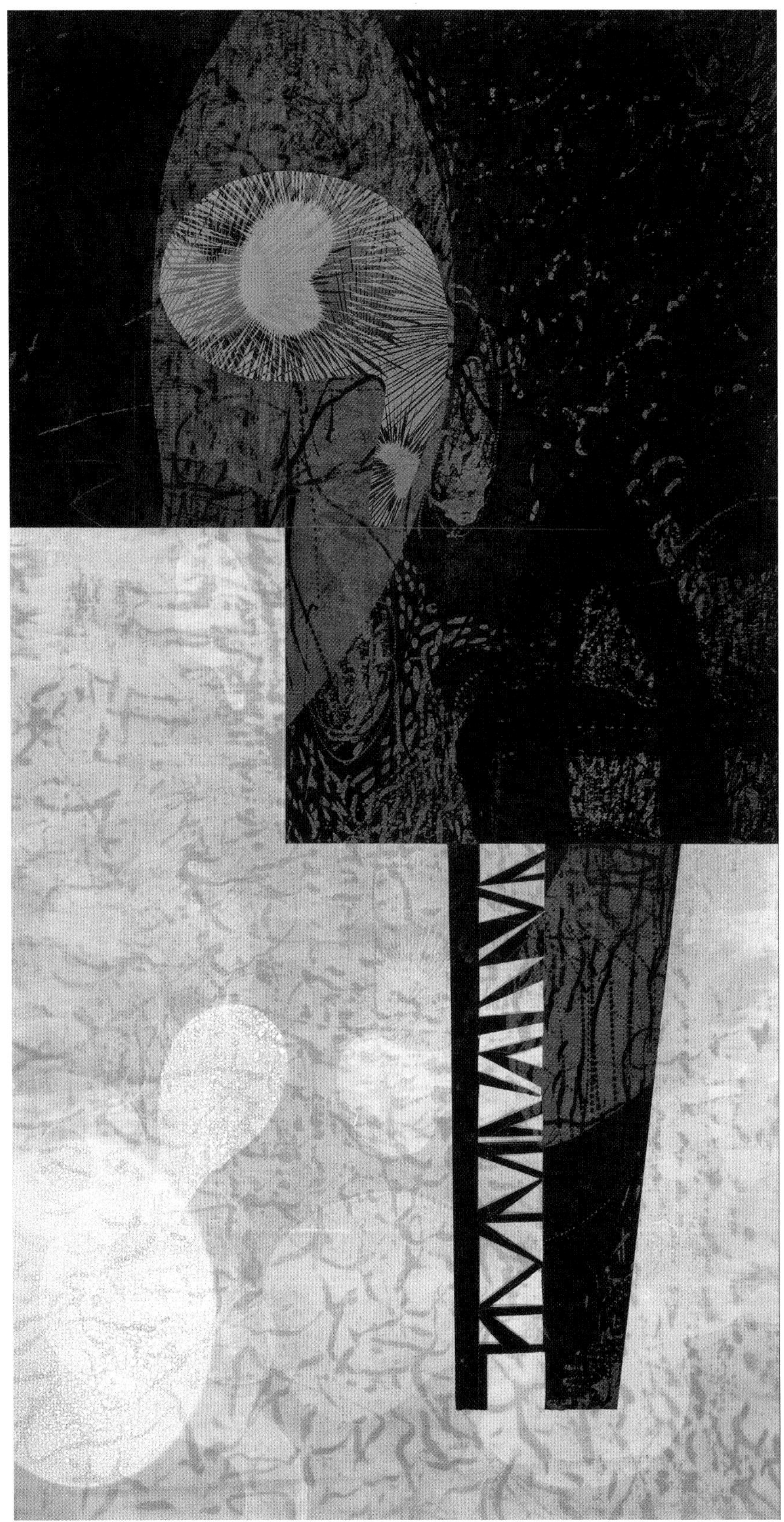

Top Bottom. Monoprint with oil-based inks, woodcut, stencil, and collage. 42" × 22". 2016.

ROBERTO JUAREZ

New York, New York

Using sacred geometric structures (*vesica piscis*—intersecting circles of equal size), I build grids that crisscross one another and combine to achieve new forms. Abutting and entangling this geometry and creating a juxtaposition of flat and deep space and figure/ground are loosely painted brush marks and washes of color. Back and forth, reverse and inverse, I create visual systems of contrasting parts.

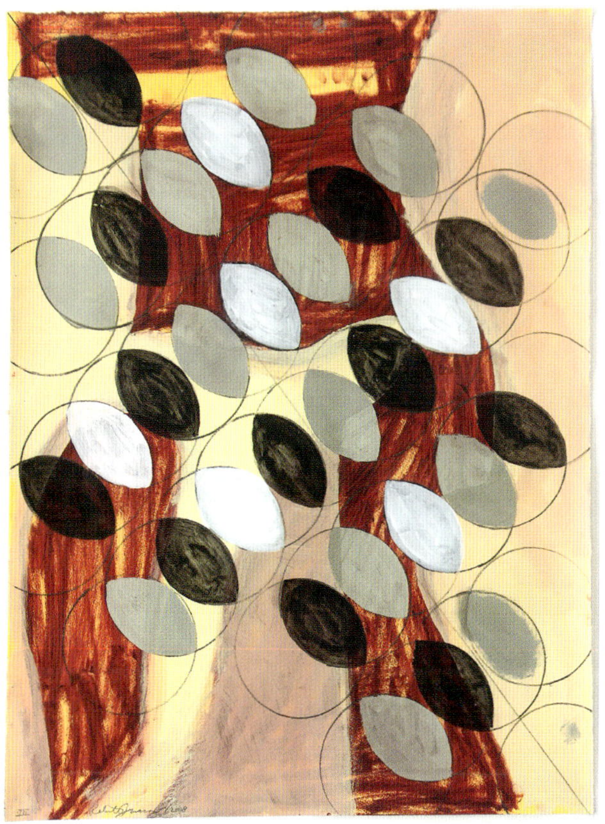

Italian VP VII. Monoprint with oil-based inks and hand coloring. 32" × 24". 2008.

ALL PHOTOS ARE COURTESY OF BUD SHARK. PUBLISHED AND PRINTED AT SHARK'S INK BY BUD SHARK.

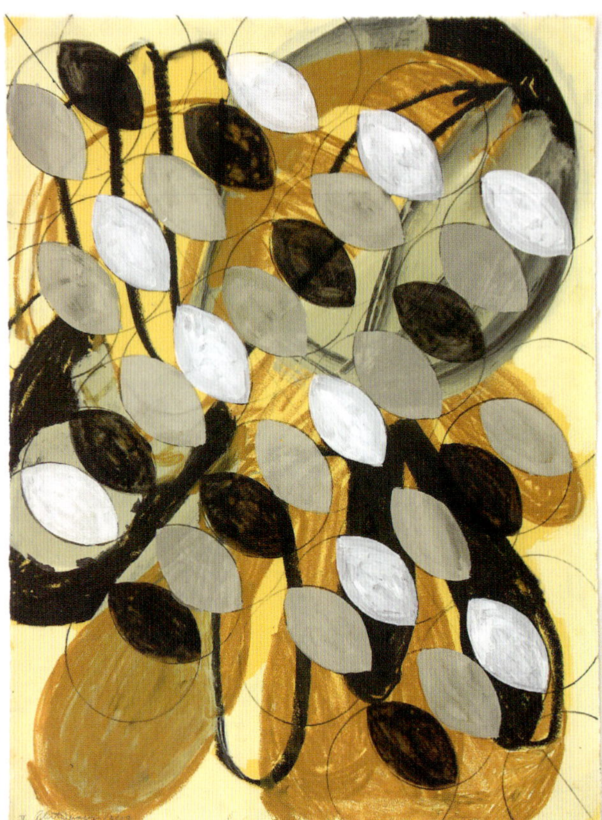

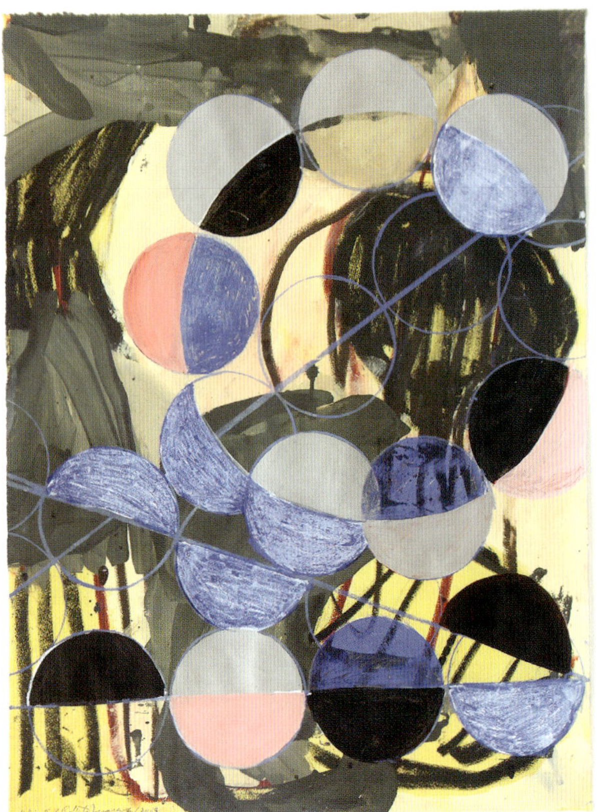

Italian VP VI. Monoprint with oil-based inks and hand coloring. 32" × 24". 2008.

Helio II. Monoprint with oil-based inks and hand coloring. 32" × 24". 2008.

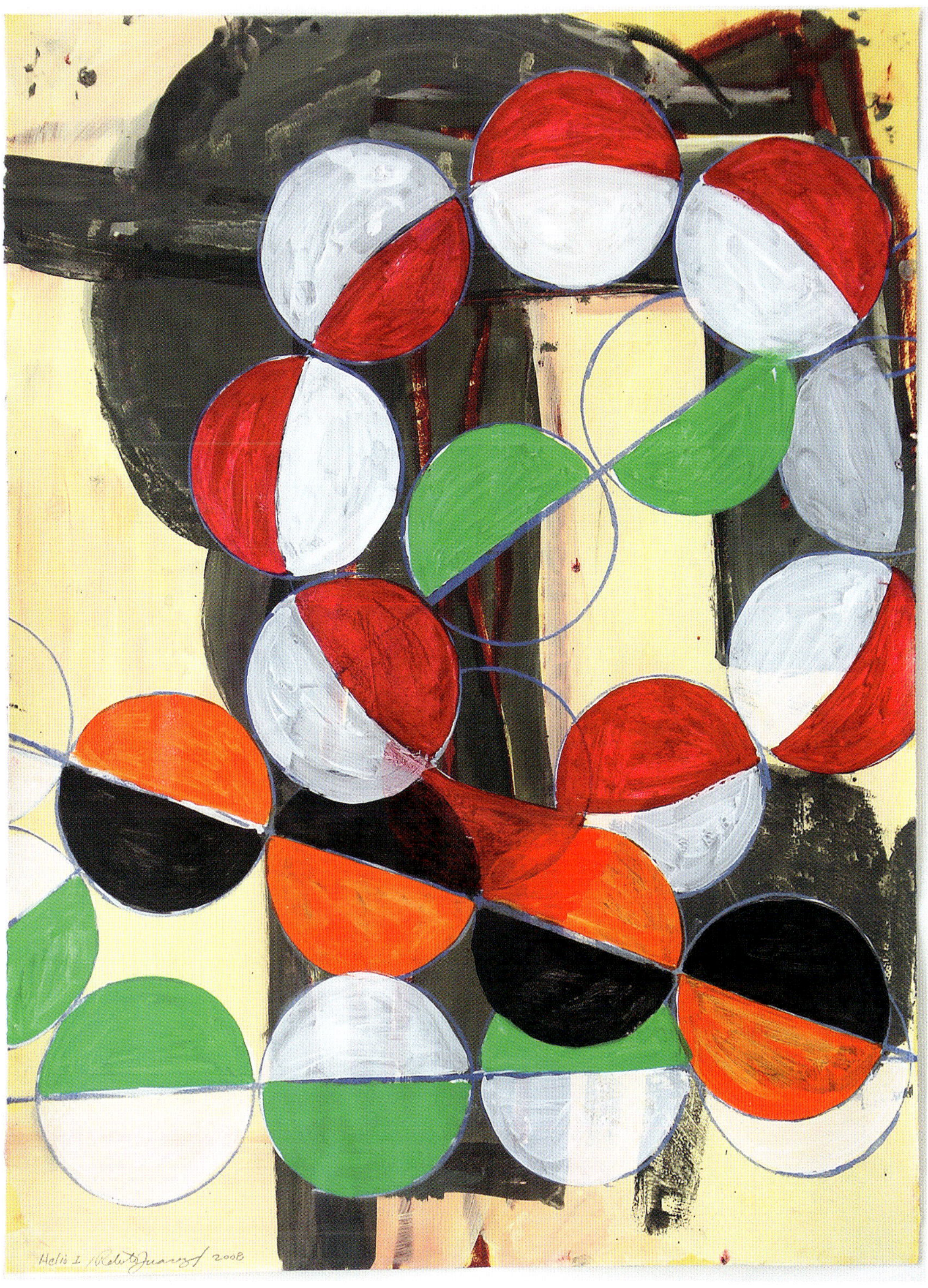

Helio I. Monoprint with oil-based inks and hand coloring. 32" × 24". 2008.

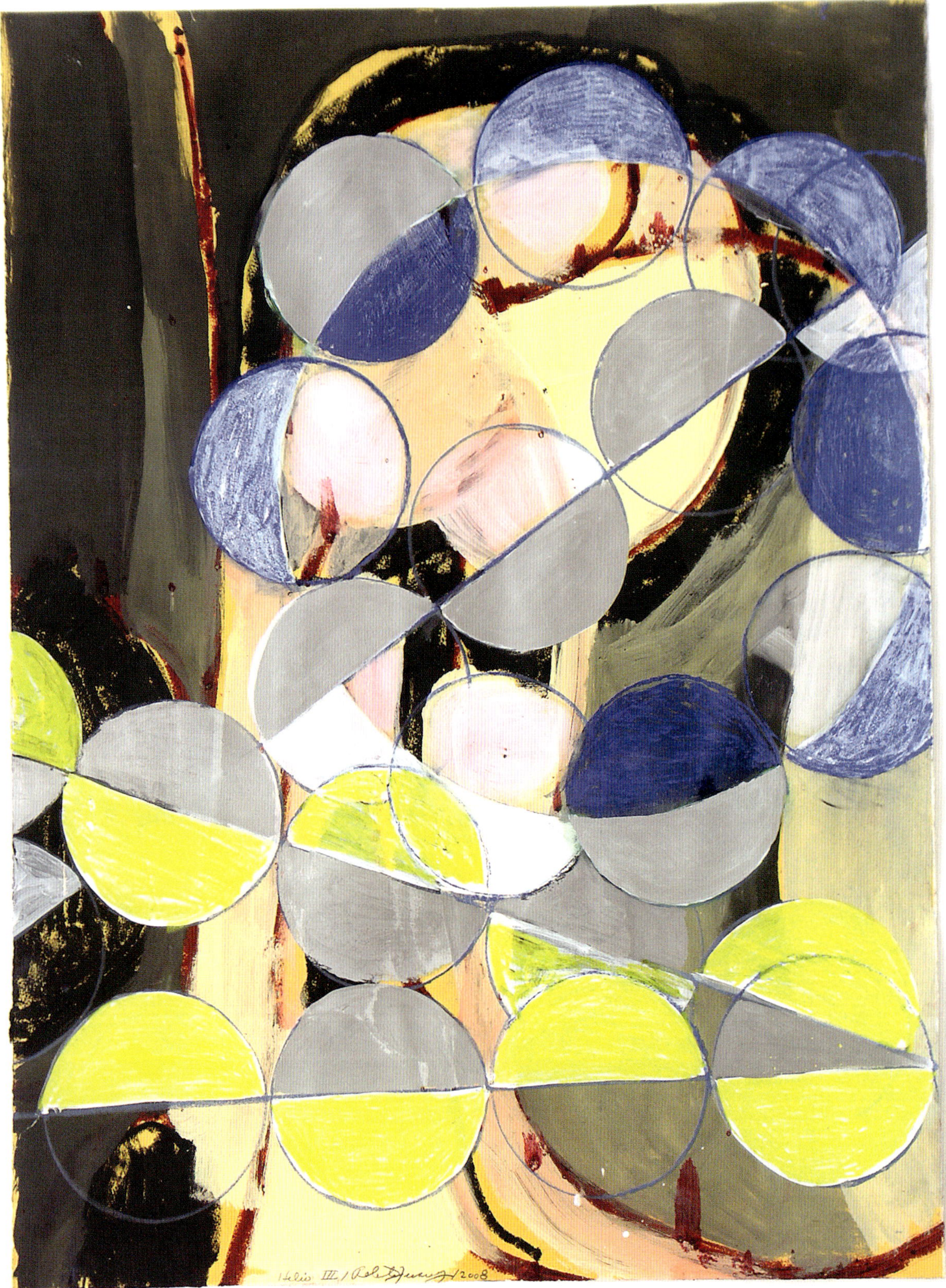

Helio III. Monoprint with oil-based inks and hand coloring. 32" × 24". 2008.

JANE KENT

New York, New York

I have been making unique prints as an essential part of my work for decades. I use ad hoc methods of producing single prints as the way to develop ideas for all aspects of my work: drawing, prints, painting, and artist's book. I combine stencils, templates, gouache on mezzotint grounds, and any other direct method I can dream up of arriving at an image that is "printed" but not a multiple. When making monoprints, I consider this flexible way of working as an essential first step to making the prints unique.

These monoprints were made using cut stencils. I printed layer over layer as a way of generating images otherwise unforeseen. I started working with thirty sheets of paper over a period of four weeks. I built them as if in an assembly line: adding, covering up, and constructing each image with shapes over shapes until I arrived at new surfaces, new images, and a new world.

Bottom Top. Monoprint with oil-based inks and stencils. 24" × 18". 2012.

ALL PHOTOS ARE COURTESY OF JEFFREY STURGES. PUBLISHED AND PRINTED BY THE ARTIST AT MCDOWELL COLONY.

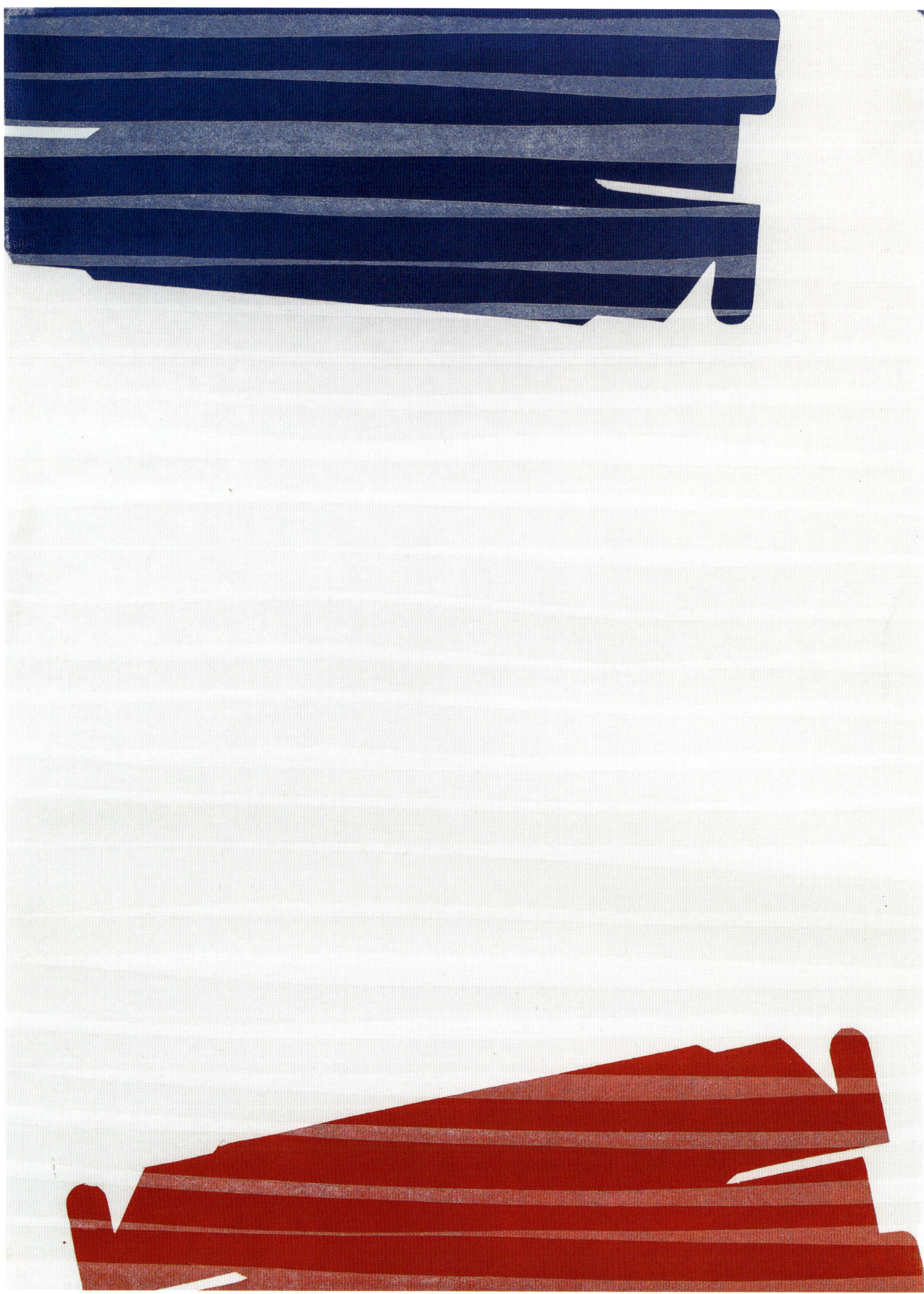

Avenue Blue and Red. Monoprint with oil-based inks and stencils. 24" × 8". 2012.

FLAG. Monoprint with oil-based inks and stencils. 24" × 18". 2012.

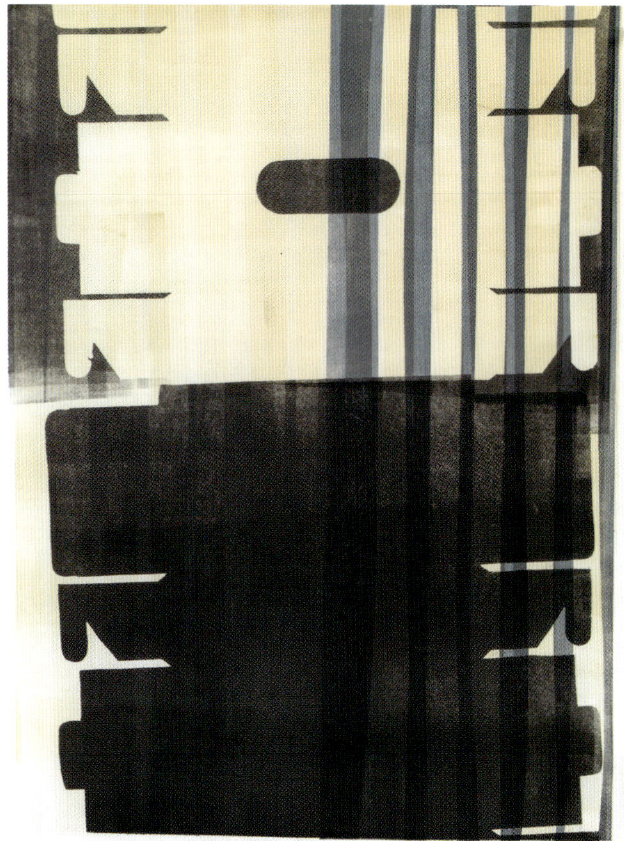

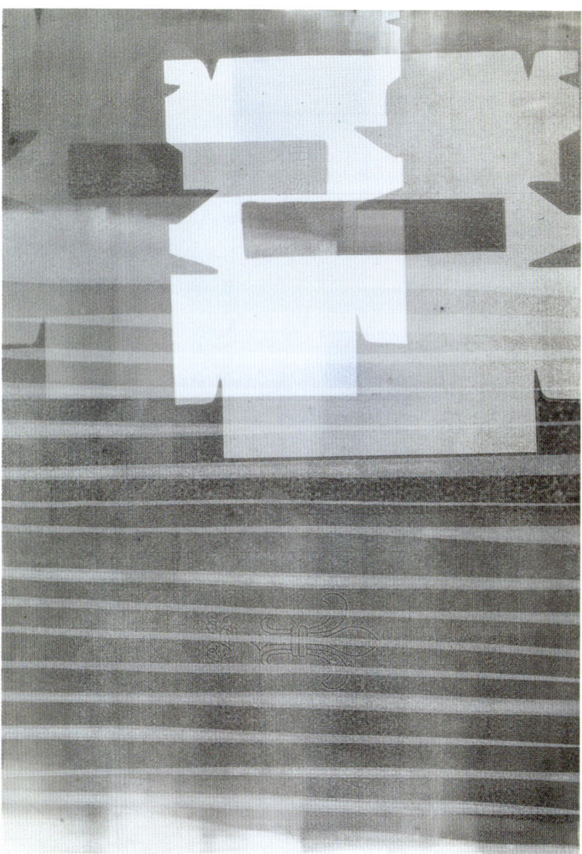

Half Fast. Monoprint with oil-based inks and stencils. 24" × 18". 2012.

Inside the Upside Down. Monoprint with oil-based inks and stencils. 24" × 18". 2012.

CATHERINE KERNAN

Somerville, Massachusetts

The premise that human memory and the experience of spaces are dynamic, mutable, and interactive and recur in ever-evolving cycles of repetition and variation underlies most of my work. Oppositional scales of control and serendipity, order and chaos, perception and obstruction, and description and suggestion guide my choices.

I have abandoned the depiction of a particular place on the earth, preferring to work in an abstract, improvisatory way, drawing on internalized experiences in a process of experimentation and controlled accident. Working at the interface between printmaking and painting, using large-scale woodblocks in unorthodox ways as a transfer tool, I build images layer by layer both by offsetting and removing ink on plastic plates. Once offset, the options for viscosity rolls, wiping ink away, and additive painting are multiplied. I deliberately avoid predicting the outcome but always stay keenly in tune with the medium. I am no longer a purist; interruption and interference with the "perfect transfer" are integral to my process.

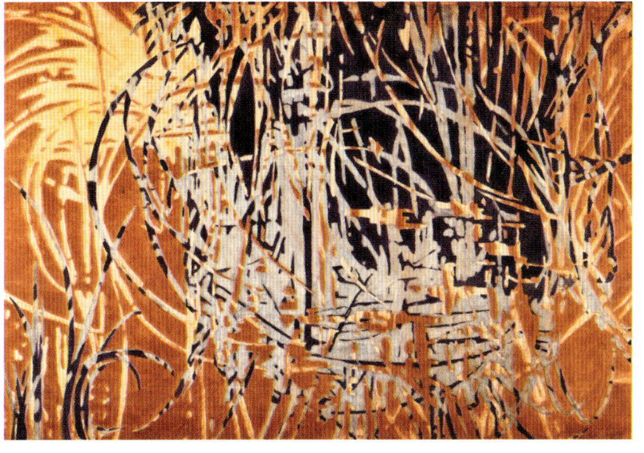

Circling the Center #7. Woodcut monoprint with Akua soy-based inks. 30" × 44". 2016.

ALL PHOTOS ARE COURTESY OF SUSAN BYRNE. PUBLISHED AND PRINTED BY THE ARTIST AT MIXIT PRINT STUDIO.

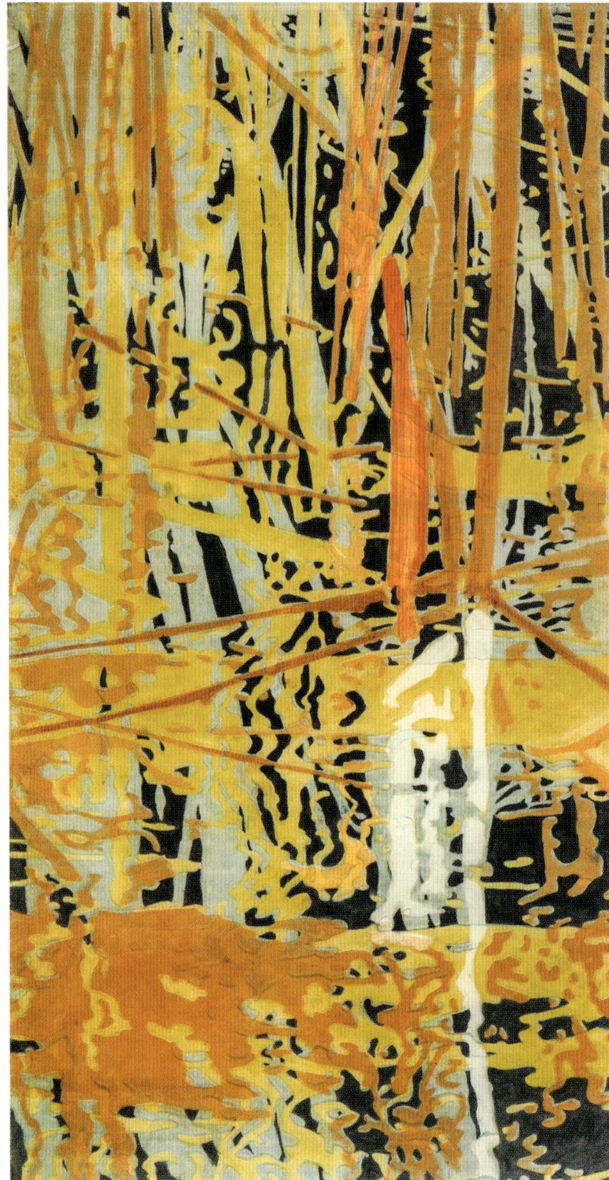

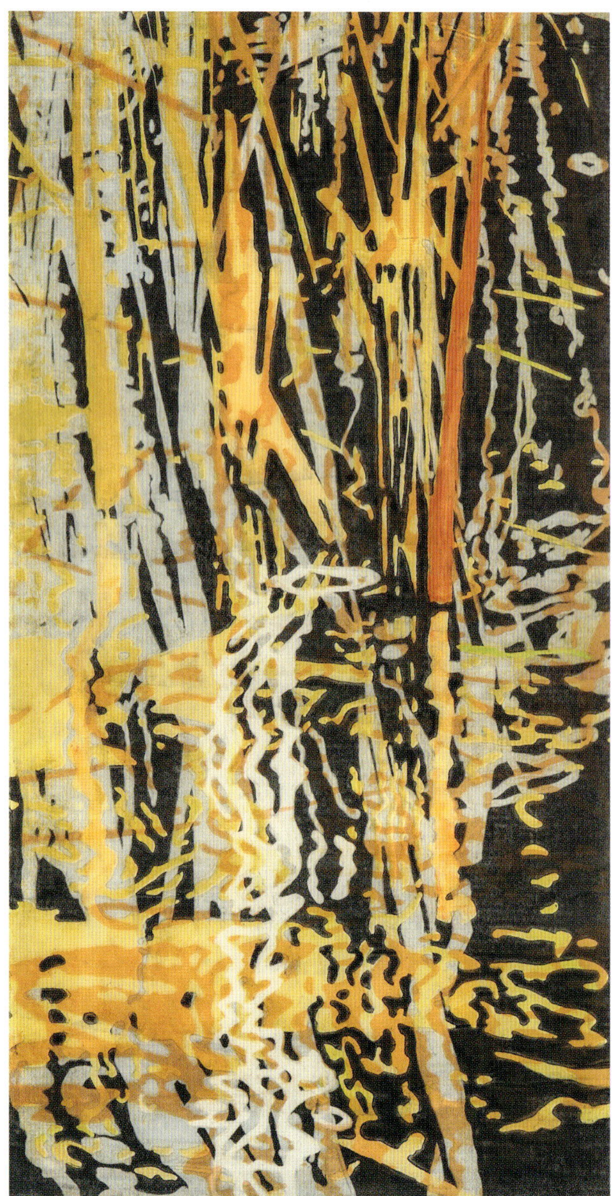

Tracking #6. Offset woodcut monoprint with Akua soy-based inks. 55.5" × 29.5". 2017.

Tracking #7. Offset woodcut monoprint with Akua soy-based inks. 55.5" × 29.5". 2017.

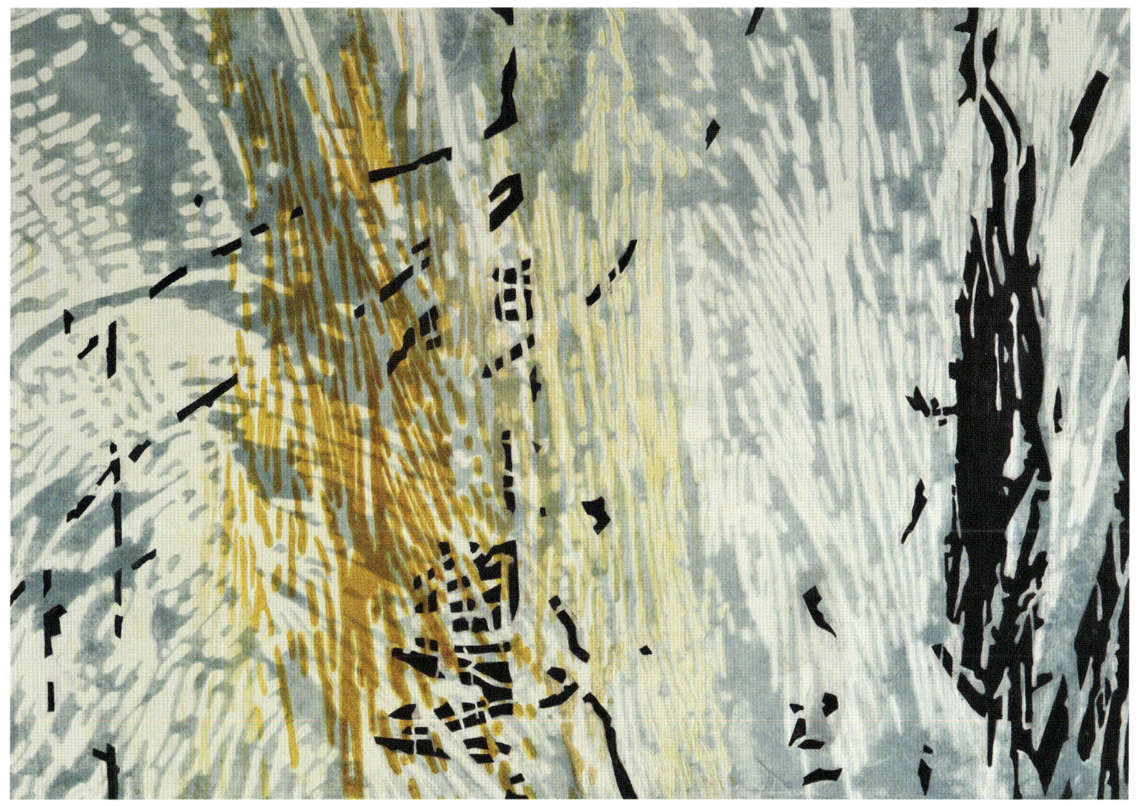

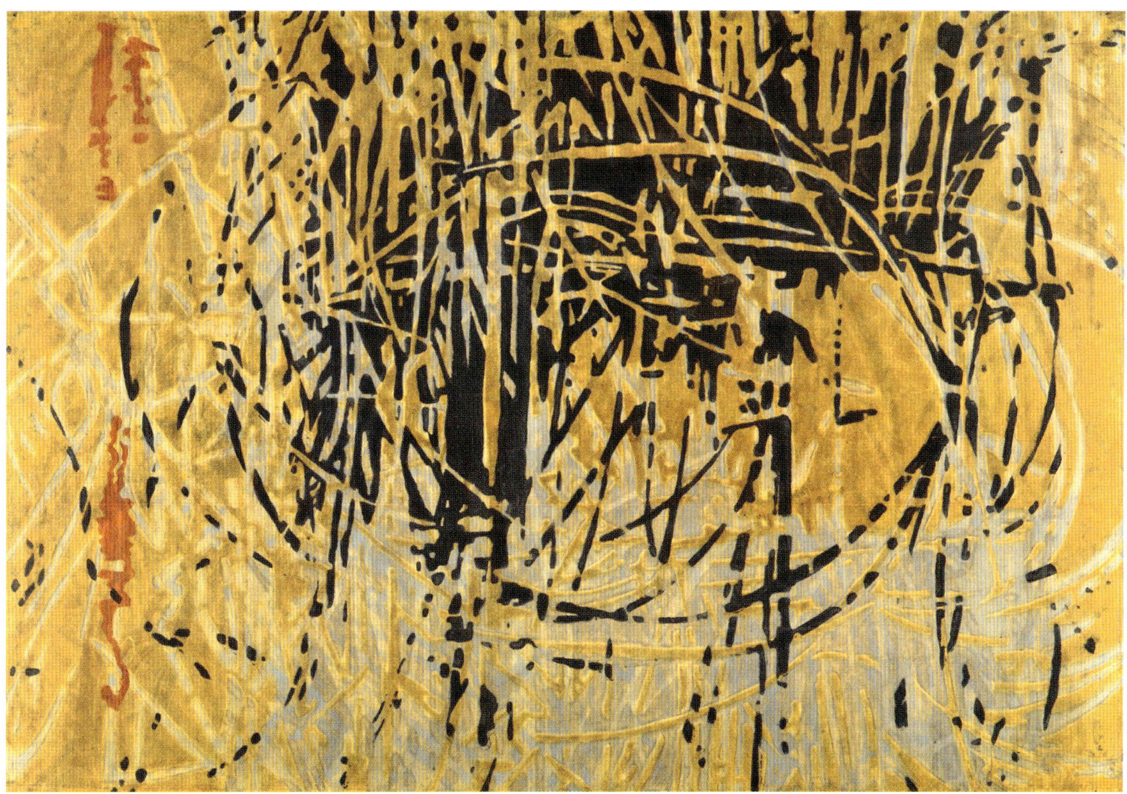

^
Circling the Center #9. Woodcut monoprint with Akua soy-based inks. 30" × 44". 2016.

v
Breathing Space #10. Woodcut monoprint with Akua soy-based inks. 30" × 44". 2015.

KAREN KUNC

Lincoln, Nebraska

My mixed-media monoprints offer visions of other worlds and vulnerable environments, suggesting edgy natural order and beautiful disasters. The richly layered information in each work evolves from unique printings from woodblocks, silkscreens, etchings, mezzotints, photopolymer relief plates, and stencils, along with various applications of shellac, acrylics, gouache, and sumi ink, on Japanese papers. There is a material richness and contrast between printed effects and painterly directness. Such effects exhibit a Printed-ness, my coined term, which is the need for and recognition of how printing happens and seeing that a mark has been transformed by printing and transferal means; there is a physicality to the ink and surface qualities.

I often begin with transparent impressions from my woodblocks, playfully layered in colors and patterns, using "ghost" residues or pressure printing with stencils to launch something onto paper for further response. I search in my source library of used blocks, stencils, and plates for the right response and allow the work to evolve with fluid hand touches that echo the eye movements through printed layers.

In this way, my approach to making monoprints mirrors the content of evolutionary forces that recognizes human and natural destruction and benevolence, especially in our time of climate change with unknown consequences. There is a poignancy to these newly vulnerable, or toxic, evolving worlds of microbes, seedlings, corals, gaseous pools, and distended flora—the sweep of such imaginary places—that are discovered in my studio investigations.

Smog Rain. Monoprint with oil-based ink from woodcut and polymer relief plates, screen print with oil base ink, with graphite and shellac, gouache, and watercolor hand coloring on Japanese paper. 17" × 56". 2010. *Photo courtesy of John Nollendorfs*

Fermentation. Monoprint with oil-based ink from woodcut and polymer relief plates, monoprint from stencils and Plexiglas plate, with gouache and watercolor hand coloring on Japanese paper. 17" × 56". 2010. *Photo courtesy of John Nollendorfs*

Aqua Regia. Monoprint with oil-based ink from woodcut, mezzotint, and polymer relief plates; monoprint from stencils and Plexiglas plate; with graphite and shellac, gouache, and watercolor hand coloring on Japanese paper. 17" × 56". 2010. *Photo courtesy of Larry Gawel*

Red Tide. Monoprint with oil-based ink from woodcut and polymer relief plates, monoprint from stencils and Plexiglas plate, with gouache and watercolor hand coloring on Japanese paper. 17" × 56". 2010. *Photo courtesy of Larry Gawel*

PUBLISHED AND PRINTED BY THE ARTIST AT CONSTELLATION STUDIOS.

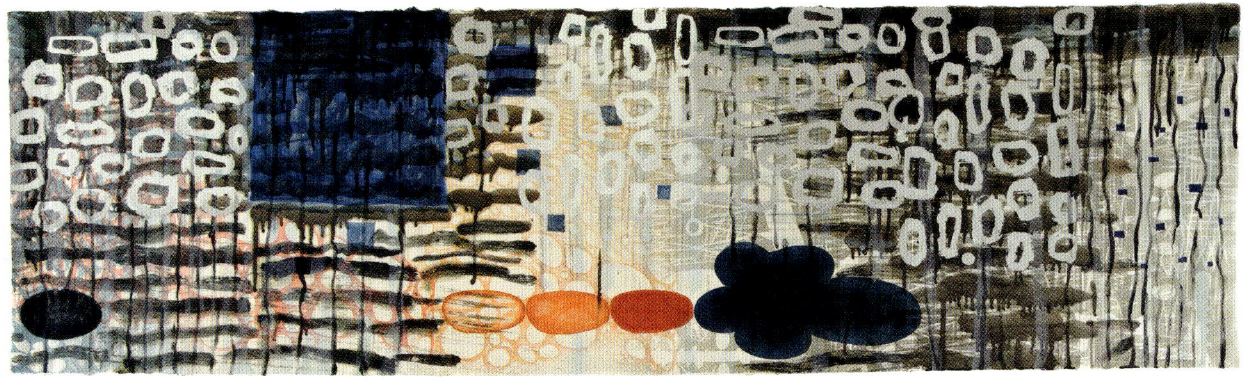

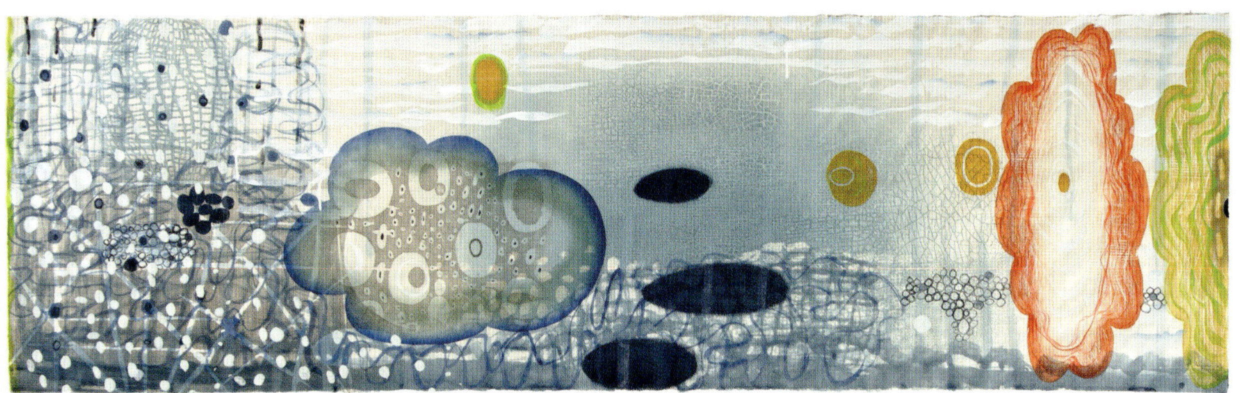

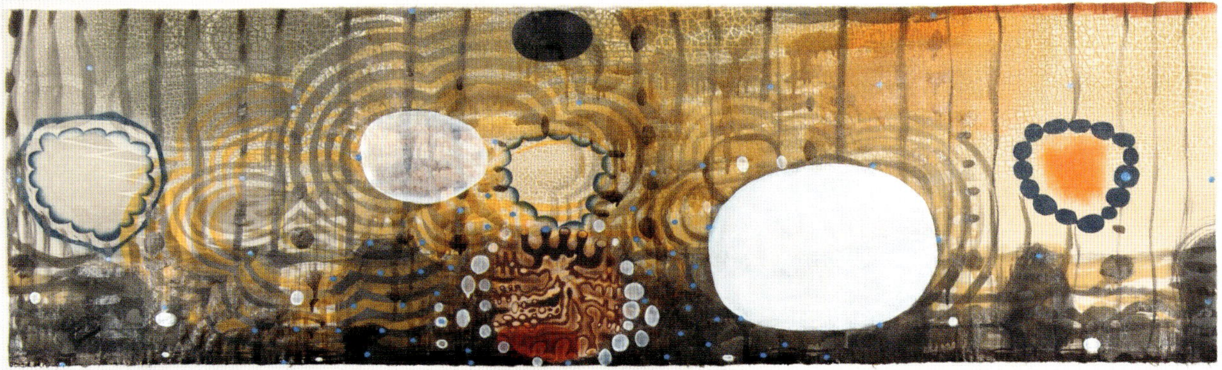

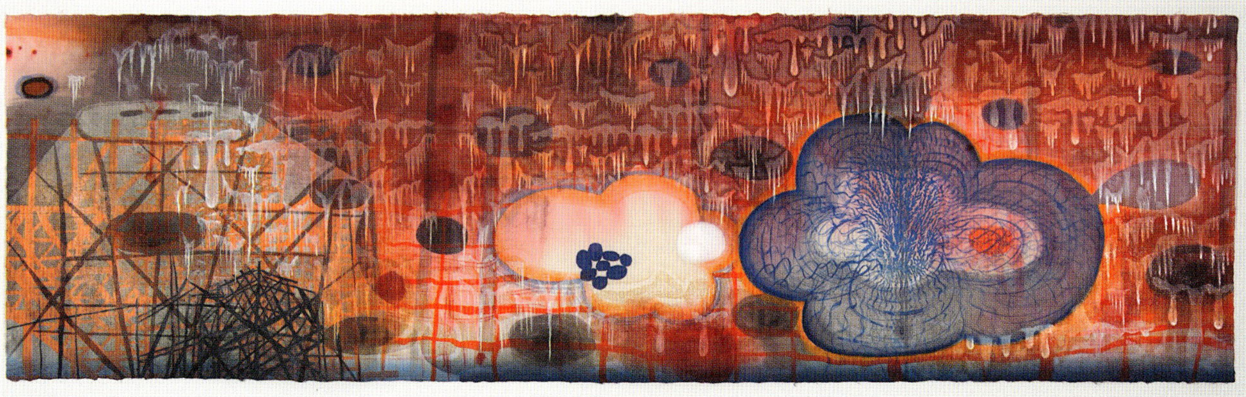

ROBERT KUSHNER

New York, New York

I began these prints by selecting pages from my stash of antique papers from around the world. The paper compositions were then collaged onto white Rives BFK paper and became the backgrounds for the monotypes.

I painted images of the plumeria, hibiscus, and coffee flowers, tangerines, and lemons on Plexiglas plates, using thinned lithography inks. These were then printed onto the paper collages. Many of the monotypes are embellished with gold leaf.

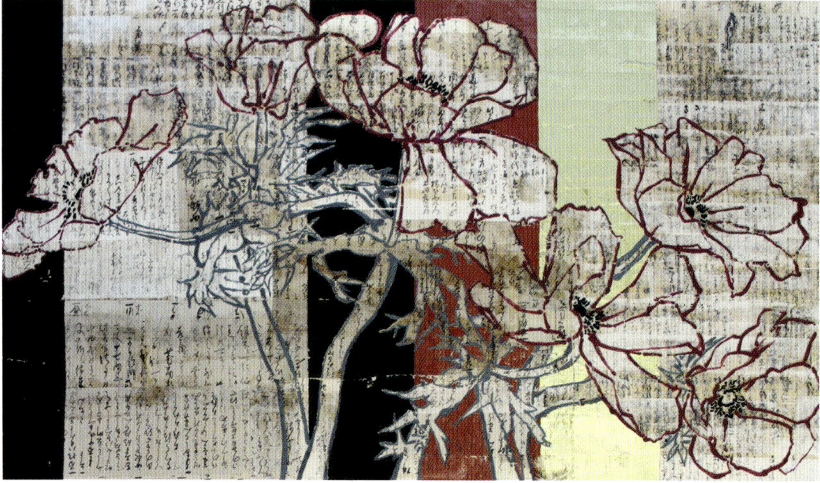

Red Anemones. Monoprint with twelve silkscreen colors (variable) on antique paper collage. 34" × 60". 2015.

ALL PHOTOS ARE COURTESY OF TAMSIN DOHERTY OF BRAND X EDITIONS. PUBLISHED BY BRAND X EDITIONS AND THE ARTIST. PRINTED AT BRAND X EDITIONS BY STEVEN SANGENARIO.

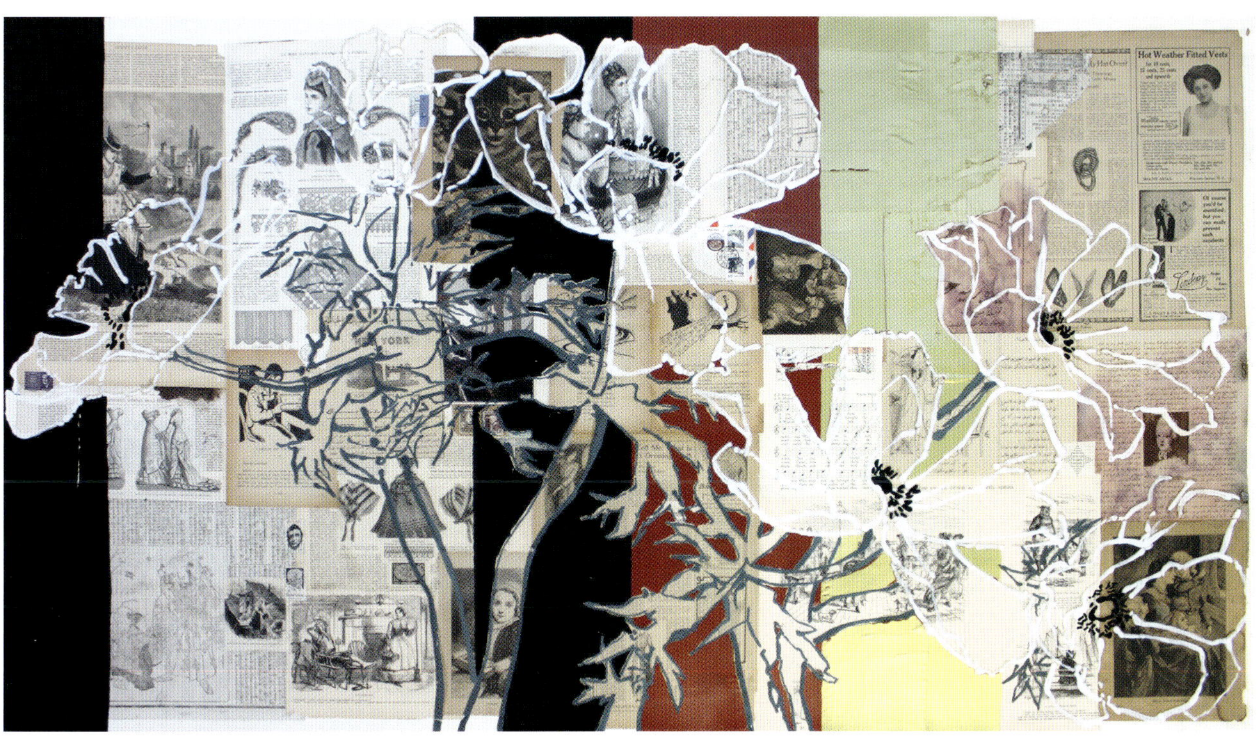

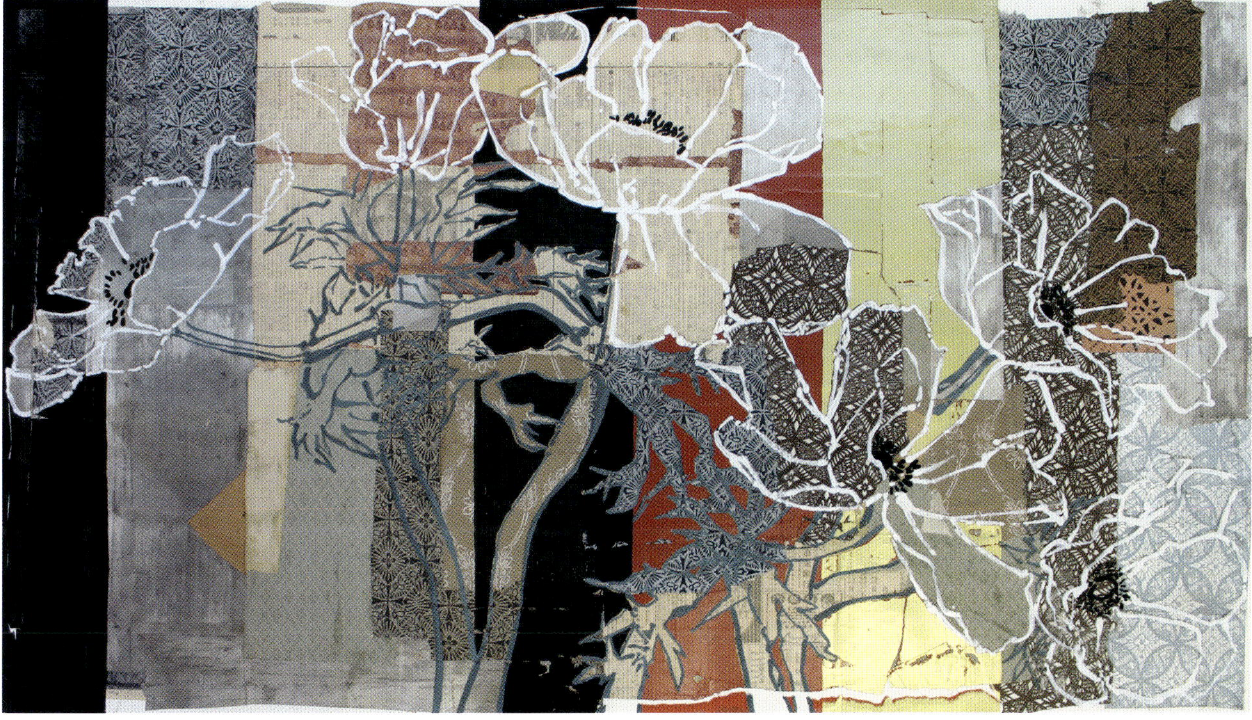

Λ
New York. Monoprint with twelve silk-screen colors (variable) on antique paper collage. 34" × 60". 2015.

V
Byobo II. Monoprint with twelve silk-screen colors (variable) on antique paper collage. 34" × 60". 2015.

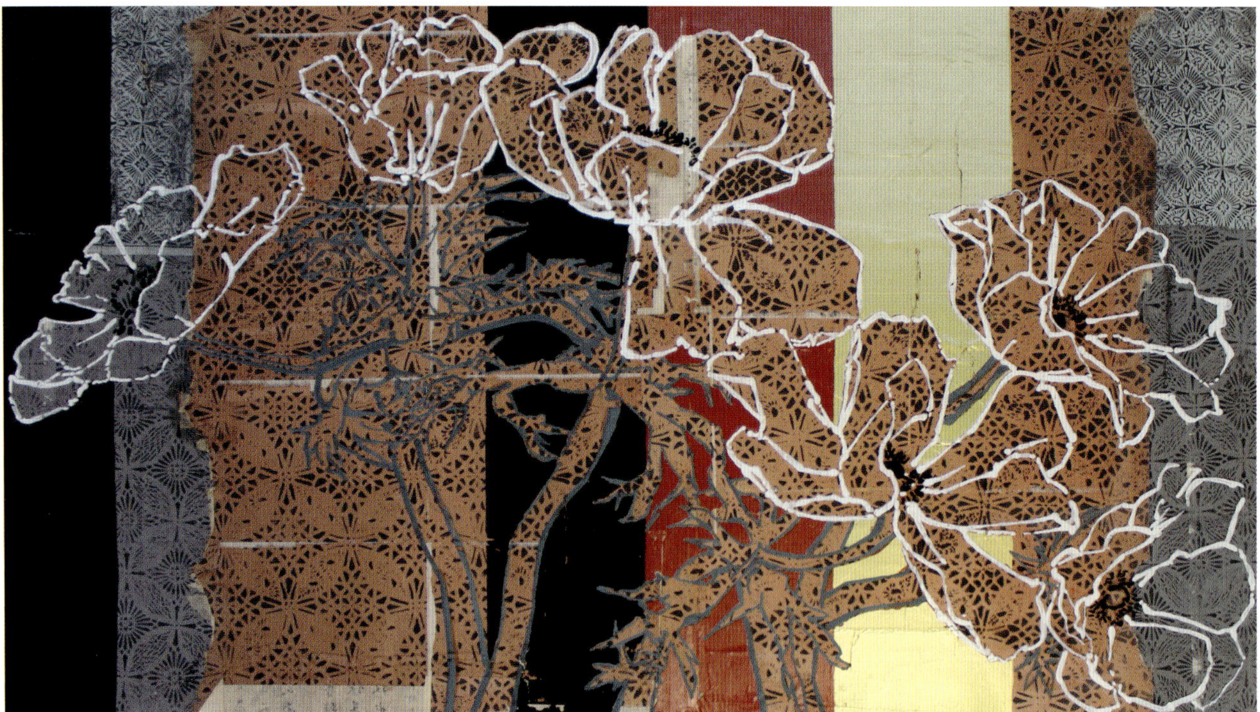

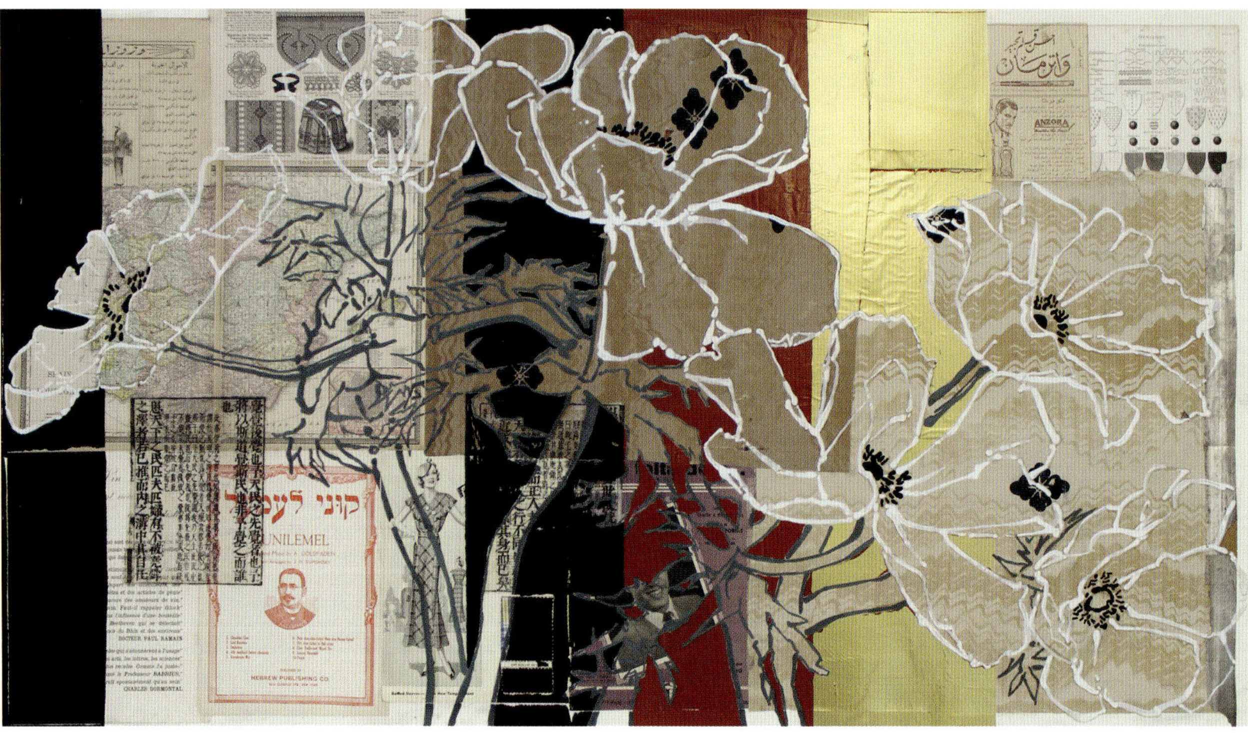

∧

Byobo III. Monoprint with twelve silk-screen colors (variable) on antique paper collage. 34" × 60". 2015.

∨

Kunilemel. Monoprint with twelve silk-screen colors (variable) on antique paper collage. 34" × 60". 2015.

EMILIO LOBATO

Denver, Colorado

For a little over twenty-five years, I have been making monotypes. I have enjoyed every minute of it, and someday the magic of it might begin to make sense to me. Every print session, every print, has been an opportunity not only to express but to continue to learn. As a nonobjective painter, I have found that monotype feels like a natural (logical?) extension of my creative practice. There continues to be a mystery to the process that both challenges and delights. There is an immediacy and unpredictable quality that I am attracted to. In my long artistic career, making monotypes is both alchemical and profoundly satisfying.

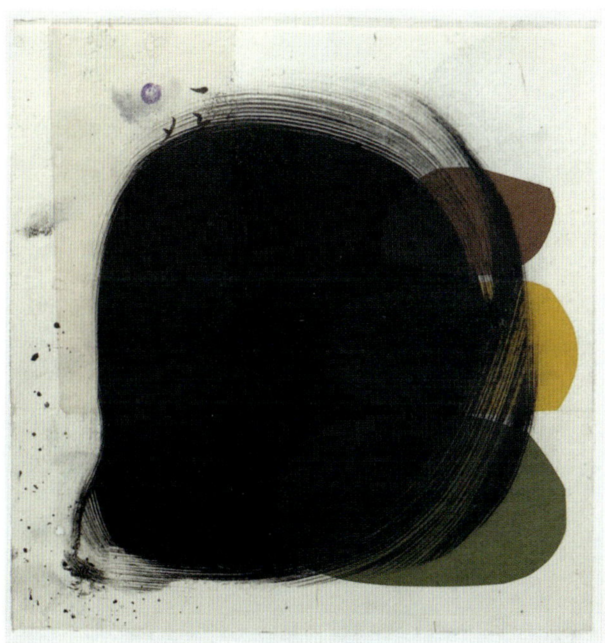

Luna Negra (Black Moon). Monoprint with oil-based inks, monotype, and chine collé. 8" × 8". 2009.

ALL IMAGES ARE COURTESY OF NICK RYAN, WILLIAM HAVU GALLERY. PUBLISHED BY THE ARTIST. PRINTED BY MICHAEL COSTELLO AT HAND GRAPHICS.

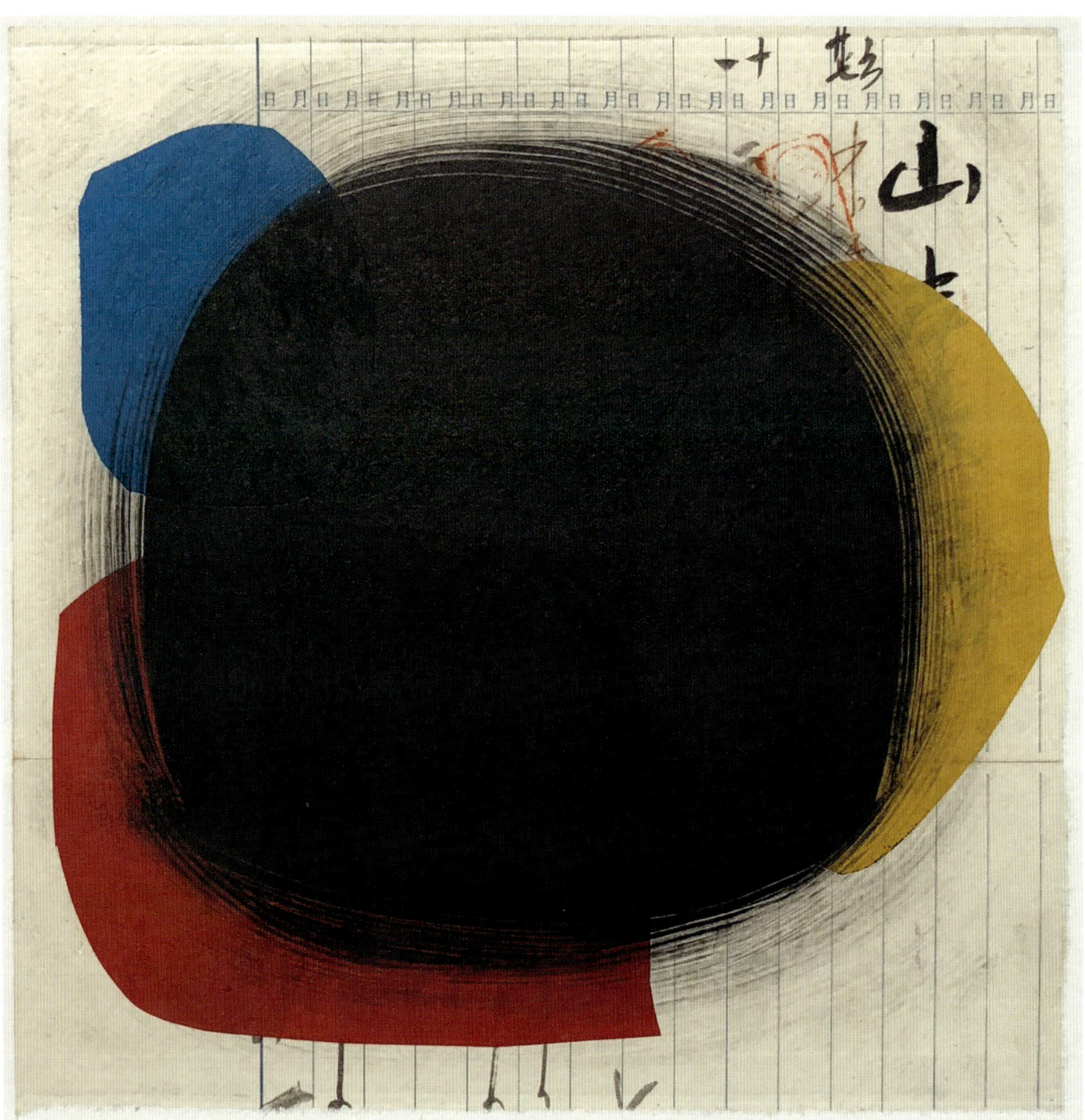

Anillo de Saturno (Rings of Saturn).
Monoprint with oil-based inks, monotype, and chine collé. 8" × 8". 2009.

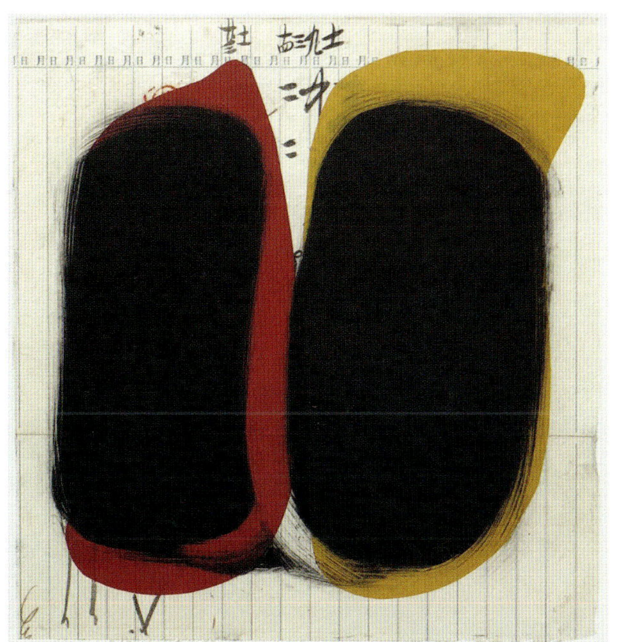

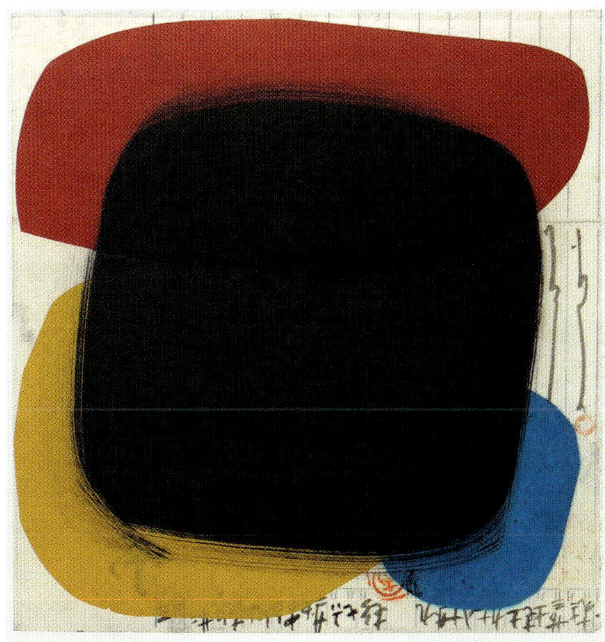

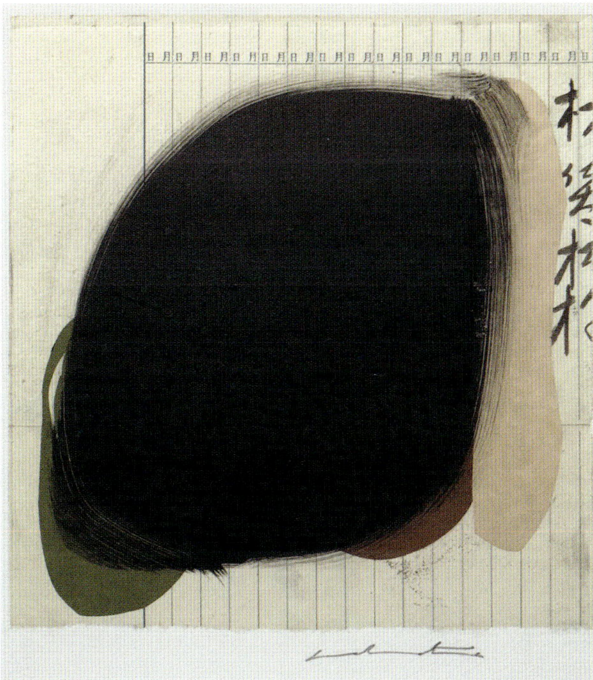

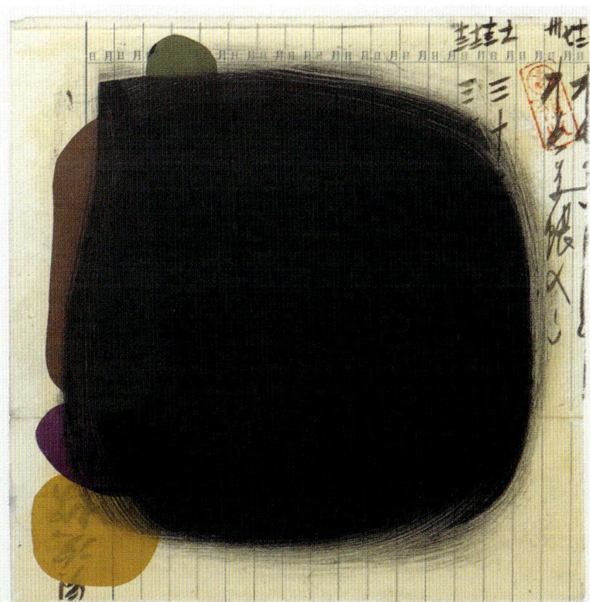

Cojones. Monoprint with oil-based inks, monotype, and chine collé. 8" × 8". 2009.

Las Primarias (Primaries). Monoprint with oil-based inks, monotype, and chine collé. 8" × 8". 2009.

Rendija (Crevice). Monoprint with oil-based inks, monotype, and chine collé. 8" × 8". 2009.

Rincon Oscuro (Dark Corner). Monoprint with oil-based inks, monotype, and chine collé. 8" × 8". 2009.

JENNIFER MARSHALL

Brooklyn, New York

These botanical prints bring together my fascination with the beauty of plants and the ability of monotype processes to capture the texture and intricacy of nature's drawing. My involvement with this subject began with a love of painting and drawing outdoors. Later, having a studio in proximity to plant specimens in their native habitat, and a press nearby, I brought the outdoors inside. The studio became a tended garden as I gathered seasonal leaves and branches from the world around me. I have been inspired by the work of naturalist and illustrator Maria Sibylla Merian and the cyanotypes of Anna Atkins. I am fascinated by the idea that something as simple as a single fern or branch of eucalyptus can convey a sense of place and time.

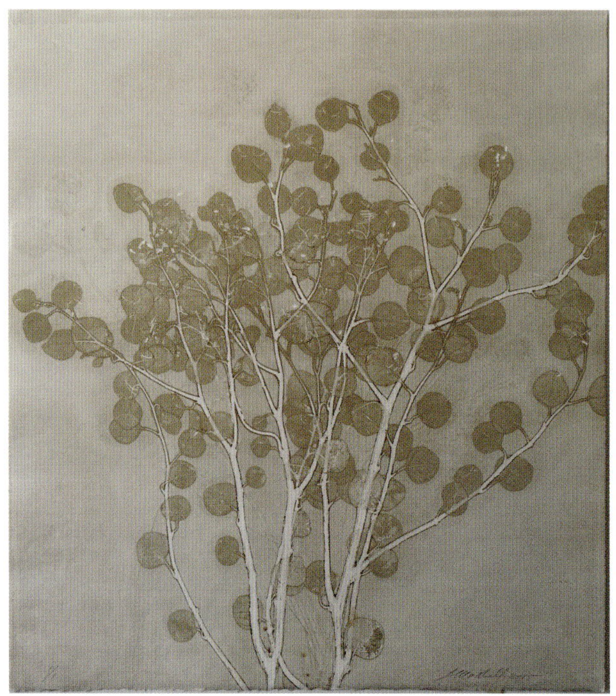

External Determination. Monotype. 21" × 19". 2015.

ALL PHOTOS ARE COURTESY OF ANDREW MOCKLER. PUBLISHED BY JUNGLE PRESS. PRINTED BY ANDREW MOCKLER AND JENNIFER MARSHALL AT JUNGLE PRESS.

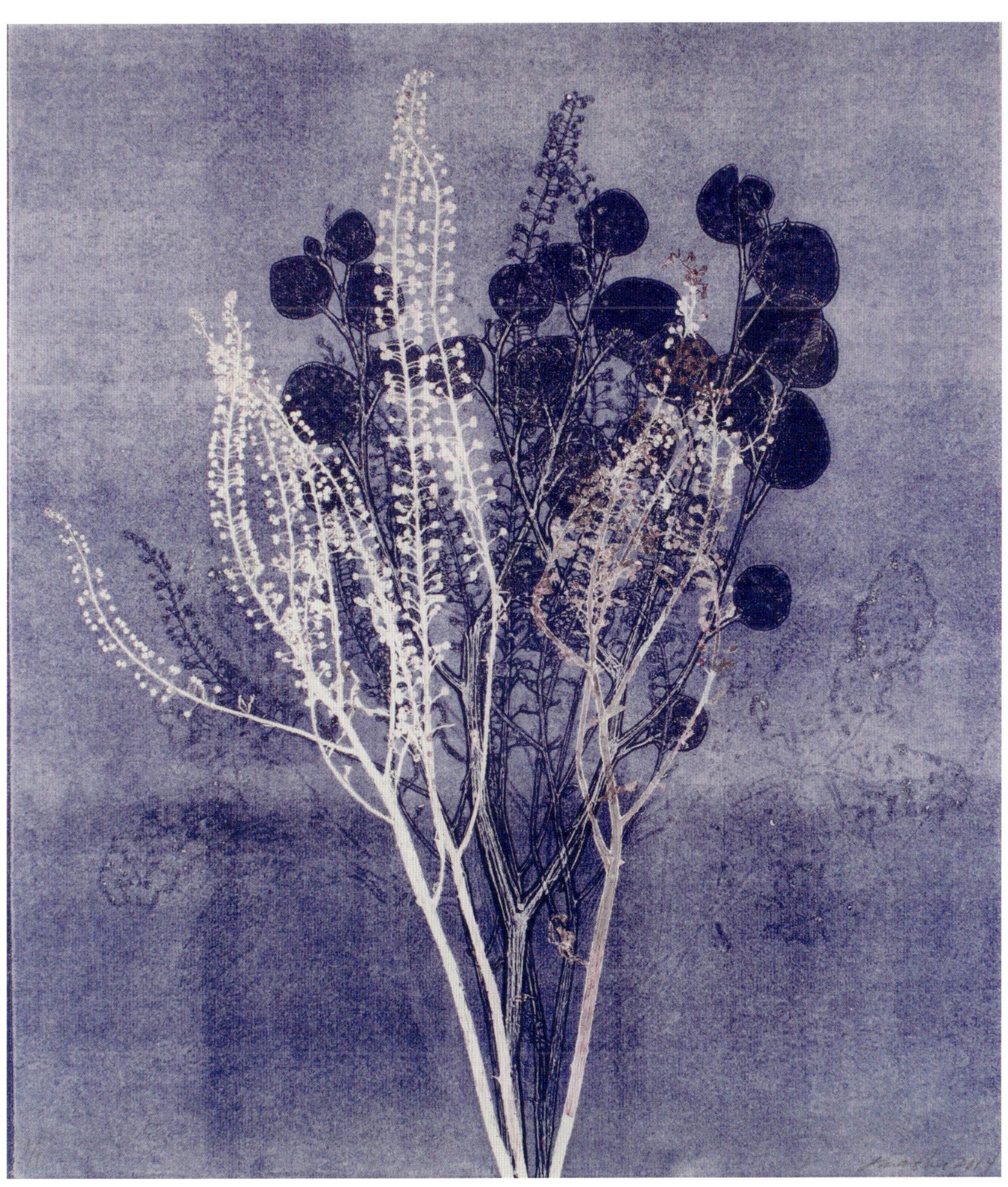

External Determination. Monoprint. 15" × 11". 2014.

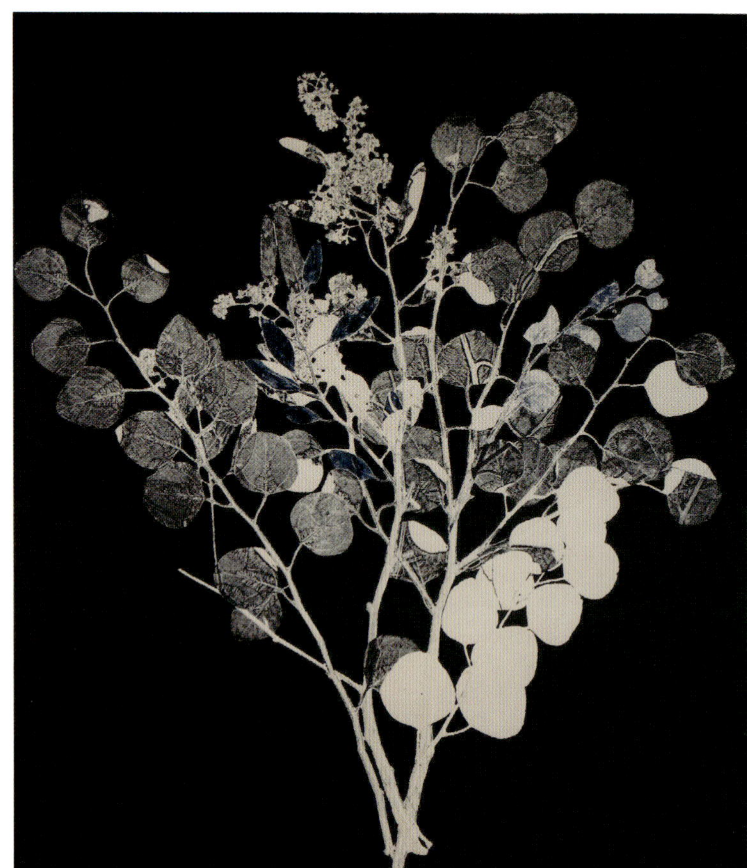

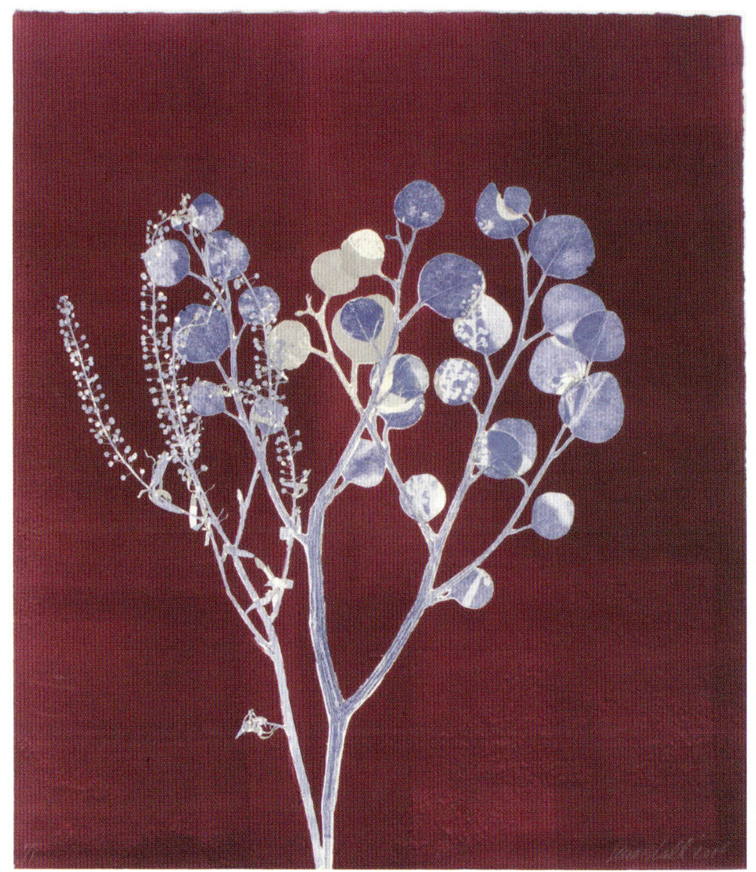

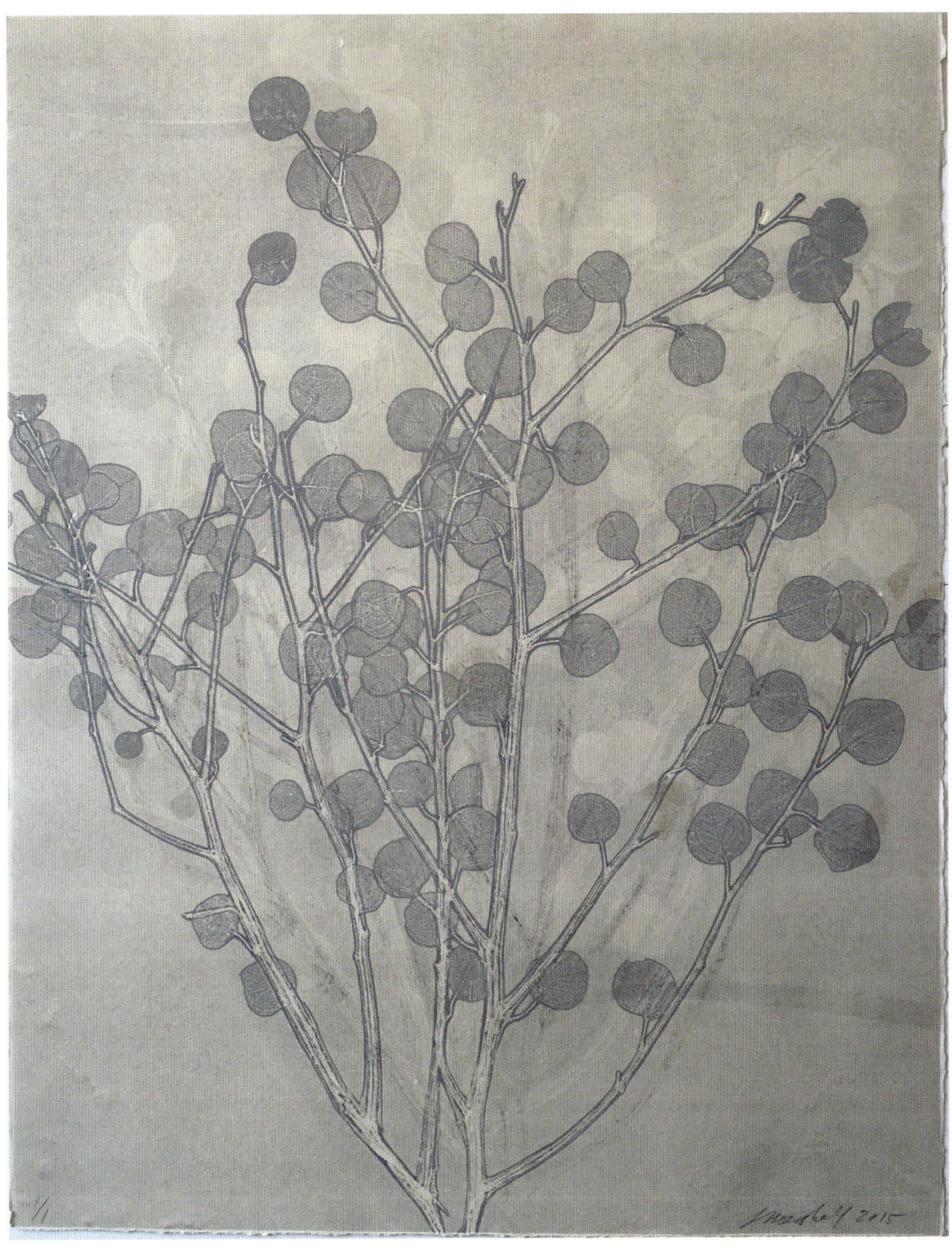

<
External Determination. Monoprint.
21" × 19". 2015.

External Determination. Monoprint.
15" × 11". 2014.

External Determination. Monoprint.
21" × 19". 2015.

RYAN MCGINNESS

New York, New York

I am interested in the push and pull between the figurative and the abstract. Starting from photographs of my wife and daughters, I created sequences of drawings, each time stripping away details to reveal essential geometric lines and forms, a process that eventually resulted in eight monochrome images depicting a mother holding her children. The prints consist of at least three of these hieroglyph-like images printed one atop of the other in my trademark saturated and neon inks, as well as shimmering gold and silver. The layering makes the original pictograms harder to decipher, while drawing the viewer's attention to isolated details revealed in the process.

Mother & Child #1. Screen-print monoprint. 40.5" × 27.75". 2015.

Mother & Child #31. Screen-print monoprint. 40.5" × 27.75". 2015.

Mother & Child #33. Screen-print monoprint. 40.5" × 27.75". 2015.

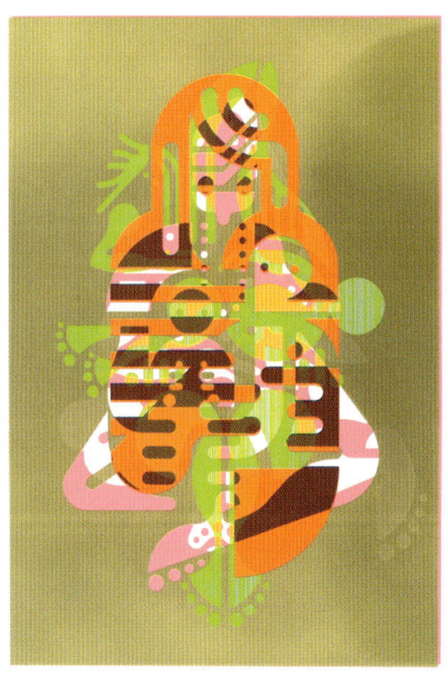

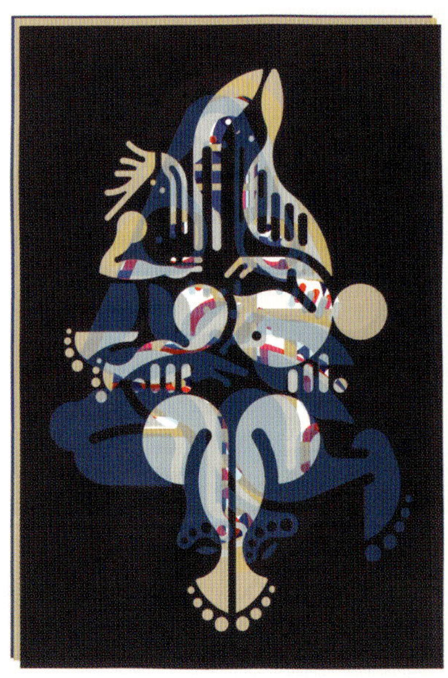

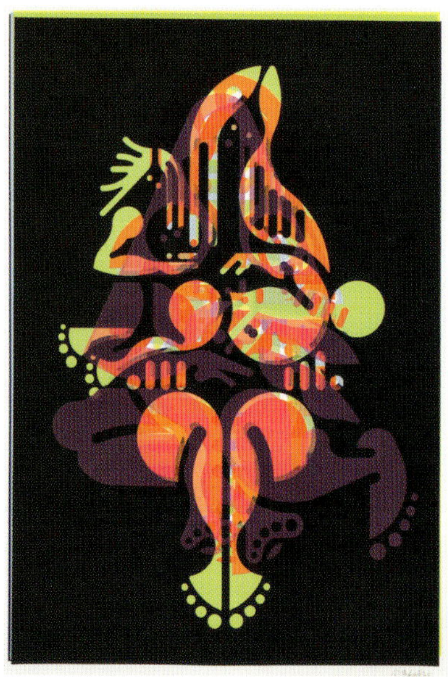

PUBLISHED AND PRINTED AT LOWER EASTSIDE PRINTSHOP BY ERIK HOUGEN AND MARCO LAWRENCE.

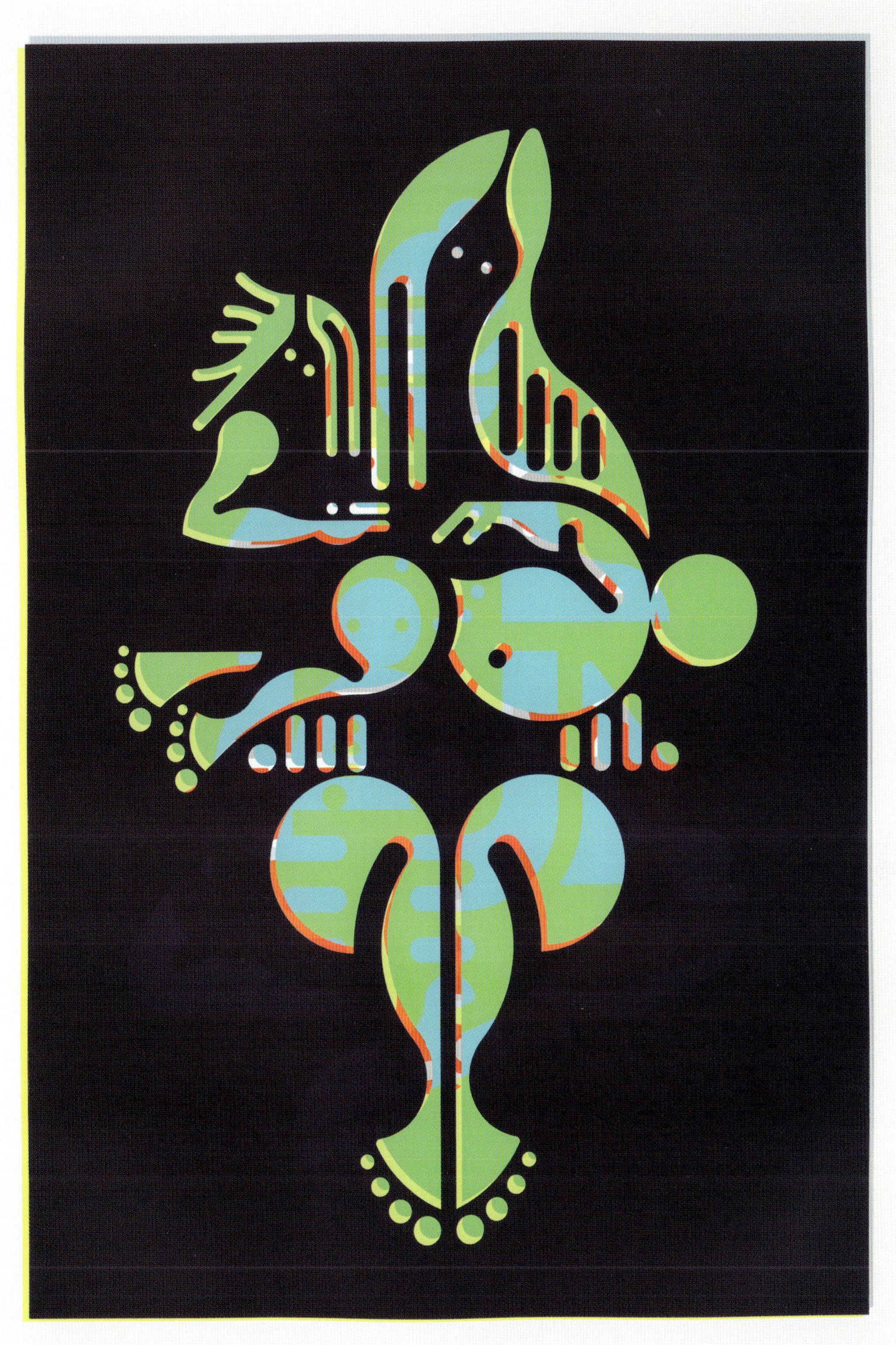

Mother & Child #7. Screen-print monoprint from a series of 50, unnumbered. 40.5" × 27.75". 2015.

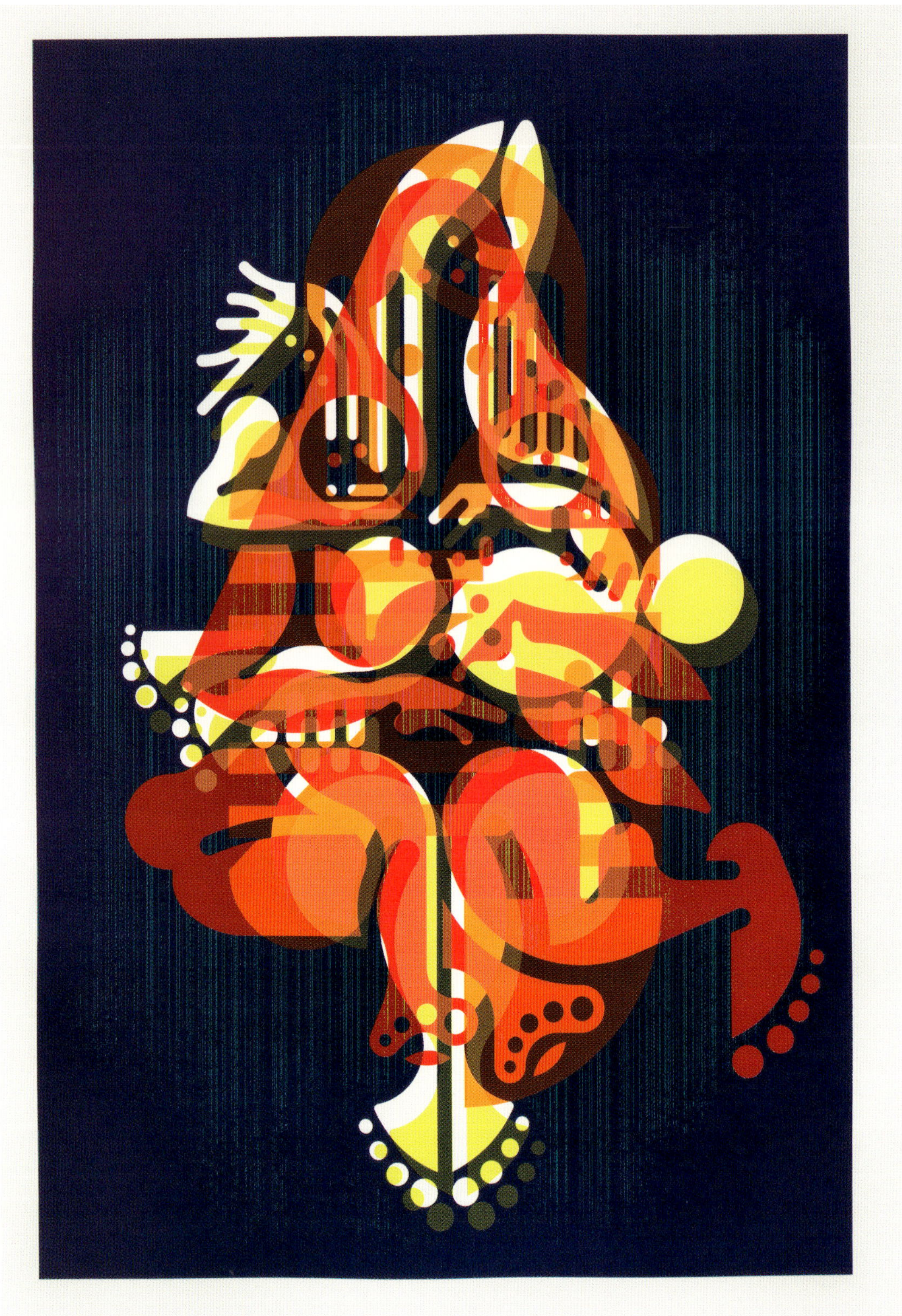

Mother & Child #14. Screen-print monoprint. 40.5" × 27.75". 2015.

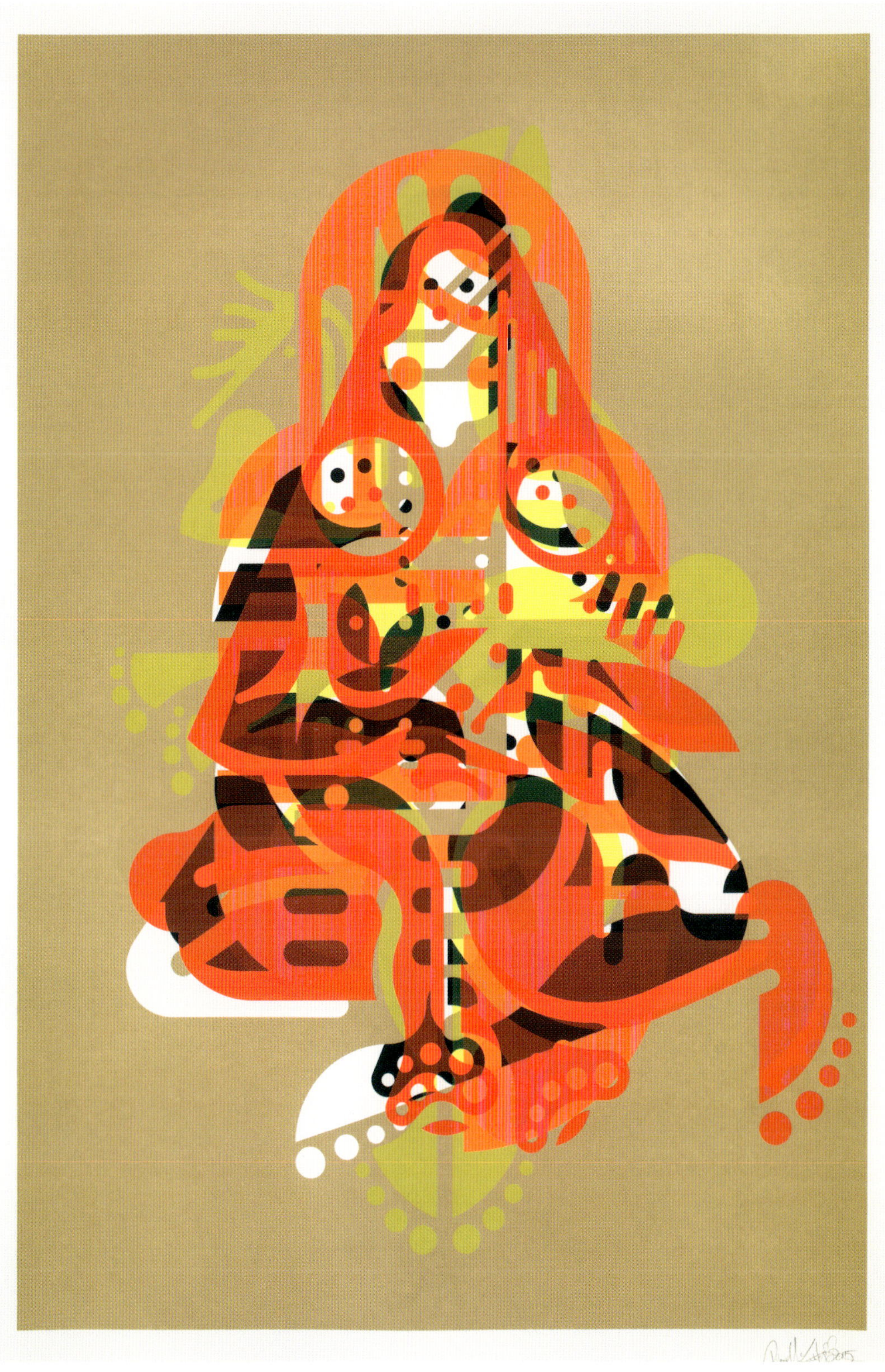

Mother & Child #44. Screen-print monoprint. 40.5" × 27.75". 2015.

MATT NEUMAN

Brooklyn, New York

Monoprint is that shaded zone in my artistic identity Venn diagram that emerges between painting and printmaking. The processes give me the freedom to push painterly chaos within the design structure of printmaking. I embrace repetition, but my interest has never been in producing editioned print runs. Frequent color changes and mark making between print layers allow me to think like a painter but execute as a printmaker as I make my way through multi-block sets in carved relief. My process mines printmaking for its repeatability and then squeezes it for variety in the pursuit of uniquely finished works.

My fascinations and explorations are focused on basic geometric interactions where color is the primary protagonist in the work. The compositions are born from my basic need and instinctive tendency to leverage geometry as a way to organize information and make sense of space. As a platform, geometry supports my wide-ranging artistic tangents and forays inspired by a host of other interests. Influences such as physics, origami, space-time, and the infinite have crept into my thoughts and have been guides in the pursuit of pointed spatial experience.

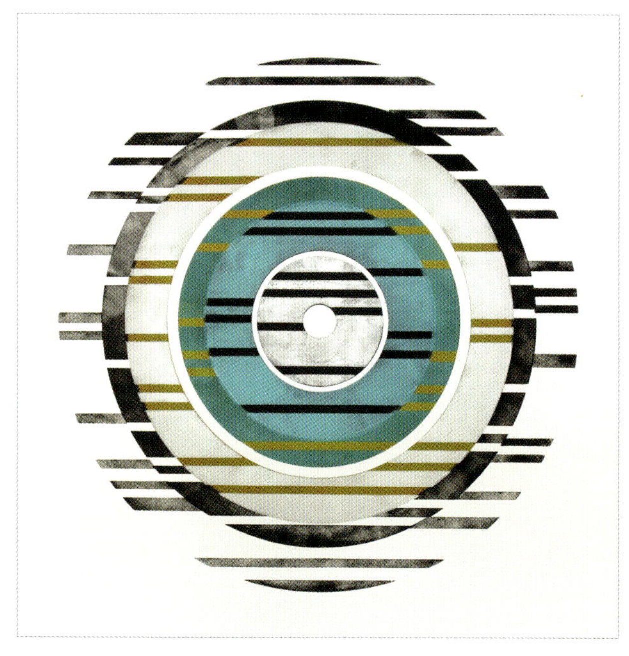

Circle Print #51. Woodblock monoprint with oil-based inks. 29" × 36". 2011.

PUBLISHED BY ASTERISK PROJECTS. PRINTED BY THE ARTIST.

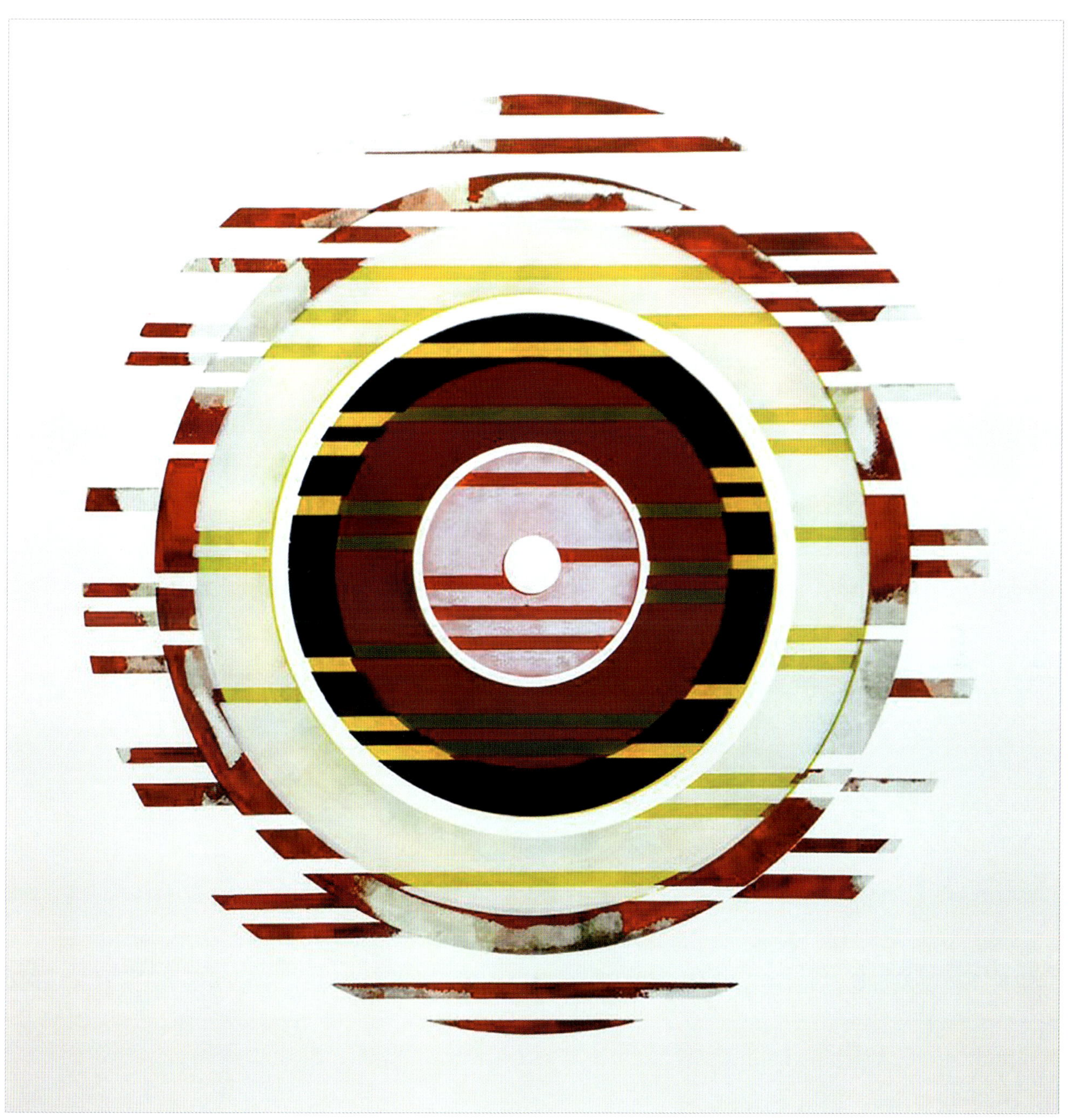

Circle Print #47. Woodblock monoprint with oil-based inks. 29" × 36". 2011.

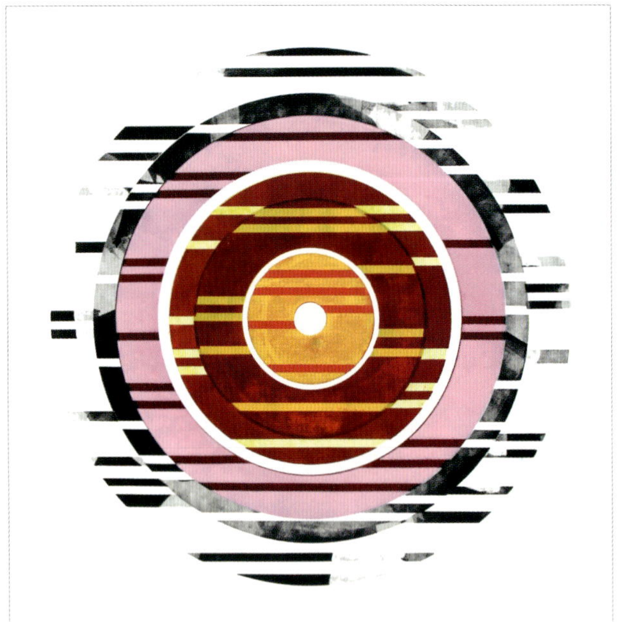

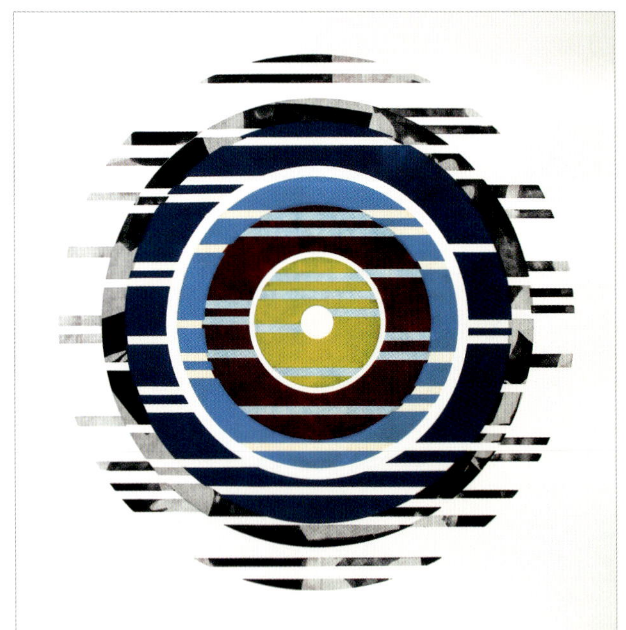

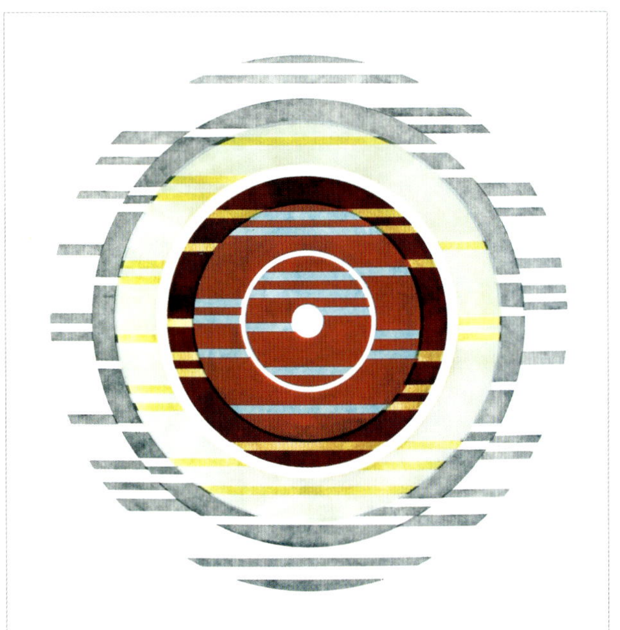

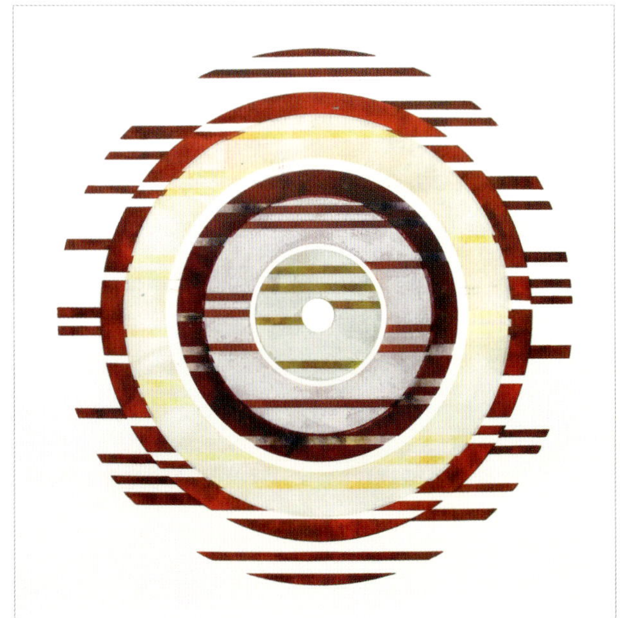

Circle Print #54. Woodblock monoprint with oil-based inks. 29" × 36". 2011.

Circle Print #58. Woodblock monoprint with oil-based inks. 29" × 36". 2011.

Circle Print #60. Woodblock monoprint with oil-based inks. 29" × 36". 2011.

Circle Print #61. Woodblock monoprint with oil-based inks. 29" × 36". 2011.

JOHN NEWMAN

New York, New York

I use monotypes as an extended form of drawing. I often take quick sketches, photographs, and manipulated photographs with drawing and scan them into a computer. The computer allows me to immediately see differing possibilities for these images in terms of proportion, rotation, isolating a detail, or inverting black and white. I then duplicate these images and use the copying machine as a kind of printing "plate." I add a little gum arabic to water, gently sponge the image, and carefully roll on ink or oil paint, which attaches itself to the toner. If I have a press, I can get better resolution . . . but I often print them by hand with a spoon.

I use these monotypes as a way to see multiple possibilities for an image I am working on . . . and I also use them as an understructure for further drawing as well. These very basic studio prints seem to reside halfway between drawing and sculpture, which offers a wonderful opportunity for me as a vehicle for "research and development."

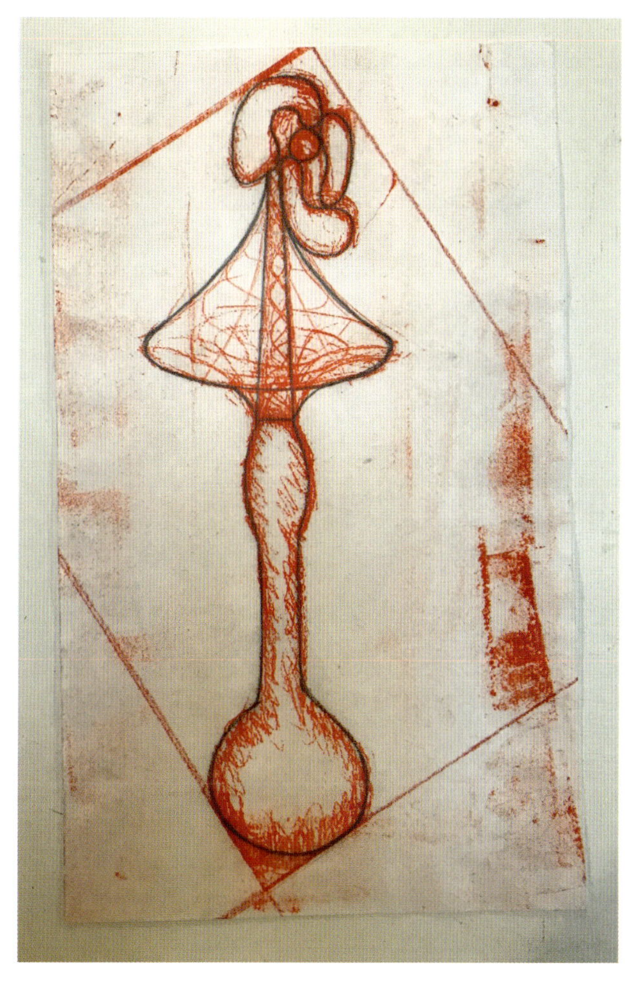

Study for Standpoint and Going Gray. Monoprint with oil-based inks. 10.25" × 6.25". 2012.

PUBLISHED BY ASTERISK PROJECTS. PRINTED BY THE ARTIST.

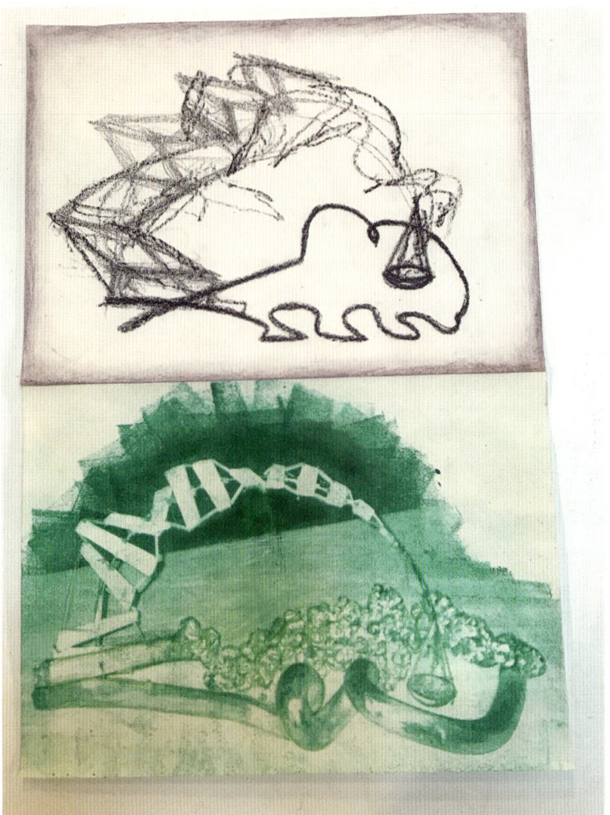

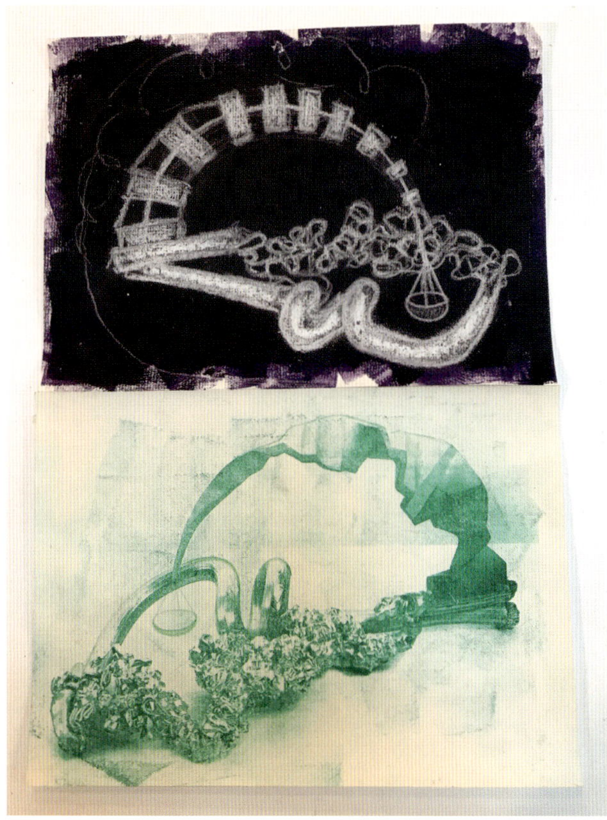

Study for Lute, Line and Level #1. Monoprint with oil-based inks. 14.5" × 10". 2010.

Study for Lute, Line and Level #2. Monoprint with oil-based inks. 14.5" × 10". 2010.

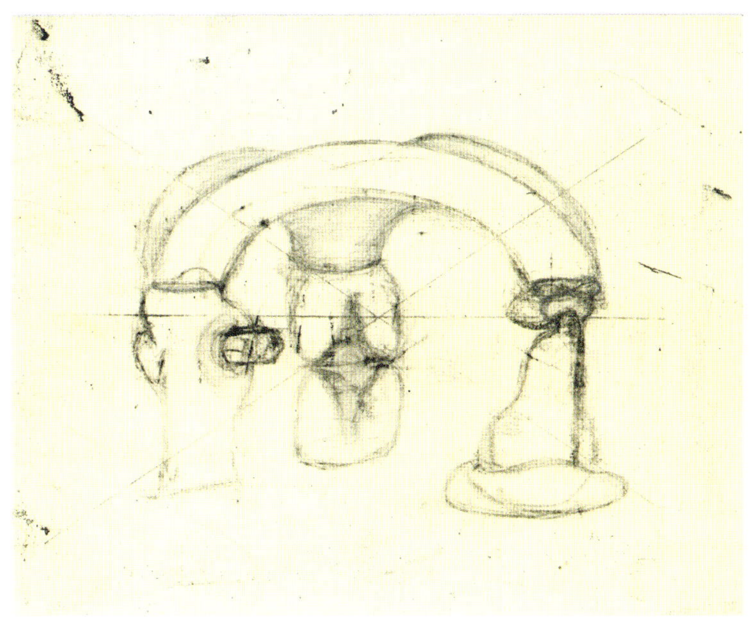

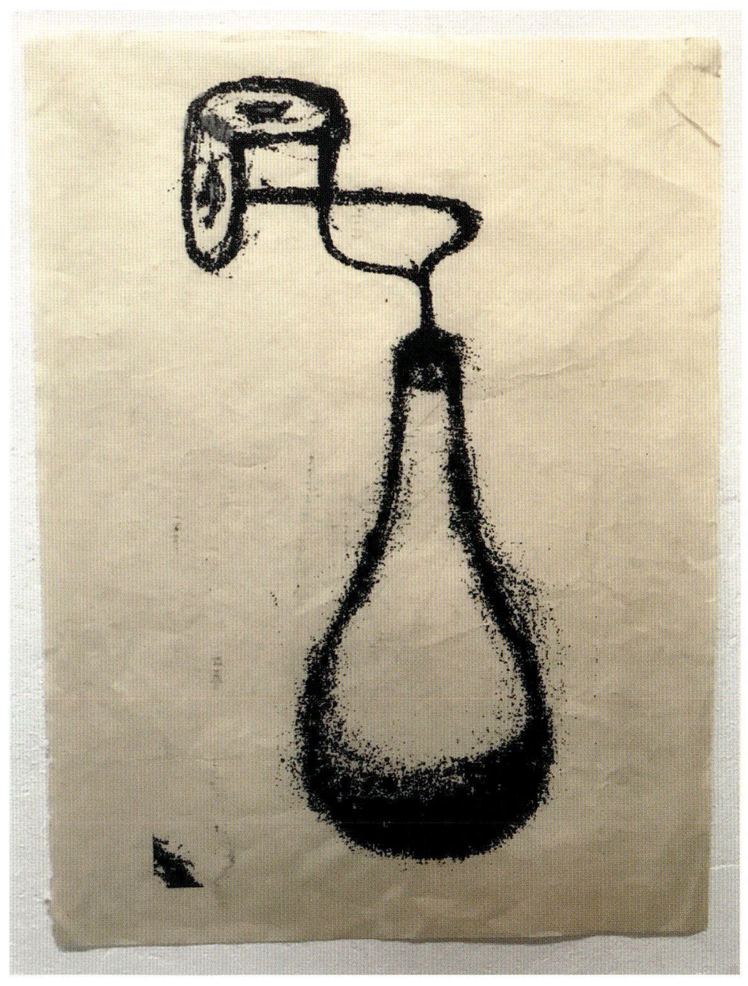

^
Study for a Blue Light Holds the Distance. Monoprint with oil-based inks. 10.25" × 6.25". 2013.

v
Study for Light and Lace Maker. Monoprint with oil-based inks. 11" × 8.5". 2012.

ROY NICHOLSON

Sag Harbor, New York

My solar plate varied-edition monoprints from the Toxic Garden (Sweet Pea) series began as a collaboration with master printer Dan Welden to demonstrate the versatility of his pioneering printmaking technique. We made nineteen unique prints from one image plate and one blank to produce a wide range of tonal and expressive effects. The blank plate was painted on, wiped out, and otherwise manipulated like a regular monotype. It was then combined with the matrix, which was also manipulated in several ways to make a series of varied-edition monoprints.

Plants that are both toxic and beautiful are the primary motifs in my most recent series of paintings and prints. The ironically named Sweet Pea, which can paralyze when ingested, is the source of imagery that abstracts the plant's complex morphology.

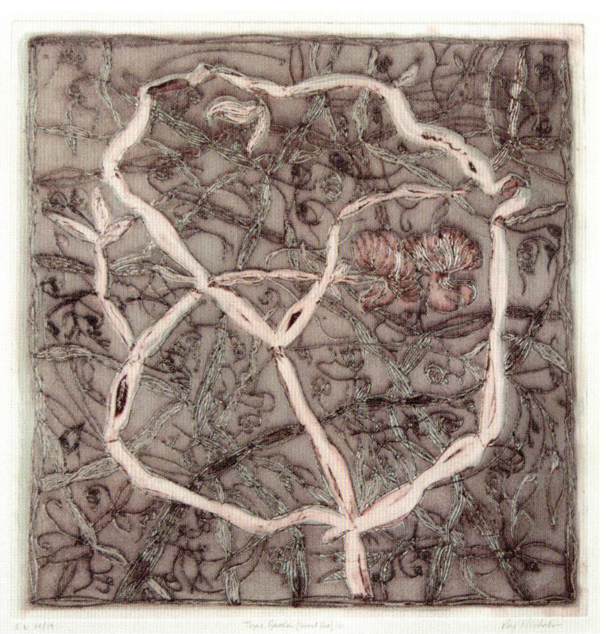

Toxic Garden (Sweet Pea) 10. Monoprint with oil-based inks and Solarplate on Johannot paper. Edition Variable 10/19. 16" × 16". 2013.

>

Toxic Garden (Sweet Pea) 5. Monoprint with oil-based inks and Solarplate on Hahnemuhle paper. Edition Variable 11/19. 16" × 16". 2013.

Toxic Garden (Sweet Pea) 9. Monoprint with oil-based inks and Solarplate on Hahnemuhle paper. Edition Variable 9/19. 16" × 16". 2013.

ALL PHOTOS ARE COURTESY OF SHEILA GUTTERIDGE. PUBLISHED BY THE ARTIST. PRINTED BY THE ARTIST AND DAN WELDEN AT HAMPTON EDITIONS.

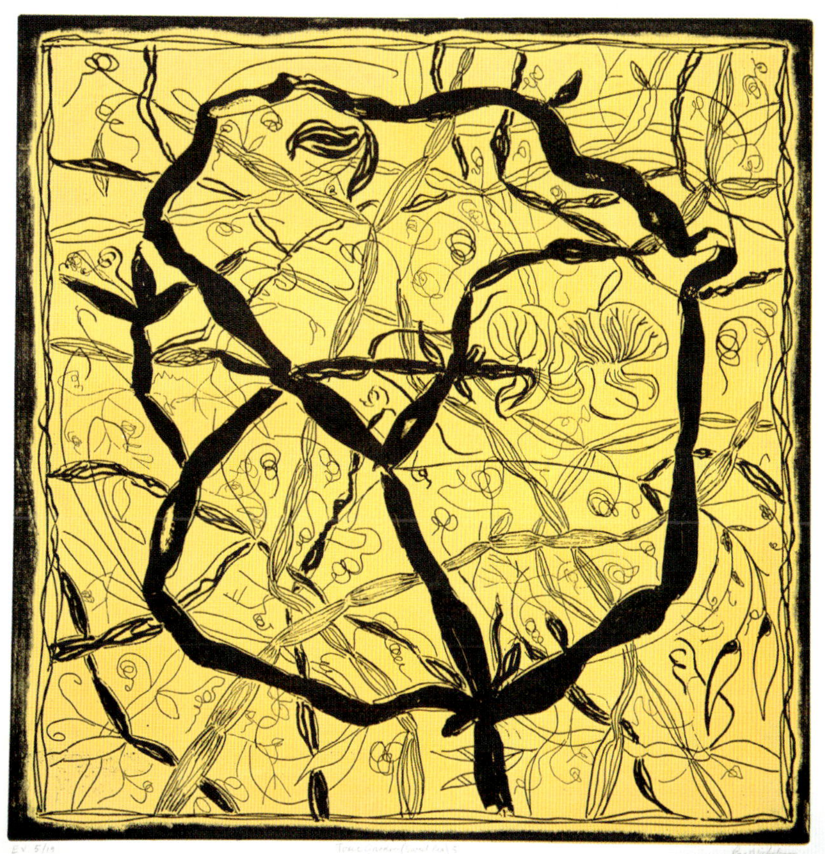

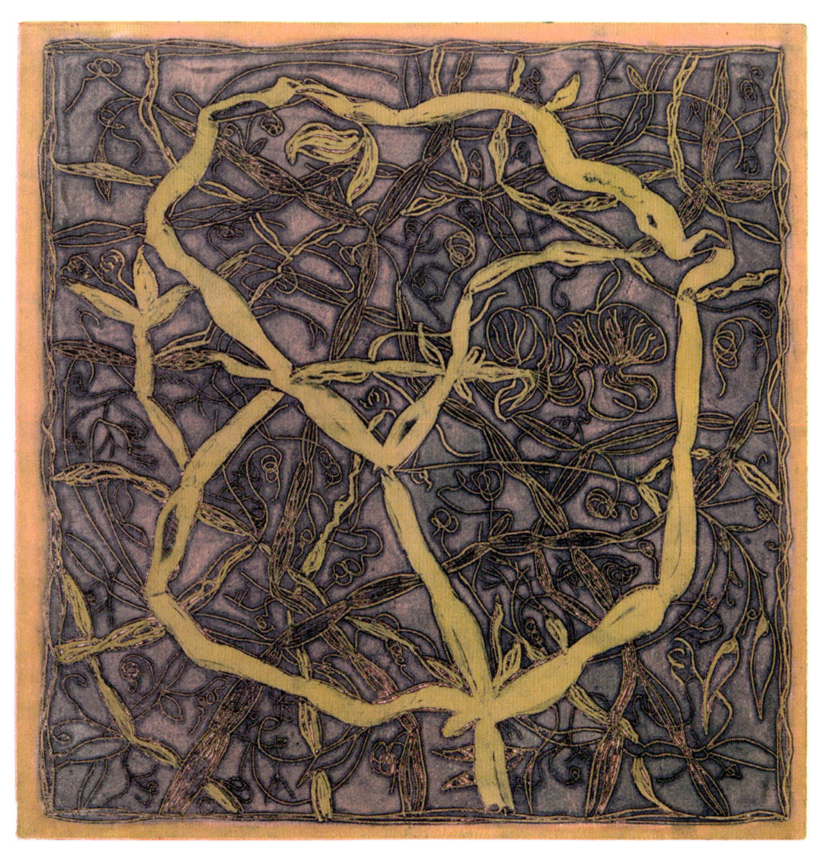

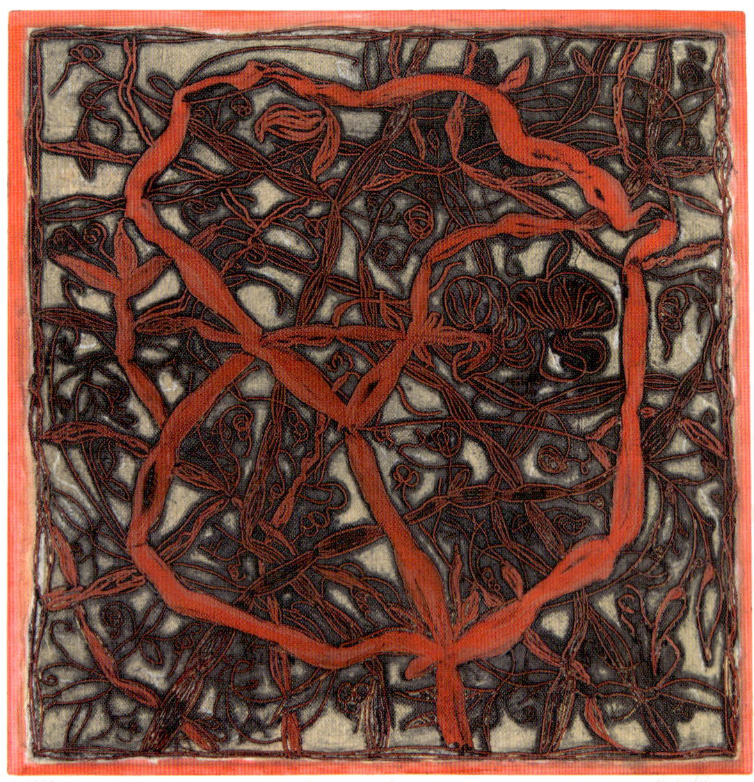

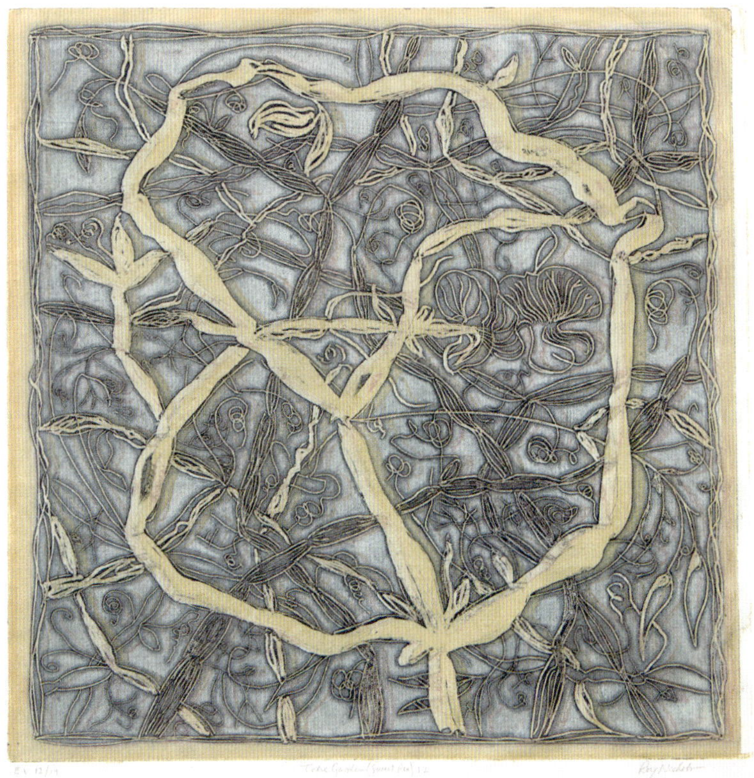

∧
Toxic Garden (Sweet Pea) 6. Monoprint with oil-based inks and Solarplate on Johannot paper. Edition Variable 6/19. 16" × 16". 2013.

∨
Toxic Garden (Sweet Pea) 12. Monoprint with oil-based inks and Solarplate on Johannot paper. Edition Variable 12/19. 16" × 16". 2013.

DEBRA OLIN

Somerville, Massachusetts

In my monoprint and woodcut collages, I begin with one composition and create stencils to explore the range and variety available through simple printmaking processes. My interest is not with creating an edition but rather with exploring the possibilities of a singular image. The question I am most eager to investigate is "What if?" What kind of texture will register with this fabric? What are the various materials on hand for making a line, a mark, or a repeating pattern? By working in a monoprint series, no decision need negate an alternative direction. All possibilities are open for discovery. I am collaborating with the press, and there is often a wonderful surprise when the paper is lifted off the plate.

These prints are from a series titled Every Protection. The work was inspired by the Jewish Ethnographic Program, a questionnaire developed in 1914 by writer, socialist, revolutionary, and ethnographer S. An-sky* and disseminated throughout the Russian Pale of Settlement. These questions covered every aspect of life from birth to death and beyond. My particular interest was in those questions concerning pregnancy and childbirth. An-sky's research included 283 queries on this topic alone. There are superstitions and precautions taken in every society to guard the pregnant woman and the newborn. Some of An-sky's questions contained provocative phrasing such as "Is there a belief that one must not place a child in front of a mirror until he gets his first teeth?" An-sky's study reveals a familiarity and breadth of knowledge that charged my imagination and inspired me to create this body of work.

**Shloyme Zanvl Rappoport (1863–1920), known by his psyeudonym S. Ansky (or An-sky), was a Jewish author and playwright, also known as a researcher of Jewish folklore, a polemicist, and a cultural and political activist.*

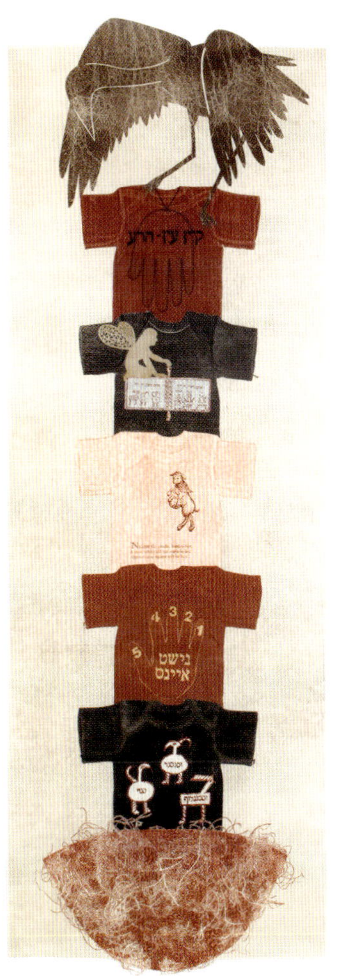

T-Shirt Totem. Monoprint with oil-based inks and collage. 69" × 24". 2010.

BILL KIPP IS THE PHOTOGRAPHER OF ALL IMAGES. PUBLISHED AND PRINTED BY THE ARTIST.

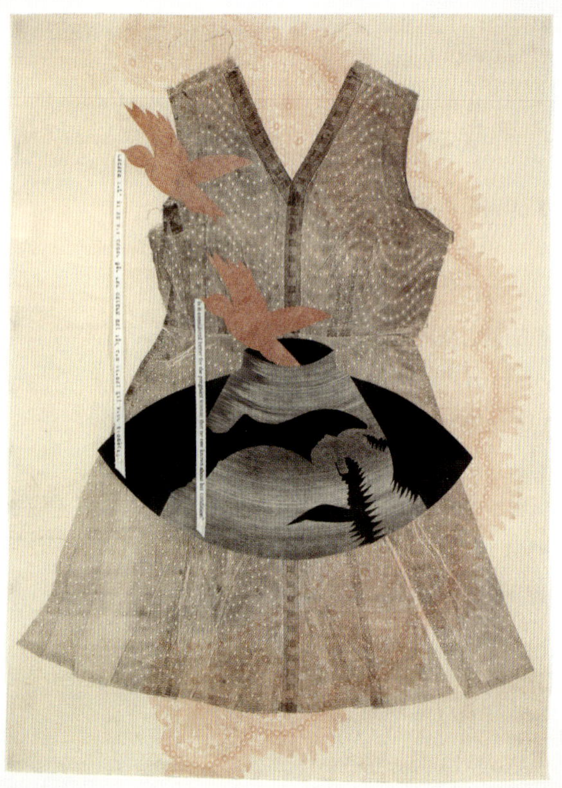

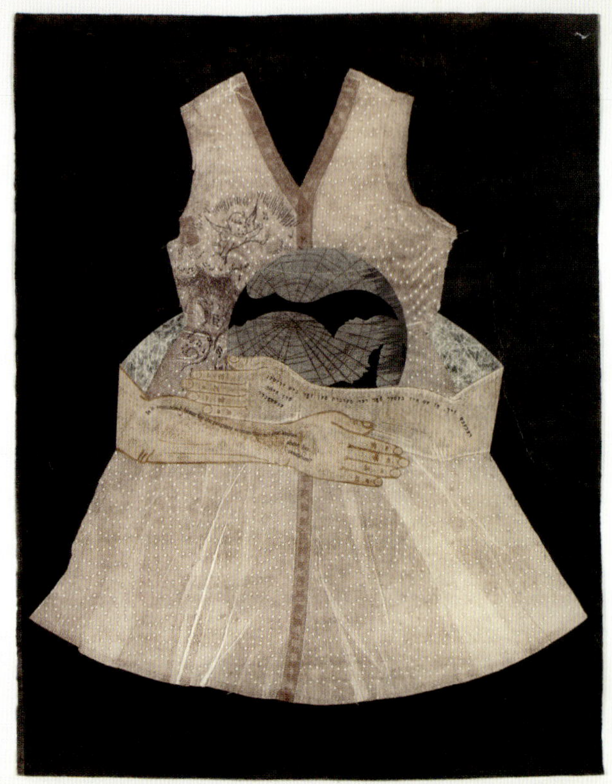

Eyelet, Vessel, Birds. Monoprint with oil-based inks and collage, ribbon. 46" x 34". 2011.

Eyelet with Angel. Monoprint with oil-based inks, collage, and wax. 48" × 38. 25". 2011.

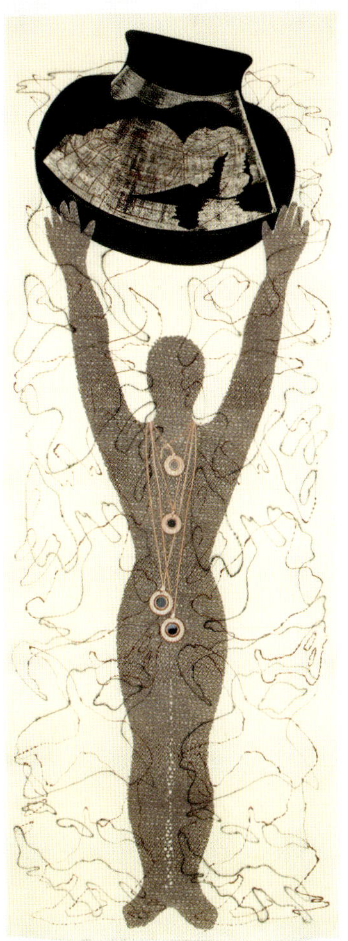

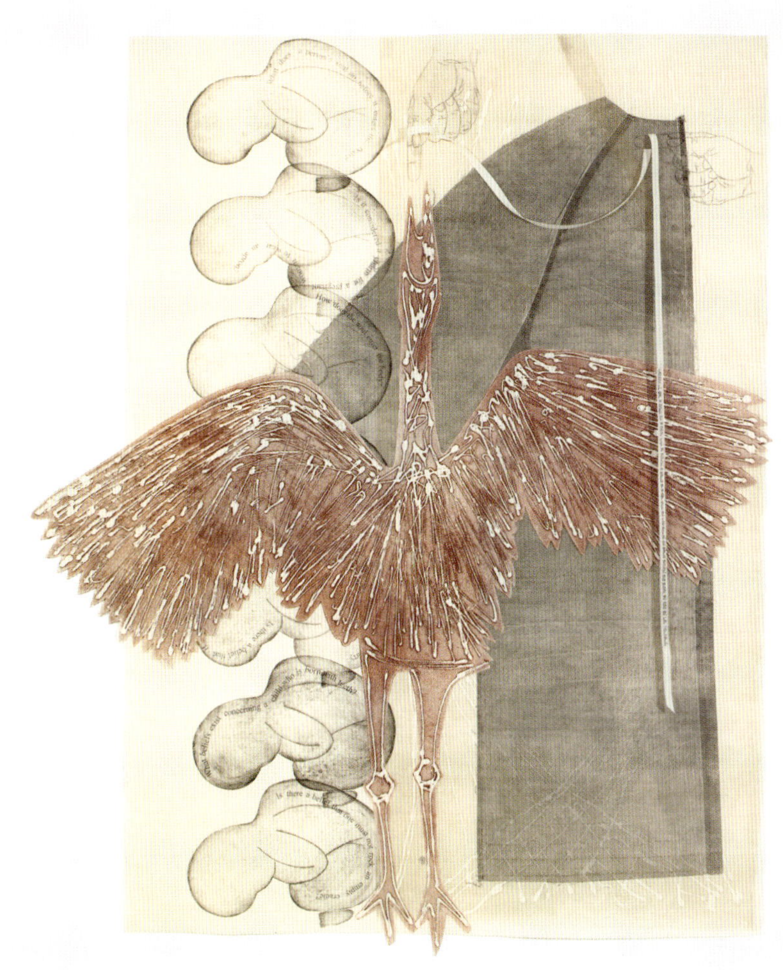

Out of Harm's Way. Monoprint with oil-based inks, collage, and mirrors. 64" × 24". 2009.

Totem of Questions. Monoprint with oil-based inks, collage, and ribbon. 53" × 45.5". 2011.

RON POKRASSO

Santa Fe, New Mexico

In the 1980s, as monotypes gained popularity, I began making intaglio plates with space for monotype to bring the compositions to completion. These repeatable matrices served to focus and vary the images with monotype. The variable editions evolved into unique impressions—monoprints—usually in a series with monotype and chine collé supporting the intaglio mark.

As I adopted more painterly approaches, the imagery from intaglio plates became elements in larger compositions. Simultaneously, I began to use multiple plates and combinations of techniques for the particular nuances and contrasts they bring to the final image.

Photopolymer plates replaced etching as my source of matrices, and digital applications are now quite prominent in my work. Working with monotype, chine collé, drawing, painting, collage, and assemblage, I have endless combinations of ways to resolve my compositions. Printmaking is no longer an end in itself. With many tools at my disposal I will choose what is most efficient and effective to produce desired results.

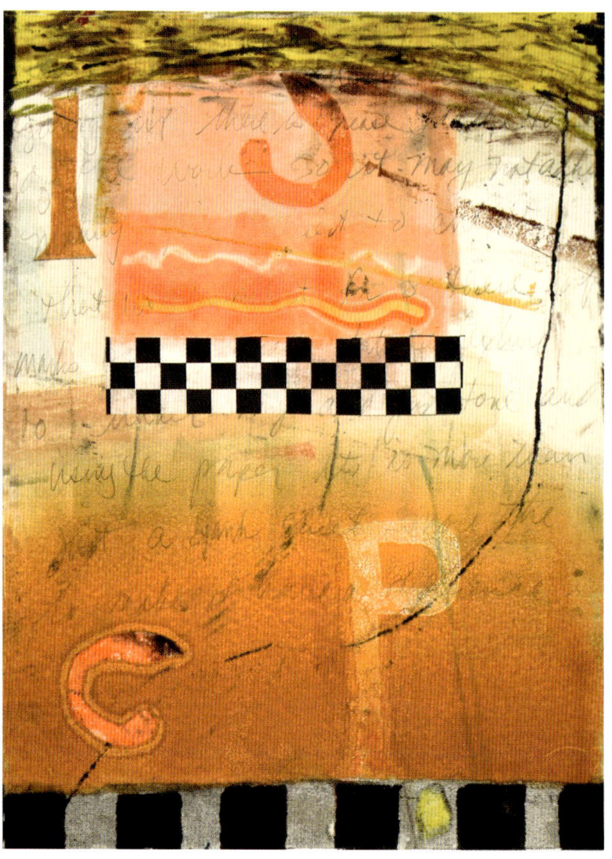

Fun with A Checkerboard. Monoprint with Akua soy-based inks, chine collé, and drawing on paper. 16" × 12". 2012.

PUBLISHED AND PRINTED BY THE ARTIST AT GALISTEO STREET STUDIO.

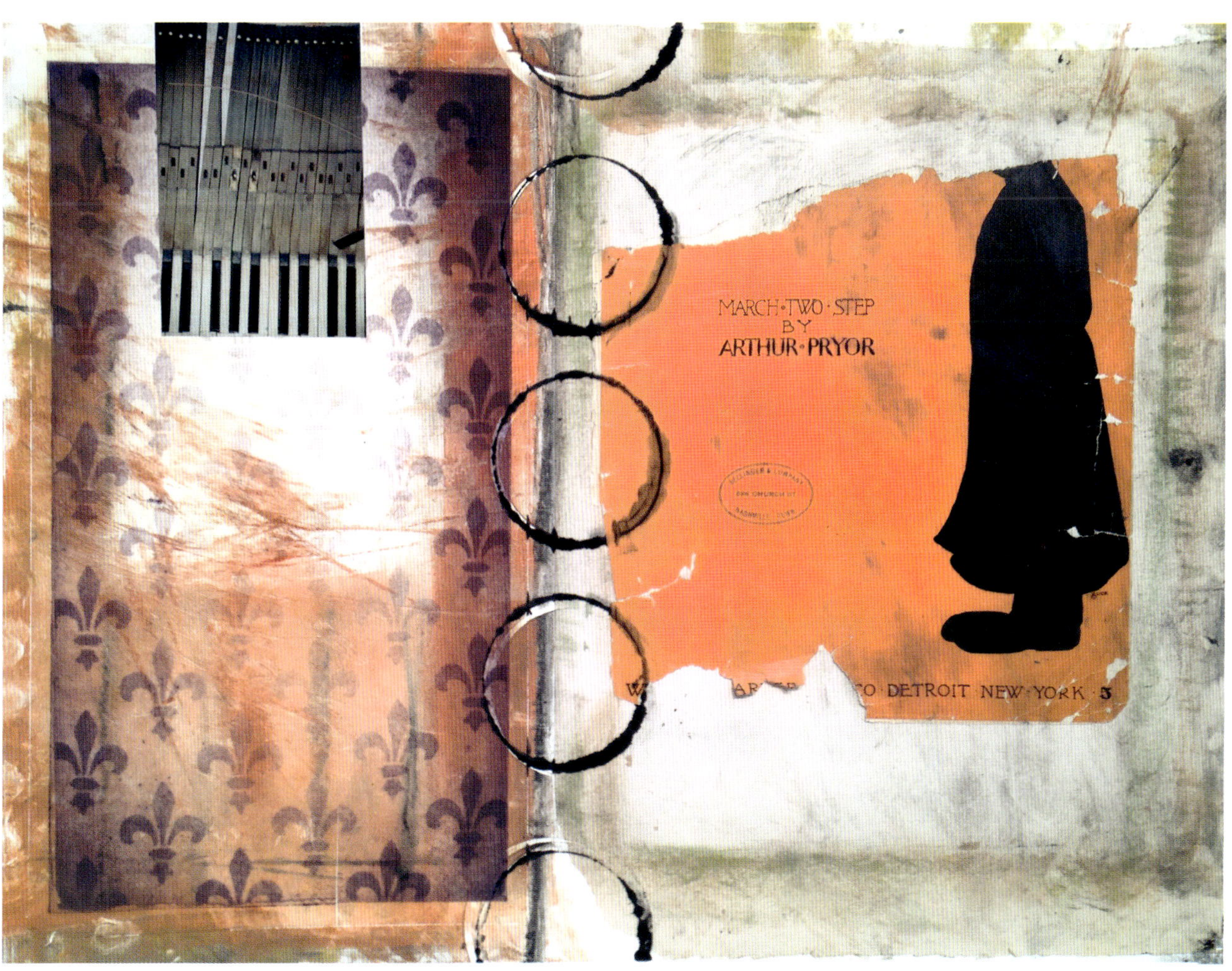

March Two Step. Monoprint with Akua soy-based inks, intaglio, chine collé, and photo collage on paper. 18" × 24". 2015.

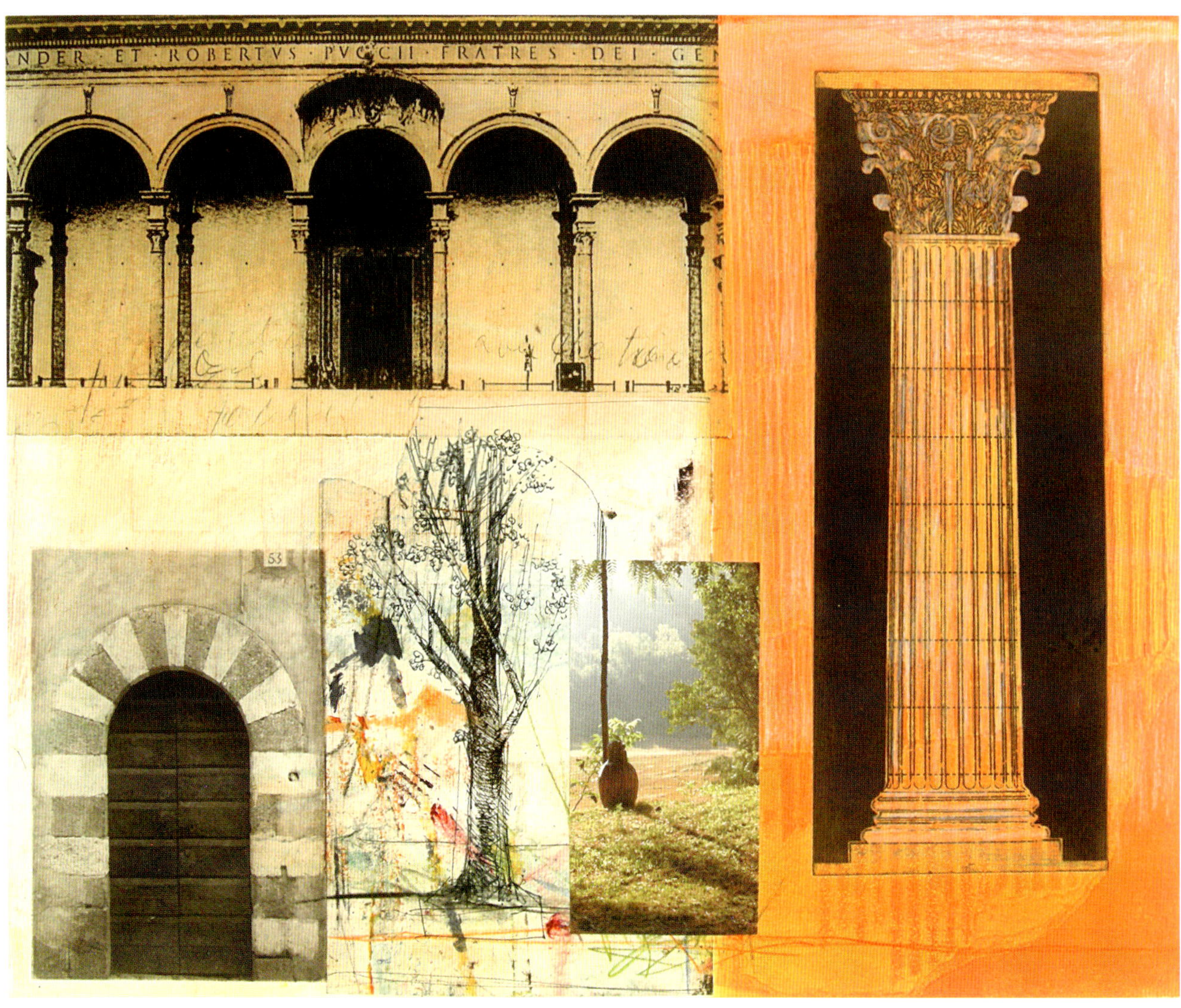

Sights and Scenes. Monoprint with Akua soy-based inks, intaglio, digital inkjet, drawing, chine collé, and collage on paper. 16" × 20". 2007.

>

Pretends to Be Winged Victory. Monoprint with Akua soy-based inks, intaglio, and chine collé on paper. 16" × 24". 2014.

Mechanical Performance. Monoprint with Akua soy-based inks, intaglio, and chine collé on paper. 16" × 22". 2011.

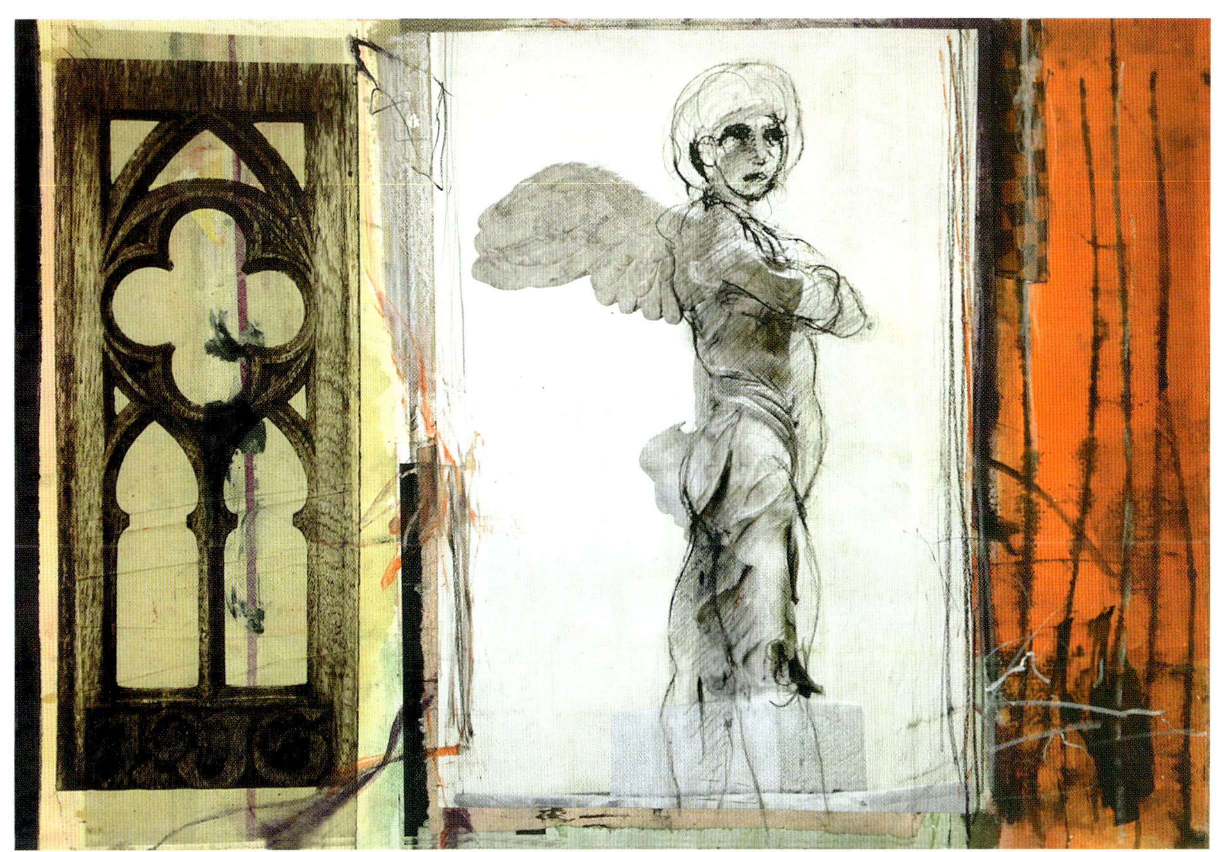

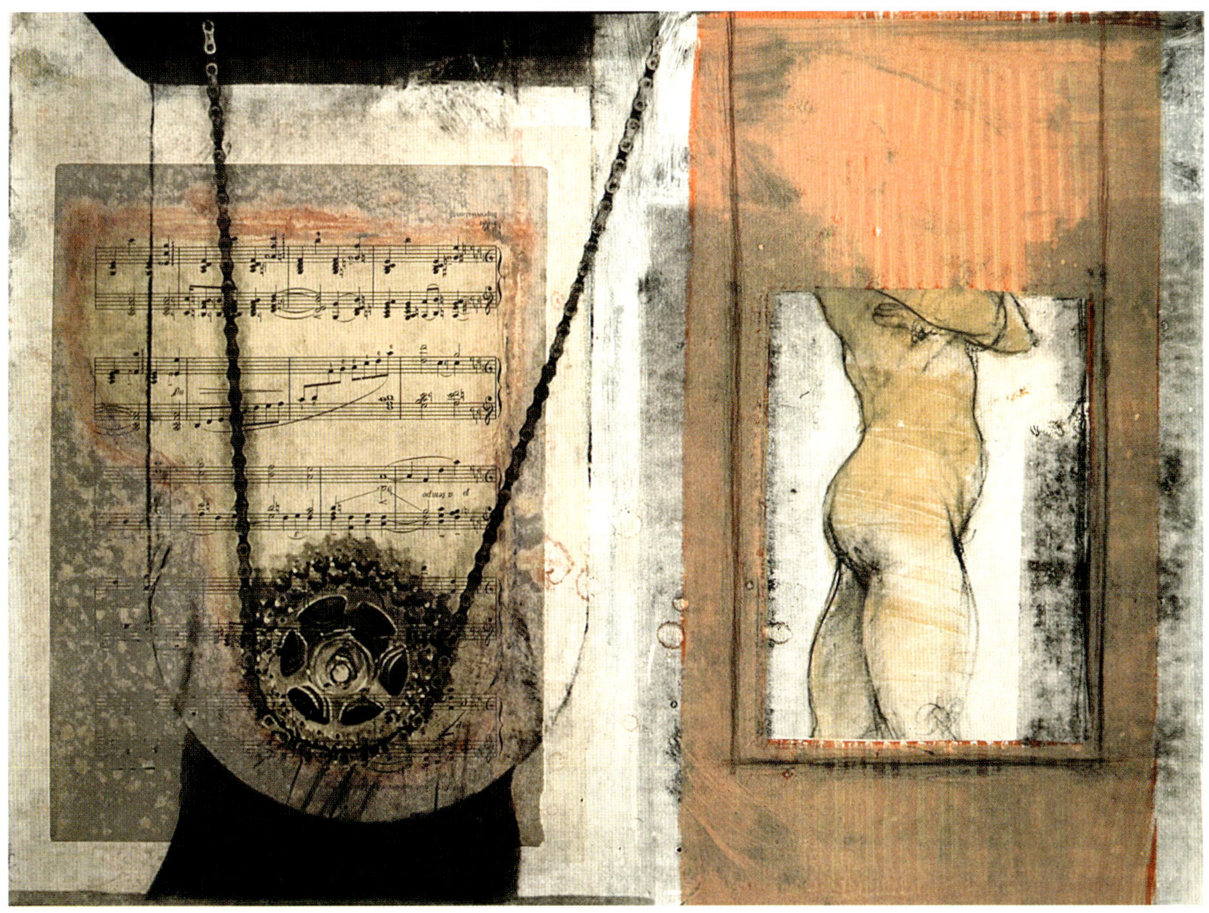

WENDY PRELLWITZ

Cambridge, Massachusetts & Peconic, New York

As a source, the interplay between water's fluidity and the solidity of built forms functions as metaphor for the intangible juxtaposed with the concrete "here and now." This duality is akin to holding onto things to feel grounded, while being immersed and connected to the unknowability of it all. That said, some of my monotypes are purely a celebration of water's movement and reflected light.

The geometric shapes reference structures and imply a viewpoint of "here versus there" as well as a diminishing perspective to direct the view out over the water to the "beyond-ness" of the sea, out of oneself and into the unknown.

To develop the plates, I use direct mark making, overrolling with varying viscosities of ink, stencils, textural transfers, and screen-printed elements to generate patterns that evoke water. Wood patterns transferred from raised-grain plywood, weathered docks, and woodcuts create a sense of water movement to reference growth patterns and the interconnectedness of things. The often unforeseen results of monoprint and the option of working into ghosts keep me loose and experimental.

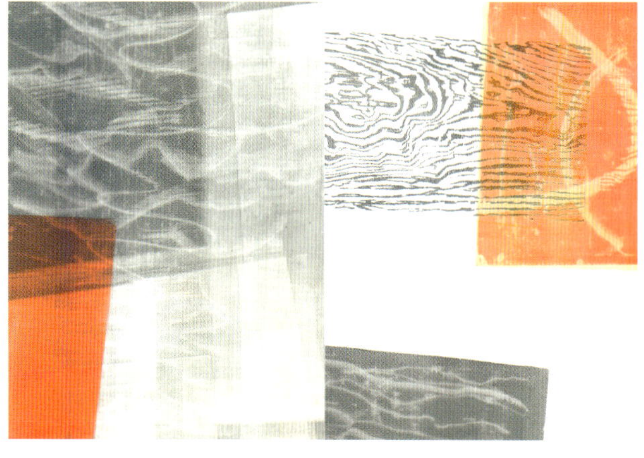

Divergence Diptich. Monoprint with Akua soy-based ink and woodcut on Revere Silk paper. 30" × 44". 2016.

PUBLISHED AND PRINTED BY THE ARTIST AT MIXIT PRINT STUDIO.

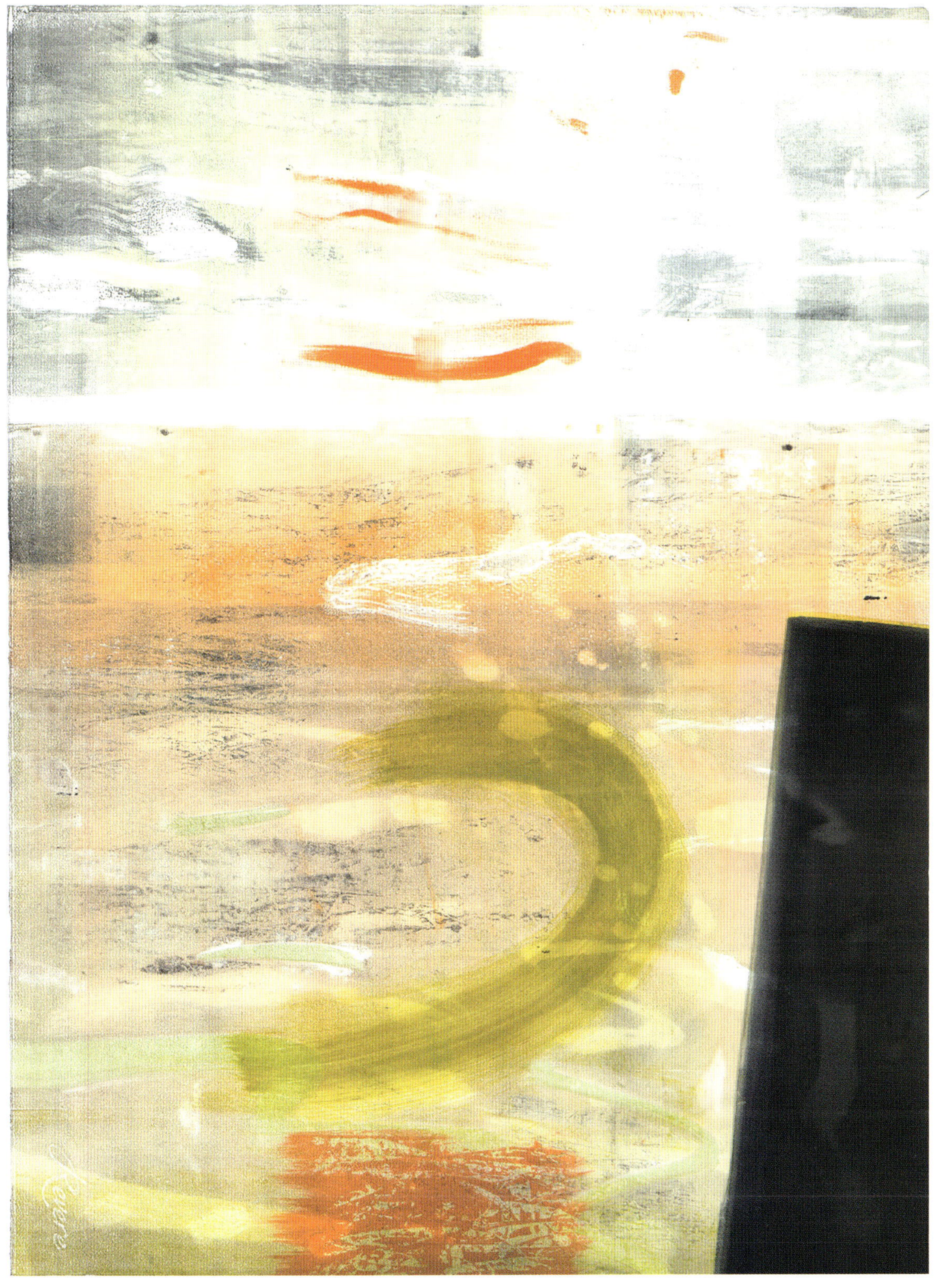

Moon Rise. Monoprint with Akua soy-based ink and woodcut on Revere Silk paper. 30" × 22". 2015.

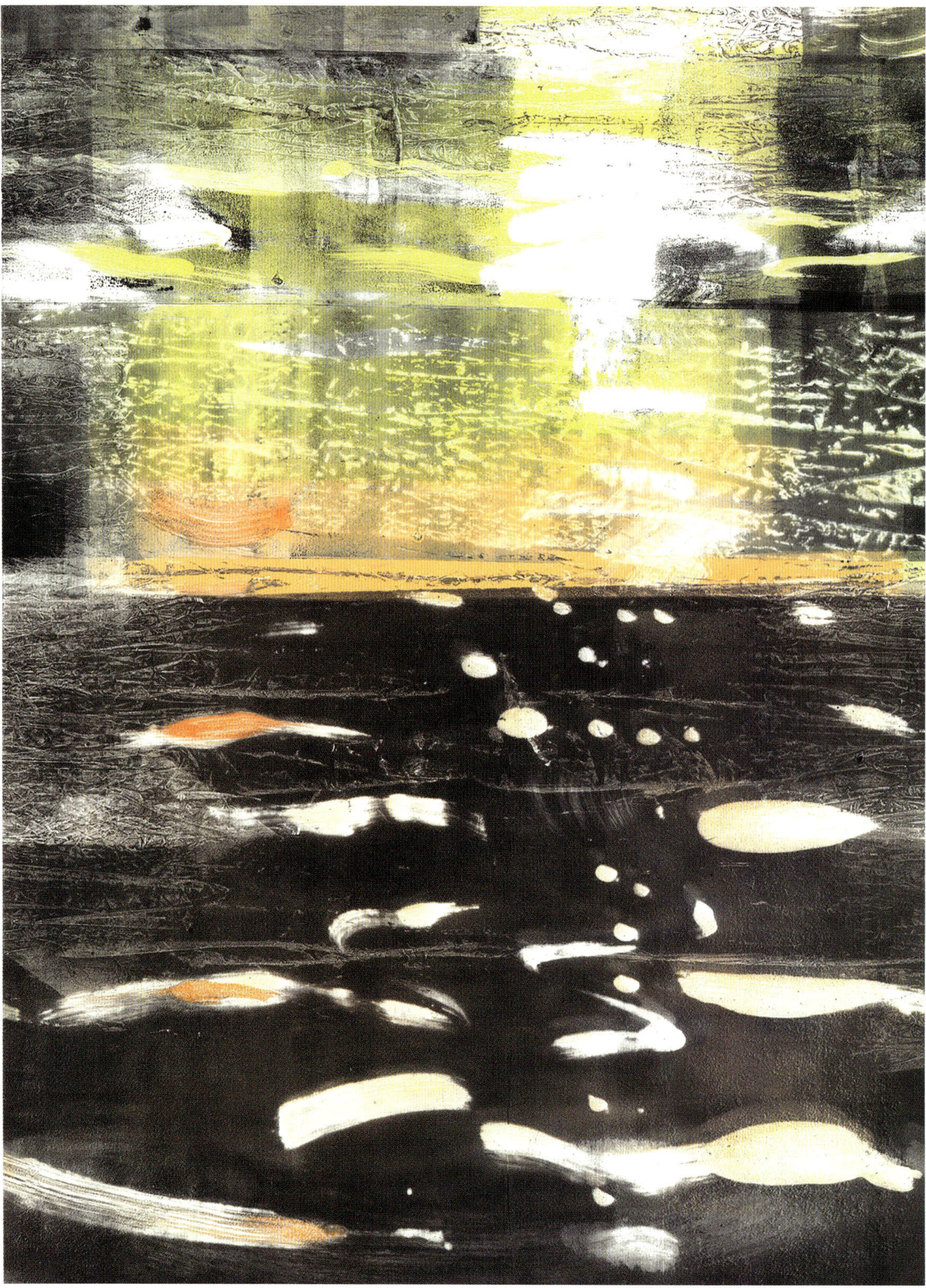

10 First Light No. 1. Monoprint with Akua soy-based ink and woodcut on Revere Silk paper. 30" × 22". 2015.

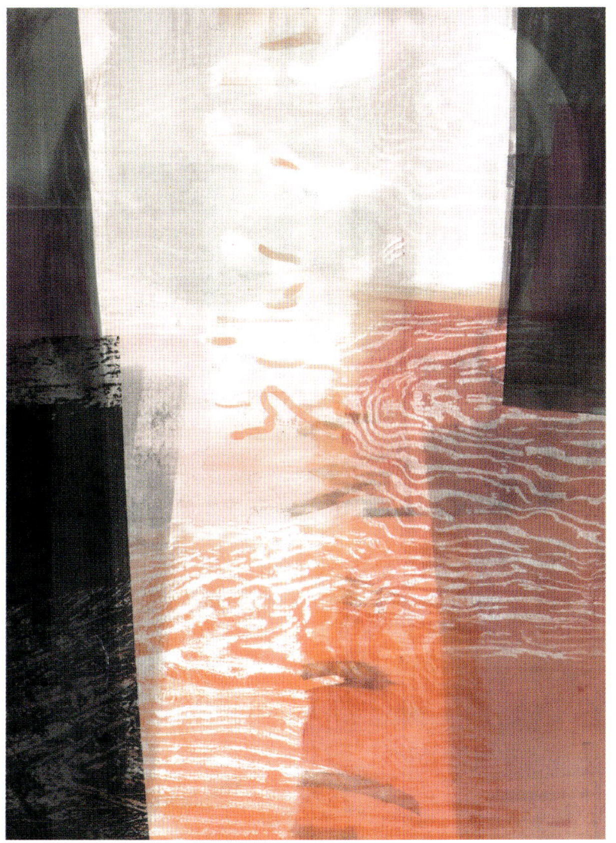

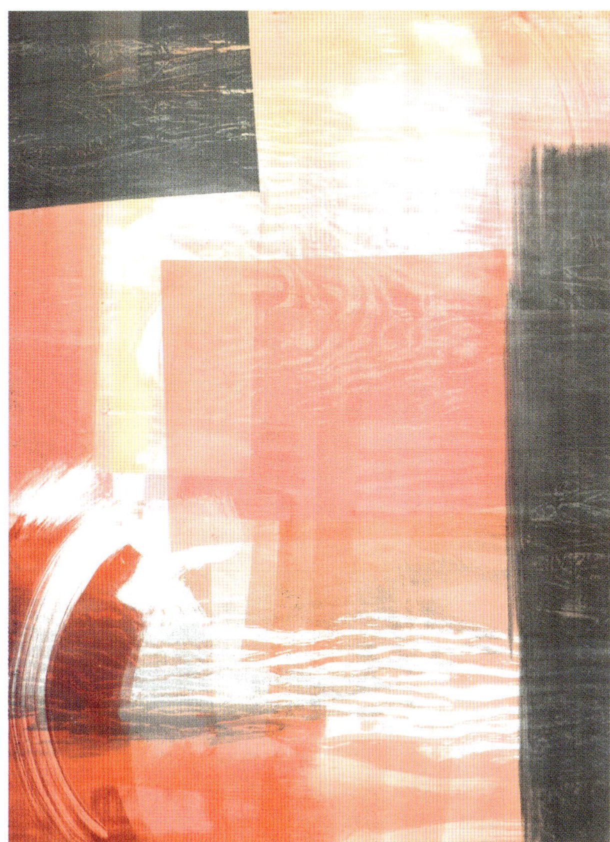

Here and There #3. Monoprint with Akua soy-based ink and woodcut on Revere Silk paper. 30" × 22". 2015.

Here and There #7. Monoprint with Akua soy-based ink and woodcut on Revere Silk paper. 30" × 22". 2015.

SARA GREENBERGER RAFFERTY

Brooklyn, New York

Inspired by the graphic photographs of Herbert Matter, Man Ray, and Jaroslav Rössler, as well as my family's history in the garment industry, I tested many articles of clothing before committing to a drop-waist dress I regularly wore fifteen years ago. Using soft ground, I imprinted the dress on a grid of ten plates, directly translating a soft, three-dimensional object into a two-dimensional surrogate. The physical quality of the resulting embossed grid, which composes and then divides the dress form, lends the print a sculptural quality.

With assistance from the printmakers at Wingate Studio, I experimented and grappled with the traditional intaglio process and its crossovers with my usual modes of making that involve industrial and digital processes. The violence of the press and how it forces ink into paper attracted me. This became central to the making of the image, and the means by which the elements of the piece—monoprint, chine collé, etching, and transfer prints—were united. Inkjet transfers of to-scale zippers create visual nuisances on the intaglio print, a constellation of deconstructed polka dots that hover over the dress. The unified pairings create conversations about consumerism, domesticity, and the body.

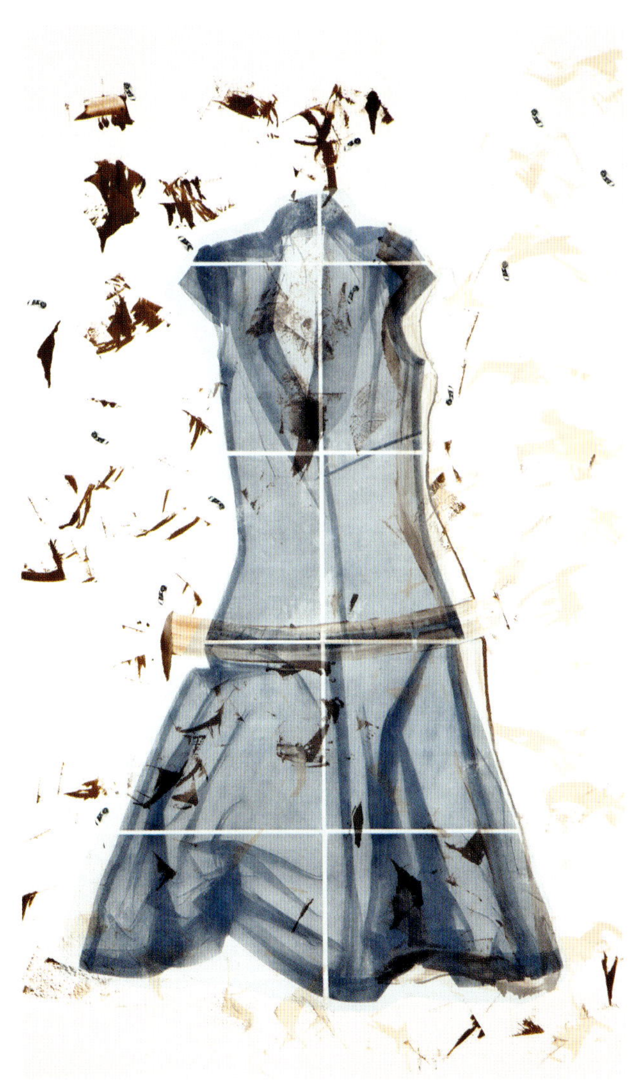

ALL PHOTOS ARE COURTESY OF ALYSSA ROBB. PUBLISHED AND PRINTED BY THE ARTIST AT MIXIT PRINT STUDIO.

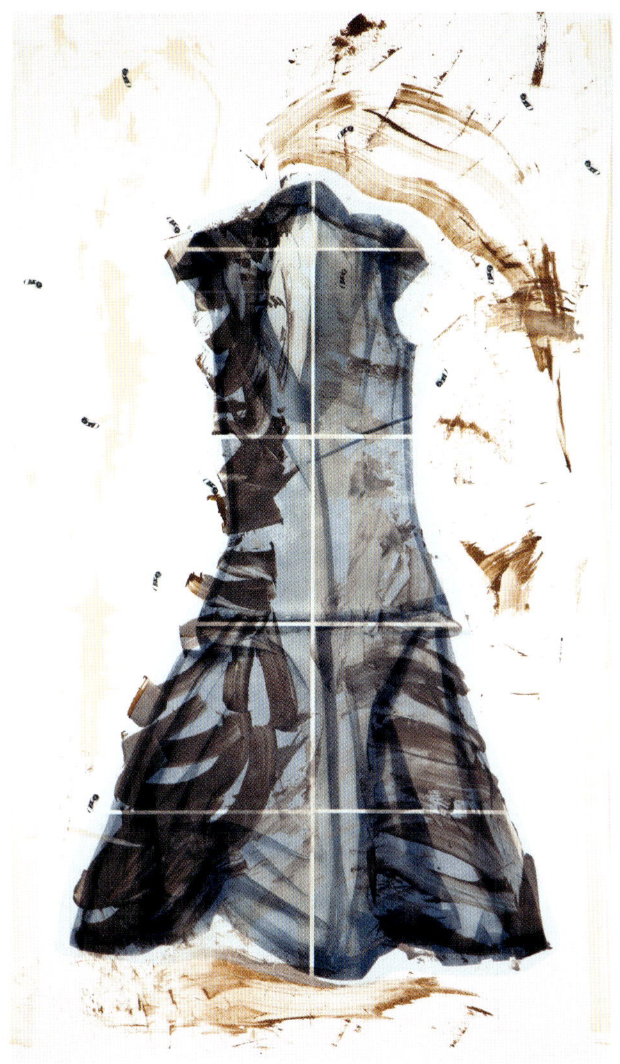

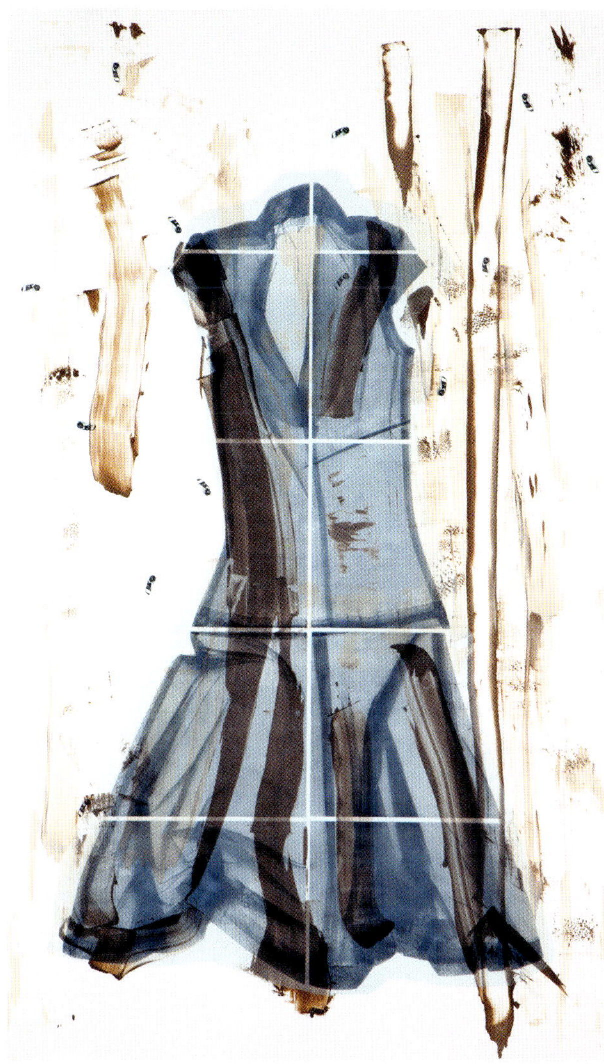

<

Paynes I. Monoprint with oil-based inks, soft ground intaglio, chine collé, and inkjet transfer prints. 61.5" × 36". 2016.

Paynes III. Monoprint with oil-based inks, soft ground intaglio, chine collé, and inkjet transfer prints. 61.5" × 36". 2016.

Paynes V. Monoprint with oil-based inks, soft ground intaglio, chine collé, and inkjet transfer prints. 61.5" × 36". 2016.

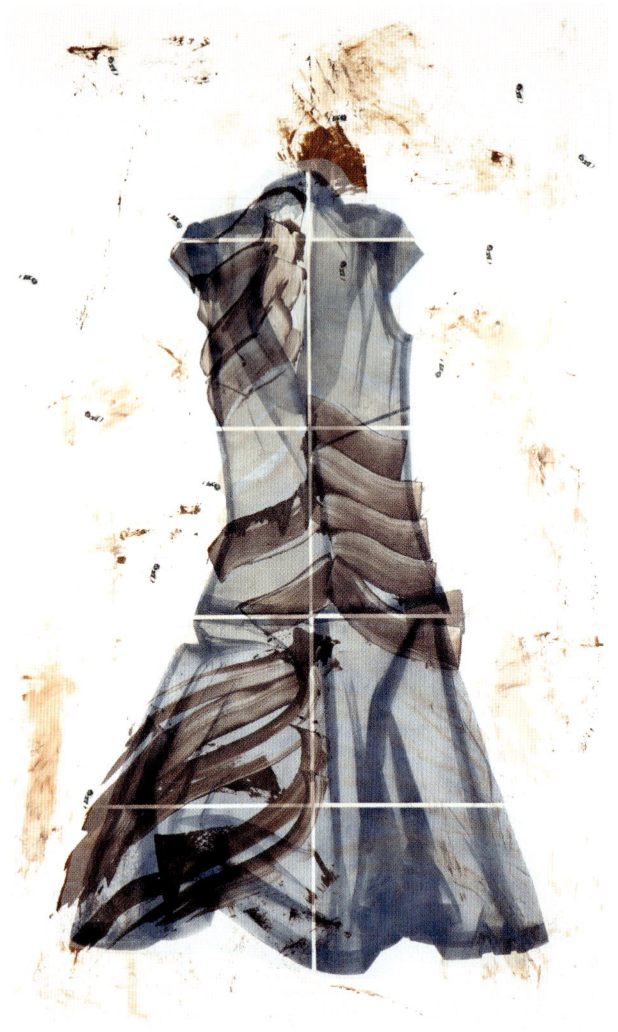

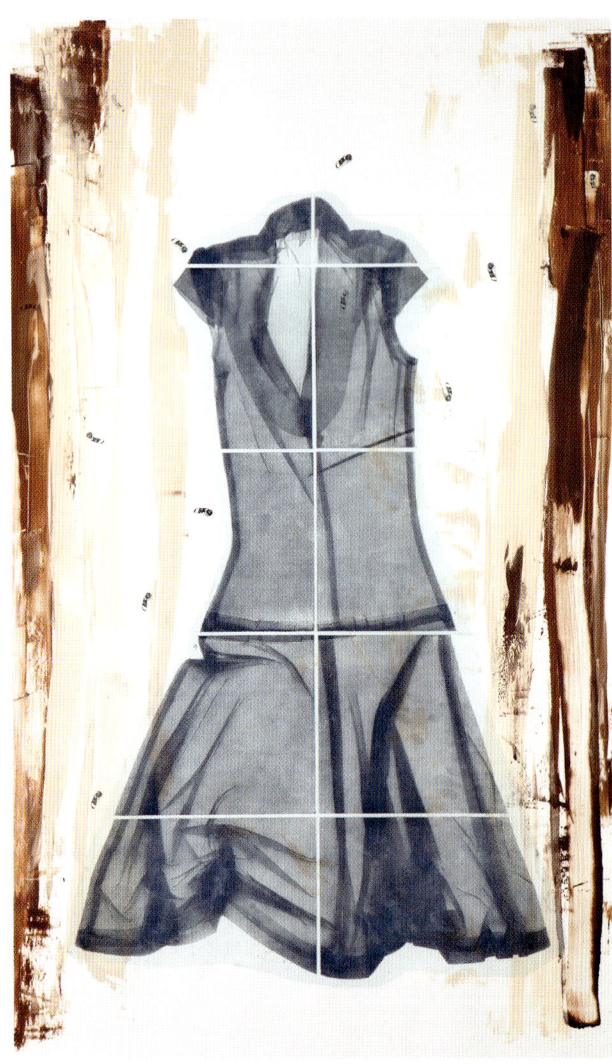

Paynes VI. Monoprint with oil-based inks, soft ground intaglio, chine collé, and inkjet transfer prints. 61.5" × 36". 2016.

Paynes VII. Monoprint with oil-based inks, soft ground intaglio, chine collé, and inkjet transfer prints. 61.5" × 36". 2016.

JENNY ROBINSON

San Francisco, California

Coming from a family of engineers, I have always been interested in the physical appearance and structural elements of our urban surroundings. I respond to location by documenting how time and the environment have affected the physical landscape.

I start my printing process by applying layers of transparent ink on Plexiglas plates, creating rich, saturated colors as a backdrop for the drypoint, which is printed last. This way I create monoprints in small editions that are rich with color and heavy with ink, suffusing them with a tactile, physical quality that reflects their subject matter.

Harrison Street Billboard. Monoprint with oil-based ink, monotype, and drypoint intaglio on BFK Rives paper. 32" × 49". 2009.

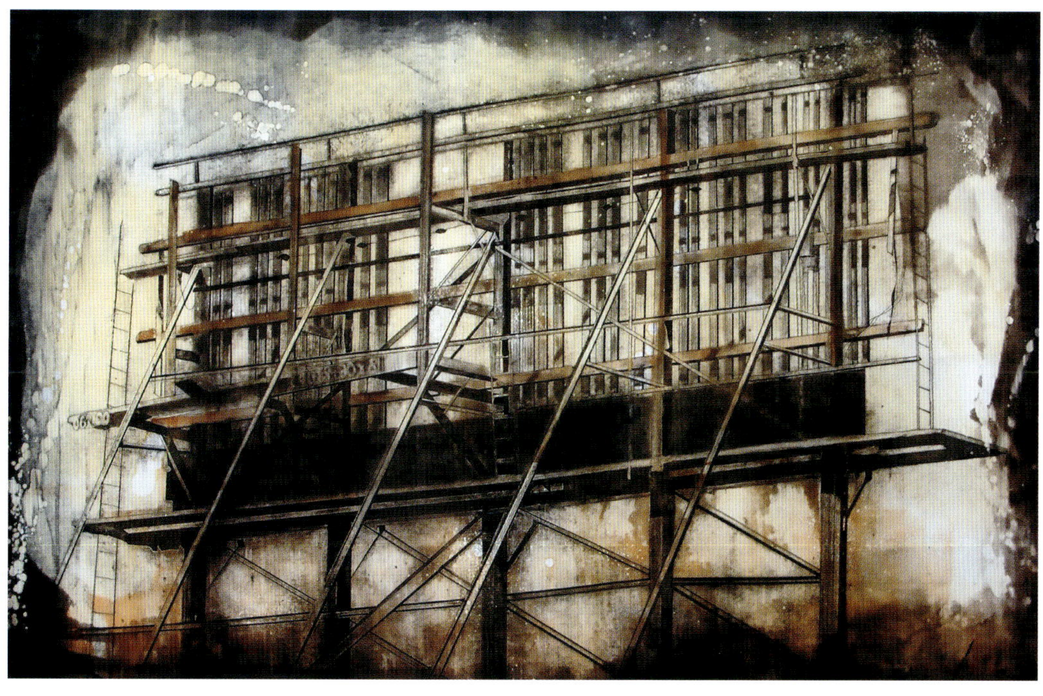

PUBLISHED AND PRINTED BY THE ARTIST AT KALA INSTITUTE.

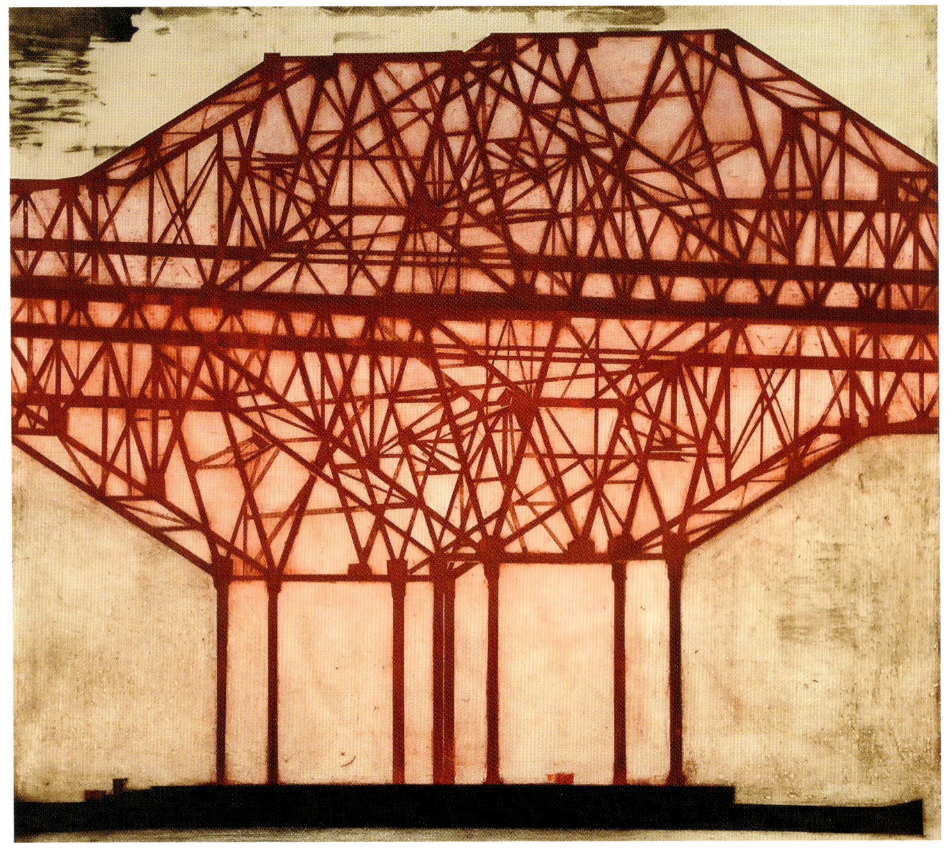

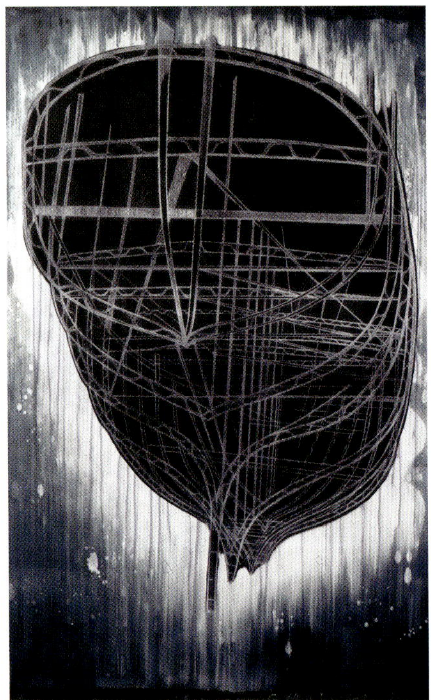

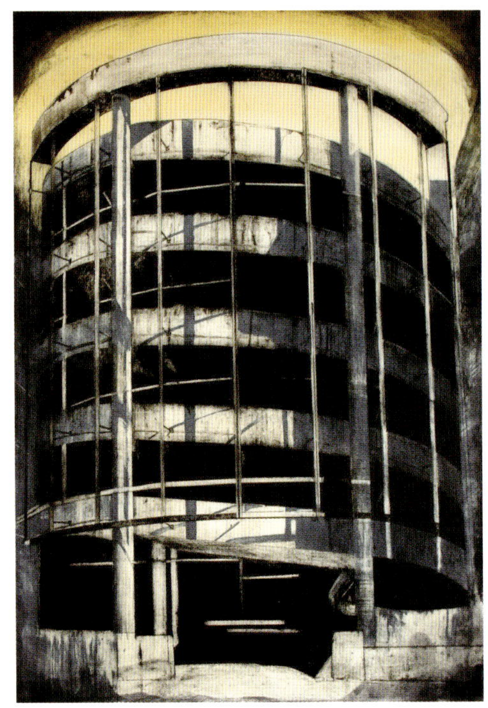

^

Infrastructure #1. Monoprint with oil-based ink, monotype, drypoint intaglio, and collage on Okawara Japanese paper, backed with Sekishu. 52" × 47". 2013–2016.

Stern Facing Forward. Monoprint with oil-based ink, monotype, and drypoint intaglio on BFK Rives paper. 56" × 35". 2017.

Garage Light. Monoprint with oil-based ink, monotype, and drypoint intaglio on BFK Rives paper. 50.75" × 36". 2013.

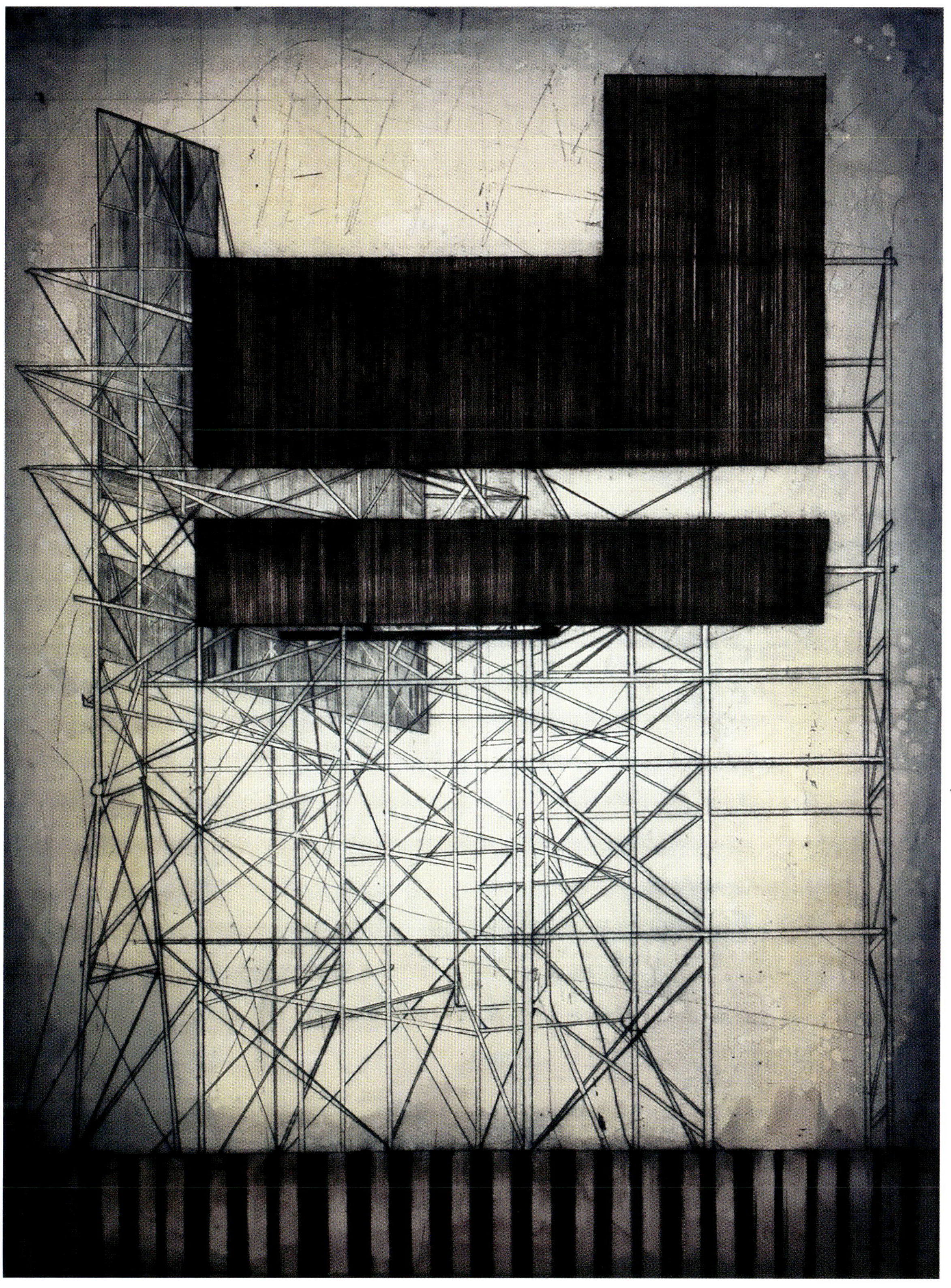

Above L.A. Monoprint with oil-based ink, monotype, and drypoint intaglio on BFK Rives paper. 51" × 34". 2017.

RON RUMFORD

Philadelphia, Pennsylvania

During a 2013 residency at the Ballinglen Arts Foundation in County Mayo, Ireland, I began a course of reinvention, seeking a more open direction and new forms for my process-driven work. Returning to Ballinglen in 2015 and 2016, I also returned to origins as a way of knowing myself better. This was key to recognizing essential motivations guiding me through the renewal evident in the work I've done since. These monoprints express in the best possible way my process of discovery, invention, and transformation.

Sheets of strong yet malleable Japan papers are printed with layers of inks transferred via color rolls, chine collé, drypoint, collagraph, and relief. Despite careful planning, what comes through the press is always a surprise and an indicator of what additions or changes might come next. Each print is built as a sequence of choices about color and technique as one step leads to the next. Faith and intuition guide the journey to a stopping point, a place where something unexpected comes into being, bearing a richness and clarity that is more than the materials of their making.

Cricket Pitch. Monoprint diptych with oil-based ink, monotype, drypoint intaglio, and collagraph with chine collé. 33.25" × 44.75". 2017.

Tackstem. Monoprint diptych with oil-based ink, monotype, drypoint intaglio, and collagraph with chine collé. 23.75" × 35". 2017.

PUBLISHED AND PRINTED BY THE ARTIST.

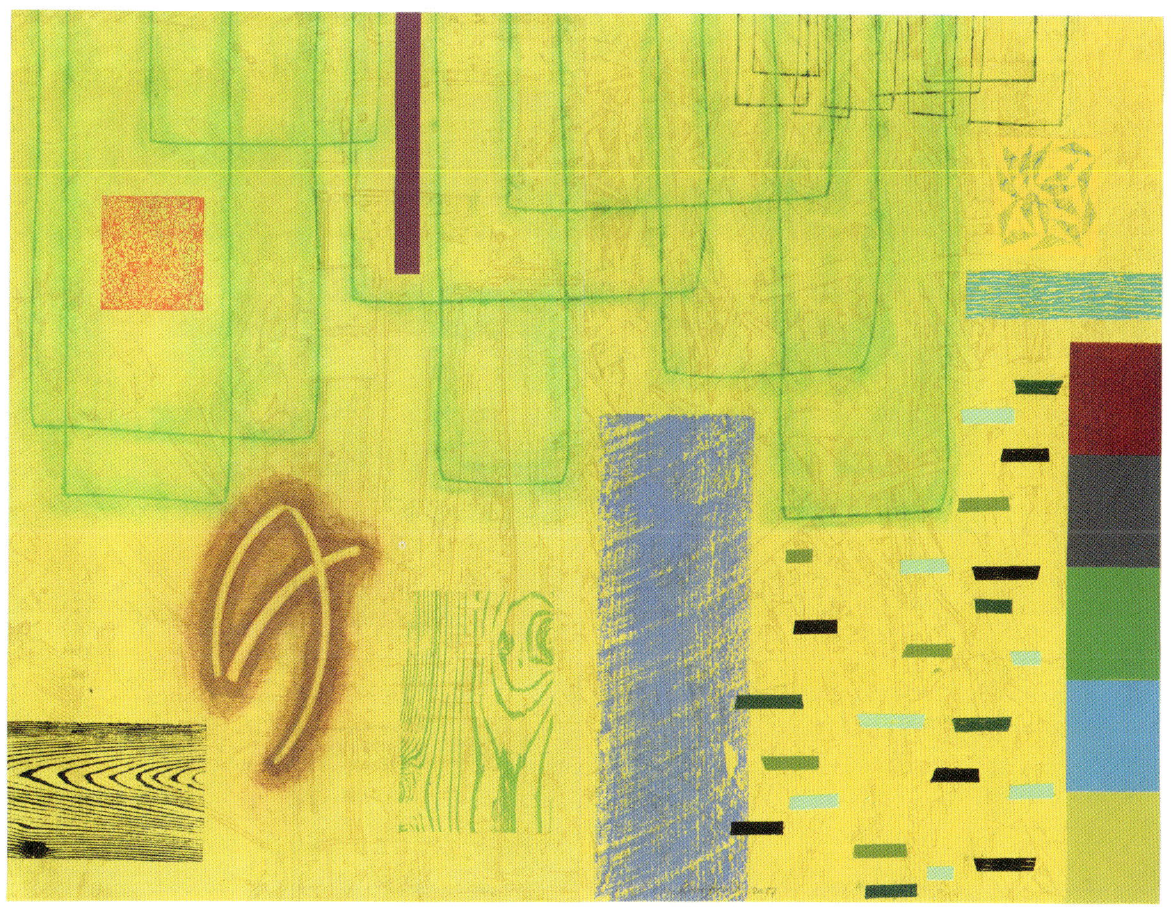

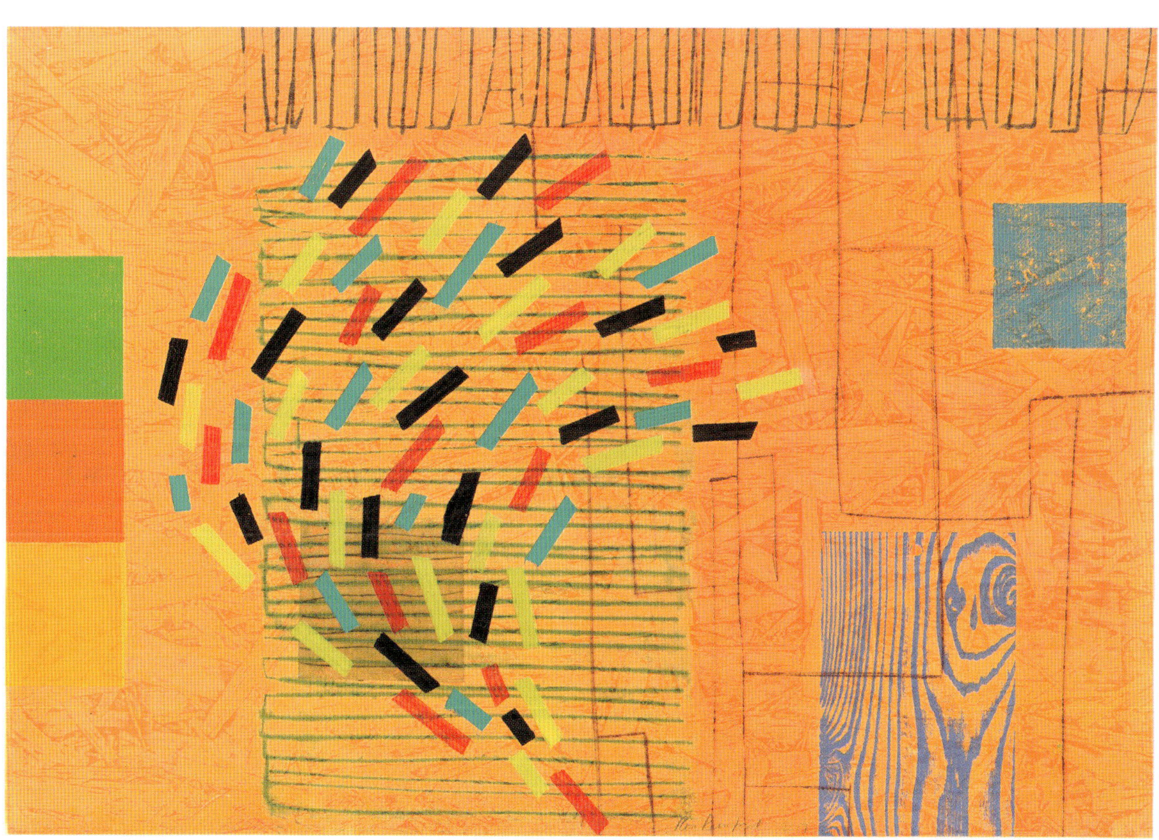

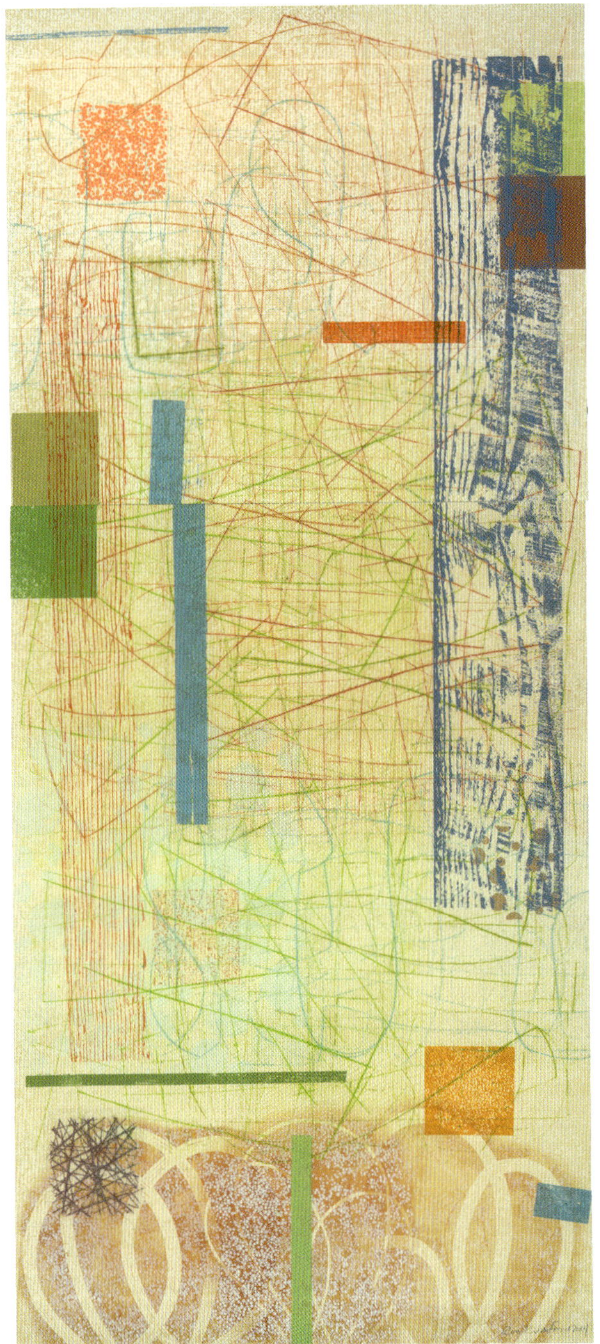

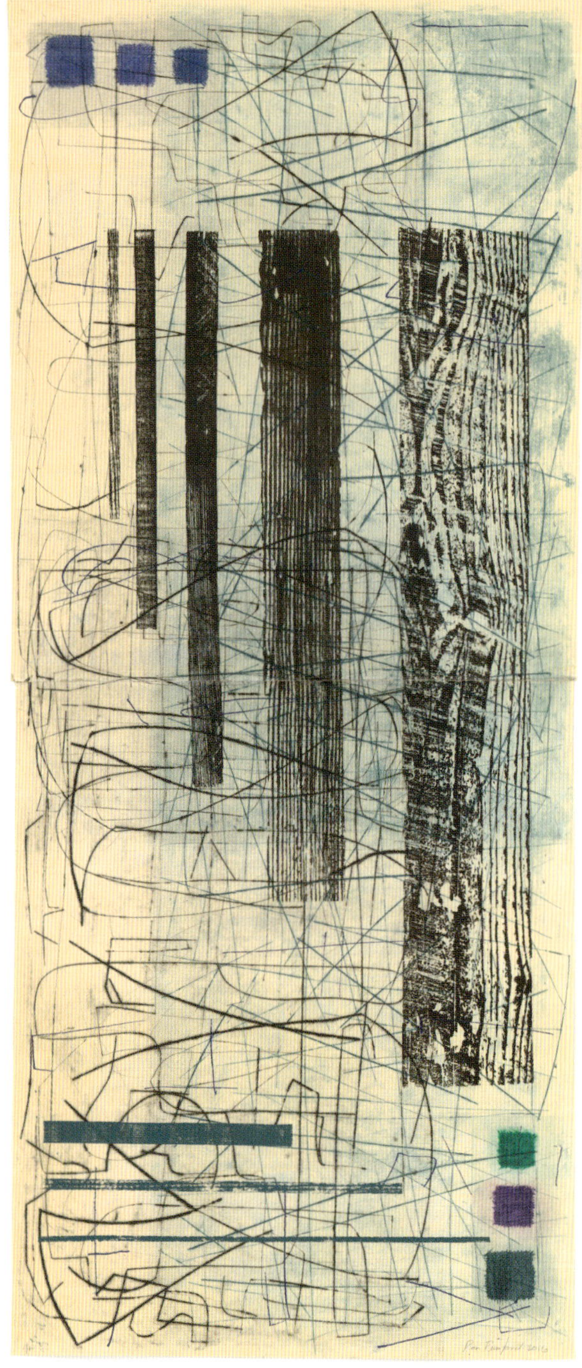

Tipping Point. Monoprint diptych with oil-based ink, monotype, drypoint intaglio, and collagraph with chine collé. 60" × 26". 2014.

Border. Monoprint diptych with oil-based ink, monotype, drypoint intaglio, and collagraph with chine collé. 60" × 26". 2016.

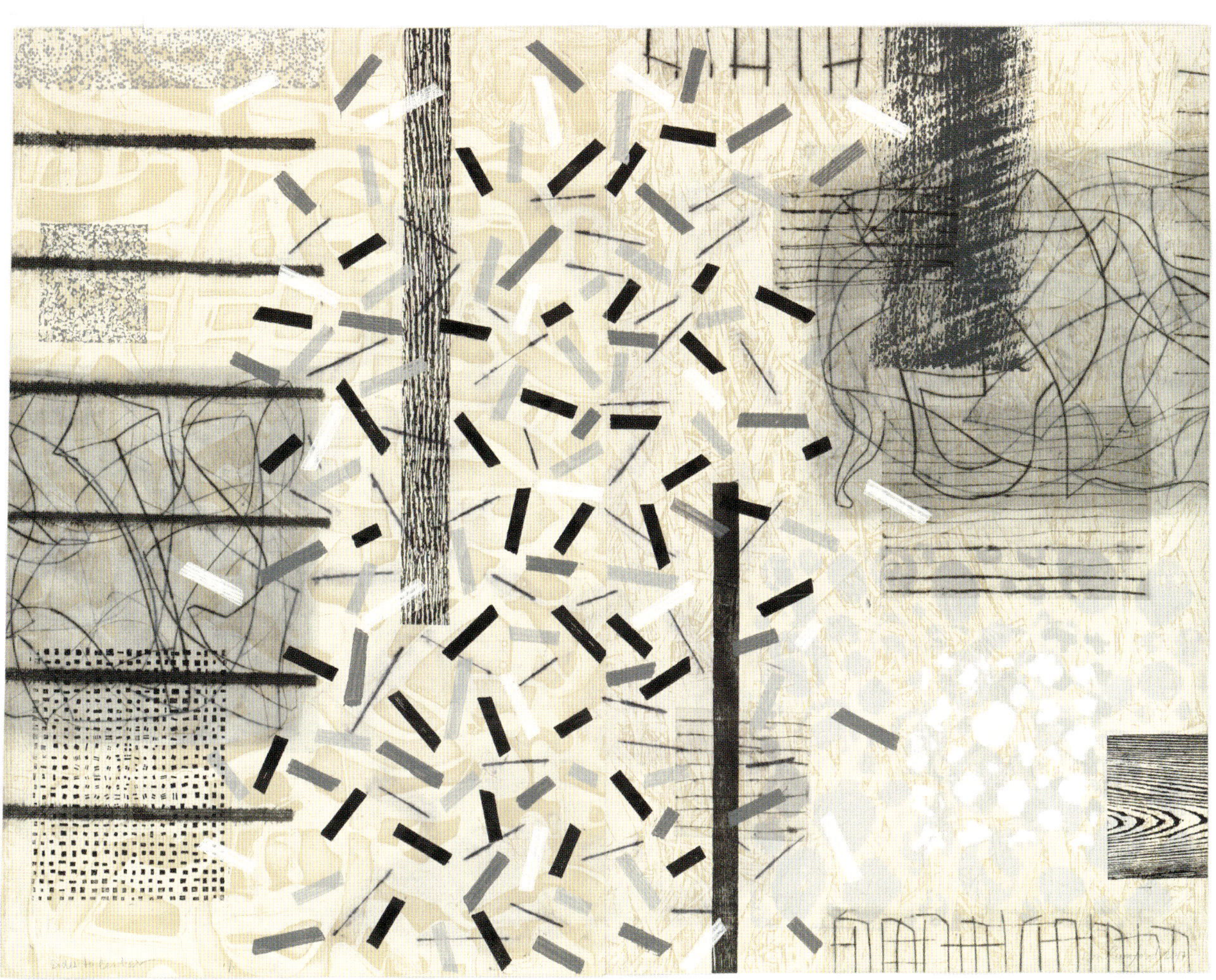

Sides to Center. Monoprint diptych with oil-based ink, monotype, drypoint intaglio, and collagraph with chine collé. 34" × 44". 2017.

JOHN SCHIFF

New York, New York

My work *as* an architect has influenced my work as a printmaker. As an architect, I was interested in order and structure. In my printmaking, I begin with order and structure, using an alphabet I invented. The alphabet is made of "letters" constructed based on the Golden Section and the Fibonacci series. Over time, I expanded a limited number of letters by adding mirror images, negative shapes, and changes of letter scale. The letters are cut out of Mylar or cardboard or made into rubber stamps. I have accumulated a growing family of shapes (thousands) with the same DNA growing exponentially.

Generally, I sketch the print I intend to make, using the sketch as a guide or as a reference point. The resulting print, however, frequently has a surprise in it, some unpredictable effect that happens during the printing process. I use these accidents, exploring the opportunities they present and incorporating them with intention in future work. Each print is source material, and I move forward unencumbered, hoping to make something inventive and new. My work is nonrepresentational, releasing the work from any associations.

My interest is in the tension between the accidents, which are spontaneous and unpredictable, and the inherent structure of the letters. The goal is to produce images that are deliberate, controlled, refined, and orderly, operating on the same page where decisions are subjective, intuitive, impulsive, and free.

ALL PHOTOS ARE COURTESY OF JOEL BIAZZO. PUBLISHED AND PRINTED BY THE ARTIST.

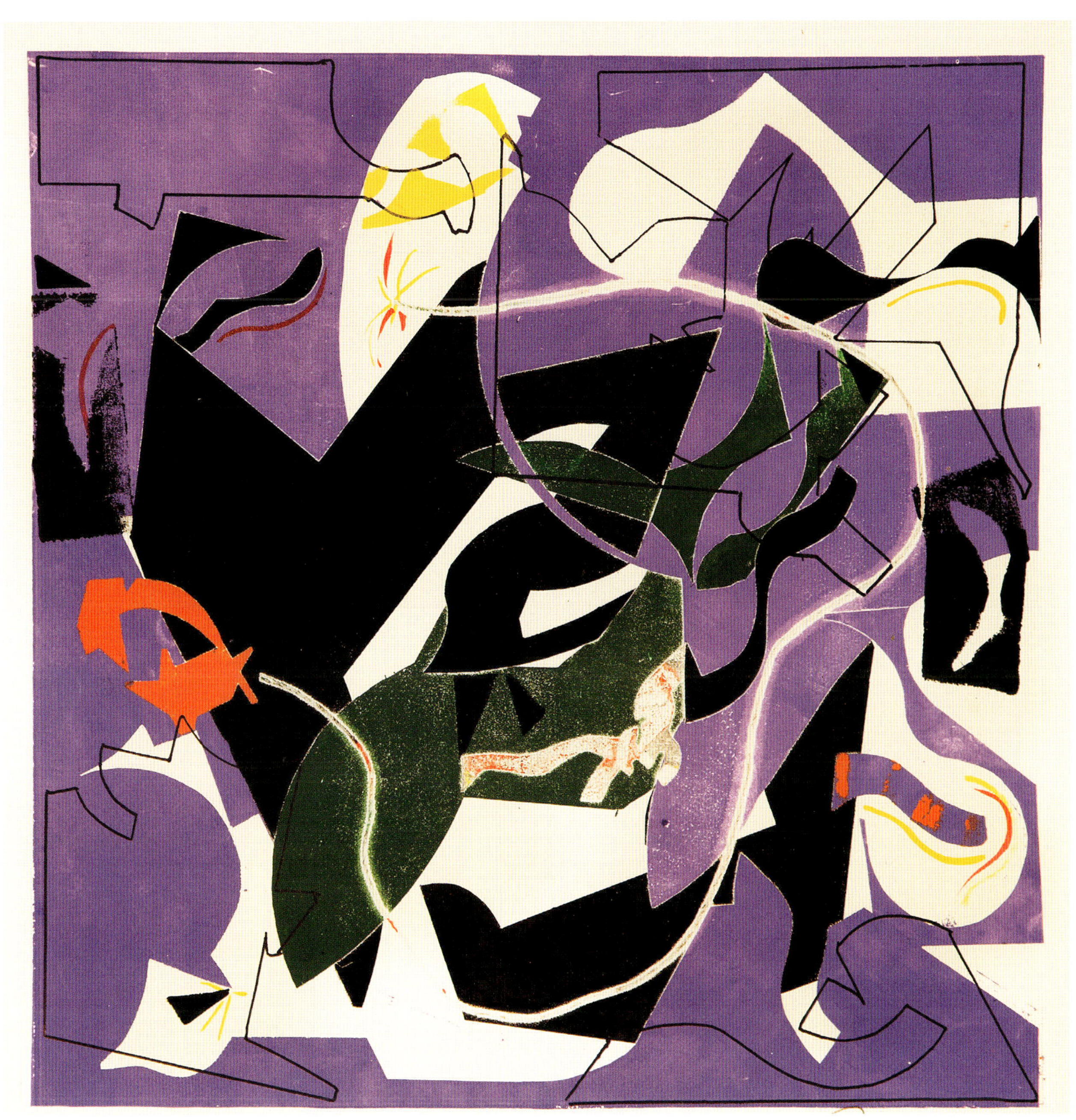

Luminary Reflection. Monoprint with Speedball water-based ink, monotype, and stencils on BFK Rives paper. 19.5" × 23.5". 2016.

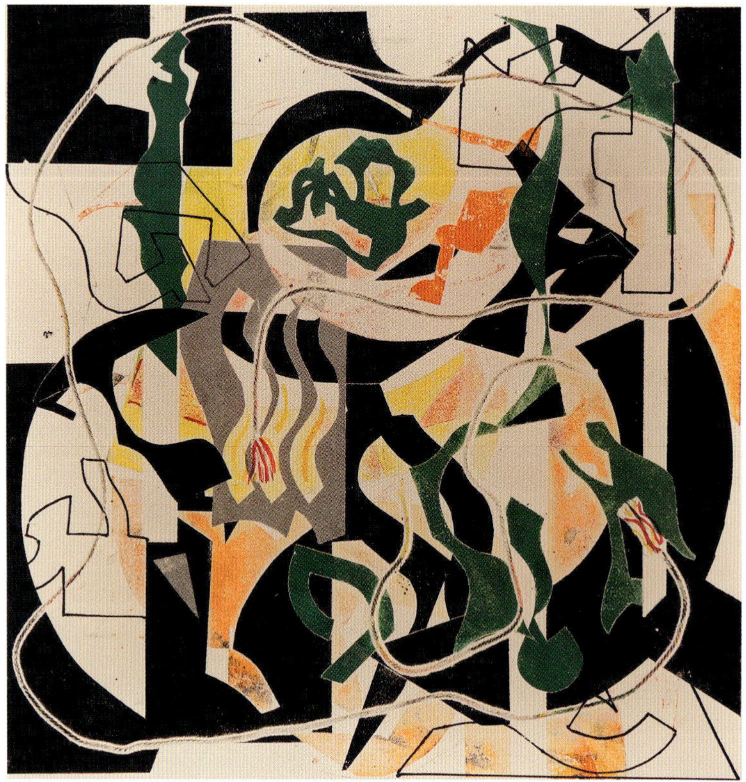

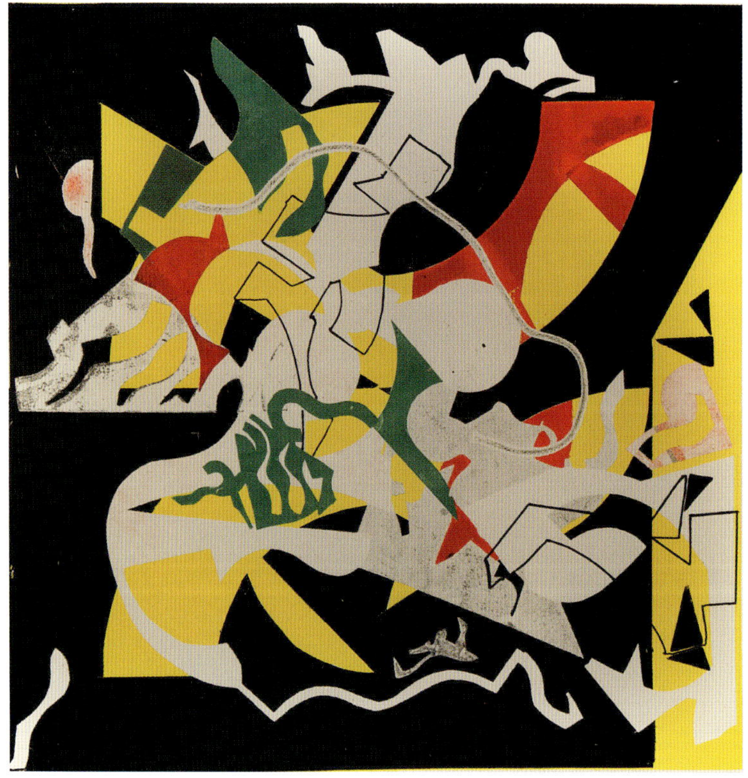

^
Upward Curving Path. Monoprint with Speedball water-based ink, monotype, and stencils on BFK Rives paper. 19.5" × 23.5". 2017.

v
Splendour of Night. Monoprint with Speedball water-based ink, monotype, and stencils on BFK Rives paper. 19.5" × 23.5". 2016.

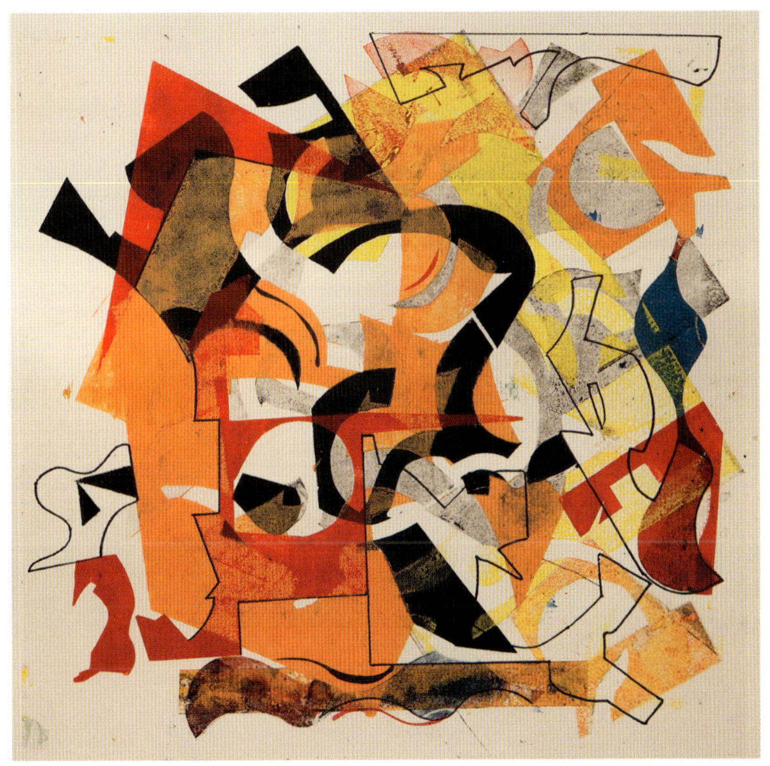

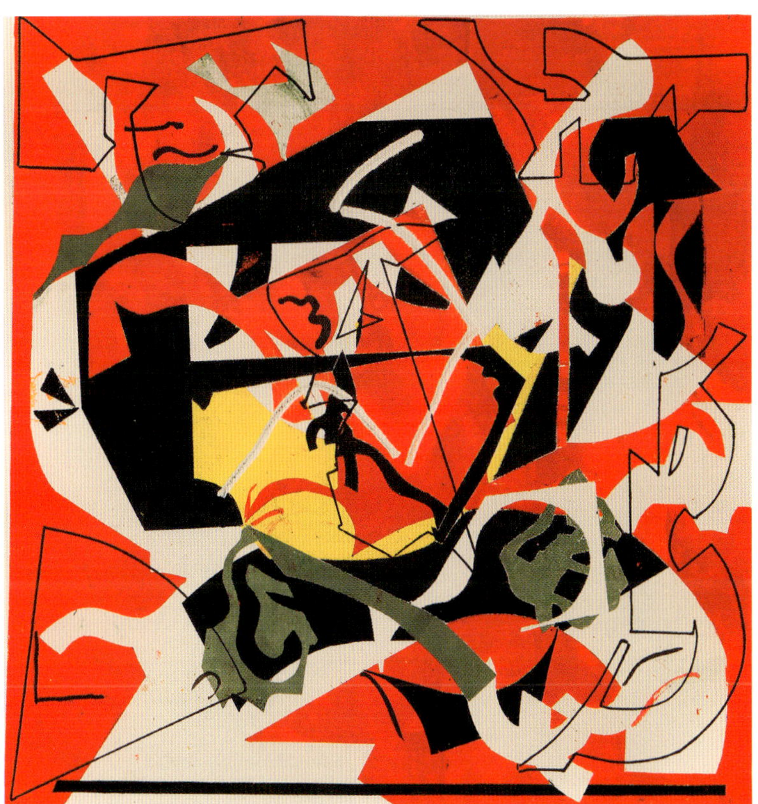

^
Infinitesimal Brevity. Monoprint with Speedball water-based ink, monotype, and stencils on BFK Rives paper. 19.5" × 19.5". 2017.

v
Tranquil Inscrutability. Monoprint with Speedball water-based ink, monotype, and stencils on BFK Rives paper. 19.5" × 23.5". 2016.

HEDDI VAUGHAN SIEBEL

Cambridge, Massachusetts

The processes of monotype and monoprint dynamically shape my visual ideas about place and story. The practice invites me to go deeper into my imagination: to seek sensations rather than depictions of my subjects; to build a metaphoric landscape by cutting and layering together variations of etched plates of copper and brushed wood with monotype stencils.

My fascination with the Arctic originates in the story of my grandfather's failed attempt at the North Pole in 1903–1905 with the Ziegler Expedition, and his years marooned on the Franz Josef Land islands in the Russian Arctic.

How would it feel to be living in such a place during the midnight sun? I asked myself when I first began the life-size Midnattsolen series. In response, I formed a place from geologic markers that explorers had cited in their records as locations to cache supplies or build camps for survival. The cut intaglio plates of a bluff, a worn volcanic core, and a glacial boulder emerge like actors upon the undulating, rocky beaches and moody woodblock and stenciled skies of the Arctic. In each print a celestial luminary shines—one for each of the twenty-four hours of the day. Displayed together, the series forms a large-scale, immersive installation.

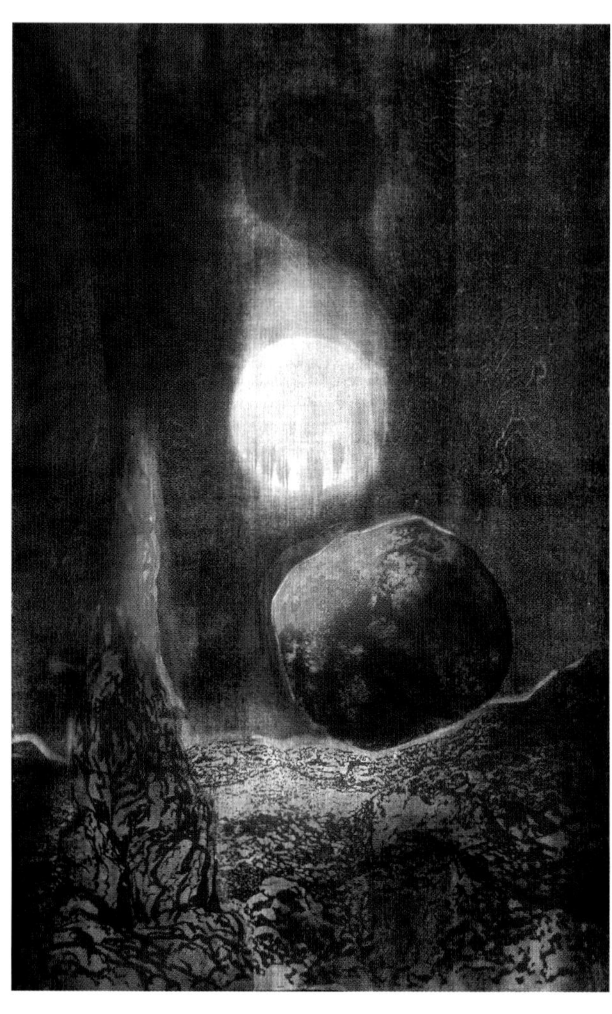

Midnattsolen. No. 1 from series of 24, monoprint with oil-based ink, intaglio, and brushed wood with monotype stencil on Okawara paper. 60" × 39". 2003.

ALL PHOTOS ARE COURTESY OF DAVID CARAS. PUBLISHED AND PRINTED BY THE ARTIST AT MIXIT PRINT STUDIO.

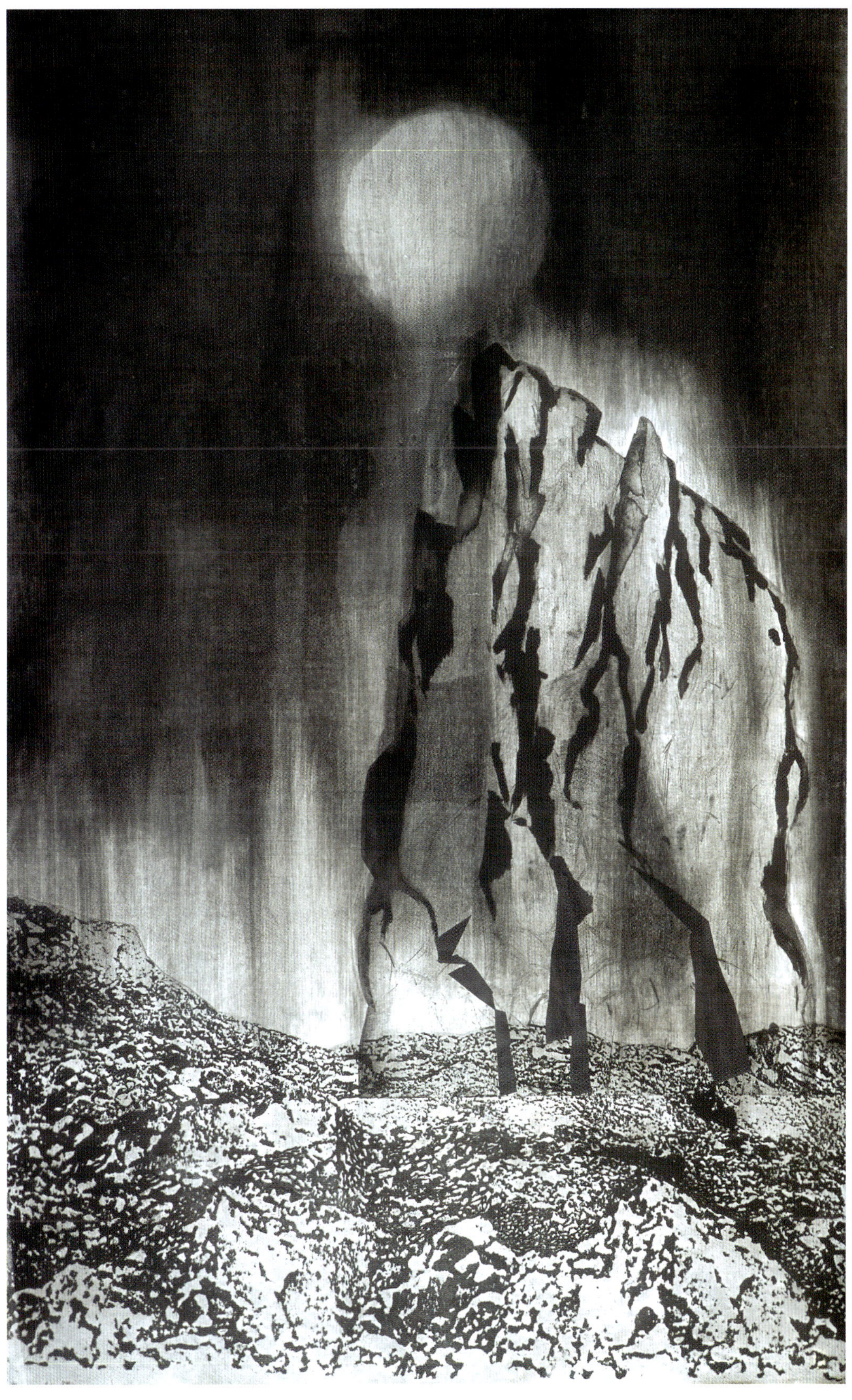

Midnattsolen. No. 2 from series of 24, monoprint with oil-based ink, intaglio, cut paper, and brushed wood with monotype stencil on Okawara paper. 60" × 39". 2003.

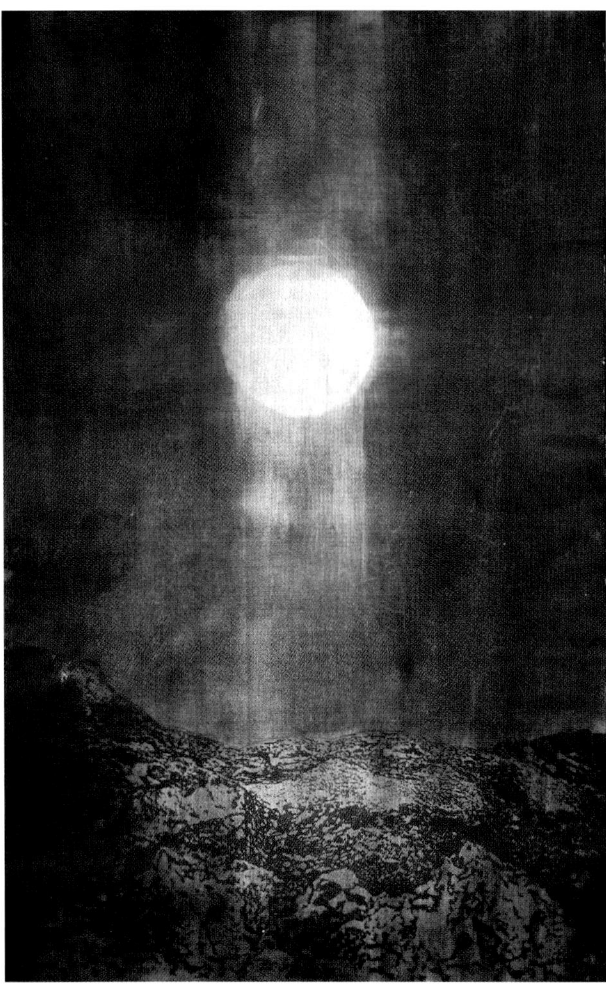

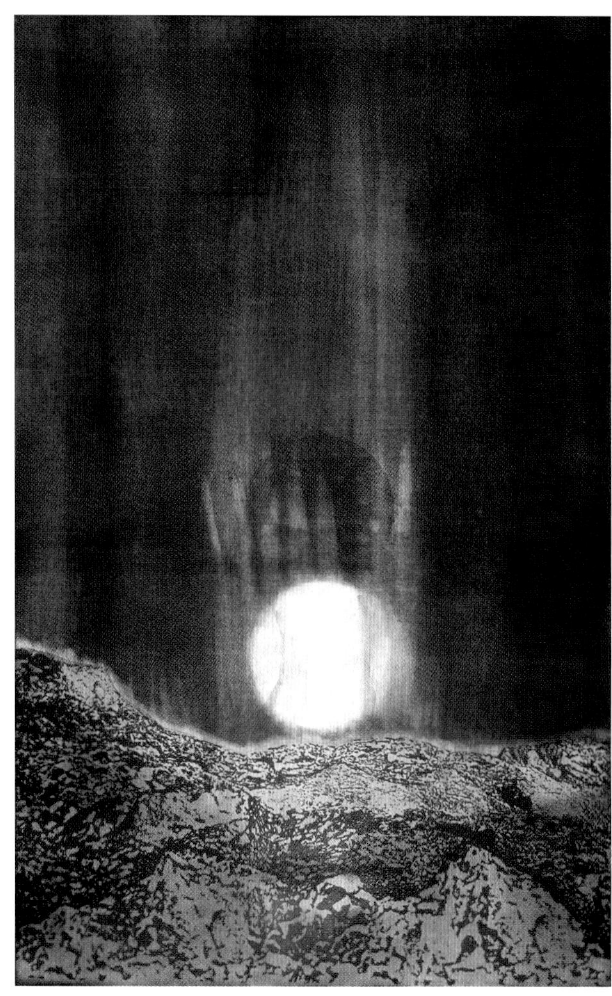

Midnattsolen. No. 3 from series of 24, monoprint with oil-based ink, intaglio, cut paper, and brushed wood with monotype stencil on Okawara paper. 60" × 39". 2003.

Midnattsolen. No. 5 from series of 24, monoprint with oil-based ink, intaglio, cut paper, and brushed wood with monotype stencil on Okawara paper. 60" × 39". 2003.

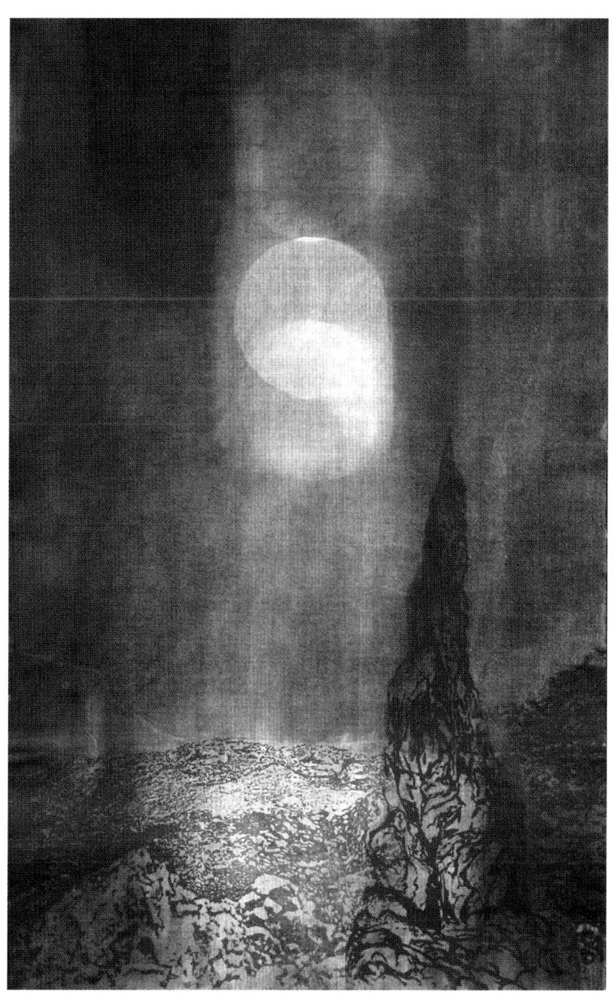

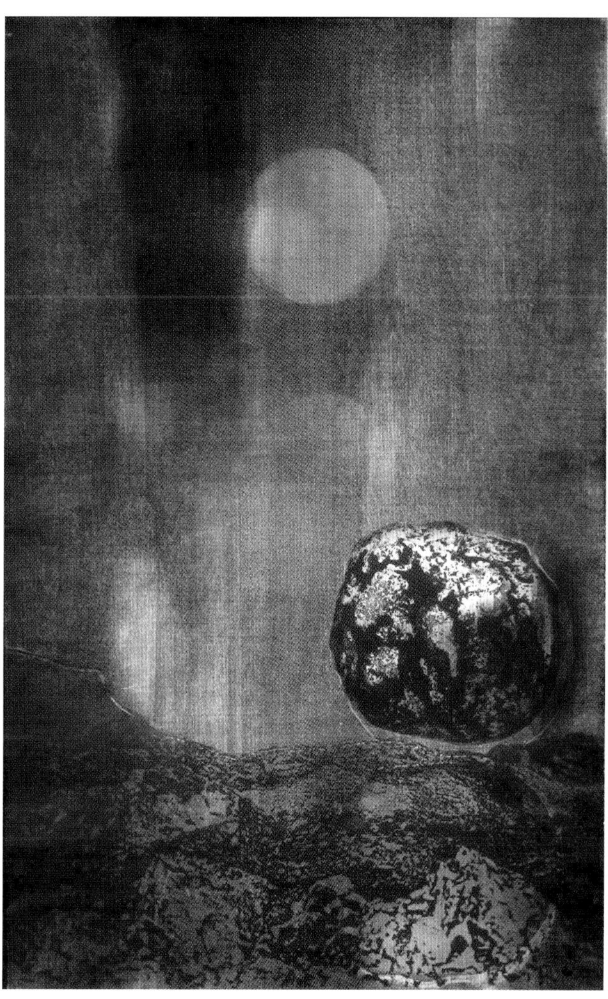

Midnattsolen. No. 8 from series of 24, monoprint with oil-based ink, intaglio, cut paper, and brushed wood with monotype stencil on Okawara paper. 60" × 39". 2003.

Midnattsolen. No. 9 from series of 24, monoprint with oil-based ink, intaglio, cut paper, and brushed wood with monotype stencil on Okawara paper. 60" × 39". 2003.

ROBERT SIEGELMAN

Boston, Massachusetts

Although many of my prints have been the product of experimentation with the media itself, the underlying concept for the work is to use printmaking itself as a personal drawing medium. My early prints are noted for their whimsy and a sense of the lyrical. Later prints range from the nearly ephemeral to large, bold, and gestural. All of my work references the autobiographical. My newest letterpress prints are made from the scanned pages of my private journals.

To Frieda. Letterpress monoprint with oil-based ink, drawing, and collage. 9" × 6". 2017.

Shoes for Men. Letterpress monoprint with oil-based ink, drawing, and collage. 9" × 6". 2017.

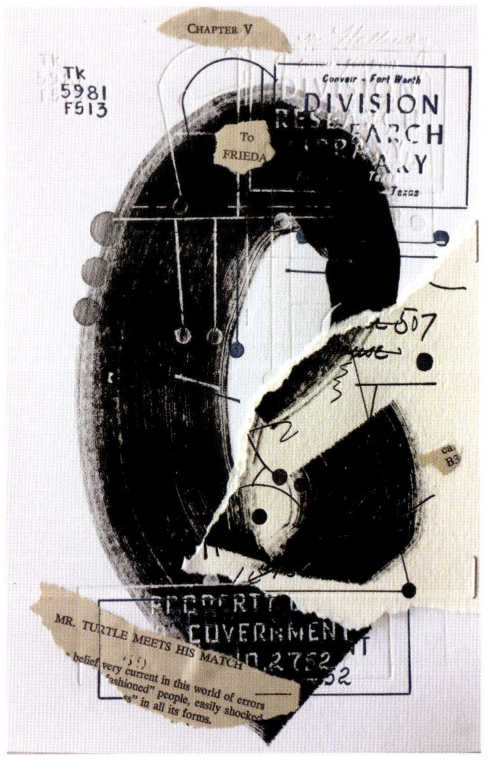

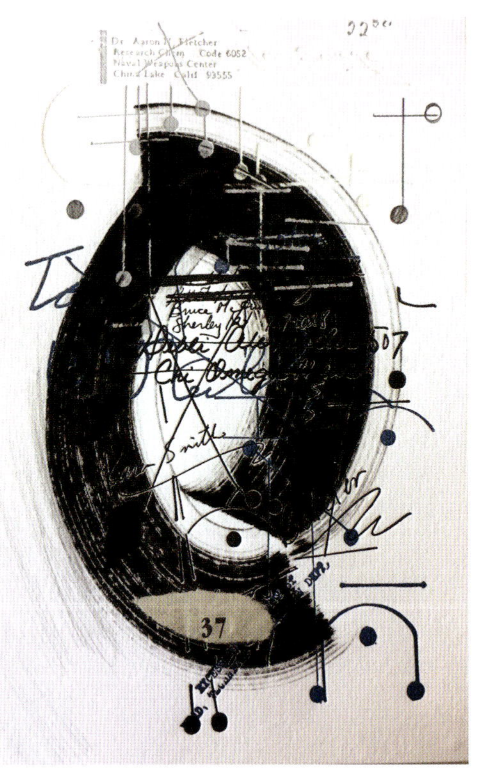

PUBLISHED AND PRINTED BY THE ARTIST WITH ROB CHARLTON AT GOOSEFISH PRESS.

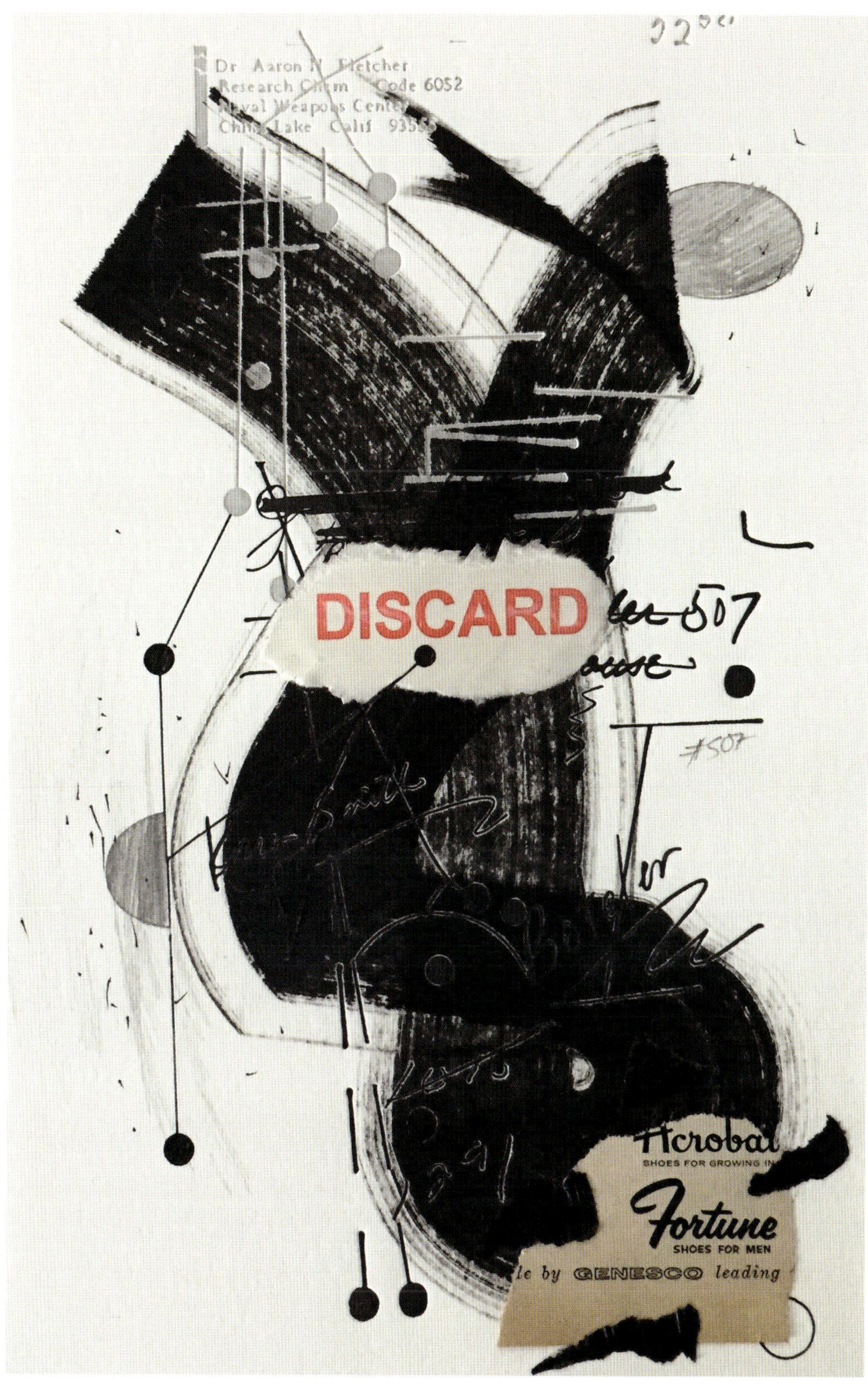

Dr. Fletcher. Letterpress monoprint with oil-based ink, drawing, and collage. 9" × 6". 2017.

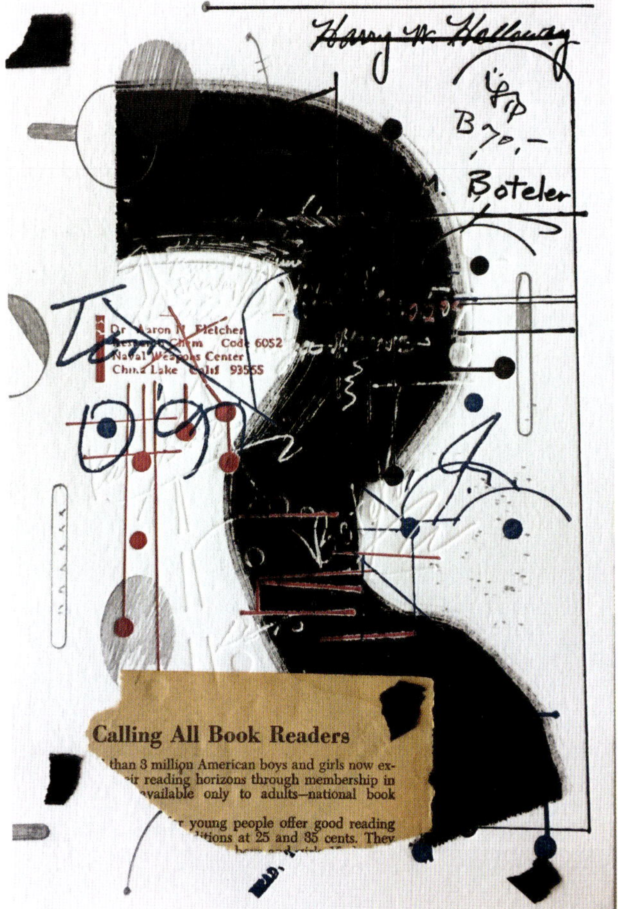

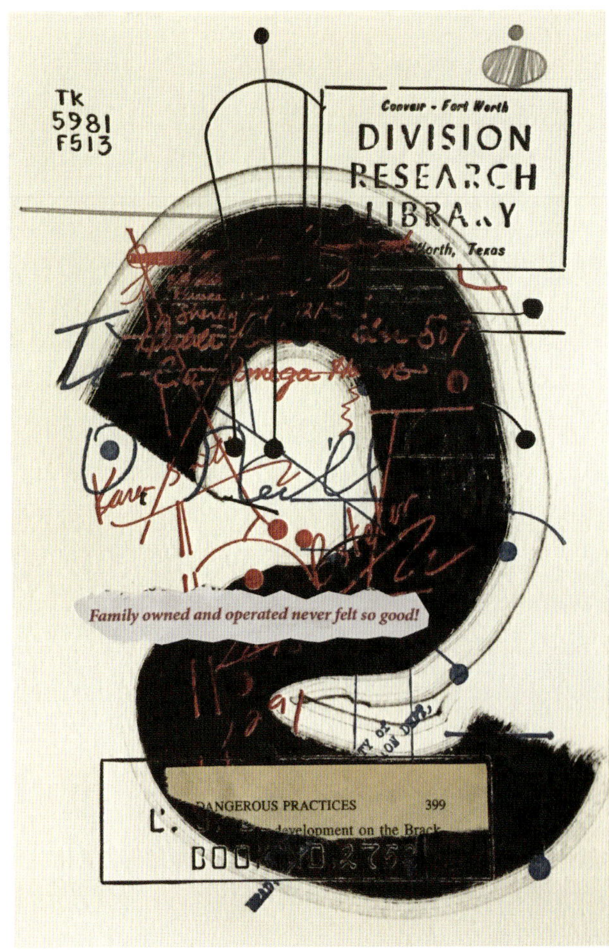

American Boys and Girls. Letterpress monoprint with oil-based ink, drawing, and collage. 9" × 6". 2017.

Dangerous Practices. Letterpress monoprint with oil-based ink, drawing, and collage. 9" × 6". 2017.

JOYCE SILVERSTONE

Amherst, Massachusetts

I am drawn to monotype's visual language, especially the openings that come from the unwilled and accidental. Over time, I discovered some of the traditional printmaking methods for describing space, using fades, transparency, texture, and linear marks to build, remove, and imply place and movement. Central to my vocabulary is drawing, and I appreciate how qualities of touch and presence are conveyed in transfer drawings. I am interested in exploring body metaphors, contained forms and openness, edges that are boundaries and connectors, and my own attunement to forces of the natural world.

I like having many pieces going at once and having them up and around the studio so I can live with them for a while. When I see one that I can work back into, where I can make some formal discoveries if I make small shifts in composition, color, or shape, I know that another one on the wall has something to do with the piece on the table. I like having the group around to inform each other.

For the prints represented here, I took my time to get the feel of the image by printing multiple plates: line plates, color plates, and plates that carry forms and textures. Each move in the printing process required me to reconsider the context of the images in relation to each other, as their chance interactions built with each additional running of plates through the press. I was on a search for the juxtapositions that felt distinctly true and right.

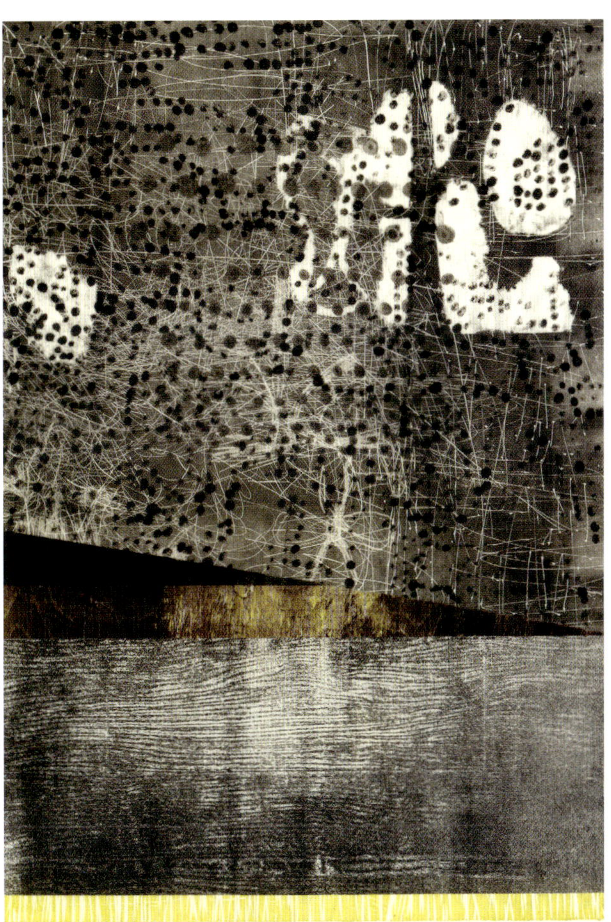

Vertical Angle. Monoprint with Akua soy-based inks, collagraph, and relief monotype printed on Revere Silk and Masa papers with Akua intaglio inks. 30" × 22". 2016.

PUBLISHED AND PRINTED BY THE ARTIST AT ZEA MAYS STUDIO.

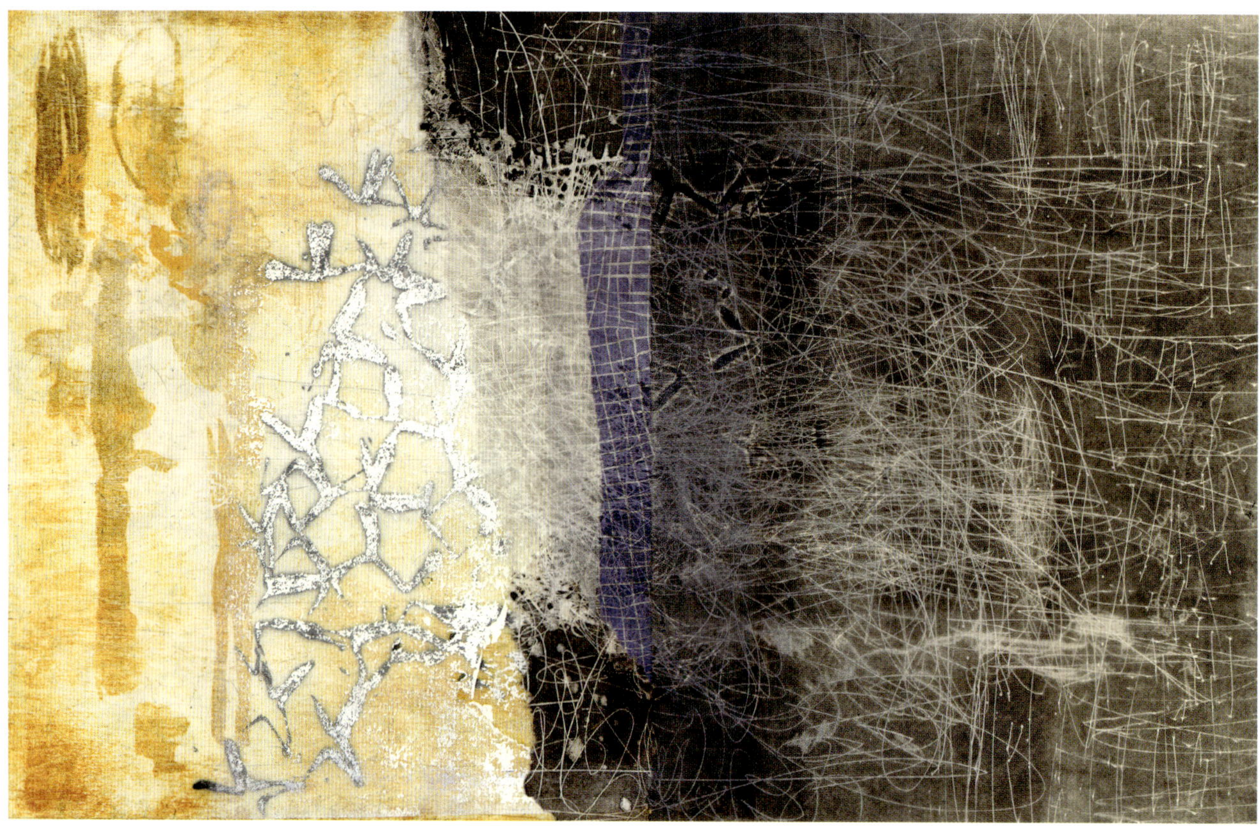

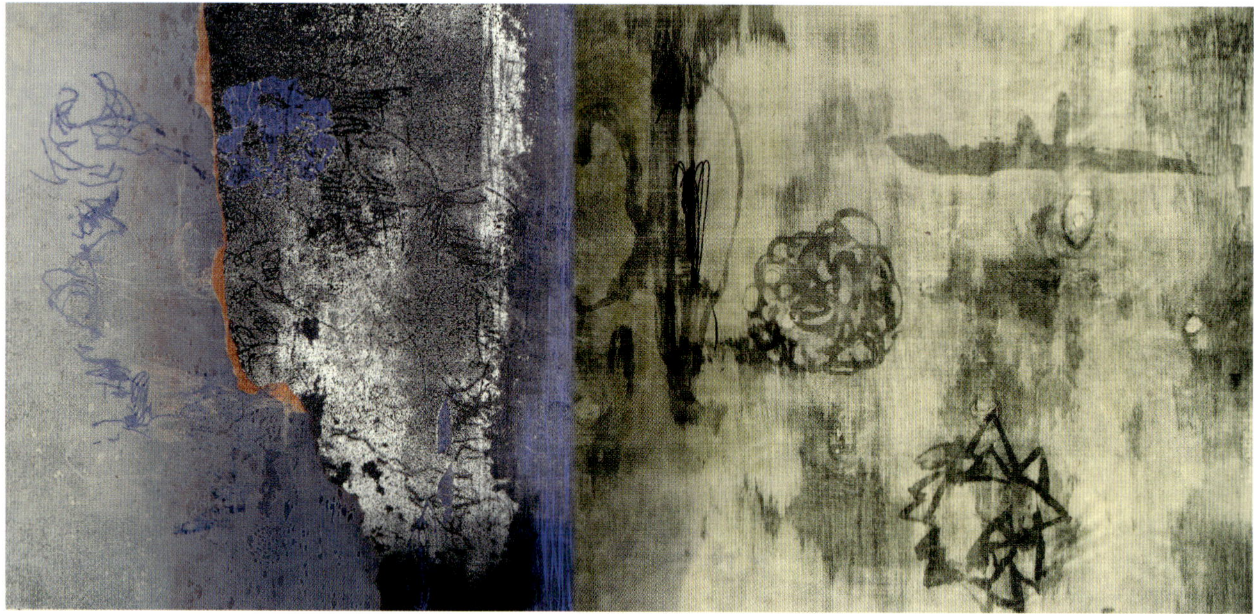

Λ

Gold Flock. Monoprint with Akua soy-based inks, collagraph, wood lithograph, relief monotype, and collage printed on Masa, Revere Silk, and Gampi papers with Akua intaglio inks. 22" × 30". 2016.

V

Blue Wood Litho. Monoprint with Akua soy-based inks, monotype, and wood lithograph printed on Masa and Revere Silk papers. 22" × 30". 2016.

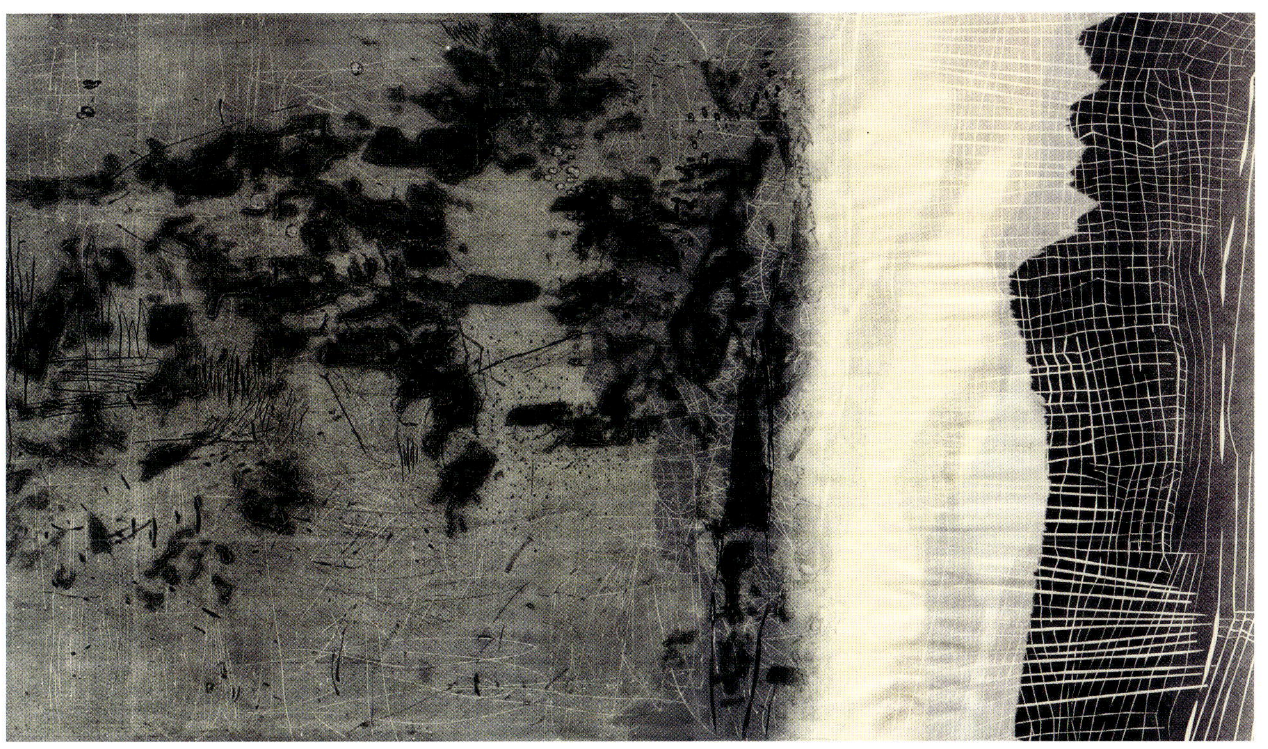

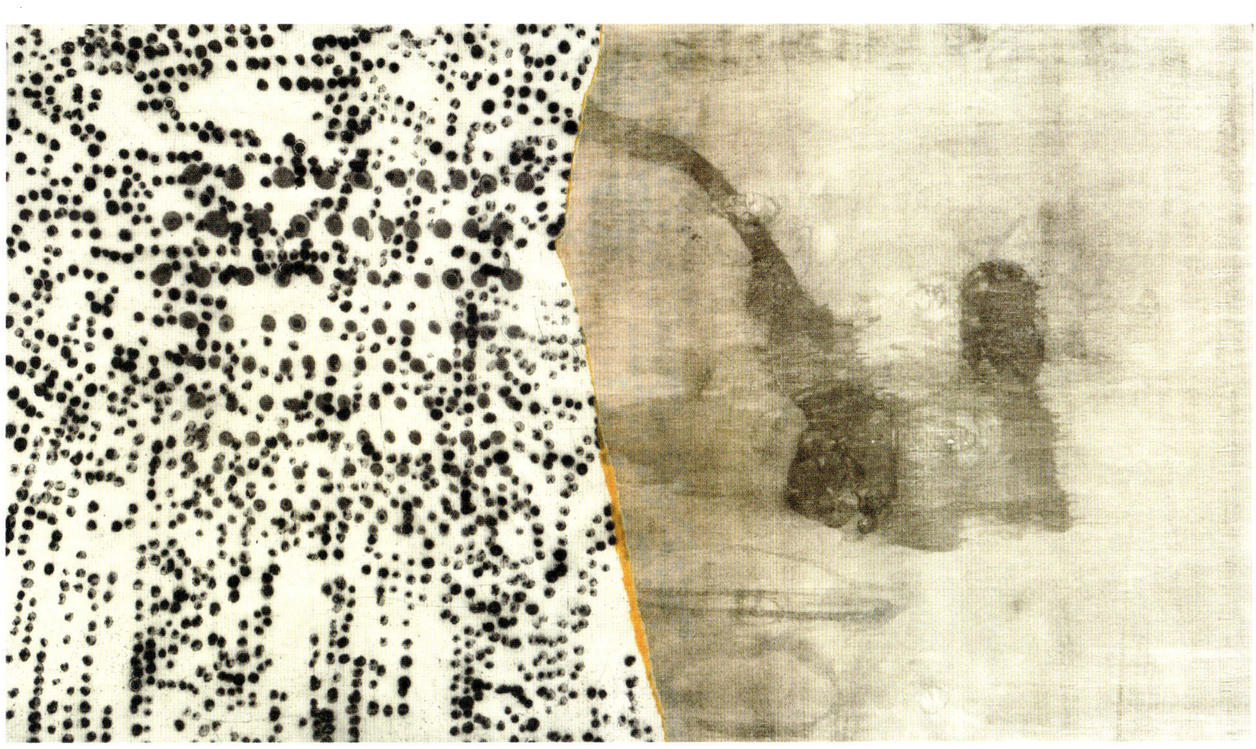

Λ

Black Collagraph. Monoprint with Akua soy-based inks, collagraph, and relief monotype printed on Masa and Rives papers with Akua intaglio inks. 22" × 30". 2017.

V

Congruent Pair. Monoprint with Akua soy-based inks, collagraph, and wood lithograph monotype printed on Revere Silk and Masa papers. 22" × 30". 2017.

STEVEN SORMAN

Red Wing, Minnesota

There is something both odd and wonderful about monotype. It seems odd to paint on one surface only to move it to another. The image, however, does not arrive at its new venue as verbatim translation. As weather changes from place to place, you leave one atmosphere to enter another. You can engineer many of the move's aspects, yet much of where you end up just happens as unpredictably as the weather.

Monoprint works for me both as preamble and postscript. Numerous proofs are printed and assembled in singular configurations before I choose one to edition. Over time I accumulate many additional uneditioned proofs, which I frequently reconsider and revisit. Although these monoprints are often composed from the ingredients for or leftovers from editioned pieces, they are often pieces printed just once only because I wanted to see what something might look like.

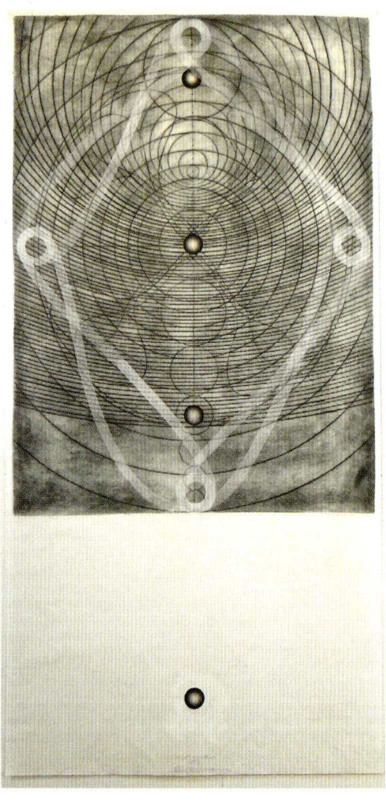

not really. Monoprint with oil-based inks, drypoint intaglio, collage, and hand painting on linen. 61" × 31". 2009.

PUBLISHED AND PRINTED BY THE ARTIST.

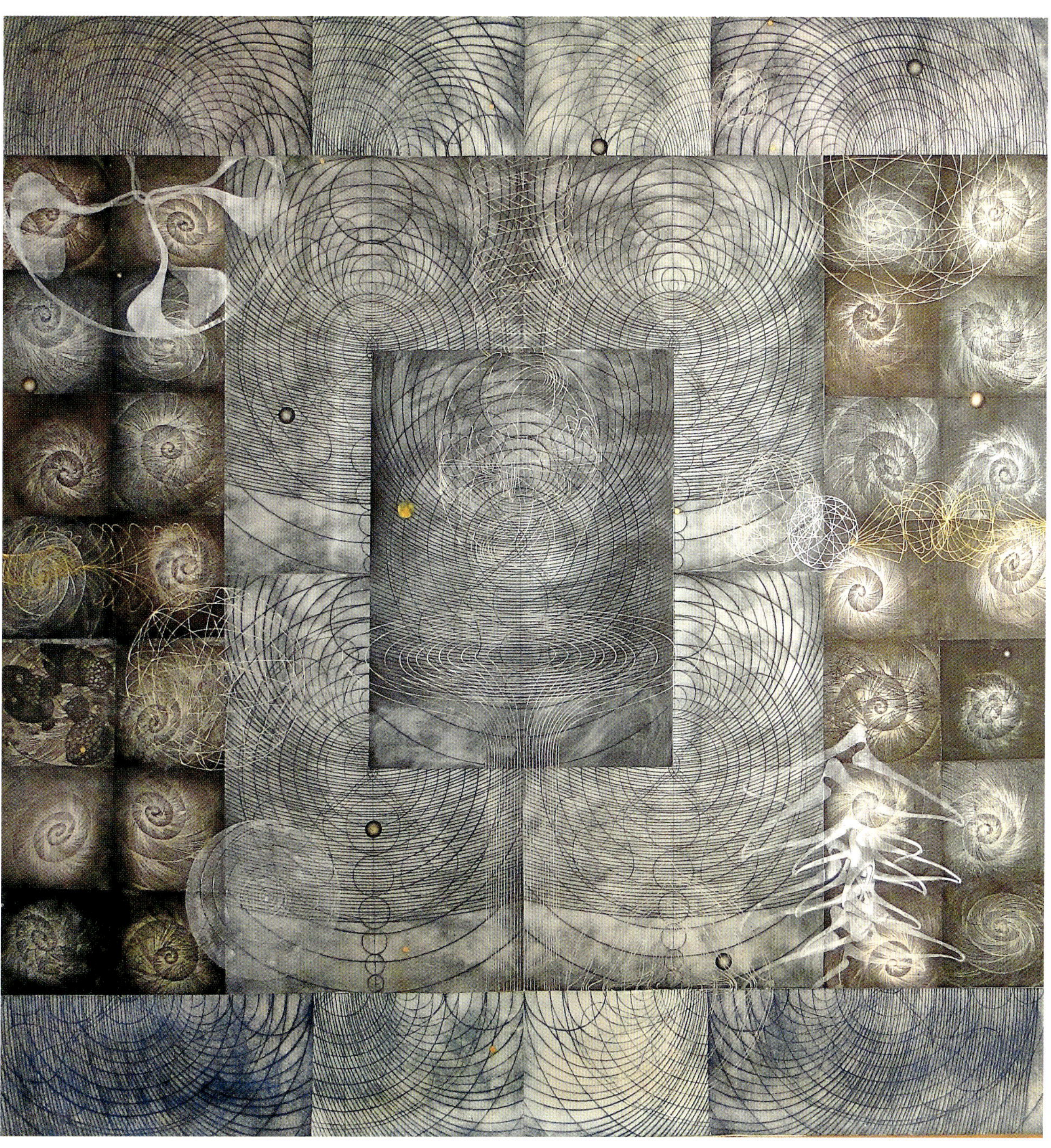

is was will be, detail (center panel 9' × 8'). Monoprint with oil-based inks, monotype, drypoint intaglio, etching, and hand painting on linen. 9' × 39'. 2010.

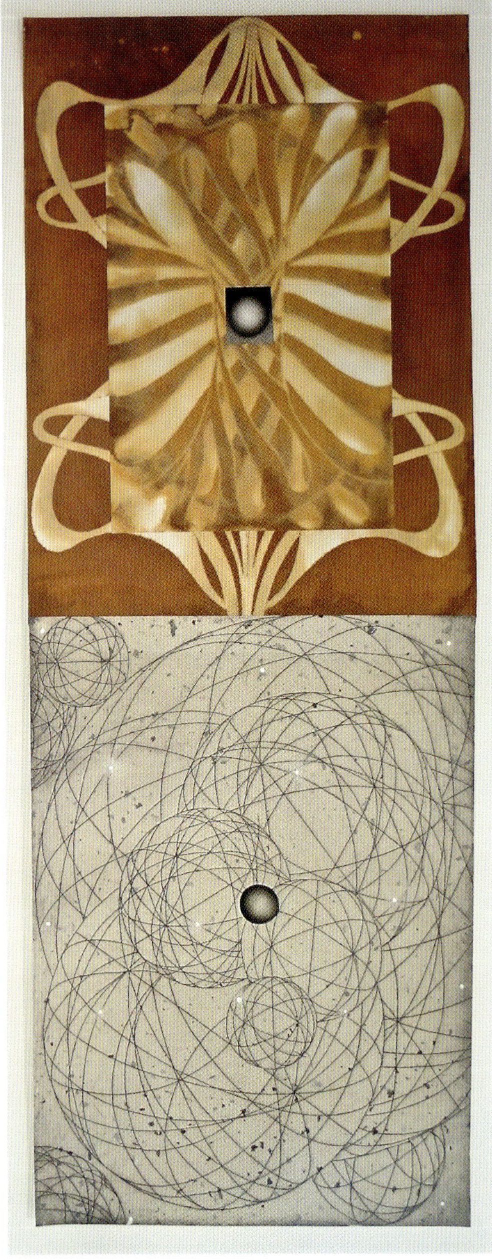

wherein which. Monoprint with oil-based inks, rust transfer, etching, and photopolymer intaglio on Japan papers. 48.5" × 17". 2008.

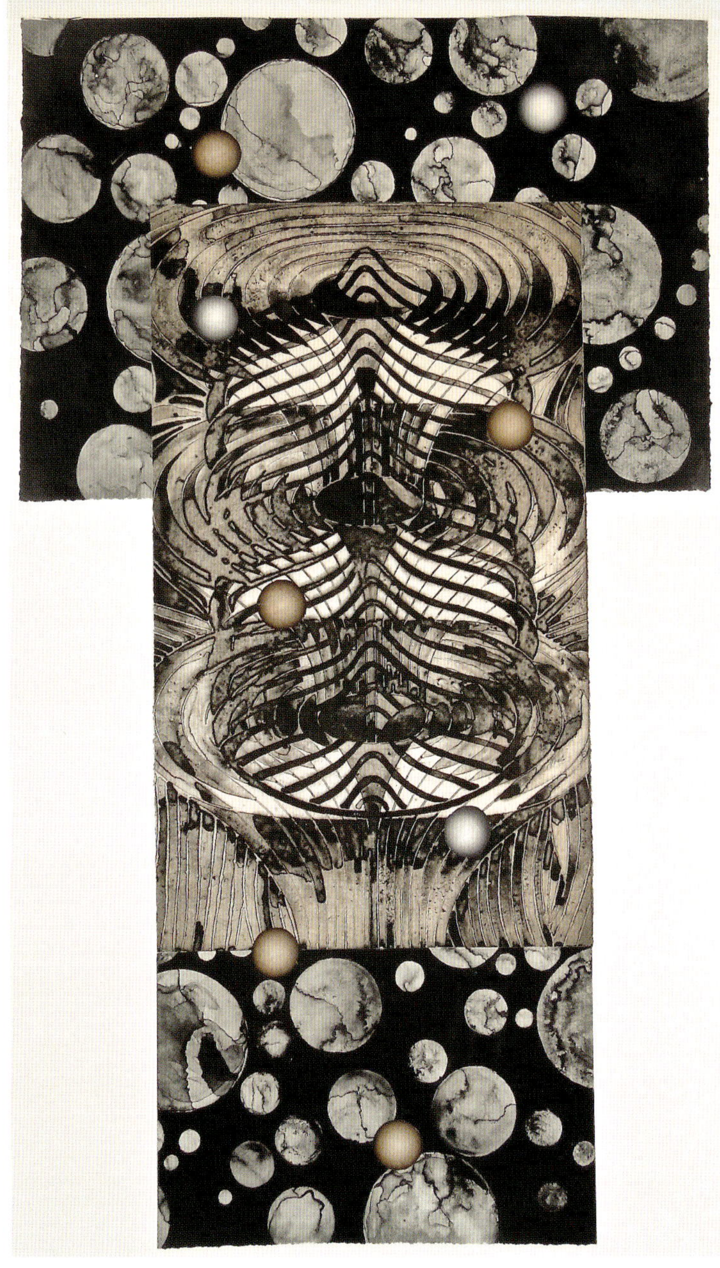

from time to time. Monoprint with oil-based inks, photopolymer intaglio, and collage on various papers. 37.62" × 22". 2017.

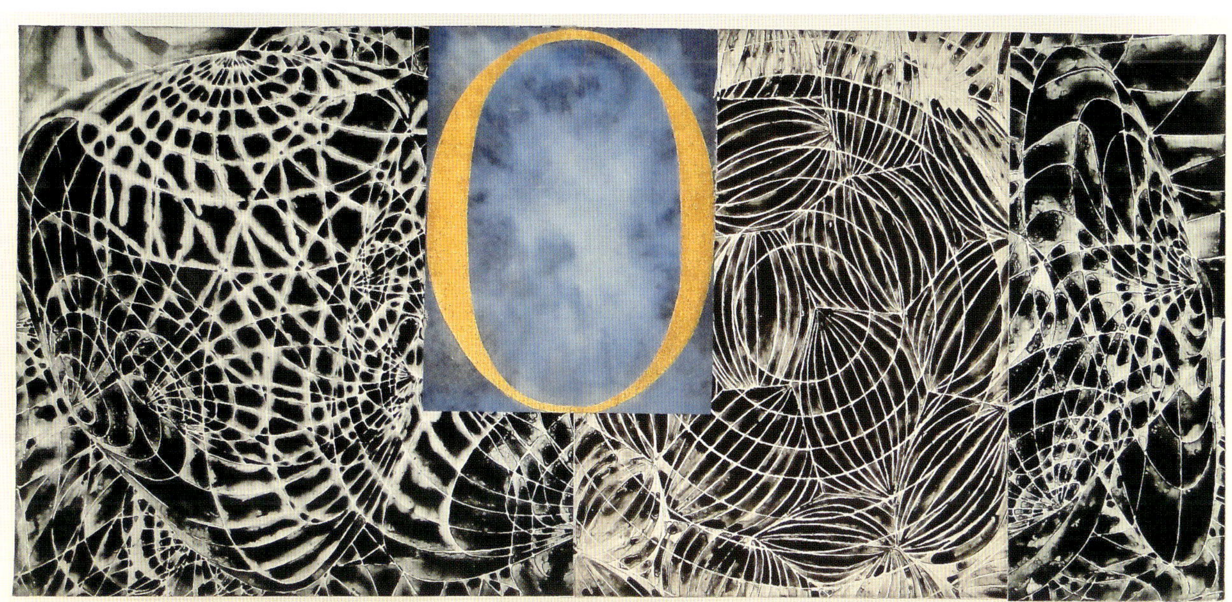

armspan. Monoprint with oil-based inks, woodcut, photopolymer intaglio, and collage on various papers. 16.037" × 36.12". 2017.

CAROLYN SWISZCZ

St. Paul, Minnesota

Art making allows me to settle into gray areas where I can explore conflicting feelings about situations and place. Assembling pleasing compositions gives me deep satisfaction and great joy. But what I'm most motivated by is the power that art gives me to transform my surroundings and imbue day-to-day life with magic and purpose. Painting a picture of a building is my way of anointing it, allowing me to believe I have the powers of consecration. In so doing, my subject and I become part of a large and important story, one that makes me feel less vulnerable to being forgotten.

My subjects are chosen intuitively from places I visit, both nearby and far-flung. What they have in common is usually loneliness, a touch of humor, and (I hope) some grace. There is a similar tension in the way I work, employing equal amounts of control and surprise. Trace monotype, masking tape, linoleum prints, watercolor monotype, and rubber stamps are some of the techniques I use in my paintings. When a print comes off the press it's a treat—like Christmas morning. I keep this moment in mind as I'm making a composition, trying to devise new ways the material can offer surprises.

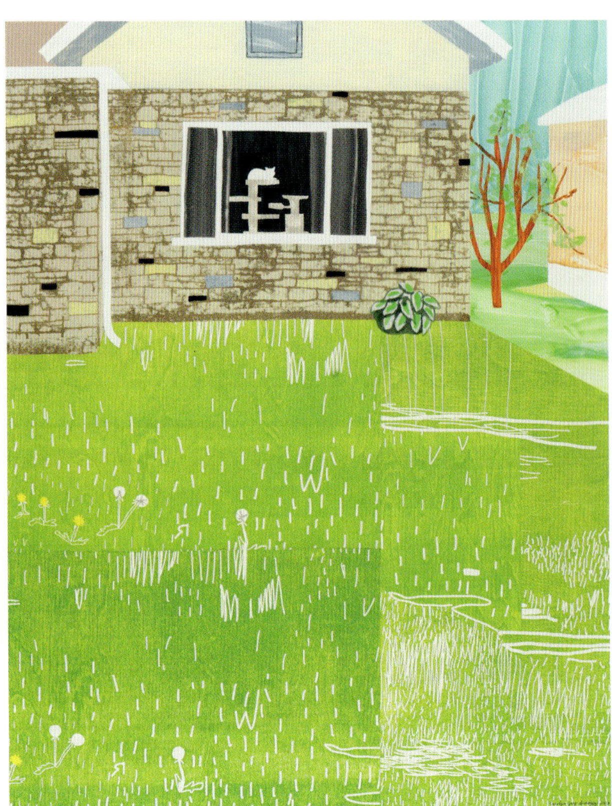

Cat Tower. Watercolor monotype. 32.5" × 25.5". 2018. *Photo credit: David Kern*

PRINTED AND PUBLISHED BY HIGHPOINT EDITIONS.

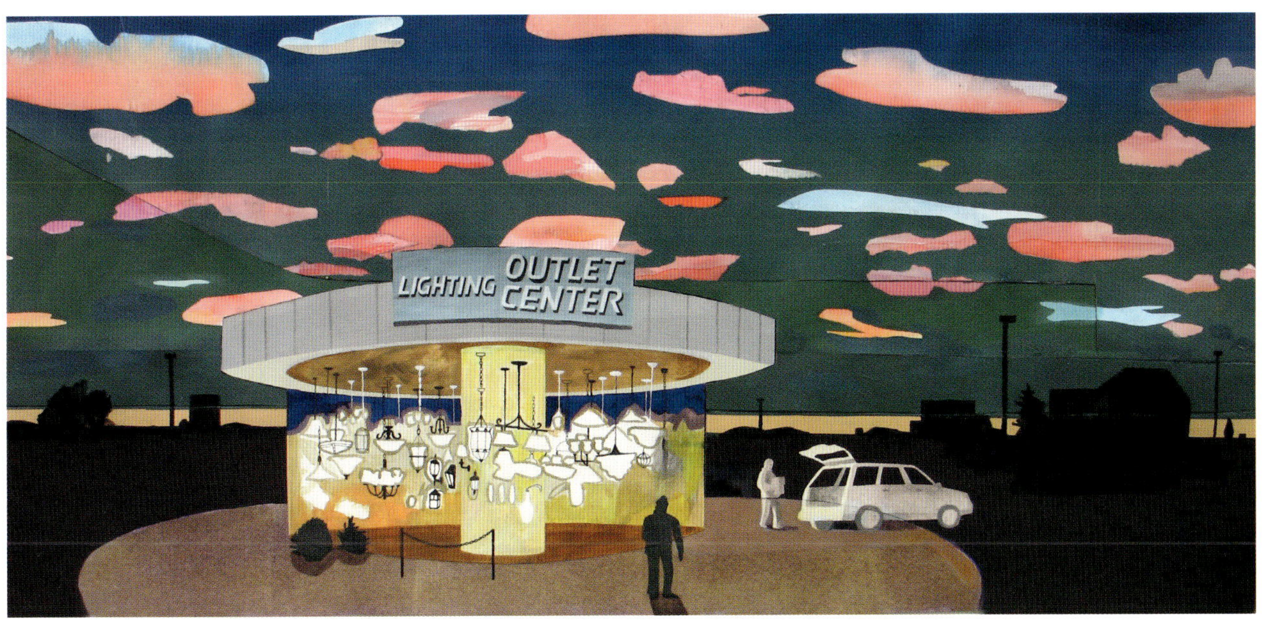

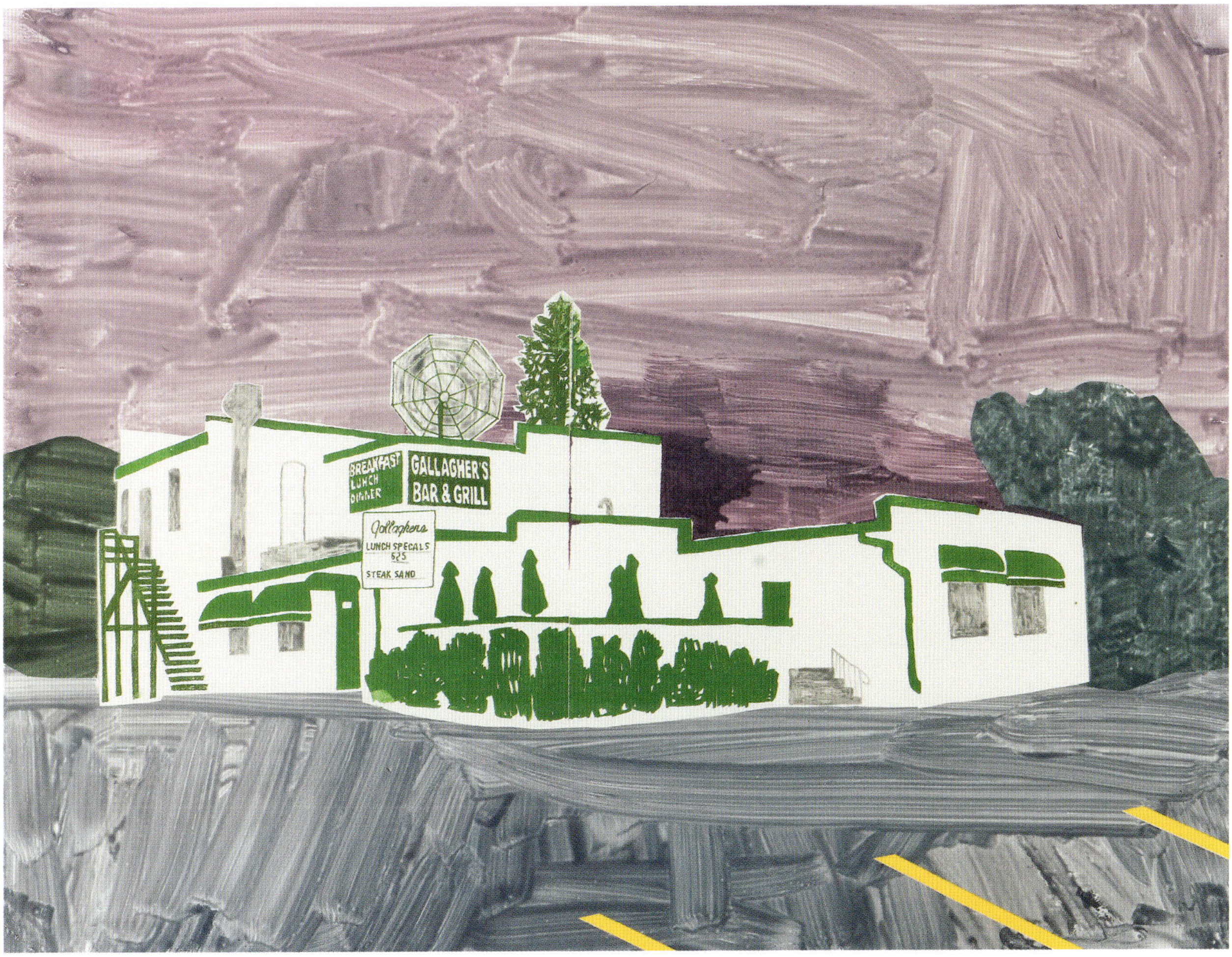

^
Lighting Outlet, Golden Valley, MN. Monoprint with oil-based inks, monotype, watercolor, hand coloring, and collage. 19" × 41". 2006. *Courtesy of Highpoint Editions*

v
Gallagher's #2. Watercolor monoprint. 17.62" × 23.62". 2017. *Photo credit: David Kern*

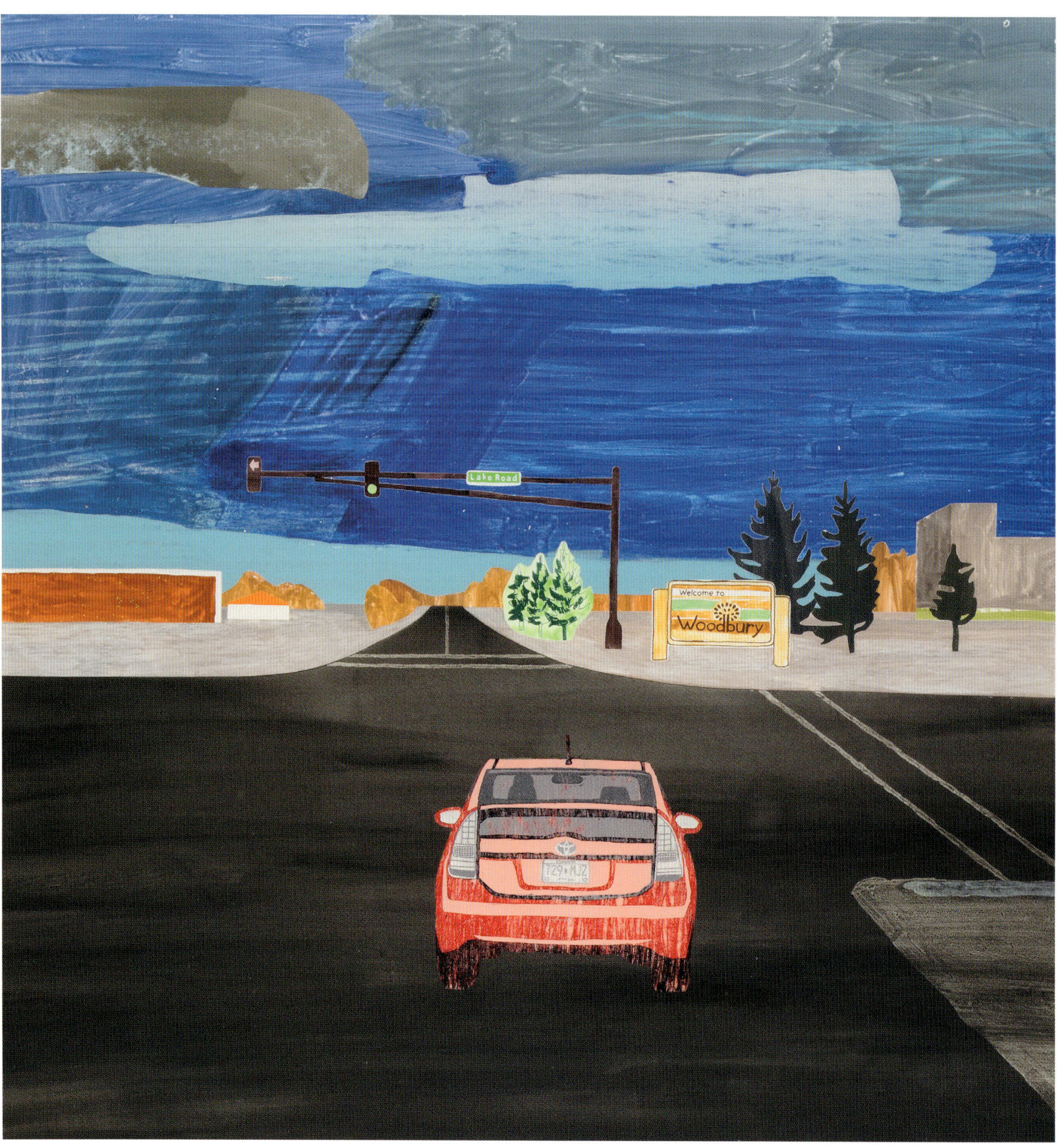

Welcome to Woodbury. Watercolor monoprint. 35.5" × 34.5". 2017. *Photo credit: David Kern*.

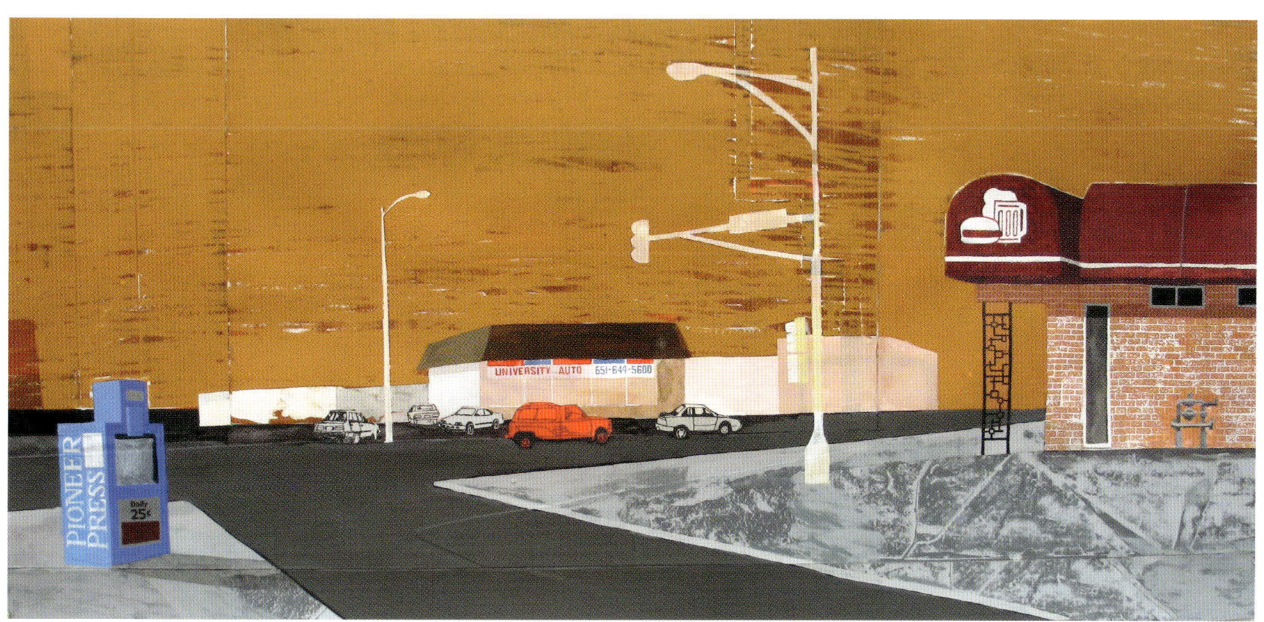

University & Hampden Avenues, St. Paul, MN. Monoprint with oil-based inks, monotype, watercolor, hand coloring, trace monotype, screen print, rubber stamp, and collage. 19" × 41". 2006. *Courtesy of Highpoint Editions*

DAN WELDEN

Sag Harbor, New York

When I set out to work, there is no image in mind, but the vision unfolds as the work evolves. It usually begins with simple forms and marks with broad areas. It then becomes more refined and delicate and knits itself together through line.

I am a process-oriented, experimental artist, interested in materials and techniques that explore the landscape of my mind. My drawings, paintings, and prints evolve from the idea of linear pathways echoing from the tracks of animals in nature, the fissures in rock palisades, and the patterns created by my hands becoming playful with a variety of tools.

Learning to read a printing plate before inking is similar to me sensing the log before wielding the ax. Creativity for me means being aware and feeling what resonates in front of me and responding with marks, colors, and textures.

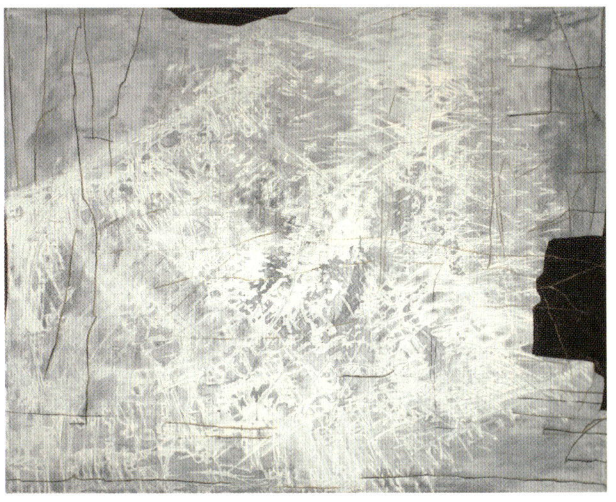

Glacial Hunger. Monoprint with oil-based and Akua soy oil–based inks, and Solarplate intaglio on Hahnemühle paper. 25" × 32". 2015.

>

Red Pepper Massage. Monoprint with oil-based and Akua soy oil–based inks, screen print, Prismacolor pencils, and Solarplate intaglio on Hahnemühle paper. 33" × 42". 2014.

On Thin Ice. Monoprint with oil-based and Akua soy oil–based inks, and Solarplate intaglio on White Crow handmade paper. 10" × 14". 1999–2016.

ALL PHOTOS ARE COURTESY OF NINA M. SOUTHER. PUBLISHED AND PRINTED BY THE ARTIST AT HAMPTON EDITIONS.

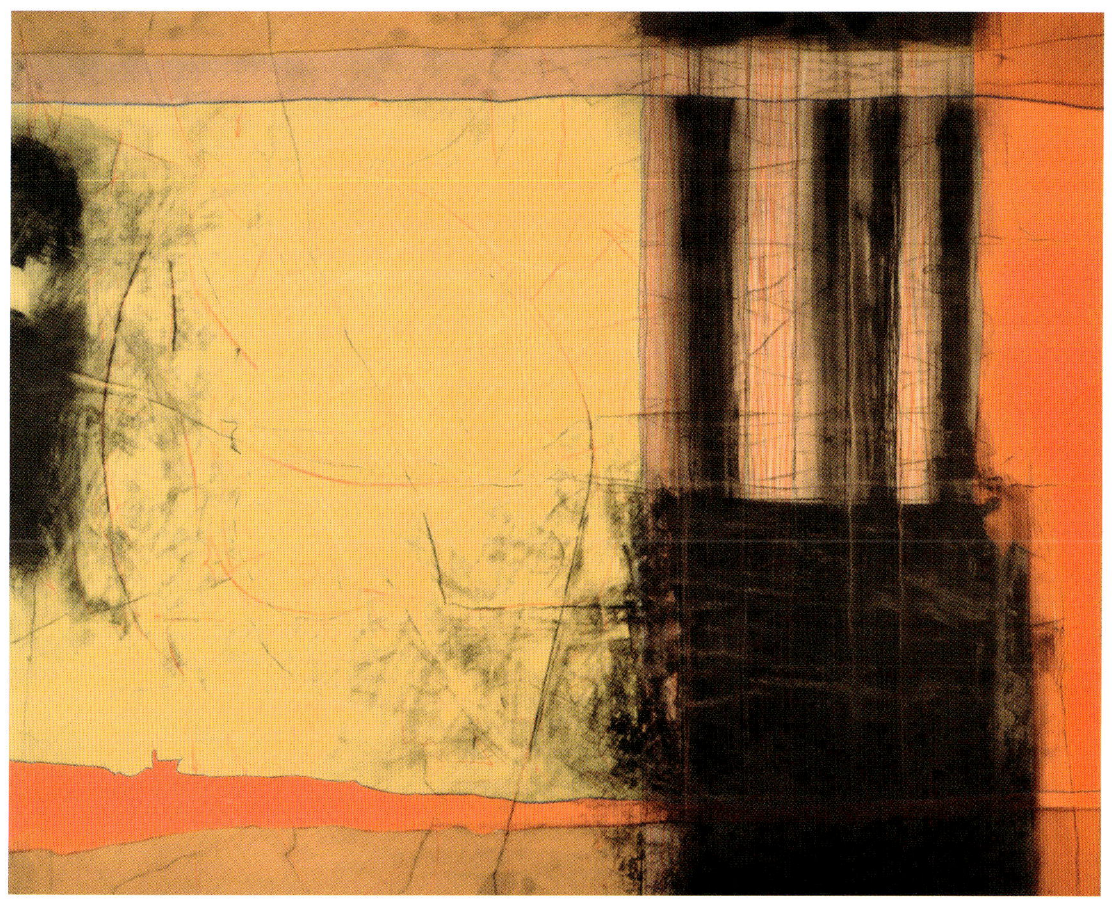

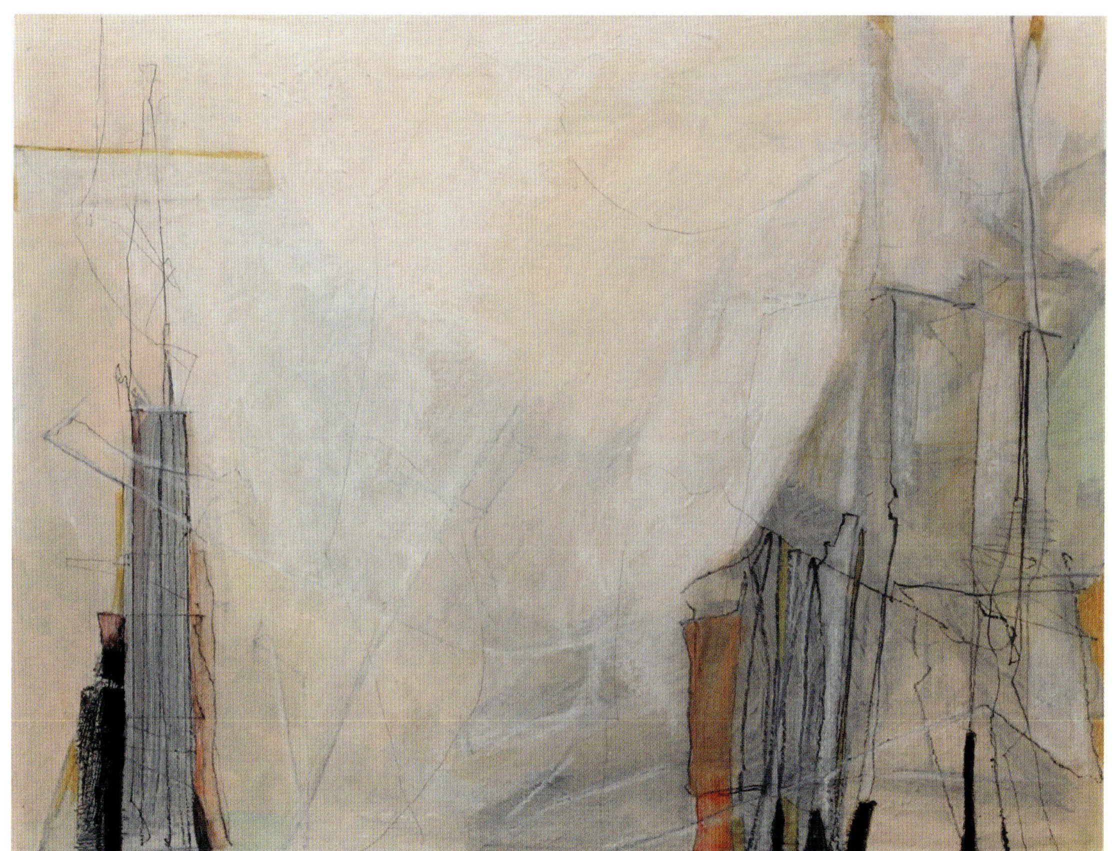

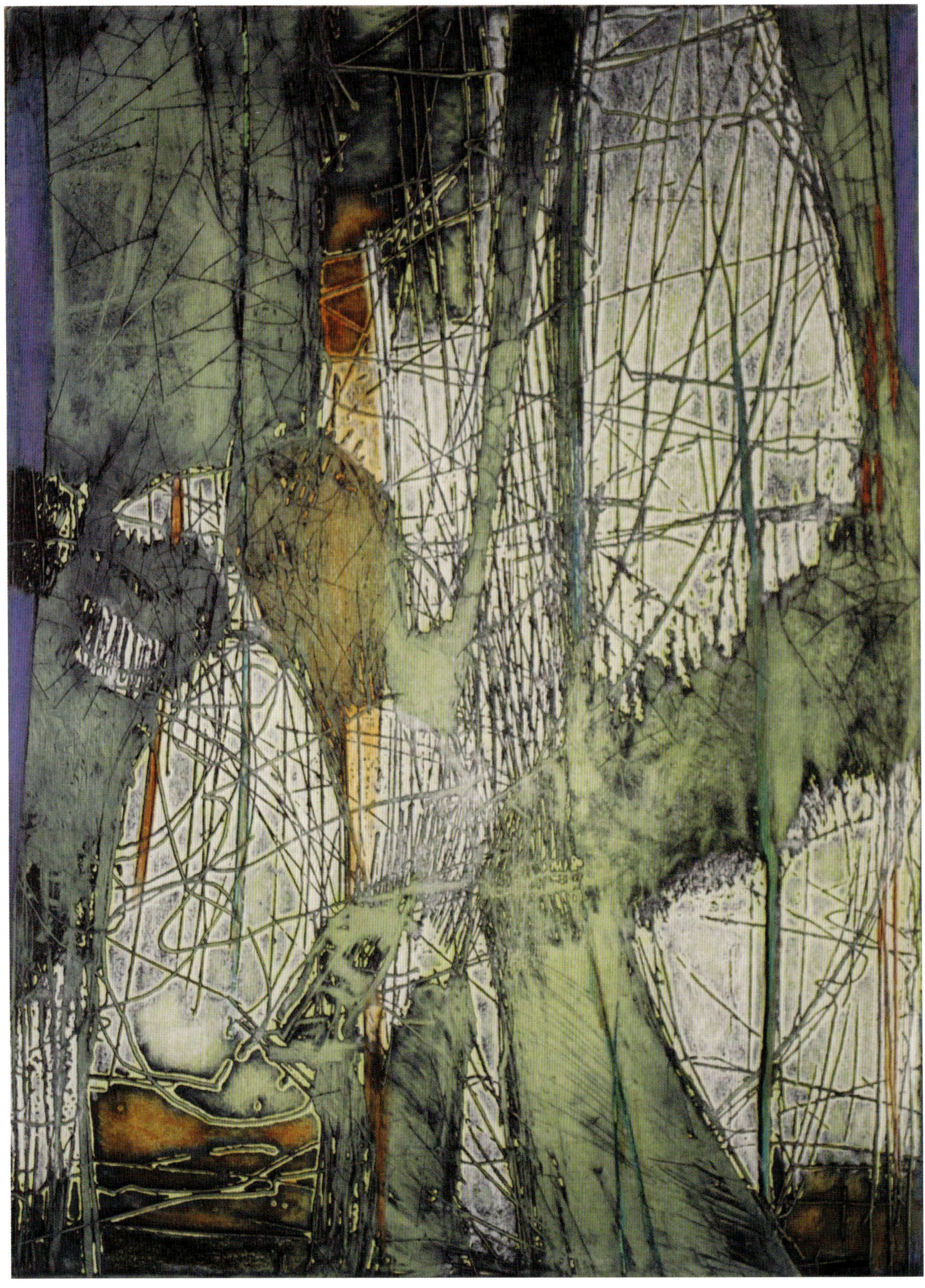

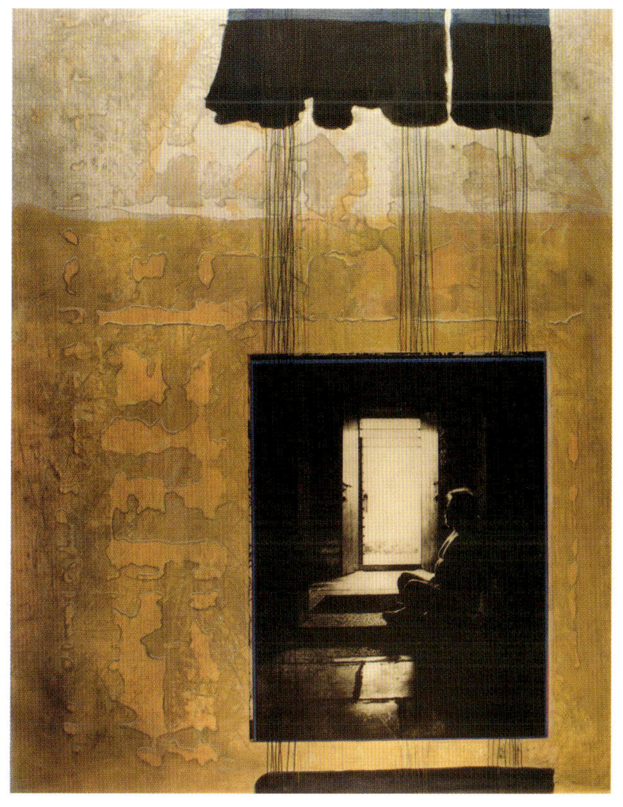

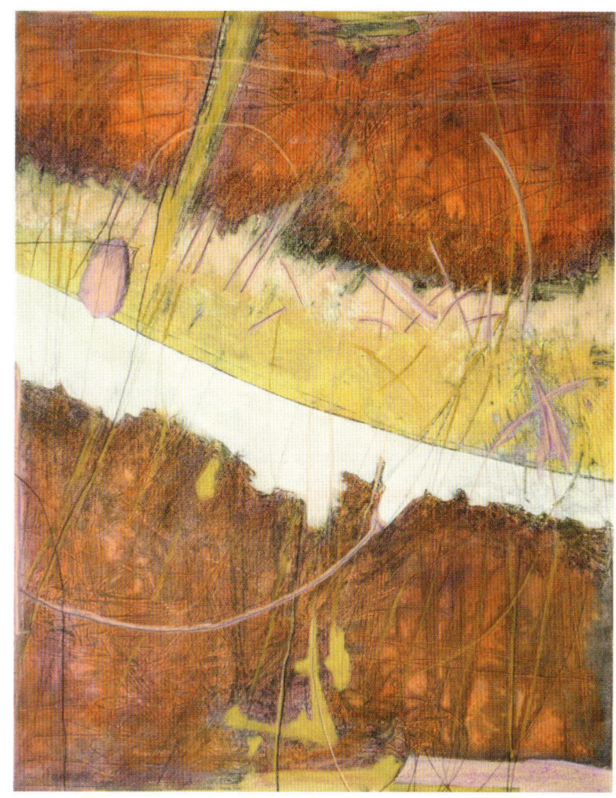

<

Nantucket Brambles. Monoprint with oil-based and Akua soy oil-based inks, and Solarplate intaglio on Hahnemühle paper. 16" × 12". 2017.

The Threads of Living. Monoprint with oil-based and Akua soy oil–based inks, screen print, and Solarplate intaglio on Hahnemühle paper. 41" × 33". 2015.

Santa Fe Ethos. Monoprint with oil-based and Akua soy oil–based inks, and Solarplate intaglio on Hahnemühle paper and ink. 20" × 16". 2017.

JOHN WILLIS

West Hartford, Connecticut

All of my prints use two blocks: a linoleum relief block and a monotype block. I use either a Universal #1 Vandercook proofing press or a Dufa flatbed offset press in making my monoprints. Both presses allow for perfect registration, which means I can execute multiple runs on each print. My completed prints can easily have six to twelve runs of relief or monotype printing. I use monotype techniques both on the monotype and relief block. The fine graphite-looking lines on the prints are actually created by drawing on the monotype block with graphite and then using tint base to turn the graphite into ink. The exacting process allows for editions of five to twelve prints, unusual for monotypes.

The prints that list "constructed materials" involve cutting and adhering monotype-printed paper to complete the prints. The process permits varied editions after the fixed matrix and monotype have been printed.

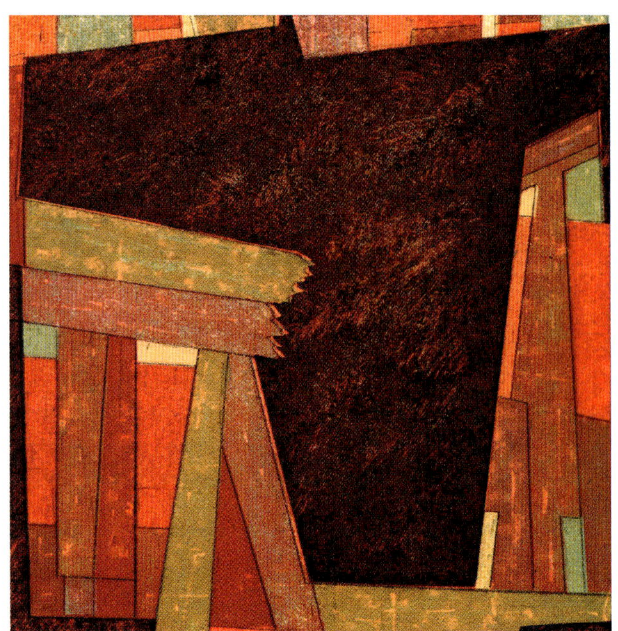

Contentious Journey VII. Monoprint with oil-based inks, monotype, and relief on letterpress and offset presses using constructed materials. 7" × 7". 2009.

PUBLISHED AND PRINTED BY THE ARTIST.

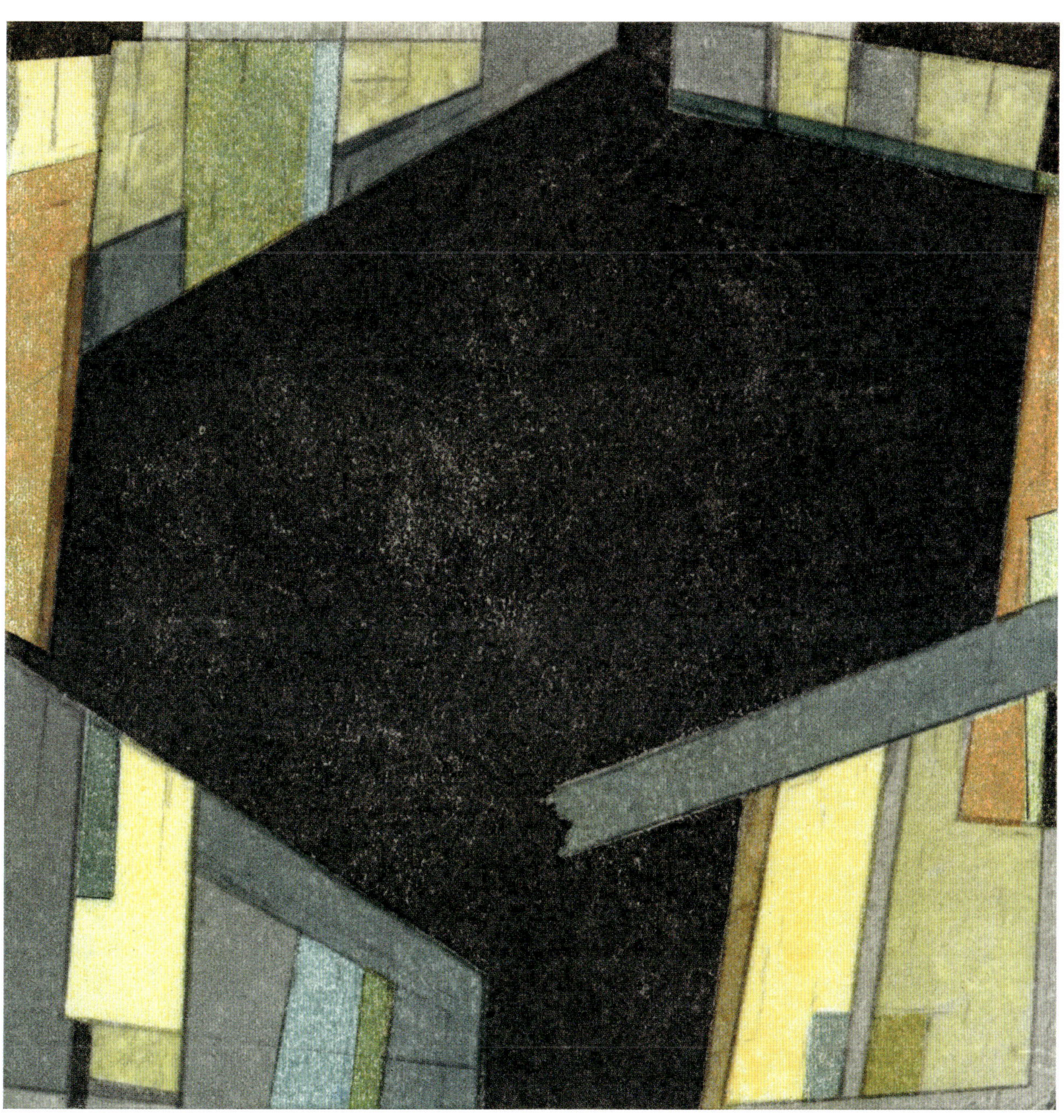

Uncertain Moment VI. Monoprint with oil-based inks, monotype, and relief on letterpress and offset presses using constructed materials. 7" × 7". 2009.

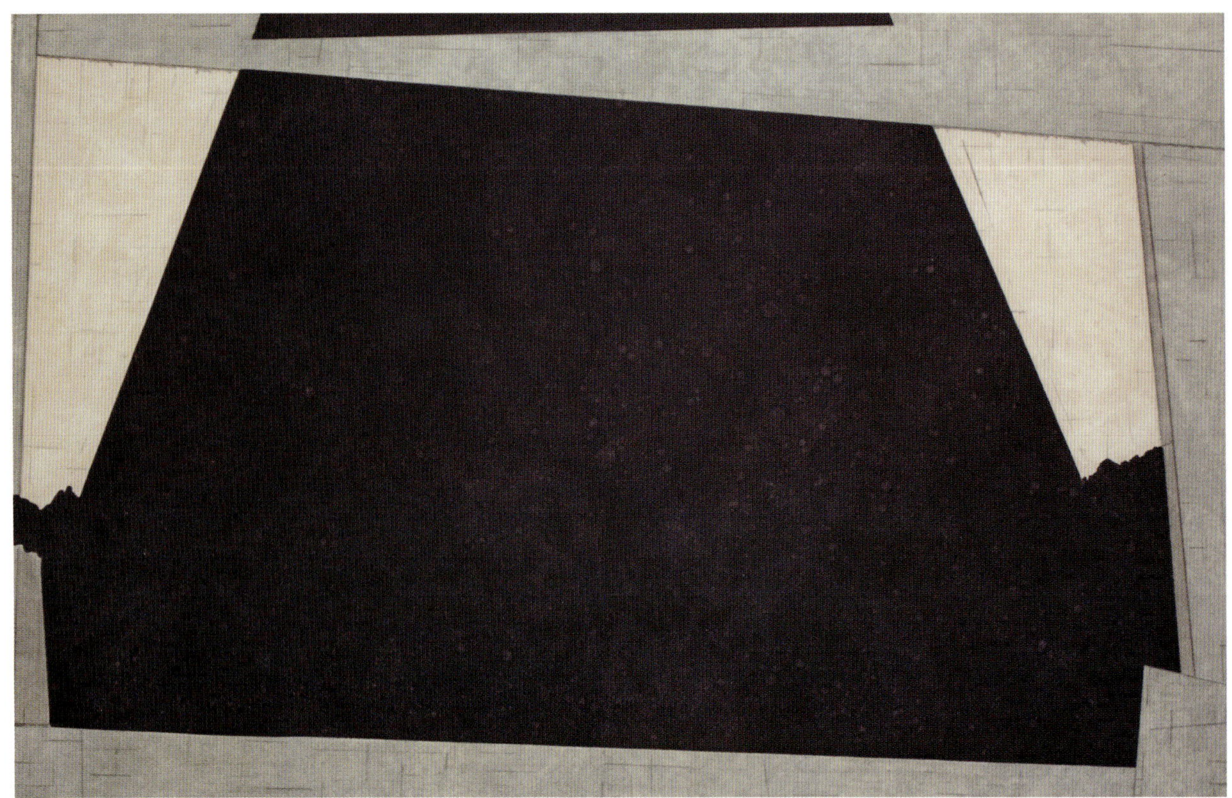

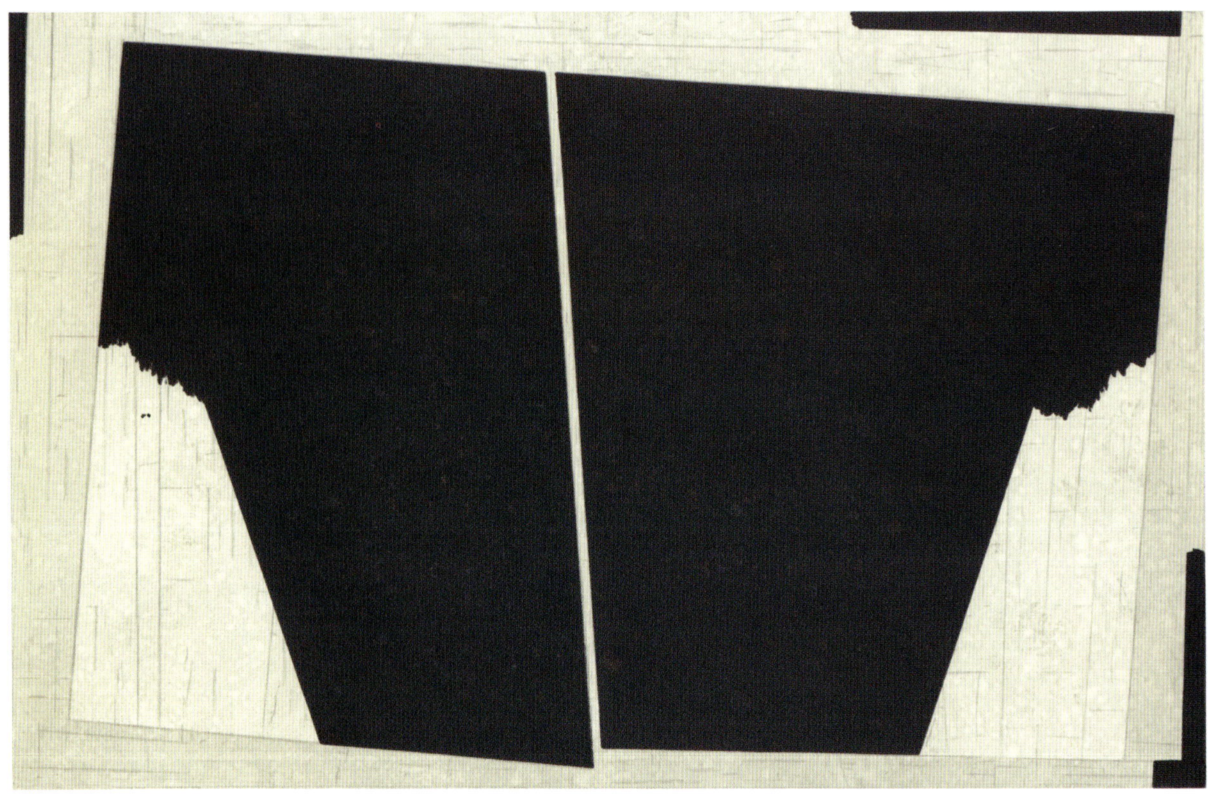

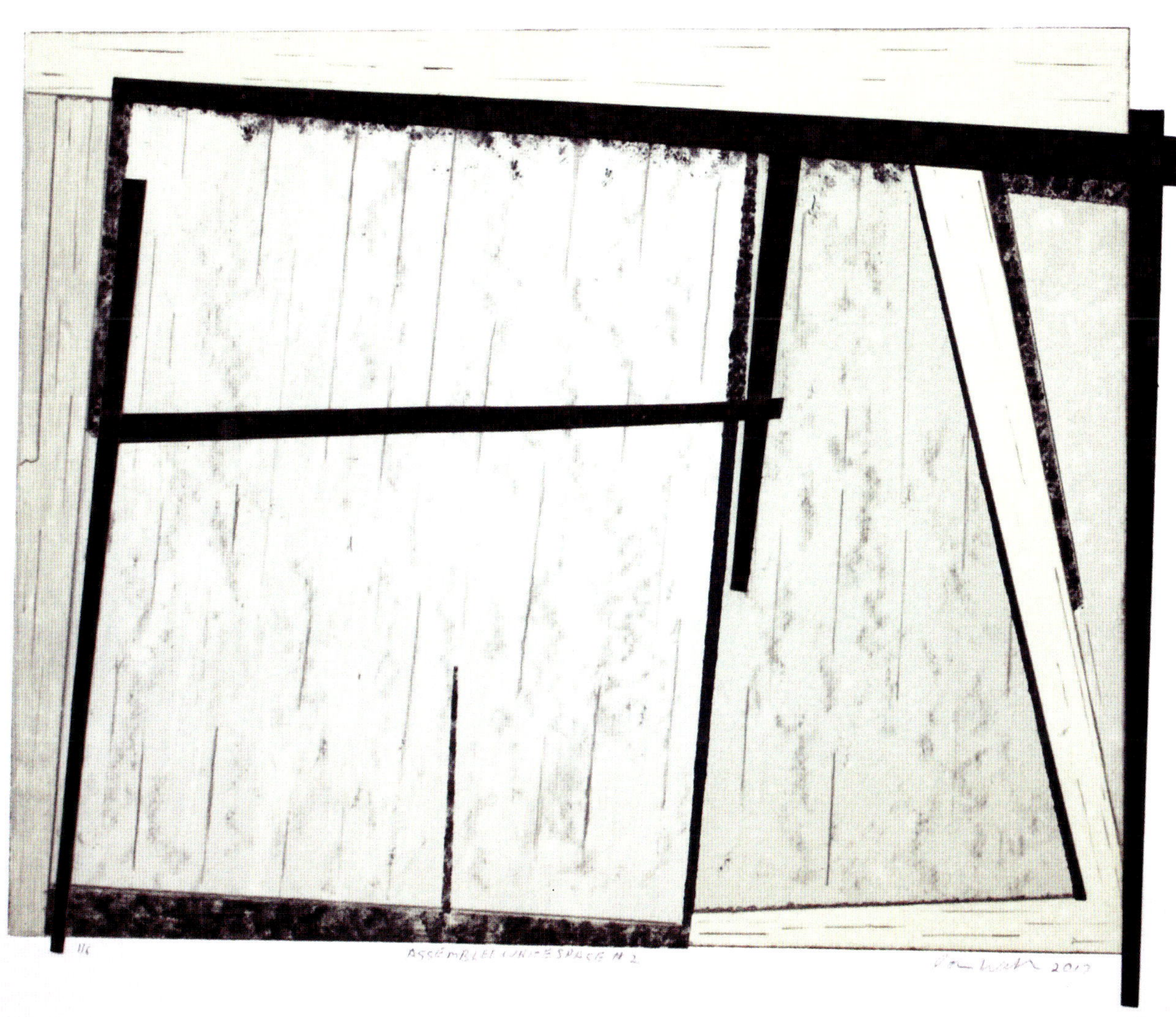

<
Conflicted Space #16. Monoprint with oil-based inks, monotype, and relief on letterpress and offset presses using constructed materials. 10" × 16". 2016.

Conflicted Space #1. Monoprint with oil-based inks, monotype, and relief on letterpress and offset presses using constructed materials. 10" × 16". 2015.

Assembled White Space #2. Monoprint with oil-based inks, monotype, and relief on letterpress and offset presses using constructed materials. 8" × 10". 2017.

NINA WISHNOK

Somerville, Massachusetts

We are constantly moving back and forth between the particular and the general, from daily interactions with each other and the world, to intellectual or emotional processing and reactions. These two threads—literal and abstract—inform each other, and visually I try to depict the fluid boundary between the two. Drawing from collected imagery such as natural and man-made forms and structures, my work explores the themes of inner/outer life, generic/individual, and micro/macro, and how these pairings relate to space, structure, systems, and networks—both literal (physical, mechanical) and abstract (social, emotional, personal). I often explore this by placing recognizable images within ambiguous visual environments or by introducing visual contrasts such as regular and irregular, organic and mechanical, representation and abstraction.

I work mainly in printmaking because I love the way it plays an active role in producing a finished piece. I tend to mix techniques such as woodcut, paper lithography, intaglio, trace monotypes, and encaustic. I enjoy working in the space between planning and accident, and I like the mental shake-up that happens when a visual detail is recontextualized or images or colors are combined in unexpected ways.

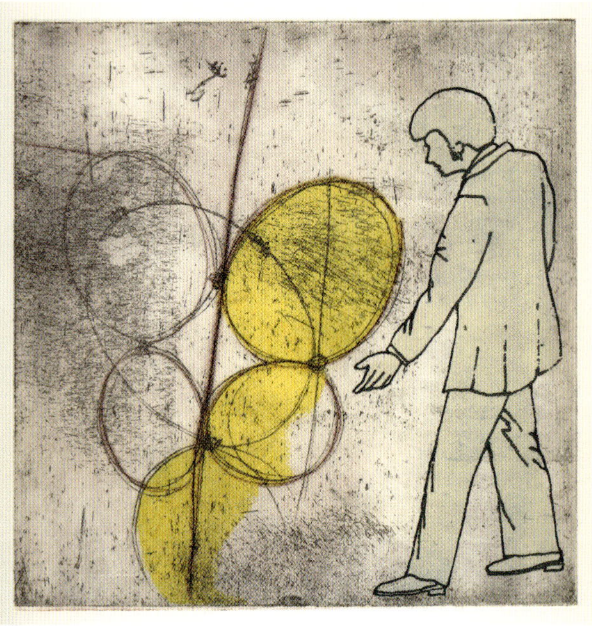

Into the Under iii. Monoprint with oil-based inks, etched and drypoint intaglio, stencil, and paint. 8" × 8". 2007.

PUBLISHED AND PRINTED BY THE ARTIST AT ABRAZOS STUDIO.

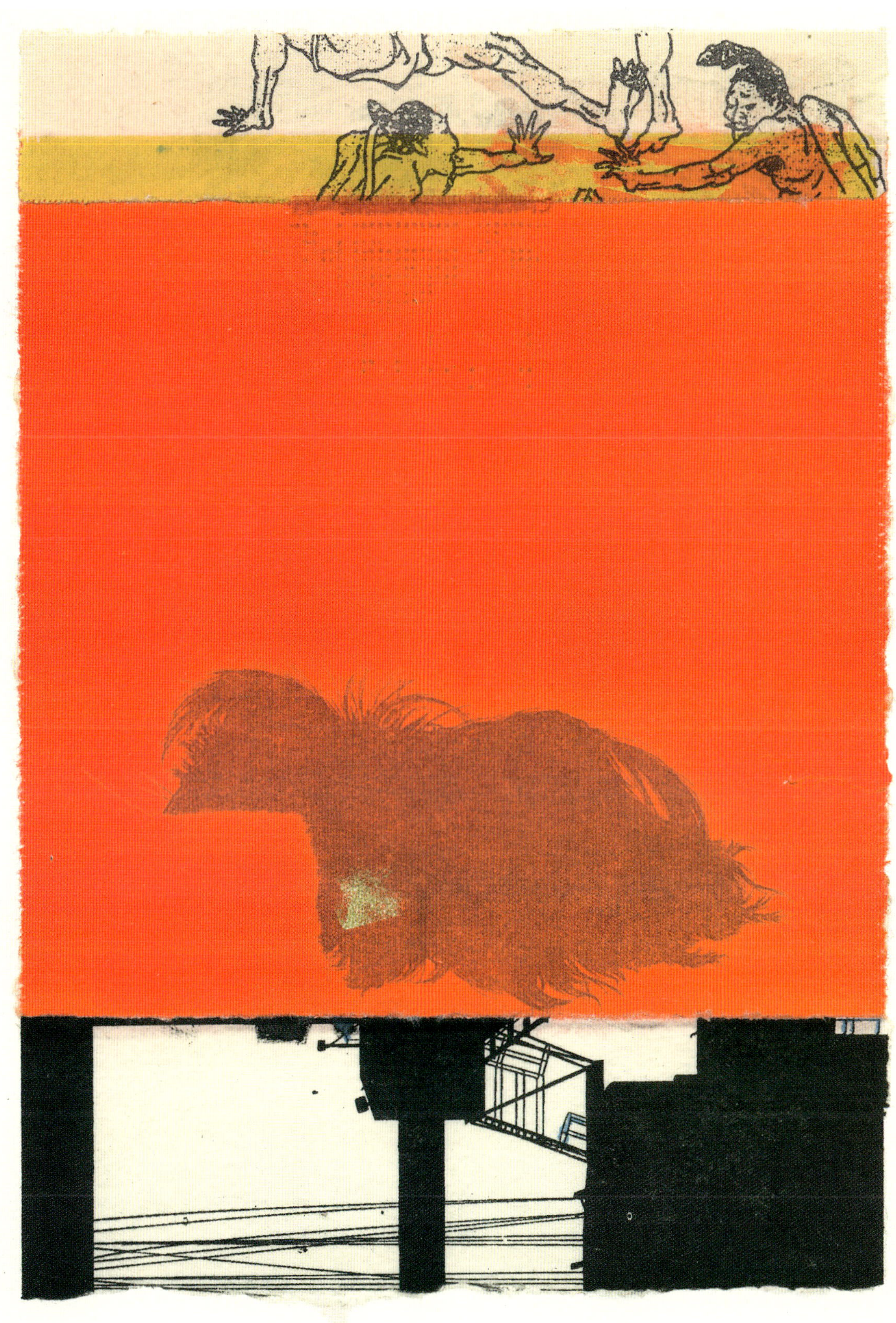

Where Is What viii. Monoprint with oil-based ink monotype, collage, woodblock, drawing, paper lithography, and chine collé. 8.5" × 6". 2016.

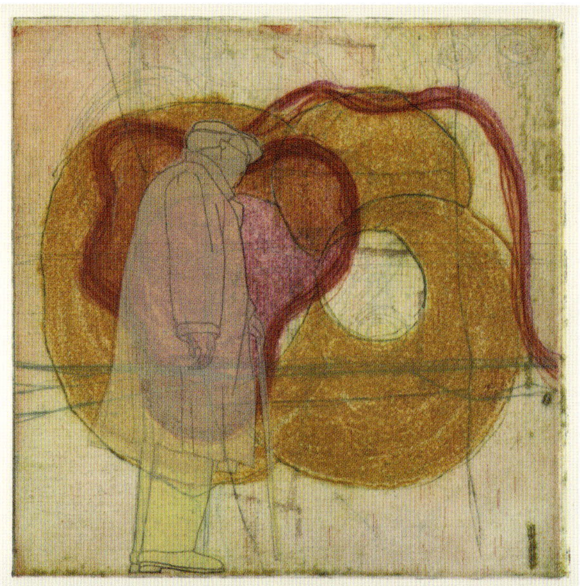

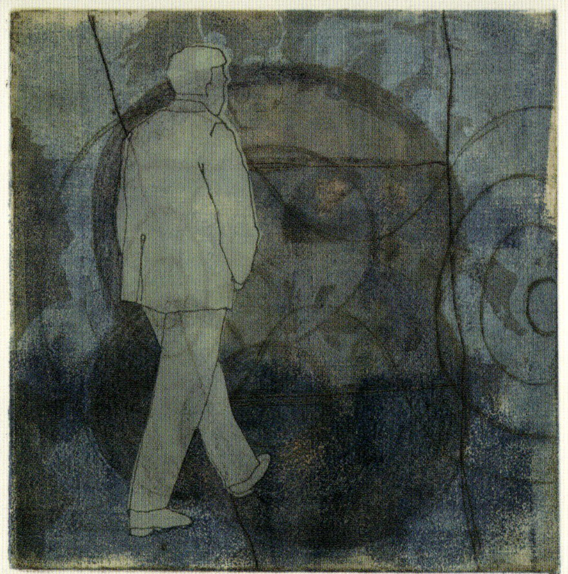

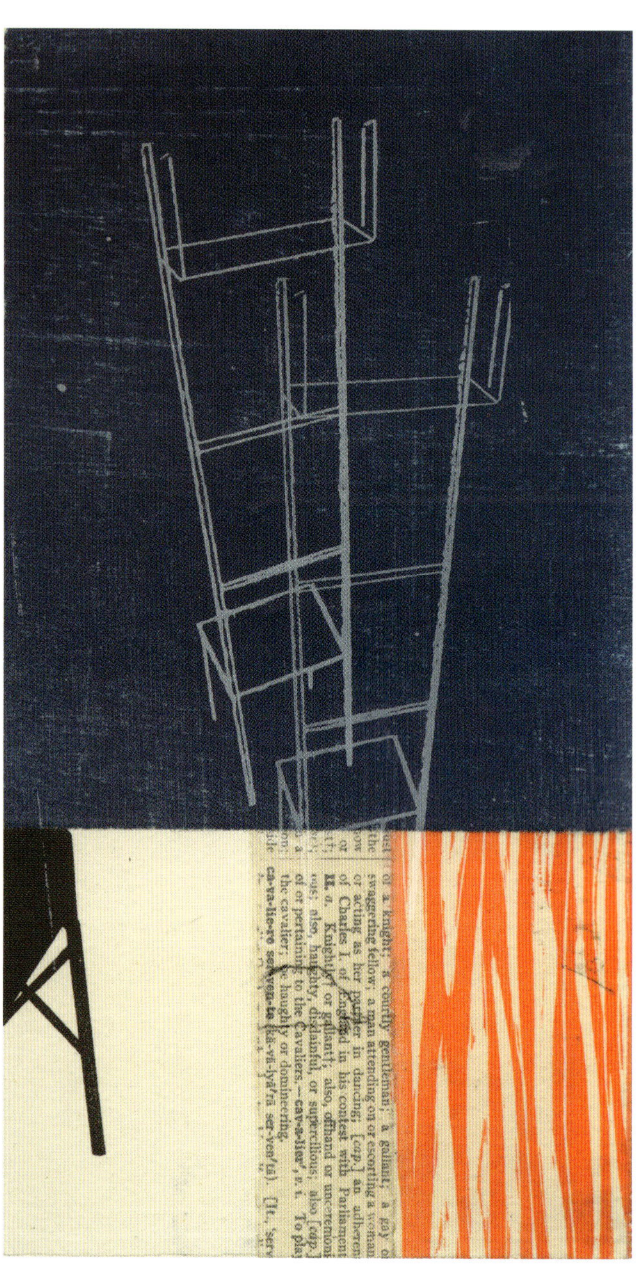

^

Into the Under i. Monoprint with oil-based inks, etched and drypoint intaglio, stencil, and paint. 8" × 8". 2007.

Into the Under ii. Monoprint with oil-based inks, etched and drypoint intaglio, stencil, and paint. 8" × 8". 2007.

Where Is What i. Monoprint with oil-based ink monotype, collage, woodblock, drawing, paper lithography, and chine collé. 9.25" × 5". 2016.

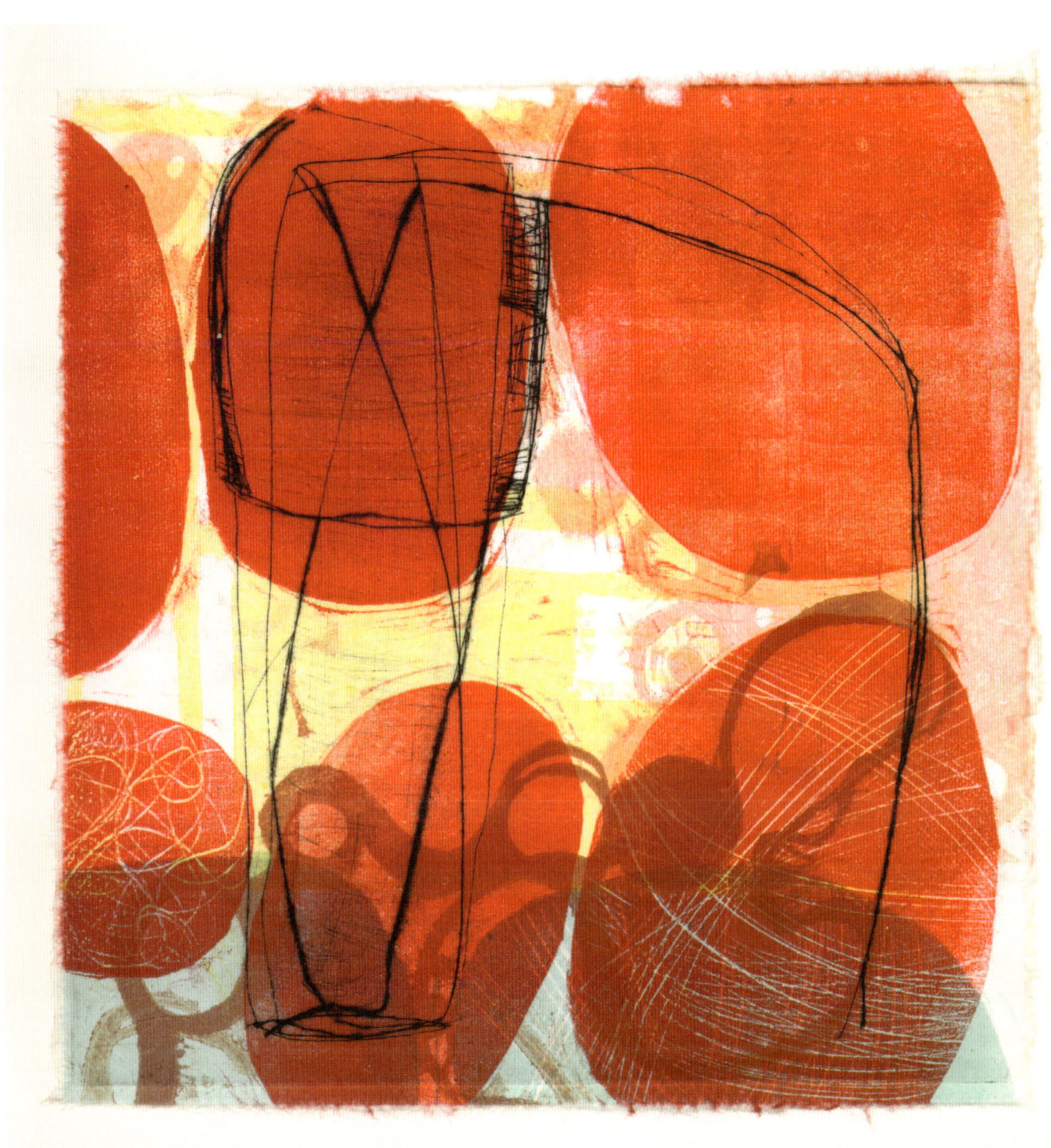

Close Up Reach Out 2. Monoprint with oil-based inks, etched and drypoint intaglio, stencil, paint, woodblock, and chine collé. 7.5" × 7.5". 2005.

ARTISTS' CONTACT INFORMATION

Rita Ackermann
www.hauser&wirth.com

Eric Aho
www.dcmooregallery.com

Neal Ambrose-Smith
www.indianspacepainters.com

Gregory Amenoff
www.gregoryamenoff.com

Sarah Amos
www.sarahamosstudio.com

R. Anthony Askew
www.sullivangoss.com

Peggy Badenhausen
www.peggybadenhausen.net

Andrea Belag
www.andreabelag.com

Chris Beneman
www.chrisbeneman.com

Richard Bosman
www.rbosman.com

Katherine Bradford
www.canadanewyork.com/artists

Brad Brown
www.bradbrown00.com

Beth Campbell
www.bethcampbellstudio.com

Jen Cole
www.jennifercoledesigns.com

David Cost
dwcpoet@icloud.com

Gregory Crane
www.gregorycraneart.com

Paul DeRuvo
www.paulderuvo.com

Valentina DuBasky
www.valentinadubaskey.com

Inka Essenhigh
www.paceprints.com

Liza Folman
www.lizafolman.com

Deborah Freedman
www.deborahfreedman.com

Nancy Friese
www.nancyfriese.com

Jane Goldman
www.janegoldmanart.com

Dirk Hagner
www.dirkhagnerstudio.com

Keiko Hara
www.keikohara.com

Sue Heatley
www.sueheatley.com

Shara Hughes
www.paceprints.com

Bill Jacklin
www.bjacklin.com

Constance Jacobson
www.constancejacobson.com

Joel Janowitz
www.joeljanowitz.com

Meghan Allynn Johnson
www.meghanallynnjohnson.com

Roberto Juarez
www.robertojuarezstudio.com

Jane Kent
www.janekent.net

Catherine Kernan
www.catherinekernan.com

Karen Kunc
www.karen-kunc.com

Robert Kushner
www.robertkushnerstudio.com

H. Peik Larsen
www.hpeiklarsen.com

Nancy Lasar
www.nancylasar.org

Judith Linhares
www.judithlinhares.com

Markus Linnenbrink
www.markuslinnenbrink.com

Emilio Lobato
www.williamhavugallery.com

Eva Lundsager
www.evalundsager.com

Jennifer Marshall
www.junglepress.com

Ryan McGinness
www.ryanmcginness.com

Carrie Moyer
www.carriemoyer.com

Matt Neuman
www.mattneumanartist.com

John Newman
www.johnnewmanstudio.com

Roy Nicholson
www.roynicholson.com

Debra Olin
www.debraolin.com

Wendy Orville
www.wendyorville.com

Robert Andrew Parker
www.davisandlangdale.com

Ron Pokrasso
www.ronpokrassoworkshops.blogspot.com

Wendy Prellwitz
www.wendyprellwitz.com

Sara Greenberger Rafferty
http://sgrstudio.info

Jenny Robinson
www.jennyrobinson.com

Ron Rumford
www.ronrumford.com

John Schiff
www.johncschiff.com

Susan Schmidt
www.susanschmidtart.com

Richard Segalman
www.maryryangallery.com

Stuart Shils
www.stuartshils.com

Heddi Vaughan Siebel
www.heddisiebel.com

Robert Siegelman
www.gallerynaga.com

Joyce Silverstone
www.joycesilverstone.com

Steven Sorman
www.stevensorman.com

Carolyn Swiszcz
www.carolynswiszcz.com

Donald Traver
www.donaldtraver.com

Chuck Webster
www.bettycuninghamgallery.com

Dan Welden
www.danwelden.com

John Willis
www.johnwillisstudio.com

Nina Wishnok
www.ninawishnok.com

Sharon Wolpoff
www.sharonwolpoff.com

GALLERIES, STUDIOS, AND MUSEUMS

The work of the artists featured in this book can be found at these galleries, studios, museums, and collections.

Galleries

13 Forest Gallery, Arlington, MA
BCB, Hudson, NY
Brian Morris Gallery, New York, NY
Brooke Alexander Gallery, New York, NY
Cantor Gallery, College of the Holy Cross, Worcester, MA
Carla Massoni, Chestertown, MD
Chandler Gallery, Maud Morgan Arts Center, Cambridge, MA
Chiaroscuro Gallery, Santa Fe, NM
Cotuit Center for the Arts, Cotuit, MA
Craig Starr Gallery, New York, NY
Davidson Galleries, Seattle, WA
DC Moore Gallery, New York, NY
Dolan Maxwell, Philadelphia, PA
Edward Thorp Gallery, New York, NY
Elizabeth Harris Gallery, New York, NY
Elizabeth Leach Gallery, Portland, OR
Flatrocks, Gloucester, MA
Flinders Lane Gallery, Melbourne, Australia
Gallery NAGA, Boston, MA
Garth Greenan Gallery, New York, NY
George Lawson Gallery, San Francisco, CA
Harmon-Meek Gallery, New York, NY
Indigo, Santa Barbara, CA
IPCNY, New York, NY
Jason McCoy Gallery, New York, NY
John Berggruen Gallery, San Francisco, CA
Kerry Schuss, New York, NY
Klaus Von Nichtssaggend Gallery, New York, NY
Mark Borghi Gallery, New York, NY
Mark Moore Gallery, Santa Monica, CA
Marlborough Gallery, New York, NY
Mary Boone Gallery, New York, NY
Mary Ryan Gallery, New York, NY
MASS MoCA, North Adams, MA
Mike Weiss Gallery, New York, NY
Nikola Rukaj Gallery, Toronto, Canada
Rachel Uffner Gallery, New York, NY
Rhona Hoffman Gallery, Chicago, IL
Safe Gallery, Brooklyn, NY
Soprafina Gallery, Boston, MA
Stephen Kasher Gallery, New York, NY
Stewart & Stewart, Bloomfield Hills, MI
Susan Eley Fine Art, New York, NY
Valerie McKenzie Gallery, New York, NY
Van Doren Waxter Gallery, New York, NY
VanDeb Editions, Long Island City, NY
William Havu Gallery, Denver, CO
Zuccaire Gallery, Stony Brook, NY
Zürcher Studio, New York, NY

Studios

10 Grand Press, Brooklyn, NY
Center for Contemporary Printmaking, Norwalk, CT
Center Street Studio, Milton, MA
Crown Point Press, San Francisco, CA
David Knut Projects, New York, NY
Dieu Donné, Brooklyn, NY
Dover Press, North Andover, MA
Echo Press, Bloomington, IN
Fourth Dimension, Santa Fe, NM
Highpoint Printmaking Center, Minneapolis, MN
International Print Center, New York, NY
Jungle Press Editions, Brooklyn, NY
Kala Art Institute, Berkeley, CA
Lower East Side Printshop, New York, NY
Phaidon Press, London, UK
Shark's Ink, Lyons, CO
Smith Andersen Editions, Palo Alto, CA
Tamarind, Albuquerque, NM
Tandem Press, Madison, WI
Tyler Graphics, Mt. Kisco, NY
VanDeb Editions, Long Island City, NY
Vermillion Editions, Minneapolis, MN
Wildwood Press, St Louis, MO
Wingate Studio, Hinsdale, NH
Zea Mays Printmaking, Florence, MA

Museums & Collections

American University Museum, Washington, DC
Arkansas Museum of Art, Little Rock, AR
Art Institute of Chicago, Chicago, IL
Baltimore Museum of Art, Baltimore, MD
Bode Museum, Berlin, Germany
Boise Art Museum, Boise, ID
Boston Public Library, Boston, MA
Butler Institute of American Art, Youngstown, OH
Center for Contemporary Graphic Art, Tyler Graphics Archive Collection, Fukushima, Japan
Cleveland Museum of Art, Cleveland, OH
Currier Museum of Art, Manchester, NH
Danforth Museum of Art, Framingham, MA
De Young Museum, San Francisco, CA
DeCordova Museum, Lincoln, MA
Denver Art Museum, Denver, CO
Des Moines Art Center, Des Moines, IA
Detroit Institute of Arts, Detroit, MI
DIA:Beacon, Beacon, NY
Fine Arts Museum, San Francisco, CA
Frick Museum, New York, NY
Ft. Wayne Museum of Art, Ft. Wayne, IN
Grand Valley State University, Allendale, MI
Hammer Museum, Los Angeles, CA
Harvard University Art Museums, Cambridge, MA
High Museum of Art, Atlanta, GA
Hirshhorn Museum, Washington, DC
Hood Museum of Art, Hanover, NH
Houston Museum of Fine Arts, Houston, TX
Kirkland Art Museum, Denver, CO
L'Orangerie, Paris, France
La Specola Anatomical Collection, Florence, Italy
Lundt Museum of Art, Spokane, WA
Mead Art Museum, Amherst, MA
Metropolitan Museum of Art, New York, NY
Minneapolis Institute of Art, Minneapolis, MN
MoMA, New York, NY
Museo Fortuny Palazzo, Venice, Italy
Museum of Contemporary Art, San Diego, CA
Museum of Fine Arts, Boston, MA
National Academy Museum, New York, NY
National Gallery of Art, Washington, DC
New Britain Museum of American Art, New Britain, CT
Oquinquit Museum of American Art, Oquinquit, ME
Oriental Art Museum of Ca' Pesaro, Venice, Italy
Palace of Legion of Honor, San Francisco, CA
Peabody-Essex Museum, Salem, MA
Phillips Collection, Washington, DC
Power Museum of Art, Sydney, Australia
Ridley Tree Museum of Art, Santa Barbara, CA
Samuel Dorsky Museum, New Paltz, NY
San Francisco Museum of Modern Art, San Francisco, CA
Santa Barbara Museum of Art, Santa Barbara, CA
Singapore Art Museum, Singapore
Smithsonian Museum of American Art, Washington, DC
Springfield Art Museum, Springfield, MO
St. Louis Museum of Art, St. Louis, MO
Toledo Museum of Art, Toledo, OH
Tufts University Art Collection, Medford, MA
Uffizi Museum, Florence, Italy
Victoria & Albert Museum, London, UK
Wake Forest University, Winston-Salem, NC
Whitney Museum of American Art, New York, NY
Yale University Art Gallery, New Haven, CT